The Forest of Taboos

The Forest of Taboos

MORALITY, HUNTING, AND IDENTITY AMONG THE HUAULU OF THE MOLUCCAS

VALERIO VALERI

with an introduction by

JANET HOSKINS

THE UNIVERSITY OF WISCONSIN PRESS

The University of Wisconsin Press
2537 Daniels Street
Madison, Wisconsin 53718

3 Henrietta Street
London WC2E 8LU, England

1 3 5 4 2

Printed in the United States of America

Library of Congress Cataloging-in-Publication Data
Valeri, Valerio
The forest of taboos : morality, hunting, and identity among the Huaulu of the Moluccas / by Valerio Valeri.
534 pp. cm.
Includes bibliographical references and index.
ISBN 0-299-16210-9 (cloth : alk. paper)
ISBN 0-299-16214-1 (pbk. : alk. paper)
1. Huaulu (Indonesian people)—Psychology.
2. Huaulu (Indonesian people)—Ethnic identity.
3. Huaulu (Indonesian people)—Hunting.
4. Taboo—Indonesia—Maluku.
5. Maluku (Indonesia)—Social life and customs. I. Title.
DS646.66.H82V35 2000
306′.089′99222—DC21 98-48152

To Sylvana and Artemisia

From Daddy

To suppose that animals first entered the human imagination as meat or leather or horn is to project a 19th century attitude backward across the millennia. Animals first entered the imagination as messengers and promises.

J. Berger, *About Looking*

La définition de l'animal comme une chose est devenue humainement une donnée fondamentale. L'animal a perdu la dignité de semblable de l'homme, et l'homme, apercevant en lui-même l'animalité, la regarde comme une tare.

G. Bataille, *Théorie de la religion*

Let's have a banana sandwich, I said. . . . I am not building a case for the vegetarians who might be too soft for the formula we were conceived in and have to work out of; I will eat meat, only I don't want to see it happen, not anymore, not once more, I don't want to hear the sound. When life changes to death in that very small instant it is an explosion against the mind that can never be rebuilt.

C. Bukowski, *Living on Luck: Selected Letters 1960s–1970s*

Psittacus, Eois imitatrix ales ab Indis . . .

Ovid *Amores* 2.6.1

A thing whose very nature is to be lodged in something else cannot exist where the base is lacking—and it is the character of a reflection to appear in something not itself.

Plotinus, "Impassivity of of the Unembodied," *The Enneads*

I claim that a person is not like a Cartesian Ego, a being whose existence must be all or nothing. A person is like a nation. In the true account of identity over time, these two kind of entities go together.

D. Parfit, *Reasons and Persons*

CONTENTS

Illustrations xi

Maps xii

Introduction by Janet Hoskins xiii

Preface xxi

CHAPTER ONE
In the Heart of the Forest, at the End of Trade Routes
3

CHAPTER TWO
Taboo in Anthropology
43

CHAPTER THREE
Maquwoli in Huaulu
114

CHAPTER FOUR
Zoology and Meatology
169

CHAPTER FIVE
Before Virtue
325

Notes 417

Bibliography 482

Index 503

ILLUSTRATIONS

Looking down at the Huaulu village 6
Walking in between the two rows of houses 7
Young girl fetching water 32
A member of the Huaulu clan 34
The author standing in the village center with a friend 41
Young mother from Nisawele, married to a Huaulu man 121
Hari, dancing at his initiation 130
Ratifala making an ataman (fork) 171
Hunters butchering a deer carcass 175
Young boy bringing food from the forest 182
Head of the clan of wife-takers 210
Fishing on the Sapulewa River 274
Young girl playing an arapapu/stringed instrument with a tame cockatoo beside her 281
Sick man and shaman 296
Pitere with an older relative 316
A hunting party shooting arrows 345
The village temple (luma potoam) 369
Young men dancing during the initiation ceremony 379
Recently initiated young man with bamboo headband 389
Young man wearing the red turban of manhood 396

MAPS

Map hand-drawn for the author to guide his travels through the interior 2
The Moluccan islands of Seram, Buru, Ambon, and Banda 10
Four cultural groupings of central Seram 18
Villages of central Seram 18

INTRODUCTION

This book is the result of a quarter century of engagement with the forest-dwelling people of Seram. It is based on a total of 40 months of field research, spread over a period of 20 years. It is also the result of a long intellectual trajectory, which led its author from philosophy into anthropology and history, and from Italy to France and finally to the United States in order to pursue these interests in different institutional settings. Although it was finished and submitted during his lifetime, the book is being published posthumously, just over a year after his death on April 25, 1998, at the age of 53. As his wife, I had promised him that I would see this book through the stages of publication, and I want to add a few brief words about the importance that it held in his life. To do so, I will draw on some of his own autobiographical writings, which describe the problems and questions that drove him into the forests of Indonesia and brought him back to the libraries of Chicago.

Valerio was born on August 4, 1944, in the small town of Somma Lombarda, near Milan, Italy. It was the last year of the war, and the Germans were occupying Italy; his father was active in the resistance, and his mother was taking refuge in her ancestral home after spending a colonial childhood in Libya. By the time he reached school age, the family had moved to North Africa, where his father, a philosopher, worked as a cultural attaché at the Italian embassy in Tripoli, and his mother returned after the war to see what had happened to the country in which she had grown up. When he was an adolescent, they moved again to Istanbul. Valerio later reflected that these childhood experiences helped motivate his turn to anthropology: "A youth spent in 'exotic' countries had given me a personal brand of attraction/repulsion for the exotic (this means that I looked for the exotic in places more distant than those where I had failed to experience it) and a deeply ambivalent identification with a country—my own—whose attempts to move into the imperialist camp had been defeated by older imperial powers. Perhaps, by choosing to be an anthropologist I wanted to deny that I felt on the borderline between those that make anthropology and those who are made by it."[1]

Valerio was initially trained in philosophy at the Scuola normale superiore, the prestigious Italian academic institution in Pisa, where he was admitted in 1964, after ranking first in a nationwide admission examination. While he was a student in Pisa, he published a series of articles about a new field which was not yet fully developed in Italy—anthropology, especially the theories of exchange of Marcel Mauss and

Claude Lévi-Strauss.[2] His first encounter with Lévi-Strauss had occurred in the train station in Genoa as he prepared to travel from his family home back to boarding school in Venice. He picked up a slender volume called *Totemism,* which had an appealing graphic design on its cover, and began to read it, and by the time he had finished it, he was, as he later wrote, spellbound: "I could not fully understand why, but one reason seemed that Lévi-Strauss thought like a philosopher but did not really speculate or work on introspection like the philosophers with whom I was acquainted. . . . But I felt ambivalent towards Lévi-Strauss' structural method of analysis. Sometimes it seemed deeply illuminating, sometimes it seemed to me that Lévi-Strauss was at his best when he forgot it, or used it as a pretext for validating his intuition or giving his magnificent imagination free rein. Thus his attempt to describe semiotic phenomena as permutations of a system of oppositions, as a mathematical group of transformations, seemed on the whole problematic—more a poetic device than an explanatory one."[3]

Intrigued but still critical, Valerio read more of anthropology in Pisa and eventually made plans to travel to Paris in 1966, to study under the direction of Claude Lévi-Strauss. His teachers in Pisa urged him not to forgo the promising career in academic philosophy that he had started for a discipline heavily identified in Italy in the sixties with the "positivistic and imperialistic sins" emphasized in the United States only in the eighties and nineties. As Valerio tells us, "When I decided to become an anthropologist, in Italy, in the mid-sixties, it was a professionally suicidal decision. Not only did anthropology have no academic recognition, but it did not have it because it had been deprived of intellectual and political legitimacy. . . . I had to ask myself then, and I have to ask myself even more today, what could have driven me so powerfully to run against the current. My honest answer is that—beside my intellectual convictions—I cannot give a reason that does not seem to me mystified, since I feel that obscure motives were at work in me. All I know is that I was deeply attracted to the idea of field-work and that, as a result of this, the experience was both satisfying and traumatic for me when it occurred. I have attempted to sort out these conflicting feelings ever since."[4]

Fieldwork, heavily mythologized as a "solitary act of heroism" performed by an isolated scholar among the savages, drew Valerio to anthropology and was essential to the "epoch of ethnographic optimism" which characterized his early training in Paris.[5] During a childhood illness, Valerio had read an early traveller's account of the Spice Islands of Indonesia, and he developed an interest in the Moluccas that was motivated both by the reported complexity of their marriage systems and the dualistic characteristics of their cosmology.

Valerio finished his philosophy dissertation in Pisa on Lévi-Strauss' theory of kinship and exchange[6] and continued his anthropological training in Paris, preparing a second dissertation on Hawaiian mythology and social organization.[7] He came to focus on the problem of the subject's intention and the context of its enunciation, all of which he found absent from French structuralism in the sixties and seventies—"the issue . . . of whether Lévi-Strauss, together with many other thinkers of the time, was justified in turning the critique of the unitary subject into a total eradication of the subject from analytical practice. The problem was, of course, that in order to give the subject a certain causality, however relative, one must give it a certain autonomy, make it something more than a mere surface of structures, a point of their uneasy and conflicting intersection."[8]

During this period, Valerio came to terms with the fact that while eradication of the subject was the key problem to be resolved in anthropological thinking of that time, its reintroduction could not be "a theoretically easy matter."[9] He became attracted to the work of Louis Dumont because he underlined the importance of hierarchy as a mental structure (rather than merely a social or political one) and because he seemed to provide a powerful reflecting lens for the ideological premises that we unconsciously bring to the study of all societies. Dumont argued that hierarchy cannot be understood without the reflexive deconstruction of its contrary—individualism.

"While I readily agreed with this point," Valerio wrote, "I felt increasingly resistant to its mechanical application—by Dumont and especially by his pupils. Was any reference to the subject in the analysis of, say Huaulu or Hawaii—the societies which I studied—to be branded as a mere projection of individualist ideology? Could the notion of hierarchy, vague as it is, exhaustively account for the way of thinking and acting of Huaulus or Hawaiians or—indeed—south Asians? And correlatively, was it legitimate to identify the autonomous subject of modern philosophy with the individual, as Dumont constantly did? Was a history of the triumph of individualism an adequate account of the notion of the subject—or, for that matter, an adequate account of modern society? Did Dumont's style of analysis retreat from some of the advances of structural analysis by presenting a homogenized description of ideological systems instead of identifying multiple structures in their internal and external transformations? And what ethical and political outcomes should one draw, finally, from Dumont's relentless critique of modernity as individualism?"[10]

Valerio came to explore these theoretical questions in two very different contexts—the strongly hierarchical society of ancient Hawaii, reconstructed through studying historical documents, accounts by travellers and indigenous commentators, and ritual texts in Hawaiian itself; and the much more egalitarian Huaulu, living in the rain forests of central Seram at the end of the trade routes. One project allowed him to look at the development of hierarchical ideas over time, in a series of related transformations, while the second afforded him the experience of intensive fieldwork in a small-scale society, previously unstudied by anyone else.

Valerio first visited the island of Seram in 1971, when he began his initial period of fieldwork (25 months) in the company of his first wife, Renée Valeri. They started their research in Piliyana, in southern Seram, and then heard of a more traditional group, the Huaulu, living in the central highlands. After eight days of hiking through the interior, they came to Huaulu and decided to establish their longer-term research there. The Huaulu were the only people in the Seramese highlands to have preserved their original religion and system of taboos, and for this reason they had achieved a quasi-mythological status throughout the region. They also had complex forms of marriage exchange, a village organization and regional organization that was classically dualistic, and a still-vital form of shamanism. Valerio and Renée stayed until 1973, collecting materials that were originally intended to produce a book dealing with mythology, marriage, and exchange.

After completing his dissertation based on Polynesian library research, Valerio had intended to devote himself to writing several volumes of the Huaulu ethnography. But there was interest in publishing his Hawaiian work (intended to appear in the series to be published jointly by Cambridge University Press and the Maison des sciences de l'Homme), and he wanted to revise it before publication. In 1976, he was invited to come to teach in the United States, at the University of Chicago, where another distinguished scholar of Hawaii, Marshall Sahlins, was preparing a series of books on ancient Hawaii. The task of teaching a series of new and demanding courses in a foreign language (at this point, his third major scholarly language) was also daunting. The Huaulu ethnography was not forgotten (in the period 1976–85 he published three major articles on marriage systems, as well as eight more theoretical articles on anthropological concepts prepared for the Italian *Einaudi Enciclopedia*), but for a long time it took second place to his intensive, and increasingly comparative, work on Polynesian materials.

Then, in 1985, Valerio published his first major book: *Kingship and Sacrifice: Ritual and Society in Ancient Hawaii* (translated into English and totally rewritten for the University of Chicago Press). The very same year that he finished the largest project of his Polynesian work, he also travelled to Indonesia to revisit the Huaulu. He arrived, 12 years after his previous fieldwork in May 1985, and invited me to come visit him there for two months in July and August 1985. I was doing my own postdoctoral research on the Indonesian island of Sumba, and was very curious to see these people who had come to occupy such an important place in his life. The project that he was returning to work on at the time focussed on shamanism and knowledge, looking at the connection between individual involvement in religious activity and more encompassing forms of understanding. In 1986, Valerio did another two months of fieldwork in Huaulu, and in 1988 he stayed for six months (during which time I joined him again for two months). His last trip to Indonesia was in the summer of 1990, when he was joined by his son, Tancredi Valeri.

In writing up his ethnography, Valerio planned to publish three separate monographs. This first one, focussing on the relations between people and animals and the moral system that implicated them, was the only one he was able to finish in virtually all details. He submitted it to publishers in November 1997 and in February 1998 was able to sign the contract to publish it with the University of Wisconsin Press. I agreed to work with the editors to see the project through. The second, titled Blood and Money: Being and Giving in Huaulu Society, focusses on the relations between men and women and also on questions of pollution, property, and value. It was the subject of the last course he ever taught at the University of Chicago, and the almost-finished manuscript is now being prepared for publication by Rupert Stasch and Martha Feldman. The third projected volume, titled Learning a Huaulu Myth: Reflections on Knowledge in Huaulu and in Anthropology, may eventually be published in some other form.

The theoretical problem of the constitution of the social subject continued to motivate these new interpretations of his Huaulu ethnography, pushed in the eighties and nineties to react against new efforts to deconstruct or limit the unitary subject. If the notion of culture was founded on the transcendental subject, then would critiques of the unitary character of culture necessarily imply the dissolution of the unitary subject? Valerio resisted the current fashion toward eradicating the subject in some new and different way from that of Lévi-Strauss: "I do not need to stress the paradoxical moral and political consequences of the rejection of humanism which results from the rejection of the unitary and autonomous subject on which it is based. The 'postmodern' claim that this humanism is intrinsically totalitarian and that only its destruction guarantees an end of totalitarianism, struck me and continues to strike me as dangerously naive at best. Any discourse, even that of a total decentering and fragmentation, can serve as support of totalitarian power as soon as it becomes exclusive or simply hegemonic. The form of power is not a mere translation of the form of discourse—and vice versa. The ideology of the unitary subject, just like that of the fragmented one, is compatible with opposite power effects. Moreover, and more importantly, those who contested, or, like Foucault, were soon to contest, the alleged totalitarianism of the concept of the universal man, implicitly used their own notion of what being a man authentically consists of, in order to denounce its violation. The connection between humanism and the idea, mythical as it is, of the universal subject, is not so easily lost even in the discourse of those who denounce its alleged totalitarianism. Man is not quite dead even in those who proclaim his demise."[11]

These ideas and unresolved conflicts turned Valerio into an anthropologist and remained the deeply personal questions that he has explored in all his theoretical and ethnographic writings. He has frequently insisted on cleavages and conflicts between different structures, practices, and language games, generally eschewing any reified notion of culture (a term he used sparingly in any case). But he also reacted against an equally reified view of diversity and heteroglossia. As he said: "Diversity does not exclude commensurability: on the contrary, it requires it. Otherwise differences would not be intelligible and significant to different actors and thus would not be socially effective."[12]

The problematic of universality, however unfashionable it may seem in the late nineties, has also never been lost from sight. Universals are both evanescent and inescapable, and so Valerio's writing has also been haunted by the interplay of the Freudian unconscious and the local, public language games that anthropologists study—as testified by some of his earliest[13] and some of his latest[14] writings. He remained fascinated by the subtle and often paradoxical relationship between the most intellectual and the most pragmatic in human life, writing, "I would like to see my work as a continuous exploration of such extremes as practical and intellectual, conscious and unconscious, universal and particular."[15]

Valerio's Indonesian ethnography has not been readily accessible to most readers because it is scattered through publications in three different languages (English, French, and Italian), often published in peripheral locations (such as the Netherlands and Norway) and not readily available in the United States. A partial effort to rectify this will be the publication of a collection that I am editing, entitled *Fragments from Forests and Libraries*,[16] which will also include a wide selection of field photographs. Some previously unpublished articles will also be included in this collection, but *Forest of Taboos* is without doubt his most important work on the Huaulu to be published so far. I am also putting together a second collection, Rituals and Annals: Between Anthropology and History, which is composed of his published pieces on Polynesia (many of them translated from French or Italian) and will include a preface by Marshall Sahlins.

A word should be said about the difficulties of preparing a manuscript for publication after its author's death. I have tried, wherever possible, to follow Valerio's original intentions and to make only those changes which were necessary for clarity or consistency. Valerio was not able to prepare his own bibliography because of the special conditions of his illness, so that bibliography was compiled by me, during his lifetime, from card files and some computerized lists of references.

The system he developed for transcribing the Huaulu language was a highly individual one which reflected his own views on the language but which he gradually modified, trying to bring it more into conformity with the systems used for other Manusela languages by linguists like James Collins and Rosemary Bolton. I have corresponded with them, as well as with Roy Ellen (the ethnographer of another Seram people, the Nuaulu), to resolve certain questions of consistency, but finally I have generally tried to use the most recent and frequent form of transcription that Valerio used. With only four months of field experience in Huaulu, I could recognize certain terms (and distinguish the local language from Bahasa Indonesia or Ambonese Malay) but do not feel qualified to make delicate semantic or orthographic distinctions.

In the last year of his life, Valerio decided to modify the spelling of *maquwoli* (taboo) from *makhuwoli,* to conform with Collins' observation that this sound is probably a voiceless uvular stop, which is generally written in the International Phonetic Alphabet with [q] rather than [k]. Other words (such as *oko,* "shrimp") he continued to write predominantly with the [k]. I have chosen for this publication to omit the [kh] spelling (which I interpret as an early stand-in for the [q]), but to preserve the [k] in those cases where it appears consistently.

He also decided to spell a number of words with a double [ss], which could be used to indicate a long consonant, or more likely simply to designate the softer [s] (as in Italian spelling) as opposed to the [z] sound. Several of these words (such as *lilipossu,* "menstrual hut") I was quite familiar with and even had, so to speak, a direct experience of, so I am reasonably confident of this statement. Whatever its merits, my own experience in transcribing previously unwritten languages on Sumba is that any transcription system is highly personal and idiosyncratic, so it seems best simply to make it clear that these were *his* idiosyncracies, and at the time of his death there was no other foreign scholar who had a comparable command of the Huaulu language.

The research on which this book is based was supported by a number of funding agencies, which should be recognized for their contribution to the long-term study of this remarkable group of people. Initial fieldwork in 1971–73 was supported by the Wenner-Gren Foundation and the Association franco-suédoise pour la recherche. Archival research in the Netherlands in 1974–75 was supported by a fellowship from the Dutch government and from the Ministère des affaires étrangères in France. Postdoctoral research in Paris from 1975–1978 was funded by the Centre national de la recherche scientifique. The

Guggenheim Foundation provided a fellowship for travel and research in 1982–83, as did the Social Science Research Council. Fieldwork among the Huaulu in 1985 was funded by the Institute for Intercultural Studies and the Research School of Pacific Studies, Australian National University, as well as the Social Science Research Council. Fieldwork in 1986 was funded by the Lichtstern Research Grant Program of the University of Chicago. Fieldwork in 1988 was supported by the Wenner-Gren Foundation and once again the Lichtstern Research Grant. The process of preparing this research for publication was facilitated by fellowships from the Institute for Advanced Study, School of Social Science, Princeton, New Jersey (1990–91), and the Getty Research Institute for the History of Art and the Humanities, Santa Monica, California (1995–96). Valerio also held visiting teaching and research appointments during this period at the Research School of Pacific Studies, Canberra, Australia (1985), the Institute for Social Anthropology, University of Oslo, Norway (1992), and the Scuola normale in Pisa, Italy (1994).

The manuscript was read in full by John Bowen, Roy Ellen, Martha Feldman, Signe Howell, J. Stephen Lansing, Rosalie Robertson, Marshall Sahlins, Salvatore Settis, and myself, most of whom offered comments and suggestions, only some of which Valerio was able to respond to during his lifetime. In the process of preparing this manuscript for publication, I have received valuable assistance from Tom Bauman, Rebecca Bryant, Sebastian DeGrazia, Roy Ellen, Martha Feldman, Rupert Stasch, and Robin Whitaker (of the University of Wisconsin Press). I wish to express my gratitude to all of them, and I hope that the posthumous appearance of this volume (and those that follow it) will allow a larger number of people to appreciate the particular combination of wide-ranging intellectual interests and the passion for details, theoretical sophistication, and personal engagement, which were so characteristic of Valerio's work.

Janet Hoskins

November 1998

PREFACE

One does not have to stay long in Huaulu before one hears the word *maquwoli,* "taboo," as I think it should be translated. A child seizes a fruit and brings it to his mouth; his mother raises her voice in alarm and warns: "Tepi, ia maquwoli," "Don't, it is taboo." A worried old woman looks at her fingers, spying the progress of leprosy, and wonders aloud if her condition is the consequence of having eaten at some point in her life spotted cuscus combined with shrimp or bird meat combined with the larvae of a beetle, both of which combinations, she says, are maquwoli. The ethnographer attempts to photograph an innocuous-looking but curious object hanging from a rafter, and he is stopped by a cry: "Ia maquwoli." A cricket jumps inside a house at night and people scramble to put all the lamps out and to cover a pregnant woman, screaming excitedly: "Ia maquwoli poto," "It is very taboo." A couple of men in a philosophical mood complain, not without pride, "Ita Huaulua maquwoliem poto," "We Huaulu people have a lot of taboos," while older men, referring to the alleged laxity of the younger generation, mumble pessimistically, "Ita maquwoliem leussi, tepire hakii nika," "We don't have any taboos left, they have all been thrown away" and point to the dire consequences: the signs of decay, the weakening of Huaulu, the low fertility rate, the frequency of illness. But a nearby shaman will praise one of his patients: "Emaquwoli oho, pinamutua anam!" "She keeps the taboos [that go with my medicines] well, the little old lady!"

Intrigued, the ethnographer pays more attention, makes systematic inquiries, asks about every possibly imaginable combination that may be declared maquwoli. Yet the subject will soon prove to be inexhaustible; the explanations given to him, puzzling; the knowledge of botany and zoology required to identify the species involved, beyond his powers. Time will pass, he will leave the field, ruminate at home, reproach himself bitterly for not having asked the obvious questions that now leap to his mind, return to the field several times to ask those questions. At each new visit he will secretly hope that no new taboo will come his way, he even stops asking, and yet he stumbles onto at least a couple every day. He will grow as bitterly philosophical as those old men whom he first heard many years before complaining about the present inexistence of taboo, but regret under his breath that they were not quite right.

Yet that ethnographer, who is I now writing these pages, is confronted with the necessity of making sense of the thick forest of taboos that threatens Huaulu (and, he feels, himself) from every side. However incomplete my knowledge of this seemingly infinite, and perhaps even indefinite, subject is, I cannot hope to convey a sense of what Huaulu culture is all about without identifying some basic principles underlying taboo's rich efflorescence and, more important, without bringing the reader face to face with the demon that so powerfully drives it.

In everyday English the word *taboo* is used to refer to prohibitions of an absolute character, usually with religious or social sanctions, rather than legal or merely legal ones. The anthropological use of the term encompasses the above meanings but is much wider than they are. A taboo is the index of certain peculiar dangers incurred by entering into contact with certain peculiar things or persons. The dangers are usually physical (characteristic disease or misfortunes) but may also be of a more conventional nature (ritual disqualification, and so on). They are due to powers intrinsic to the thing or person that is taboo.[1] These powers react automatically, although their effects may take time to become apparent. Indeed, it is characteristic of taboo that whether contact has occurred intentionally or not is irrelevant: usually all transgressors are equally struck and suffer the same consequences. The striking power itself is usually conceived as devoid of will and even of personality; in fact, it is often left undefined. Any will that it may possess is suspended or not exercised with regard to the field of taboo, where its power reacts automatically and inexorably, "with the same ruthless indifference to motive as a typhoid germ."[2]

The main questions that have exercised anthropologists ever since Frazer and Robertson Smith turned taboo into a subject of inquiry are: How do the dangers associated with taboos differ from ordinary dangers, given that the form of their manifestation is usually similar, that is, physical? What lies behind these judgments of dangerousness, and why are they associated with impersonal or scarcely personal forms of agency? Are taboos reified moral rules ("prohibitions") taking the appearance of objective dangers, or are they the formal statement of incompatibilities (between substances, acts, times, spaces, and so on) which are determined by a poetic logic of analogy with pragmatic implications? What kind of rules are they? Do they prescribe unconditionally like norms, or are they of a conditional character, of the form "If you want to avoid x or achieve y, then avoid z"? Are they moral or instrumental, or do they blend these two aspects inextricably? Does taboo constitute the sum total of the regulation of conduct in certain societies, or does it coexist everywhere with other forms of regulation, invoking different concepts (e.g. responsibility), ranges of application (e.g. purely interpersonal relationships), and sanctions (e.g. from human authorities)? In other words: How does taboo compare with what we call law and what we call ethics? And with what we call divine commandment? How do the dangers associated with the violation of taboos compare with sin, shame, and guilt? Is it possible to correlate the prevalence of taboo with certain social forms or social situations? And how do these social motivations for taboos relate to their intellectual or cosmological ones? What are the political implications of using taboo, rather than "law" or "categorical imperatives," as the main idiom of legitimate action?

These are the questions that we must also ask with regard to the Huaulu notion of maquwoli. Investigating it entails drawing on anthropological debates on taboo and contributing to them. But the tenor of these debates is often far from clear, and the various theories proposed are often mutually incompatible and in conflict with certain massive facts. A dialectical review of the principal theoretical positions on taboo will therefore be necessary. I stress the "dialectical," because the review is not a chronicle or even a history of what has been said on taboo. Rather, it attempts to put those theories in a certain logical sequence which makes a concatenation of problems and a certain possible outcome visible. Thus my dialectical review (perhaps I should say, à la Kojève, "my reasoned history") displays a significant directionality and has a cumulative effect. By moving from theory to theory by a problematic rather than a historical progression, I hope to suggest a set of solutions, which I will then develop in dialogue with my Huaulu materials.

This way of proceeding stems from a constatation: that the anthropologist's knowledge forms at the intersection of his critical dialogue with two communities—that of his fellow scholars and that of the people with whom he has chosen to live for a while but who speak in his mind and to his mind forever. These two sides of the dialogue which constitutes anthropological knowledge should receive equal weight. The anthropologist-to-anthropologist relationship should not be ignored or, worse, made invisible. Interpretive ideas do not emerge in an unmediated contact between the "field" and the "fieldworker." Between an anthropologist and his "people," his other people, those of his own intellectual (and not just intellectual!) community, stand as often uninvited—or even unacknowledged—guests. I have tried to invite them both from the outset. But first let me introduce the Huaulu, and explain how and why I came to live among them.

The Forest of Taboos

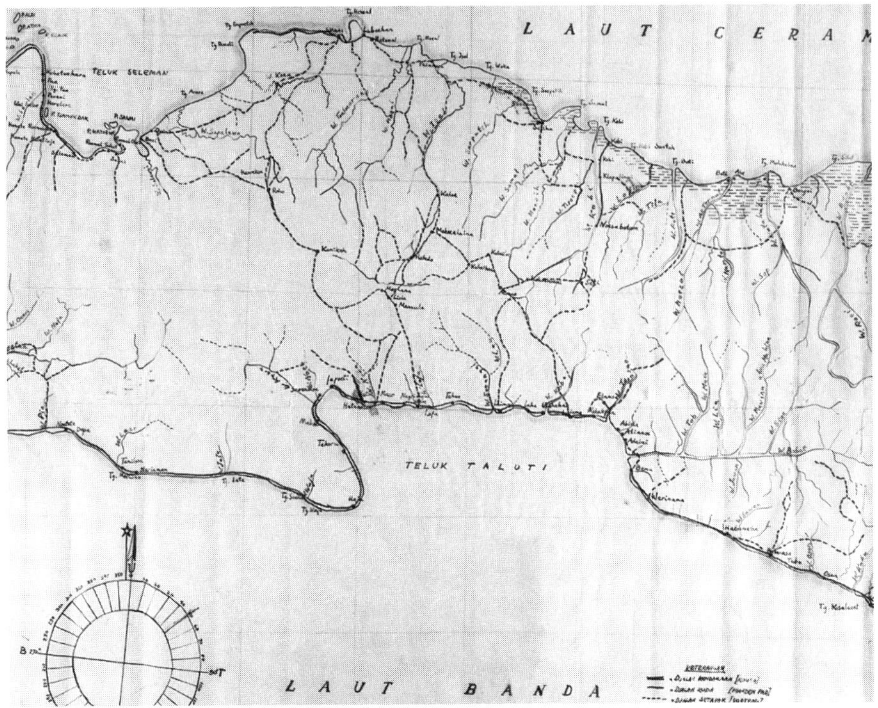

This map was hand-drawn for the author in Ambon to guide his travels through the interior of central Seram, beginning at the Bay of Taluti and ending in the Huaulu mountain village.

CHAPTER ONE

In the Heart of the Forest, at the End of Trade Routes

Sometimes, wandering in the kaleidoscope of city odors, I capture one that crystallizes by chance. Suddenly alert, I smell again. I attempt to keep it steady, trying to discover its source. And then it triumphs over all others, as an unexpected beauty suddenly sighted in the crowd crushes its monotonous ugliness. It is an odor from long ago, from far away—from the forest. Most often, it resembles the musky odor of a marsupial. But, as in the forest itself, it transmutes into another odor, and then into another; it exists in the mysterious balance of a crushed fruit, of the soil scintillating in a sunray after a rainfall, of the perpetually rotting leaves, and of the indefinite mustiness forever buried in the heart of the wooded dream. I keep inhaling avidly, fearful that each step will take me away from the smell, but hopeful that it will bring me closer to its hidden source. I feel at the anxious threshold of a backward slide in time, into the depth of a sensing self forever lost. But I never fall. The odor dissolves as soon as I open my nostrils wider to take it all in. The elusive forest hidden somewhere in the concrete jungle of Chicago has sunk again. Like the fragile radiance of the woman in the crowd, it is swallowed again in the gray stench of the city's embrace.

The forest of Seram—an ocean of ever-changing sameness. I cannot evoke it. At every conjuring trick it disappears from my page, too omnipresent to be seized.

From my field journal, Huaulu, February 27, 1972

> Of the long trip from Hatu [a village on the bay of Taluti, in southern Seram] to Huaulu I preserve a memory: the obsessive identity of the forest, the impression of walking without ever moving, of being unable ever to arrive. Only thrice the landscape widened to give us some perspective, some sense of the distance already traveled and of the distance still to travel—what we had left behind and what awaited us.
>
> The first time was on the way from Hatumete [another village on Taluti] to the pass on the Howale Mountain. Following the river Walala, which winds and falls precipitously at various points, the view opened wider and wider over the sea, and across an extremely dense forest . . . until the mist and the rain cut us off from the lower slopes, confining us to a world of mountain tops and of dripping trees. Then the second time. The sudden revelation of the other world which opened up on reaching the top of the mountain which had separated us from Manusela:[1] the lowlands covered with eternal forest, where villages we knew

> existed were lost, submersed into invisibility. And finally, the third time, when travelling from Kanike to Roho.[2] Suddenly in front of us opened a wide valley, and the mountain which runs horizontally between us and the distant blue sea was pointed out to us as the site of Huaulu.
>
> For the rest of the trip variety was given only by the alternation, in different rhythms, of identical elements: groves of monstrous bamboos, under the shade of which the clear ground was carpeted with dry leaves—clearings soft to the step, breaking with the tiresome entanglements of our usual path; rivers in whose currents we advanced, struggling, for kilometers, as they were the only open way; sticky mud reaching up to our knees in which we had to progress slowly; leeches attached to our arms and to the bleeding legs of the porters; sudden perfumes which evoked fleeting but extremely vivid culinary mirages for our hunger. . . .
>
> Thus for a week, sleeping in caves or in depressing villages built, for the most part, in the dreary "Company style," which gave them the aspect of railway towns in a western movie. Only Kanike—almost an alpine village under the crushing mass of the Binaya—and Roho seemed a faint promise of what I was hoping to find in Huaulu. From the already corrupted coast of the south to Huaulu it has been a travel back in time, to the intact culture of Seram as I had divined and dreamed of it from its sad remains, and passing through the immutable forest which protects it. I have known an unknown and unknowable forest—intense, a vegetal universe barely marked by animal signs, and by some cancelled human trace. A nature whose apparent message of eternity—illusory to the intellect, but irresistible to the imagination—gives rest from history, and releases me from the passions that still bind me to what I have left behind. Thus I am now here without regrets, freed from the past as never before. . . .
>
> Immense forest, secret language, key to the villages it envelops and to the thoughts that wander in it. Peopled of its monsters, of its gods, of animals that turn into humans . . . Without this forest in which they wander, I would never have understood the inhabitants of its sparse clearings, of villages situated in limited spaces, but within labyrinthine universes. Sometimes, their tales brought back my own, as on the upper ranges of the slope that descends to Manusela. We slid in the twilight with quiet steps among immense trees covered with yellow moss and thickened by silence—a forest of gnomes, of trolls in which the memories of childhood blended with Heine's verses—the warmth of stunned winters, of Christmases that have grown unknown to the senses.

In the forest, I thought I came face to face with time itself, or rather with what would cancel it, just like the smell I sometimes rediscover in the city.

Another memory of the forest. This time seen, not in the analogic waves of the city that stands between a lake of blood[3] and a lake of water, but through the fragility of the village, opening like a red wound in the immense green flesh.

I shall never forget the first time I saw Huaulu.

For a whole week, I had travelled through forests and mountains, along the course of rivers and more often inside them.[4] I was hastening to reach Huaulu from the south coast of Seram, where I had spent a few months in the latter part of 1971 and the beginning of 1972, waiting with increasing impatience for the rainy season to slacken and make my trip across the island possible. I was exhausted, splattered with mud, and soaked with rain.

From a little earlier in my journal, same day:

> Yesterday we arrived in Huaulu, first passing through an extraordinarily rich forest, a tropical color plate, streaked with the hues of fruit and echoing with the grunts of wild pigs. From afar, a song guided us and made us feel the presence of the village before we could see it. The voice, accompanied by the sound of an arapapu[5] (I hear it again, in this rainy and sleepy afternoon), sealed us from the villages left behind, Christian and silent. We were entering another world. . . .

Memory invades me. It is no use keeping it at bay by quoting musty pages. I cannot confine this first sighting to the past. I must let it run its course in the present, on this page.

The voice became closer and closer, winding with the widening path, which had turned left to initiate its slippery descent. Durian and kanari trees gave smell and color to the increasing proximity of the village. Suddenly the tops of coconut palms appeared, quietly murmuring in the distance, and under them the first roofs of brown thatch blending with the ocher of the village ground. I stopped, and my gaze took in the scene. Below me, the village, on the western slopes of the long hill of Sekenima, which we had seen from afar the day before and whose ascent we had begun a few kilometers earlier, rested like a gigantic eagle watching its dominions. On the left side, the overbearing chain of mountains, whose brief appearances among the trees had accompanied our progress on the crest of the hill, continued its northwesterly course, until it reached the perpendicular backdrop of the Mawoti Mountains, a somber wall against the occidental sky. Before me, and left and right, the forest extended unbroken and uniformly dark green, as far as distant hills, which could not completely hide the sea, whose fragments scintillated in the distance.

We continued our descent. The voice suddenly stopped. Silence was followed by alarmed exclamations. Walking in between the two rows of large houses on stilts, their props decorated with geometrical

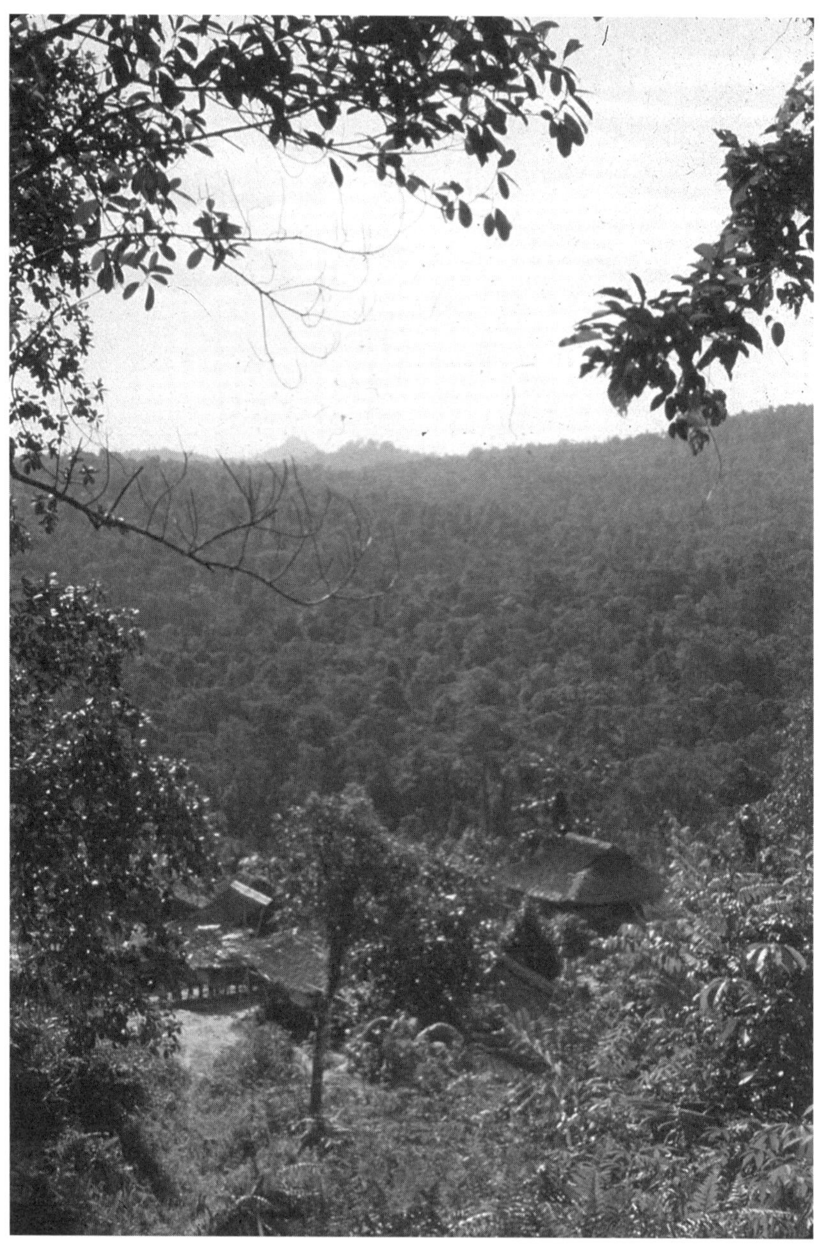

Looking down at the Huaulu village from the mountain ridge. 1985.
(Photo by V. Valeri.)

Walking in between the two rows of houses on stilts. 1985. (Photo by V. Valeri.)

motifs or with animal and human figures, we reached a gigantic hall (luma potoam, "the big house") and climbed into it while its great drum sounded in alarm, rumbled in sinister waves over the outstretched forest, calling the Huaulu back to the almost empty village. Little by little, men with faded red turbans and women curved under heavy shoulder baskets appeared out of the forest from all directions. Their lips were scarlet with the juice of betel and their hair was uncut. Our porters explained the purpose of our visit, because none of the present could speak more than a few words of Ambonese Malay (but I could follow what they said, since, as I discovered, their language was closely related to that of Manusela, which I had begun to learn in southern Seram). We were told that we had to wait for the guardian of the hall, whom they would go and fetch from the Sapulewa River, where he had been hunting for some time. They suspected us of being missionaries or perhaps traders, but told us not to be afraid: "Nowadays we do not kill anybody." Very reassuring.

The Village and the Forest: The Huaulu and the Non-Huaulu

I have quoted at some length from my journal, and let myself be carried away by the memories of my first impressions of Huaulu, for a precise reason. I wished to convey a sense of how overwhelming two oppositions at first appeared to me. One opposition was between the puny, and yet proudly defiant, village and the immense forest surrounding it on every side; the other was between the acculturated communities which I had experienced until then and Huaulu, the only people in central Seram whose members all proclaimed themselves faithful to their ancestral heritage, and still rejected, after some 70 years of state pressure, conversion to either of the established world religions (Christianity and Islam) to which their neighbors had yielded.

These oppositions are indeed fundamental, but I exaggerated them initially for a variety of reasons. One transpires from the fragments of my journal which I have quoted. Like many anthropologists of my generation (and even of the present generation, which, however, has grown too hypocritical to acknowledge the fact), I went to the field with romantic longings for cultural authenticity. I was looking for a place that would correspond as closely as possible to my image of an intact Seramese culture and, even more so, for a place which had coherently and voluntarily rejected the seductions of modern Western culture, which I then disliked more than I do now and which I wanted to escape. The Huaulu's neighbors had depicted them to me as profoundly traditional. In my months among the people in the south, I had become increasingly intrigued by their ambivalent attitude towards the Huaulu. The southern people affected superiority—as being closer to modernity and especially as members of either of the two rival "true" religions—over those benighted pagans. At the same time, they were awed by the Huaulu spirit of resistance. I began noticing a protective attitude. Clearly, many did not welcome the idea that the Huaulu could be converted too, that even the last bastion of traditional culture could disappear from central Seram.

This attitude was not without parallels in other parts of Indonesia. For example, in Muslim west Java, the Badui people are believed by their Sundanese brethren to be the descendants of the ancient rulers of the area. The Badui's alleged keeping of original—pre-Islamic—Sundanese "custom" (adat), with its "Hindu-Buddhist" overtones, enables the other Sundanese to stay away from that custom and thus to be pious Muslims while remaining, by the magical virtues of synecdoche, true Sundanese.[6] Later, I would discover that the Huaulu were used by their neighbors as custodians of ritual practices forbidden or forgotten elsewhere, but still deemed worth using whenever necessary. Thus I repeatedly saw people from Christian villages come to Huaulu to request the performance of divinations and, more frequently still, to indulge without restraint in the performance of "heathen" practices—shamanism in particular—which could exist only underground in the Christian villages farther east or along the coastal areas.

To some extent, the Huaulu shared this image of themselves as lone representatives of the past on behalf of others.[7] Indeed the image was in part justified by the categorical opposition between the Aseran-iem[8] (Christians) and Laufaha[9] (Muslims) on one side and the Mema-haem (mountain people practicing what is often called akama[10] tua, "the old religion") on the other. But they were not content with this generic identity. For on the whole, sticking to the past meant—and still means to them today—sticking to important differences from their neighbors, whom they continue to divide between enemies and friends, but always consider fundamentally different. Thus, while my dualistic longings for the authentic as against the inauthentic were initially reinforced by Huaulu and non-Huaulu alike, I soon discovered (or rather began to accept) that the reality was far more complex than this, and that, in any case, Huaulu was not as absolutely conservative as it presented itself.

As for the other opposition, that between village and forest, it proved more valid than the first, but still only part of a much wider and more differentiated picture, of a whole system of differences in which I learned to situate it. Furthermore, any temptation I might have had, against my better judgment, to connect the two oppositions, to see the traditionalism of Huaulu as a function of its apparent isolation in the middle of an overwhelming forest, was soon dispelled by the realization that Huaulu was in no way more isolated than its Christianized or half-Christianized eastern neighbors and perhaps even less. Indeed, it became apparent that to make sense of many of its traditional ideas and institutions I had to take into account the fact that the Huaulu, along with all the other peoples of Seram, had been for centuries part of a wider world and one of the end points of a wide network of trade connections, with accompanying or subsequent interventions from indigenous and nonindigenous states, which stretched from western to southeastern Asia.[11] The stubbornness of Huaulu's commitment to its tradition, to the idea of it, if not to all of its details, appeared then even more appealing and more puzzling. It was an intentional act of resistence, conjuncturally made possible by a sequence of events and strategic shifts in a central Seramese history of colonial oppression, not a passive result of "isolation." The forest isolates only those who seek to be isolated.

Divisions, Claim, and Resources

In describing Huaulu,[12] one can start from the village or from the forest surrounding it, but in either case, one must always move from one to the other. I shall start from the forest or, rather, from the territory claimed by the Huaulu, seen in the context of Seram as a whole. But to begin with, let me give a few facts that exist under Western eyes. After all, we must be able to find Huaulu in our pilot books to get there at all,

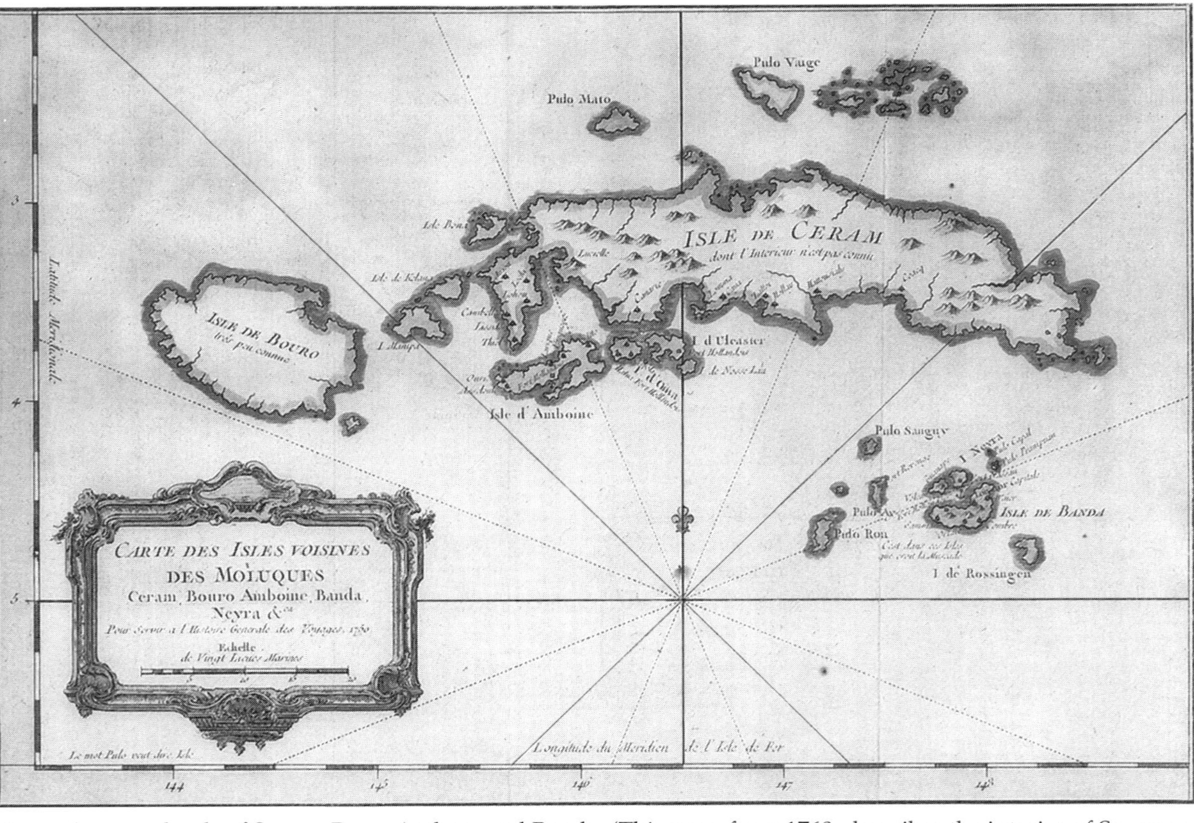

The Moluccan islands of Seram, Buru, Ambon, and Banda. (This map, from 1760, describes the interior of Seram as "unknown.")

so as to listen to its own stories, uncover its own classifications, and finally redraw our maps in the Huaulu scale.

The island of Seram, the second largest of the Moluccas (Maluku, in the national language, Bahasa Indonesia, henceforth B.I.) stretches for about 338 kilometers[13] from the sea east of Buru Island to the sea west of Irian Jaya's Onin Peninsula and has a surface of 2,478,000 hectares.[14] Of the smaller islands adjacent to it, the largest and more numerous are in the west and southwest. Among them is Ambon, whose main city (Kota Ambon) is the capital of the province of Maluku. Geographers divide the island, like Gallia, into three parts. The western part is characterized by a rugged relief and by three main basins, those of the rivers Tala and Eti (both of which flow southward into the sea) and the Sapulewa (which flows northward). Central Seram is divided longitudinally by an imposing chain of mountains, alpine in character and in geological age, which, running from northwest to southeast, comes progressively closer to the southern coast until it becomes parallel to it behind the bay of Taluti. The highest point of this chain, Mount Binaya, reaches 3055 meters. Another chain runs for a lesser span and at a lesser altitude north of the main one. The Manusela Plateau extends between the two chains. Farther north the terrain slopes and flattens in great alluvial formations, which, near the coast and particularly in the easternmost part of the region, turn into large swamps. These are alimented by the large rivers that descend from the central chain. Southwest of the mountain chain there is another land mass, also passably rugged but with lesser altitudes, particularly in its westernmost area, where the two rivers Nua and Ruwata run their courses.

Eastern Seram bends slightly toward the south and has lower altitudes than the central part. Its northern coast is as swampy as the neighboring coast of central Seram, while in the south the mountains usually reach the sea, leaving only narrow coastal strips. The two largest rivers, the Bobot (which runs from east to west) and the Masiwang (which runs in the opposite direction) are found in the south. To the southeast, and in the direction of the Kei Islands, stretches a chain of small archipelagoes: Seram Laut, Gorong, Watubela.

The climate of Seram, like that of the other Moluccas, is characterized by the equatorial monsoon regime.[15] During the summer, the wind blows from the southeast, whereas during the winter months it blows from the northwest. Passing over the seas, the winds become heavily charged with humidity, which condenses over the land, resulting in intense precipitations. Because of the island's relief, however, the south receives most of the rain in the summer, whereas the north receives most of it in the winter. The contrast is particularly striking in central Seram because of the orientation and the altitude of its principal mountain chain. Thus, over a period of 25 years, the mean monthly rainfall in Wahai (a village on the north coast) during the month of February (which is the peak of the rainy season there) was 445 millimeters, while in Amahai (south coast), it was 112 millimeters. Reciprocally in July, at the peak of the rainy season in the south, the mean monthly rainfall was 456 millimeters in Amahai and 105 in Wahai.[16] However strong the contrast between the seasons, it is rarely strong enough to warrant the title "dry season" for the period of lesser rainfall. The fact is that in Seram it rains most of the time and skies are usually overcast and gloomy. Significantly, in Huaulu I have often heard of magic for stopping the rain, but I have heard of magic for making rain only with the purpose of stopping enemies who were in pursuit. The figures say it all: in Wahai a yearly average of 2179 millimeters of rain fell over a 25-year period; in Amahai, the average was 2749. These figures refer to coastal stations and should be increased considerably to reflect precipitations in the mountain areas, which, moreover, are characterized by lesser seasonal variations and greater irregularity than precipitations in the coastal areas.[17]

The territory claimed by the Huaulu is situated in the northwestern part of central Seram, from the top of the central mountain range to the sea. It is limited, on the west side, by the Salawai River and some of its tributaries up to the peak of the Roifelu in the Mawoti Mountains, and on the east side—moving from the sea landwards—by the Ika, Sapulewa, and Umu rivers up to the Umu's mountain source behind Kanike. The extension of this territory is at least 400 square kilometers. It presents a great variety of environments. The central mountains are steep and rocky and thus are appropriately put in the category of hatu (hatuam), "stone, stone mountain." Their upper reaches are treeless owing to the cold, but afford very good hunting, with many deer, birds, and bats. The last of these nest in caves in the cliffs on the mountains' flanks. In their lower reaches the rain forest begins. It extends without interruption as far as the sea, although it gives way to mangroves (*Nipa fruticans*) and palms in the swampy low areas formed by the large rivers that delimit or cross the Huaulu territory, particularly by the delta of the largest one, the Sapulewa. The rest of the area is covered with hills or "mountains" (ulay [ulayem]), often quite steep, such as Sekenima, on which the Huaulu have built their villages for the past century or so. Among these hills meander streams of various dimensions, most of which empty into the Sapulewa. They are fished and shrimped extensively, with bow nets by women and with bow and arrows or spears by men. If the streams become shallow enough during the dry season, they are dammed and fish are stunned with munu (a sort of poison, probably *Derris elliptica*).[18] In exceptionally dry years, the Sapulewa River is fish-poisoned, but this is a very demanding enterprise that requires the cooperation of the entire village and, if possible, of neighboring villages that have some rights on part of the course of the river.

Several areas on the riverbanks are particularly favorable to the growth of "the sago palm" (ipiam[ipi]) and to its processing (the crushed pith must be washed to separate the starch from the fibers), making the vegetable a staple of the Huaulu (and of most other peoples of Seram). Therefore, sago palms are often planted in these sites, where they then propagate spontaneously. But large groves have also developed without human (or at least recent human) intervention. The lower course of the Salawai River meanders endlessly in the largest naturally propagated sago groves in Seram, to which the Huaulu lay exclusive claim, although they are extensively used by coastal peoples at the mouth of the river and along the coast to the west of it.

Because the Huaulu practice gardening (of the ladang [lawa, in Huaulu] type) to only a limited extent,[19] the areas of secondary forest (B.I., belukar; there is no Huaulu equivalent) are rare,[20] and are limited to former village sites and their surroundings or to small settlements in the forest, where people keep their hunting stations and open small tobacco or taro gardens. Only in certain areas of the north coast has deforestation begun to occur in recent years. It is due to logging, both the organized one of concessionaries and the wild one of various poachers. It is also due to the increasing number of pioneer settlements from overpopulated areas of Java,[21] the Moluccas, and Sulawesi, with concomitant gardening and creation of coconut palm plantations. But these phenomena are still occurring at the fringes of the Huaulu territory.

Apart from these small areas, then, most of the territory claimed by the Huaulu is covered with true evergreen rain forest (B.I., hutan rimba; Huaulu, airumaniam).[22] A sign that this forest is indeed the unmarked state of their territory is that there is no special name for it in the Huaulu language. It is usually referred to with the generic name for land, kaitahu. That is to say, land usually comes covered with evergreen forest in the Huaulu environment. This forest, as elsewhere in the permanently humid tropics, is characterized by three layers of vegetation: tallest trees (33–60 meters); intermediate trees (16–25 meters); younger trees and shrubs. "Continuous *stands* of single species are rare."[23] This means that a great variety of species (there are about 45,000 of them in southeast Asia according to Merrill)[24] are represented uniformly throughout the entire territory. Put otherwise, most vegetal (and consequently also animal) species are found within any relatively small radius. This makes it possible for small human populations to live off wild resources and also accounts for their tendency to fragment into small groups, each exploiting a discrete territory. It is exactly what has happened all over the hinterland of Seram, including Huaulu. In May 1988, at the time of my last visit, the Huaulu numbered 168 in all.[25] If we assume, very conservatively, that the territory claimed by them is about 400 square meters, then each Huaulu had the use of 2.38 square kilometers at that time.

Interestingly, the Huaulu do use—at least occasionally—most of this territory, although the extent of their claims is not recognized by their neighbors. Their disagreements occasionally erupt in acts of war, as happened (fortunately without loss of life) when I was in the field in 1985. However, the territory recognized as Huaulu under Dutch rule was about half of what they now claim—and most probably of what was claimed under Dutch rule.[26] This more limited territory, between the river Warana in the west, the river Umu, the mountain of Kopiafata, and the high course of the Ika in the east, and not reaching the sea, is in fact the one most frequently used by the Huaulu. We can therefore say that each Huaulu can find most of the needed resources in 1.19 square kilometers on the average. This territory offers a variety of wild resources: game, fish, crustaceans, eels, wild vegetables, sago, fruits, and nuts for food; wood, bamboos, leaves, rattans, and fibers, among other things, for building, making implements, heating, and cooking; resins for lighting; and so on. It also furnishes forest products that can be sold to or bartered with coastal traders: parrots and other birds with beautiful plumes, the skins of crocodiles and pythons, deer horns, cassowary caudal plumes, and, in the past, damar (the B.I. term for resin from *Agathis*).

Most of the food eaten by the Huaulu is wild. Indeed a combination of hot sago porridge and game or fish, sometimes accompanied by leaves or other vegetables, is the usual meal. I cannot give figures for the relative importance of domesticated and nondomesticated food resources in Huaulu. In a comparable case—that of the Nuaulu people on the southern coast—the figures are as follows: Forty percent of an estimated daily adult intake of about 3085 calories is derived from nondomesticated sources, as well as 64 percent of the protein fraction of all consumed food. Over 80 percent by weight of plant-derived food comes from sago (*Metroxylon*). Four categories of wild animals—pigs, fish, cuscuses, and deer—provide almost 90 percent by weight of animal-derived foods, and 56 percent of the male energy expenditure devoted to productive activities is spent hunting wild animals.[27]

I believe the use of nondomesticated resources is proportionally even higher in Huaulu. It certainly was so in the early seventies.[28] The life of the Huaulu thus depends almost entirely on their relationship with the forest. This relationship has a double aspect. It implies entering the forest, abandoning oneself to it to find its bounty. But it also implies exiting the forest, carving out of it a space free from it, where that bounty can be used by humans and thus transformed into something quite different from what it was. The forest must thus be present everywhere and yet absent somewhere. The physical contrast of village and forest is thus symbolic of the complex relationship of dependence and independence, identity and difference, amity and enmity, that exists between the Huaulu and their wooded environment. But ultimately, the dominant mode is dependence, the dominant feeling is helplessness. The forest seems always to claim back the spaces that humans have managed, at one point, to cut out of it.

This is best demonstrated by the sites of former villages that surround the present one, sites through which one passes daily. Those that have been abandoned most recently (the last about 1960) are still treeless, although they are now covered with tall "elephant grass" (lesalesa). The fruit trees and palms planted on the rim of the most recently abandoned site are still extant and productive. Less recent sites, however, have already been invaded by wild trees and have become quite impassable. The oldest sites, on the northwesternmost side of the Sekenima hill, which were inhabited 80 or 90 years ago, are now completely covered with gigantic forest trees, especially with strangling figs.

The forest also seems always to claim back the life it has given. People are born out of its rich soil, but they are also called back into it. The giver of life is also a giver of death, not only because the resources from the forest are obtained through a struggle that may bring about defeat and death (by being gored by a pig or bitten by a snake, by falling from a tree, by being carried away by the current in a flash flood), but also because, more profoundly, death is always inscribed in life, since all life ends in death. A basic figure thus resumes the values of the forested land for the Huaulu: that of the female, of the mother, who nurtures but also devours, who gives food which eventually turns her children into food. "The forested land" (kaitahuam) and "the island" or "domain" (nusam) are Puhum, Mother Earth, who gives birth to her children and receives them as corpses. She lies supine, her legs and arms spread out, under Father Sky, Lahatala. Her shapes—the head, east; the feet, west—can be traced in the orography of the island; they are forever before the Huaulu. "Don't you see her breasts and her belly and her right leg?" an old man, Murahaka, asked me, pointing at the mountain chain behind the village (the trunk) and at the Mawoti Mountains (the right leg). By this representation, the Huaulu territory lies between her right arm and her right leg, and includes her right breast and the right side of her trunk.

Social Classification

The forest's cruelty is not limited to the way one procures food in a struggle that may end—that eventually always ends—in oneself becoming food. It also creates a struggle for this struggle, a competition among humans for its resources. How many lisaem ("war stories") do not begin with women inciting men to destroy a neighboring people, "because they fish all the shrimps out of the rivers"? One way or another, wars are about the continuation of life, and thus about the control of the means for continuing it: about hihinaem, "the women" for reproduction; about kaitahuem, "the land," for eating (ita ae kaitahuem, "we eat the land," say the Huaulu). Life continues at the expense of other humans, just as it continues at the expense of animals, of plants, of any other living being. But it is never sure who is going to win, who is going to be predator and who is going to be prey. Out of the forest, suddenly, comes the enemy; he attacks, destroys, carries away heads as trophies. Into the forest, the Huaulu plunge to reach their enemies and do the same to them. Humans are not only outside the forest and against it, but also of it. Like all creatures, they follow its law: hunting and being hunted, killing and being killed. The fear of the surrounding forest is also the fear of this fearsome symmetry—of being attacked and of having to attack in return.

But if ultimately relations among humans, just like relations among humans and animals and all other living things, are submitted to Anaximander's iron law of balance and retribution, there are ways to regulate, displace, or even repress its operation. These are the persuasive ways of ritual and history. Only their final result need concern us here: a complex classification of the peoples of central Seram, and beyond, which indicates what kind of relationship should exist between them and the Huaulu. But to follow this Huaulu classification it is necessary to think of the peoples of Seram and their relationships, in terms of that primordial form of identification, differentiation, and communion—that is, language.

About 19 languages have been documented in Seram.[29] Recent research has established that they all belong to two main groups: one east and south of the Bobot River basin (including the small archipelagoes at the southeast), the others north and west of it, as far as the Manipa Strait in western Seram.[30] These two groups, which Collins calls, respectively, "east Seram" and "Nunusaku," are in turn branches of a proto-language, which he names proto–East Central Maluku, in contrast with proto–West Central Maluku, the hypothetical proto-language from which the languages spoken in the islands west and northwest of Seram (Buru, Sula-Taliabo, Ambelau) are derived. Both proto-languages are descended from a single source, which Collins calls proto–Central Maluku.[31]

Although linguistically speaking central Seram belongs with western Seram, culturally there are some notable differences between the two areas (along with many similarities). Ideologically at least, the two main peoples of western Seram, the Alune and Wemale, form a group apart. The Wemale are (or better said, were) matrilineal,[32] whereas the Alune are patrilineal. These and other opposed characteristics of the two peoples are considered by them as complementary, so that the two form a single whole. Another and more encompassing symbolic and political organization which set the peoples of western Seram apart was the so-called Three Rivers confederation (after the three main rivers of western Seram). This confederation played an important role not only in the ritual life of the area, but also in the centuries-long fight of the peoples of western Seram against the encroachments of Moluccan and European powers.

The inland area east of Wemale country and well into central Seram was inhabited, until the late nineteenth century, by small groups which were then moved by the Dutch to either the southern or the northern coast. Among these groups, on the north, are or were the Warasiwa, Marehunu, Herelau, Horale, Masisihulan, Ruma Sokate.[33] On the south, the most important are or were the Waramania and Yalahatani. The older literature also refers to a Patakai group,[34] which appears to have consisted of the peoples called Nuaulu (now settled on the south coast, east of Sepa), Openg, and Ruma Olate (both now settled on the north coast, in the Bay of Saleman).[35]

The most important linguistic and cultural groupings in central Seram are four. They are not all locally named or self-named but, for the sake of convenience I shall call them the Manusela, the Taluti, the Seti, and the Laufaha. The grouping that I name Laufaha, following Huaulu usage, consists of four villages on the north coast: Saleman, Sawai, and Besi on the Bay of Saleman and Wahai farther east. They are all Muslim and speak the same language, which Collins names Sawai. According to him it derives from the Three Rivers proto-language and is thus more closely related to the languages of western Seram than to the other languages of central Seram.[36] These villages are basically landless and have traditionally lived off the sea: fished, traded, practiced piracy. Their culture is close to the Islamic variety of Modern Ambonese culture. The influence of Ambonese and even of the culture of the Indonesian nation-state is particularly apparent in Wahai, which, being the capital of the district of northern Seram (Kecamatan Seram Utara), has a sizable population of civil servants from Ambon and even from other areas of Indonesia such as Java. A community of Indonesianized Chinese shopkeepers and traders also lives there.

Most of the inland area of Seram north of the mountain chain is inhabited by the linguistic and cultural grouping I call Manusela, after the name of the village that seems to have had the greatest political and ideological importance, at least in Dutch times. The named communities included in the Manusela grouping are, from west to east, Huaulu, Nisawele, Selumena, Maraina, Manusela, Makualaina, Kabauhari, and Maneo. These speak closely related dialects. Collins puts them and the so-called Patakai (which includes the Nuaulu, Ruma Olate, and Openg dialects, all closely related to one another) in the subgrouping which

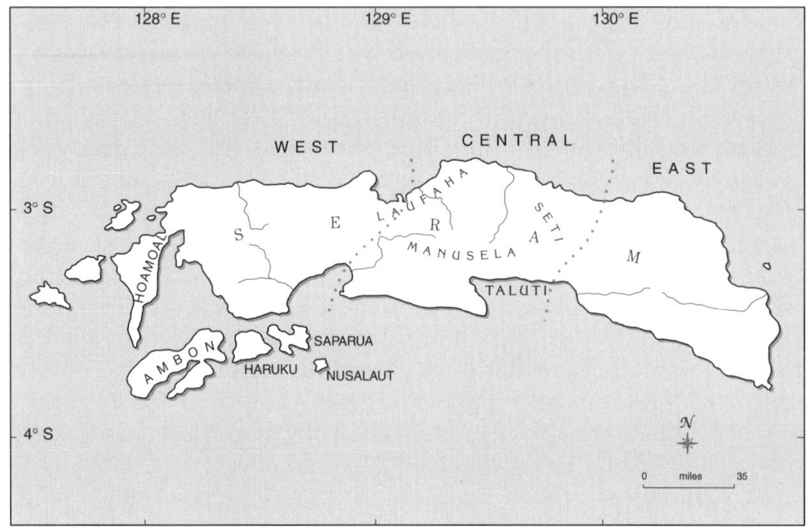

Four cultural groupings of central Seram (the grouping here called "Laufaha" are Muslims of the Sawai area, the Manusela include the Christians and pagans of the interior).

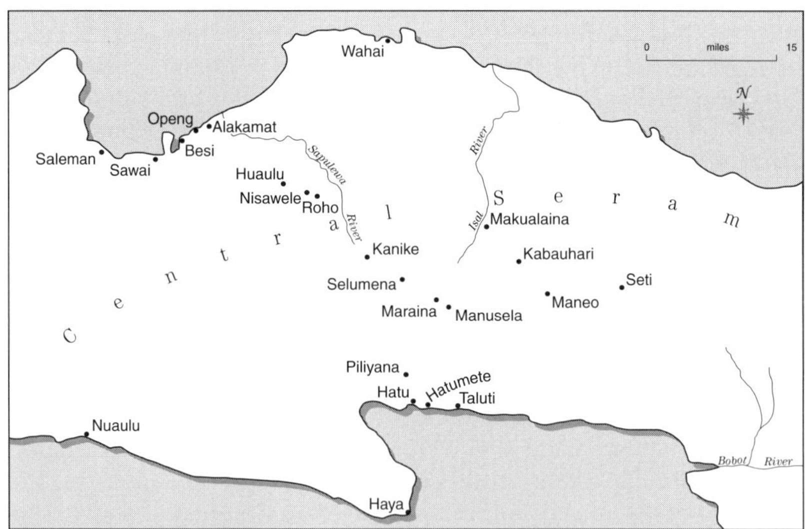

Villages of central Seram.

derives from the reconstructed "Nunusaku" language.[37] Another subgrouping, the Seti, begins east of Maneo and includes the village of Seti as well as a number of recent settlements on the north coast. This linguistic unit corresponds to my third grouping, the Seti. All inland people, whether Seti or Manusela, have much in common with regard to their subsistence economy, their material culture, their customs and beliefs, and so on. Yet the differences that exist between Seti and Manusela, particularly the linguistic ones, are strong enough to make them feel different from one another.

The fourth grouping, which I name Taluti, consists of the original inhabitants of the Taluti Bay in southern Seram and extends from the village of Haya in the west to the Bobot River in the east.[38] All these villages speak one single language, locally called Sou Nama. This belongs, along with most languages spoken on the southern coast of west and central Seram, to the "proto–Piru Bay" subgrouping of Collins' Nunusaku proto-language.[39] The reason for this distribution is probably that all the speakers of this subgrouping's language spread from the Piru area following the upheavals caused by the Hoamoal wars of the mid-seventeenth century.[40] These wars were fought by the Dutch East India Company in order to eliminate the native-controlled cultivation and trade of cloves in southwest Seram. The peoples who were pushed away by the Dutch and spread eastward along the southern coast were thus involved in trade and have preserved this character over the centuries. After the Dutch monopoly on growing cloves was lifted in 1864,[41] the cultivation of cloves (which had never completely disappeared) was legally reestablished in Seram. Since World War II, because of a steep rise in prices,[42] it has greatly expanded, and the area around the bay of Taluti has become one of the largest producers in the island. The cash economy that has thus formed has attracted many of the mountain people to the coast, and nowadays one finds numerous Manusela speakers around the bay of Taluti. However, this more recent emigration from the Manusela area was preceded by a more ancient one, limited to the hinterland of Taluti. Descendants of these more ancient emigrants nowadays live inland in small villages (Ekano and Piliyana) or on the coast near the bay (Hatumete, Amahena). The cultural interchange between the Manusela and the Taluti areas has thus existed for a long time, as local traditions also testify.[43]

Ethnographically and linguistically, we still know too little about eastern Seram to say much. Suffice it to say that there were, until recently, groups living on the upper courses of the Bobot and Masiwang rivers. These groups have now been settled on the southern coast by the Indonesian administration. Another group, the Bati, famous all over Seram, Ambon, and the adjacent islands for being witches, lives in various villages in the hinterland of some of the Muslim principalities (such as Kiandarat and Kianlaut) of southeast Seram.[44] Finally a third group, the Bonfia, is mentioned in the literature; it is now reduced to little and is probably related to the peoples of the Bobot and Masiwang rivers. The culture of the coastal villages, long involved in trade, is a variant of the usual coastal-Islamic culture of the central Moluccas and betrays numerous contributions from areas of the Indonesian archipelago farther west. There is even one settlement (Air Kasar) of Buginese origin.

The Huaulu classification of their relations with other peoples concerns principally their neighbors, of course, but it uses categories that are extensible, and occasionally extended, to the whole of Seram. Some of these, moreover, are variants of categories used rather generally by the various peoples of Seram. One case is the Siwa/Lima (Nine/Five) opposition, which is (or was) used not only in Seram but also in most of the central Moluccas and in the islands of Banda, Kei, and Aru in the southern Moluccas,[45] to partition them into discrete territorial entities. In the past, these corresponded to the highest possible level of political confederation to which autonomous political entities (such as the Huaulu, the Nuaulu, the Openg, the Selumena, and so on) could belong. Notionally, Nine and Five were eternal enemies. The opposition was thus the highest level of expression, but also of regulation, of the agonism that was endemic among all politically autonomous groups, and many other social relations, in this area of the world. Its nature, though, was and is more conceptual (a representation of social relations as essentially agonistic and of hierarchies as reversible) than political. In practice, less encompassing alignments or enmities were and are much more important. Furthermore, the opposition itself is elaborated in different ways by different groups of people. The Huaulu case illustrates both points.

Conceptually, the Huaulu combine this most diametric of all dualism with a concentric one. They say that they are "Five," and thus part of the opposition of Five and Nine, and "One" (Essa), as the center to which both Five and Nine are hierarchically contrasted. Reasons for the dual value of the Huaulu domain are found in its peculiar spatial position between the Lima and Siwa peoples of central Seram. Huaulu is located in the Lima territory, but on its boundary with Siwa territory. According to the Huaulu, all people east of them are Siwa, and all people west of them are Lima.[46] This spatial situation makes the Huaulu the "guardians of the boundary" (ita saka sifatam) between Siwa and Lima. But spatial relations here are the enduring form taken by temporal ones.

The Huaulu do not find themselves on the boundary of the two moieties by chance: they do so because they have engendered these moieties. According to their myths, they were the first human beings in Seram. In fact the island developed from their ship *Kalasiwa,* which ran aground when the bottom of the ocean, which originally covered the site now occupied by land, began rising. The stone ship is still found on one of the mountains behind Huaulu and marks the site of the first village (called Kalasiwa after the ship, or Liapoto). This is the center—as the original engendering point—of the whole of Seram. To this center came all peoples who now inhabit Seram. The Huaulu sent them either east, where they became Siwa, or west, where they became Lima. Having then descended themselves to the lower lands, they have become part of the division; but at the same time, through their continuing connection with the "navel" of the island, they transcend it, they are "One," that is, "first" in time and first in rank.

This myth thus superimposes on the agonistic and reversible world—expressed at its highest level by the Siwa/Lima opposition—a hierarchical world which is beyond and above contest and division, the world of One against the many. But it is not a world in which the Huaulu do in fact live. They are exiled from it, as they are exiled from Kalasiwa, to which they cannot return and at which they cannot even look, on pain of dying, because of a loosening of their navel knots. In actual reality, they participate in the agonistic and rival world as Lima, and are therefore vulnerable to defeat and subordination. Hierarchy exists only as longing or as an additional value—an additional bone of contention—projected onto the unstable world of incessant conflict, of the *bellum omnium contra omnes* (the war of all against all), the true jungle in which the Huaulu live.[47]

So much for the conceptualization of the Siwa/Lima dualism in Huaulu. As for the actual relationships of alliance, enmity, and neutrality that exist, in precarious balance, between the Huaulu and their neighbors, they crosscut that dualism in part. Thus some of the Siwa on the east—such as the people of Roho, of Maraina, and especially of Manusela—are their hereditary and bitter enemies. But with a few others—Kanike and to some extent Selumena—peace was established, although it is important to keep in mind that it followed a destructive period of war, to which it is always possible to revert. Indeed, during the entire span of my acquaintance with Huaulu from the early seventies to the late eighties, a state of more or less latent feud (due to an alleged murder) existed between the nominally at-peace Selumena and Huaulu. As for the other Lima, none of those immediately west of Huaulu are enemies. On the contrary, a brotherhood relationship exists with the Nuaulu, and the Openg and Besi are viewed as client peoples of the Huaulu, who allegedly saved them from destruction at the hands of their enemies. With the people farther west, enmity is supposed to have existed and to continue today, because no peace was ever made. Although these peoples (Waramania, Marehunu, and so on) are axiomatically viewed as Lima, their collective name—Fatasia, clearly derived from Patasiwa, the name for the Siwa in west Seram—betrays a different affiliation. This is not recognized by the Huaulu, however.

There is thus a certain contradiction between their current conceptualization of the Siwa/Lima system and the historical traces which their now obsolete enmity with the Siwa of western Seram has left in their tradition. This apparent anomaly aside, though, Lima peoples were not considered primary targets of headhunting raids. These were directed mostly against the Siwa, with the exception of the few with whom peace pacts were established. In any case, the Huaulu are at pains to stress that anybody, enemy or friend, can be a target in case of necessity. The law of the struggle of all against all thus enjoys an ultimate supremacy in their eyes. Everybody is a potential enemy.

Other oppositions define other forms, or possibilities, of enmity and amity. They crosscut one another and the Siwa/Lima opposition. The main ones are between ita hoto mui, "we of the mountain," and asie lau tasiam, "they of the sea/coast," and between Memahaem (followers of traditional cults) and Laufaha (Muslims). Before Christianity gained a foothold in north-central Seram in the early part of this century,[48] and before the policy of forced transfer of inland peoples to the coast was initiated, with various degrees of success, by the Dutch and continued by the Indonesian state, the two oppositions largely coincided. Mountain peoples were all pagans and in this respect all equally opposed to the coastal peoples, who participated in the pan-Indonesian coastal culture, characterized, among other things, by the practice of Islam.[49] The opposition also correlated, at least in Huaulu eyes, with that between two modes of life. The inland peoples lived as hunters and exploiters of forest resources in general. The coastal peoples were traders, pirates, and fishermen. They were, and are, say the Huaulu, landless; their domain is the sea. The opposition finds its emblem in the contrast between two main foods: wild pig for the mountain pagans, fish for the coastal Muslims. This alimentary contrast is supposed to translate into a behavioral one. The sea people are cowardly like the fish they eat, which, when wounded, flee; the inland people take after the wild pigs they eat: like them, they strike back if they are struck. This implies a superiority of the inland peoples, which is also stressed by the contrast between indigenousness and immigrant status (makasupakie, "people who came later") and by the Huaulu myth accounting for the division between Memaha and Laufaha.

According to the myth this division took place well after that of Siwa and Lima, and in western, not central, Seram. Also, it was not effected by the Huaulu people, the original latu (ruler) of Seram, but by a foreign latu, a certain Sahulau.[50] He congregated all the peoples of Seram on the mountain Nunusaku and challenged them to jump over a gigantic log. Those who could—that is, the stronger ones—became

Memahaem; those who had to pass under the tree—the weaker ones—became Laufaha.[51] As all these representations indicate, considerable tensions existed, and to some extent continue to exist, between mountain and coastal peoples, between indigene and immigrant. Mountain peoples such as the Huaulu and their eastern neighbors from Nisawele pitilessly raided coastal people, "stealing" (amana') their heads and possessions.

In other areas of Seram, however, the coastal peoples managed to control and often enslave their mountain neighbors. These destructive actions were checked only by the need that each had of the other.[52] The coastal peoples traded and still trade the products of the forest (parrots, deer antlers, resins, massoi bark, sago, dried meat), or, in certain areas, cloves and nutmeg, for the products of the external world that were and are needed by the inland people: iron, ceramics, shell, cloth, jewelry, gongs, and so on. These objects, although usually recognized as foreign, have become over the centuries consubstantial with the traditional inland cultures, since they are used in the most important ceremonial transactions, and the iron bush knives are needed for practically every activity.

Visible and Invisible Powers

The image of the forest, with its connotations of agonism and reversibility, does not mediate only the relationships between the Huaulu and the wild animals and those among other human groups. It also projects its disquieting shade on their relations with those beings that in our books go under the names of "spirits" and "ghosts." Indeed one of the first things I was told about these beings was that all, except those who have been turned into protectors and helpers, live permanently in the forest and desire, but fear, to tread the humanized space of the village, unless they find there wild trees or grass in which to hide. For this reason, the village ground is kept carefully free of such vegetation. Indeed the "spirits" would not inhabit planted trees, particularly fruit trees, wherever they are situated. The only times these beings are bold enough to enter the village are times of temporal transition (between night and day) and more generally times of categorical confusion (such as when it rains in sunshine), perhaps because these confusions evoke all others and thus also that of village and forest. But even at those times one is quite safe inside a house. This is the ultimately human space in which the wild "spirits" cannot enter, unless they invade the body of one of its inhabitants before this person can return home or the body of some animal which occasionally or habitually enters the house.

Up to now I have qualified the term *spirit* with quotation marks because, although it is currently used by anthropologists to refer to beings like the ones I am discussing here, the term is in fact misleading. The notion of spirit in our discourse is part and parcel of two oppositions which are by and large inapplicable to Huaulu thinking. One is the ontological opposition of spirit and matter; the other is the moral opposition of spirit and god (and often, more radically, of numerous spirits and one single god). The former opposition implies that spirits are immaterial. Their substance is spiritus, "breath"—what is most invisible in the visible, most immaterial in the material. Spiritual existence is understood as the existence of an animating principle without a body or outside a body. But no spirit in Huaulu has this disembodied existence, nor is it reducible to such an existence. In fact, only one category of spirits, namely the sewaem, or familiars of the shamans, are talked of as "winds" that enter into the shaman's body. However, this is not the only metaphor used (another one is that of heat), and in any case these beings have a plurality of very concrete bodies, particularly animal ones. Most of the spirits are encountered in a much more material form. Indeed this is what makes them dangerous, because one cannot easily distinguish them from ordinary animals, humans, vegetals, or minerals. Perhaps the most dangerous spirits are the so-called ghosts of the dead, which are in fact what is left of them after their breath has abandoned their body at death and has dissolved in the air. Their dangerousness lies precisely in their refusal to give up their bodily existence completely. They are, like Bram Stoker's vampires, the "undead" who prey on the living to retain their corporeal existence. And most other spirits are in fact beings in the flesh, different from humans only in their (especially moral) behavior and powers and in their propensity to confuse and mix the animal and the human forms.

As for the second opposition—that of spirits and gods (or god)—it is again too radically dualistic to apply to Huaulu thinking. It is true that a contrast exists in Huaulu between a couple of supreme beings—Lahatala,[53] or Father Sky, and Puhum, or Mother Earth—and all others, including what we would call spirits. Lahatala and Puhum are the ultimate custodians of the moral order of the cosmos, but they cannot be opposed to the spirits like the good god is to the devil, not even like their Durkheimian avatars—the collective moral order of "religion" and the individualistic disorder of "magic."[54] The Huaulu moral cosmos is rather far from the Judaeo-Christian one, certain similarities notwithstanding. Far from being the mere antagonists of Lahatala and Puhum, the spirits are allowed by them to act in malevolent ways, provided it suits Lahatala and Puhum's (ultimately moral) purposes. Thus, the spirits' action is not totally immoral or amoral, even when it is so from the point of view of their intention. More important, Lahatala and Puhum share with the spirits an ambivalent value for the Huaulu. Just one example: It is said that only a kapitane (war leader/headhunter) may dream of Lahatala; but if he does, he must provide Lahatala with the blood of a human victim before three days, otherwise he will himself be killed by Lahatala. The basic relationship with Lahatala and Puhum is thus similar to the one with the so-called spirits: their inhuman preying fury must be appeased; they can be "good" for the Huaulu only if they are "bad" for others. Lahatala and Puhum are no embodiments of the idea of absolute good. If biblical comparisons are called for, they are the gods of Abraham and Isaac, not the gods of philosophers. Far from being pure spirit, they are sufficiently involved in the flesh to desire to "eat it," as the Huaulu say.

If *spirit* is inadequate, what word should we use instead? There is no Huaulu word that encompasses the whole range of beings at issue here, so an easy (and, in truth, too easy) way out is precluded. Some anthropologists who share my worries have chosen the term *superhuman.*[55] Unfortunately this term seems inadequate too. It evokes more easily a gender-neutral version of Nietzsche's superman than the kind of beings that the Huaulu have in mind. Moreover, and granted their basic anthropomorphism, these beings also have nonhuman characters: they could as well be called superanimal or supervegetal or even supermineral (many of them are associated with mountains or large stones). Also, only certain of these beings are considered morally superior to humans; most are morally subhuman rather than superhuman. Even in matters of power, few are unambiguously superior to any human; shamans can easily scare them off or even kill them. Finally, only Lahatala and Puhum, the shades of the ancestors, and some other protector spirits are considered superordinated to humans. Otherwise, the relationship of spirits and humans is defined more correctly as one of mutual struggle than as one of hierarchy. This mutual struggle, in fact, creeps even into hierarchical relations. The Huaulu never conceive of authority or power as something to which one is merely subordinated.[56]

In many ways, the term *inhumans* is much more suitable than *superhumans* to refer to a majority of these beings, who have human characters and desires but not, the Huaulu say, hali manusia, "a human heart" (lit., "a human liver"). They lack the love and compassion that, however narrowly applied, should characterize human beings in the Huaulu view. However, the degree to which they are "inhuman" varies with their moral status, so this appellation is not general enough. All in all, I think that the least misleading, if hardly the most satisfactory, term is *occult powers.* Powers are what really qualify these beings in relationship to humans: they are defined by the effects that they produce and are interesting only insofar as they produce any. *Occult* indicates their nonpatent character without prejudging their nature. The latter is of less interest to the Huaulu than these beings' place in Huaulu cognition, than the fact that they are not immediately known or known in the way in which patent phenomena are known.[57] Indeed the Huaulu often declare themselves agnostic about the ontological status of these powers.

Still, one ontological imputation *is* stressed in their discourse: these powers are personal—they are endowed with agency. Personal agency is a character shared, in different degrees, by all living beings in the Huaulu world-view. But humans and occult powers possess it in a higher degree than all other beings. In conclusion, I shall henceforward avoid the term *spirit* and call these beings "the powers" or "the occult powers," implying that they are powers of a personal nature.

All occult powers are wild at heart. They belong to the forest even when they have been transformed by human agency enough to become compatible with the village. In fact, there is no benevolent power attached to the village or its houses or to particular individuals that was not once a malevolent power attached to the forest. The very expression *benevolent power* is fundamentally inaccurate. By threat or trickery, the ancestors of the Huaulu and some of their living descendants have managed not to change the nature of malevolent powers but to direct their malevolence against non-Huaulu, human and nonhuman alike. This is borne out by the myths that explain how these powers have been acquired. Some narrate how a conflict between a dangerous power and a Huaulu was resolved by a pact, each side yielding something. Thus one of the most powerful shamanic familiars (collectively called sewaem)[58] originated from a power who wanted to make humans become mortal. He won, but in exchange promised to cure humans for as long as they live. In other cases, it is said that the familiar of a shaman is an evil power whom the shaman frightened into submission by threatening him with a knife; now the power fights the still-malevolent powers of his own kind for the shaman.

Another common scenario is the following: A wild power establishes contact with a Huaulu and requests to be "fed" by him, usually with human victims. In exchange the power promises to provide his feeder with invulnerability. These "good" powers are thus really bad ones who use conflicts among humans to satisfy their thirst for human blood. If their Huaulu counterpart does not "feed" them, they feed on him or his relatives. Lahatala himself may act in the same way, as I have mentioned. No "moral" motives are cited for such requests, even when they come from the Supreme Being. Preying on humans is just part of being an occult power. If there is a moral to be learned from such requests it is that life cannot be had for nothing, that sacrifice is the basic moral principle of human life.[59]

"Ancestors" (ailaem) also fit the generalization that there is no good power that was not once bad, and that even good powers are good in a very relative and dangerously unstable sense. Ancestors are just one subspecies of topoyem, the dangerous "shades of the dead." But the malevolence of the dead is progressively neutralized by the passing of time. The more distant in time a dead is from the living, the more benevolent it becomes or, rather, the more moral becomes its malevolence. Ancestors protect only at a price: the obedience to ancestral mandate, which includes, once again, sacrificial killing. But the mere passing of time is not sufficient to neutralize the dangerousness of the dead. Two other conditions are necessary. One involves human agency: the performance of the appropriate funerary rituals, which separate the dead from the living or, rather, create a different and more distant relationship between them. The other involves the mode and timing of the death in the first place. The Huaulu believe that all humans are allotted a certain span of life by Lahatala. If somebody dies before his allotted time, he refuses to die fully and to give up his relationships with the living. He attempts to make his loved ones die to be reunited with them, or he persecutes the living simply out of envy and spite. Here again, ritual should take care of the problem, but it is often ineffective. A violent death—or one that is assimilated to it, such as death in childbed—has the same effect as a shortened life. Indeed, the two usually go hand in hand. Those who die such deaths become the most dangerous and cruel of all topoyem. The worst are the women who die in childbirth. They turn into powers called muluaqinaem, who seduce men, driving them mad with desire and sometimes castrating them. Also, they attempt to make women in childbed die as they themselves did.

If protecting or helping powers have an ambiguous value, powers that have undergone no transformation at the hands of humans, and have no social relationship with them, are definitely negative. As such, they all fall into the category of kinakinaem, "the evil ones." They are also unambiguously declared manusiassi. This word literally means "nonhuman," but it does not encompass all that is not human, only that which appears, or may appear, as human but is not so in reality or in full. This contrast between human appearance and nonhuman or not fully human in reality is perhaps the trait most generally shared by all occult powers, good and evil alike. Both tamed and wild powers may thus be called manusiassi. But "humanity" is a matter of moral substance, not just of visible form. Thus insofar as the evil powers take on human shape with the purpose of deceiving real humans, of covering their moral nonhumanness with the appearance of physical humanness, they deserve to be defined more than any other power by an expression that denotes the negation of being human.

In contrast, powers that have been brought morally closer to humans by the stable social pact they have with humans may sometimes be described as manusia, "human beings." These usages demonstrate that occult powers are defined by their approximations to an unmarked term that is their paragon: manusia, "humans." Either they are made humanlike by their close approximation to humanity, or they are made nonhuman by their negation of what defines humans, morally and bodily. Occult powers are not so much superhumans as parahumans, conceptual parasites on the unmarked—and thus "normal"—notion of human.[60] This is why, when encountering these powers, Huaulu typically say that they wonder: manusia te' manusiassi? "a human or a nonhuman?" *or* manusia tuniam (pinipiniam) te' kinakinam? "a true (beautiful/good/perfect) human or a bad/false/imperfect/evil one?" And they also say: Hata manusia te' koa? "Does it have a human body [as against an illusory human body] or not?" Indeed, in the anthropocentric and aestheticist thinking of the Huaulu, the possession of a "human body proper" (hata manusia) implies the attributes of "beauty/goodness" (pinipiniam), which are denied those who lack such a body, or those whose body is not limited to the human one (because they can embody animals, vegetals, minerals), or those who mix human and nonhuman traits. Physical ugliness/imperfection (which becomes apparent once one sees through their often beautifully deceptive appearances) is a sign of moral ugliness in the occult powers. The Huaulu are Platonists at heart.

The category of kinakinaem, or, as I prefer to call them, the wild occult powers, is as proliferating and metamorphic as the forest which is their elective home. This makes it difficult, indeed impossible, to stretch this category on the Procrustean bed of classification. Nevertheless a few words about the main kinds of powers it includes are necessary, because they are part of the imagined environment of the Huaulu as much as all other creatures of the forest and will thus continue to haunt the pages of this book.

I have already quoted the topoyem and their most dangerous representative, the muluaqinam. A power that has much in common with the muluaqinam in its mode of operation (seduction as a means of destruction), but a completely different origin, is the lusikinam. While the muluaqinam originates from a woman who died in childbirth, and lives in stagnant pools of water or in streams, the lusikinam is an eagle power that comes from the sky. Both of them, and all topoyem, have shifty and reddish eyes—the signs of the demonic.

The lusikinam, in turn, has much in common with the kaitahu upuam, "the lord of the land," or more exactly of a piece of land and all living forms on it, animals in particular. The kaitahu upuam may appear in human or animal form, and it chases humans either sexually (very much like the lusikinam and the muluaqinam) or in an invisible hunt which reverses the visible hunt of game by men. There are also specific masters of animals which defend them against human preying and which must be propitiated by hunters and fishermen (e.g. Okosopa, the giant shrimp which attacks the women who fish shrimps). Covenants are often established with them, so as to learn the way to obtain some of their animals. Then they become auwetem if they help with river fishing and mutuaulaem if they help with hunting and especially with trapping.

Another kind of wild power includes the atalayem, "the giants." As the kaitahu upuem rule over stretches of the forest, the atalayem lord over the tops of the mountains, inside which they live and accumulate treasures. Being anthropophagous, they prey on humans. They are human in aspect, except that they are immense and have wings to fly with. They sometimes take a fancy to a man and give him headhunting and war[61] magic. Headhunters thus have atalayem as helpers in their expeditions. Somewhat similar to the atalayem are powers called lusiem (gigantic eaglelike beings) and nasinahem. These also prey on humans, but they may seek a covenant with humans they take a fancy to. They then direct these humans to seek human victims for them, so they can eat. In this way, they become the most powerful helpers of headhunters—humans who themselves become wild and partly inhuman in the forest.

A last category of occult powers deserves to be treated apart because of its importance and its peculiarities. It is the sewaem, the familiars of the shamans. They are divided into four main classes (sewa potoem, sewa ninawaniem, sewa pukariem, and sewa laufaha or wahako' [wahakoam]) corresponding to the four kinds of shamanism in which they serve. These sewaem may be viewed as the inverse of the masielem. The latter are witches, that is, humans who take the body of animals to harm other humans—as occult powers, if untamed, do.[62] They also enter the body of humans to devour their entrails invisibly. The sewaem, in contrast, are occult powers, of various but often animal origin, who enter the body of humans to cure and protect them, and thus to chase evil powers, including witches. But a shamanic familiar can fight only itself, that is, what it once was. Thus sewaem are the best illustration of the principle that good powers are the transformation, by superior human agency, of bad ones. Indeed, sewaem may originally have belonged to any of the previously mentioned "evil ones."

For instance, four of the five most common categories of sewa potoem are: topoyem (the ancestral shades derived from originally malevolent dead), kahianaem (the transformed muluaqinaem who help childbirth instead of impeding it), mutuaulaem (the lords of animals, formally antagonists of the hunters, who now help them), and teluem (the crocodile spirits, lords of rivers, who help humans to fish poison in their domains). A fifth category is the kolalem—named and in part modelled after the konane, the northern Moluccan rulers of the states that at different times were influential in Seram (i.e. the states of Ternate, Tidore, Jailolo, Bacan).[63] This category is particularly interesting in its implication that external political powers, actually or potentially antagonistic to the Huaulu, are put in the same general category as the occult powers. They are all "outsiders" who must be tamed and given a positive value relative to Huaulu.

The interchangeability of powers in the outside is in fact a very general tendency in Huaulu. The outside, and thus principally the forest, is metamorphic. Animals, enemies, and occult powers have unstable boundaries and often blend with one another. A "lord of the land," a dead, and the detachable mattiulu, "soul," of a living may all take the body of an animal, and so may an enemy if he is a witch[64] or a powerful shaman. An animal encountered in the forest may thus be just what it looks like, or it may be anything from a dead person to a living enemy. Consequently, the forest is associated with cognitive and moral uncertainty—with the split between appearance and reality, visible and invisible—to an extent that is not experienced, or would ever be tolerated, in the village. Even in this ambiguity the forest is the elective ground of the occult, of hidden powers which escape Huaulu control and surround it menacingly. A constant struggle exists between the Huaulu and them. It has the same qualities as their struggle with animals and the Huaulu's struggle with enemies, and especially the same uncertainty and reversibility. In their relationship to animals, enemies, and "spirits," the Huaulu see themselves as predators and prey, victorious and defeated. Their goal is to be victorious as often and for as long as possible—until they inevitably succumb.

Niniani and Settlement: Equality and Hierarchy

From the relations between the village and the beings that surround and are opposed to it, let us turn to the relations internal to it. To begin with, I should mention that *village* is a gloss of the Huaulu word *niniani.* But the word has additional meanings and connotations. Like the English *village* it refers both to a physical structure and to the society associated with it. But unlike the English word, it implies political and economic (at least with regard to subsistence) autonomy. Thus *niniani* conceptually includes the sole control of a territory and is inseparable from it. Furthermore, not all settlements are considered niniani. A niniani is the embodiment of a political entity, of a people. It must therefore have a number of cult houses in which the rituals that define this group are performed.

The Huaulu themselves claim that only one single niniani should exist at any time in their territory. When, as was the case some years ago, two niniani form, an intolerable state of dissension and potential fission is said to occur. The unity of the Huaulu people must be embodied by the unity of its niniani, where all can congregate for certain rituals which require universal participation, such as the kahua dance. *Niniani* is, in sum, "village" as the ritual and political center of an autonomous people and of its territory. It is closer to our idea of capital than to that of village, really. Maybe it should be called a village-state.

Although many Huaulu live most of their life outside the village—in small shifting settlements or in more permanent ones that are now developing along the northern coast where some have planted coconut palms to make copra—most of them maintain a house there. It is in any case obligatory for each ipa (one of the lineage-like groups that make up Huaulu society) to have a house in the village, where its sacra are stored. The largest settlement not considered a niniani is found at Alakamat, on the north coast, between Besi and Openg, at about 18 kilometers from Sekenima, where the niniani is located.

When I first went to Huaulu in the early seventies only two small Huaulu families lived in Alakamat, owing to a political feud. But in the last 10 years or so, more and more Huaulu have taken up residence in Alakamat, usually for a few months but sometimes for years. None or very few admit that they are permanently settled. Indeed, most of them spend time in Alakamat only because their children have to attend elementary school in either Besi or Openg. This is also a change; when I first lived in Huaulu only a couple of children were attending school. Now about half of the children of school age attend. But sending children to school—an obligation under Indonesian law—costs money. This has forced their guardians to become involved in the coastal cash economy, at least by planting gardens with the purpose of selling or bartering their products. Some have planted coconut palms and clove trees on the sites of these gardens. These slow-growing cash crops, which had begun to give their fruits when I last was in the area in 1988, may eventually keep their owners on the coast beyond the requirements of school attendance.

Some Huaulu are thus subtly and unconsciously becoming converted to a cash economy and are planting their roots in coastal society. The effects are becoming visible in some of the youngsters, who bear certain hideous marks of Ambonization. But the more serious effect is an increasing split between the more conservative inhabitants of the mountain village (that is, the only village), many of whom refuse even to set foot on the coast, let alone to send their children to school, and the coastal ones, who are accused of selling out.

Yet Huaulu solidarity is far from broken. The kahua feast still sees the presence of all the Huaulu population, at least at its climactic moments. And many people who had seemed rooted in Alakamat have

Young girl going to fetch water in bamboo tubes. 1972. (Photo by V. Valeri.)

suddenly decided to return to the mountain for good, usually because of a misfortune imputed to living on the coast. Thus the basic flavor of Huaulu society and belief was hardly changed in the period from 1972 to 1988. Moreover, the very phenomenon represented by Alakamat could be made to fit the traditional Huaulu practice of pulsating residence, with long periods spent outside the village (in the forest or on the coast) to acquire food and more generally to make a livelihood, interspersed with other periods spent in the village, especially when important rituals take place, and also when the rainy season is at its peak. Many Huaulu still do not see that something different from this traditional pattern is taking shape in Alakamat.

As I have argued elsewhere,[65] the pulsating pattern of settlement is hardly to be explained in seasonal terms. Rather, it is one major external manifestation of the conflict between cohesive and divisive forces in Huaulu society. Its ideological counterpart is the unresolved tension, documented by the origin myths, between two images of Huaulu society, each of which may be invoked as an argument in situations of conflict. In one image, the society is an open confederation of lineages or even of households, bound together by rescindable covenants. This image is essentially egalitarian, in that every group is conceived as potentially autonomous, even when it actually is not. Dependency exists thus only as a matter of choice, of agreement: it is made necessary only by the rule of exogamy and is given some duration by the rule of asymmetric alliance.

In the opposite image, a clearly hierarchical one, society is constituted once and for all and thus closed. It includes a fixed number of complementary parts, each with its unique but unequally valued attributes, although there is some disagreement about their relative value. Furthermore, this image emphasizes less the lineages than the larger groupings which encompass them. These groupings are four: Huaulu proper, Allay, Tamatay, and Peinisa. Both lineages and groupings are called ipa in the Huaulu language and are defined as descent groups (that is to say, they are said to be constituted by the descendants of a founding ancestor). For this reason, but especially for convenience's sake, I will call the encompassed units lineages and the encompassing ones clans. The reality, particularly with regard to clans, is vastly more complex, but this complexity will have to be addressed elsewhere. The clan named Huaulu is universally recognized as the dominant one. It is so not only numerically but also conceptually, as is indicated by its title latu, "ruler," and by the fact that it has given its name to the entire society. This fact is a typical manifestation of the hierarchical formula which assimilates the dominant part with the whole. The hierarchical position of the other clans is on the whole determined by their order of arrival in the Huaulu territory after the Huaulu clan got there. But other factors enter into play, and there is intense rivalry for second position between Tamatay and Allay, although only the former can boast a title (matoke) as the Huaulu clan does. As for Peinisa, its inferiority to all others is no less unanimously recognized than Huaulu's superiority.

As this brief characterization of the two images is sufficient to show, they are not totally separate. A certain coefficient of equality creeps into the hierarchical image to make the hierarchical relationship

A member of the Huaulu clan, the dominant group. 1972. (Photo by V. Valeri.)

between Tamatay and Allay a matter of competition. Reciprocally, the egalitarian ethos of the first image is countered by asymmetric alliance which creates, and tends to perpetuate, an inequality between wife-givers and wife-takers. Yet a fundamental difference remains. The inequality created by alliance is purely relative: every wife-taker is inferior to his wife-giver, but he is himself a wife-giver relative to another group. Furthermore, the engagement in affinal exchanges of valuables reconstitutes autonomy, in a different register, over the long term.[66] Thus whatever hierarchy forms through alliance, it is countered by a global tendency to equality, enshrined in an egalitarian image of society. The inequality implied by the hierarchical image, in contrast, is not relative, although it contains at one level an element of uncertainty that translates into a constant competition. But this competition, after all, is not waged to reestablish equality (as in the reciprocal gift exchanges between affines), but rather to establish a clear-cut inequality, to figure out (once and for all) who is first. Unfortunately or perhaps fortunately, nobody ever comes out first, and so the competition goes on forever.

It should also be said that the two principles of inequality—the one based on the mythical order of arrival, the other on asymmetric alliance—may be combined, with ambiguous results. Indeed the relativity of affinal inequality may subtly undermine the absoluteness of myth-based, titular hierarchy, especially when the titular inferior is allowed to become a wife-giver to the titular superior (as Allay is relative to Huaulu). Or reciprocally, the absoluteness of titular hierarchy, especially when the titular superior is also the wife-giver (as Huaulu is relative to Tamatay), may suppress some of the subversive potential of relative inequality. These ambiguities explain the tendency to confine, as much as possible, the directionality of alliance to the level of lineages proper and to neutralize it at the higher level of the clan. In other words, there are usually no oriented affinal relationships between clans; when there are, they are assumed by the dominant lineage(s) in each clan.

Thus it is only the senior lineages of the Huaulu clan that strictly follow the rule of asymmetric alliance with Tamatay, by giving their daughters or sisters to the men of Tamatay's senior lineage. In other words, as I have indicated elsewhere,[67] the senior of one clan marries asymmetrically with the senior of another on behalf of the hierarchical identity of the entire clan, but the marriage of juniors is freer because it does not have hierarchical implications. This creates a de facto, if embryonic and fragile, hierarchy of ranks side by side the hierarchy of clans. One can see how, under the proper conditions, the hierarchy of ranks could erase the hierarchy of clans instead of uneasily coexisting with it. Such conditions have not occurred in Huaulu, so that the unresolved tension between different principles of hierarchy and, more profoundly, between hierarchy and equality, is the fundamental sociological fact about this society. It is a fact on which I had to dwell somewhat, because it is crucial for understanding certain features of Huaulu culture and of its taboo system in particular.

One may ask at this point (and I have often been asked this question) how hierarchical ideas could possibly have developed in such a small and simple society, whose form of production, largely dominated by hunting and foraging, does not seem to allow for the formation of economic surplus. The answer is that hierarchy is precisely an idea, and as such it does not need to be generated spontaneously by hard-core economic facts, with which it is evidently not necessarily related, but can be acquired through the normal process of circulation of ideas. This is to say that no Indonesian society, however simple, can be understood independently of the larger Indonesian world, where hierarchical societies have had for centuries a culturally hegemonic position even in the absence of domination.

Huaulu may be too small to have generated its ideal of hierarchy spontaneously (although it had a larger population until before the smallpox epidemic of 1917 and the influenza pandemic of 1918–19), but it has never subsisted in isolation; it belongs to the much wider world of central Seram, in both its inland and its coastal cultures, and to the even wider world of the central and northern Moluccas, as I have mentioned. Indeed the Moluccan sultans and their Portuguese and Dutch allies and successors play an important role in the imagined past of the Huaulu.

It is also well known that the Moluccas are the Spice Islands and since the sixteenth century have been part of an international trade system which has allowed the people of Seram to obtain prestigious goods such as porcelain plates, gold and silver jewelry, textiles, and so on. It is such ceremonial items, still used in Huaulu and elsewhere for affinal gifts, fines, and other prestations, that provided the wealth necessary to accumulate and deploy for political purposes. Directly or more often indirectly, most Seramese people were able to secure these items. There is no tradition in Huaulu that they ever engaged in spice cultivation and trade. On the contrary, they have a taboo on planting clove trees, part of a more general prohibition against following the coastal mode of life. While some of their eastern neighbors or the Wemale of western Seram have suppressed the memory of the external origin of this wealth and claim that it originated in Seram itself in mythical times, the Huaulu say that their ancestors obtained it from the outside, as affinal gifts or, more frequently, as war booty. Indeed the Huaulu traditions suggest that war was the main avenue for acquiring wealth, so that military prowess was the ultimate source of power, even in this respect. Internal inequality was thus made possible by unequal relations, peaceful (as in marriage) but more often warlike, with external sources of wealth and prestige.

But the role of wealth in the creation of inequality should not be exaggerated. Wealth was more important in the warlike past, when the spice trade was still flourishing, than it is now, when that trade's sources have by and large dried up. Furthermore, even in the past, knowledge was as important as, if not more important than, wealth in the creation of inequality. For one thing, knowledge (mostly of magic) was considered indispensable to wage war successfully; for another, knowledge had and continues to have economic benefits, besides the benefit of prestige.

The upshot of all this is that Huaulu society cannot be understood through a systemic approach that considers it in isolation; in fact, whatever systemic aspect there is to Huaulu society cannot be explained except as the cumulative effect of a long history. The Huaulu case (or, for that matter, the case of any Indonesian society with a documented history) shows the risks of reification inherent in any explanation through "the system."[68] Such explanations see the system as what explains the different phenomena of a society because it generates them. But the fact is that the generativity of the system at any given time presupposes events that it does not generate. And of course, it presupposes the system itself, which is not self-explanatory because it is not self-generating. On the contrary, it can be understood only as the result of a cumulative process, and thus, most unsystemically, through infinite regress. What we call system is in fact a certain order, a certain coherence, a certain predictability in the flowing of causality over any significant duration. This duration of a certain invariance should not be reified into a "something" that endures because it "generates" even what modifies it. As for these invariances or regularities, whether they are explained by logical, ideological, economic, or technological facts should be decided in each particular case.

It remains to be said that to the duality of the images of society—one hierarchical, the other egalitarian—corresponds a duality of power manifestations. On the one hand, there are titles associated with certain functions and prerogatives, reserved to certain lineages as representatives of their clans: the already-mentioned latu and matoke are the main examples. The title of latu belongs to the Huaulu clan as a whole, but its prerogatives are exercised by two officials: the Latunusa, who is the ultimate guardian of traditional law and the priest of every ritual that concerns the entire community, and the kamara,[69] who is concerned with the administration and the prosperity of the people (which he also guarantees through charismatic attributes).

It is possible that the office of kamara was introduced here by the Dutch administration, since in the narrative depiction of the past the Latunusa is complemented by a war leader (kapitane or kapitale), not by the kamara. Furthermore, the title of kapitane was an achieved one, although the members of one particular senior lineage (Issale) of the Huaulu clan were supposed to have a hereditary attitude to fighting that made them the more likely persons to achieve that status. If this hypothesis is correct, then the traditional system of rule combined achievement and hierarchical privilege to some extent.

However, a particularly important office was and still is completely achieved: that of "guardian of the community hall" (makasaka luma potoam), which represents the society as a whole and is the seat of the most important collective ritual, the kahua dance.[70] Each lineage owns a number of community hall names,[71] which entitle it to build one such hall for the entire village at a given moment. In other words, community halls are built by particularly forceful men who are able to obtain the support of the members of their lineage and of all other lineages. Besides the permanent dominance of certain lineages, enshrined in certain offices, there occurs thus the temporary dominance of a particular leader and his lineage. This second type of dominance is obviously related to the egalitarian image of society as a federation of lineages. It is true that the community house can also be built by a latunusa or a matoke but, at least nowadays, only if they are also able to form a consensus as leaders and not just by virtue of their office.

In short, Huaulu society is characterized by the coexistence and tension of hierarchical and egalitarian principles at several levels.

Colonial Connections: Long and Short

Because of the Moluccas' importance in the spice trade, a rich historical documentation exists on them since the early sixteenth century. Archival documents on northern Seram, particularly on the coastal peoples, are also numerous.[72] Huaulu itself is not named in any of them until the end of the nineteenth century, when the Dutch East Indies government began to establish its control over the inland peoples of central Seram, waging a series of wars with the Huaulu and especially with their Nisawele neighbors.[73] But the Dutch presence in the coastal areas of northern Seram was more ancient. The Dutch East India Company (VOC) maintained a small military post in Sawai from the midseventeenth century until 1799, when the company was dissolved and Holland was invaded by the French revolutionary armies.[74] Ruins of the small post still exist in Sawai,[75] and its traces survive in Huaulu histories. The Dutch did not return until 1823–24, after they managed to dislodge a nest of "pirates"[76] who, under the leadership of a certain Raja Jailolo, had sought to reestablish the sultanate of Jailolo (destroyed by Portuguese and Ternatans in 1523) in the area.[77] The strong Galelarese and Tobelorese influx into northern Seram (which still finds an echo in Huaulu traditions and practices) dates back to that time.

Upon their return the Dutch decided to establish a new military (and later administrative) post in Wahai, about 120 kilometers east of Sawai.[78] This site afforded a good harbor and easier access to the interior of the island, where the bulk of the as-yet-unsubmitted population lived. But Wahai also proved an easy target for Huaulu and Nisawele headhunters. The raids, in turn, furnished pretexts for the colonial effort of military, and eventually religious, subjugation. By the early twentieth century the internal population had been brought under control, and many of the villages in the interior had been forcibly moved to the coast, so as to be more easily policed. In 1914 the area was considered sufficiently pacified to be put under civilian rule. The onderafdeeling (administrative district) of Wahai was created. It included all of central Seram north of the tallest chain of mountains and parts of western Seram. After Indonesian independence, it lost its western part (which became the Kecamatan Taniwel) and became the present Kecamatan Seram Utara.

The recorded history of Huaulu is tied up with this administrative entity, in its Dutch and Indonesian avatars. The Huaulu and Nisawele—who were closely related in culture, although enemies—offered the strongest resistance to the Dutch presence. They thus became the principal targets of Dutch military and Christianizing efforts. Christianization was forced upon the Nisawele, because they were the most numerous, were closer to Wahai, and controlled the way to populations farther inland, such as the Selumena and the Manusela. The Huaulu obstinate resistance to Christianization was not treated as seriously by the Dutch, because the Huaulu were a lesser threat, both in number and strategic position.[79] Furthermore they were forcibly moved to a coastal site, Loulehali, to be controlled better.[80] There their population was further diminished by epidemics, particularly by the serious outbreak of smallpox in 1917.[81]

Huaulu was probably given up for doomed by the Dutch; in a census taken soon after that year only 59 Huaulu were recorded (31 men and 28 women).[82] Their number may have been underestimated, because some had managed to escape Dutch notice at the time of their forcible removal from the mountain and continued to live in isolated settlements in the forest. Nevertheless the population losses in 1917, and again in 1918–19 with the influenza pandemic, were traumatic for the Huaulu. Concluding that their ancestral powers were against life on the coast (as they still largely believe, even when they live on it), the Huaulu decided, Dutch or no Dutch, to "run back to Sekenima"—that is, to the inland area where they had been building their villages since, probably, the nineteenth century. There, they rebuilt their village in 1918.[83]

The Dutch were changing their policies at the time, allowing some of the inland people whom they had deported to return to their inland settlements.[84] Once returned to their inland location, the Huaulu were left largely to their own devices and were not further molested.[85] By the time the German ethnologist Roeder visited them in 1937, they seem to have recovered a measure of demographic strength, since their village then was larger than the present one. Soon afterwards, however, a period of constant involvement in war began for them and other inland peoples. First the Japanese occupation (1942–45), then the occupation by the RMS (Republik Meredeka Seram) guerrillas and the Indonesian army fighting them (1950–62)[86] greatly disrupted their life and their reproductive patterns. Women had to be hidden for long periods to avoid being raped by soldiers, and the population declined. Only in the early sixties was the authority of the Indonesian state established in all of northern Seram.

At the time I began to do fieldwork among them in early 1972, they had just built their first village in a long time. But administrative influence was minimal, for a variety of reasons. The district of northern Seram was quite isolated throughout the seventies. Communications with Ambon, the capital of the Moluccas, were minimal and even nonexistent during the western monsoon. That was precisely why I had to walk all the way from the southern coast to reach Huaulu. There were no roads in the entire district. Very few radios existed. The cash economy was underdeveloped, because the population was even smaller than in Dutch times and there were few resources of economic interest. Government officials were usually absent from Wahai, spending much of their time in Ambon. They did not bother to implement government policies of compulsory school attendance and compulsory practice of one of the official religions of the Indonesian state. Huaulu was left alone more than it ever had been much to the satisfaction of the Huaulu themselves.

But when I returned to northern Seram in the period 1985–88, the changes were beginning to be visible. There were still no roads from the coast to Huaulu or anywhere on the northern coast, except near Wahai. But coastal settlements, both of immigrants and mountain people, had multiplied around the coconut plantations that had been forcibly created at government command. Many Huaulu lived at Alakamat, close to the Openg and Besi peoples, who are heavily influenced, respectively, by the Christian and the Islamic variants of the metropolitan Moluccan (one should say Ambonese) culture. Some commercial logging had begun in the coastal areas, and there was talk of imminent large-scale logging inland. Such logging had already begun east of Wahai, where the government was maintaining a migration project, involving the relocation of a large number of landless Javanese peasants and not a few criminal elements. A natural park was created in the mountain areas for purposes of preservation and tourism. But it also seemed an excuse for the destruction of all other forest areas, including much of the Huaulu territory. With cash-cropping, cash had become more abundant. Radios and cassette players had become more numerous in Alakamat, but were still rare, and rarely tolerated, in the mountain village. Some even claimed they were to be considered taboo.

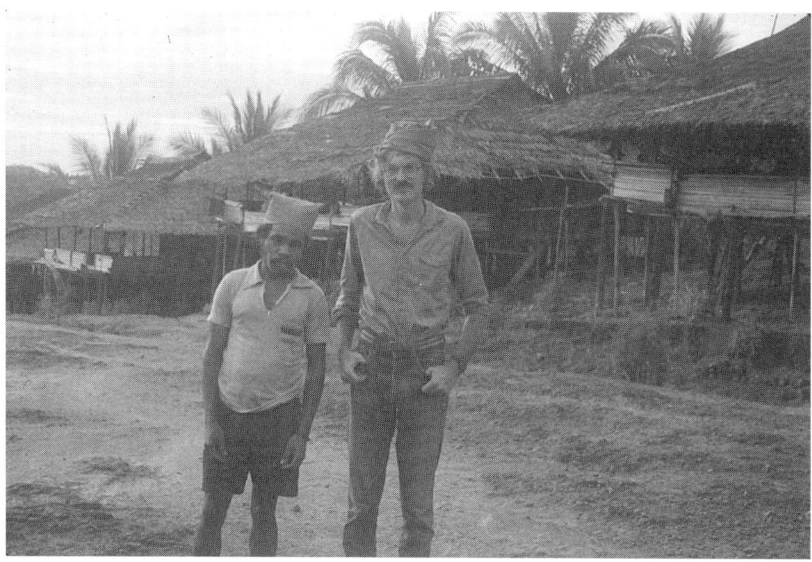

The author standing in the village center with a friend. 1985. (Photo by J. Hoskins.)

The most ominous development was a first step in the implementation of state religious policy. A couple of months before my arrival in 1985, three families of American missionaries, from the notorious New Tribes Mission, had settled in Alakamat. Their corrugated iron–roofed, comfortable bungalows dwarfed the rather miserable-looking coastal houses of the Huaulu. The Huaulu were puzzled by the presence of these rich strangers, who had not revealed their purpose and seemed to spend most of their time snorkeling. Although they had forbidden the Americans to take up residence in the mountain village, the Huaulu seemed inclined to take economic and political advantage of the Americans' presence on the coast, without yielding an inch as far as religion was concerned. The missionaries themselves seemed confident that the daily spectacle of the healthy middle-class life they offered—that is, one heavily oriented toward consumerism—would be sufficient, in the long run, to persuade the Huaulu of the superiority of Christianity or of their own brand of it, one which involved quoting Reagan more than the Bible. In 1988 the missionaries had made no inroads yet and had not even managed to learn the Huaulu language. But they had managed to incur the enmity of local Muslims, who were demanding their removal.

Owing to a variety of historical circumstances, then, the Huaulu escaped forced Christianization and excessive administrative intervention, first from the Dutch colonial power, then from the Indonesian state, at least until the midseventies. Even the developments of the eighties had not managed, up to the time of my departure from the field in 1988, to change much of their practices and ideas, especially in the mountain village. I was myself surprised by this relative conservatism over almost 20 years. Huaulu has remained an exception in Seram[87] and even more so in the national Indonesian context. Although, or perhaps because, it belongs to an area of the world that has had a long experience of external contact and influence, Huaulu has managed to keep a large degree of cultural and even political autonomy. It has been helped by the forest, as well as by its indomitable spirit of resistance and by its cleverness in exploiting the opportunities created by a history made in equal parts of neglect and colonial and postcolonial divide and rule.

The exceptional status that twentieth-century history has created for Huaulu has turned it into something that often gives its culture the support of many changed (but not completely changed) neighbors. The reason is that these neighbors see, or wish to see, in Huaulu their own lost, and often regretted, form of life. Indeed the passing of time increases the sense of similarity over the sense of difference in the mountains of central Seram. Or so it did at the time of my various periods of fieldwork in the seventies and eighties. I myself became convinced that even in the past this whole mountain area dependent on Manusela included a series of variations in a common set of practices and beliefs.[88] So the factual exceptionality of keeping the practices and beliefs of one's version has sometimes been turned into the conceptual exceptionality of representing a whole system for those who held, and want to remember and occasionally practice, their own versions. Huaulu is (or was in the late eighties) both a unique living present and a "representative of a common past." Having figured this in its multiple peripheries, I finally managed to defeat all my resistances and warnings against going to them and concentrated my fieldwork there.

CHAPTER TWO

Taboo in Anthropology

As I gnawed on the roll, I came to a stop once more, this time before a sausage shop. I stared at the sausages hanging and spoke to them silently: "You were once alive, you suffered, but you're beyond your sorrows now. There is no trace of your writhing or suffering anywhere. Is there a memorial tablet somewhere in the cosmos on which it is written that a cow named Kvyatule allowed herself to be milked for eleven years? Then in the twelfth year, when her udder had shrunk, she was led to a slaughterhouse, where a blessing was recited over her and her throat was cut."

I. B. Singer, *The Certificate*

Taboo and Danger

Aquinas' dictum that "God is the author of the evil that punishes, but not of that which defiles"[1] summarizes the Christian view that a radical opposition exists between sin and defilement, and between moral and physical evil, which in turn corresponds to the ontological opposition of God and the world. However much the stains of the body may provide metaphors for those of the soul, a gulf exists between the physical and the metaphysical, a gulf which symbolism can bridge only partly and only to aid minds afflicted by the debility of concreteness.[2] The anthropological reflection on taboo starts with the constatation that such radical dualism as postulated by philosophical Christianity can rarely be found beyond it or beyond similarly minded thought systems.

The "savage," says Frazer, does not distinguish between what pertains to the gods and what pertains to the world, between spiritual and physical evil, between the holy and the unclean or polluted: he confuses them all under a single notion of "danger,"[3] which corresponds to a single, amoral sentiment—fear. Robertson Smith echoes these views, writing that holiness (in the sense of restrictions in the relationship with the divine) and uncleanness (which he defines as "supernatural dangers . . . arising . . . from the presence of formidable spirits which are shunned like infectious disease") are two kinds of taboos around which "in most savage societies no sharp line seems to be drawn."[4] Indeed even in more advanced nations (such as the Hebrews) "the notion of holiness and uncleanness often touch."[5] The reason is that in both cases "certain restrictions" lie on people's use of things "and contact with them, and that the breach of those restrictions involves supernatural dangers. The difference between the two appears, not in their relation to man's ordinary life, but in their relation to the gods."[6] Holy things are not free to man because they pertain to the gods; unclean ones are shunned because they are hateful to the gods. Yet this theocentric perspective, as instantiated by Leviticus and especially Deuteronomy, reformulates a more ancient combination of "religious" and "magical" motivations for taboo—the former predicated on "respect" for the gods, the latter on "fear" of so-called supernatural powers. Moreover, following Frazer, Robertson Smith believes that the magical motivations are the only, or the dominant, ones in the earlier stages of man's evolution.

This view that taboo and the danger of pollution (the latter considered as an automatic reaction from the tabooed object or person) cover the same ground has become commonplace. It is found among the latest theorists as much as among the earliest successors of Frazer and Robertson Smith. For instance, Durkheim writes that a taboo is a prohibition justified by the sacredness of what is prohibited, and this sacredness, in turn, is embodied by "puissances redoutables qui . . . réagissent contre tout ce qui les offense avec une nécessité automatique, tout comme font les forces physiques."[7] Years later, he complicated matters by distinguishing religious and magical "prohibitions" (a term which he now preferred to *taboo*) and by reserving the mundane notion of "danger" to the latter, although he recognized that the notion of pollution could apply to the former as well.[8]

Not long afterwards, Radcliffe-Brown interpreted the food taboos of the Andamanese as expressions of the belief that "food may be a source of danger unless it is approached with circumspection," that is, by respecting certain prohibitions and practicing certain avoidances.[9] Like the later Durkheim, Radcliffe-Brown did not like the term *taboo* because of its local (Polynesian) connotations. He preferred *ritual prohibition.* He also preferred *ritual sanction* or *undesirable change in ritual status* to *pollution.* Nevertheless his definitions of these expressions can be easily retranslated into the plainer language of his forefathers: "A ritual prohibition is a rule of behaviour which is associated with a belief that an infraction will result in an undesirable change in the ritual status of the person who fails to keep that rule. This change of ritual status is conceived in many different ways in different societies, but everywhere there is the idea that it involves the likelihood of some minor or major misfortune which will befall the person concerned."[10]

Radcliffe-Brown's harshest critic, Steiner, goes back to the old terms. After having written that "taboo is an element of all those situations in which attitudes to values are expressed in terms of danger behaviour," Steiner goes on to say that "through contagion [i.e. pollution] there is social participation in danger, and social relations are describable in terms of danger."[11] These definitions reflect a sociological interpretation of taboo, but in connecting taboo, danger, and contagion,

Steiner does not depart from anthropological tradition. This tradition is also followed by a number of contemporary scholars: philosophers (such as Ricoeur), classicists (such as Dodds, Moulinier, Vernant, and Parker), and especially anthropologists (most notably Douglas, whose book on taboo is significantly entitled *Purity and Danger*).[12]

This near uniformity on the basic definition of taboo must raise some suspicion. It is probably made possible by a certain ambiguity or even equivocation in the use of terms. *Taboo* is used interchangeably with *prohibition, avoidance, sign of danger,* and even *obligation.*[13] *Pollution* is treated as equivalent to *contagion, automatic reaction, misfortune, uncleanness, impurity, sacredness, mystical retribution,*[14] and so on. These loose usages are worrisome because, quite obviously, the terms overlap but are by no means equivalent in either intension or extension. Misfortune may not take the form of uncleanness. Contagion may not take the form of a misfortune, which once it has occurred cannot easily be remedied, but the form of a more abstract, and conventionally controlled, disqualification (for instance, one may be barred from entering a temple, but the performance of a special sacrifice on one's behalf removes the disqualification immediately and entirely). The "transgressor" may in fact not be a transgressor at all, since a taboo may merely be the signal of a danger in establishing contact with a thing rather than the imperative proscription of such contact.[15]

At the highest level of generality, we may wish to use the least specific terms possible. But, clearly, not all the terms mentioned are equally good because they are not equally general. *Contagion* may be better than *pollution,* which belongs to an idiom of *dirt* less generally widespread than may be thought. And *automatic reaction* may be even better than *contagion,* because it does not imply indefinite spreading. Neither conveys a sense that the contamination it refers to is different from ordinary, nonsymbolically loaded forms of contamination. But then, are we sure that such a difference is actually recognized or that it is so sharp as to warrant separate terms? After all, the whole field of taboo is characterized by the blending of the physical and the moral. *Any* form of contamination may be interpreted in "moral" terms. No perfect term exists, of course. And the use of one term instead of another (for instance, *signal of danger* instead of *prohibition,* or *mystical retribution* instead of *pollution* or *contamination*) may depend on the interpretive framework adopted, as we shall see shortly. We should at least not forget that these terms are loaded with our own cultural metaphors and that they may not all be appropriate, particularly when we move from abstract generalities to concrete analyses of ethnographic facts. Doing otherwise would mean ignoring the idiomatic differences that exist among and inside the societies we study and using these societies to stuff the same old worn-out potato sack of "primitivism."

Another term that may correspond to rather different phenomena is, of course, *danger.* From Frazer to Ricoeur, *danger* has been attached to a single sentiment—fear or loathing.[16] Even Douglas, as we shall see, connects the danger that motivates taboo with a sort of fear of disorder, of things out of place. But while fear is certainly present, it may not be the only component of the attitude that exists toward things regarded as taboo. Respect may in fact be the primary feeling, while fear may focus on the consequences of not following the taboo—the fear of punishment. Of course the two feelings become commingled, as in "the fear of God," and fear may even become the more important motive in following the taboo. But that is no reason for confusing them.

In sum, *danger* should be used as a convenient label to refer to a variety of motivations for the attitudes of precaution and avoidance that characterize taboos, but its reification into a single property shared by all things taboo needs to be avoided. It is illegitimate to argue, as Frazer and Robertson Smith did, that "savages" do not distinguish between "unclean" and "holy" simply because, by using a single term for both or even by acting in similar ways toward them, they emphasize the relational property which they both share: it is dangerous to approach them. In fact, the quite different reasons that things may be considered dangerous are usually recognized even if they are not given names of their own.[17]

More important, what appears as a case of lack of distinction may in fact be a case of marking, that is, of emphasizing one term of an opposition (the one that requires most care because it is the most dangerous or because it does not belong to the ordinary state of things) over another. Silence does not automatically entail nonexistence: as in music, what is silent may exist by contrast with what is sounded. It is not because one names only the unclean that one knows only the unclean or is unable to differentiate it from the clean. More generally, it is not because one emphasizes the negative—as what is more dangerous—that one does not recognize the existence, or even the primacy, of the positive and of the sentiments and attitudes attached to it. Indeed, it may well be that the emphasis on the negative that finds its expression in taboo is perhaps less a function of a morality based on fear alone than a phenomenon of markedness.[18]

Magic or Abnegation?

If anthropologists seem to agree (perhaps lexically more than conceptually, as we have just seen) on the general definition of *taboo* as something that has to do with the danger of "pollution" or "contamination," they sharply disagree in their interpretations and explanations of the phenomenon. One major, and classical, disagreement concerns the degree to which local statements regarding the reasons for taboos should be taken at their face value. Usually, the reasons anthropologists are given by their informants are highly pragmatic and framed in a seemingly materialistic idiom. There are, they are told, certain incompatibilities in the world. To become involved in them is undesirable because they have destructive effects. I was told by many Huaulu, for instance, that eating crocodile induces skin disease, because the skin of crocodiles resembles that of people with skin disease. Other relations are not so direct, but on the whole the idiom of taboo (or at least of food taboos) is often reminiscent of a homeopathic sort of medicine and more generally of magic. It is this magical aspect that Frazer emphasizes and turns into a general theory of taboo.

"The whole doctrine of taboo, or at all events a large part of it," he writes, "would seem to be only a special application of sympathetic magic, with its two great laws of similarity and contact."[19] If the contact of *x* with *y* will produce *z*, and if the occurrence of *z* is not desired, then one avoids the contact. Taboo, in sum, is negative magic: "Positive magic or sorcery says, 'Do this in order that so and so may happen.' Negative magic or taboo says, 'Do not do this, lest so and so should happen.' The aim of positive magic or sorcery is to produce a desired event; the aim of negative magic or taboo is to avoid an undesirable one. But both consequences, the desirable and the undesirable, are supposed to be brought about in accordance with the laws of similarity and contact."[20] For Frazer, then, taboo has a self-evident pragmatic reason to exist. Its pragmatic efficacy, moreover, is justified by a strong belief in the regularity of the world: "The magician does not doubt that the same causes will always produce the same effects . . . the element of caprice, of chance, and of accident are banished from the course of nature."[21] This faith in the lawlike character of nature, Frazer tells us, is sound; what is unsound is the representation of the causal laws in terms of similarity and contiguity. This representation owes its existence to the uncontrolled projection of the fundamental laws of psychology—that is, the laws of association—onto the world. So the distinctiveness of taboo, like that of all magic, lies for Frazer in its falsity: "If the supposed evil necessarily followed a breach of taboo, the taboo would not be a taboo but a precept of morality or common sense."[22]

There are some obvious problems with this dissolution of taboo into magic and into the laws of the association of ideas. First of all, even if we admit Frazer's view that all there is to taboo is a misapplication of the laws of association, is this misapplication to be explained exclusively by ignorance or, as a revised form of Frazerism[23] would have it, by the absence of a scientific ideology, that is, of norms for controlling and testing associations among phenomena? Such a claim rests on a very intellectualist view of taboo—as merely the application of a "theory." But the belief in analogic relationships among certain phenomena may be based on more than cognitive deficiencies and may even be largely independent of them. It may also be motivated by emotional processes. Emotions and desires travel easily along the paths of analogy and contiguity. This point was made by Freud and Malinowski, among others, although it long predates them, since we already find it in Spinoza and Hume. Thought, in elaborating causal connections from analogic or contiguous ones, may be guided by desire rather than guiding it, contrary to what is implied by Frazer.

In any event, Frazer's theory should imply that taboo covers all phenomena to which the laws of association are mistakenly applied. And yet this is clearly not the case. Typically, and cross-culturally, taboo has certain elective affinities. It seems to concern preponderantly the body in its exchanges with other bodies (through eating, reproducing, bleeding, excreting, decomposing) and to define certain basic social rules involved in those bodily exchanges or symbolized by them (for instance, the taboos on murder and incest, both of which are usually symbolized by a polluting flow of blood). Taboo also seems to be involved in the avoidance of sacrilege, that is, of improper relations with divinities and their appurtenances. Frazer's "technological" and "intellectualist" theory of taboo does not in the least explain these elective affinities. It just takes them for granted. For instance, it assumes as a matter of course that the important place of bodily phenomena in taboo results from a universal interest in health. But is the propensity of taboo to cluster around the body to be explained only by this interest? Is it not the case, rather, that the body and its processes have symbolic values attached to them and that, through them, the interest in health is turned into a springboard for other interests, of a moral and social nature? Does the body stand for itself in a self-evident, commonsensical way?

We have come to the crucial issue. That taboo belongs to the same mental universe as magic—because both are characterized by associations through analogy and contiguity (although the specific tropes involved are much more complex than appears from Frazer's analysis)—does not mean that taboo is to be explained just as a form of magic, that it exists only to satisfy certain pragmatic concerns. That this is not the only or even the principal reason it exists becomes apparent as soon as we go beyond Frazer's generalities and attempt to identify the particular associative chains that account for a particular taboo. Associations involve more than two terms and their ostensible physical properties—they involve the terms' meanings. To explain why the spilling of the blood of a certain person in a certain context is "polluting" and thus tabooed, we must take into account all the significations of blood, of the causes of its flowing out of the body, of the persons and places involved. In sum, we shall have to consider the association of a substance (blood) and of a person (the spiller of blood) in the context of a whole complex of ideas and practices. And among these we shall find much more than the pragmatic concerns of abstract individuals. We shall find moral ideas about legitimate and illegitimate killing; we shall find a preoccupation with the intangibility of certain social relations; and so on.

Our view of the motivations of the taboo may thus have to go in a direction opposite Frazer's. It will seem to us that the taboo on spilling blood is to be explained not by a mistaken application of the law of contiguity, resulting in the belief that contact with blood is polluting, but by the fact that the flowing of this liquid indexes the violation of a social rule—not to kill—and points inexorably to its transgressor. The empirical fact that a murderer is often splattered with the blood of the person he has killed is the ground for a symbolic generalization—a sign of the state of unpunished murder. The moral concern—the prohibition of killing—is primary. The polluting character of blood is its accessory. It is a mistake to call it a mistake, then. It is a case of symbolic, not magical, thinking. But of course symbolism, to become sufficiently persuasive, had to become literal and material enough to elicit a real concern for one's bodily well-being. Hence the pragmatic dimension of the taboo on spilling blood. It is a derivative dimension, however. To explain it by a magically induced concern with not becoming polluted would be to confuse the individual motivations for following a rule with the cause of the rule as such.

One can also point out that even when taboo is primarily concerned with bringing about pragmatic effects it may do so less through magical than through moral devices. For instance, among many hunting peoples (including the Huaulu) it is taboo for the hunter to eat the meat of the animal he has killed himself. Otherwise the supply of meat is believed to come to an end. The efficacy of the taboo in this case cannot be explained by sympathetic magic. Rather, it is explained by a logic of exchange. By giving up something (by not eating his own meat out of respect for the animal), the hunter receives something else (an abundant supply of meat to exchange with others). Analogously it is often the case that "chastity is the starting-point of magic."[24] Taboo, in sum, may be more than avoidance: it may be a minimal form of sacrifice. This example shows that there is not necessarily a conflict between the moral and pragmatic aspects of taboo.[25]

A symbolic and sociological approach to taboo was first developed by Durkheim. His basic argument is that taboo is not a kind of technique but a kind of law. It is a religious prohibition, namely a prohibition justified by a power (which Durkheim calls "sacredness") intrinsic to what is prohibited. Durkheim's argument is both functional and symbolic. Certain rules (such as the incest prohibition) are too fundamental to be enforced by human agency or by human agency alone.

They must be associated with forces that are as infallible and as unchallengeable as physical forces.[26] But these forces, says Durkheim, derive from society itself and in fact symbolize it. Their force is ultimately the force of society legislating over itself or, rather, over its members.

For instance, the force that motivates and sanctions the incest prohibition is the sacredness of the clan's blood. This blood represents the life of the clan and is therefore imbued with the respect that its members feel for it. The respect is extended to the women of the clan, who carry its blood and thus its life, and it makes sexual relations with them out of the question.[27] Hence these women must be given away; one must marry exogamously relative to the clan.[28] The same sacralization (i.e. through institutionalized respect) explains why it is prohibited to shed the blood of a member of one's own clan. Analogously, the blood that flows out of women at menstruation and childbirth must be avoided.[29]

Respect thus produces sacredness. But the power that respect attributes to the clan also includes the ability to defend itself, to react against those who defy it. The blood that represents this power can thus turn against those who approach it and "pollute" them.[30] Fear mingles with respect. The resulting ambivalence is objectified, that is, transferred to the sacred itself. Hence the confusion of the holy and the unclean noted by Frazer and Robertson Smith. Menstrual blood is an object of both respect and horror because it is sacred.[31]

Symbolism thus helps explain sacredness. It also explains the contagiousness of the sacred. Durkheim views it as the reinforcement (matching the greater force of the sacred itself) of a common psychological property: the tendency to find oneself again in all objects with which one has been associated: "Nous mettons quelque chose de nous-mêmes partout où nous passons: l'endroit où nous avons posé le pied, où nous avons mis la main, garde comme une partie de notre substance, qui se disperse ainsi sans pourtant s'appauvrir. Il en est du divin comme du reste. Il se répand dans tout ce qui l'approche; il est même doué d'une contagiosité supérieure à celle des propriétés purement humaines, parce qu'il a une bien plus grande puissance d'action."[32] In other words, the idea of contagiousness is to be explained as a result of the arbitrariness of symbolism—an arbitrariness or even an instability which, as Durkheim will explain better later,[33] increases with the intensity of the emotional state in which the subject finds itself. Religious emotions, being extremely intense, must not be allowed to spread too far and wide, hence the necessity of taboos, of rules of separation of the primary objects of religious emotion (i.e. the sacred) from all other objects, that is, from the "profane."

This view of contagion as spreading arbitrarily, by virtue of mere contact and independently of the properties of the things that come in contact with one another, is quite unsatisfactory. It throws away even that minimum of constraints inherent in Frazer's thesis that contagion follows the paths traced by the laws of association of ideas. Durkheim's view of contagion as totally unstructured and unselective is not borne out by ethnographic reality. Contagion does not go without a minimum (and often a maximum) of classification, as we shall see.

In *Les formes élémentaires de la vie religieuse,* Durkheim generalizes the explanation given for the incest taboo in 1896. Just as this taboo enforces—through separation—respect for the sacredness of the clan's blood, so all other religious prohibitions are motivated (and at the same time enforced) by some sacred power. The purpose of religious interdictions or taboos is to keep the sacred rigorously separated from its opposite, the profane.[34] The profane is not free from prohibitions, though. Only, these have nothing in common with the prohibitions of religion. They are, rather, the rules of Frazer's "negative magic," for which Durkheim now makes room. While religious prohibitions are "categorical imperatives," linked to the highly moral idea of sin, "magical prohibitions" are "des maximes utilitaires, première forme des interdits hygiéniques et médicaux."[35] They are linked to the notion of danger, which involves judgments of appropriateness or inappropriateness[36] of contact, not moral evaluations. The field of taboo is thus cut across by an extremely rigorous opposition of sacred and profane, to which corresponds an equally rigorous opposition of religion and magic.[37] For in Durkheim's view magic is a kind of individualistic and utilitarian appropriation of the forces and qualities of religion.

But Durkheim's separation of taboo into two sharply differentiated, indeed antithetical, classes is highly artificial. The fact is that a majority of taboos cut across the boundary that he traces. Respect and fear, as he himself had indicated in his earlier essay, are not so easily disentangled from one another. What he calls "magical prohibitions" have moral components; and, vice versa, what he calls "religious prohibitions" have magical aspects, not to speak of a component of appropriateness and inappropriateness. "Religion" is not all categorical imperatives, just as "magic" is not all pragmatic individualism. In fact, the very usefulness of a contrast between magic and religion is doubtful in a society like Huaulu or even in the Australian societies discussed by Durkheim.

The artificiality of the opposition of religious and magical prohibitions is aggravated by the almost exclusive reduction of the former to the avoidance of sacrilege, that is, of the mixing of sacred and profane.[38] Durkheim must, of course, recognize that there are prohibitions which derive from the incompatibilities that exist among different kinds of sacred beings (and which are therefore closer to the "magical" taboos, one must presume), but he dismisses them as unimportant and underdeveloped.[39] Also, by reducing all taboos, magical and religious, to prohibitions, Durkheim unduly homogenizes them. Even by his own account, it seems difficult to accept that magical taboos are anything but signals of inappropriate conjunctions, rather than prohibitions. One is not bound to follow them. There is, in sum, a certain conflict between the general claim that "danger" equals reified prohibition and the view that magical taboos belong to the realm of pragmatic recipes.

Durkheim's near reduction of religious prohibitions to the normative separation of sacred and profane is a consequence of his theory that the sacred is the social in symbolic (i.e. reified) form. The preservation of the integrity of the sacred, he argues, is the preservation of the integrity of society. But the latter is possible only if its individual members are prepared to sacrifice their "natural appetites"[40] constantly to the common good. The first and most fundamental form of social practice is thus renunciation, with the acceptance of suffering that goes with it. Religious prohibitions, with their avowed end of reproducing the sacred in its separation from the profane, are the symbolic coat taken by this "ascetic"[41] imperative which survives all changes in belief, because "il fait partie intégrante de toute culture humaine."[42] All positive forms of religious cult presuppose this "negative" form and are made possible by it.[43]

Durkheim's point that "religious interests are nothing but the symbolic form of social and moral interests"[44] and its corollary, that ritual practices are nothing but the symbolic form taken by the devices for reproducing those interests, are taken up again by Radcliffe-Brown. But not without some reformation: both the sacred and its opposition to the profane are consigned to the dustbin of anthropology's history. Radcliffe-Brown uses instead the more neutral, but also vaguer, notion of "ritual value," which dissolves the contrast of religion and magic. In his essay on taboo, the definitions of *ritual value* and more generally of *ritual* turn out to be rather tautological. He writes: "Anything . . . which is the object of a ritual avoidance or taboo can be said to have ritual value."[45] One could as well say that anything that is hated has hate value.

To make any sense of ritual value, we need to know what ritual is in the first place. But Radcliffe-Brown defines ritual—or its "primary basis"—as "the attribution of ritual value": "The primary basis of ritual . . . is the attribution of ritual value to objects and occasions which are either themselves objects of important common interests linking together the persons of a community or are symbolically representative of such objects."[46] The circularity is total. We still do not know what ritual value is or what ritual is, except that they are in some way connected with important social interests. This is indeed a prudent form of

Durkheimism; perhaps it could be called Durkheimism with an English face. To find a more satisfactory definition of ritual and of why certain objects acquire ritual value, we must turn to an older work of Radcliffe-Brown's: *The Andaman Islanders.* There a "rite or ceremony" is said to be:

> an action required by custom, the performance of which on appropriate occasions serves to keep alive in the mind of the individual a certain system of sentiments necessary for the regulation of conduct in conformity to the needs of the society. By it the individual is made to feel (or to act as though he felt) that his life is one of continually repeated dangers from which he can only be preserved by conforming to the customs of the society as they have been handed down by tradition. He is made to feel that the eating of food is not merely the satisfaction of an animal appetite, but an act of communion, that the food itself is something "sacred" (if we may use the word in the sense of the original Latin "sacer").[47]

The argument is more thoroughly Durkheimian here, down to the use of the term *sacred* (although its Latin sense is emphasized). Ritual is a kind of customary action defined by its function, which is to create in the individual a habit of dependence on the society. The primary form of social control is the manipulation of sentiments. The most powerful sentiment is fear, so it is no wonder that the category of the dangerous has such prominence in ritual. Indeed the minimal form of ritual is taboo, that is, the avoidance of the socially dangerous.

This particular line of functionalist reasoning is developed in the essay "Taboo," where Radcliffe-Brown argues that all social rules must have sanctions or reasons. These may be "moral" or "legal" or "ritual." So ritual is like morality and law in that it consists of rules, but differs from them in the matter of sanctions. In ritual, the sanctions, in their "simplest form" at least, consist of misfortunes, of physical events.[48] In essence, Radcliffe-Brown's point is anti-Frazerian in the extreme, as he himself notes.[49] The mundane goal of avoiding misfortune by avoiding certain contacts or other actions should not be taken at its face value. The connection between the two events is not causal, and the meaning of the action is not technical.[50] Rather the connection is symbolic and the action is moral.

For instance, the Australian aborigines believe that if they talk to their mothers-in-law, their hair will turn prematurely gray.[51] Frazer would interpret this connection in causal terms. Being older than their sons-in-law, mothers-in-law have gray hair; thus if you stay in too close contact with them, you turn gray-haired too. Contact is enough to produce contamination because of the principle of homeopathy—a false notion of causality. By this account, however, anybody who comes in contact with gray-haired women should get gray hair. In reality, only sons-in-law do. This indicates that the rule of avoidance between mother-in-law and son-in-law is the primary fact. Mothers-in-law are to be avoided, because avoidance is a conventional expression of respect. A natural fact (gray hair) with some symbolic connection with what is to be avoided (the mother-in-law), and with what is sufficiently undesirable to function as a deterrent, is picked up to stand for the transgression of the rule. The rule becomes ritual, it seems, when it disappears in its symbol, when the symbol becomes completely objectified (to such an extent that the native view may provide grist for the mill of a Frazerian interpretation). People act morally, not because they follow rules for their own sake, but because they are afraid of certain putative consequences of not following them: premature senescence, high fevers, leprosy, or whatever. In the same vein, many people under the rule of law obey it because they are afraid of punishment and see no other reason for lawful behavior.

This is, somewhat embellished and worked out more completely, Radcliffe-Brown's argument about "ritual avoidances" or taboos. It can certainly be accepted as the best account of many taboos or even of the major aspect of most taboos. But it is as reductionist as the Frazerian argument it attempts to displace. For it leaves out one major fact: the reification of rules results in a world of substances with sympathies and antipathies, compatibilities and incompatibilities, which acquire a life of their own. In other words, the idea of contagion may indeed derive from the reification of the idea of sanction, but once it exists, it may become relatively independent of its origins. By extension and generalization, it may end up working in a Frazerian, amoral, way. The similarity of one reified sanction to other things that are not sanctions, that do not symbolize anything moral or social, may be sufficient ground for annexing them to the realm of taboo. They are to be avoided too, but no direct connection exists between these avoidances and the rule whose sanction originally attracted them into that realm. In sum, a "symbolic" interpretation and a "magical" interpretation of taboo are not necessarily in contradiction. On the contrary, a certain coefficient of magical thinking is the necessary correlate of the reification of moral rules.

But magic or no magic, it is clear that Radcliffe-Brown seriously underplays the logical and cosmological aspects of taboo. To reduce the notion of danger to that of the socially valuable, without the intermediation of concrete cultural concepts and arguments about the objects that are tabooed and their relations with other objects and with human subjects, results in accounts that are both extremely contrived and indeterminate. The inadequacy of Radcliffe-Brown's approach is shown by his own analysis of Andamanese food taboos. It does not allow one to predict adequately which species are going to be tabooed or to motivate their dangerousness adequately.

Radcliffe-Brown notes to begin with that for the Andamanese "the eating of food is dangerous"[52] and thus a focus of taboos. His explanation for this generic dangerousness of food is that eating furnishes the most intense and primordial experience of the moral power of society over the individual.[53] Eating is, of course, the most important act in human life. But it is also the one for which one depends most on others and for which this dependency is experienced earliest—in the child's relationship with its parents. Indeed Radcliffe-Brown argues that this first experience of dependency colors all subsequent ones. Food, being thus imbued with the power of society over the individual, has an eminent social value.[54] This great social value implies an ambivalent attitude on the part of the individual, however. On the one hand, what one obtains by submitting to the social will and its rules is gratifying. On the other, it evokes frustration of individual desires, since obtaining those good things hangs on the fulfillment of certain burdensome obligations. Food is thus dangerous because it is a good that has a price and can always be lost if one does not pay that price. Its dangerousness, one may say, stems from the debt that we all owe to society.

As a general explanation of why food is so imbued with moral values and ambiguities, this argument is acceptable. The problem is that it reduces the symbolic value of food to a single dimension: its "social value." As a result, the concrete objects that serve as food are differentiated only quantitatively, by the degree to which they all symbolize this social value.[55] But objects are related to one another and to the human subjects who consume them through a complex logic of qualitative differences and identities, not just through quantity. "Society" exists only in these complex relations, which involve cognition and classification and ideas about forces and agencies, not as a disembodied abstract value that is symbolized in different degrees by concrete objects. The relationship of the abstract and the concrete is not to be conceived in Radcliffe-Brown's Durkheimian way. Society is the notion of the categorical dependence of the self on the other, together with all its conditions and results. But this whole complex does not come as an amorphous experience of moral power. Rather, it is experienced as the sense of an order, underlying the interrelationship of concrete objects of experience, human and (insofar as it involves human relationships) nothuman, and inseparable from them.

Radcliffe-Brown's propensity for reducing the question of difference to a quantitative one of intensity is demonstrated by his explanation of the fact that "not all foods are equally dangerous"[56] in the Andamans. He claims that the rough scale of dangerousness which he produces is explained by two principles: "those foods that are difficult or dangerous to procure are considered more dangerous than others"; "the foods that are most prized are regarded as being more dangerous than those that are less prized."[57] Thus the dugong, the most difficult to obtain and the most prized, is also the most dangerous. The fat of animals is a delicacy and is therefore considered dangerous.

But the two principles are too approximative and hardly explain the ranking. They explain even less the inclusion or exclusion of certain items in the list, because these are determined by categorical, not merely quantitative, variations. For instance, it is not stated that the livers of sharks, stingrays, and *Plotosus* are delicacies like fat; yet they are included among the dangerous foods. This cannot be just because they come from animals that are dangerous and difficult to obtain; otherwise all their meat would be equally dangerous. Conversely, it cannot be the value of liver in general that explains its inclusion in this case; otherwise, the liver of all animals would be dangerous. To explain why the liver is singled out in these three animals, we would need to know more about their larger signification, as well as that of the liver as an organ.

One may well ask, for instance: Are fat and liver the foci of taboo because they are good to eat? Or is it because they represent the life of the animal to a higher degree than its flesh, and it is the transformation of the living animal into meat that constitutes the real danger addressed by taboo? The fact that all taboo foods are of animal origin, with the exception of two vegetables (yams and *Artocarpus*), furnishes a further indication that this transformation, rather than mere social value, is indeed the case. The vegetable exception may find its explanation in Leach's reinterpretation of Andamanese cosmology, where he shows that, for reasons that need not detain us here, vegetables are taboo only because of their association with interstitial times in the seasonal cycle, whereas animal foods are taboo at all times to some extent but more particularly so during transitions of the life-cycle or in cases of murder, sickness, and so on.[58] In any case, it is doubtful that Radcliffe-Brown's own criteria explain the inclusion of those two vegetables in the list of taboo foods. They are not dangerous to obtain like large and resisting animals (or like honey, an animal product that is also taboo and is protected by the bees), and they are not particularly good to eat. Indeed they are eaten mostly during the season of famine and are thus probably associated with scarcity.[59]

It seems probable, in sum, that much more is involved than a mere two-dimensional, utilitarian (how good is it? how difficult is it to get?) classification.[60] In particular, what seems involved here is an idea that is rather typical of hunting peoples, and one which we shall find in Huaulu too. It is the idea that animals, particularly the larger and more anthropomorphic ones that are at the top of the taboo list (dugongs, pigs, turtles, monitor lizards, civet cats), share many of the characters of agency and personhood with humans. This makes them moral subjects and not mere utilitarian objects. The danger of eating them consists then in the conflict between their utilitarian use and their moral status. The living animal remains attached to the meat and attempts to exact a revenge. So if these animals represent the overwhelming moral power of society over its members, it is in a very different sense from the one recognized by Radcliffe-Brown. The society in question does not quite stop at the physical boundary of human and animal. Humans and animals, especially humanlike animals, are part of the same ultimate moral universe—both of them as subjects, not the ones as subjects and the others as objects.

At least two major facts show that this line of interpretation is justified. The first is that the five animals (wild pig, turtle, dugong, monitor lizard, and civet) that are the strongest foci of taboo have a human origin in Andamanese mythology. Pigs and turtles are transformed humans, and the dugong originates from a pig roasted by a man.[61] The monitor lizard and civet are the two most important of primeval beings that represent the coincidence of human and animal, since they bear animal names but have human attributes.[62] The second major fact that confirms my interpretation is that the eating of the animals listed by Radcliffe-Brown, in particular the five most important ones, is said to be dangerous because it gives the eater the body odor of the animal he eats.[63] In this way the eater becomes liable to be "hunted" by dangerous spirits, as if he were the animal.[64] This belief indicates that the living animal is still evoked by its flesh, even some time after it has been eaten. The belief may also betray the fear of a revenge by the animals (in the form of spirits?) if they can recognize their own odor in the body of a human eater. A moral law of reciprocity between human and animal may be expressed here: to eat means to be eaten. So one must avoid detection from the avenging spirits when one eats.[65] To this purpose, the body is painted with "clay" (odu).[66] The interesting fact is that the patterns of these paintings are evocative of the animal eaten.[67] Moreover, turtle-eating is accompanied by a dance which imitates the movements of the turtle in the water.[68] Radcliffe-Brown himself recognizes that these practices index "solidarity with the species."[69] But he misses the reason for this, especially why one manifestation of this solidarity (imitating the *living* animal on one's body or with one's body) must obliterate another one (smelling like the meat of the *dead* animal). The reason should be clear in my interpretive framework: those who are guilty of reducing the animal to meat can erase the stink of animal death that threatens them with death in return only by imaginatively and symbolically reconstituting the living animal. The identification with the living animal, in sum, is made in order to overwhelm the identification with the dead one. This also explains a belief that seems otherwise rather paradoxical, namely that the bones of killed animals are, contrary to their flesh, not dangerous but protective.[70] Radcliffe-Brown explains this belief with the same generic principle of ambivalence: things that have social value are dangerous if used improperly, beneficial if used properly. The explanation ignores the evidence that the dangerousness of eating living animals precedes the regulations that create a proper or improper use and in fact is what motivates these regulations in the first place. Eating is *always* dangerous, but the danger can be neutralized by a ritual transformation. At the end of this process of transformation, what is left of it—and left permanently—that is, the bones of the animal, represents danger fully neutralized and the highest testimonial to the human power to control the forces that threaten human existence. There is, thus, no mere ambiguity between the beneficent and maleficent aspects of food, but a profound asymmetry. This asymmetry is the whole point of the ritualized eating of animals and of the taboos that accompany and punctuate it in the Andamans.[71]

Repression or Classification?

The preceding discussion should have shown that whether taboo is magic or morality, or both, it cannot be explained without reference to the cosmological ideas and the classification of things that exist in particular societies. Realizing this fact has prompted a number of anthropologists to develop a "classificatory" theory of taboo. But before I turn to some variants of this theory, I must discuss Freud's version of a view which is also found in Durkheim and Radcliffe-Brown. This is the view that taboo, being essentially proscription, is the expression of a renunciatory or repressive form of morality. The two issues, that of classification and that of renunciation/repression, will prove to be closely intertwined.

Freud attempts to use his theory of the unconscious to account for the two aspects of taboo to which his predecessors attracted attention: ambivalence and contagion. A taboo, he says, is a prohibition against powerful "longings." These are repressed but not suppressed: they continue to operate unconsciously. Hence the ambivalence attributed to the object of the prohibition is in reality an ambivalence of the subject. One is afraid of violating the prohibition, and yet one desires to violate it. But this ambivalence remains unconscious and is apparent only in a reified form—as a combination of attractiveness and loathsomeness in the object. As for the contagious power attributed to the tabooed object, it has its source in the unconscious ability to camouflage the object of desire through displacement, that is, symbolic substitutions.[72] Moreover, the fear of contagion from persons who have violated a taboo is in reality the fear of falling prey to the temptation to do the same; it is the contagiousness of bad example. Finally, "the fact that the violation of a taboo can be atoned for by a renunciation shows that renunciation lies at the basis of obedience to taboo."[73]

Some similarities between Freud and Durkheim are obvious. Both identify taboo with renunciation; both view contagiousness as symbolic displacement. Moreover, both view the ambivalence of what is tabooed as the reification of an ambivalent attitude toward it. But their interpretations of the reasons for this ambivalence are different. For Durkheim (and Radcliffe-Brown) the ambivalence stems from the overwhelming power of society over the individual's consciousness. Society is both crushing and exalting; it curbs the individual even as it multiplies his power. Freud, in contrast, links the ambivalence more directly with the coexistence of desire and renunciation, which, in his view, is the essence of taboo. It is not that a reified society has an ambivalent status in the individual consciousness, but that desire and the law that limits and molds it coexist at two different levels; the one is repressed in the unconscious, the other is foregrounded in consciousness. Desire is always rebellious to the law even when it is curbed by it. Both Durkheim and Freud, in sum, locate the ambivalence in a process of individual consciousness, but the process and the tension that defines it are defined differently. It is worth stressing, however, that at bottom Durkheim's theory is no less psychologistic than Freud's.

Freud's view of taboo as a renunciation that is accepted not so much voluntarily as through the process of repression, whereby the subject acquires to some extent a loathing for what he or she in fact desires, runs into certain difficulties with the evidence. The first difficulty is one it shares with all other theories which postulate that taboo is exclusively a form of morality. Indeed, in Freud's view, taboo is the first form of conscience, which he defines as "the internal perception of the rejection of a particular wish operating within us."[74] I do not need to repeat what I have already said about the impossibility of identifying all taboos and everything about taboo with moral rules. What has to be stressed here is that the attitude to taboos often seems remarkably free of that "fearful sense of guilt" which Freud thinks is inherent to taboo because of its moral character. On the contrary, the objectification of the prohibition, its reduction to a danger in its object—a danger which is therefore incurred whether one acts voluntarily or not—makes for deresponsibilization. Moreover, we shall see that, at least in the Huaulu case, transgression is usually not conscious and is discovered only *ex post facto,* through the interpretation of misfortune. The violation of a taboo is seen more as an involuntary misstep than as a willful sin or a conscious lapse. It therefore involves very little sense of guilt and certainly not much of a "conscience." This is all the truer when no particular desire is felt to exist, contrary to Freud's hypothesis, for the object of the taboo.

The second major difficulty of Freud's theory is precisely his postulate that taboo must always be understood as what counters a positive desire for the thing tabooed. For those who, like Freud, identify taboo with prohibition in the strict sense, the presence of such desire must be a matter of course. What is the point of forbidding something if it is not desired? But then one is also forced to assume that when no desire for what is tabooed can be detected, the taboo cannot be a prohibition to begin with. Freud's way out of this is, of course, to assume that desire is present, only it is not immediately recognizable. It has become unrecognizable in the process of its displacement, which coincides with its repression. Behind the ostensible object of taboo, one must therefore seek its real object, and there one finds desire. Freud's escape from the difficulty is thus to resort to the same "argument by symbolism" used by Durkheim and Radcliffe-Brown to explain the discrepancy between native consciousness and learned interpretation.[75]

But there is a twofold problem with his use of the argument in the case of taboo. On the one hand, some of the most "repressive" taboos do not erase the consciousness of the desire for what is forbidden—quite the contrary. Thus, in Huaulu, it is taboo to have sexual intercourse with a classificatory sibling, but the desire for having it is often quite conscious and not infrequently acted out. What makes this regulation a taboo is not that the desire for transgression is unconscious, but that the satisfaction of this desire is believed to contain its own "curative" poison, its immanent sanction.

On the other hand, it is extremely hard to find any trace of desire, hidden or otherwise, in a large number of taboos. For instance, in Huaulu it is taboo to let certain species of frogs jump into a house. The reason is that such an event imperils the life of those who inhabit the house, owing to certain incompatibilities between those species of frogs and the house. Were we to explain this taboo in the Freudian way, we should have to assume that the taboo counters a strong desire for the frog to enter the house and to bring havoc there. A sign of this desire should be an ambivalent attitude to the frog or, rather, to its presence in the house. Yet I can find no trace of such ambivalence. The frog's presence is simply loathed, and the Huaulu belief in the incompatibility of house and frog, or rather of what they represent (a human order vs. an antihuman disorder), is a sufficient explanation for the taboo. In sum, not all taboos are to be explained as the repression of a desire, nor are all desires repressed by a taboo unconscious.

Freud's theory, then, cannot be applied to all taboos—far from it. But the linkage of taboo and ambivalence that this theory stresses is quite real in many cases. However, Freud's attempt to reduce that ambivalence to a spontaneous emotional reaction that arises in the face of prohibitions of desired objects should be rejected, because this ambivalence—along with all that gives shape to the desires involved in it—preexists the subject, is socially produced, and must be learned. But again it should also be recognized that desire and ambivalence and other emotional formations associated with taboos do not have merely a cultural existence. One learns them, but one is also deeply responsive to what one learns. Or rather: one is not as responsive to all one has to learn, and this differential response is not without consequences for what continues to exist as something to be learned.

At one time, in one place, for some people, certain cultural conventions make more sense than others. The part of the subject, and even of what is rebellious to cultural constructions in his or her experience, is not without importance in social and cultural reproduction. The spontaneous reproduction of certain formations is not so easily separated from its programmed reproduction. Social and cultural reproduction, as I have argued elsewhere,[76] works by taken-for-granted but noninstitutionalized processes as much as by institutionalized ones. Furthermore, Durkheim's separation of collective psychology and individual psychology is unwarranted—and contradicted even by his own explanation of the sacred, as we have seen. There are no two kinds of mental processes, only ideas that are more or less shared, more or less institutionalized or even institutionalizable. The subject and his or her reactions should therefore not be seen as purely passive and shapeless—a soft wax on which the social unproblematically imprints itself.[77]

Two anthropologists, E. Leach and M. Douglas, have contributed more than any others to the classificatory theory of taboo. I begin with Leach, because his work makes the continuities between this theory and earlier approaches, in particular that of Radcliffe-Brown, clearer. The first thing to remark about what Leach has called "Leach's theory of taboo" is that it considerably widens the notion of taboo to include any kind of "prohibition, explicit and implicit, conscious and unconscious."[78] This allows him to treat in the same analytic framework phenomena like aversion, disgust, judgments of inedibility or unmarriageability (due to danger or to a sense of propriety), and formal prohibitions—in sum, the whole spectrum of socially shared avoidances. Such avoidances are in turn viewed as symptomatic of the general classificatory status of their objects. Leach's extremely encompassing definition of taboo is useful insofar as it allows us to recognize that social regulation shades from the formally prohibited to the merely habitual, from the telling of a commandment to the instillation of a dislike.

But there is another side to the coin. For by focussing exclusively on what makes all forms of avoidance identical—namely their identical result (for instance: not eating a certain substance)—the crucial differences that exist among them in bringing about that result are obliterated.[79] Take, for instance, the difference between stated and unstated prohibitions. In Leach's analysis of English or Kachin taboos, this difference makes no difference.[80] For him it is just the same rule, except that it operates from two different places—consciousness and the unconscious. But do we really have the same phenomenon in two different forms, or two different phenomena altogether? To me it seems that there is a crucial difference between the two cases. When the rule is formally stated ("you shall not eat pork"), the substance is considered edible; it would be eaten if the rule did not exist. But when the rule (if it can be so called) has turned into an emotional state, a dislike or even a disgust ("pork is disgusting," "pork is harmful"), then the substance is considered inedible, and there is no need to taboo what is inedible and what nobody may want to eat anyhow.

It makes no sense to apply the term *taboo* to a situation in which there is no conflict, or at least potential conflict, between the spontaneous attitude to an object—attraction or simply lack of fear or aversion—and the attitude that is prescribed or recommended by a rule. One may object that there are formally expressed taboos about things that are considered disgusting anyhow, such as the flesh of pigs among Jews and Muslims. But in these cases the aversion is simply a redundant introjection of an explicit commandment. Without the commandment, the aversion would soon reduce or disappear. This implies that some degree of subterranean attraction for pork exists. In other words, we do not have suppression, but repression, of desire, and thus also an ambivalent attitude to the desired object. Overtly the thing is detested, but covertly it is also desired. In fact, the prohibition must encourage a sense that its object is desirable; otherwise obeying it could not have the religious signification it has (i.e. renouncing the satisfaction of one's desire in order to fulfill God's will).[81]

In sum, while one must applaud Leach's methodological decision to consider all attitudes toward animals in English and Kachin cultures (for this is the subject of his 1964 essay) as part of a single system or framework, one cannot accept his attempt to justify it by reducing taboo to the minimum common denominator of all phenomena that have the avoidance of those animals, and more particularly of their meat, as an effect. Taboo is not just avoidance, even if it cannot be separated from the phenomena of like and dislike, from the habitual or aesthetic judgments of edibility or inedibility that are its bedfellows. Taboo would seem to imply a conflict between a rule that excludes or limits the use of an object and a feeling or even an idea that, without that rule, the object would be used, or used indiscriminately, or, at the very least, approached carelessly.

Having clarified Leach's definition of *taboo*, we are in a position to examine his theory of the phenomenon. Leach's point of departure is a very general claim about cognition: "We can only arrive at semantically distinct verbal concepts if we repress the boundary percepts that lie between them."[82] Taboo is a manifestation of this kind of discriminatory repression which is necessary to the functioning of conceptual thought: "Taboo serves to discriminate categories in men's social universe . . . in so doing it reduces the ambiguities of reality to clear-cut ideal types."[83] Our perception of the world as consisting of discrete things is the result of "a simultaneous use of language and taboo. Language gives us the names to distinguish the things; taboo inhibits the recognition of those parts of the continuum which separate the things."[84]

Taboo, in sum, consists of the repression of interstitial states produced by the application of discrete conceptual classes on the continuum of experience. These interstitial states seem to have a tendency to pop up and undermine the work of classification by confusing adjacent categories. Hence their association with "sacredness," that is, with powers that are both contaminating and ambiguous. Taboos are indeed rules for the avoidance of such powers, as taught by the classical theories. But in inducing us to avoid the sacred, or to keep it separate in the Durkheimian sense, taboos in reality keep the destructive powers of confusion at bay and help maintain the unambiguous categorization that is a prerequisite of successful communication.

What are we to make of these claims, and how does the theory relate to the concrete phenomena of taboo? In connecting the ambivalence and contagiousness of the tabooed with the phenomenon of repression, Leach sounds superficially like Freud, although he confusingly uses *repression* and *suppression* interchangeably. Indeed he writes that "what is suppressed becomes especially interesting" and "a focus of . . . anxiety," as "variously described by anthropologists and psychologists."[85] But it is not at all clear why the repression of perception should have the kinds of effects that the repression of desire (as in Freud's theory) has. Desire is a force, energy directed to an object. We can understand, therefore, that it resists its repression, that it appears as a power that constantly risks overstepping its boundaries. And we can also understand, therefore, its ambiguous character.

But is perception such a force or energy? Is it so intentionally and obstinately driven to its object that it actively resists its repression? Granted that perception is not passive, it cannot alone bear the burden of explanation that Leach gives it. Its power must be increased by association with some interest or desire. It is not so much the case that a raw perception sets itself against the cultural categories in between which it exists as that the "in between" is itself invested with some value, that it derives its power from somewhere else. This somewhere else need not be Freud's desire; it may be culture itself, which invests the interstitial with mediating or subversive functions, as Leach himself shows in his concrete analyses. But then these analyses indicate that the general theory cannot be sustained: the mere contrast of "empirical" and "conceptual" explains neither the powers of the interstitial nor the need for tabooing it.

In fact, there seems to be an inherent conflict between Leach's theory in its most general formulation and the presuppositions of his actual analytical practice. In the latter, there is never a question of repressing raw percepts that are intermediate or residual relative to distinct cultural categories. The question, rather, is that of repressing the free and careless use of objects that are as clearly categorized as any other. In other words, taboo concerns not intermediate percepts but intermediate categories with as full a conceptual status as the categories in between which they are situated. Furthermore, taboo represses neither percept nor concept—but limits and regulates human action vis-à-vis the objects included in those "intermediate" categories.

What allows Leach to mask the conflict between his explicit and implicit theories is a rather loose use of terms, combined with clearly empiricist or even nominalist presuppositions. Thus he writes indifferently of taboo as repressing "boundary percepts that lie between" verbal categories[86] and as "apply[ing] to categories which are anomalous with respect to clear-cut oppositions."[87] Only the presupposition that categories are mere names for the percepts that they contain allows Leach to treat percepts and categories interchangeably and to slip from a theory of taboo as repression of intermediate (and thus uncategorized) percepts to a theory of taboo as "applying" to what is in fact categorized and has not, therefore, a purely perceptual, interstitial reality. And only the vagueness of the term *repress* allows him to reduce the reality of taboo as a rule of human action to the theory of taboo as what subdues percepts that do not fit "categorization."

It seems obvious not only that the "cognitive" theory of taboo has little in common with Leach's own analysis of concrete taboos in the classificatory and symbolic mode, but also that it has rather absurd implications. For by this theory, there should be a taboo for every categorical discrimination, since it is impossible to think, except in the most empiricist frame of mind, that there are any categories that perfectly fit perception. Indeed Leach himself excludes there being any, since he says that the conceptual is discontinuous, whereas the perceptual is continuous. But if there were a taboo for every categorical distinction, then the number of taboos in any culture would be enormous, which is clearly not the case. In fact taboos cluster around certain areas of categorization, as Leach himself has to recognize at one point.[88] And their importance and extent vary considerably from culture to culture.[89] Leach's theory of cognition would seem to require the suppression,[90] not the repression, of the perceptions that do not fit categorical distinctions.[91] But then the theory cannot explain the existence of taboos, which have no reason to exist if there is nothing to repress. This is perhaps one reason Leach uses *suppression* as if it were equivalent to *repression.*

But a more radical issue can be raised with regard to the basic functional presupposition of "Leach's theory of taboo" in all its incarnations. Is it really true that categories must be so clear-cut (as Leach claims) that no ambiguity can be tolerated?[92] It does not seem that this is the case. Ambiguity, the use of conflicting principles, and so on, abound in folk classifications without either of the two consequences predicted by Leach, namely a breakdown in communication or an efflorescence of taboos. Nor is the fact surprising, since various theoretical developments have made us aware that the taxonomic, Aristotelian model of discrete and hierarchically related classes implied by Leach is more the exception than the rule.

The more frequent classificatory procedures are continuous rather than discontinuous: they situate items by the degree to which they approximate a prototype (so that an item may be related to different prototypes at the same time);[93] they relate series of items horizontally, by multiple and variable traits linking them in chains, rather than by their common possession of the same list of features (family relations or polythetic classes);[94] or they relate them genealogically (genealogical or cladistic classifications).[95] In such classifications, ambiguities and interstitial entities cannot be an issue, since there are no clear-cut categories to begin with.

But if such is the case, the value of a theory that identifies taboo with the repression of the ambiguous, the interstitial, the anomalous, and so on, *in any classification* must be very small. The only way that the theory can be saved is by giving it a much more limited and determined application than it has in Leach. That is to say, it must be limited to those cases in which, for whatever reason, there is a demonstrable interest or purpose in keeping distinctions as clear-cut as possible. Taxonomic classification could be one such case. Yet it does not seem that a taxonomic interest is sufficient as such for generating taboos.[96] This empirical observation ruins Leach's cognitive theory of taboo altogether. Taboos tend to appear not in connection with any particular type of cognitive interest but where more vital interests are involved, where the terms to be kept distinct correspond to fundamental moral and cosmological incompatibilities. This point is fully supported by my analyses of Huaulu taboos below, but may also be demonstrated with reference to the English, Kachin, and Andamanese taboos which are discussed by Leach in his essays.

Just as he conflates different kinds of distinctions, and different kinds of reasons for having them, so Leach conflates different kinds of phenomena that undermine those distinctions and therefore motivate taboos according to his theory. Thus he equates anomaly with intermediacy or interstitiality,[97] ambiguity,[98] mediation,[99] and so on. But these terms are not equivalent and cannot even be said to be different manifestations of the same phenomenon—at least not in all cases. For instance, anomaly is not necessarily the same thing as something intermediate. Pink is intermediate between red and white, but it is not anomalous; mediocre is intermediate between good and bad, but is far from being anomalous—alas. Also, there are different kinds of anomalies: an anomalous species is not the same thing as an anomalous event, and it does not have the same mental (and emotional) implications.

An anomalous species is a permanent challenge to our classification, but being permanent it is also familiar and thus does not challenge our perceptual habits and expectations. It can challenge only a specific taxonomic sensibility, which is perhaps not as pervasive as Leach seems to imply. In contrast, an anomalous natural event (for instance, an eclipse or a thunderclap when the sky is cloudless) is an assault on perceptual habits and expectations shared by all. The shock of confusion it produces is repeated at every occurrence. One never gets used to it. Therefore it is anomalous both in classificatory terms and in perceptual ones. So, if there is a connection between taboo and anomaly, one should expect more numerous and stronger taboos around thunderclaps and eclipses than around anomalous species like certain amphibians and so on. I shall return to this complex issue in the Huaulu context; in any case, what I have just said suffices to suggest that one cannot equate the perceptual and the categorical in the manner of Leach.

In sum, while there may indeed be a connection between taboo and anomaly, it is much more complex than postulated by "Leach's theory." Also, a less loose use of *anomaly* may well show that it is not as pervasive as claimed by him. And even with this loose use, a substantial residue remains which is unaccounted for by the theory or plainly in conflict with it. A few examples from Leach's own analyses of concrete taboo systems illustrate these points. The analyses, as Leach himself points out, are really the development of certain strands already present in Radcliffe-Brown. One strand we have already seen, for it is the most prominent in Radcliffe-Brown's own view: the idea that values should be classified by degree and, more specifically, by the degree to which they represent the moral power of society. This idea is transformed by Leach[100] into the more fruitful one that categorization is made by reference to a hidden center: namely the human group and more particularly the category of the Self. Thus in his analysis of English classifications of animals with regard to edibility and of people with regard to marriageability, Leach is able to show that the same structure, based on degrees of closeness to self, is apparent.

In the realm of marriageability, those who are very close ("true sisters") are unmarriageable and sexually inaccessible. The next class is defined by those who are kin but not very close ("cousins"). Marriage with them is prohibited, but sex may be tolerated. An even more distant class is that of neighbors who are not kin. These are potential affines. Finally there is the most distant class, that of enemies, with whom no social relations (including marriage) are possible.[101] Four structurally analogous classes of animals exist: (1) "those who are very close—'pets,' always strongly inedible";[102] (2) tame animals that are not very close—"farm animals" who are edible only if immature or castrated; (3) field animals—"game"—which live under human protection but are not tame, and are edible in sexually intact form but only at certain seasons; and (4) "remote wild animals—not subject to human control, inedible."[103]

Thus it is not the case that the more distant an animal, the more edible it is, and the more distant a person, the more marriageable he or she is. The edibility or marriageability of a particular item is determined by an opposition and not just by a gradation. Or rather the gradation moves from one opposite to the other, from self to nonself, from friend to enemy, from humanly controlled to uncontrolled, and so on. This warrants, in Leach's view, the use of his anomaly or intermediacy thesis. Between two opposites stands an intermediate or mediating term, which becomes "taboo-loaded."[104] Thus in between the opposites "man"and "not man" stands the "ambiguous . . . intermediate category" of "man-animal," which includes pets. And in between the opposites "friendly" and "hostile" stands the intermediate category "friendly-hostile," which includes game. This intermediate situation is the reason taboo attaches to both pets and game in English culture.

The gist of the analysis is that animal species and categories of humans form a classification that is generated by a series of hierarchically ordered oppositions. The final product is a series of categorical distinctions between self and nonself, which is the most encompassing opposition. "Taboo serves to separate the SELF from the world, and then the world itself is divided into zones of social distance," corresponding to the basic categories indicated above.[105] Taboo maintains these divisions by focussing on the animals that are intermediate between them.[106]

But this account is clearly unsatisfactory. To begin with, it does not explain why taboo takes different forms and different intensities. Why, for instance, are pets fully taboo while game is so only seasonally? More important, the account is at odds with taboos' (in Leach's own wide sense of the term) association with opposites and with identicals (or similars) even more than with intermediaries. Human is inedible to human because all humans, at least with regard to edibility, are members of the same category into which an English Self puts himself. But the most distant animals—those that are classed as fully wild (lions, giraffes, or whatever)—are also inedible. Neither can be construed as intermediate or anomalous in Leach's sense. Moreover, it is possible to argue that pets are taboo, not because they are intermediate between human and nonhuman as such, but because they are associated with humans. Only one side of their intermediate character, the human side, makes them inedible. Hence the association of taboo with intermediacy is an artifice of the analysis. Its artificiality becomes even more evident when we move from edibility to marriageability. Here there is little doubt that it is not intermediacy but relative identity that determines taboo in English culture. I may not marry those who are like me or the opposite of me; I may marry only those whose status is "mixed"—neither too close nor too distant—that is, precisely those who should be taboo according to Leach's theory.[107]

However subtle and enlightening in several respects Leach's analysis is, it ultimately fails because, in the process of reducing the axis of proximity/distance to a set of mediated binary oppositions, it fails to recognize a basic point. In each opposition (self/nonself, human/animal, tame/wild), one term is markedly superior to the other. This inequality is one of the generating factors of taboo, precisely because taboo is not merely a cognitive fact but also a fact of evaluation. Even intermediacy, it seems, is more frequently associated with taboos when it blends and confuses terms that are antithetical in value and not merely in logical opposition. In sum, Leach may be missing the whole (hierarchical) point of taboo precisely when he seems to get close to it.

Critical conclusions converging with the above are prompted by Leach's reanalysis of Andamanese ethnography. Here again, the debt to Radcliffe-Brown is patent and acknowledged.[108] Radcliffe-Brown had noted that the special signification of certain animals, such as the monitor lizard and the civet cat, in Andamanese thought is to be explained by their anomalous position in the basic classification of species by habitat. The Andamanese distinguish three basic habitats: water, land, and the tops of trees. Each forms a separate world to which all animals that belong to it are confined. But the monitor lizard and the civet are exceptions. The monitor lizard is an exception because "it is equally at home in the trees, on the ground, and in the water of a creek. It is in a way free of all the three divisions of the world."[109] The civet cat cannot live in water, but it can run on the ground and climb in the tops of trees.[110] Their anomalous positions in the three-tiered cosmos explain, in Radcliffe-Brown's view, their association as husband and wife and their totalizing role in myth: "In some of the tribes the monitor lizard is regarded as the original ancestor not only of the Andamanese, but also of all the animals, including the birds of the forest and the fishes of the sea."[111]

Leach generalizes this brilliant observation and transfers it from the realm of myth to that of ritual. Indeed he attempts to show that anomaly is the source of animal taboos in the Andamans.[112] But this is clearly the case only for certain animals, although it remains to be demonstrated that anomaly is the only reason for tabooing them. Other taboos do not seem to have any particular connection with anomaly, however construed.[113] Moreover, some animals, even when we may succeed in construing them as anomalous with regard to some classificatory principles, appear to be taboo because of their prototypical status in their cosmic tier. A case in point is the triad of turtle, pig, and bee—animals which, by Leach's own admission, are prototypical (as sources of food) of their habitats—sea, land, and the tops of trees, respectively.[114] Leach explains the taboos on eating turtle and honey with what he thinks is their anomalous status with regard to various classificatory principles.[115] These principles, however, are only postulated. They may or may not be part of Andaman culture. There is no direct evidence one way or another. Moreover, Leach does not say that the pig is an anomalous animal for the Andamanese, and nothing shows that it is. Yet this animal is as great a focus of taboo as the other two, if not greater. Prototypicality, therefore, seems a more plausible candidate than anomaly as a source of taboo when the triad turtle-pig-honey is concerned. If this is so, it is possible to conclude that taboo contributes to the life of categories not only indirectly, by focussing on the species that straddle them and thus seem to threaten them, but also directly, by focussing on the species that are prototypical of them. The triad suggests more than this, though. It also suggests that prototypicality, just like anomaly, is not alone capable of motivating taboo. It must be conjoined with other values which are of more direct human interest and which point to a classification based on degrees of closeness to SELF rather than on cosmological zones or taxonomic principles. Indeed, what singles out pig, turtle, and bee, *even as prototypes of their cosmological zone,* is their value for humans[116] and also, no doubt, their similarity to humans in various respects.[117] This anthropocentric and sociocentric dimension, which played an important role in Leach's 1964 essay on English taboos, seems lost from sight in the 1971 essay on Andamanese taboos.

As we have seen, a possible minimal definition of *taboo* is "avoidance of pollution." Taboo and pollution imply one another in this definition. But which one is the primary concept? There is little doubt that taboo is primary for both Radcliffe-Brown and Leach. For Radcliffe-Brown, it is primary because prohibitions logically precede their sanction. In other words, the avoidance of pollution is a secondary and subjective motivation in taboo: it equals the avoidance of a sanction which in itself does not motivate the prohibition. The latter finds its motivations elsewhere, in the social structure and its functional requirements. For Leach, taboo is primary because it is its repression of experience that gives birth to the very idea, and fear, of pollution. Once again, the overt, subjectively meaningful reason for taboo—the avoidance of pollution—is viewed as purely derivative. Taboo exists because it is the necessary complement of categorization.

Douglas's own position on this issue is somewhat ambiguous. At her most structural-functionalist, she follows Radcliffe-Brown in considering pollution as a sanction, and thus as presupposing the taboo it sanctions. Thus she writes that an offense (for instance, the murder of a kinsman) "is treated as a pollution . . . when the sanction is . . . couched in terms of a misfortune that falls upon the offender without human intervention."[118] The functionalist corollary of this definition is that pollution is an idea that arises as an ersatz for direct human punishment[119] when the latter is impossible, either because the "political organization is not sufficiently developed" or because "it is developed in such a way as to make certain offenses inaccessible to police action."[120]

In another, more cognition-oriented, view, Douglas makes pollution primary but only by giving it some of the properties that taboo has in Leach. Indeed, she views pollution as an aid to "imposing system" in the face of "an inherently untidy experience."[121] "Repression" of what is experientially residual begins before taboo sets in. It takes the form of a judgment that the residues of order are dangerous for order and thus are to be avoided by those who participate in that order. Douglas claims that such judgment is not fundamentally different from the old and still common English idiom of *dirt,* as in Lord Chesterfield's definition: "matter out of place."[122] For in this acceptation, *dirt* "implies two conditions: a set of ordered relations and a contravention of that order. . . . Where there is dirt there is system. Dirt is the by-product of a systematic ordering and classification of matter, in so far as ordering involves rejecting inappropriate elements."[123] This could be called the housewife's view of pollution.

Douglas's emphasis on pollution derives from her attempt to link more closely together what motivates taboo and what functions as its sanction at the same time. The argument is that what is rejected acquires some rejecting power of its own. The repelled becomes repulsive and *makes* repulsive by contact. Or, to put it in Chesterfieldian terms, the dirty dirties, thereby punishing those who enter into contact with it. But one problem in equating the disorderly rejects of classification with the power to sanction any disorderly rejection of what is proscribed (taboo) is that it skips too many logical passages. It reifies both order and disorder to such an extent that it is at odds with the essentially relational nature of taboo. To give just one obvious example, the claim that only the dirty dirties conflicts with the belief that pollution may also be induced by *inappropriate* contact with eminently clean sources of order, such as gods, sanctuaries, sacred objects, and, in many parts of the world, rulers or priests.[124] The reason is not that the notions of purity and impurity are confused in the notion of sacredness, but that pollution is a much more relational notion than Douglas makes out.[125]

The disorder of which pollution is the sign is not so much the residue of generic order-making as the violation of a system of specific compatibilities and incompatibilities. The subject is not polluted by its running into "residues of the classificatory system" which are extraneous to it, but by its disregard of the implications of the classificatory position in which it finds itself. What is polluting to some is not so to others. And what is polluting at one time and place is not so at another. The basic shortcoming of Douglas's theory—at least as formulated in 1966—is that it does not incorporate the subject of pollution, let alone make it central.

The view that pollution is to be explained, purely and simply, as the reification of the disruptive power that "inappropriate elements" have on the system that has "rejected" them is thus far too crude. As we shall see, and as Douglas herself has come to recognize over the years, even the phenomena that this view captures (anomalies and so on) do not assume polluting powers before they carry some symbolic load, and are thus integrated into some other classificatory grid, or symbolic process, from the one that has "rejected" them. To speak of "the system," of "form," or of "order" as if they were one monolithic thing is thus quite inappropriate. There are many coexisting orders of classification; what is residual to one may be central to another. In any case, it seems questionable to reduce the complexity and variety of powers that are implicated in "pollution" and "taboo" to mere residues of, or resistances to, order-making. There is a strand in Douglas's theory[126] that seems to go back less to Durkheim's than to Hume's (and de Brosses's) account of religion. She shares with the latter two the view that religious concepts focus on the unexpected, the residual and the anomalous.[127] Only, for her such anomalies and residues are determined by reference to arbitrary classifications and not to mental habits that are the result of experience. Also, she views the focus on the residual as a means to reinforce and clarify the systemic by contrast. So, by way of her functionalism, she is a Durkheimian after all.

In any event, Douglas's definition of *pollution* as "misfortune" cannot be fitted so easily with her definition of it as "dirt." If misfortune is some kind of naturally occurring, intrinsically harmful event such as a disease, a crop failure, or a death, it can hardly be construed as a residue of classificatory order, especially in the matter of its dangerousness. The connection between a taboo and the misfortune that follows its violation is often arbitrary, as Marett noted long ago against Frazer.[128] The main criterion for the choice of a misfortune as a threatened sanction is its power as a deterrent. Thus the choice leans toward what is most fearsome. For instance, leprosy is treated in the Talmud virtually as the universal sanction.[129]

Of course leprosy can also be construed as a particularly serious form of "dirt" attaching itself to the skin. But then it is not dirt as a residue of ordering (unless the transgression of a taboo is itself defined, quite tautologically, as a residue of ordering),[130] but dirt as a metaphor of the transgression sticking to the transgressor, "unwashable" until it is expiated. This points to there being more to the image of dirt than Douglas says. Dirt may also function as a metaphor for the relationship of the offender to his offense or to the offended.[131] It may also symbolize the inappropriate mixing of something with another thing that is incompatible with it. Douglas not infrequently recognizes some of these additional meanings, particularly "mixing." But then it is unclear to me how she can stretch them on the Procrustean bed of her general formula for dirt—that is, a "residue" or a "byproduct" of system-making.

Another reason for doubting that Douglas's two definitions of pollution—as dirt and as misfortune—are necessarily equivalent or convergent is that her functional claims do not apply equally well to both of them. Indeed, it seems to me that—paradoxically in view of her formulation of them in connection with "misfortune pollution"—these claims apply much more cogently to "dirt pollution." The reason is that dirt, for all its overlappings with misfortune, differs sensibly from misfortune in that it is much more abstract and imaginary.[132] As Douglas herself points out, dirt is very much in the eyes of the beholder.[133] As such, it can automatically and immediately be attributed to an object or a person whenever necessary, by virtue of a conventional fiat: "Whenever x does y, then x is z," where z stands for *dirty.* This makes it a very powerful sanction in itself. To feel dirty in the eyes of everybody else; to feel, in addition, polluting to them; and to be excluded from social intercourse or even from the performance of certain necessary acts (particularly of a ritual nature) are punishment enough. Misfortune may or may not follow in due time, but it is obviously just an additional threat that is a further stimulus to get rid of the stain by conventional, ritual means, as is usually possible when this ideology of pollution as dirt is dominant.[134]

Contrast this with what happens with misfortune pollution (and I know this firsthand from Huaulu). A misfortune is not an event which is produced in a fully conventional way. The only thing that the community can produce is an interpretive connection between event and transgression. But it is usually an a posteriori and hypothetical connection, often traced many years after the fact. The transgression itself is usually also hypothetical: it is invoked as an explanation for some serious or recurring misfortune that cannot be explained in less morally burdensome ways. Since a disease, a death, or some big loss is a very concrete and threatening event, it seems paradoxical to have to say that any one of these is less effective, as a deterrent, than some imaginary "stain," some "dirt" which attaches to an offender only in the eyes of the beholder. Yet a pollution that reveals itself only at some later, indefinite moment, or that may not reveal itself at all, cannot be taken as seriously as something that is allowed to exist immediately because of its imaginary and conventional (if reified) character. It is therefore unsurprising, although by and large ignored by Douglas,[135] that the most developed and paradigmatic of pollution systems are those that have been built on the semiabstract notion of dirt-pollution. Obvious examples are fourth- and fifth-century B.C. Greece,[136] the India of Hinduism and its caste system,[137] and postexilic Israel.[138] Indeed the last of these furnishes the best exemplification of Douglas's notion of dirt, perhaps because it is the hidden source of her theory in the first place.

This is not the place to proceed any further on these issues. But what I have said should indicate that it is necessary to look a bit more closely at the notion of pollution. Many different phenomena—perhaps too many—are put under its capacious mantle, especially by Douglas. Yet its usual definitions and its proclaimed functions fit certain phenomena more closely than others. One can even make a case for pollution as a relatively abstract, essentially ritualistic notion, so that the mere use of misfortune as sanction would not be sufficient to speak of pollution. For that, disease would have to be the consequence of "dirt." But then, "pollution" or not, the essential interconnectedness of all these phenomena, and their common reliance on notions of contagion and impersonal powers, should not be lost from sight. Terminological usage is less important than conceptual precision and awareness that, even inside the same society, different notions of action and reaction and different images of their workings apply to different spheres of life. Huaulu will provide us with many examples of precisely this coexistence.

Although Douglas's theory, in its most general formulation, states that pollution arises from what is residual in terms of *any* type of classification, in practice her most novel and stimulating contribution lies in associating pollution with what is out of place in terms of *one* particular kind of classification—namely taxonomy.[139] A taxonomy, to borrow Sperber's neat formulation, is "a hierarchical classification in which at each level of the hierarchy all the categories are mutually exclusive."[140] In other words, each item can belong to one category and only one category in this classification. In a zoological taxonomy, for instance, an individual belongs to only one species, a species to only one genus, and so on. If any of these items has attributes, each of which belongs to different categories by definition, it is said to be anomalous in terms of the classification based on those categories. Suppose, for instance, that the category of water animals is defined by the attribute "lives only in the water," whereas the category of "land animals" is defined by the attribute "lives only on land." Then turtles, crocodiles, and frogs are anomalous in terms of these two categories because they belong to both: although they live mostly in the water, they are also found on land. An animal is also anomalous if it is the only one in a category not to have one of the set of attributes that defines the category. For instance, the pig is defined as an anomaly in the Bible because it is the only one among the animals with cloven hoofs that does not chew the cud. This is precisely why, says Douglas, it is polluting and thus taboo for the Hebrews.

Of course, one may well wonder why, in the presence of animals that do not fit the definition of the categories, the definition of the categories is not modified to fit the animals, so that they cease to be anomalous. For instance, why is the definition of the category of water animals as "animals that live only in the water" not changed to "animals that live in the water, but not exclusively"? Or why is the attribute "chew the cud" not eliminated from the definition of the category of animals with cloven feet, so that the category can include the pig? These questions raise the basic issue in the anomaly theory of pollution. Unfortunately, they are not questions that Douglas herself asks, let alone answers. But before we turn to this basic issue, on which the whole theory of pollution as taxonomic anomaly rests, it is necessary to find out if the theory is at least capable of accounting for all the facts. That is to say, is it possible to show that everything polluting is taxonomically anomalous and everything taxonomically anomalous is polluting?

In practice, the question can be formulated in a narrower form: Are all taboo animals anomalous and, conversely, are all anomalous animals taboo? The reason one can concentrate on this narrower question is that animals are, among all the things that are the objects of taxonomies, the more likely to be connected with ideas of pollution and thus with taboos. So if the theory fails with regard to animals, it fails altogether. On the other hand, if it stands with regard to them, that does not prove that it stands with regard to all other kinds of beings that happen to be taxonomically anomalous. For there is nothing in Douglas's formulation of her theory to explain what she implicitly acknowledges by giving the animal taboos of the Hebrews and of the Lele as its main illustrations—namely the tendency of ideas of pollution and accompanying taboos to focus on certain kinds (such as animals, particularly viewed from the point of view of their edibility), but not on others. Taxonomy alone cannot explain this selectivity, since the latter is not a taxonomic phenomenon in the first place. Of this, more anon. For the moment, let us inspect Douglas's principal illustration of her thesis.

This illustration is provided by her analysis of the animals that are declared "abominations" in Leviticus 11 and Deuteronomy 14. Both these texts begin by defining the edible animals par excellence ("the ox, the sheep, the goat, the hart, the gazelle, the roe-buck, the wild goat, the ibex, the antelope, and the mountain-sheep," Deut. 14:4–5) by their combination of two taxonomic characters: they "part the hoof" and "chew the cud." The animals that have either of these characters but not both are declared "unclean." Thus the camel, the hare, and the rock badger, which are all said to chew the cud but not to part the hoof, are unclean. So is the swine, which parts the hoof but does not chew the cud (Deut. 14:7–8). Then the texts mention the denizens of water. Of these, only those that have fins and scales are declared edible; all others are unclean (Deut. 14:9–10; Lev. 11:9–12). Then follows a mere list of tabooed birds, without any taxonomic identification (Deut. 19:12–18; Lev. 11:13–19), after which both texts mention insects, but each to somewhat different effect. Deuteronomy (14:19) is categorical: "And all winged insects are unclean for you; they shall not be eaten." Leviticus (11:20–25) declares that "all winged insects that go upon all fours"[141] are taboo except those "which have legs above their feet, with which to leap upon the earth"—namely the locust, the bald locust, the cricket, and the grasshopper.

Deuteronomy stops with the insects; Leviticus (11:27–42) continues with other animals. First it mentions the quadrupeds "that go on their paws" (predators?). Then it lists the weasel, the mouse, the great lizard, the sand lizard, and the chameleon. Finally, it condemns "every swarming thing that swarms upon the earth," that is, any terrestrial animal that has no feet or "many feet."

Faced with this list, many commentators since antiquity have given piecemeal explanations of the most diverse sort. Douglas condemns them all because "they are neither consistent nor comprehensive."[142] She claims that the only acceptable interpretation is one that finds a single systematic principle for them all, and she thinks that she has found it. All the taboo animals, she argues, are anomalous in terms of a taxonomic order, which is itself viewed as an expression of divine order. To eat anomalous animals is to eat animals that contravene God's order; it is to go against him and thus to be "unholy." It is eating "dirt" in the Chesterfieldian sense. Holiness is taxonomy. The cult of God is a taxonomic cult.[143] The God of Abraham and Isaac may not be the God of the philosophers, but he certainly is a God of taxonomists, maybe even of a follower of Aristotle.

In essence, Douglas's interpretation (and, one may argue, her whole theory of pollution and taboo) is the generalization of the principle by which the priestly text begins—namely the one which allows us to discriminate between ox, sheep, goat, and the wild animals that resemble them, on the one hand, and camel and pig on the other. The two groups of animals represent, respectively, holy and unholy food. In fact, the first includes most of the animals that are the appropriate sacrifice to God.[144] The principle is indeed taxonomic. But two questions immediately arise. The first is whether the principle generates the taboo or is just a key in the zoologist's sense—that is, a device by which certain traits are arbitrarily selected to be able to identify and thus also distinguish species for practical purposes. The second is whether the generalization of this principle to all abominations is warranted.

As several critics have observed, in *Purity and Danger* Douglas violates her own precepts of comprehensiveness and systematicity in interpretation because she leaves out what most clearly does not fit her view: the birds.[145] She writes: "Birds I can say nothing about because, . . . they are named and not described and the translation of the name is open to doubt."[146] This is a very lame excuse. In fact, it is no excuse at all, because if the sacred text gives no reason for tabooing an important category of animals, contrary to what it does for most others, then this must be significant. It must mean that either there is no principle to the list, or the principle presiding over it is quite different from the one of taxonomic anomaly that the priestly authors of Leviticus and Deuteronomy foreground. Indeed, anomaly is not prevalent among these birds,[147] some of which (eagles, falcons and so on) seem, on the contrary, archetypal of birdness.[148] On the other hand, as three interpreters[149] have independently felt, most of these birds have in common a feature that "stands out a mile,"[150] and which they share with the animals "that go on their paws":[151] they are carnivorous.[152] Thus the principle of anomaly alone is not able to account for the entire list of abominations.[153]

To be fair to Douglas, though, it must be said that, viewed as a source of pollution, carnivorousness may be construed as dependent on anomaly.[154] Indeed carnivorous animals feed indiscriminately "on other creatures which may themselves transgress the category-rules or be unclean in other ways. If the contents of their stomachs are abominable, so are they themselves."[155] But is the fear of indirectly eating anomalous animals the only, or even principal, reason for shunning carnivorous animals? Or is it their carnivorousness as such that is the truly objectionable trait, as claimed by the high priest Eleazar in the letter of Aristeas and by Philo?[156] In *Purity and Danger* Douglas denies that it is,[157] but Soler has shown otherwise.[158] In fact, his interpretation implies that the objection to carnivorousness motivates even some of the taboos that Douglas views as motivated by anomaly exclusively.

Soler sees the rules of Leviticus and Deuteronomy as the end point of a mythical development that reveals their meaning. He notes that "Paradise is vegetarian," that at the beginning of time Yahvè gives only herbs and fruits as food for humans and animals alike (Gen. 1:29–30). Meat is reserved for only him, as sacrifice, because only he can take the life that he has given.[159] Only after the Flood, having decided that humans are intrinsically evil, and thus inevitably violent, Yahvè allows them to eat meat (Gen. 9:3). But an element of the antedeluvian order is preserved: blood, which contains the life of the animals, remains a preserve of God. Thus the context in which it becomes lawful marks the eating of meat negatively. The third and final stage is reached with Moses, who introduces the distinction between lawful and unlawful animals. This distinction is made necessary by the Covenant that separates the Jewish people from other peoples. They will keep pure by eating pure animals (Lev. 20:24).[160]

But what makes it possible to discriminate between pure and impure animals? Soler identifies two criteria of purity. One is that animals must conform to their "ideal model," that is, be without defect or mixture. Here he is in full agreement with Douglas: anomalies are impure, both at the level of the individual[161] and at the level of the species. But another criterion, unrecognized by Douglas, is that animals must be vegetarian, in conformity with Creation's plan, as revealed by its origins.[162] This is, in fact, the most important criterion. Anomaly is only derivative, at least as far as the most important groups of animals are concerned. Soler's analysis of the paradigmatic pure meat according to Leviticus and Deuteronomy shows why. This meat is furnished by the animals that "part the hoof" and "chew the cud," as we have seen. But these are not just any taxonomic traits. They index the feeding habits of the animals that display them. As Soler notes, the hoof (in the cloven form it assumes in the most familiar of herbivorous animals) is implicitly opposed to the claws or nails. Animals that do not have claws or nails lack the organs for preying on other animals. However, not all animals that part the hoof are exclusively herbivorous. The pig also eats meat and, moreover, is a ferocious animal in its wild state.[163] Thus, to be extra sure, after having established that an animal has hoofs and then parts them, one must find out if it possesses an additional trait: rumination. Only ruminating animals give an absolutely compelling proof of their vegetarianism.

The starting point of the classification is thus not a decontextualized taxonomic impulse. There is a basic, mythically expressed ideal: vegetarianism. From this ideal humans have lapsed, although they preserve a trace of it in the refusal to consume a meat that is not vegetalized, so to speak, by its complete separation from what is most animal—blood. Furthermore, the ideal survives, in even more displaced form, in the view that the purest meat is furnished by a fully vegetarian animal, by an animal whose meat is just transformed vegetal, as Héritier puts it.[164] Taxonomy enters into play, not as an autonomous principle, as the expression of an ideal of classificatory order that is entirely responsible for generating the opposition of the pure and the impure, but first and foremost as a key,[165] that is an aid for inferring from some easily identifiable traits whether an animal is herbivorous or not.

Taxonomy presupposes, in other words, something that is nontaxonomic. Furthermore, as Douglas herself admits, it presupposes the existence of prototype animals rather than explaining why they acquire this prototypical status. Indeed, the herbivorous ideal exists[166] embodied in the three animals that happen to be associated with the pastoralist's mode of life that is the biblical ideal: the cow, the sheep, and, to a lesser extent, the goat. It is these animals that furnish the materials for the analysis which results in their definition by two principles (parting the hoof and chewing the cud), which are then used as a key to establish the lawfulness or unlawfulness of other animals. Thus all wild animals that part the hoof and chew the cud are declared lawful because of their similarity to the prototypical domesticated animals. Those which either part the hoof but do not chew the cud or chew the cud but do not part the hoof are—wild or domesticated—unlawful. An opposition of pure and impure that may seem the result of a worship of taxonomy in the guise of God[167] turns out to be an a posteriori justification of the presupposed status of a domesticated, herbivorous animal. In other words, in this case at least, taxonomy is not the generative principle of taboo. Taxonomy intervenes as a "rationalization"[168] or, better, as a way of rendering a part of the factual (the animals of the herd) normative by generalization.

That taboo is generated by a normative classification by means of prototypes, rather than by a taxonomic impulse proper, is shown even better by the remaining taboos. On these, Douglas's and Soler's analyses converge. Both point out that the interpretation of these taboos must be based on the "three-tiered cosmos"[169] that is presented in Genesis. The book divides the world into earth, waters, and firmament. To each of these tiers corresponds one and only one proper kind of animal life: "In the firmament two-legged fowls fly with wings. In the water scaly fish swim with fins. On the earth four-legged animals hop, jump or walk. Any class of creatures which is not equipped for the right kind of locomotion in its element is contrary to holiness. Contact with it disqualifies a person from approaching the temple."[170]

Thus inhabitants of the water that do not swim, such as shells, are taboo. So are those that live in the water like fish but walk like terrestrial animals, such as crustaceans.[171] Terrestrial animals that crawl, creep, or swarm are also taboo, because they do not use the "right" form of locomotion; indeed, they do not have four feet but too many or none.[172]

Furthermore, "eels and worms inhabit water, though not as fish; reptiles go on dry land, though not as quadrupeds; some insects fly, though not as birds."[173] Of the winged insects, those that hop (a legitimate form of terrestrial locomotion), but not those that crawl, are lawful.[174] Finally, the weasel, the mouse, the crocodile, the shrew, various kinds of lizards, the chameleon, and the mole may be taboo because they walk on all four, although they have "hands" but not "feet."[175]

These interpretations may be questioned in certain particulars, but on the whole the pattern seems clear: the Bible rules out as unclean every animal that is "anomalous" in terms of the prototypes it chooses in each tier of the cosmos. The association of anomaly with tabooed uncleanness is thus not what is problematic in *Purity and Danger*'s theory, although, as we have just seen, anomaly alone cannot explain all the taboos or all the components of taboo. What is problematic is the view of what generates anomaly. It is said to be the consequence of an autonomous, universal classificatory impulse. However much Douglas recognizes, in particular analyses, that classification cannot be separated from evaluations and pragmatic givens, her general thesis in *Purity and Danger* is framed exclusively in terms of pure taxonomic reason. The mind imposes order on the world and does not tolerate ambiguities. One thing is either *x* or *y*; it cannot be both. The reason for this is supposed to be a kind of horror of ambiguity as such.[176] The problem with such a view is that it confuses logical rigor with normative rigidity.

If classification were guided by logical rigor alone, it would probably generate no anomaly. The logical impulse can hardly be satisfied by such simple-minded and obviously selective generalizations as "all land animals are four-footed and either walk, or hop, or run." It is a fact of observation that this statement is untrue. Hence it would have to be revised to allow it to encompass the terrestrial animals that do not have four feet, and so on, instead of excluding them and leaving them hanging out, so to speak, of the classification. Or it would eliminate the very category of terrestrial animals altogether, as too wide and heterogeneous. Or it would use prototypes in nonexclusive, and thus nontaxonomic, ways; it would use them as terms of comparison, as devices for situating species or genera by their degree of approximation to a paragon. Such use would exclude the very notion of anomaly, since it would exclude the very idea of exclusive classes. Indeed, it seems that most actual folk classifications of biological species attempt to be comprehensive rather than exclusive. Exclusivity, and thus rigidity, begins when being one way instead of another acquires some symbolic value and some moral consequence. Then classification reflects not so much a descriptive impulse as a normative, moral one. It reflects the way the world should be rather than the way it is.[177] It is a protest against reality rather than an account of it.

A good example is furnished by the animals that are prototypical of pure food—those that part the hoof and chew the cud. The normative power of this combination does not lie in any yearning for classificatory neatness per se, but in the normative/ideal character of the mode of life represented by these animals and, beyond it, in a yearning for the moral perfection of the original, prelapsarian vegetarianism mandated by God, which they also represent. As for the animals that are normative for each tier of the universe, their normativeness concerns less the other animals than the Hebrews themselves. Just as the Hebrews are prototypical among humans, the "chosen people," so the birds are prototypical among the creatures of the air, the fish among the creatures of the water, and the quadrupeds among those of the earth. And just as the Gentiles represent the antithesis of the Hebrews in the human world, so the anomalous creatures in each of the three animal realms represent the antithesis of their "normal" counterparts. By eating the "normal" animals and avoiding the anomalous ones, the Hebrews reproduce themselves as distinct and superior. In sum, the use of rigid prototypes in animal classification is not the result so much of a descriptive impulse as of an interest in the rigid separation of a human group (the Hebrews) from all others through the separation of their food, since one is what one eats.

Thus, if there are normative ideals to be found in the animal world, they are really normative ideals for humans, not for animals.[178] The classification of animals that is found in Leviticus and Deuteronomy is not an all-purpose one, in all probability. It is a classification for the purposes of eating and touching. The rules for eating and touching animals are not a side effect, a mere application, of a taxonomic enterprise; they orient that enterprise because they are its end. The issue is not "given this classification, what should we not eat?" but "if we are to eat so as to reproduce our identity, what classification?"

This does not mean, of course, that the classification of animals is a mere projection of the classification of humans. The relationship of the two is much more complex than that. Observational facts have their integrity and do contribute to explaining why it is that certain animals and not others are chosen as prototypical. Birds are the most frequent of sky animals and are the best adapted to their environment. Analogously, fish are the most frequent of water animals. And, as Hunn observes: "If animals with cloven hooves were equally likely either to chew or not chew their cud, it seems unlikely that one combination of characters should be seen as exceptional and the other normal."[179] Yet that would not in itself be sufficient to equate the more frequent combination with the pure and the more infrequent with the impure. For that to happen, the animals that represent one combination must be associated with humans, indeed, have a semihuman status, as we have seen.

Thus the observation and classification of animals neither precede the classification of humans nor furnish a model for it, or vice versa. Rather, they coexist in a complicated dialectic. This dialectic is, moreover, inflected by purpose. Classifications vary in form and rigidity (and thus also in the degree to which they produce anomalies or evaluate them), depending on whether they are used to discriminate between animals for symbolically loaded purposes (edibility, sacrificiability) or merely for purposes of recognition, identification, and so on. It is an error to postulate—as Douglas seems to—that a single, all-encompassing, and context-free classification exists in each society. Taboo has its own reasons that reason does not know, as I hope to show in greater detail in the analysis of the Huaulu case.

Soon after the publication of *Purity and Danger,* Bulmer pointed out that Douglas's taxonomic criterion (that is, one based on physical and behavioral characteristics alone) was insufficient to account for the anomalous status of animals like the pig among the Hebrews and the cassowary among the Karam of New Guinea, whom he had himself studied. He argued that the purely taxonomic definition of the pig's uncleanness in Leviticus sounds more like a rationalization than a motive. He showed that the cassowary's "special status" in Karam classification is due to this animal's peculiar position not only in taxonomy but also "in culture, or cosmology, at large."[180] In particular, he suggested that the cassowary obtains that status because its relationship with humans is viewed as analogous to humans' relationship with their married-out sisters and with their patrilateral cross-cousins.[181]

The rather Leachian point that the classification of animals is not independent of the classification of kin and the classification of space was also made by Tambiah in his analysis of northeastern Thai taboos.[182] On the strength of that analysis, Tambiah concluded that "simple intellectual deductions from a society's formalized scheme of animal categories will not take us far unless we can first unravel the core principles according to which people order their world and the valuations they give to the categories. . . . In my analysis the core principles lie in the domain of primary social interests and values connected with the ordering of kin, incest and marriage, and conceptions of social distance."[183]

Acknowledging that these and other criticisms (including some that I have mentioned above) are justified, Douglas has attempted to modify her general theory, and especially her analysis of Hebrew taboos, accordingly. First of all, she has shown that the animals that are fit for the human table are part of a hierarchy at the top of which are the animals that are fit for the altar, that is, for sacrifice. Then she recognizes (without mentioning Soler) that what makes some birds taboo is the fact that they are predators.[184] This means, she points out, that they eat meat with blood, thereby violating another rule (blood cannot be consumed), which she had previously left out of consideration. Finally she notes the obvious analogy between the rule of separation of pure and impure animals and the rule of separation of pure and impure people (Hebrews and non-Hebrews and different categories of Hebrews).[185]

Much is made of the connection between the Hebrews' insistence on social boundaries and their intolerance of anomalies,[186] but anomalies are, by and large, still taken for granted. Thus Douglas does not quite make the point I have made, namely that the rigidity of the opposition of Hebrew and non-Hebrew largely accounts for the creation of anomalies to begin with.[187] Indeed, it creates a preference for a morally (but not descriptively) satisfying classification by rigid and thus exclusive prototypes as against a classification more sensible to actual diversity and thus more flexible and encompassing. But we must not forget that it is a classification of animals as food and thus, from an anthropocentric point of view, not of animals per se.

Another problem that Douglas faces in her later essays is that the Hebrews' consistently negative reaction to anomaly, which in *Purity and Danger* she supposed to be "the normal one,"[188] is very far from being such. Her own field research among the Lele of Zaire provides the example of a highly anomalous animal, the pangolin, with highly positive connotations. She therefore attempts to account for the variations in the reaction to anomaly (and never, incidentally, for the variations of the degree to which anomaly is produced or recognized) in terms of her newly found emphasis on the social correlates of natural classifications. A positive evaluation of anomaly, she claims, correlates with a positive evaluation of exogamous alliance, such as is found among the cross-cousin-marrying Lele, whereas a negative evaluation of anomaly correlates with a negative view of exogamy and an insistence on endogamy, such as probably occurred among the Hebrews around the time of the Exile and subsequent Return (sixth and fifth centuries B.C.), when the Priestly Code (of which Leviticus is a part) was put together.[189]

Unfortunately such simplistic correlations between typological abstractions lead Douglas from the Scylla of pure taxonomic reason to the Charybdis of Durkheimian reductionism. To her examples, one can pose innumerable counterexamples, and especially the observation that positive and negative evaluations of different anomalies coexist in the same society.[190] For instance, Lewis points out that only one species of pangolin is given ritual value by the Lele, although both are anomalous. Only an analysis of classifications in the totality of their social and cosmological contexts can explain why anomalies are given positive or negative values (both of which, incidentally, can lead to tabooing them) in each case. Such analysis would also confirm what should by now be clear—that anomaly is far from being a necessary correlate of any form of classification[191] and, a fortiori, the only and necessary source of taboo. Douglas now acknowledges the latter point.[192] But then, if taboo does not mark only "those experiences which defy classification," and if those experiences are not necessarily equated with "dirt," Douglas's original theory stands in ruins. More persuasive, but incomplete, is the later theory, which includes anomaly in the more generic principle of improper mixing.

Identity and Difference

As I mentioned at one point, the exclusive linkage of taboo with categorical intermediacy or anomaly leaves out precisely what epitomizes taboo in both popular and anthropological discourse: the taboos on incest and cannibalism. For it seems highly artificial or even impossible to explain these taboos as proscriptions of the categorically anomalous or interstitial. A sister is proscribed as a sexual object not because she is intermediate between self and nonself (a marriageable cross-cousin may also, and in fact more appropriately, be defined as such), but because she is categorically *identical* to self, because she belongs to a category (clan, lineage, or consanguineous group) to which ego also belongs. Analogously, the flesh of human beings or of fellow members of one's group is forbidden not because they are categorically intermediate between human and nonhuman or between friend and enemy, but because they unambiguously belong to the category—human, or Huaulu, or whatever—in which the ego places itself. Also, as I pointed out in my critique of Leach, pets or even domestic animals (as in Huaulu) are taboo to eat not because they are "intermediate" between self and nonself, but because they have a component that is identical to oneself. These taboos, then, seem to point to an irreducible principle: the avoidance of the identical, the proscription of associating—at least with regard to eating, reproducing, and having sex—two terms that are in some crucial respect considered the same.

This principle of avoided identity, as I would call it, has recently been carried beyond incest and cannibalism by some anthropologists who have turned it into the cornerstone of a general theory of taboo which stands in stark contrast with that of Leach and Douglas. Their ultimate inspiration is Durkheim's essay on the prohibition of incest. As I mentioned earlier in this chapter, Durkheim argues that this prohibition[193] is due to the sacredness attributed to the blood of one's clan. This sacredness creates a horror of confronting that blood as it flows out of the bodies of members of the clan. It therefore discourages wounding or murdering clanspeople. It also discourages sexual intercourse (and a fortiori marriage) with clanswomen, who because of menstruation and childbirth (and presumably also defloration) "spend so to speak part of [their] life in blood."[194] The theory that exogamy derives originally from the horror felt for menstrual blood has been effectively criticized by Lévi-Strauss.[195] But Durkheim's focus on blood should not obscure what this substance stands for in his view: the identity of a group.

The theory can therefore be translated into more abstract terms. The horror of contact with one's blood in another person is really the horror of contact with oneself in this other. Durkheim's theory of the prohibition of incest may thus be viewed as the misguidedly concrete expression of a principle of dissimilation that applies in many contexts and not just in sexuality: the identical cannot associate with the identical. It is precisely on this principle that the theories of taboo of Héritier and some others are based.[196]

Héritier claims that "a balance between two ideas" is found more or less in all societies: (1) contraries may attract or repel one another, depending on the context; (2) a balance of the contraries "is necessary to the harmony of the world, of the individual, of the social order."[197] Taking Greek thought as a paradigmatic example, she asserts that perfection consists in an optimal proportion of as many contraries as possible. "In contrast, the accumulation of the identical always triggers a loss of balance, an *excess*."[198] This accumulation may be sought in exceptional cases (for instance, in medicine, to reestablish a balance when one of the contraries is weakened),[199] but is ordinarily avoided. Héritier's thesis is, in sum, that taboos maintain the balance of the world by proscribing the reinforcement of either of two contraries which is brought about by the summation of two or more identical (or equivalent) terms. For instance, the association of two hot things or of two cold things is proscribed in order to maintain the balance of hot and cold. The taboo on incest belongs to the same logic: in order to reproduce certain relationships of contrariety in the social world, it proscribes the marital and even sexual association of people who are categorically identical.[200] A number of objections can be advanced against this theory, which, in the attempt to account for the incest taboo in terms of the cosmological system, in fact turns the incest taboo into the paradigm of all taboos. First of all, a "Greek" model of cosmology—that is, one that emphasizes the balance of contraries—is not relevant for all cultures.[201] But even where it is relevant, it does not exhaust all principles of order and cannot account for all taboos. The alternative "accumulation of the identical"/ "balance of the contraries" is everywhere too simple a principle of explanation. The association of terms of the same category is more often than not neutral; it becomes bad only under conditions that must be spelled out and that are not necessarily the imperative of preserving a balance of contraries.

For instance, people of the same category (let us say, kinsmen) should always associate. The accumulation of the identical is unproblematic and even prescriptive in their case. It is proscribed only when certain types of relationships—sexual intercourse, violence resulting in bloodshed, eating—are involved. One cannot have sex with, wound, kill, or eat people who are "identical" to oneself. The reason is that these relationships are appropriate among contraries but inappropriate among identicals. And they are inappropriate because they are all, more or less, in contradiction to the basic equality or solidarity that should exist among the members of the same category ("kin" or whatever). Penetrating, wounding, devouring are strongly asymmetric acts that require a high measure of otherness and, more important, of subordination. A sister is too much like me to be my wife, a kinsman is too much like me to be my victim, and a human is too much like me to be my food. So the "accumulation of the identical" per se is not a sufficiently precise principle. For a prohibition to arise, there must be a basic incompatibility between the prohibited act and the axiomatic relationship that exists between agent and patient. The particular should not violate the general; or the more contingent, the more necessary.

Just like the association of identicals, so the association of contraries may have to be avoided. Héritier recognizes as much, since she says that contraries may repel and not just attract each other. But in practice she hardly pays attention to contrariety—and, indeed, to difference—as a source of taboo, although its existence undermines her general point that taboo is about the avoidance of identicals. In fact, taboo is neither about the avoidance of identicals nor about the avoidance of contraries per se. It is about what makes identicals and contraries incompatible under certain conditions. Among such conditions are specific acts. The relationships involved in such acts should not contradict more important, axiomatic relationships that exist between two terms. For instance, if the relationship of contrariety is the axiomatic one, relationships that imply similarity or identity are ruled out, especially in the same contexts. An example is provided by the Huaulu rule that everything that pertains to menstrual blood and everything that pertains to war should not associate. In particular, men who leave for war should not have sexual intercourse with women. Also, a man whose wife menstruates should not go to war.

These taboos would probably be explained by Héritier as instances of the proscription of the accumulation of identicals (women spill blood by menstruating and giving birth; men, by killing enemies).[202] But this explanation would miss the basic fact: the hierarchical contrast between spilled blood as such and the mode and sense of its spilling. The latter, which determines contrariety, is more fundamental than the former, which implies identity. The association, especially in intercourse, of man and woman contradicts the contrast in value between their bloods by mixing them. The taboo arises in this case, then, because a relationship that implies identity is in contradiction to a more important relationship which implies contrariety. This case is thus the exact reverse of the case of incest, in which a relationship that implies otherness and especially subordination (sex and even more so marriage) is felt to be in contradiction to a more important relationship that involves identity and basic equality (sibling solidarity).

These two examples show that taboo is exclusively concerned neither with the accumulation of identity nor with horizontal relations of contrariety. Rather, it seems often to be concerned with a hierarchical conflict between identity and contrariety (or simply difference) in the various relationships that exist between terms. For it must be clear that rarely are the relationships between terms defined exclusively as identical or different. On the contrary, the key to taboo lies first and foremost in the recognition of the multiplicity of relations and the conflicts that it occasionally produces, which amounts to saying that Héritier's and Leach's (or Douglas's) approaches should be reconciled.

If in Héritier the principle of avoided identity is, at least nominally, the counterpart of a principle of balance of contraries and thus of difference, in Testart it becomes absolutely primary. For him, taboo is concerned solely with disjoining a substance from itself,[203] and thus with creating difference where lack of difference is implied.[204] In the earlier formulation of Testart's doctrine (1985–86), only one substance was in fact said to be involved in taboo—blood[205]—because that substance is, more than any other, "good to think"[206] an "identity underlying an apparent difference,"[207] since "it represents what all living beings have in common."[208] From this Testart inferred that insofar as other substances are involved, they must be involved because they stand for blood.

The argument seems to be that since taboo is about the separation of identicals, and since blood is the substance that represents identity better than any other, any substance that is involved in taboo must be so only as an imperfect approximation to blood; hence, it symbolizes blood—it is really blood in disguise as far as taboo is concerned.[209] This is, of course, a very curious argument. It takes for granted what must be proven to begin with: that taboo is only about the separation of identicals. It also assumes that identity is always necessarily substantial. Finally, it takes the peculiar (neoplatonic) view that the imperfect must signify the perfect. The possibility that different substances have their own autonomous significations and that these significations, rather than their alleged approximation to the signification of blood and thus to blood itself, have something to do with why they are involved with taboo is not considered by Testart, or it is considered only so far as to declare that such significations are superficial and unimportant or even that they mask the real (essential) ones.[210]

At any rate, what explains the generalization of the incest taboo to all taboos, namely the principle that blood should not be associated with blood, identical with identical? The answers provided by Testart do not seem as consistent or satisfactory as one may wish. But even they imply, albeit unwittingly, that there is no ruling out the summation of identicals if some fundamental difference is not implied—if the "identicals" are not, in fact, also different. Testart notes that because blood—a substance that signifies the identity of all living beings—"is contained in a bodily container which is distinct from that of another living being,"[211] it allows one to think of individuality against the background of that identity. He then proceeds to say that blood flowing outside its container is "good to think" of the transgression or transcendence of limits—the violation of an established order.[212] These transgressive flows, as he notes, may signify creation (as in reproduction) or destruction (as in wounding/killing), but in both cases they stand in opposition to contained, canalized blood, which signifies their preservation in the same state in which they had existed previously.[213]

But if flowing blood evokes the breaking down of the distinction between different bodies, and more generally of an established order of differences, then the taboo on associating blood with blood (and thus, necessarily, bloods that flow out of different parts of the same body or out of different bodies) is not the expression of an irreducible imperative to separate same from same, but is instead a means of protecting an established difference. Testart sees only the avoidance of identity,[214] not the preservation of difference, making that avoidance significant, by his own account.[215] The point may be reinforced if we move beyond the only difference that Testart seems to recognize in blood: that given it by its various containers. In fact, blood is differentiated also by the modalities and causes of its outflow. The blood that flows spontaneously out of the body of a woman who menstruates or gives birth does not have the same value as the blood that flows out of the wound inflicted in an enemy, or an animal. Testart boldly declares that no system of representations ever saw a difference between the blood of game and the blood of women,[216] yet the ethnographic record seems to prove otherwise. In Huaulu, for instance, large bleeding animals (or their meat) are not dangerous to menstruating women, but menstruating women are dangerous to them or, more pertinently, to their bleeding—that is, to success in hunting.[217] The separation of the two bloods is reciprocal but not reciprocally motivated.

In fact, as we shall see, full symmetry never exists between any two qualitatively different bloods that are separated by taboos in Huaulu. They are not mutually dangerous or equally dangerous to one another. This fact cannot be explained if categorical differences between these bloods are not taken into account and if the taboos are merely reduced to the avoidance of the summation of blood with itself. Furthermore, these bloods are separated not simply from one another, but also—and again differentially—from the village, which I am not prepared to view as, or merely as, a "latent" symbol of blood. Hence, Testart's idea that all there is to the taboos of blood is a dissimilation of the same from being united with itself ("même d'avec le même") seems to me a terrible simplification. Even leaving aside the idea's obvious disregard for native formulations, we see that it does not account for all the facts, indeed for the most important fact—the asymmetric relations of categorically different bloods. Furthermore, if the taboo is about separating blood from blood, why is it that, in Huaulu as in many other societies, bleeders of the same category are not separated? Why is it that Huaulu women can menstruate in the same hut, and hunters and headhunters can spill blood together? Obviously it makes no sense to view blood as a mere symbol of indifferentiation. Blood is itself categorically differentiated, and these differences do matter to taboo. On the other hand, it is true that difference exists in a less evident, more notional form for blood than for most other things. Hence it is more easily threatened and must be more strongly reaffirmed by taboo. This may be one reason for the almost universal proliferation of taboos around blood. The many perceptive things that Testart has to say about the symbolic role of this substance may then be incorporated into a theory more sensitive to the interplay of difference and identity in taboo.

Ultimately, Testart's explanation of the principle of "avoided identity" (as I call it) is sociological. At the basis of "primitive communism" (which largely coincides for him with hunting societies) there is a principle of dissociation of producer and consumer. Thus it is extremely frequent (Huaulu is no exception) that the hunter cannot consume the game (or the most important game) that he himself kills. He must give it to others and he is dependent on others for his meat. A system of alimentary reciprocity, analogous to matrimonial reciprocity, is thus generated.[218] In both cases, one is separated from something (meat) or somebody (sibling) that is assimilated to one. Better than any other substance, blood allows one to think this underlying identity between hunter and game, brother and sister. The rule of separation from one's product is thus reified and translated into a rule of separation of blood from blood.[219] Blood cannot be summed. The principle is then generalized to all blood, and in fact to everything that has some connection with blood.[220]

Clearly, Testart ends up by reconciling Lévi-Strauss with Durkheim. Lévi-Strauss's explanation of exogamy is put in hematological, and thus Durkheimian, shape. But then a leap occurs that is neither Lévi-Straussian nor Durkheimian. Testart generalizes from the taboos of exogamy and what may well be called exophagy to all taboos. The symbol of devalued identity, or failed differentiation—that is, blood—

inundates the entire universe of taboo and drowns in the process whatever classificatory differences may preexist the flood. Taboo does not separate different from different, Testart keeps insisting, but only identical from identical, and thus blood from blood. But for this generalization of blood, and for the corresponding devaluation of classificatory difference, no convincing motivation is offered. Blood is not, after all, Marx's generalized commodity, although Testart seems to treat it as such—that is, as money.

Perhaps the problem with Testart is that, by dint of a vaguely Marxian detour, he allows himself to be more Durkheimian than Durkheim himself, since he reduces the entire perceived universe of "primitive communism" to a mere projection of the social (itself reduced to the rule of reciprocity) in its reified (bloody) state. But however socially influenced, the classification of the world has its integrity, which cannot be ignored, not even by taboo.

Recently, Testart has attempted to resolve some of the empirical and conceptual difficulties of his theory by reformulating it.[221] He now views the principle of avoided identity as an a priori condition of symbolic efficacy and thus as independent of any specific social base. Moreover, he has ceased to connect the expression of identity with blood exclusively. It is the idea of substance, rather than any specific substance, that allows one to think about identity. Instead of saying that blood should never be summed with blood, he now says that a substance should never be summed with itself. Nevertheless, blood retains a privileged status as the best substance with which to think identity. Finally, Testart claims that the conjunction of identicals is ambivalent and not just negative; it may therefore be sought as much as avoided. The real issue, he says, is how to avoid its negative consequences while benefitting from its positive ones.

Thus the theory of taboo becomes part of a more general theory of symbolic efficacy, which Testart uses to account for everything from cosmogonies to magical operations. All his interpretations of such phenomena consist in finding an "S structure" (where the *S* of *sang* has become the *S* of *substance*) at work in them. This structure consists of the "transgressive" conjunction of two terms which share the same substance or which have both been in contact with it, together with the negative and positive consequences of a conjunction, in addition to the devices for neutralizing the negative ones.

Testart is certainly right to point out that one cannot separate negative from positive effects, and thus phenomena of avoidance such as taboo from their opposites (e.g. magical or mythological associations of what should not otherwise be associated). But he is just as unconvincing now as before when he attempts to prove that only the association of identicals is efficacious, whether negatively or positively. The same criticisms that apply to the view that taboo is really about summing blood with blood apply to his view that symbolic efficacy (which in its negative form corresponds to taboo) is about adding a substance to itself. Just like the "incest" view of all taboos, the "incest" view of all symbolic efficacy is made possible by an extreme form of reductionism which disregards the relational attributions of identity and difference by local classifications. By devaluing or denouncing the latter as misleading, Testart begs the question of whether the "substantialism" he attributes to symbolic thought is not in fact a figment of his own decontextualized analysis of the "substances" employed by that thought. Only by separating a substance from the specific contexts and relations in which it is used can he claim that it has the same and identical symbolic value in all of them—indeed that it is this identity exclusively which is ground for symbolic use. Substances thus become essences—that is, substances in the Aristotelian sense.

Testart's reduction of all symbolic efficacy to the principle of identity forces him into a worse predicament than ignoring the differences that exist among discrete forms of the same substance. He must also treat different substances as if they were the same. Indeed, whenever native statements attribute symbolic efficacy to a difference, not an identity, of substance, Testart is at pains to demonstrate that such differences are either mere appearances or secondary formations. His favorite argument for treating two different substances as "really" one is that they have the same effect. He argues, in sum, for the identity or similarity of the cause with the effect.

But the problem is that in the symbolic world, even more than in the physical one, the same effect can be produced by different causes. Furthermore, the argument that some differences of substance are secondary formations rests on the claim that these differences result from the polarization of the negative and positive effects of the conjunction of a substance with itself. However, such a derivation remains largely a postulate, to which Testart gives credibility mostly by a tortuous piece of myth analysis. Both arguments ultimately presuppose a radical devaluation of native statements.

In fact, Testart goes so far as to claim that these statements always "mask" the "veritable reasons"[222] of belief and even that they take "forms contrary to their ideological reality."[223] But it is not clear what the motivations for these distortions may be, nor through what processes they occur. If the relationship of a substance with itself is really what propels symbolic thought, why should it manifest itself as the relationship of two different and indeed contrary substances? Why should the avoidance of the identical present itself as the avoidance of the different? The need to separate positive and negative consequences can hardly account for this total reversal of the "true" nature of the symbolic.

Testart's theory of taboo, and more generally of symbolic efficacy, seems completely at odds with the usual structuralist and functionalist theories, particularly those of Leach and Douglas. While they stress the preservation of difference, he stresses its creation from the negation of identity. Their presuppositions are dualistic, his are monistic. Identity is for them secondary, for it presupposes a system of differences, but for him the opposite is true: identity is primary and difference is derivative. Indeed, the S structure is first and foremost a requirement of dissimilation, just like the incest taboo. At the same time assimilation—again, just like incest—may be necessary and even inevitable in certain contexts, particularly in making sense mythically of the world. Thus most of Testart's 1991 book is dedicated to an analysis of cosmogonies which show the necessary interdependence, and even relativity, of the conjunction and disjunction of substances.

Rather than being mutually exclusive, the two theories seem to me in need of each other, as I have already remarked with regard to Héritier's version. The Leach-Douglas theory fails to account for the "incestuous" component identified by Héritier and Testart. But the reduction of all taboos and indeed of all symbolic efficacy to this single component (and to issues of substance) is misguided. Difference is clearly primary and irreducible in a number of phenomena. Testart's attempts to prove that it is not are based on unconvincing arguments and questionable assumptions.

If difference and identity are inseparable and equally important, the crucial issue must of course be: At which point in their articulation do the twin notions of taboo and pollution become applicable? Or, put another way: Which of their articulations constitutes a threat, and why? An interesting attempt to answer this question through a theory of personal identity has been sketched by Gomes da Silva.[224] His starting point is Héritier's approach to the issue of the incest taboo. He agrees with her reduction of the problematic of incest to that of the articulation of identity and difference,[225] but notes that her views are doubly inadequate. First of all, she does not take difference as seriously as identity (or similarity). She treats difference as a mere limit of identity—the point where identity or similarity cease to exist.[226] She therefore privileges identity in her theory and, as I myself have noted, all but ignores the issue of "wrong" combination of differences. Second, she conceives of identity too narrowly, as "consanguinity." Gomes da Silva has an easy time in demonstrating that even the examples that she herself invokes prove that much more general notions of identity are involved, and that excessive difference in marriage or sexual relations may be as polluting as excessive similarity. Clearly, even "incest" (that is, taboo and pollution as they apply to sexuality and reproduction) cannot be viewed as a matter of mere "accumulation of identity."

So what is the common principle underlying the two apparently opposite principles of the accumulation of the identical and the combination of the excessively different—or, as I would like to call them, of excluded identity and excluded difference? For Gomes da Silva these are two faces of the same reality: the relationship with the other is indispensable to the constitution of the self, because the other presents the self with an image of himself in which a social relation is entailed. This requires neither too much similarity nor too much difference. The social self is destroyed by images that evoke excessive isolation or excessive opening up, and thus by images provided by an other who is either a replica of oneself or too different from oneself to be comparable at all: "A la crise d'identité où je me trouve plongé aussitôt que l'autre devient un semblable, répond celle qui me frappe lorsque l'autre retombe dans l'indifférence ou, ce qui revient au même, lorsqu'il me dérobe sa présence, son image, ses différences. Il s'agit alors non plus d'éviter des similitudes excessives, mais de prévenir des disjonctions dangereuses."[227] By this interpretation the idea of pollution (that is, of an existential threat to one's identity) intervenes to reestablish the proper balance of identity and difference in a specific social context.[228] It marks off either an intolerable proximity or an intolerable distance.

Nevertheless Gomes da Silva—just like the predecessors he criticizes—seems to see a privileged connection between pollution and excessive similarity. For instance, he writes that "le langage de la pollution énonce, chez les Trobriandais, les règles de l'identité sociale: il recrée un écart différentiel lorsqu'une proximité intolérable est affirmée."[229] And the lesson that he draws from several examples is that "certains des dispositifs de la pollution ont pour fonction d'imposer des règles à l'univers des similitudes."[230] Finally he uses the Indian case to assert that complete strangers are beyond the rules of pollution, which presupposes comparability and thus, fundamentally, similarity.[231]

So it seems that while Gomes da Silva's theory requires a symmetric treatment of similarity and difference, his practice is once again skewed in favor of similarity, if less so than that of Héritier. Is this because pollution does tend to concentrate on similarity relations (as we would expect, if for very different reasons, both from the Héritier-Testart approach and from the Douglas-Leach approach) or because of Gomes da Silva's selection of empirical cases? It may well be that there are cultures where the question of identity is posed principally in the sphere of similarity, so that pollution concepts do not apply beyond it. One instance is the Hindu case treated by Gomes da Silva. But there are cultures where the outsider is equally at issue and where he or she may be as polluting as, or more polluting than, the insider. Judaism and the French aristocracy from the late sixteenth to the early eighteenth century[232] may serve as examples.

The more crucial issue raised by Gomes da Silva's views, however, is another one. Can the notions of pollution and taboo in all their manifestations be fully or directly explained by his account of identity, that is, by the mere dialectic of self and other? The answer depends in part on the kind of extension that can be given to this dialectic. To explain food taboos, for instance, the constituting other would have to include animal and vegetal species. But then, can these be said to enter the sphere of taboo simply because they symbolize a human other who is either too close or too distant? Or do the relations of natural species have their integrity; do they form an order which humans have to respect even if it symbolizes nothing human? How far does anthropocentricism have to go? Unfortunately, as it stands, Gomes da Silva's theory—just like that of Héritier—is deficient in two respects: it is not clear how it applies to relationships between humans and nonhumans, and it does not explain why certain spheres of activity or experience are imbued with ideas of pollution whereas others are not. Presumably those that are imbued with such ideas have more to do with the constitution of identity than those that are not. But we would like to know why and how.

"Totemism" has long provided anthropology with the ground on which the interrelationship of human and nonhuman aspects in the dialectic of self and other (and thus also in the creation of identity) can be apprehended. In its classical form, which associates exogamous groups with natural species conceived as their ancestors, as well as with various ritual practices, the concept has long been abandoned. But it survives as a descriptive term for a variety of relations between social units and natural ones (particularly animal and vegetal species). The most famous formulation given to totemism in this sense is that of Lévi-Strauss. For him, it is solely a phenomenon of classification. Moreover, it is based not on a term-to-term relationship between social units and natural units but on the relationship established between two series of differences: differences among natural species and differences among social species. Rather than saying that moiety *x* is related to eaglehawk and moiety *y* is related to crow, he says that moiety *x* is related to moiety *y* as eaglehawk is related to crow. In other words, totemism is invariably systemic and differential: the individual signification of a species is irrelevant; any species would do, provided it would sustain a difference with another one.[233]

No doubt this "phonological" view applies well to certain cases, but does it exhaust the complexities of animal and human relationships? Even in the paradigmatic case of eaglehawk and crow, which is borrowed from Radcliffe-Brown's discussion of certain Australian societies,[234] more than a mere difference between two series is involved. As Fortes notes, following Radcliffe-Brown, eaglehawk and crow are the two chief meat-eating birds of Australia. They are thus perceived as analogous to the meat-eating aborigines. Furthermore, the two birds relate to meat inversely: the eaglehawk hunts, the crow scavenges. The common element between animal series and human series is thus a principle of rivalry and complementary opposition, not one of mere difference where the nature and behavior of the two species is irrelevant.[235]

Lévi-Strauss himself contradicts his general proposition, at least on the human side of the relationship, when he writes: "When nature and culture are thought of as two systems of differences between which there is a formal analogy, it is the systematic character of each domain which is brought to the fore. Social groups are distinguished from one another but they retain their solidarity as parts of the same whole, and the rule of exogamy furnishes the means of resolving this opposition balanced between diversity and unity."[236] Here, the system involves not just difference but also a dynamic balance of diversity and unity whose key is to be found in the principle of exogamy. Exogamy so conceived is very close to the incest taboo as conceived by Héritier and Gomes da Silva, but also close to the plain old principle of complementary opposition of British social anthropology. Yet Lévi-Strauss's momentary recourse to the idea of dynamic balance is much more limited in scope than is the case with any of these other authors.

On the social side, it is limited to a social structure based on the principle of exogamy or else (as Lévi-Strauss mentions elsewhere in *The Savage Mind*) on food exchanges that extend or substitute for exogamy in securing the "interlocking of social groups with one another."[237] On the natural side, the principle is completely absent, and it is not specified what provides the unity in difference, unless it is a higher-level taxonomic class. For instance, "birdness" is the unity against which all its specific differences (the bird species that function as totems) are measured. The problems are, of course, that totems are rarely all of one genus and that it remains to be demonstrated that taxonomy is the only or even the most important principle in totemic classifications. In any event, Lévi-Strauss's statement implies that there may be important differences between natural and social series with regard to their systemic character. Saying that only the differences between the elements of the two series are analogically comparable, then, may well be saying that only what is trivially common to any classification is comparable. Far from demonstrating that totemism is just about the comparison of pure differences, the proposition may indicate that Lévi-Strauss has focussed on what is less important about totemism, that in the search for excessive generalities he has missed the interesting complexities of the phenomenon.

Among such complexities must also be reckoned, of course, the numerous cases in which the relationship between social unit and natural unit is not a function of any systemic principle whatsoever or a function of those in which, whatever the systemic principle involved in the choice of a species over another, the one-to-one relationship between a human unit and its natural counterpart becomes more important in mental and social practice than the systemic one. Lévi-Strauss recognizes that such one-to-one relations may take over in certain cases, but declares them debasements of totemism or transformations of it in the direction of "caste."[238] This is a curiously essentialist way of looking at totemism, however. Why should these phenomena be less representative than those that correspond to Lévi-Strauss's definition? Why not modify the definition or, better, acknowledge that totemism is a rather heterogeneous family of phenomena, which cannot be reduced to any essence, however abstract, such as the analogical relationship of two series of differences?

In any case, the issue is not simply that totemic classifications are more complex and heterogeneous than Lévi-Strauss makes them. It is not even just that the contingent, the idiosyncratic, and even the aleatory play a far greater role in totemism than he is prepared to admit. The issue is also that identity is never a matter of pure classification, but a matter of relationships in which the subject is engaged through more than his or her contemplative activities—that is, relationships that are both pragmatic and moral, together with the internal process of identification or distancing.[239] The principle of balance between similarity and difference, for instance, is not one that may be reduced to its taxonomic expression. It involves total relationships between human subjects and between them and their natural correlates, whatever the mode and reason of their correlation.

Lévi-Strauss's treatment of taboos is symptomatic of his inability to view little more than classificatory concordances and oppositions in the "totemic" family of phenomena. He views taboos as redundant or alternative[240] to the main totemic fact—namely the constitution of a series of "natural" signifiers for a series of "cultural" signifieds (i.e. social units).[241] Either taboos reinforce the semiotic power of natural species by attracting attention to their special status, or they take the place of those species by creating their own discontinuities. In other words, either I do not eat kangaroo so as to indicate that kangaroo is my totem, or I do not eat them so as to create a difference between me and those who do eat them. Either the taboo signifies the totem which signifies the group, or it signifies the group directly. Naturally Lévi-Strauss, with his habitual ingenuity, provides much more complex examples than this of the interrelationship of totem and taboo,[242] but the basic thesis remains untouched: taboo creates a "signification" which is reduced to the creation of a social difference, or rather a difference of social units.

No doubt taboo may be what Lévi-Strauss says it is. Nonetheless many taboos and even food taboos have nothing to do with totemism or the totemic function of differentiating social units (including categories and individuals). Even with regard to the latter function, the mere semiotic difference between one taboo and another may be far less relevant than the moral difference created by the specific "burden" of each. This is the case in Huaulu, at least.

Furthermore, it is erroneous to assume that people are necessarily aware of the totems and taboos of others, although this is precisely the assumption required by the differentiality thesis propounded by Lévi-Strauss. The point has been noted for peoples as different as the Dinka and the Tallensi.[243] Among both, differences among descent groups are sufficiently sustained by names or by positive practices[244] visible to all. Negative practices, by their very nature, are more elusive: one cannot learn from mere avoidance, since avoidance becomes apparent only if its object is already known. Moreover, avoidances or other forms of respectful behavior reserved for totems often concern species or events that are rarely encountered. In any case, one does not seek to know or to know precisely what is not of direct concern to one.

Taboos, whether they stem from totemic relations or not, are mainly of interest for the negative consequences that follow from their violation. These need concern only their owners. It is precisely this differential interest, and therefore knowledge, that the communicational theory cannot explain. But both are perfectly intelligible if totems and taboos are seen as moral phenomena concerning only particular subjects, and especially as phenomena of self-identification. Not that internal and external identifications are separable. On the contrary, they need one another. But the cultural emphasis is on the first, as is indicated, for instance, by the Huaulu reluctance to invade the sphere of another person's being by seeking to know his totems, his taboos (and not infrequently his names), even when they are not secret.

Lévi-Strauss assumes that the universe of the savage mind is a universe of communication and thus that the key for the interpretation of all institutions lies in their communicative structure and function. But for many institutions, or aspects thereof, this is true only in a negative sense, because they are based on the blocking of communication and the withholding of information. Therefore a purely classificatory interpretation of identity constitution seems inadequate, since it presupposes that every participant in the system has full information on its elements. In fact, the subject assumes an identity vis-à-vis himself and others less by the trivial fact that he wears certain publicly recognized badges of identification than because something of himself is withdrawn from others, is uniquely his, or is uniquely accomplishable by him.

This dual character, both inward- and outward-looking, is even stronger in taboo than in totemism. For taboos characteristically concern the body, which is radically individual and personal, even when they identify groups in Lévi-Strauss's classificatory sense. This is particularly true of food taboos because, as Fortes observes, eating is a very social act, indeed the most common and pervasive after speaking, and yet a "peculiarly individual activity. Everybody must eat for himself."[245] It is not an act that anybody else can do for us. It is therefore uniquely ours even when it takes place in a collective context and is imbued with indices of our position in that context.

Eating thus joins the social and the personal. But it also joins the human and nonhuman in complex oppositions and identifications, since it consists in turning animal or vegetal bodies into my own body. Food taboos indicate all these dimensions—human to human, human to nonhuman, collective to personal—in the process of constitution of identity. For they introduce contrasts between the eater and other eaters and between the eater and the beings which are eaten. These contrasts may be motivated by identification (as when food taboos concern totems) or by repulsion (as when they concern animals or vegetals which are viewed as inimical to the identity of the eater). Identifications and repulsions are, in turn, explained by the properties attributed to the various edible things, and not merely by their differences.

Food taboos are thus far more complex than Lévi-Strauss's "totemism" and cannot be viewed merely as appendages or alternatives to it. They imply a dialectical relationship between internalization and externalization (for which the very process of eating, digesting, and excreting furnishes an apt model) and between intrahuman and extrahuman relations, not the simple concordance or "formal analogy" of separate series that is stressed in Lévi-Strauss's analysis. In any case, even when the idea of totemism as analogy between two systems of differences applies, it does not apply in the way postulated by Lévi-Strauss in his most "Marxist" moments, that is, as a communicative superstructure resting on an autonomously motivated system of infrastructurally determined social differences.[246] As Lévi-Strauss himself recognizes at his best, totemism is not just a system of signals used to communicate preexisting identities, but is also part and parcel of the very process through which those identities are constituted in the subjects who assume them.[247]

An interesting attempt to develop a subjective perspective on taboo—that is, one that takes into account taboo's role in creating a sense of personal identity and agency—has been made by Alfred Gell. He emphasizes the constitutive character of taboo even at its most Lévi-Straussian, that is, as a diacritical sign. For Gell, taboo does not signal a self that preexists it; it *is* a form of existence of the self:

> The "I" does not stand apart from the world in placing a portion of it under a variety of interdictions: it is present only in the network of intentionalities which bind it to the world, its contours outlined in the

> very substance of the world. Taboos on eating, on killing, on sexual intercourse, on looking at, touching, etc., together circumscribe a "hole" in the texture of shareable intersubjective reality which, privileged with respect to a specific individual, constitutes his soul, or ego, or personality. Taboo does more than express the self: it constitutes the self.[248]

In other words, personal identity consists in a difference from other humans which coincides with a difference in their relationship with the world.[249] But the latter is not merely semiotic. Objects are not merely socially recognized signs of socially recognized subjects, as in Lévi-Strauss. They are also objects of different experiences for different subjects, and it is these different experiences that constitute their personal sense of identity. An account of taboo that leaves out this experiential, "intentional" relationship with the object leaves out much of the phenomenon. It makes it impossible to apprehend the dialectic of internal and external identifications, of personal and collective discrimination, which sustains the existence of the self and which taboo helps bring to existence.

But Gell wishes to go beyond a diacritical approach to taboo, however modified. He argues that if the ego[250] consists in "a network of relations, having its origin in intentional acts," then it is necessary to ask, What are the form and dynamics of this network in a particular culture? In fact, he wants to find out what the place of taboo is in a "culturally specific personality system."[251] Taboo cannot be separated from its opposite, "lapse." Various types of oscillation from one to the other constitute the processes through which personality is formed in the New Guinea people which Gell uses as an example.

One such process is that of hunting and its corollaries. Among the Umeda, as is the case with many other hunting peoples, it is taboo for men to eat the game that they themselves have killed. They therefore give it to their allies (in the sense of "affines") to eat. Sexual intercourse with the women of the allied groups is apparently the reward for these gifts of meat. But to be able to hunt again men must separate themselves from women and ascetically retreat to the forest. Gell sees in this sequence a dialectical alternation of dissipation and asceticism, of consumption and renunciation, through which the interaction of ego and world plays itself out.[252] He also sees an interplay of paradigmatic and syntagmatic relations which determines the specific content of taboo. He argues that the three stages of the sequence are paradigmatically equivalent. Killing, eating, and sexual intercourse are all forms of *tadv*, a term to which Gell refuses to attribute a "basic" meaning (although some would argue that its proper, against figurative, meaning is precisely "to eat"). When paradigmatically equivalent acts follow one another, as in the above process, the subject cannot have the same relationship to them. Because one form of tadv ("eating" game) follows another one ("killing" game), the man who kills—say, a pig—cannot eat it. Participating in one activity excludes participating in another activity that is its paradigmatic equivalent.

But this motivation of taboo with what sounds like an application of Jakobson's theory of the poetic function[253] seems hardly satisfactory to me. To begin with, the alleged motivation of taboo is itself left unmotivated. Why should the subject relate in opposite ways to paradigmatically equivalent activities? Gell's only attempt to answer the question is contained, almost as an afterthought, in a footnote. Moreover he refers there to a single dimension of the application of the principle, namely to the relationship of what he calls "planes of *tadv* relations . . . that is, the plane of the individual's own sexual-gustatory-aggressive experience, the planes of his vicarious experience, his dreams, myths, sociological constructs, etc."[254] He sees these planes as having different degrees of generality. Dreams, myths, and so on, "generalize" experience and thus have a metaphoric relationship with it. The principle that one cannot relate at the same time with different planes, suggests Gell, is really a "framing device" which maintains a separation between "'metaphors of experience' and what is *meant*." And he concludes: "The metaphor of *tadv* relations, which generalizes the ego-world interaction (eating, aggression and sexuality) at the same time motivates an Umeda preoccupation with keeping separate in reality what metaphor unites in terms of a cognitive paradigm."[255]

But even if we accept this as an explanation for the opposite relations (taboo or lapse) that exist vis-à-vis the same (or equivalent) elements as they exist in different "planes," we are still unable to account for the polarization found inside each plane, and particularly in the "lived" one. Why should I not eat the pig after I have killed it? The only possible way to account for this taboo in terms of Gell's theory is to do precisely what he says cannot be done, that is, to consider one meaning of *tadv* as metaphoric and another one as literal. Killing is metaphoric "eating"; that is why it should be maintained separately from literal eating. But then what explains that there is lapse and not taboo with regard to sexuality, which is again paradigmatically equivalent to killing according to Gell's theory? The difficulty here exists in whether sexual intercourse is given metaphoric status or not. And it exists not only from the point of view of the men who have done the killing, but also from that of the women who have done the eating. In fact, there seems to be a double reason for sexual intercourse to be taboo between them. Yet this is precisely where there is lapse rather than taboo.

Quite clearly, the coexistence of these opposite behaviors is due to a more complex principle of syntagmatic organization than the principle of incompatibility between different terms of a paradigmatic chain. This more complex principle is precisely the oscillation between asceticism and abandon, activity and passivity, of which Gell speaks so eloquently. But then if this principle dictates that there should be taboo at one stage and lapse at another, it does not explain why the taboo should be on the pig's meat and the lapse on the woman's flesh. Gell's principle of paradigmatic incompability can claim only to explain one, as we have seen, which means that, in fact, it explains neither.[256] In my opinion the problem is not so much that Gell has not presented a convincing account of the interrelationship of, syntagmatic and paradigmatic structure as that the idea of exhaustively accounting for the situation by this interrelationship is misguided to begin with. It artificially homogenizes phenomena that seem to have rather diverse and multiple motivations and consequences.

Take the so-called paradigm which encompasses killing, eating, and having sexual intercourse. This is constructed on the basis of the use of a single word (*tadv*) to refer to these activities. We are told that the word refers indifferently and in the same way to any of them, but this seems improbable,[257] and in the course of his analysis Gell in fact admits that some uses are metaphoric. In any case I see no reason to reduce the relationship of these three acts to a single, identical dimension. Killing may be comparable to eating in certain respects, but the two things are quite different in others. And the difference between both of them and sex is even greater. But the real issue is another one.

Is it mere identity or identity *and* difference which determine the legitimate sequencing of acts—whether an act is appropriate or inappropriate at a certain point? In a way, Gell seems close to Testart in privileging identity at the expense of difference. We have seen that there are serious problems with leaving the tension of identity and difference out of the picture. In any case, does the taboo on eating the game one has killed result from a perceived equivalence of eating and killing, or instead from an equivalence of killer and killed? Gell himself begins his discussion of Umeda ideas of taboo by saying that they have "everything to do with avoiding eating one's own self."[258] All taboos, in sum, are taboos of autocannibalism, directly or indirectly.

But then it seems that Gell pays less attention to the idea that external objects are taboo because they evoke the self than to the idea that they evoke the self because they are taboo for it. Indeed, in his interpretive scheme the relationship between the self and its correlative objectives is mediated by a grammar based on such principles as that of the syntagmatic incompatibility of the terms of a paradigm.

Granted that the relationship between the self and the objects that stand for it in the world is not independent of the cultural "grammar," the latter is not independent of the properties of those objects (that is, their aptitude to symbolize aspects of a particular identity) and especially of the totality of their lived relationship with subjects. It seems to me very difficult to derive the identification of the hunted pig with his human hunter (which Gell repeatedly mentions) as a mere offshoot of the identification of eating with killing. It is a much more particular relationship, and one that can be understood (at least if I can judge from Huaulu) only by reference to the total experience of the hunt.[259] Nor can one leave out of the picture the relationships with other humans in the form of a distributive rule with regard to the consumption of meat. By separating producer from consumer, the taboo on eating one's own kill perpetuates human relationships through relationships with animals.

It is therefore obvious that many different reasons for the taboo exist. This overdetermination rules out any single-principle, grammar-like interpretation. For the same reason, it is difficult to postulate a perfect symmetry between taboo and lapse when they concern rather different activities such as food and sex. Moreover, the alternation of taboo and lapse in the specific example considered by Gell may better be explained by a logic of reciprocity (a sort of exophagy complementing exogamy and linking affinal groups with one another) than by a "syntagmatic structure" necessary for the existence of the subject. The point is that different things are going on at the same time, and they cannot be reduced to a single logical organization. A certain tendency toward the semiotic homogenization of a complex reality may indeed be at work in Umeda taboo, but it is a tendency and not an achieved result which allows us to disregard its persistent heterogeneity.

Gell is certainly right to point out that taboo, by carving out a part of the world, carves out a self. But he neglects to add the implication: that this self must then be located in the body. For what are the relations between object and subject that taboo regulates? Principally eating, touching, and penetrating, as in killing and having sex. All these involve the body as desiring, that is, as feeding on its objects, consuming them. Even gazing may be the expression of a desire to consume, and this is why it often enters the province of taboo. Moreover, these relations do not simply imply that the subject exists as a body. They also imply a certain homogenization of subject and object. A subject that exists through its consumption of objects must itself become an object. Reciprocally, the objects of consumption must be given the status of bodies when they are not already fully endowed as such (as are sexual partners or human victims). In sum, a subject conceived as feeding on its objects, as principally endowed with a corporeal existence like theirs, runs the risk of losing itself in them: they invade it and undermine its identity. The totemic view of taboo which Gell still fundamentally shares with Lévi-Strauss makes him miss this crucial element of corporeality inherent in taboo. More important, it makes him miss the dialectic that ensues from a corporeal conception of the subject—a dialectic of which taboo is an expression and to which it provides a response.

This element of corporeality is instead stressed by others—although usually from perspectives different from the one which I have just outlined—and I will develop it in due time. For instance, Anna Meigs has revindicated the body-centeredness of the notion of pollution and thus also, by implication, the body-centeredness of the notion of taboo, in an ethnographically based critique of Douglas and Leach. Meigs shows that Douglas's equation of "out of place" and "polluting" is unwarranted. The "cognitive discomfort experienced when confronted with ambivalence, ambiguity, or anomaly" is very different from the fear of pollution which is felt when decaying living matter or matter that is subject to decay as soon as it leaves the body—such as semen, blood, sweat—threatens to gain access to our body and thus to make it decay and die too.[260]

Meigs is undoubtedly right to emphasize that among the Hua of Papua New Guinea[261] and among modern North Americans pollutants are "substances which are perceived as decaying, carriers of such substances and symbols of them."[262] And it is quite likely that the unwanted invasion of the body by decay-inducing substances furnishes the basic model of pollution everywhere. Yet Meigs is insufficiently attentive to the possible expansion of this basic corporeal model in directions that bring the idea of pollution away from the exclusive focus on decaying substances or their "symbols." She reifies her own definitions and runs against actual usage, even in her own culture, when she introduces a rigid separation of "pollution" and other forms by which harmful substances intrude into the body or into things assimilated to the body. For instance, she denies that the modern use of *pollution* to refer to the contamination of water, air, and the environment is justified: "These substances which are dangerous to our bodies but which are not decaying and which do not arouse revulsion properly fall into the category of poisons."[263] I am not sure that pollution of water by sewerage or chemicals does not elicit revulsion; in any event, the case could as well be used to argue that it is wrong to separate the basic ground of pollution from all its possible extensions. Pollution cannot be imprisoned in Meigs's definition, because that definition is merely differential[264] and as such it does not contain all the aspects of the basic ground that may be used for its metaphoric extension.

One aspect that is left out is the notion of the undermining of bodily integrity by an incompatible substance. This is the aspect that underlies the notion of pollution in the environmental sense and also in many of its religious senses: pollution of a sanctuary, of a ritual object, of a priest or god, by contact with an incompatible person, animal, plant, or substance that does not have to be decaying or to evoke decay. These uses of the notion of pollution (exemplified, for instance, by the

Greek *miasma* or the Sanskrit *asauca*) usually also imply a further metaphoric extension, even more abstract in kind, of the basic corporeal model on which Meigs focusses exclusively. This extension results in the notion of inappropriate mixing, of loss of distinctiveness. Here *pollution* is used to describe the passage from purity, in the sense of "without mixture," to impurity—precisely the area covered by Douglas's, Leach's, and many others' analyses of pollution. Granted that this area is not necessarily identical with pollution, it must also be recognized that it always overlaps it, and not just in the limited way considered by Meigs (of which more anon). Indeed, it is curious that she never talks of the relationship of the notion of pollution with the notions of purity and impurity.

One can also point out that, when applied to food, Meigs's way of tracing the distinction between polluting and poisonous or merely harmful can be quite misleading—even, it seems to me, with regard to American culture. For it is by no means the case that the distinction falls where she puts it or is as clear-cut as she says. Junk food is harmful, even poisonous, but one can also argue that, for people of a certain class or with certain social pretenses, it is polluting in the sense that eating it (or at least being seen eating it by one's peers) undermines those pretenses because it is morally demeaning. Indeed the integrity of a certain identity rests on forms of consumption appropriate to that identity. Junk food is not unhealthy for just your physical body; it is even more unhealthy for your cultural body, since it is the food of culturally devalued people ("health" being an index of superior knowledge and morality in American society).

There is nothing here that does not recall pollution in more exotic locales. There as here, pollution consists not only of an undermining of the body by decaying substances, but also of an undermining of one's identity as expressed in bodily terms, and thus as defined by the inclusions or exclusions of certain substances in or from the body. In fact, it seems to me that there is no such thing as a purely asymbolic pollution. Harmful intrusions into the body, even if they concern decaying substances, can rate as harmful only if they have nothing to do with our sense of identity. The reason that certain bodily substances are viewed as polluting is precisely that, coming from inside other people, they intimately belong to them, and thus undermine our own intimate sense of self when they enter into contact with us. Their decay and decay-inducing properties are secondary: they simply reinforce a fear of loss of identity and integrity which *already* evokes death.

In sum, although Meigs correctly identifies the ground of pollution as bodily, she does not correctly identify the attributes of that bodiliness that warrant talk of pollution. For her that bodiliness is largely physical, and thus pollution remains an unanalyzed revulsion—in fact, a mere instinctual reaction to the phenomena of bodily decay.[265] Cultural symbolism intervenes for her only as a modification of this basic reaction and in order to explain that contact with the bodily excretions of others may be desired instead of being resisted.[266] She argues that contact is "easily accepted if not desired" when the relationship with the excreting person is positive, resisted when the relationship is negative: "One shares a glass, even a fork, with a friend. Victors in a field sport embrace each other's sweating bodies. Saliva and sweat are freely exchanged in love-making." Generally speaking, "bodily emissions may have positive as well as negative powers. Which power obtains in any specific instance is determined by the relationship."[267]

This analysis is far too simplistic, however. It does not explain how the existence of a "positive relationship" can turn an otherwise spontaneous feeling of disgust into its contrary. Nor can it explain why certain bodily products remain polluting, however positive the relationship with their producers. North American lovers or sportsmen are not supposed to exchange excrement, although they may exchange other bodily substances. Also, Meigs dispenses a bit too quickly with the essential ambivalence of bodily emissions on which Leach insists.[268] This ambivalence does not simply consist, as she says, in the fact that the same bodily emissions can be positive or negative depending on the interpersonal relationship involved. It is inherent in the unique ability of these substances, with their flows in and out of the body, to reflect the contradictory relationships of abandon and resistance, permeability and impermeability, through which the self is constituted in its relationship with others.[269] This contradictory coexistence is present in some measure in all relationships, positive or negative. Indeed love, which Meigs qualifies as an unambiguously positive relationship, may be seen as flirting with precisely that loss of identity which we fear most, but also desire most, and which is evoked by the mixing of the innermost bodily substances. To be penetrated, invaded, just as to penetrate, to invade, is to bring down the boundaries of self and other, to experience the shudder—and pleasure—of self-annihilation, of a death that is no death. Love is, perhaps, a controlled form of fear, playing with the catastrophe of pollution by circumscribing it in a space and time hidden from the all-seeing eye of society and its relentless dictate of personal integrity.

In sum, it may well be that ambivalence, rather than the instinctual fear of decay that Meigs postulates, is the crucial feature of bodily emissions. It makes them ideally suited to represent the fundamental ambiguities of a subject constituted by both separation from and communion with the other. In any case, it is not enough to say that these substances are polluting where their access to the body is not desired.[270]

Only when they are not desired because they undermine the symbolic body—the subject—can they be said to be polluting.

The point that what is at stake in pollution is the integrity of the subject is developed by Julia Kristeva.[271] To follow her argument, it is necessary to keep in mind the opposition that she makes between "semiotic" and "symbolic." Kristeva uses *symbolic* to refer to the phenomenon of signification as described by Husserl, namely as an act of predication whereby object and transcendental subject are simultaneously constituted. She opposes the "symbolic" in this sense to the "semiotic"—the realm of significant articulations which are logically anterior to sign and predication and which, therefore, lack the stability and coherence provided by the transcendental consciousness.[272]

In her psychoanalytic perspective, influenced by Lacan, the semiotic is constituted in the prelinguistic stage of development, when the child is still an appendix of the mother or feels imperfectly distinguished from her. It is through her, because of the frustrations and interdictions that come from her, that the child learns to divide its body like a territory "avec zones, orifices, points et lignes, surfaces et creux où se marque et s'exerce le pouvoir archaïque de la maîtrise et de l'abandon, de la différenciation du propre et de l'impropre, du possible et de l'impossible."[273] Over and against this prelinguistic topography of the body, which is based on maternal authority, is built the linguistic order which is acquired in the phallic phase (shared by both males and females)[274] and is associated with paternal laws. Through language and the resolution of the Oedipus complex, humans acquire a distinct and stable subject that is the correlate of a stable system of symbolic distinctions—culture. "Si le langage, comme la culture, établit une séparation et, à partir d'éléments discrets, enchaîne un ordre, c'est précisément en refoulant cette authorité maternelle et la topographie corporelle qui les jouxtent."[275] What happens when the "paternal" symbolic order does not sufficiently repress the "maternal" semiotic order, when a subject that is the function of language does not completely displace a presubject that exists in the instability of the semiotic differentiation of the body—and of the differentiation of one's body from that of the mother? What happens is the phenomenon of ritual pollution, which Kristeva interprets as a transposition into the realm of the symbolic of the borderline separating "the territory of the body from the signifying chain":[276]

> A travers le langage et dans les institutions hautement hiérarchisées que sont les religions, l'homme hallucine des "objets" partiels—témoins d'une différenciation archaïque du corps sur la voie de l'identité propre qui est aussi l'identité sexuelle. La *souillure* dont le rite nous protège, n'est ni signe ni matière. À l'intérieur du rite qui l'extrait du refoulement

> et du désir pervers, la souillure est la trace translinguistique des frontières les plus archaïques du corps propre. En ce sens, si elle est object chu, elle l'est de la mère.[277]

Pollution is what Kristeva calls *abjection:* a loss of the symbolically, linguistically founded subject, a fall into its presymbolic stage, where the subject becomes lost in the object instead of constituting itself by standing against the object.[278] The potential for this dissolution exists as soon as a symbolic order constitutive of human subjectivity exists. Hence pollution is a universal phenomenon: "on le rencontre dès que se constitue la dimension symbolique et/ou sociale de l'humain."[279] It is a defensive ideology, enshrined in rites: "ces rites religieux ont pour fonction de conjurer la peur chez le sujet, d'engouffrer sans retour dans la mère son identité propre."[280] And this fear is all the greater in societies where, for whatever reason,[281] the symbolic "exclusion imperative," associated with male power and constituting "collective existence," is relatively weak. Then the "abject or demonic power of the feminine" "n'arrive pas à se différencier comme *autre,* mais menace le *propre* qui sous-tend toute organisation faite d'exclusions et de mises en ordre."[282]

For Kristeva, who echoes here Freud's *Moses and Monotheism* and *The Future of an Illusion,* the history of morality is that of a progressive reinforcement of the "male" principle of symbolic differentiation and order as against the "female" principle of indifferentiation (or, what amounts to the same, of a merely semiotic, pre-predicative, differentiation). This evolution is correlated with transformations of both principles. Kristeva postulates a primitive stage in which pollution exists in a very "material register": as "le mélange, le flux, le non-conforme convergeant vers ce lieu 'impropre' dans tous les sens du terme qu'est le vivant maternel."[283] At this stage, impurity is fundamentally "dirt," and the pure seems to be defined merely as separation from this dirt. The next stage, which Kristeva identifies with Mosaic law and more specifically with the Levitican abominations, is characterized by a more abstract conception of impurity, matching a more abstract conception of the pure: "la souillure sera maintenant ce qui porte atteinte à l'unicité symbolique, c'est-à-dire les simulacres, les ersatz, les doubles, les idoles."[284]

In other words Kristeva, following Douglas, interprets the biblical system of food taboos as a symbolic statement on the nature of God. God is one as the taxonomic logic of his creation is one: "la loi . . . est une taxinomie."[285] To respect this order and shun the species or individuals that violate it, is to be holy—that is, separated, differentiated in logical fashion, like God himself. The unholy is the unseparated, the confused, the logically heterogeneous—in a word, the polytheistic. In sum, in this conception the "maternal," with the risk of regressive dissolution it evokes for the separated subject, is overlaid by the risk of a dissolution of "paternal" logical distinctions. Food provides the bridge between the two. The world as food can easily stand as a transformation of the mother as food. A loss of distinction between lawful and unlawful food can thus be seen as metaphoric of a more primordial loss of distinction: that between child and mother.[286] Conversely, keeping one distinction implies keeping the other. Moreover, the giving up of an "impure" food matches the giving up of an impure part of oneself—one's prepuce, viewed as the symbol of one's attachment to the mother.[287]

Accepting the food taboos is thus accepting "castration": a distinction in one's body that correlates with a system of distinctions outside it,[288] in what may be desired, eaten both literally and metaphorically. This acceptance is to be "pure" of the feminine, like God the Father himself. Refusing the food taboos is becoming a baby again—inseparable, indistinguishable from mother. It is to suckle again, to be soiled again—to become impure like mother herself, dripping milk, leaking blood. This is why Kristeva affirms that all the Levitican taboos "s'étayent sur l'interdiction de l'inceste," in the psychoanalytic sense, of course.[289]

A further development occurs, according to Kristeva, when the Christian notion of sin substitutes the Levitican notion of pollution. While Judaism externalizes abjection, Christianity internalizes it. Impurity has its source *in interiore homine,* not in some animal or people outside him. It is to demonstrate this point that Christ violates all taboos.[290] This reversal of the source of danger, from outside to inside, correlates with a transformation of orality. Levitican orality is linked with eating; Christian orality is linked with speaking. "Not what goes into the mouth defiles a man, but what comes out of the mouth, this defiles a man" (Matthew 15:11; see also Mark 7:15).

Abjection can thus be purged only by "good" speech, speech addressed to a God who is himself "good speech."[291] Situating the impure in oneself, making it intrinsic to one's being, means reconciling the subject with what is maternally derived in it, since impurity is always maternally derived according to Kristeva. In this sense, Christianity is a revanche of the maternal principle over the paternal one.[292] But if the maternal principle is reconciled with the subject, it is not rehabilitated. The biblical logic of separation survives as a separation in the universe of speech. The speaking being is "brisé entre deux potentialités, la démoniaque et la divine."[293] Sin and salvation exist in a dialectical contest, in an eternal argument between God and Satan.[294] But this contest exists inside the subject; it is not between subject and object, as in Judaism. In sum, the Christian notion of sin, by situating the source of evil in the subject, in the *act* by which it chooses its objects, rather than in the objects as such, completely reverses (in theory at least) the Judaic notion of pollution. Lepers can be kissed and prostitutes embraced. It is not touching them, but refusing to touch them, that is polluting, in the sense of sinful.[295]

Kristeva's attempt to combine Freud, Douglas, and Soler is not without interest. It is indeed likely that some of the forces identified by psychoanalysis (particularly the ambivalent relationship with the mother) are at work in the biblical notions of pollution. After all, the Old Testament is dominated by a God the Father who seems to view such phenomena of motherhood as menstruation and childbirth as particularly inimical to himself, since he excludes them from his cult as polluting. One may even speculate that they are polluting to God because they rival his creative power, and as such threaten his status as the one and only creator. Motherhood may indeed be intrinsically polytheistic. This perhaps explains why it is the first woman, Eve, who forever turns man into a rebel against God in the garden of Eden.

It is also possible that the same forces can be found to underlie the notion of pollution in other cultures, although in forms different from the biblical ones. But of course, there is much more to pollution than its possible psychological appropriations[296] or motivations. Kristeva would no doubt concur with this in principle. But she never attempts to work out the relationship between the actual sociological and classificatory aspects of the notions of pollution and taboo, on the one hand, and their purported psychological foundations, on the other. Yet it would seem that without working those relationships out, some of her crucial claims on the psychological signification of the dietary rules cannot be sustained in any credible way.

Take, for instance, the claim that all pollution ultimately refers to the regression of the subject to its presymbolic relationship with the mother. This interpretation is obviously more credible for certain biblical taboos (like the one on seething the meat of an animal in its mother's milk) than for others. If it applies to other taboos it does so only very indirectly, through a series of mediating steps. Kristeva herself never provides them. She is content with the very general postulate that because taboos are about food and dirt, they must also be about the relationship with mother as feeder and toilet trainer, however indirectly. I doubt that the necessary intermediate steps could be provided for many taboos. Even if they could, they would raise the question, What is more important in determining the taboos—their ultimate, purely unconscious referent, or the multiple sociological, classificatory, and historically situated referents indicated by those "intermediate steps"?

Even if taboos have a psychoanalytic dimension, it is hard to accept that that dimension is equally important in all or is even the most important one in any. The undermining of the subject for which taboo provides a defense has to do with much more than a regressive relationship with the mother, even if it may ultimately be modelled after that relationship. The reason is, of course, that the subject is constituted by the entire spectrum of objectual relations dictated by the cultural order (whether or not this order is to be identified with the "father principle," as Kristeva assumes). The violation of any such prescribed objectual relation is polluting, that is, undermining for the subject, whenever it violates a culturally defined, but strongly embodied, subject, as I have indicated. There is no need to suppose that in all cases pollution implies reference to the maternal in its precultural or anticultural identification. Pollution is the idea of an invasion of the symbolic body, and as such it can refer to primordial experiences, but it also, and more often, refers to more advanced ones: getting sick, being poisoned, contracting a skin disease (an experience which seems particularly important in the biblical context[297] but also, as we shall see, in the Huaulu one), being allergic to something, getting dirty, becoming glued to viscous substances (as in Sartre's famous description), and so on.

Nevertheless, I would agree with Kristeva that the relationship with the mother does play an important archetypal role in the ideas of menstrual and excremental pollution. And I agree with the reasons she gives for this: in the usual process of constituting the subject, the separation from the mother, whose body is both first object and first presymbolic articulator of sense,[298] is a fundamental, but never fully completed, stage. This is what makes the incest taboo and all its equivalents so important in human culture. However, it is one thing to say this and another thing to say that all taboos are ultimately equivalent to or modelled after the incest taboo. This is where I part company with Kristeva, just as I did with Testart.

Indeed, it is curious that both end up producing an incest theory of taboo from a theory of the incest taboo. Although their reasons for it are quite different, I feel that some of my objections to Testart can be extended, *mutatis mutandis,* to Kristeva. It must be recognized, however, that Kristeva's view of taboo does not have the rather decontextualized formalism of Testart's view. The incest taboo is not turned into the model of all taboos by reducing it (and them) to the abstract formula (A + A). Rather, it is claimed that the differentiation of objects develops from and correlates with the differentiation of the subject from its primordial (maternal) object. Classificatory taboos are thus functionally but not formally equivalent to the incest taboo in Kristeva's view.

The most fragile aspect of Kristeva's construction is undoubtedly her tracing of an evolutionary sequence from a "primitive" notion of external pollution[299] to the internalized pollution of Christianity, through the Levitican notion of pollution—external to, but redeemed by, taxonomy. Christianity has indeed a more subjective bent than Judaism and, a fortiori, than Hebraism. But the relationship between the two religions at the time of the formation of Christianity, not to mention their subsequent parallel history, is too complex and multilateral to be viewed as one of succession. Kristeva perpetuates "the image of the timeless Israelite," which has been justly decried by Feeley-Harnik.[300] The most serious problems lie, however, with Kristeva's view that what she calls the taxonomic approach of taboo in the Old Testament is an extraordinary innovation.[301] This unique status accorded to Hebrew taboos implies that the taboos of all other cultures cannot be explained taxonomically and must be relegated to the rather shadowy first stage of Kristeva's evolutionary scheme.

This claim is doubly questionable. First of all, that the Levitican taboos can be explained only by reference to taxonomy is very much open to question, as we have seen. They simply lack the unity, coherence, and exclusively logical nature postulated by Douglas (particularly in *Purity and Danger*) and exaggerated by Kristeva to be so explained.[302] Second, the taboos of all other cultures are no different in this respect. They are as "taxonomic" or untaxonomic as the Levitican ones. If there is a difference it lies in the fact that the taboos of the Hebrews were codified at one point (indeed, it seems, quite late) by priests of a certain lawyerly cast and thus given a certain formal and principled shape. The radical difference postulated by Kristeva is in any case unacceptable in that it consigns all taboo systems except the Levitican one to a sort of shadowy and unformed existence, devoid of classificatory reason. She exaggerates the cult of logic among the Hebrews and ignores its counterparts among the numerous non-Hebrews of the world. Indeed, even in form, the Hebrew classification of animals in terms of the three-tiered universe (heaven, earth, and water) is extremely common.[303]

It would be a pity, however, if the failings of Kristeva's evolutionary construction were to blind us to some of her achievements with regard to the understanding of the phenomenon of pollution. She injects a subjective and developmental dimension into the exclusively classificatory perspective of structuralism. Her point that pollution is the cultural form taken by what threatens the subject because it has to do with its precultural stage—that it is the presymbolic making itself felt in the symbolic—rings true. But it does not sound like the whole truth either.

Personally, I would prefer to see pollution as arising from a more general and less psychologically specific phenomenon than Kristeva thinks. I would say that the culturally articulated subject (the subject constituted in the discursive predications made possible by the symbolic order of culture) fears its loss in the inarticulated that haunts it, precisely because it constitutes itself by standing against the inarticulated. Of this resisting inarticulate, the body, particularly the constantly moving and transforming body which we experience in its processes of ingestion, excretion, reproduction, transformation, and decay, is the strongest expression. The body is not only a substance to be legislated upon, to be turned into grist for the symbolic mill, but also a constant source of nonsense undermining the affirmation of sense. Whether this resisting body is also connected with the infantile experiences invoked by Kristeva, whether the contrast of the semiotically unstable body with the symbolically stable subject corresponds to the contrast of the maternal and the paternal, as she says, matters little in the end. A subject symbolically constituted, but necessarily located in the body, must be haunted by the fear of its disintegration through the body, since it constantly experiences the body's resistance to the subject's symbolic ordering of itself. The embodied subject's fear of disintegration through the body and by the body is the ultimate basis for the notion of pollution.

Taking Stock

Other contributions to the theory of taboo could be considered. But what we have considered so far is sufficient to take stock and ask ourselves what we have learned that will help us find our bearings in the thick forest of Huaulu taboo. It is not without premeditation that my discussion has moved from magic to the body and from collective classifications to the subject's development and constitution. This general direction should already be sufficient to suggest my basic point: that the phenomenon of taboo and the various dangers that motivate it must be apprehended at the points of articulation and confrontation of the subject and the conditions—symbolic and presymbolic—of its existence.

For all her failings and the intrinsic fragility of her psychoanalytic approach, it is the great merit of Kristeva to have insisted that taboo and pollution are centrally concerned with the subject. The subject is not given; precisely because it is developed and constituted through a process that moves from the presymbolic to the symbolic, from instability to stability, and from asociality to sociality, it is constantly haunted by the possibility of its collapse. The subject's integrity has its base in the integrity of its participation in the symbolic and thus also, ultimately, in the integrity of the symbolic. That the loss of that integrity is represented in bodily terms and viewed on the model of disease—that is, as a vulnerability of the body to external agents capable of invading it and annexing it—results from the subject's existence in concrete form principally in the body and through the body. In other words, the subject is symbolically constituted, first and foremost, by symbolically articulating the body with other, external bodies. The greater the embodiment of the subject, for whatever reason, the greater its potential permeability to external bodies. The greater, also, the potential that any material undermining of the body (disease, etc.) be interpreted as the undermining of the subject. The line between symbolic and material danger is thus blurred. Potentially, any disease can be read as a pollution, and any pollution can turn into a disease.

The strong embodiment of the subject also implies that it is intrinsically difficult to differentiate sharply between bodies that are subjects and bodies that are mere objects. This has important consequences for taboo, blocking or limiting the consumption of natural species that are endowed with strongly subjective character. To eat them, or to eat them without neutralizing that subjective component, would mean undermining one's subject through the intimate presence of another one. More generally, if subject and object are not radically distinguished, being invaded by external agencies must acquire the signification of a potential shattering of one's subjective identity. One loses more than one's health: one loses one's distinct being.

The focus of the language of taboo and "pollution" on the body as carrier of a subject that is constituted by symbolic classification should be made evident by the concern of the symbolic classifications with food, excretions, and the processes of transformation and decay of the body that are principally associated with taboo and pollution. A taboo usually marks some event or situation that is likely to threaten the integrity of the body as the seat of the integrity of the subject. But of course, this integrity of the subject may in turn depend on the integrity of a certain external object, as determined by the classificatory system at large. If the focus of interest of taboo, then, is ultimately the subject, it does not exclude—indeed, it must include—all classifications of objects that have any bearing on the subject. My integrity may depend on the integrity of a sanctuary, a god, an animal, an authority. Furthermore, an embodied subject necessarily tends to embody itself beyond the limits of its body. This is particularly true of powerful people, but every subject participates in objective correlatives, analogues, or metonymies of itself on whose integrity its integrity depends.

Thus pollution, although focussed on the subject, modelled on the body's permeability to external objects, and principally concerned with the substances and processes where this permeability is located, may stray very far from them. It may, moreover, become entangled with all kinds of medical and magical theories and practices where they exist. Furthermore, it may be used to enforce rules, to shore up or even express hierarchical relations, and so on. The more generalized the idiom of pollution and the practice of taboo, the more numerous their significations and uses become. For this reason, the theories that we have discussed are not necessarily incompatible. The incompatibility arises when they turn the aspect of taboo on which they focus into the essence of the phenomenon and exclude all the rest. I prefer for my part to acknowledge that phenomena of great variety can go under the headings of "taboo" and "pollution." This variety and multivalence should be recognized, particularly when it is sanctioned by native categories that cover a lot of ground (such as Huaulu maquwoli or Wemale holiate or Polynesian tapu/kapu).

If taboo is seen as an idiom, it must stand to reason that it can say a lot of different things. Nevertheless, it is also necessary to stress that if taboo has no rigid essence, it also has a basic focus from which it cannot stray too far without losing its power and relative distinctiveness. This focus is provided by the embodied subject, as I have indicated. It is sometimes present only in the background or as a silent party to what occurs, but it always makes itself felt one way or another. Indeed, this is indicated by the fact that pollution truly disappears as an operative concept only when the subject becomes completely disembodied—when, as in the Christianity of theologians and philosophers, it becomes vested in speech alone. Then the subject (even if it preserves some connection with its body) loses all connections with other bodies. Or better, such a radical distinction is introduced between subject and object that the subject ceases to be at risk in its objects. Or so it likes to believe.

CHAPTER THREE
Maquwoli in Huaulu

Ita Huaulua ai maquwoli rupa-rupa.
(We Huaulu have taboos of all kinds.)

Idioms of Taboo

The Huaulu render their word *maquwoli* with the B.I. word *pemali,* which is usually translated as "sacred, forbidden, taboo."[1] Indeed *maquwoli* seems to cover many of the notions that "taboo" has in anthropological discourse. But to establish its signification, truly as well as how it stands in relationship to the various theories we have just examined, requires investigating all the forms and contexts of its use and their conceptual, ideological, sociological, and experiential underpinnings. A full definition of *maquwoli* can be, therefore, only the final result of our analysis, not its first step. What can the first step be, then? This choice is the most difficult, because it presupposes the greatest number of alternatives. Only the cumulative effect of all the choices that follow the first one allows us to say retrospectively that it was the right one.

Having tried many different beginnings, I have found that the most productive one is a discussion of a number of linguistic facts about *maquwoli.* All too often, a word is immediately translated without paying attention to the actual forms of its use in language. These include its grammatical uses (the way the word appears in sentences), and its contrasts, parallels, or partial overlappings with other words that belong to the same universe of discourse. Ignoring these forms risks unconsciously using our own. This may produce serious distortions, because a word is more than a peg for attaching a number of dictionary-like "meanings." If *meaning* is defined as all the choices that have gone into an utterance, then it must include grammatical and discursive choices besides lexical ones. We must therefore be aware at the outset of how *maquwoli* functions in sentences, with which kinds of grammatical forms it is compatible or incompatible, and what words overlap or contrast or are otherwise associated with it. This initial discussion does not require a precise lexical definition of *maquwoli.* Suffice it to keep in mind that the Huaulu feel it is equivalent to *pemali,* as glossed above.

Maquwoli, like many Huaulu words, can be used as a noun, a verb, or an adjective. When it is used as a noun, it may take the definite or the indefinite form. The indefinite form consists of the stem followed by a numeral (e.g. maquwoli essa, "a taboo"). In the definite form the stem is suffixed with *-am* in the singular and *-em* in the plural;[2] for instance: maquwoliem laite, "many taboos"; maquwoliem leussi, "there are no taboos left" or "the taboos are ended"; ita Huaulua rahe maquwoliem laite, "we the Huaulu people have many taboos"; eme kae maquwoliem, "he eats taboo things." With some words, the shift between the indefinite and the definite forms necessitates a change in spelling [e.g. *topoi, topoyam/-em; sui, suyam/-em*].) When it is used as an adjective, it is appended to the noun that it qualifies, and the suffix *-am* or *-em* is added to it to indicate that it forms a single syntagm with the qualified noun. Examples are: luma maquwoliam, "the taboo house" (a special house in which the most sacred objects of the community are kept), and alalosa maquwoliam (a tray for ritual offerings of betel nut).

The most frequent uses by far are verbal. *Maquwoli* is found in the form of a stative verb of which the thing taboo is the subject, or in the form of an intransitive or relative verb of which the person concerned with taboo is the subject and the thing taboo is the object. Transitive uses, and more specifically the causative form, are conspicuously absent. An example of a stative use of *maquwoli* is: amuni ia maquwoli, "that is in the state of taboo" or, more briefly, "that is taboo." An example of an intransitive use is: emaquwoli oho, "he [observes] taboos well" (i.e. he relates scrupulously to his taboos). Much more frequent is the relative use, examples of which are: amuni ita Huaulua ai maquwoli poto, "that thing we Huaulu observe as a strict taboo"; amaquwoli eme, "I am in a taboo relationship with him" (i.e. he is taboo to me); ita maquwolire, "those are taboo to us." As these translations show, there is no verbal use in English that may directly render the intransitive and relative uses of *maquwoli.*

The relative construction always focusses on the person for whom the taboo exists, whereas the stative or adjectival constructions leave him or her implicit or refer to an indefinite person; therefore, the latter constructions tend to be used more often in contexts where it is necessary to emphasize what is taboo and the seriousness of a certain taboo. In contrast, the relative construction is used more often when people voice their particular concerns or when they are explicitly or implicitly differentiated by their taboos—in other words, when taboo functions as a system of social classification.

All the above uses indicate that the notion of maquwoli is primarily relational. The fact is made most evident by the relative construction, of course, but it is also implied by the other ones. When *maquwoli* functions as an adjective or as a stative verb, it does not describe the intrinsic property of a thing, a predicate that defines it as a substance (something that exists independently of any relationship). Rather, these uses, like all the others, signify an incompatibility between subject and object which depends on *both,* but is the choice of neither, and especially not of the subject.

I have said that there are no transitive and particularly causative uses of *maquwoli.* This means that a sentence of the type "*x* makes *y* maquwoli" is an impossibility, whether the making of maquwoli refers to the institution of a rule or to the bringing about of a provisional state of taboo in something (usually by applying a rule). There is only one specialized word that can be used as a verb to refer to tabooing: *soko.* But its use is limited to the temporary tabooing of possessions: trees (or rather, their fruit or resin), traps, gardens, land, houses, and even people.

Soko conveys the idea of crossing or forking. Used as a noun (*sokoam*), it may refer to a "tree fork" (hala soko hua) or a "road fork" or "crossroads" (hala soko tolu). It may also refer to the most common signal employed to keep people off property. The signal is made by inserting a cross-piece of bamboo or wood into a notch made in a stake driven into the ground. The word *anasokoam,*[3] but sometimes also *sokoam,* refers to the protective magic put in the taboo sign to keep trespassers at bay. Because this magic makes an object automatically dangerous to touch, it bears comparison with the power that makes something or somebody maquwoli. Indeed, as we shall see, the basic meaning of *ia maquwoli* is "it carries an intrinsic danger." Furthermore, the dangers of objects that have been sokoi (which are for the most part edible) are usually identical to the dangers of edible objects that are *maquwoli.* In both cases consumption may result in some disease which eats the victim's skin or his flesh.[4] The name of any of these diseases, or of the supposed agent of retribution (usually some dangerous snake),[5] identifies each anasokoam.[6] We thus have an anasoko (or soko) mainase (the mainase is, in the language of Openg, from which the charm was borrowed, the Pacific boa [*Candaia carinata*][7] called hinaheheam in Huaulu), an anasoko (or soko) mulalam (the mulalam is the most dreaded poisonous snake),[8] an anasoko (or soko) asualiam (the asualiam is the cassowary, an ostrichlike bird which vicious spirits often take as a body), an anasoko (or soko) husuimatam (*husui* refers to boils or yaws), and so on. Just by approaching such anasokoem, one is struck by them. Therefore, crude images of the magical agents are sometimes used as signals, in order to warn would-be trespassers or passersby of the specific danger they incur.

Anasokoem are used only to fence off objects, never persons. Persons are put off limits (i soko asie: "they put them off limits") not by secret, privately owned magic but by public rites. Thus bride and bridegroom are sokoi, "fenced off" (that is, primarily, made off limits for the sexual and a fortiori matrimonial pursuits of third parties) by putting certain prescribed ceremonial gifts (strings of glass or metal beads on the bridegroom, sarongs on the bride) on their shoulders while uttering aloud a formula (upete ea leusi, akumamayam, "you won't call my name again, my son-in-law/brother-in-law" for the bridegroom;

upete ea leusi, akuhihinaotoam, "you won't call my name again, my daughter-in-law/sister-in-law" for the bride).

The verbal uses of *soko* and *maquwoli* are in complementary distribution, then. While *maquwoli* is found only in stative, relative, and generally intransitive forms, *soko* can function only as a causative verb that has a human agent as subject and a prohibited thing or person as object (as in the examples given above). A thing can never be said to be in a state of soko or to be soko relative to somebody; it can only be said that somebody made it soko, as in *i soko nuweam,* "they put a taboo on a coconut palm," or *i soko sawahuwae,* "they made the two spouses taboo." This is also why *soko* does not exist in adjectival form, and as a noun it properly refers to the physical *sign* (the stick with a cross-piece), although this sign can also stand for the magic (anasokoam) whose presence it signifies. But grammatical complementarity is not matched by semantic complementarity. Things are not maquwoli because somebody sokore them; nor are things that people sokore maquwoli. For instance, it is never said that a tree that has been sokoi (put off limits) is maquwoli. The only case known to me in which something, or rather somebody, that has been sokoi also acquires maquwoli status concerns the wedding rite mentioned above. Indeed, as the very formula used should suggest, personal names are said to become maquwoli as a result of the rite, and through the name taboos all other affinal taboos (on the sharing of betel, of food, of sex, and so on) are also instantiated. As somebody put it to me, speaking of his sister-in-law: "Amaquwoli eme taka holuholu i soko asihua," "She is taboo (maquwoli) to me since the time long ago when they tabooed (soko) them both [i.e. her and her husband]." Thus in this case *soko* and *maquwoli* are semantically complementary. A sister-in-law is maquwoli for her brother-in-law because somebody has sokoi her. Maquwoli is the effect and sokoi is the cause.

How can this anomaly be explained? Probably by the mixed character of the area to which it applies—alliance. Alliance concerns people as property (hence the use of *sokoi*) and people as carriers of prescribed relations (defined by *maquwoliem*). But people instantiate maquwoli only insofar as proprietory rights in them are transferred, through the i sokoi rite. Hence it can be said, although I think in a manner of speaking, that the maquwoli state is caused by a sokoi act in this case.[9]

Granted that a sentence of the type "*x* makes *y* maquwoli" is a grammatical impossibility and that maquwoli usually cannot be the result of the tabooing that is designated by *sokoi,* is it possible to describe the making of maquwoli by means of some periphrastic expression? As we have seen, *maquwoli* may refer to a rule or to the particular state that is the result of the instantiation of a rule. For instance, a taboo rule is: When the kahua feast is not held, it is taboo that the drums of the village temple rest on the floor; they must hang on the rafter until they are ritually lowered to mark the beginning of a new feast. Conversely, when the feast is on, it is taboo to raise the drums. The raising of the drums at the end of the feast, or their lowering at the beginning, is the bringing about of particular states of maquwoli by instantiating the above-mentioned rule. Now there is no periphrasis that allows one to say "*x* makes *y* maquwoli" when this refers to the making of a rule, that is, when *y* stands for a class of phenomena; but it is possible to say, or rather to imply, by means of a periphrasis, that "*x* makes *y* maquwoli" when *y* stands for a state which is brought about by the application of a rule. In other words, in the sphere of taboo to make is always to enact. "Enacting" is indeed the meaning of the verb *(k)opa(i)*—the most common designator of "*making*"—when it is followed by the word *maquwoli.* Thus the frequently used expression *eme kopai ia rahe maquwoliem* means "he enacts its [the ritual event's] taboos" (i.e. he sets the taboo state on or lifts it from particular things at particular times according to the taboo rules).

Another common way to refer to the action of setting taboos according to the requirements of a ritual "script" is to use an expression which literally refers to the action's most significant material correlate or effect. Take, for instance, the expression *i tulu ia rahe maquwoliem,* "they make its [the kahua feast's] taboos descend." It refers to the rite whereby the elders, led by the Latunusa, inaugurate the taboos that are in vigor during the kahua feast. The rite is named after its most significant correlate: the lowering of the drums from the rafters to the floor of the village temple, where they can be beaten.

The tabooing of something for somebody (usually in the course of a ritual) can also be designated by expressions that literally mean "conveying/giving" or "communicating" the taboo. An example is: *anakoram eme rui sewaem rahe maquwoliem si mulitam,* "the senior shaman gives/transfers the taboos of the familiars to the junior shaman." The expression refers to the tabooing of various foods that are incompatible with shamanic familars. Instead of *tui/rui,* "give/transfer," one can use a more concrete verb: *sali,* "to say/communicate" the taboos. This points to the fact that the taboos are set by saying them: leuw tep'u kae *x, y,* . . . , "then don't eat *x, y,* . . ."; or leuw ia maquwoli *x, y,* . . . , "then *x, y,* are taboo to [the familiar or, as it is also claimed, his medicines (aitotuem)]." Similar expressions are used for the tabooing of various foods, or baths, or whatever by the shaman to his patient. The untabooing is also effected by a simple declaration: *leuw ia maquwoli leussi,* "then it ceases to be taboo," although this applies only to the patients; the shamans have to go through a more complex rite when some of their own permanent taboos are occasionally lifted after a distinguished career.

One could argue, of course, that these "taboolings" and "untabooings" are such only in a manner of speaking, since all that the shaman does is state to his patient what the taboo happens to be. In a way, this is precisely the point: maquwoli is never made; it always preexists the actions that concern it. All the same, there is more than communication in communication. By "declaring" the taboo, the shaman actually inaugurates the requirement of its observance. So in a sense he makes the thing taboo for a particular person at a particular moment, although his making depends on a rule not of his own making. His contribution to the taboo's concrete existence is made even more evident by the removal of the taboo. For here saying that the taboo ceases to apply does not register a fact but it creates it. Indeed, it is the shaman's decision. Nevertheless, this contribution of agency is not explicitly recognized in the expressions used. Either one says that one enacts the taboos, or one describes the enactment; but one cannot use the verb *maquwoli* to say, simply and straightforwardly, that one "tabooes" something. This is true of the creation of a particular taboo state through the application of a rule, just as it is true of the creation of that rule.

Maquwoli has no direct antonym, no special word that signifies the absence of taboo, as in Polynesian languages *noa* is the antonym of *kapu* or *tapu.* One simply adds the negative suffix *-ssi* to *maquwoli* to refer to its contrary. Thus, the expression *emuni ita maquwoliressi* means "we have not a taboo of those," and *ia maquwolissi* means "it is not taboo." Certain expressions of more general import can occasionally be used to indicate the absence of taboo. For instance, *amuni koni* may mean "that's not taboo," besides more generally meaning "it is possible," "it is within the possibilities." The expression *maasiki* (*maasire* in the plural), from the verb *maasi,* means "it is allowed," and thus also "not taboo." The choice of *koni* or *maasi* has different connotations which have some bearing on the definition of *maquwoli.* If *koni* is chosen, the implication is that *maquwoli* stands for a material obstacle, since *koni* indicates possibility in the sense of "can," not "may." If *maasi* is chosen, the implication is that *maquwoli* refers to a prohibition, since *maasi* means "it is allowed," "you may." We shall have occasion to discuss this ambiguity at some length.

Another very general expression, *pinia* or *amuni pinia,* "it is good/beautiful/harmless," may be used to refer to the absence of maquwoli in things (never in persons), particularly with regard to edible species, lands, and so on. Reciprocally, that these things are in a state of maquwoli may be indicated by saying that they are "bad," that is, either *piniassi* (not good) or *kina'* (bad in the more restricted sense of "malevolent" or "evil").[10] It is also possible to say that shamanic familiars or their medicines are pinia or piniassi, depending on whether their use for curative purposes entails few and light taboos or many and grievous ones.

How does one talk about following or not following taboos, being careful or not about them, and so on? The most general expression for following taboos closely parallels the English one: *ita lulu maquwoliem,* "we follow the taboos" (*ita lulu maquwoliemussi* in the negative). But the more common expression is more concrete. It combines the verb for an action with *lulu maquwoliem,* as in *eme kae lulu maquwoliem,* "he eats following [taking into account] the taboos." The corresponding negative sentence may be obtained by adding *-ssi* at the end of the positive (*eme kae lulu maquwoliemussi*) or by adding *maquwoli* to the verb as an object (*eme kae maquwoliem,* "he eats taboo things"). But there is a semantic difference between the two forms. In the sentence *eme kae maquwoliem, maquwoliem* means "taboo *things,*" as I have just indicated. But in *eme kae lulu maquwoliemussi, maquwoliem* means "taboo as *rule*" (since it is "followed"). The coexistence of these two sentences reflects the already noted coexistence of two attitudes to taboos: one emphasizes the fact that it is a rule of action; the other, the fact that it is a property of certain objects relative to certain subjects.

To indicate the general habit of care and preoccupation with regard to taboo, one can say either *ita maquwoli oho,* "we follow/respect taboos well [as a matter of habit]," "we are scrupulous with regard to taboos"; or *ita mane maquwoliem,* "we know/are aware of taboos" (sometimes abbreviated to *ita mane,* awareness of taboo being the epitome of awareness pure and simple). The equivalence of the two expressions—that is, of "knowing the taboos" and "habitually respecting the taboos"—should not be taken as a mark of intellectualism,[11] or as an indication that statements of maquwoli are just statements of fact.[12] It is simply the recognition of the obvious fact that knowing the taboos is the main condition for following them. It also reflects a notion of knowledge wider than the purely propositional (or even procedural)[13] one which we use as a matter of course. The Huaulu notion of knowledge covers much of what we call consciousness, with its accompanying phenomena of attention and intention. Thus "to know taboos" means "to respect" them in practice, because that respect requires a heightened state of awareness, a preoccupation not only with the rules of taboo, but also with the contexts of their application and with whether one is violating a taboo without realizing it. For such notion of knowledge as consciousness, our separation of *knowledge* and *will* makes little sense. If we seek comparisons to understand this Huaulu notion of "knowing/respecting taboos," we should rather look in the direction of *religio*—that is, as the term is interpreted by Cicero,[14] who, for once, was right about an etymology. Indeed, Benveniste[15] has approved Cicero's derivation of *religio* from *relegere,* "to return once again to a previous choice,"[16] so as to check on its correctness, "to be meticulous," in the spirit of ritual, when relating to dangerous powers, divine or otherwise.[17] Such meticulousness obviously presupposes the habit of heightened awareness and self-awareness that the Huaulu identify with respect for taboo.

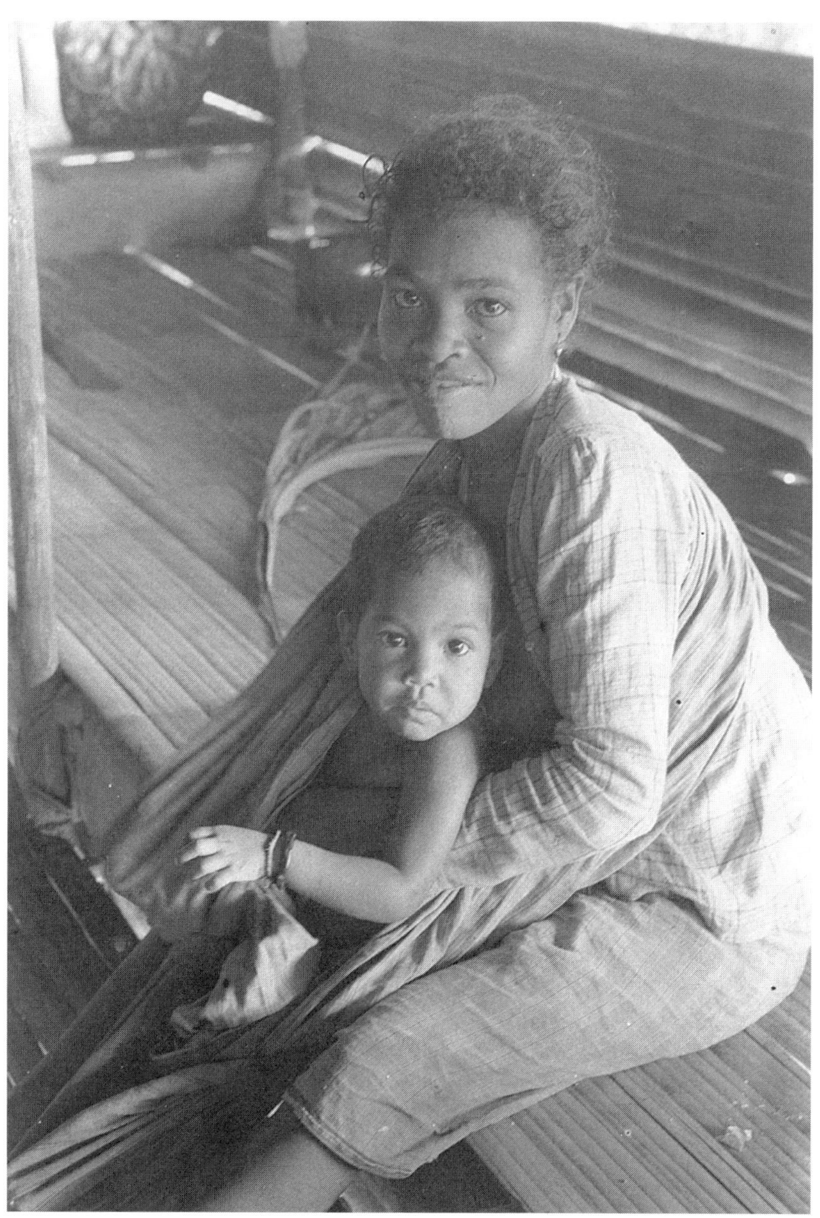

Young mother, originally from Nisawele, who married a Huaulu man and had his child. She agreed to follow Huaulu taboos when she moved into the mountain village. 1972. (Photo by V. Valeri.)

This meticulousness or scrupulousness in matching one's actions with the taboos—and thus also in identifying the objects, events, and situations to which the taboos apply—is viewed as a sign of orderliness, as can be inferred from the words that qualify, adverbially for the most part, the way an action is carried out without concern for taboos. The words are: *takaruwa* (meaning "with unreflective spontaneity," "without restraint"), *wela* (meaning "in a disorderly manner"), *taluwa* and *sala* (both of which mean "in the wrong way," "erroneously," "falsely").

Takaruwa or *takaruwani* is a composite word, formed by *taka* (a prefix indicating the habitual character of an action) and *ruwa* or *ruwani* (self). It literally means something that comes spontaneously from the self, out of an inner impulse, and therefore signifies an action done without reflection or care, unregulated or even unruly. For instance, *a ae takaruwani* means "I eat as it comes," "I eat without taking any rule into consideration," "I eat anything." Or, to quote a Huaulu friend of mine who felt freed from the restraints of affinal taboos because of his second marriage: "Leuw ausawa holuam nika, a loqi takaruwa," "but then now that I have married a new wife, I chew betel without following any rule" (so at least he claimed). *A ae wela* means much the same thing as *a ae takaruwani,* although *wela* has a more generic sense of "disorderly." The expressions *tepi omi una wela* and *tepi omi una takaruwa(ni)* are interchangeable and heard very frequently: they are used to exhort people "not to act" (tepi omi una) without a sense of limits, in a disorderly, careless way, and more specifically, not to act without keeping the taboos in mind.[18]

Although sentences in which the verb is qualified by *takaruwa(ni)* or *wela* indicate a generic habit of carelessness with regard to taboo in general, the use of the qualifiers *taluwa* and *sala* imply the violation of a specific taboo—a specific mismatch between the subject and the object (or rule) of its action. Thus the expressions *a ae taluwa*[19] or *a ae sala* mean "I have violated a food taboo," "I have eaten the wrong food" (in terms of taboo rules). Therefore, their statement is often completed by the mention of the food involved (just as the statement of a taboo is often paralleled by the affliction that ensues from not respecting it); for example: A ae sala asualiam, "I have violated the food taboo of the cassowary" (lit., "I have erroneously eaten cassowary," "my eating of cassowary meat was erroneous"). It is important to note that the words *taluwa* and *sala* refer more generally to actions that misfire, such as failure to hit a target (e.g., a ana sala, "I missed the target with my arrow"),[20] or hitting an inappropriate target (e.g., a hita taluwa, "I cut [myself] by mistake").[21] Objective inappropriateness is thus emphasized more than the voluntary or involuntary character of the action, although *sala,* contrary to *taluwa,* is also used to refer to actions that the actor performs while knowing that they are wrong. Also, contrary to *taluwa*, which can be used only adverbially, sala can be used as an adjective (as in *assauw sala amuni*, "that wrong/mistaken speech") and as a noun (as in *sala amuni*, "that wrong," "that mistake"). Much is made of the contrast between an "objective" notion of wrong like sala, where *wrong* means principally "mismatch," "disagreement,"[22] and the Judaeo-Christian notion of sin.[23] But it is interesting to note that both *chattat*, the more frequent of the biblical words translated as "sin,"[24] and its Greek counterpart (*hamartema*),[25] literally mean, just like the Huaulu word *sala*, "missing the target."[26] Even more interesting is the fact that, when the Huaulu have borrowed a word that, in the Indonesian language, means "sin," they have recovered some of its more ancient Sanskritic meaning, which has little to do with the modern notion of sin. I am speaking, of course, of *dosa*,[27] which has become *rosa* in the Huaulu language and which is used mostly in shamanic contexts (shamanic language borrows heavily from several languages, including B.I. and Ambonese Malay, henceforth A.M.). Judging from these uses, *rosa* means *both* what is inappropriate according to the rules of maquwoli and the afflictions that follow from this state of inappropriateness.

Thus the common expression *ita tana rosaem* (lit., "we take rosaem in") means being on the receiving end of a misfortune which may be due, not just to one's own transgressions, but also to the maleficent activities of others (such as sorcery, which is taboo among Huaulu) or to chance encounters with ominous events. The emphasis is clearly not on responsibility but on misfortune, not on the person who bears the blame but on the one who bears the trouble. People are visited not only by the sins of their fathers, but also by those of their enemies. There will be much to say about this. What matters here is that *rosa* means less "sin" in the sense of intentional rebellion against divine law than "trouble"—trouble that has to do with ritual matters which largely overlap with the notion of maquwoli. "Trouble" is precisely one of the two basic meanings of *dosa* in Sanskrit (the other is "bodily humor").[28] Paired with *vas* (in the expression *vas-dos*) it still means "misfortunes due to ritual errors" in Sri Lanka.[29] In Pali, *dosa* means "hatred"[30] (which motivates sorcery, say the Huaulu). The near-recovery of some of the original meaning of *dosa*, reversing its modern Indonesian transformation, is clearly the result of an entirely local process of convergence due to the appropriation of a sin word by a culture that knows no sin—or almost.[31]

More important in this context is to stress that the term *rosa* is the only negative counterpart of *maquwoli* that has its same extension, and more. Indeed, it refers to all that *maquwoli* signals should not occur and to the misfortunes that follow from those occurrences—in a nutshell, to all taboo-related "trouble." *Sala* is not as efficient as *rosa* in this respect, since its most frequent use is adverbial, in connection with as many verbs as there are actions that can go wrong. Next in frequency are its adjectival, stative, and exclamative uses. As a noun, *sala* is used much less frequently and in a more restricted sense than *dosa* (it does not include misfortune). Therefore, it is not surprising that shamans had to borrow a foreign word to create a noun that would give some unity to the domain of ritual "trouble," which is their main professional interest. But *rosa,* however convenient it may seem and however great the prestige of shamanism, has not yet acquired wide currency in everyday discourse.

The Meanings of *Maquwoli*

We have gathered, so far, that maquwoli is a relational notion, that it points to dangerous incompatibilities which are not supposed to be made by an agency and, a fortiori, man-made (except when they result from the prescribed application of general rules, themselves unmade, to particular situations). Humans can only take them into account, which means that they must exert extreme care in knowing them, keeping them in mind, and establishing in what situations they apply. But these are preliminary inferences from various grammatical facts and idioms. To progress further, we must determine what exactly is stated by stating that something is maquwoli. The following exemplify the main kinds of maquwoli statements one is likely to hear:

1. Iyaem pohi manuem ia *maquwoli,* ia koloputi, "[Eating] fish and fowl together is *maquwoli,* it gives leprosy."
2. Ilauwam ia kusu lumam pohi ia haku hiliam ia maquwoli; masa luma upuam maata', "It is maquwoli that the ilauwa frog enters the house and touches the pillar; the master of the house will die."
3. Hari e maquwoli ipiam taka eme hua potonasi, "Hari [a man] has been in a maquwoli relationship with sago since he was a small child."
4. Ita Huaulua ita malamala humani ia maquwoli, "It is maquwoli for us Huaulu people to practice sorcery against one another."
5. Tutu roa potona amuni, ailaem ia putani i rahe maquwoliem tepiire hakii nika, "When it rains that much, [it means that] the ancestors are crying over the fact that their maquwoliem have been abandoned."
6. Akafhuaniam tutu ita kopai ia rahe maquwoliem sehu, pohi ohoa naunan, "When we have accomplished all the maquwoliem of the kahua feast, everything is all right [i.e. there are no more dangers]."

Before attempting to explain what the word *maquwoli* means in each of these statements and what they all suggest when taken together,

I must define some of the terms that I shall use in my analysis. Two kinds of statements can be distinguished: descriptive and prescriptive. The former describe a state of affairs, the latter prescribe what should be done. Some statements are statements of rules, that is, of regularities. There are likewise, therefore, two kinds of rules: descriptive and prescriptive. Descriptive rules are empirical generalizations; that is, they describe a regularity that exists independently of the effect that stating the rule may have. Prescriptive rules bring about a regularity through the statement of the rule, that is, by influencing people's actions. Prescriptive rules are of two kinds: conditional (or optional) and mandatory (also categorical imperatives; obligations). Conditional rules are rules of the type "if you want *x*, then do (or do not do) *y*." Mandatory rules are such that "the fact of the rule's existence becomes a reason for action."[32]

I also need to distinguish two kinds of actions: actions that are necessarily intentional, and actions that can be either intentional or unintentional. A necessarily intentional action is an action which can exist only by being accomplished on purpose, such as beating a dog with a bush knife or practicing sorcery (to take two examples of actions that are maquwoli). Neither of these actions can occur unintentionally—sorcery because it consists in following a certain number of "scripts"; beating a dog with a bush knife because, by definition, beating someone qualifies as beating only if it is done intentionally, as against hurting him by, say, stumbling over him. However, intentionality is not a necessary condition of occurrence for many other actions. Eating remains eating, speaking remains speaking, whether it is intentional or not. Intentionality is not a necessary part of their definition. Hence I call them actions that can be either intentional or unintentional.

Theoretically, a third kind of action could be added: actions that can be defined as wholly unintentional, such as sneezing when somebody leaves the house, stumbling while leaving the house, and so on. Yet there is no limit to imitative power: one can fake a sneeze and stumble on purpose. So I feel that there is no need, at least for my purposes here, to create a third category separate from the second, which includes all the acts that can exist, both intentional and unintentional, and not exclusively those that are unintentional.[33]

Armed with these definitions, let us turn to the six statements above. The first exemplifies the most common kind of maquwoli statement one may encounter. Its form is that of all taboos that concern touching, consuming, or otherwise appropriating an object. The statement obviously points to a rule, but what kind is not clear. All rests on the translation of *ia maquwoli*, the expression that links the antecedent (eating fish and fowl together) to the consequent (gives leprosy). If *ia maquwoli* is translated as "it is forbidden," then the statement is obviously a prescriptive rule, indeed, a mandatory one. If *ia maquwoli* is translated as "it is dangerous," then the statement is a descriptive rule: it says that a regular connection exists between eating fish and fowl together and contracting leprosy. The two interpretations are not necessarily exclusive. For the second does not specify the reason for the regular connection between antecedent and consequent, and the first does not specify the reason that eating fish and fowl is forbidden. Thus it is possible to suppose that the reason the Huaulu regularly connect the two phenomena (mixing fish and fowl, leprosy) is that, because the first is forbidden, the second is meted out as a punishment. It is as if we say, "It is dangerous to murder people, for one risks ending up on the electric chair." The regular connection between antecedent and consequent is a fact that can be described, but the reason for the regularity is that murder is against the law and the law is sanctioned by capital punishment. The regularity is produced by a norm and its sanction, but it is an empirical regularity nonetheless. Thus statement 1 may be interpreted as a descriptive rule, and yet imply a mandatory one. But even if the second interpretation is taken to imply nothing more than an intrinsic connection between the mixing of fish and fowl and the contracting of leprosy (that is, the same kind of connection that exists between ingesting a poison and getting sick), it is not necessarily in conflict with the first. For it may well be that eating fish and fowl together is forbidden *because* its intrinsic effect is leprosy. In other words, the rule consists in an injunction to protect oneself against the possible negative consequences of eating dangerous food. The implication is that maquwoli is a prohibition predicated on a duty of self-preservation. It represents an ancestral mandate to avoid death and malady, for the sake of preserving the society's strength and continuity, for instance.

In sum, even if *ia maquwoli* is translated as "it is forbidden," it does not necessarily mean that statement 1 should be translated as "eating fish and fowl together is forbidden; *therefore* it gives leprosy" rather (or any more) than "eating fish and fowl together is forbidden, *because* it gives leprosy." On the other hand, if *ia maquwoli* is translated as "it is dangerous," statement 1 must be translated as "eating fish and fowl together is dangerous, because it gives leprosy." But then this translation says nothing about the reason that leprosy follows from eating fish and fowl together; it may well be that the connection is intrinsic or that it is provided by a prohibiting and sanctioning agency. Let us also note that while statement 1 is explicitly prescriptive if *ia maquwoli* is translated as "it is prohibited," it is implicitly prescriptive even if *ia maquwoli* is translated as "it is dangerous." For, obviously to say that something is dangerous is to imply that it is better avoided.[34] There is no obligation to do so, however; that is, the implicit prescription is conditional. It says, "If you do not want to contract leprosy, don't eat fish and fowl together." Thus the prescription implied by saying "it is dangerous" is very different from the prescription implied by saying "it is forbidden"; the former is like a doctor's prescription.

This exercise in laying bare the ambiguities of statement 1 may seem frivolous. Wouldn't the ambiguities be resolved if the statement were situated in the wider context to which it undoubtedly belongs? The answer is that when the ambiguities are resolved, they are resolved in different ways in different contexts, and these resolutions correspond to the possibilities that I have delineated. But there is no reason to postulate that the ambiguities are always resolved or that they must be. Indeed, in most cases it seems that statements like number 1 are best translated in the least committal way and therefore—we have just shown—as descriptive statements with prescriptive implications of the conditional kind. Indeed, the usual, everyday attitude of the Huaulu toward their taboos is highly pragmatic and rather agnostic. This means that on the whole they treat maquwoli statements as statements of fact, signals of regularly occurring dangers that had better be avoided. Only when there are powerful motivations for further progressing in the interpretation of taboo-related misfortunes do they abandon this matter-of-fact, pragmatic approach, often with the help of their shamans.

If there were any doubt that the primary, or most extensive, meaning of *ia maquwoli* is "it is dangerous," it would be dispelled by statement 2 in my sample. Here, *ia maquwoli* can be translated as "it is dangerous" but can hardly be rendered as "it is forbidden," since it concerns an event (the entering of a certain kind of frog into a house) which is not produced by human action and which is hardly in the power of humans to avoid, or only minimally so. Moreover, even if we admit that there is a prohibition against letting frogs into the house, it is clearly impossible to view the misfortune following that entrance as the sanction of the prohibition. It is, rather, that the misfortune, as the intrinsic effect of the frog's entrance, is the reason for the prohibition. If there is obligation, in sum, it is an obligation not to incur an objective danger. But it does not seem to me that one wishes to avoid the presence of frogs in the house because it is mandatory to avoid it; it is, rather, that one wishes to avoid the presence because of its effect. Statement 2 is primarily descriptive ("the entrance of frogs into houses is dangerous"); the prescription it implies is of the conditional type ("therefore, if you do not wish to be dead before the end of the year, do not let frogs into the house if you can help it"). But precisely because there is not much one can do in practice, the practical consequences of the statement are not as important as its descriptive content. An event is used to predict the future occurrence of another event (or conversely, the latter is used as evidence that the former may have occurred, unbeknownst to all). In other words, *maquwoli* refers here to negative omens, to dangerous events that cannot be avoided (although they can perhaps be ritually countered), and not to dangerous actions that can be avoided or perhaps to forbidden ones, as was the case with the first statement.

That *ia maquwoli* signifies here "it is dangerous" in the sense of "it is a bad omen" is confirmed by the explanation given for the anomalous presence of frogs in the house. It is due, I was told, to the detached mattiulu, "life-principle," of the householder or somebody else in his family. The mattiulu seizes the frog and forces it into the house as a sign of its as yet unrecognized flight from its owner's body. What better proof of this than its constraining an animal body to act like a human one (i.e. seeking the company of humans in their houses)? Indeed, the event is one of many similar ones that are commented upon with the statement *(ia) mattiulu nika,* "he has lost his life-principle." If nothing is done to reintegrate the mattiulu into his owner, he will die. Clearly, then, the frog is dangerous in the sense that it is a sign of danger, but a sign which is also in some way an efficient cause, since, if it is avoided or ritually voided, the danger is also avoided or voided. There is nothing strange about this conflation of omen and taboo, which is also found elsewhere.[35] It is justified by the fact that *ia maquwoli* primarily means that an event "is dangerous [to a human]" whether the event is an effect of human action or not.

The little prescriptive component that one may discern in the judgment ia maquwoli when it is applied to the entering of frogs into the house disappears altogether in other cases. For instance, it is said that it is maquwoli that chickens utani (cry) rather than tutukoho (cluck). If they do cry, then "we shall die" (masa ita maatae). There is absolutely nothing one can do about the way chickens behave vocally, so *ia maquwoli* here is a purely descriptive statement, without any prescriptive implication. It simply means "there is a danger that we will die." But whether something can be done to avoid an ominous event or not, the interesting question is whether people do indeed try to do something or simply comment on the event. In the case of frogs, I can testify that when a frog is heard on a tree near the house people do try to chase it and that if the frog enters the house they scramble to avoid the more ominous outcomes by blowing out lamps (so that the frogs will not be attracted to them), covering pregnant women, putting clothes away in closed containers, and so on. In other cases, though, people are totally passive observers. One such case which I witnessed was at a burial. It is maquwoli if a dry leaf falls into an open grave at the time of the burial. People watched one slowly fall into it, commenting on the event with concern, but they did not attempt to avoid it.

It seems, then, that *ia maquwoli* signifies primarily an objective mismatch: a dry leaf is mismatched with an open grave; a frog, with a house and its inhabitants; a certain vocal utterance of chickens, with the village and its inhabitants; and so on. The mismatch has negative effects; hence, notice of its dangerousness is given. The same is true of the mismatch between a certain food, or combination of foods, and a certain eater. The difference is that in this case, contrary to the other ones, the mismatch occurs in a human action (eating), and it is therefore in the power of humans to avoid it to a certain extent. Then, although ia maquwoli is exclusively, or almost exclusively, a descriptive rule in statement 2 and others which corroborate it, in statement 1 it is a descriptive rule with prescriptive implications. It therefore means both "it is dangerous" (whatever the reasons for its dangerousness) and "do not do it if you do not want to risk the danger."

And now the case of the statement 3, which long puzzled me in the field. I was once sitting at a meal with some Huaulu friends when I noticed that one of the people eating with us, a young man called Hari, did not eat sago porridge as we all did. The sight of a Huaulu not eating the staple food was so unusual that I could not help wondering aloud. My friends replied, "Emaquwoli ipiam," which I mentally translated as "he has the taboo of sago." I knew that some varieties of sago are taboo when taking certain medicines. So I asked if some curer had given this taboo to Hari. No, I was told, he was born with it. Since the earliest age, he had not been able to bring himself to eat any sago in porridge form; he had a strong aversion to it and was made sick by it. My puzzlement arose from my assumption at that time that maquwoli was to be translated as "prohibition" in every case as a matter of course. Therefore, one could not include in it a case of allergy, as Hari's "maquwoli" of sago seemed to be. Later I discovered that Hari's case was not unique. Another man, Hayele, was said to have this "taboo" on sago. Indeed, his aversion to it went so far that he would not even touch sago palms. It is true that Hayele was a mumanu, a "madman"; but several perfectly normal people listed similar idiosyncratic "allergies" among their maquwoliem, side by side with what I regarded as legitimate taboos. This forced me to question my assumptions about the meaning of *maquwoli* and to accept what I knew but had long resisted accepting: that the Huaulu spoke about a good many of their taboos, especially food taboos, as so many allergies, cases of objective mismatch with intrinsic bodily consequences, rather than as prohibitions accompanied by sanctions.[36] If many taboos were viewed as collective allergies, allergies of entire categories of people, then it made sense that individual allergies, such as the one Hari was born with, could be called taboos.

It must be said, however, that the comparison with allergies holds only up to a point in Hari's case and similar ones. An allergy is characterized by a bodily reaction that affects the health or well-being of a person. It need not be associated with feelings of disgust or aversion for the thing that causes the allergic reaction, although these feelings may develop with time. Conversely, aversion or disgust need not be associ-

Hari, the young man who has the taboo of sago, holding a wooden sword and dancing in the village square at his initiation. 1973. (Photo by V. Valeri.)

ated with allergic reactions. Hari definitely felt disgust for sago porridge, but I am not clear what other allergic reaction he experienced apart from nausea. It seems rather difficult to draw a line between strong disgust that "makes one sick" and allergic reaction. So in the end I am unclear about the basis of comparison between such strong aversions as Hari's to sago and the institutional avoidances called maquwoliem. Does it lie in the presence of the allergic reaction (an equivalent of the negative bodily consequences of violating a taboo) or in the strength of the aversion (an emotional equivalent of the strong reasons for avoiding an object in taboos proper)?[37]

The basis probably involves some of both, but it is difficult to say because my Huaulu friends are unable to articulate their reasons or even to understand my questions on this matter. They know that a condition like Hari's is to be described as ia maquwoli, but they don't know why, or rather they know it intuitively, not discursively. It is not a question that they ask themselves, so it is not one that they can answer when the ethnographer asks it. In any event, statement 3 illustrates a fact of some importance: the judgment ia maquwoli is not applied exclusively to institutional avoidances, but is occasionally extended, with quasi-Freudian insight, to individual obsessional behavior.[38]

Putting these statements 1, 2, and 3 together, then, one may conclude that maquwoli evokes to the Huaulu a strong incompatibility between subject and object, which takes the psychological form of either spontaneous aversion (Hari's inability to eat sago, however much he would otherwise like to), or a rationally motivated fear (of leprosy, in the case of fish and fowl; of death, in the case of frogs). The latter is the prevalent, ordinary sentiment associated with maquwoli; the former is rare.

One can eat a taboo food unintentionally and still pay the consequences; a strong allergic reaction such as Hari's is also unintentional; and the entrance of frogs into houses is an event that humans don't have the power to bring about or even to avoid. In contrast, maquwoli in statement 4 concerns something that exists only as intentional action, namely sorcery. By definition, one does not involuntarily lapse into sorcery; one must want to practice it in order to do so. It is a necessarily intentional action. So when the Huaulu say that it is maquwoli for them to practice sorcery against other Huaulu, *maquwoli* does not simply mean "it is dangerous if it happens to you" (as in statement 2). It means "it is dangerous if you do it, so don't do it." This *don't* may be predicated on a conditional rule that appeals to self-interest (you will endanger yourself, because the action is intrinsically dangerous for the doer, because it carries its own punishment, or because the victim will take his revenge on you), but it may also be predicated on something else—namely on the idea that it is wrong to harm other Huaulu, and even more wrong to do so in the hidden and sneaky way of sorcery, without taking responsibility. It is not just harm to oneself, then, but also harm to others, and to the principle of solidarity that binds the Huaulu, that is evoked by maquwoli here. Therefore there is little doubt in this case that *ia maquwoli* also means a categorical prescription: it enjoins one not to do something because it is bad in itself (piniassi, "not good/beautiful"),[39] at the same time as it is bad for the doer, since he may get sick or be attacked for doing it. When faced with the issue of whether or not to practice sorcery against a certain person, an individual Huaulu actor may pay more attention to the possible consequences for himself than to the possible consequences for his victim, whom he presumably wants to harm. But when talking of this prescription in general terms, its categorical character is emphasized: it is viewed as a prohibition. Accordingly, the danger involved in violating the stated rule, which one may want to avoid out of mere self-interest, is the danger of punishment. But then the questions arise: What makes this prescription categorical, and what is the agency of punishment?

An answer to both questions is suggested by statement 5. Here *maquwoli* is used as a noun, designating all the rules that "belong to" (i rahe) the ancestral powers (ailaem), and in whose preservation these powers have a vested interest. In the discursive context exemplified by statement 5, then, maquwoliem are commands that rest on the relationship of dependence between ancestors and their descendants and which reproduce that relationship. They say, "You will not do this because *we* say so, and if you do it, beware, we will make you sick and even make you die." The meteoric form taken by the ancestors' sadness at the lack of respect for them, to which the disregard of their commands testifies, is proof of their power to minister punishment in the "objective" form of sickness and other misfortunes. In sum, the ancestors are here the source of both the authority of taboo and the sanctions that follow on their violation. Rain, thunder, lightning, disease, famine, and sterility are punishments and reminders; they carry the voice of ancestral command to those who have become deaf to it.

In sum, on the basis of the first five statements, we can conclude that the main signification of the word *maquwoli* is negative. *Maquwoli* means: it is dangerous to do it, therefore don't do it; it is dangerous when it occurs, so it should not occur; don't do it—the ancestors don't want you to, and they will remind you by sending an affliction. It also signifies an avoidance due to a very strong, but idiosyncratic, inner compulsion with certain bodily reactions, rather than an avoidance due to very powerful reasons, as is normally the case. But not doing certain things implies doing others, so that paradoxically a few "don'ts" are able to stand for many "dos." This is precisely what happens in the cases exemplified by statement 6. There, maquwoliem—that is, the institutionalized avoidances that are part of every Huaulu ritual—stand for the ritual as a whole. That is to say, maquwoliem in this sense are both negative and positive prescriptions. Indeed, there is no other word for "ritual" in the Huaulu language. When one needs to refer to the kahua ritual, one says *akafhuaniam rahe maquwoliem,* "the prescriptions [lit., "negative prescriptions"] of the kahua." When one refers to sewa pukari ritual, one says *sewa pukariam rahe maquwoliem,* or else uses a more specific, descriptive expression, such as *i napa sewaem,* "they wait for the shamanic familiars [to come]."

The use of *maquwoliem* to refer to entire rituals, in their negative and positive aspects, is thus a typical case of markedness, in which the part stands for the whole. But why is it the negative that stands for both itself and the positive, and not the other way round? Why this preference for negation at the expense of affirmation in the definition of *maquwoli?* The tendency is very general in Huaulu culture, but here two reasons seem to carry the greatest weight. One is that not doing can be more easily defined and circumscribed than doing, so it becomes the most marked element in action. The other—and the decisive—reason is that there is an essential equivalence between taboo and ritual in general. Ritual is primarily viewed as the avoidance of danger (never mind that its existence is in fact responsible for at least some of the dangers that it is supposed to fend off);[40] thus taboo, which is the minimal form of avoidance of danger, is also ritual in minimal form.

We can now return to another meaning of *maquwoli,* illustrated by statement 5. When *maquwoli* is used, as it is there, as a noun in the plural form and as an object of possession, it basically means "custom," "the entire set of traditional rules and practices according to script that one has to follow to be a Huaulu." *Ita Huaulua rahe maquwoliem,* "the maquwoli of we the Huaulu people/we Huaulu as a people" is pretty much equivalent to what in other parts of Indonesia is called adat and perhaps even to what is beginning to be called "our culture" (kebudayan kita) or "our tradition" (tradisi kita), under the influence of anthropology. The equation of maquwoliem and custom is again a phenomenon of markedness: the most remarkable part, the one to which one must pay most attention—that is, the negative part—stands for the whole. But it is important not to forget the connotations that this part lends to the whole. It turns custom into a mandate, into an obligation to be Huaulu in a certain way—the way of the ancestors. The Huaulu can truly be Huaulu only if they, in the words of the oracle to Zeno, "take the complexion of the dead" or, as they themselves say, *ita leku mutuaniem koni,* "it is well [or all goes well] if we replicate the ancients." But then they hasten to add, sadly, *mahi ita wahi mutuaniem leussi,* "but we are not like the ancestors any more." This condition of decay from the state of potency and health in which the ancestors found themselves is assimilated with the loss of the "knowledge" of taboos, that is, of the ability to practice them in their pristine rigor.

The exemplary statements that we have just considered show that *maquwoli* has a wide variety of meanings—from "danger" to "prohibition," from "strong innate aversion with allergic reactions" to "ancestral custom," from "negative omen" to "ritual." As we have seen, some of these meanings are derived from the more basic ones through generalization or analogy. Thus "ritual" is the extension of "negative prescription"; "ancestral custom" is the extension of "ritual" and even of "negative prescription"; and idiosyncratic allergies can be viewed as maquwoliem by analogy with those collective allergies that food taboos appear to be. Nevertheless, an impression of heterogeneity and disparateness remains. I am prepared to argue that it is mostly due to our own presuppositions. For us, it makes a lot of difference whether an event is an action or not, or the result of an action or not, and whether the action is intentional or not. All our morality is based on such distinctions. We tend to define events more by the way they are produced than by the way they affect people. Thus for us having a frog jump into our house is in an ontological category radically different from doing something, and doing something intentionally is also different from doing something unintentionally. Also, doing something "wrong" is, for us, different from doing something "bad," that is, such that it negatively affects our welfare.

But all these differences, although they may be taken into account in other areas of Huaulu culture, are irrelevant in the area of maquwoli.

The term may apply indiscriminately to an intentional or to an unintentional action, to an event that is the effect of a human action and to one that is not, and to "wrong" and "bad." What is common, then, to all these phenomena that warrants calling them with a single term, *maquwoli?* Could it be that we have only a series of linked meanings here that do not all share a single feature? There are indeed linked meanings, but there is also—I think that I have said enough to show it—at least one common feature that happens to be the one to which the Huaulu themselves give the greatest importance. All situations that are said to be maquwoli for somebody are *dangerous* for him or her. Yet to translate *maquwoli* as "dangerous" and leave it at that will not do. For what is dangerous is not coextensive with what is maquwoli. While all things maquwoli are dangerous, not all things dangerous are maquwoli. Maquwoli, then, must indicate a special kind of danger. But what kind is it? Two apparently contradictory answers are suggested by our examples. One is that the danger indicated by maquwoli is the danger of punishment for violating an ancestral mandate. By this interpretation, the meaning "dangerous" is implied by the meaning "prohibited" in maquwoli. And yet this answer cannot apply to a number of dangers that are indexed by maquwoli. In what way, for instance, can the danger represented by an event such as the "crying" of chickens be interpreted as a punishment, since the crying of chickens cannot be the object of a prohibition? Indeed, as applied to this event, *ia maquwoli* can be only a descriptive, not a prescriptive, statement.

The second answer is that the danger indicated by maquwoli arises from a mismatch between subject and object or subject and action. By this interpretation, the meaning "dangerous" is implied by the meaning "mismatched" in maquwoli. This answer covers such maquwoli events as bad omens; it also covers most of the other cases insofar as they can be interpreted as allergies in an extended sense. For instance, it can easily be claimed that a food is dangerous to eat not because it is prohibited but because "it does not agree with" the eater. Indeed the expression *ia kana sala* ("it does not agree with," "it does not go well with," "it does not fit") is commonly used by the Huaulu to describe such cases of maquwoli. The problem with this answer is that it does not account for the dimension of prohibition, of "wrong," that is unmistakably present in certain cases, even when they are commonly described as cases of mismatch, of "badness," at the more superficial level. Indeed, all taboos, whatever they are, can be said to assume a prohibitional dimension in certain contexts, that is, when they are considered as what the ancestors did—and therefore what their descendants should also do, not only for the sake of their own health, but also for the sake of respecting the ancestors, of following in their footsteps.

There is thus no intrinsic incompatibility between the two views of the sources of danger. But this does not mean that the choice between the two is indifferent. The view that danger is the correlate of a mismatch is clearly more basic. There are at least two reasons for this. The first is that most collective maquwoliem are not arbitrary in their content and in the consequences (or, if one wishes, sanctions) that are attached to them. Whether they are conceived as ancestral mandates or as descriptive rules with conditional prescriptions attached, their basic motivation is a mismatch that is to be explained by the classificatory system. In a sense, the ancestors are a useless hypothesis to account for the maquwoliem. Maquwoliem are inherent in the structure of the cosmos as conceptualized by the Huaulu. They have been learned from experience and reasoning, over countless generations, including the present one, which has added several to the list. This is precisely why, as we have seen, "knowing taboos" is equated with following them. Hence the second reason why the "ancestralizing" view of maquwoli is not as basic as what I would call the "naturalizing" view. Ancestors are never presented as the authors of taboos. It would even be impossible to say so in any straightforward way, as we have seen. Taboos, or at least taboos as rules, just *are;* they can be known but not made. Their association with the ancestors, then, is primarily through knowledge. It is the ancestors who first discovered most taboos and first taught them; and it is through the transmission of this knowledge, generation to generation, that the taboos have reached the present generation. So, although the domain of taboos is permeated with the ancestral presence, although one motivation for following taboos is that by so doing one pays respect to the ancestors who practiced them and from whom one learned them, the ultimate source of the taboos is not the ancestors, or anybody else. Taboos are beyond any agency to make, it seems.

Nevertheless, a closer look at this ideology reveals that things are not so simple. Precisely because the ancestors have a vested interest in the continuity of the system that they themselves practiced, the ancestralizing view is not redundant relative to the naturalizing view. It is not surprising, then, that ancestral agency is recognized more strongly in the consequences of violating taboos than in the definitions given to them. Indeed, the more intractable or serious taboo-related afflictions are, the more pervasive the presence of that agency. Mismatching thus becomes colored with guilt; and its supposedly automatic consequences (may) take on the appearance of punishment.

But before we can get to this, and thus to realizing the intrinsic ambiguity of this Huaulu view of taboo, we must delve further into the question of taboo-related danger.

Danger and Taboo

If we take "dangerous mismatch" as the basic definition of *maquwoli,* we must still add what kind of mismatch it is, because any connection between two terms that, because of their properties, has negative consequences for either, or both, can be said to be a "dangerous mismatch." For instance, bad mushrooms are dangerous to eat because they do not agree with the human stomach—but they are not identified as maquwoli.

The thesis that I shall put forward is nothing surprising in light of the discussion of taboo in chapter 2, and especially its conclusion. Contrary to ordinary dangers, maquwoli dangers result from symbolic mismatches—mismatches that depend on what subject and object stand for in terms of a categorical structure that gives them value and signification. That is to say, the maquwoli action or event stands for a relationship between subject and object that contradicts their identity as determined by categorical affiliation. The dangers of maquwoli are dangers of identity by association, if I may say so. I am what I eat, those I eat with, have sex with, speak with, those whose blood I shed, and those with whom I shed it. Therefore in eating, having sex, speaking, and, in sum, interacting with what is not me but is in some way implicated in what I am or can be, I run the danger of losing myself, of undermining my embodied identity.

To identify what makes certain things "dangerous" in the maquwoli sense, therefore, is to identify what it is about them, or rather about certain ways of relating to them, which evokes the undermining of the subject. It is, in a sense, to investigate the symbolic constitution of the subject through the symbolic unraveling of its body—a body inseparable from certain negative or positive, but especially negative, relationships with other bodies. Because of the immense ground covered by maquwoli, the task is immense. I shall have to concentrate on one single, exemplary domain of maquwoli: that of meat and therefore also of animals. I hope that this intensive study of meat and animal taboos will reveal certain general principles of maquwoli and will make it possible to raise the question of how these principles apply to other typical domains of maquwoli.

Before turning to the symbolic motivations of particular maquwoli, I must discuss a number of general features which differentiate maquwoli dangers from ordinary ones. All these features are symptomatic of the symbolic nature of maquwoli. They are also the features to which the Huaulu themselves pay most attention, since they have to do with the concrete misfortunes which the Huaulu wish to avoid or to counter. It is here, I think, that we must begin, because it is here that the Huaulu's own recognition of the identity-determining (and therefore symbolic) character of maquwoli is highest, however indirectly and however much in distorted or reified form. But a couple of terminological observations and stipulations are in order to begin with.

Although maquwoli covers dangerous contacts irrespective of

whether they occur as a result of human action or not—so that perhaps the best possible general translation of *ia maquwoli* is "a contact between incompatibles should not occur, otherwise a misfortune will also occur"—by far the most frequently accepted meaning of the expression is "it should not be done." In other words, most mąquwoliem concern mismatches whose occurrence depends on human action. As such, they correspond closely to the usual anthropological definition of *taboo* (meaning "an intrinsic incompatibility with intrinsic consequences of an undesirable kind"). This is why, from now on, I shall use *taboo* as a translation of *maquwoli,* except when inappropriate. Then I shall use the required English equivalent (*bad omen, ritual,* and so on) or the word *maquwoli* itself.

Second, there are no Huaulu equivalents for the English words *misfortune* and *affliction,* which I will be using in my discussion. There are, however, at least two expressions for *disease,* a word which I shall also use. The most common is *hatanilouwam* (*-em* in pl.), which literally means "pain in the body." The other expression is *hatanipiniassi.* Literally, it means "bad/ugly body." But in fact it refers to chronic disease, or to a permanent bodily impairment, or even to "sickliness"—to a propensity to contract maladies.

The words *danger* and *dangerous* also do not have exact equivalents. The adjective piniassi, "not good" (i.e. having bad effects), and the verbal expression *ita mutaui,* "we are afraid of it," are used instead. Although these expressions are more general than *danger/dangerous,* they include the same ground covered by it and, like it, they do not differentiate between maquwoli and non-maquwoli contexts. This is a sufficient reason for using the convenient term *danger,* especially since it is the one that has widest currency in anthropological discourses on taboo. Nevertheless, the fact that the Huaulu language inscribes what we can appropriately call "dangerous" onto wider notions with their own resonances and connotations should never be lost from sight. *Piniassi,* "not good," is a more strongly evaluative term than *dangerous.* It ranges from "not useful," "not promoting well-being," to "evil" in the sense of something or somebody that is deliberately out to do harm. As for *mutau* it means not only "to be afraid" but also "to respect" (and even, sometimes, "to admire," "to be amazed by"). As we shall see more and more, respect is never too far from fear in the realm of maquwoli.

Diagnostic Misfortunes

In some cultures, the effect of the violation of all taboos is a special state common to them all, and is identified by one or more technical expressions. Famous examples are *miasma* (pollution) and *agos* (consecration, in the sense of being engulfed in or by a god's wrath) in ancient Greek;[41] *tame* (impurity) in Hebrew;[42] *najas* (defiled), *hadath* (affected), *junub* (precluded) in Arabic;[43] *asaucya* (impure) and *asauca* (impurity) in Sanskrit.[44] These terms are usually paired with positive counterparts, thereby indicating that they stand for the privation or diminution of normal or ideal states.[45] Such verbal abstractions are completely absent in Huaulu. The consequences of taboo violation are seen not as "impurity," with certain correlative afflictions or ritual exclusions or both, but as directly certain, more or less characteristic misfortunes and diseases.[46] Indeed, a taboo is usually enunciated together with the disease or misfortune that follows from its disregard (as in *ia maquwoli, ia koloputi,* "it is taboo, it gives leprosy"). Moreover, the enunciation of the disease can stand for that of the taboo (for instance, the previous expression may be abbreviated as *ia koloputi,* "it gives leprosy"). Thus, the role played by an abstract word elsewhere is played, at a much lesser level of generality, by these misfortunes, under which classes of taboos group themselves. It remains to be seen, though, if certain of these misfortunes do not display traits that are reminiscent of the notion of pollution as used both in the above-mentioned cultures and in anthropological literature.

The specificity of taboo-related misfortunes varies. Some are generically indicative of some sort of "trouble," including taboo violation. Others are merely diagnostic of taboo violation in general. Therefore, both kinds need to be determined further, usually through various forms of divination (the most frequent being shamanic). But a number of misfortunes, especially diseases, are highly diagnostic of relatively well-delimited classes of taboo violations. Since these misfortunes and the corresponding taboos play the greatest role in everyday life, I shall consider them in more detail. First, a brief mention of the more generic kinds of taboo-related misfortunes.

Premature death of one kind or another, or the occurrence of phenomena that may produce it, is a strong indication of a serious taboo violation. Even if other causes are at work, taboo violation is usually the root cause that makes one vulnerable to the others. Any chronic or severe misfortune that strikes an individual or a group (especially the entire community) may be interpreted as the consequence of taboo violation, most likely as chronic or as collective as the misfortune itself. The most characteristic of these misfortunes are: epidemics, infertility, an increase in infant mortality, systematic and generalized lack of success in hunting, trapping, and fishing, excessive or anomalous thunder (with the ensuing possibility of people or houses being struck by lightning), torrential rains (with accompanying flash floods and people possibly being washed away and drowned), and other catastrophic meteorological or elemental phenomena (such as eclipses, earthquakes, tidal waves).

Although all these phenomena must be subjected to further interpretation to determine what specific taboo violation, or series of taboo violations, causes them in particular instances, some have their own elective affinities. Eclipses and earthquakes are usually attributed to incest among true relatives, or to the violation of the secrecy or accuracy rule on sacred knowledge, or to serious errors in the performance of the most important rituals of collective interest. As for tidal waves, the only case I heard of was attributed to the violation of perhaps the most stringent of all Huaulu taboos: the ban on bringing the Leautuam (the supreme palladium in war) in the vicinity of the sea. The Huaulu were forced into this violation when the Dutch, early in this century, relocated them to the coastal site of Loulehali. There the village was allegedly destroyed by a tidal wave caused by the Leautuam's anger at seeing the "blue blue ocean" (tassi maramaraa). As a consequence of this event and a terrible epidemic, the surviving Huaulu returned to their inland abode.

Again, excessive thundering, lightning, and rain[47] (all linked phenomena, as the Huaulu well understand)[48] may be generically related to the violation of many taboos of ancestral concern, and even to phenomena (such as soul loss) that are not related, or are not necessarily related, to taboo violation. But typically these phenomena are attributed to the violation of a number of taboos that regulate the relationship between the Huaulu and two categories of others that occupy an intermediate position between enmity and amity—namely pela (members of a community of former enemies with whom a brotherhood pact was established) and wild animals. Examples of such taboo violations are sexual relationships with pela, laughing at wild animals, "cursing" (sero) by mentioning sexual relationships with animals, putting human clothes on them or generally treating them as humans, combing oneself in the presence of a freshly killed animal or even its meat.

Finally, epidemics, famines, and so on, because they strike the entire community, must perforce index some serious collective transgression, and thus usually point to the failure to undertake or adequately perform prescribed community projects, such as rebuilding the village hall (luma potoam) or the village shrine (luma maquwoliam) and performing the rituals connected with them. However generic, this correspondence suggests that there is at least a diagrammatic relationship between the social range of an affliction and the social range of the corresponding maquwoliem. This relationship is usually the starting point for much more complex determinations.

And now to the misfortunes more specifically connected with classes or families of taboos. Those that recur more frequently are as follows:

1. The malahau disease, whose symptoms are reminiscent of what we call consumption, strikes those who violate a number of taboos

among relatives, particularly the taboo on sexual (and a fortiori matrimonial) relationships with "true relatives"[49] (as against mere pela)[50] and the taboo on uttering the name of a close dead relative. In addition, malahau is one of the possible consequences (indeed the most frequent one) of violating affinal taboos (uttering the name of affines, partaking of food from the same pot with them, partaking of lime from the same container with them).[51]

2. Skin diseases that end up "eating" the flesh—koloputi (leprosy),[52] kekuem (tropical sores),[53] husuyem (yaws)[54] result from eating taboo meats.[55]

3. In men, persistent coughing, spitting or vomiting blood, shortsightedness and even blindness, general weakness, and a distended belly are due to their contact, however indirect, with menstrual and parturitional blood, which are highly taboo.

4. In women, dysmenorrhea, loss of hair, cross-eyes, false pregnancies, miscarriages, and loss of fertility are due to disregard of the taboo on contact with everything and everybody connected, however indirectly or symbolically, with human blood ritually shed by men. By extension, the same effects follow in women when they make contact (or improper contact) with any ritual activity or knowledge or object that is associated, like those involving that shedding, with the reproduction of the community as a whole, and thus also with its founding past.

5. In men, any tabooed misuse of the same rituals, knowledges, names, and objects has the following diagnostic effects: being bitten by the deadly mulalam snake[56] or by a centipede, falling from trees and cliffs, being gored by a wild pig, wounding oneself (and often dying of the ensuing hemorrhage), being snatched away by crocodiles, bitten by pythons, killed by headhunters, and, more generally, "falling in war." These misfortunes are considered typically male, as is shown, for instance, by the fact that they are all mentioned together in the prayer for a boy's initiation.[57] Indeed, most of them are not likely to happen to women, who do not usually climb trees or rocks,[58] do not hunt with bow and arrow, do not go to war,[59] do not use the large bush knives that are the source of some of the worst accidents, do not walk in front of a party in the forest (and are therefore less likely to step on snakes or centipedes).[60] Although some of these misfortunes (such as being bitten by crocodiles or snakes, or being drowned, or being killed by headhunters), just like other typically male ones (such as tuberculosis or chronic cough), can also strike women, they are matched with the violation of a precise class of taboos only when they strike men. Retrospectively, in what is remembered and narrated to illustrate the power of these taboos, women disappear because symbolically these taboos do not fit them.[61] Indeed, I heard a lot about men's coughing and spitting

blood, or about men who died because of snake bites, but very little of the kind, if anything at all, about women.

6. Stiff knees (probably due to arthritis) and "short breath" (due to asthma, tuberculosis, angina pectoris), both of which impair locomotion, are the consequences of violating the taboo on uttering the name of living kinsmen[62] in the parental and grandparental generations.

7. Difficult deliveries, sometimes resulting in death for the mother and usually also for the child, occur when the child is the fruit of an extramarital relationship or one with a taboo relative.

What links particular misfortunes to particular taboos? Or, to put it otherwise, why is it that in each case it is precisely that set of misfortunes and not another one that is involved?

Fear and Sense

The Huaulu tend, at least in practical contexts, to treat the relationship between the taboo violation and the misfortune that is its effect as an empirical one. It is supposedly a fact of observation that whenever one eats taboo meat *x* one gets yaws, just as it is a fact of empirical observation that whenever one eats bad mushrooms, or drinks water mixed with crushed *Derris elliptica* (munu), one dies. This pragmatic view is all one needs to stay alive and well. But paradoxically it is made possible by a premise from which it fails to draw some crucial consequences, and by ignoring one variable: memory.

The premise is one of temporal elasticity in taboo-related causal relations. When a taboo is violated, it makes little difference whether the temporal interval between cause and effect is short or long, although it is an "empirical" fact that it tends to be long.[63] It is therefore unpredictable, or much less predictable than in the ordinary causal relations that are taken for granted or even conceptualized, in everyday action. To take the bad (poisonous) mushroom example again, one bases one's decision not to eat it on the assumption, backed by experience, that whenever anyone eats it, he or she becomes sick and dies after a short time. But if one eats a taboo mushroom—that is, one that would be good to eat were it not for the taboo—the effect may follow immediately, or may follow after months or years, or may not follow at all.

It is precisely this elasticity which allows one to reconcile experience with the belief that taboo violation is the cause of certain misfortunes. This reconciliation is further aided by an unconscious phenomenon—the selectivity of memory. To understand why, we must realize that taboo works more often as an a posteriori system of interpretation of misfortune than as an a priori system of norms.[64] When people get certain diseases or experience other misfortunes that are conventionally associated with the violation of a taboo, they (or others for them) invoke it as a cause. If I get yaws, then I must have eaten a kind of taboo meat that induces yaws. Indeed, the onset of a symptomatic disease triggers a process of anamnesis, usually aided by a shaman (or, in the Huaulu view, by the powers who possess him and speak through him). Some violation at some point in life is always likely to be found. On the other hand, even if one is aware of having violated a taboo, one soon forgets all about it if there are no immediate consequences. Under these conditions, a regular connection between cause and effect is likely to be the dominant impression. It is an impression that would be destroyed if records were to be kept.

Besides being temporally elastic and characteristically delayed, the causal link is not infrequently undetermined in the realm of taboo. Take, for instance, the male violation of the taboos that concern the ritual shedding of human blood and other activities of communitywide significance. The possible consequences form a fixed and finite set but seem very disparate: being bitten by a snake, falling from a tree, drowning, and so on. There is no way of predicting one instead of another. It is in fact a matter of indifference which one occurs; they are interchangeable. There is, of course, indeterminacy in many ordinary causal relations, but in none is it as pronounced as it can be in the field of taboo (although the degree of indeterminacy usually varies with the class of taboos).[65] Do we have to assume, then, that this relative looseness of the cause-effect relationship in taboo situations indicates that it is fundamentally arbitrary? Or better said, do we have to assume that the choice of misfortunes to be attached to taboo violations is exclusively motivated by the deterring power of the effect, so that any effect that is fearsome enough—dying from a fall, or from snake poison, or from a wound—is as good as any other?

Undoubtedly fear plays a role in all of this. It is not insignificant that some of the most important taboos, those that have most to do with the existence of the community at large, are connected with the danger of a sudden and terrible death or with cataclysmic events to which the Huaulu react with fear and awe. But fear is not enough. It cannot explain why certain particularly terrifying diseases (such as elephantiasis) or truly disgusting ones (such as ringworm, or kolikoliam), which turn the afflicted person into a social outcast unable to find a spouse[66] are not among the taboo-related afflictions. Fear is complemented, modified, and even countered by sense, and sense, I would argue, is provided for the most part by analogic correspondences between misfortunes and taboos (besides obviously indexical ones such as those that indicate the gender of the transgressor).

Consider, for instance, the contrast between the "sudden-death" misfortunes due to a violent encounter (a poisonous snake, a wild boar, and so on) and the diseases or dysfunctions that are curable or that cause death only over a long period of time. In both cases, one is overwhelmed by an extraneous power, since disease is understood as an intrusion. But the overwhelming, and the resulting total passivity of the victim, is much more radical in one case. Furthermore, in one the whole body, indeed the whole life, of the victim is immediately involved; in the other, the disease begins in an organ or part of the body, eventually spreading to the whole through a process which one hopes to stop or even to reverse. This contrast between kinds of misfortunes no doubt parallels a contrast between the corresponding taboos. What are degrees of overpowering on the side of misfortune are degrees of encompassment on the side of taboo. One must yield to the whole (the taboos on which the reproduction of the entire community rests) more totally and unconditionally (*perinde ac cadaver,* one is tempted to say jesuitically) than to the parts (the taboos that protect lower-level categories and relations, whose violation affects only particular organs). Analogously, cosmic upheavals (such as eclipses, earthquakes, and tidal waves) are more encompassing phenomena than mere bodily diseases; thus they tend to correspond to more fundamental taboos. In sum, a rough diagrammatic relationship seems to exist between the contrast of misfortunes and the contrast of taboos: an absolutely overwhelming misfortune matches an absolutely encompassing taboo. Furthermore, because diseases are the most distinctive of all misfortunes, lower-level taboos, which concern specific (particular?) categorical distinctions, are connected with diseases more often than with other kinds of misfortunes.

Beyond these analogic correspondences between broad kinds of misfortunes and broad kinds of taboo violations, more precise and more telling analogies can be found. For instance, all "sudden death" (or "sudden overpowering") misfortunes consist of striking reversals of the subject-object relation in typical male activities. Instead of shedding the blood of enemies, Huaulu men shed their own blood, or their blood is shed by enemies. Wild boars kill them instead of being killed by them; they fall while they are intent on climbing (usually for hunting or headhunting purposes); and so on. In short, their action misfires, and from agents they turn into patients.

As we have seen, misfortunes from the sky (violent storms with lightning, thunder, and floods) concern two basic categorical distinctions: that between marriageable and nonmarriageable communities (pela and non-pela) and that between animal and human. Incest with a pela conflicts with brotherhood with a community of former enemies and therefore threatens to re-create a destructive return to the state preceding brotherhood—one that made possible sex and marriage, but also war. Laughing at animals, insulting them with curses that mention copulation with them, and putting clothes on them are all acts that threaten an even more profound contrast: that between animal and human. This is rather evident for the act of dressing animals in clothes; but it is also implied by the other two acts, since sex—even in the form of a verbal reference to it—is legitimate only between humans, and so is laughter. I shall return to these points in more detail later. What matters now is that it is not symbolically irrelevant that the punishment for threatening these categorical distinctions descends from heaven to earth. It is not just that heaven is associated with the ancestral powers that are particularly interested in sanctioning some of the taboos that contribute, so to speak, to constituting the community. It is also, and more important, that rain and thunder/lightning seem to confuse heaven and earth, that is, things that should stay separate more than anything else, because their separation is the most primordial, the one from which, as the origin myth teaches, all other separations ensue. Thus the threatening of two cardinal separations threatens an even more radical separation. The cosmos may come apart if some of its partitions are ignored by humans.

A similar message is conveyed by eclipses, earthquakes, and tidal waves. These are all cosmic mixtures[67] which parallel inappropriate mixtures in the human sphere (such as incest among true relatives),[68] the conjoining of the Huaulu palladium with the sea (evoking the collapse of the contrast between inland and coastal peoples), the revealing of secret knowledge to strangers,[69] or whatever other inappropriate conjunction may threaten the Huaulu community as a whole.

Even more striking parallels exist between skin diseases and meat taboos. More precisely, leprosy is the outcome of disregarding the taboos on the combination of certain meats;[70] all other skin diseases are the consequence of eating a single forbidden species of animal. There are several points of comparison between skin diseases and forbidden meats. The most obvious one is pointed out by the Huaulu themselves as one reason certain meats are taboo: because they come from animals whose skin is reminiscent of a skin disease.[71] As we shall see in detail later, this spontaneously "Frazerian" explanation is "superficial": it displaces onto the surface of the animal a number of deeper reasons for the taboo. But the point is that it is precisely through this displacement that the correspondence between cause and effect, between the body of the animal and the body of the human, becomes apparent, and that the disease can become the signature of the taboo. Symbol piles upon symbol.

The more general correspondence between cause and effect, though, is based not on the visual aspect of the skin affected by the disease, but on the mode of operation of the disease. As "one eats the wrong flesh" (eme kae sala ayokuam), "so" (leu) "yaws [or tropical sores] eat him" (husuyam [kekuem] kaei). The implied correspondence between the two "eatings" is reinforced by the use of a single word, *ayoku,* to designate human and animal flesh (or meat) in the Huaulu language. There is thus a very striking correspondence between cause (eating a tabooed flesh) and effect (being eaten in one's flesh by disease). And there is more than a correspondence: because the disease is the reversal of the taboo act, or rather is the taboo act applied to the agent, it signals that a norm of reciprocity applies to the relations between certain animals and the Huaulu. Through the threatened effects of its violation, the taboo gives reasons for itself: it indicates that it follows from the participation, in certain contexts, of animal and human in the same moral community.[72]

Other correspondences between skin diseases and the taboos they index are subtler. For instance, I believe that there is an analogy between the intensely social act of eating, which is always open to public scrutiny in Huaulu, and the extremely patent character of skin disease. Even more to the point, just as skin diseases—which are considered visually and olfactorily repulsive by the Huaulu—tend to isolate the afflicted person socially, so the violation of food taboos (which are for the most part meat taboos) has antisocial connotations. Carelessness with food means carelessness with people, since one usually shares food with them. Moreover, as we shall see in detail later, a great number of food taboos have to do with the integrity of social categories. In sum, just as proper eating indexes proper sociability, improper eating indexes a lack of sociability that must be as patent to the rest of the community as a disease that invades the visible surface of the body. Furthermore, the disease's movement from surface to inner flesh may evoke the dependence of an individual's identity, reified into bodily integrity, on his publicly perceived image. Through a disease that moves from skin to flesh, in sum, the eye of the other is introjected as an inner eye. Of this eye, of this gaze that defines the self through its bodily image, one cannot easily be rid. It sticks to the surface of the body; it is extraneous to it and yet part of it, like dirt that cannot so easily be washed away. And indeed, this is what skin disease is: a stronger form of dirt, of something that has become mixed with some other thing to which it does not, and cannot, belong without undermining that thing—a metaphor of the altered state of the person that is the consequence of the violated taboo. Much more than dirt, skin disease spreads, penetrates, occupies the body, makes itself felt, urging itself upon consciousness through the body it devours, devouring like this consciousness.

Something similar can be said of the other, and much more serious, devouring affliction called malahau. As I have mentioned, this affliction is reminiscent of what used to be called consumption. Susan Sontag has thus summarized the nineteenth-century image of consumption (TB): "In TB, you are eating yourself up, being refined, getting down to the core, the real you." Thus she has contrasted it with the twentieth-century image of cancer: "In cancer, non-intelligent ('primitive,' 'embryonic,' 'atavistic') cells are multiplying, and you are being replaced by the non-you. Immunologists class the body's cancer cells as 'nonself.'"[73] The Huaulu view of malahau involves no refining process but strikingly parallels the notion of "eating yourself up." In fact it makes it quite literal, because it sees consumption as the ultimate consequence of an insatiable hunger that finally prompts the person afflicted to devour himself internally, to eat himself up. But this process also has much in common with Sontag's definition of cancer (leaving aside, of course, the "primitive" cells and so on), for it is not spontaneous. Rather, it is the consequence of an invasion from the outside (usually attributed to the ancestors of the offended affines) that turns the body (and thus the self) against itself. So malahau is both consumption and cancer, both eating oneself up and being eaten by the nonself. The same can be said of leprosy and the other skin diseases that are the effect of eating the wrong meat. These resemble cancer as defined by Sontag, and yet they also resemble her consumption, because being eaten for eating the wrong kind of flesh is an indirect form of self-eating.

In sum, malahau and leprosy, yaws and so on, utilize the same basic image, the image of a self that is turned against itself, that becomes the agent of its own destruction, under the influence of a punishing nonself. Malahau differs from leprosy and the other skin diseases only to the extent that the main transgression to which it corresponds—incest and thus the undermining of one's dependency on the other par excellence, the affine—can be viewed as a stronger and more direct form of "self-consumption" than the consumption of wrong meat. Indeed, incest is viewed as "eating" an object that is wrong because it is lelakissi, "not other"—a replica of oneself.[74] By refusing to "eat" the "other" (lelaki), that is, to marry or have sexual intercourse with traditional affines, the subject can "eat" only itself. Hence the "consumption" component, the self-devouring, is emphasized in malahau. It is nevertheless triggered by the rejected affines, who are its ultimate cause. Hence it also involves an element of "cancer," of invasion of self by nonself. However, the latter is obviously dominant in leprosy, yaws, and so on, which make literal what is metaphorically implied by the ingestion of a meat at odds with the self—an irreducible nonself that cannot be digested but digests its eater.

In both cases, one undermines one's embodied identity with a form of consumption that undermines the system of differences on which that identity evidently depends. But the disease associated with "kinship" taboos symbolizes self-devouring much more directly than the diseases connected with meat taboos, signaling that sexual reproduction (which involves interhuman relations) is more intimately connected with identity than eating meat (which involves the more distant relationship between humans and animals). In any case, both kinds of disease make it evident that the body cannot survive (and reproduce) except by being subordinated to the cultural laws presiding over the desires of the flesh, among which the desire for flesh (in its two forms, alimentary and sexual) is primary.

That a taboo-related affliction must evoke the taboo object is also shown by "short breath" and stiff knees, which are the two possible effects of uttering the tabooed names of kinsmen in the parental and grandparental generations. As the Huaulu note, the effects of an impaired breathing apparatus and stiff knees are the same—loss of locomotion[75]—and it is through this common effect that the two kinds of misfortune are associated. Its practical consequence is that the afflicted person had difficulty procuring food by hunting, fishing, gathering, and so on. One also has difficulty—and this is of special or exclusive interest to males—defending oneself or participating in war. A man's whole life and ability to fulfill his obligations toward relatives are diminished. These afflictions therefore function, just like malahau, as reminders of the person's dependency—in his very body, in his very life—on the integrity of his relations.[76] Given the great place that bodily articulations have in Huaulu symbolism, I would also venture the hypothesis that an analogy may be perceived between the impairing of a vertical articulation of the human body (the knee) and a vertical articulation of the social body (the generation structure of kinship).[77]

Both kin taboos and meat taboos have to do with ayoku, "flesh," and perhaps this explains the striking symmetry that exists between the effects of their violation. While meat-taboo-related afflictions reach the inner flesh starting from the visible surface of the body, suggesting perhaps that one's integrity depends on a double other—the animal whose flesh becomes one's flesh, the fellow human whose gaze becomes one's internal gaze, one's socially mediated bodily image—kin-taboo–related afflictions move in the opposite direction. They start from the invisible inner parts of the body (lungs, bones, and so on), and they eventually become visible on the surface through exhalation and locomotion (in malahau, also through the state and tonus of the whole body), that is, through dynamic signs, not static and purely visual (and olfactory) ones such as skin diseases are. This shift from the outer to the inner as the principal location of the affliction seems to confirm the point that one is more intimately and fundamentally dependent on relatives than on animals and the undifferentiated public. What attacks vital organs and bones and (in malahau) consumes the whole body from the inside is more threatening and more radical, not to mention more irreversible, than what attacks the surface of the body and the flesh immediately below it.

A number of afflictions are thought to be related to taboo violations because they make patent the loss of categorical difference with which taboos are associated. This is particularly true of the taboos that concern the difference between man and woman, and thus also of "male" and "female" things. For instance, men who improperly handle sacra connected with war and other male-defining activities may suffer distended belly—a misfortune that indicates they have threatened their difference from women, which ultimately rests on the use of those sacra, and have thus become womanlike. Indeed they are derisively dubbed aila mahahiem, "the pregnant gentlemen," and it is not unusual to ask them when they are going to give birth. Conversely, improper contact by women with some of the same things that evoke maleness results in a loss of their femininity and thus of their desirability: crossed-eyes (the Huaulu ideal of feminine beauty is not Venusian) and loss of hair afflict them. Such improper contact may also result in a condition of swollen belly without pregnancy, that is, a form of false femininity that matches the false femininity of certain male transgressors.[78]

But since it is principally by flows of blood (the blood of menstruation and parturition in women; the blood of circumcision and murder in men) that male and female are contrasted, it stands to reason that most afflictions resulting from threats to that contrast consist of "wrong" flows of blood. It is absolutely taboo for men to enter into contact with menstrual blood or menstruating women, however indirectly. If they do, they run a very telling danger: their throat and lungs are attacked, they cough persistently, and they may end up spitting blood. This bleeding from the respiratory apparatus matches female genital bleeding. It symbolizes the feminization of a male who has become mixed up with what is most female. One bleeding turns into the other because much of the menstrual contamination affects men through the mouth, since women prepare food and betel nut, of course,[79] but also, and more indirectly, since women may step over betel spittle expectorated by men.[80] In this way, the throat and, through the throat, the lungs are attacked by the extraneous blood spilled from women's genitals. Hence the persistent coughing and, eventually, the revealing hemorrhage. The main point is that the impairment of the respiratory apparatus implies the impairment of the two major kinds of activities that make a man a man and thus differentiate him from a woman: the blood-spilling activities of hunting and headhunting, and the social and ritual activities that involve "speech" (souwam). Men contaminated by menstrual blood are unsuccessful in both kinds of activity, when they are not altogether barred from them. Thus the spitting of blood condenses in a single powerful symbol the invasion of masculinity by femaleness at her most characteristic, and therefore most incompatible with maleness. The same "unmanned" state is also indicated, if less pointedly, by the generic debility and slowness that contact with menstrual blood is supposed to induce.[81] Note that here too, just as in kin-related taboos, much emphasis is put on locomotion, as the epitome of activity, especially of a male kind. Menstrual taboos and kin taboos thus converge in some of their ultimate effects. The convergence is not surprising, since menstrual taboos maintain gender difference, which is the foundation of all other differences in the realm of kinship. Moreover, blood is as important in the conceptualization of kinship as it is in that of gender. Blood, as the currency of all relatedness, animates all these taboos with an idiom of respiration: walking, speaking, acting.

The misfortunes suffered by women who enter into contact with men as shedders of blood, that is, as warriors and so on, and with any of their paraphernalia, symbols, and representations in that capacity, are symmetric to those suffered by men who enter into contact with women who shed blood in menstruation or parturition. Just as men can't stop spitting blood, so women can't stop menstruating—or rather, they have inordinately "long and irregular periods" (poture melekae). In sum, an improper flux of blood in each sex is induced by an improper contact with the flux of blood that is distinctive of the other sex. Here again, afflictions are interpreted as effects of taboo violation insofar as they recall what is violated, and thus make the sense of the taboo patent (and persuasive) through suffering. If suffering can be related to taboo, then, it ceases to be senseless. It is no less painful for being meaningful, but there is at least a justification for it. Like Dante's Hell, in sum, this particular Huaulu hell is dominated by the law of "contrappasso" (dictating that the punishment must fit the crime).

The most serious and distinctive forms of taboo-related death in men (by falling, being bitten by snakes, self-inflicted wounds, etc.) have a counterpart in the most serious misfortune in women: death in childbed. Indeed, a parallelism is established between the latter and falling to one's death: women who die in childbirth are referred to as pukue ria ninianiam, "fallen in the village." Death in childbirth has many causes, but always involves the violation of some sexual taboo. A difficult childbirth (which may often end in the death of both child and mother) is also attributed to the father of the child being a sexually taboo man for the woman. Even distantly incestuous relationships may be the cause of frequent miscarriages, or still-births, or infant mortality (usually through "consumption," the malahau disease). The burdensome consequences of sexual misconduct, then, afflict women most, whereas the burdensome consequences of ritual misconduct afflict men most.

Taboo-related afflictions may point not only, or simply, to the object of taboo, but also to the organ with which the transgression has been committed. Furthermore, by impairing that organ, or even the whole body of the transgressor, the afflictions may block the further commission of the transgression. For instance, it is said that if one tells sacred stories during daytime (it is taboo; they should be told at night), one contracts husuyem (yaws or boils) on one's buttocks. This affliction can be understood if one keeps in mind that the expression *ita malimaliamae,* "we sit continuously," designates any activity of deliberating, narrating, and so on. By attacking the buttocks of the improperly "sitting" person, disease points to the nature of his impropriety and at the same time makes its continuation impossible, since the afflicted person cannot sit. Another example is the loss of teeth as a consequence of the taboo on mixing the bland meat of marsupials with the tangy lime or the hot chili (an obvious mismatch). Here again, attention is directed to the organ of commission, and its impairment impairs all eating and thus also the eating that is taboo (although it must be admitted that in this case the effect is too general not to make the opposite consequence possible: once the teeth are all gone, people feel free to violate the taboo). Blindness, which is one of the possible consequences of entering into contact with menstruating women, again impairs the very organ of commission, since women in that state should not be looked at.[82] Chronic coughing is one possible consequence of violating the food taboos of the sewa potoam and the taboo on mixing menstrual blood and food. Thus the affliction points to the organ of commission, and by blocking that organ, it makes the repetition of transgression more difficult. Finally, the premature death of those who represent a taboo mixture between Huaulu and non-Huaulu radically eliminates that mixture by eliminating them. An example is the death of children who attend school, particularly beyond elementary level, when one really learns something of reading and writing. Such attendance is said to be taboo because literacy is incompatible with being a Huaulu, that is, the member of an oral culture which should stay so by ancestral mandate.[83]

We have seen, in sum, that some afflictions and other misfortunes unequivocally signal taboo transgression, because they are considered its results. But these afflictions typically concern taboos that have to do with categorical status. When taboos define a goal-oriented action, then, it is the action's failure, whatever that happens to consist of, that signals their violation. Therefore in such cases it is much more difficult to infer the taboo violation from the unwanted event as such.[84] Nor is there an analogic relationship between the event and the taboo. It is only because the event is situated at the end point of an action defined by certain taboos that it counts as the consequence of the violation of those taboos. The relationship is mostly indexical.

Categorical and situational consequences may, of course, be combined, indeed they are in most rituals. Both may also be combined with social consequences. These are rarely corporal punishments,[85] less rarely fines (which may have to be paid to the party offended and endangered by a taboo violation),[86] and more frequently various forms of social exclusion or even ostracism. In particular, taboo violation may disqualify a person from performing an act or participating in an activity. For instance, a shaman who is aware of having violated a taboo, and even more so one who is known to have violated it, cannot perform shamanic rituals until he has ritually remedied the consequences of his violation. In this case, one does not wait for an affliction to discover the violation or to take it seriously, for an immediate consequence looms: the failure of the ritual performances (or, what amounts to the same, the failure of the shaman to make people believe in their efficacy). Analogously, a man who is aware of having been contaminated by a menstruating woman, either because he has disregarded the taboos that separate her or because he is married to her (in which case the contamination is inevitable), will automatically bar himself (and in any case be barred) from active participation in such activities as headhunting or war, formal negotiations, shamanism, using secret knowledge, telling myths, and so on. The reason is that his effectiveness is greatly diminished in all these fields; indeed, he may risk death if he engages in some of them.

In a majority of cases, however, social exclusion becomes necessary only after the onset of telltale afflictions and only if these are capable of impairing other people or the community as a whole. For instance, if a person is bitten by a snake or a centipede but does not die (or is not yet dead), he or she cannot return home without first undergoing a remedial ritual, which consists in eating a small, specially prepared packet of "baked sago" (umulu). In principle, the reason one waits until an affliction declares itself before segregating or excluding the transgressor (or before performing remedial rites) is that most transgressions are inferred a posteriori from the affliction; but in practice, it is often the case that one—and even the community at large—is reluctant to take action on taboo violations if no bodily consequences, and thus no actual signs of danger for the community, are apparent.

However, there is a taboo violation that has an immediate social consequence of a supremely serious kind: it requires the disbanding of the village association for a while. This is the taboo of bringing back to the village the corpse, or any personal object, of a person who died a premature and violent death, such as from falling, being gored, bitten by a poisonous snake, struck by lightning, and so on. If this taboo is violated, even by mistake, the village must be abandoned, and its site becomes forever uninhabitable.

In conclusion, we have seen two things. The first is that a kind of disease totemism exists which makes it possible to differentiate the more important classes or families of taboo. The second is that this totemism alone cannot fully differentiate the field of taboo-related dangers from that of ordinary dangers. Therefore, other, less immediately evident, parameters must now be considered.

Agents and Patients

In the previous section we have seen that certain diseases with differential and analogic potential, and with a fair amount of deterrent power as well, have become associated with certain kinds of socially significant objects and relationships. The diseases have thus lent their dangerousness to the objects and relationships, which have become maquwoli as a result. But danger does not flow in one direction only, from the bodily to the social. It also goes the opposite way. The fearsomeness of the misfortunes that are exclusively associated with taboo objects also depends on them. A disease is feared not just as such, but also in some measure because it signifies the power of the things, relations, or persons whose taboos have been violated. Physical suffering becomes inextricably blended with moral suffering: beyond the rotting flesh, the coughing, the bleeding away of life, one comes face to face with the pain that comes from others, and thus also face to face with oneself as a moral person. From symbolizing diseases we must therefore move to symbolized moral relations—to the subjects and objects implicated in taboos and to their interconnections. Only in this way will the true extent of the difference between ordinary dangers and taboo-related dangers become apparent.

I begin with an obvious difference between the two which also emphasizes the moral character of taboo. Ordinary dangers are universally incurred by all humans by virtue of their having the same body. When such dangers are specific to some subset of humans it is because this subset is defined by the possession of particular organs and functions (as in the case of males and females), or because of particular vulnerabilities or conditions due to age. Occupational difference may, of course, imply that one category or class of people is more likely to be exposed to certain dangers, but not that their bodies are intrinsically more vulnerable to these dangers than the bodies of those who follow a different occupation. In contrast, taboo-related dangers do not, or not usually, have the same universality. They are selective vis-à-vis the social identity of the subject, even if that identity is embodied, substantialized, and thus superficially indistinguishable from that of the universal human body implicated by ordinary dangers. Taboo-related dangers, in sum, differentiate subjects; ordinary dangers leave them undifferentiated. A taboo food is capable of "poisoning" only certain categories of subjects; a poisonous food is capable of poisoning anybody. Furthermore, contact with the same taboo object may have quite different negative consequences for different categories of subjects.

The first generalization is illustrated by menstrual blood, which is dangerous for initiated males but not for uninitiated ones and for women. Conversely, human blood ritually shed by initiated males is not dangerous to them but is to women and uninitiated males. An illustration of the second generalization is provided by sacred objects whose mishandling has different consequences for males and females. These examples show that what is involved in taboo-related dangers is not the physical body, but embodied identity. They manifest the different responsibilities of men and women (men kill and women give birth) and at the same time their complementarity. They are motivated by moral relations and sustain them by using the body—its organs, its substances and functions—as their symbols. Clearly, and as the analysis of the symptomatic misfortunes also revealed, the difference between ordinary dangers and taboo-related dangers is that the latter stand for something else and cannot be accounted for without this symbolic valence. Or more precisely, ordinary dangers may also be symbolically motivated, but if so, what they stand for is very different from what taboo-related dangers stand for. What the latter stand for is something that has some profound connection with the moral identity of a subject, with his rights and duties vis-à-vis others and himself, which an ordinary danger does not have. More of this, and of the relativity of the dangers of taboo, later.

There is another remarkable difference between ordinary dangers and the dangers of taboo. Ordinary dangers are incurred either through one's own acts or through those of others. For the acts of others to endanger us, however, we need to be in physical contact, mediate or immediate, with the dangerous situation. Such contact is wholly unnecessary, indeed irrelevant, when taboo-related dangers are involved. Then I may suffer the consequences of somebody else's taboo violation, not because I actually participate in what he does or I am around when he does it, but because I participate in what he *is*, because I am his relative or because, as his partner in a certain relationship, I help define him. I may be 100 miles away, and still I will suffer the consequences. In this sense the danger of taboo violation is like the danger of revenge for murder between two descent groups. I may be the victim of revenge whether or not I have had anything to do with the murder, simply because I am a relative of the murderer. And as in that case, the actual perpetrator need not himself suffer any consequence. Indeed it should be clear that I suffer the consequences of somebody's taboo violation not because this somebody suffers them to begin with and then contaminates me. On the contrary, I often suffer these consequences instead of him. And even when I may suffer them together with him, it is because of a relation, not a contamination—because we are in some way inseparable.

Let us look more closely at these two possibilities: suffering together with the taboo violator, and suffering instead of him. Either or both can be realized in certain cases. For instance, when a taboo shared by all members of a lineage is violated by any of them, the violator alone, or the violator and any other member of the lineage, or any other member alone, or all of them together, may suffer. All these possibilities are in a sense equivalent, since the sharing of danger is the sharing of a relationship; the taboo is more about this sharing than anything else. But it is striking that in actuality two types of persons tend to suffer the consequences of taboo violation most, even when they are not responsible for it: those who are entrusted with ritual office, and those who are defined as "weak," or rather, "not strong" (kuruessi). For instance, the person who is entrusted with the performance of the ipa's sewa potoam may become seriously ill or fall from trees and so on if anyone violates one of the taboos which the sewa potoam requires all members of the ipa to follow. At a communitywide level, the violation of taboos may have dangerous consequences for the guardian of the community hall. Limule, for example, its guardian during my sojourns in 1985 and 1988, complained that his daughter's miscarriage and his own persistent weakness were due to his fellow villagers' reluctance to repair the hall (it is taboo to let it fall into disrepair). I had heard similar complaints in 1972–73 from Pulaki, the guardian at that time. Obviously people in positions of authority become the scapegoats of taboo transgressions because they are most responsible for keeping order in their group, and because they are in direct contact with the occult powers—ancestors and sewa—who have an interest in those taboos. So in a sense the shifting of danger from transgressor to person in a position of authority manifests the true referent of taboo, which is a hierarchical relation. The danger which the taboo signals is both a danger to that relation and a way to give reality to it. Indeed, one may even say that the relation is reproduced by being endangered.

Hierarchy is also revealed as the true referent of these taboos when danger displaces itself in the opposite direction, from superior to inferior, or rather, from strong to weak. This is a possibility that exists for all taboo violations. The Huaulu believe that, like all misfortunes, the misfortunes that follow from violating taboos are more easily incurred by the weak than by the strong. But they follow in ways that are quite different from those of ordinary misfortunes. If they do not manage to affect the transgressor because she is too strong, they move on to her (but usually his; men are supposed to be stronger than women) weaker relative, simply because he or she is a relative. In other words, taboo-related misfortune follows a social path quite unknown to ordinary misfortunes: it displaces itself along kin lines. The relatives more often affected are the weaker dependencies of the transgressor: wife and children. The weaker they are, the more they suffer for what they have not committed. Once again, we see that the dangerousness of taboo requires a symbolic translation in order to be understood. Here, it stands for the equivalence of relatives, but also for their inequality in a hierarchical structure. The "weaker" are in reality the subordinate (wife and children); they pay for the "strong," who are in fact the superordinated. But at the same time the latter suffer through the suffering of the former. The strong are motivated to act properly, then, not out of fear for themselves, but out of care for significant others. They are, in a way, above taboos; yet insofar as they care for their weaker dependents, they are below them for reasons higher than fear, which is the moral springboard of the weak. Needless to say, this theory is also a device whereby the discrepancy between the location of misfortune and the location of taboo transgression may be neutralized. If it is the wife who suffers, even though it is the husband who transgresses, it must be because they are in some respect equivalent and yet also unequal. Kinship dogma is vindicated in vindicating taboo dogma.

Suffering alone the consequences of somebody else's taboo violations is not just a possibility, but a *necessity,* in a number of other cases. Two kinds of cases may be distinguished. In one, the taboos must be followed by both partners in a relationship, but only one of them suffers if either of the two violates the taboos. In the other kind, the taboos are as unshared as the danger of violating them: the person who suffers the consequences is different from the person who was supposed to keep the taboos.

An example of the first kind is offered by shamanic treatment. During a cure or a prophylaxis, both the shaman and the patient must follow the taboos that go with the medicines used. A violation by either affects only the patient.[87] While the sharing of the taboos indicates the bond between patient and shaman, then, the nonsharing of the dangers inherent in their violation indicates the dependency and subordination of the patient vis-à-vis the shaman. At the same time this asymmetry makes the shaman a more responsible person than his patient: he does not violate taboos out of concern for his patient and also, it must be admitted, out of concern for his reputation as a conscientious curer.

The most striking examples of the second kind (neither taboos nor dangers are shared; one partner in the relationship follows the taboo, the other partner suffers the consequences of its violation) are found in the conjugal relationship. If the wife violates the sexual taboos that go with her status, the husband (especially if he already finds himself in a dangerous situation, such as a war or a hunt) will suffer any of the usual set of serious consequences: he will wound himself, be bitten by a mulalam snake or a crocodile, gored by a boar, killed in war, and so on. The same will result ("before eight days have passed") if she lets fall to the floor the piece of likitotu leaf that she must put in her hair bun every time she cooks sago porridge for her husband (this rite symbolizes the wife's continuing subordination to her husband). Other examples are found in the intrinsically dangerous situation of departure from the village for a trip of long duration or, in the case of a guest, for a homebound trip. Then, if anybody in the house other than the person who is about to leave eats or sneezes or plays the war drum or sheds tears, or if anybody leaves the village at the same time as the traveller without accompanying him, or if anybody inquires from him when he plans to leave or speaks badly of him as soon as he has left (all of which are strictly taboo), misfortune strikes the traveller (who will be bitten by a poisonous snake, fall from a tree, and so on), not the transgressor.[88] Not only do these dangers differ from ordinary ones in that they *necessarily* fall on somebody other than the person who acts; they also and more profoundly differ from ordinary dangers in that their symbolic roots are explicitly recognized. Indeed, the above taboo violations are described as an "abandoning" of the husband by the wife, of the departing person by those who stay home (i taki holi ala eve, "they abandon him"). One partner "turns his back on the other" (titikalu eme), as is also said.

One may well ask why it is the innocent partner rather than the guilty one who pays the consequences. But such a question betrays a misunderstanding of the taboo and projects onto it the view that morality is essentially a matter of justice. If the taboo is not about the danger of incurring guilt, but about the danger of losing my relationship with somebody, then only if this somebody is in danger of dying am I in danger of losing my relationship with him. On the other hand, were I to die, the basic reason for having a relationship to begin with would come to an end. Hence, punishment cannot be suffering in the body, but suffering the loss of somebody. Yet things are not so clear-cut after all. For here too morality may work through concern for the other, rather than simply through concern for oneself, as in so many other taboos. This concern, though, is usually not very far from its opposite: lack of concern or even hostility. A wife may wish to get rid of her husband (indeed, she is often accused of this intention), as a host may also wish to get rid of a guest. Not surprisingly, such ambivalence is at its strongest in the taboos that involve the most ambivalent relationships, such as conjugality, and when the social bond is loosened by a departure.

In conclusion, taboo-related dangers may differ from ordinary dangers because one risks the former independently of physical involvement with their cause and simply by virtue of some social relationship with a person who is physically involved with that cause. This shows that, although these dangers pass for dangers of things, they are in fact dangers of social relationships. Because these relationships are symbolized by things and are attached to physical dangers, they have themselves acquired the character of things. Yet they are recognizably still not quite things, since they operate with a logic which is not truly that of things.

The Sources of Danger

Even more important, if at times less immediately apparent, is another difference between ordinary dangers and taboo-related dangers. Ordinary dangers come from the dangerous objects alone, but taboo-related dangers may come from a variety of occult sources which complement the object or take its place entirely. The degree to which this happens depends on the definition of the taboo action. If the action consists in the appropriation of an object, particularly through ingestion, then the cause of the ensuing misfortune tends to be identified with some badness intrinsic to the object as such. The basic model is that of poison, and in this sense there is little overt difference between the etiological discourse of taboo-related misfortunes and that of ordinary misfortunes.

But if the action does not consist in the appropriation of an object or is not principally defined by it, the poisoning model of misfortune retreats to the background or cannot apply at all. This is particularly the case when the misfortune consists in the misfiring of an action (for instance, falling from a tree, being unsuccessful in the hunt) or in its reversal, such as when the object becomes the subject (cutting oneself with a bush knife, being gored by a wild pig, killed by an enemy, etc.). Because of an implicit principle that the cause and effect must be homogeneous, an action can go wrong only because of another action. In other words, the source of the misfortune tends in this case to be identified with an agent—not with a poison but with a person of sorts. This amounts to saying that most of these misfortunes are explained by the intervention of malevolent occult powers.

It is also clear that the same principle of homogeneity between effect and cause ensures that the more interpersonal or socially significant a taboo is, the more likely it is that the misfortune following its violation is attributed to an agency both personal and social in character. In the extreme, this agency may even be a living person—the offended party. Take the case of the violation of such interpersonal taboos as those that regulate the relationship of affines. One of these taboos is that an affine cannot utter the name of other affines. If he or she does, there will be an immediate request of compensation from the offended party (the owner of the name). The payment of a fine is a sine qua non for purposes of social peace; but it also preempts punishment in the form of misfortune, which is supposed to come from the ancestors of the offended party. The case where punishment takes the form of a fine to be paid to a living party is rare, however, and by and large limited to affinal relationships. Normally, the violation of interpersonal taboos or in any case of socially significant ones is punished with misfortunes inflicted by nonliving humans, that is, by ancestors and ultimately by the pair Lahatala and Puhum, who are the first and most important ancestors. However, this does not always or even frequently mean that they mete out the punishment directly. In fact, their intervention usually consists in withdrawing their protection from their "children," who then become vulnerable to the attacks of malevolent occult powers. These powers are precisely those who make actions misfire or who turn the agent against himself or who transform the agent into patient.

These powers are in a permanently hostile relationship with humans. Their malevolence is usually indiscriminate, although in certain cases they have some good reasons to be angry. For instance, as we shall see in the next chapter, the "lords of the land" usually attack humans because they kill the lord's animals or appropriate the resources of the forest in large quantities. Analogously, the powers who preside over fishing (auwete) or trapping (mutuaula) are believed to turn the humans' hand against their own bodies, thereby provoking often lethal hemorrhages, out of anger for the war humans wage on the powers' "children" (the animals). Most powers, however, are totally amoral. For instance, one of the most fearful misfortunes, death by fall, usually from trees, is explained as the work of mulua awaem. These perverse "little girls" sit on a branch above a man who is climbing a tree and stick out a leg which deceptively looks like a branch. When the man attempts to seize it to continue his climb, they quickly pull it back, and he falls to his death. They seek his death by this deception, because their insatiable sexual appetite requires a constant supply of male companions in the form of ghosts.

But whether or not the attacking power has some moral ground of its own, its action is given a moral signification in its ultimate governance by the ancestors, who decide on its success or failure. If a Huaulu has violated a serious societal taboo, the ancestors may decide to let one of these powers to have its way against him. This is how it happens that men who have mishandled the society's sacra, or the most important rites that are the concern of ancestors, meet their death by fall, or by self-inflicted wounds, or by being bitten by a snake, gored by a wild pig, and so on. Naturally, ancestral intervention may take a more direct form, but this is comparatively rare, partly because the ancestors are given the more exalted role of *dei otiosi,* partly because their benevolence is ideologically foregrounded.

The etiology of taboo-related misfortunes thus shades into two different directions that transcend the domain of taboo. One is that of "poison," where tabooed objects do not prima facie seem to operate differently from any other kind of harmful objects. The other is that of misfortune due to attacks from malevolent occult powers. Many of these attacks are attributed to taboo violations, but many others are not. Even when a taboo violation is considered the main reason for the afflicted person's vulnerability to attack, other reasons are usually invoked as well. In sum, when the problem is to identify the source of affliction, taboo is only one—if usually the most important—among many different interpretive tools. Nevertheless, even the most reified of all taboo-related dangers differ from ordinary, nonsymbolic ones, in that they too are ultimately subject to ancestral governance, as is indicated by the possibility of praying to the ancestors to be freed from the consequences of taboo violation, even when this violation concerns food. Indeed, causality has a hierarchical structure, which is more prominent the more it concerns human values and interests. The amoral or imperfectly moral world of incompatibilities, antagonisms, hostilities, desires and malevolences in which the Huaulu participate, and from which they seek protection through their taboos, has its autonomy, but it is only relative. Ultimately cause and effect, especially when they concern the human world, are governed by essentially moral forces—the ancestors of the Huaulu, and above them the ultimate ancestral pair, Lahatala and Puhum, who continue to govern, however distantly and indirectly, the cosmos they originally brought forth.

Dangerous Objects

If we take a synoptic look at the misfortunes that strike the individual transgressors of taboos, we cannot fail to notice that these misfortunes are for the most part reducible to three basic images: being "bitten" or "eaten," bleeding, being blocked. Altogether, these images modulate a single theme—that of passivization, indeed of loss of a characteristic activity, ultimately resulting in death. Evidently, both power and difference are threatened in taboo violations.

The "biting" image is instantiated, needless to say, by the bite of snakes or centipedes or crocodiles or bush knives,[89] and by the strike of a lightning bolt.[90] The closely related "eating" misfortunes are, equally obviously, consumption (malahau, which, as we have seen, is conceived as a form of self-eating), leprosy, and other skin diseases that are said to "eat" their victim. The bleeding misfortunes are, in men, tubercular diseases of the lungs, and in women, dysmenorrhea and other kinds of "wrong" losses of blood from the womb (miscarriages, parturitional hemorrhages that cause death). Finally, the "blocking" misfortunes are those that impair locomotion (asthma, stiff knees) or delivery (difficult or unsuccessful childbirth).

Obviously, some misfortunes reflect more than one image. For instance, self-wounding evokes being "bitten" or "eaten" by the knife and bleeding to death. Death due to failure to deliver a child[91] can be seen as both a case of blockage and one of bleeding. A few misfortunes fit one or more of the basic images, but are notable for directly evoking the general theme of "passivization." One case in point is death from falling. It may be viewed as being "eaten" by the land[92] where the misfortune occurred (indeed, such land is said to be "not good" and becomes taboo) or as bleeding to death. But these images rather pale in comparison to that of the fall, which evokes a sudden, catastrophic loss of control. It must also be stressed that the principal metaphor of misfortune is that of "being eaten," since all diseases, and in fact all death-causing misfortunes, are represented as eating agents in Huaulu speech usage: lilaham kae eme, "lightning ate him"; tutaam kae eme, "the bush knife/sword ate him"; koloputi kae eme, "leprosy ate him"; mulalam kae eme, "the mulala snake ate him"; and so on, are common expressions.

"Bleeding," "blocking," and "eating" can be identified as so many fundamental areas of taboo. Bleeding misfortunes correspond to bleeding taboos, as we have seen. The consequence of violating the separation of incompatible forms of bleeding (vaginal in women, sacrificial in men) are debilitating forms of bleeding for both sexes. Blocking misfortunes (blocking of locomotion and blocking of child delivery) define an area that clearly corresponds to our notion of consanguine kinship (particularly the asymmetric structure of generations) and that the Huaulu identify as "nonotherness"—the sharing of something, usually blood, but also milk, name, property, and so on. Eating misfortunes correspond to two kinds of offenses against two kinds of others on whom one's bodily incarnated identity depends: animals and affines. If one eats (i.e. destroys, literally or metaphorically) these others, one is eaten in return or one literally eats oneself (as in malahau). Not surprisingly, the violation of the incest taboo is followed by both an eating affliction (malahau) and a blocking affliction (difficult or impossible childbirth), that is, by afflictions that are characteristic, respectively, of the affinal and the consanguine domains, because the violation undermines them both.

The least clear-cut case seems to be that of the next in kin of eating, namely biting. It corresponds to a variety of maquwoliem whose only common feature seems at first to be that they are somehow fundamental, in that they are associated with the "core" ritual practices and knowledges on which the reproduction of the community as a whole rests. This in itself would justify the association with the most terrible image—that of the death-inflicting "bite." But let us look more closely at the practices and knowledges in question. What domains of experience do they in fact cover, and how do these domains relate to those of the other taboos?

The most important of these practices (and related knowledges) all have to do, directly or indirectly, with the violent shedding of human blood by males. Indeed, there is hardly a ritual or a sacred object of collective significance that does not require the ritualized (one can even say sacrificial)[93] shedding of blood and that does not help effect it. These areas, then, are identical with those which women cannot approach or sometimes even mention without incurring dysmenorrhea or other forms of damage to their reproductive powers. Men, on the contrary, must be active in them, but in appropriate ways. Otherwise they are "bitten," usually to death. A second important area corresponding to these biting misfortunes is that of the sewa potoam, as we have seen. This form of shamanism was traditionally intertwined, in the most serious situations, with headhunting and thus with the spilling of human blood for sacrificial purposes. In any case, the sewa potoam is considered as of a piece with headhunting rituals and related practices which still survive (such as the kahua feast and initiation), in that they are the most ancient and fundamental core of Huauluness. Ita kaluara pohire, "we have come out with them," as the Huaulu say. They are thus strongly associated with the image of the continuity of the community and its founding ancestors. Knowledge (in the form of narratives, ritual scripts, and so on) of matters pertaining to all these domains is considered equivalent to them and is therefore protected by taboos that are associated with the same "biting" misfortunes. Finally, these misfortunes are associated with a number of taboos that seem central to social interaction at large. Most notably, this interaction is associated with taboos that concern food in general (as against the exclusion of certain species as food), such as climbing over food, falling asleep near food, eating while somebody departs, and so on.

All in all, it seems that biting afflictions correspond to domains of taboo in which food and blood dominate in cementing social relations. Moreover, these domains are strongly associated with the continuity of Huaulu as a distinct society and with ancestrality as its expression: the ancestors, as former practitioners of the taboos and as their custodians, are never far from these domains. Indeed, most of the sacrificial practices they include allow one to propitiate the ancestors and to avert their devouring wrath. As the Huaulu put it, "If we do not feed them [with "people" or "blood"—the two expressions are equivalent] they feed on us."

In sum, blood and food seem the principal ingredients, or at least the common denominators, of a lot of these taboos. Why? In this book, I will be able to answer the question at some length only for food, in fact mostly for meat, to which I shall turn in the next chapter. But I must preliminarily, and very briefly, review both some of the reasons taboo has an irresistible attraction for these two substances and some other kinds of phenomena. And I cannot avoid starting with a few words on food, which condemns me to anticipate some of the points to be developed in the next chapter.

The elective affinity of food and taboo is as strong in Huaulu as anywhere. Food taboos are the most numerous of all taboos and, what is more important, those with the greatest incidence in everyday life. They are also the most intimate, so to speak, since—as I keep repeating in company with Fortes—one cannot delegate one's eating to others. Thus it is in eating that the Huaulu child first encounters the obstacle that he or she will later learn to call maquwoli. And it is invariably to these taboos that he or she will refer, once grown up, to illustrate maquwoli and decry its burden (monue poto! "they are very heavy!"). The number and importance of food taboos reflect the exceptional dangerousness that Huaulu thought attributes to ingestion, a dangerousness ultimately due to the fact that eating amounts to reconstituting oneself by assimilating others—that one is what one eats and that what one eats is not, ontologically speaking, radically different from what one is. Because the Huaulu self is profoundly embodied, anything that affects the body may affect the self. And because animals and plants are not just the source of symbolically inert substances, but are also symbolic values made flesh, eating them can reinforce or undermine the eater's entire being, and not just his or her physical body. This is particularly true of eating animals, for the rather obvious reason that animals are closer to humans than plants are and are therefore more easily and frequently invested with human attributes or symbolic values that are of import to humans. This, along with the fact that the Huaulu hunt and fish a great deal, is precisely why a majority of food taboos are meat taboos.[94] If we are to understand Huaulu meat taboos, and more generally all their animal taboos, we must abandon our mental habits about animals. John Berger has put it very well: "To suppose that animals first entered the human imagination as meat or leather or horn is to project a 19th century attitude backward across the millennia. Animals first entered the imagination as messengers and promises."[95]

Eating is unproblematic only where the human subject is radically separated from the body and where animals, especially, are wholly denied a subjective identity and agency. This is the Cartesian solution, which I shall discuss in the next chapter. In this perspective, one can never be what one eats, because one can never eat what makes one what one really is, that is, a soul, a rational being. Hence, the precondition of this total differentiation of animal and human, which accounts for the utilitarian reduction of the animal, is the radical opposition of soul and body, of *res cogitans* and *res extensa*. This opposition implies, in turn, the animalization of the human body *qua* body or, to put it otherwise, the reduction of all bodies, including the human one, to the same mechanical order of nature.[96] Much of chapter 4 of this book is an attempt to recover the drama of eating in an enchanted world as it displays itself in Huaulu, and to justify the points I have just made. It will also attempt to go beyond the point that food (and especially animal food) is potentially dangerous in a universe of embodied subjects and to determine what makes particular species actually dangerous, and thus taboo, as food for particular subjects. It is unnecessary to anticipate the results of this analysis here, for what matters at the moment is to show that the idea of maquwoli has a propensity to become associated with certain kinds of objects, and thus also with the areas of experience in which these objects are constituted. But it must by now be expected that just as the afflictions that are connected with taboos symbolize their objects, so these objects symbolize attributes that are incompatible with subjects. It may also be expected that two sources of these attributes are recognized: the animal or vegetable itself, either as a member of a species or as an individual; and the human through which the food reaches the potential eater, for food is also imbued[97] with the qualities of those who procure, prepare, and share it.

The second major area of maquwoli is blood. The basic reason is that this substance combines contradictory values, which all stem from a very simple fact: blood is both contained and spilled. Primordially, when blood is contained it evokes life; when it is lost, it evokes death. Blood may also evoke identity and its loss, again through the contrast of containment and spillage. Contained blood evokes a distinct identity because it is the only substance of the body which is found identical in all of its parts and gives them all the same life. But then the flow of blood outside the body must evoke the loss of that distinct identity, and in any case the loss of its precondition: the distinction between inside and outside. Blood is fluid and thus easily mixed with other lost or shed bloods. Even if there is no physical contact between them, all shed bloods look the same or not different enough. Hence, the substance that is said to be the very basis of the distinctive unity of a person, of a group, and even of the human species, is also fundamentally indistinguishable in different persons, groups, and even species. Loss of blood may thus represent loss of identity at various levels. If it occurs—and it is inevitable, even socially prescribed, that it does in certain cases—it must be circumscribed, avoided, controlled, or compensated. The deployment of these various strategies explains the extreme richness of blood-related practices in Huaulu. They are described in full in another book.[98] A few observations will suffice for the moment.

From the general principles just stated, it obviously follows that blood becomes dangerous when it flows out of the body. But there are, of course, various modifying factors. Not all flows are equally dangerous, and in any event all dangers are relative.[99] Three kinds of shed blood are particularly dangerous: menstrual and parturitional blood; the blood of slain enemies; and the blood of the three main, and the most blood-filled, game animals—wild pig, deer, and cassowary. In different degrees and forms, these shed bloods are all incompatible with, and thus dangerous for, one another. They are also dangerous for the village[100] and must be kept separate from it, or require special transforming rites and precautions. To explain these foci and configurations, it is necessary to take into consideration what each flow of blood stands for and the entire complicated context in which it occurs. The primordiāl facts about blood that I have outlined, then, are not sufficient to account for the specific blood taboos, just as the primordial facts about eating are not sufficient to explain why certain foods are taboo and others are not. But these facts do explain why it is in the realm of blood, just as in the realm of food, that maquwoli most frequently and insistently chooses its objects.

Besides shed blood, the other forms of dangerous blood outflows are connected with sexuality, in marital and nonmarital forms.[101] Sex is indeed the means through which the distinctive blood of a group may be lost to others, particularly through women. This outflow is made inevitable, indeed prescribed, by the rule of exogamy, which thus subverts the idea of groups whose identity is based on a single, unmixed blood. It subverts it but does not erase it. This creates a first danger: the sexual association of the identical bloods of two siblings, which stands for the temptation of unmixed group identity, of utter autonomy (isolation) from other groups. But in substituting mixed blood for pure blood as the basis of group identity, exogamy creates another danger: the converse danger of a confusion of identities between groups. This danger must be neutralized by re-creating separation through other means. One means may consist of emphasizing purely paternal blood. Another is the adoption of a solidarity based on sharing name, property, ancestral powers, and so on, rather than blood. These solutions coexist in unresolved tension. But the most powerful means—powerful because it endures by biting into the trivialities of everyday life—is taboo. When taboo cannot apply to the actual transfer of blood-based identity, then it must apply to its metaphoric equivalents: the bloodlike spittle of betel-chewing can never be mixed among affines; personal names (the other lineage-based source of identity) cannot be uttered; and so on.

One way or another, blood flows, and thus taboos have to do with the reproduction or reconstitution of life. This is evident for the exogamic and affinal taboos just mentioned and also for menstrual and parturitional taboos. But it is no less true, albeit in a more metaphoric and perhaps mystical sense, of the bloody activities of men.[102] These are not merely pragmatic defenses and offenses, but are also viewed as part of a sacrificial cult in which men transcendentally ensure their reproduction and that of their game by "feeding humans" or "feeding blood" "to the ancestral powers" (ita umanaki ailaem), as they say. It is true that the flow of blood indexes the indissoluble connection between life and death, but then this is what reproduction also indexes, according to the Huaulu. They point out that when the ancestors were still immortal, they did not reproduce; and that when they began dying, they began reproducing. It was all decided long ago, when human fate took shape, as the origin myth of death explains. Two sewaem, Hahunusa and Olenusa, quarrelled and quarrelled over their plan for mankind. Olenusa wanted mankind to be like stone: to endure forever, albeit unproductively. Hahunusa, instead, wanted humans to be like banana trees: to be soft and short-lived, but to have many "sucklings" (ananiem, a word related to anaem or huwenanaem, "children").

The ambiguities of sexual reproduction, its evocation of death in life, of a life perennially spoiled by death, go a long way toward explaining why sex is so often taboo, especially when life is put at risk in dangerous transitions and in all other ritual activities where life is conquered at the price of death. Thus sexual intercourse is rigorously taboo for those who participate in a headhunt and for their wives; for those who undergo the male initiation or initiation into a shamanic cult; and for everyone during the entire sailoa, an apotropaic ritual connected with headhunting and now discontinued. We can add sex to blood and food (two phenomena with which it has much in common anyhow and with which it exchanges metaphors) in the catalogue of taboo's elective affinities. We can also add other phenomena entailing the loss of internal substances or loss of control—sneezing, laughing, speaking loudly, quarrelling—to the same catalogue, for these are strictly taboo in many ritual events and in other transitional situations (such as departures).

The ambiguities of blood, then, teach us about analogously ambiguous substances or activities that exert a powerful attraction for taboo. Beyond these ambiguities, they force us to confront another area of taboo which is traced by "the corpse" (wailuam) and its transformation, topoi, "shade of the dead." The Huaulu view the corpse as dangerous because it drags the living into death. It makes them, in a sense, partly dead. As they formerly participated in the dead person's life, so now they participate in her or his death. The closer this participation (as is the case for the widow or widower,[103] the children or parents, and other relatives), the greater the danger.[104] The preexisting relationship between the living and the dead must therefore be severed[105]—and, it is hoped, a new one constructed. The new relationship, however, does not come into being that easily and may never materialize, especially in the case of people who die a premature and violent death and are thus full of resentment for the survivors. Then "the shade of the dead" (topoyam) remains as dangerous as the corpse. But even properly transformed, the dead remain dangerous because they maintain a powerful pull on the living. They want, the Huaulu say, the persons they were attached to, or other persons who now catch their fancy, to die so as to become their companions. For not only are the dead full of regrets about life, and thus positively envious of the living, but also they feel alone. It is not just the hatred of the dead but also their love that is dangerous for the living. In fact, the distinction between love and hate loses its meaning in the relationship between living and dead.

Because the corpse pulls the living with itself, it is absolutely necessary to separate it from food, for otherwise death will enter the body of the living through the process of ingestion and digestion. Hence, for as long as the corpse is not buried in the forest or put into some hole in a tree or in a cliff, it is taboo to cook and eat in the village. As I have mentioned, the greatest danger is represented by the pukupukuem, the shades of those who fell to their death. If their bodies, or even anything connected with them, are brought into contact with the village, the latter is permanently endangered and must be "fled" (as the Huaulu say). The bodies of "those who fell in the village" (pukue ria ninianiam), that is, of women who died in childbirth, are also very dangerous, but in their case, it is sufficient to perform special funerary rites (similar to those that are performed for the true pukupukuem in the forest) to render the village safe again.

During the mourning period, the shade of the dead is supposed to return to its house at certain intervals. Its presence involves various taboos, in particular that of burning lamps and fire in the house. As we shall see in the next chapter, the dead person can appear in the form of certain animals, which are then taboo to harm.

As these beliefs suggest, the pull of the dead on the living is the pull of sentiments and bonds that survive death and cannot quite adjust to it. Taboos cut into the ensuing confusion of the living and the dead and work to control it, if they do not help to resolve it by forcing the living to keep the dead—that is to say, their thoughts of the dead—at bay. This is not psychologizing, but recognizing that one of the mainsprings of the life of institutions is their emotional aptness for individuals, their ability to "work" for them.[106] But more profoundly, these taboos confront the effects on human life of the idea of its inevitable end in death, revived by each death, and most powerfully by the rotting and fly-covered corpse. Life and death are ultimately inseparable, but this fact cannot be faced continually without making life psychologically impossible. Taboo must keep the dead apart from the living so that thoughts of death do not continually mix with thoughts of life.

Another major area of taboo concerns all occult powers, besides the dead,[107] on which the Huaulu depend and from which they may be threatened. These powers manifest themselves in concrete phenomena, and it is these that are tabooed. The normal attitude toward them is complete avoidance; but this gives way to more selective precautions whenever it is necessary, or unavoidable, to establish contact with them. From avoidance we may thus move to full-fledged ritual interactions, but these are still marked by the idea of avoidance: they are doings made possible by not-doings.

The concrete phenomena in which the occult powers manifest themselves are quite varied: species of animals or plants and even individuals thereof (more of these later); metereological phenomena (such as thunder and lightning, high winds, torrential rains, yellow light, "black clouds at sunset" [eteliaem]); kinds of speech (for instance, myths or chants that speak of these phenomena and ultimately originate with them); sites in space (for instance, former settlements, especially the earliest ones high in the mountains, rocks or caves or groves); periods in time (the founding past as reactualized during the performance of certain rituals or narratives); certain sacra (collectively called luma upuem, "the masters of the house") and the buildings or parts thereof where they are housed; human persons (such as shamans or headhunters or the Latunusa, when their bodies becomes imbued, or even invaded, by the occult powers); and so on. To these extremely varied and numerous manifestations correspond accordingly varied and numerous taboos. But note a fundamental fact: The presence of taboos indicates a relatively regular and predictable relationship between these powers and the Huaulu. Where there is no trace of such a relationship, of at least an implicit pact with *A* which allows a person to predict "if I do not do *x* to *A*, *y* will not happen to me," there is no taboo. Taboo cannot exist without the postulate of a certain regularity, however minimal, in the phenomena. This regularity derives from a tacitly or explicitly agreed to coordination between beings equally characterized by agency—living humans and the dead or other kinds of occult powers. It is a regularity, then, that has a certain moral dimension. We shall have to return to this.

Many more areas are, of course, covered by taboos, but on closer examination most of these areas appear to be motivated by or derived from the primary ones that I have mentioned. This is the case, for instance, with various taboos in effect between relatives or between people with different ritual functions and with taboos regulating the organization of the house or the village and the often shifting relationships of various people to those organizations. These shifts are sometimes associated with transitional or liminal periods of time which are themselves marked by taboos in Huaulu, as in so many other societies, as classically recognized since van Gennep.[108] But in Huaulu at least, or rather from a Huaulu point of view, transitions as such are less motivating than the opposites between which one moves. These opposites are usually found in the principal areas of taboo which I have just mentioned.

Even intuitively, these areas define classes which appear to be interrelated and to overlap in various ways. Moreover, some of them, in certain respects at least, may be further reduced to more encompassing classes. For instance, food taboos and taboos that have to do, directly or indirectly, with reproduction (and thus with blood) can be seen as two sides of the interchange between the inside and the outside of the body: food taboos concern substances that enter the body, whereas reproductive taboos concern substances that come out of it—taboos of ingestion and taboos of excretion, one may say. One must immediately add, however, that the excretion only of life-giving substances (blood and semen, which is transformed blood and further transforms into the blood of a fetus), and not of waste, is marked by taboos. For instance, while it is taboo to shed menstrual blood in the village, it is improper and aesthetically unattractive, but not taboo, to defecate in it. Thus the two classes of taboos correspond not to the two stages of the digestive cycle, but to the two complementary modes of the production of human life: the reconstitution of individual bodies through the metamorphosis of the other into the self, and the multiplication of the self through reproduction.

Another way of looking at the taboos makes it possible to collapse three classes into one: the taboos of digestion, reproduction, and death have in common their focus on what is animal in humans. They therefore circumscribe an area of darkness produced both by the overlapping of two categories (animal and human), which, as we shall see, should ideally be kept distinct, and by the resistance of "animal," unintentional processes to human intentionality and action. All these taboos, therefore, have to do with the body as the battlefield of the social and the natural.

Finally, all classes of taboos may be seen as focussing on a more general conflict: that between human action (that is, the intentional activity of living human agents in the present) and the nonhuman conditions of its existence and realization, of its success or failure, or of its constitution in the first place. Indeed, both the occult powers of one class and the empirical powers of the others (that is, powers that we would be tempted to call supernatural and natural, respectively, if such categories were applicable without further discussion of the Huaulu way of thinking) are such nonhuman conditions.

CHAPTER FOUR
Zoology and Meatology

nature, eccentricities and possible impossibilities
B. Stoker, *Dracula*

La hiérarchie des choses est plus complexe que la hiérarchie des hommes.
G. Bachelard, *La philosophie du non*

"I like the steak because whenever you bite it, it bites you."
Artemisia Valeri, four-year-old daughter, once at the table

The Meat Paradox

Coming to Huaulu from the comparatively meatless east, through whose scarce vegetables and sparingly shared sago we had passed with some disappointment, my wife and I were pleasantly surprised by the sudden opportunity to turn carnivorous afforded us by our new hosts. Huaulu hospitality, founded on a seemingly inexhaustible supply of meat and other food, amazed us. We were compelled by local custom to eat several meals a day, for the villagers vied with one another to invite us to what we continued to view as breakfast, lunch, and dinner. Indeed, one of the first expressions of the Huaulu language we learned was *i tika asie,* "to invite to share a meal" (lit., "they call them"). We began observing with some worry yet another roof enveloped in the kitchen smoke, since it usually announced that the mistress of the house, or perhaps some of her children, would come to us with a serious and somewhat mysterious air and say in a low but solemn voice: "Bapak, Ibu, homa ala ita ae," "Father, Mother, come let us eat." Politeness, we soon learned, demanded that we should at first ignore the message or appear rather surprised, somewhat annoyed even, upon hearing it. After a while, however, we had to get up and meekly follow our proud host through the village and up to her house.

Fortunately or—as we sometimes thought—unfortunately, this period of overfeeding did not last much beyond the inauguration of our own house. At that point we ceased being the guests whom everybody wanted to honor and establish good relationships with. We became another household and had to fend for ourselves. We could only watch with some envy the occasional visitor being overfed the way we ourselves had been.

The experience provided some mental nourishment too. We were immediately introduced to some basic facts and values of Huaulu life—

most obviously to the fact that food mediates social relationships and can even constitute them. Thus friendship was almost literally forced down our throat by just about everybody in the village. We also became aware of the Huaulu propensity to show off by claiming unlimited abundance of food. "Eat, eat," they would say, "otherwise the food will rot." The rotting of food because "there are not enough people to finish" (manusia ia sapassi; B.I.: manusia tidak sampai) is axiomatic in any Huaulu feast, especially when there are guests from outside the society. At the same time it is acknowledged that much food remains uneaten by the guests because the hosts use hunger-suppressing magic against them. An admission that the proclaimed abundance can be spurious, that famine remains a possibility—or at least that this possibility is secretly feared. And also, more important, an admission of the hostility which lurks under the cover of hospitality. Indeed, the voracity of the guests is denounced as soon as they have turned their back to the leftovers of the food they have often been forced to gorge upon.

Even more striking was another ambivalence. As we learned from experience and from proffered commentary, a true meal is hardly conceivable without ayoku. The word refers to the flesh of any edible animal, fish included. Therefore, *meat* will be used here in this extended sense, unless otherwise indicated. Ideally, ayoku should be complemented by ipia kouwam, "hot sago" (A.M.: papeda), that is, the mush which results from throwing boiling water onto a solution of sago flour and water and stirring it until it acquires the necessary homogeneity and transparency. Each of the commensals picks some out of the same pot by rolling a "wooden fork" (atamam) in the mass, much as Italians do with their own helping of spaghetti, and immerses what sticks to the fork into a broth or sauce made by boiling some meat. Thus seasoned, the mush is brought to the mouth, which has previously been filled with a morsel of meat or vegetable. Eating sago without meat is inconceivable.[1] My wife early on realized this at the cost of some mortification. She once asked a friend for a few packets of "cold mush" (ipia peteam), for which she had developed a rather inexplicable passion. She was chagrined to see that her request was tantamount to begging for meat. Her friend, having no meat in the house, felt obliged to send for some from another house. Only then was the sago, with its usual complement, handed to her.

While sago cannot be eaten without meat, it is possible to eat meat without sago—that is, with some mulama (tubers or plantains or other products of the garden) or with some cooked fruit (such as durian or jackfruit), or even without anything else, in a plain smoked state. This asymmetry indicates that meat is the most important and indispensable food. Indeed, it is in every respect at the top of the scale of alimentary values. The Huaulu have a true passion for meat. If they cannot eat it,

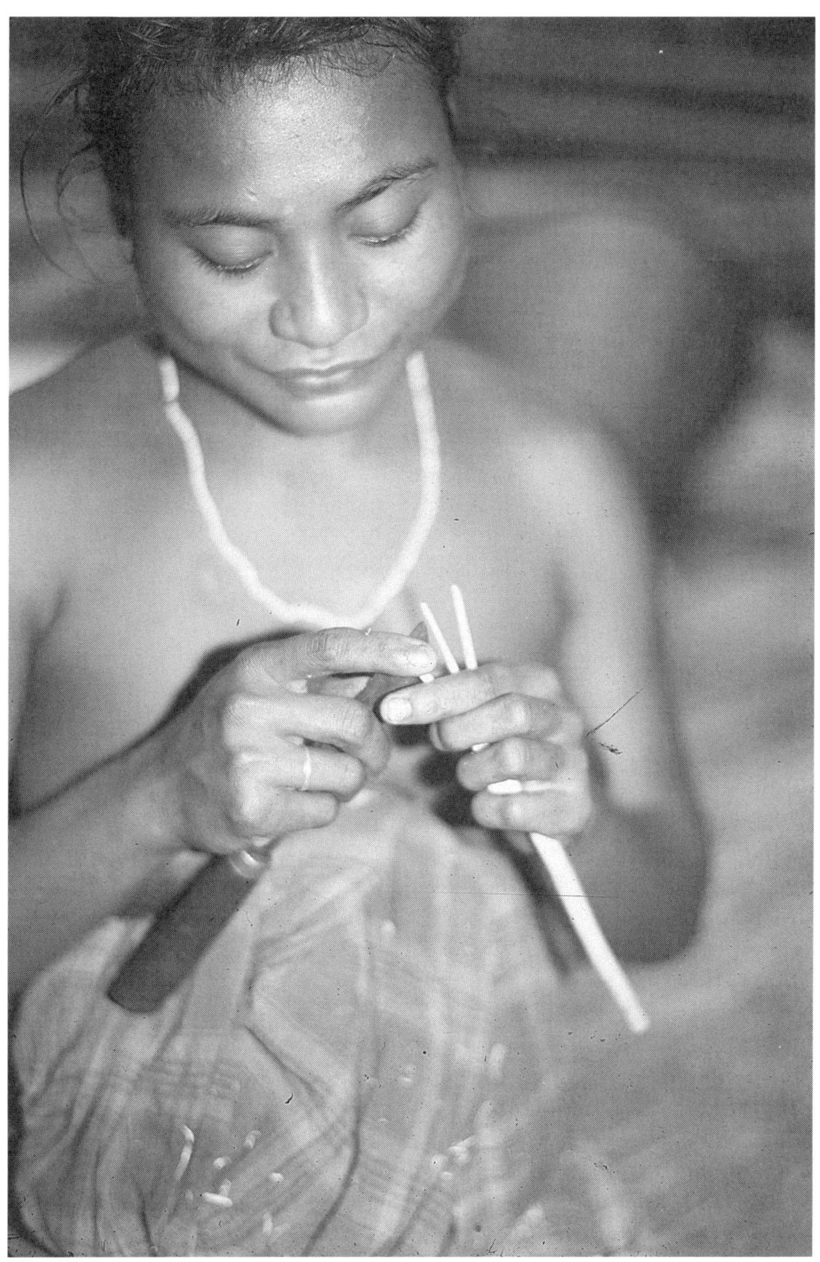

A young girl, Ratifala, making a wooden fork or ataman, used to eat sago mush. 1973. (Photo by V. Valeri.)

they feel hungry and weak. However much they may eat of other stuff, they long for meat—especially pork, venison, cassowary, and marsupials—or at least for shrimp or fish. It is considered "shameful" (ita mukae) to offer a meal with little or no meat. Again, we realized this early on, since the few times we were invited to a meal with little meat, the hosts kept repeating apologetically: "Ayokuemussi," "There is no meat." A husband who is not a good enough hunter to provide his family with a steady and abundant supply of meat is guaranteed to be nagged and held in contempt by his wife. Repeated and habitual failure to provide meat is even grounds for divorce.

Yet we were amazed that for all this passion for meat, so many animals were considered dangerous to eat. Indeed, our gastronomic wanderings through virtually all households soon made it clear that there scarcely was an animal whose flesh was not taboo to somebody. This paradox seemed to betray a profound ambivalence: the most desired food was also the most feared. Further proof of the dangerousness of meat was afforded us a few weeks after our arrival, when we had our first opportunity to witness the butchery of a wild pig fallen into a "spring-trap" (supanam).

Kalahei Tamatay had checked his spring-traps the day before and found a boar killed by one of them. He had put the carcass in a stream, fastening it with a pole held by heavy rocks so that it would stay underwater, to slow putrefaction and to avoid excessive damage from predators and insects. Returning to the village, he had sent word to a number of people, including us, that he would "go fetch the pig" (lipe hahuam) the next day, and wouldn't they be of the party? The next day, we all followed Kalahei to the place where he had left the pig. What I observed left me puzzled and somewhat shaken. I admired the surgical precision with which the carcass was cut up, but the admiration could not suppress the nausea provoked by the gore and blood and smell, which attracted thousands of large green flies. I felt much less happy than I had until then about the abundance of meat that had welcomed us. All around me, the Huaulu seemed perfectly unconcerned and went about their work. It was easy to imagine that they saw only meat in the animal, whereas I was beginning to see the animals in all the meat I had eaten. Yet I had to notice a number of phenomena that did not agree with my presumption. To begin with, Kalahei, the owner of the spring-trap that had killed the pig, did not participate in the butchery, which was performed by a classificatory sister's son of his, and in fact did not touch the carcass at all, except once briefly the head. Then I was surprised that for once the people were serious and never laughed, whereas my experience thus far had been that being together and joking were inseparable for the Huaulu. I also noticed that the women did not approach the carcass, but waited at some distance behind the men's backs. Finally, having attempted to take a picture at the scene, I was stopped rather sharply by a youngster who claimed that it was taboo to do so. Indeed, the principal butcher, Pitere, confirmed that it would have provoked thundering, and Koholio, one of the helpers, said that a flood would follow.[2] As I would increasingly learn, these phenomena were signs of anger coming from the kaitahu upuem, the masters of the territories inhabited by the game and thus also the "owners" of the animals. It was for not angering them that people avoided laughing in the presence of animal carcasses and even of "fresh, uncooked or unsmoked meat" (ayoku holuholuam). And it was to propitiate them that the skulls of the animals killed were put on tree branches as offerings and that the owners of the traps that struck the animals did not eat their meat and even avoided butchering it if possible.

All this left me wondering. If the Huaulu really felt unconcerned by having to kill to eat, if they saw animals only as meat on feet, why this fear of angering the masters of animals, why these offerings, renunciations, and restraints even in the presence of fresh meat? Why could one abandon seriousness only after the meat was cooked? Was it because only cooking made the living animal disappear completely from its flesh, by turning the redness of blood into the brown of mere meat?

These questions were renewed, and the conflicting impressions that accompanied them were reinforced, a dozen days later, when I participated in my first hunting expedition on the Sapulewa River, at about seven kilometers northwest of the village. The six days spent on this hunt, in the company of nine men, were the most memorable introduction to Huaulu meatology[3] I could have hoped for. They were also very fortunate for my ethnographic destiny in Huaulu, for, as I learned many years later, we had remarkable luck in hunting, which made the Huaulu infer that my presence among them was auspicious.

Several things struck me during this hunt. First of all, it was an all-male affair, characterized by a lot of camaraderie but also competition. The competition aspect sometimes took over and became an end in itself, a game, as when people had a shooting contest. This made me understand better than anything else that hunting was, for men, much more than procuring meat; it was a way of testing and asserting one's total worth. The fight with the animal was never very far from the fight with other men. Indeed, I heard more than my fair share of hunting stories told around the campfire, and I later learned that boasting about one's hunting abilities and those of one's dogs is men's favorite form of self-expression, because to be a good hunter is to be a good man, period. Moreover, hunting being a noble activity, it is one basis of two acts of hierarchical discrimination: of men from women, and of "great men" (manusia potoem) from lesser or "ordinary men" (manusia piaseaem).

One amusing result of this connection of greatness with hunting was the avoidance behavior I noted in Pulaki, the guardian of the village hall and my host until our house was built. It had already struck me that Pulaki boasted about his hunting abilities and about his not bothering to cultivate a garden, since people would bring vegetables to him to reciprocate for all the meat he gave them. During the hunt, however, Pulaki seemed to avoid being put to the test of his boasting. In fact, most of his actions those days seemed to be dictated less by the technology of hunting than by that of power. Both on the way to the Sapulewa and on the way back, he avoided journeying with our party. He was thus able to join us with tales of all the game he had met on his way but barely wounded or missed. On the Sapulewa itself, he was my shadow, and this allowed me to notice that he never ran after animals and hardly used his arrows. All of this did not hinder him from boasting that our luck (that is, the luck of others) was due to his special powers. I realized, in sum, that his hunting abilities were more of the metaphysical than the physical kind, but also that, in a sense, this was proper in a "great man" daily involved with the ancestral powers residing in the village hall.

When so many social and political games are played around game, one can expect the image of the human other to become intertwined with the image of the animal. It is the animal, after all, who is the proof of, who witnesses through its own death, the hunting ability of men. In fighting animals, one fights men, and in fighting men, one fights animals. It immediately seemed to me that there was ground here for an almost inevitable urge to anthropomorphize the animal, and perhaps even to animalize the human. This blending of hunter and hunted was in any case made evident in the course of the hunt. It was a battle of wits and strengths, in which the animals—especially the male ones—were more than a match for the humans. Indeed, most of our victims were the more vulnerable females and their little ones; the only male we got was a deer that had been gored to death by another male deer in a duel over a female. Just as in war, or rather in the war stories I would hear throughout my residence in Huaulu, the really honorable preys of hunting were the adult males, not the females or the children. The intelligence and courage of animals—virtues which the Huaulu esteem most in humans—were constantly before us those days, especially when we used the most common hunting technique on big rivers.

That technique consisted in posting ourselves at various neighboring fords on the side of the river opposite the one where some others "brought the dogs" (i sonai wassuem). We expected that the dogs, smelling deer or cassowaries, would pursue them and that the game would try to cross the river to shake the dogs off. But we could see that the animals understood the ruse perfectly and would not try to cross the river unless they were sure of escaping us by their superior speed.

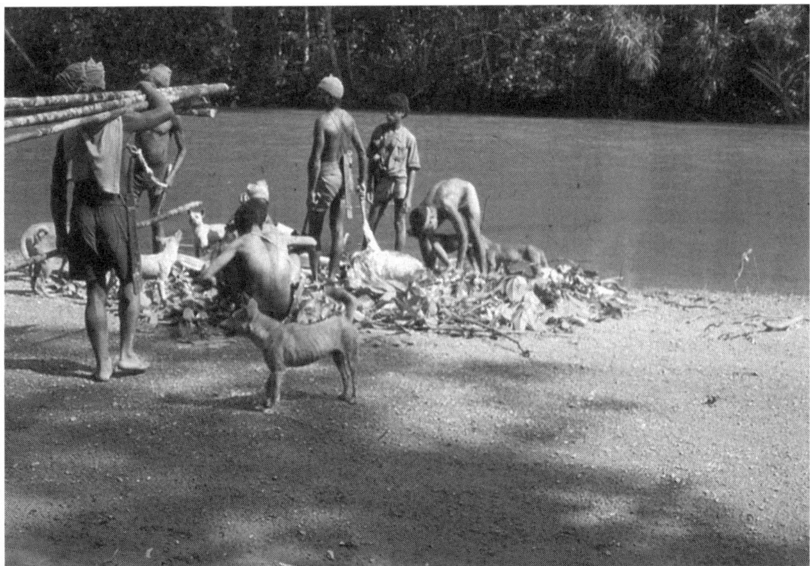

Hunters prepare to bring a deer carcass home by butchering it outside the village. 1972. (Photo by V. Valeri.)

It became painfully clear, after a while, that the deer which attempted the fording were mostly females and their fawns. The fawns did not run as fast as the stags before the dogs, and their mothers attempted to save them by leading them across the river, in the hope that they would make it across the gauntlet of hunters. This desperate move—dictated by a motherly love that seemed as human as a woman's love for her children may seem animal—created another, but less valued, connection with humans.

I was also impressed by the ferociousness of wild pigs and the fear—indeed, the respect—they inspired in my fellow hunters, not to mention in me, who had been warned I should climb a tree as soon as I saw a boar coming (fortunately none did, for I could not have climbed the gigantic trees that surrounded us). Yet for all the signs of fellow animality or fellow humanity, even intimacy, that the hunt revealed, the Huaulu seemed pitiless, if always serious (it was, again, taboo to laugh), in dealing with the animals. But then they could be pitiless precisely because the animals were like enemies—because they had been vanquished fair and square. One must kill to live; there is no escape from that. The animals themselves were teaching us that lesson, since we surprised two goring each other for a female in order to reproduce and since the pigs, at least, were quite ready to kill us to save themselves.

But the law of the true jungle is not like the law of the asphalt jungle from which I came—tender in theory, brutal in practice. I was not entitled to call the Huaulu cruel, since I had grown up eating steaks by studiously ignoring the horror that preceded them. Thus I made a point of being as hardhearted (from my point of view) as I thought the Huaulu were. I even ate a piece from a fetus which had been extracted from one of our female victims and which I had expected, and especially hoped, would be taboo to eat. And I remember gnawing at a leg of half-smoked venison which had been offered me (a misunderstanding on my part, since I should have cut a few slices and passed the leg on; but my appetite gave rise to the admiration and applause of all present, which shortly afterwards made it difficult to declare myself unable to finish the piece off).

I was not long in discovering that Huaulu pity took other forms than those I would have expected on the basis of my own cultural premises and habits. Not the emotional and hypocritical ones of those who like their roast seasoned with the assurance of "humane killing" (how too human this "humane" is!), but the more straightforward ones of rituals based on the recognition that eating means killing and therefore incurring an unquantifiable debt with the killed. This was in any case the light in which the conventional acts I had already witnessed increasingly began to appear to me: the hunter's avoidance of "his own" meat (which necessitates a complicated logistics to keep different animals separate on the smoking racks), the offering of skulls, blood clots, and sometimes genitals to the lords of the land, and the almost constant avoidance of laughter, which, like the buzzing flies, and the half-burnt, half-rotten smell, was a constant reminder of the pervasive presence of the animal behind the meat.

I do not wish to run ahead of myself. I will return, and at some length, to these rites, positive and negative, and to the representations and experiences that surround and sustain them. But I had to introduce the reader to my discussion of animal taboos by providing an immediate sense of the paradoxes from which they ultimately grow and which immediately confronted me in those happy and yet sad hunting days on the shores of the river, when we had fun being men in killing and pursuing animals like us, and then eating them in astounding quantities, but at the same time felt compelled to accomplish the acts of respect and renunciation laid down for us by past generations, so that we would continue to be human just when we most ran the risk of turning bestial.

Eating and Ambivalence

How can we explain the ambivalence of meat? Why is this most valued of all foods also, quite often, the most dangerous? There are many angles to this question and thus also to its answer. It is tempting to view the dangerousness of meat as the negative side of its high evaluation. The more we desire a thing, the more we are afraid of its power over us, and the more, thus, we attach a dark side to it. Moreover, this spontaneous mechanism of desire control is inseparable from a social process. Because our strong desire threatens to separate us from the others, limiting it reduces the risk of social disruption and at the same time teaches us that we depend on others more than we depend on things. Or, put otherwise, it teaches us to desire the approval and affection of others more than the enjoyment of objects. It puts the social world above the world of objects. We could interpret in this way, for instance, the idea that the meat of the animals which provide the most desirable and abundant meat (pig, deer, and cassowary) is extremely dangerous (and thus maquwoli) to the hunter or trapper who has killed them. Indeed, this taboo implies that he must give the meat of his kill away, that his hunting can only be altruistic, and that he himself is dependent on others for eating meat. In sum, the meat of others is not dangerous; one's own meat, which creates the possibility of socially unmediated eating, of gorging oneself without thinking of others, is.

There is some truth to this view. But it can hardly explain everything in the scenes which opened this chapter. How can it explain, for instance, the fact that it is always taboo, for everybody and anybody, to laugh or joke in the presence of animals, edible or not, and of fresh meat? Or that certain parts of the larger animals, particularly their skulls, should be given to beings who are said to own them? Obviously, these acts concern more the relationship between animals and humans globally than the relationships among humans, let alone the issue of antisocial desire for meat.

But more important, the view is unable to explain why—however ambivalent meat always is—positivity dominates in certain meats, negativity in others, while still others are neutral. Indeed, there is no regular correlation between the desirability of meat and its dangerousness. Certain meats are not particularly desirable, and yet they are viewed as highly dangerous. Others are highly desirable, but not particularly dangerous or then only to those who are responsible for the animal's death. Clearly, another and more important kind of logic is at work here than that of raw desire for meat and its social control.

To understand this logic and why it eventuates into a profound ambivalence vis-à-vis meat (an ambivalence that manifests itself in a proliferation of taboos but also in the attribution of positive moral qualities to the flesh of certain animals), we must start from the more primordial ambivalence inherent in the act of eating as such. Eating is a pleasurable activity, but it is also an intrinsically dangerous operation, since it consists in making oneself by assimilating what is nonself. Of course, this dangerousness is inherent in any form of self-making. Humans cannot relate to themselves without relating to what is external to them and is thus potentially beyond their control. Their whole existence consists in appropriating an unfriendly world to make a friendly one. But in no other activity is this paradox as extreme as in eating, in which the nonself is brought into the most intimate possible relationship with the self: it enters the body to become one's flesh. One is what one eats.

This elementary experience of transmutation creates a special sensitivity to the qualities of food and its compatibilities or incompatibilities with the self, especially when, as is the case in Huaulu, no radical contrast between body and soul, the "physical" and the "spiritual," exists. Then eating is not just the matching of hunger and what can best satisfy it, or even the agreement of taste and tasty, but the fateful encounter of two total beings with all their significations attached. This is not all. For eating confronts not only a human eater and a nonhuman eaten. That relationship is usually mediated by a third party who is a fellow human: the person from whom one receives food, with whom one eats or avoids eating. The compatibilities or incompatibilities that exist among humans thus reflect on the food they eat. It is a further paradox of eating that in this ultimately solitary act (ultimately solitary because, as Fortes so perceptively noted, one must do one's eating oneself) one constantly experiences the intrusion of others, and must therefore come face to face with oneself.

Food, then, evokes danger or safety for a subject insofar as food is capable of evoking attributes that correlate negatively or positively with him as a total being. We should therefore expect that the greater this evocative or symbolic potential is in a food, the greater its potential for carrying positive or negative attributes. Animals, because of their anatomy, physiology, and behavior, are perceived as closer to humans than to vegetals. The animal kingdom can function as a mirror palace for the subject. Is it surprising, then, that not only in Huaulu, but worldwide, animals tend to be more symbolically significant than vegetals, and thus more frequently viewed as carriers of negative and positive qualities for the eating subject?

What is, at first sight, somewhat more surprising is that the negative qualities are so much better articulated, and in fact more numerous, than the positive ones. There is a plethora of animal taboos, and indeed practically every animal is taboo for somebody in Huaulu. But there are few animals that are symbolically marked in a strongly positive sense; most are simply neutral, or else ranked in terms of gustative categories rather than in terms of their contributions to the subject. Among the few positively marked animals the most important are wild pigs, deer, and cassowaries, that is, the game which is largest, most vigorous and mobile—qualities that are viewed as desirable in humans too. Their meat is supposed to give strength, but also to provide the eater with moral qualities. This is particularly true of the wild pig.

As I mentioned in the first chapter, a frequently repeated Huaulu saying is that the Memahem (pagan, mountain people who live off the forest) are like the wild pigs they eat: if attacked, they attack in return. In contrast, the Laufaha (Muslim, coastal dwellers who live off the sea) are like the fish they eat: if attacked, they flee. In other words, Memahem such as the Huaulu absorb courage from the wild pig; Laufaha such as the people of Besi and Sawai absorb cowardice from the fish. Truly, then, one is what one eats. But one is, even more, what one does not eat. Identity establishes itself more by opposition to food than by identification with it, more by avoidance than by election.

How can we explain that negative qualities are much more marked than positive ones? Why is it that only one side of the ambivalence of meat is well articulated? Why is loss or undermining of identity in the objective form of eating the wrong kind of food so much more marked than the perpetuation of identity through regular eating of the right kind? The answer should be obvious, but it is at the very heart of the ideology of taboo. What is to be avoided—the dangerous—deserves more attention and thus precise signalling than what is to be welcomed. The latter simply continues, or reinforces, one's being, but the former undermines it. Loss is more noticeable than continuous possession. This is precisely why identity is reproduced more by not eating than by eating, more by negation than by affirmation. We shall have to return to this fundamental asymmetry of the negative and the positive in the constitution of the subject.

"Animal" and "Human"

Precisely because animals are our next of kin, because they offer a ready mirror for human attributes, for virtues and vices, taken together they raise a problem of self-definition for us: to establish where the difference between animal and human lies is to define what it is to be human. Underlying the symbolic utilization of the various animal species relative to various human subjects is a symbolic utilization of animality in general relative to humanity in general. In this process of comparative definition, analogy and contrast are necessarily intertwined, but the emphasis may be put on one or the other type of relation. In other words, the boundary between animal and human, and the very definition of these categories, may be traced more or less sharply.

We ourselves come from a tradition where animals and humans have been radically opposed on ontological grounds—that is, on the grounds of the soul/body distinction. One way or another, we are all heirs to Descartes in this. He has left us with some outmoded furniture, which we have put in a dark corner but still occasionally use to support our plates when we enjoy our steak or roast. We had better become aware of this mental inheritance, because it is the single strongest obstacle to understanding food taboos and meat taboos in particular.

Descartes believes that granting a soul to animals is an error second only to the error of denying God.[4] Animals are for him pure machines, and as such devoid of any signification beyond their utility. This cleavage is logically related to another one, that of soul and body in humans. Together, they run counter to any possible problematic of taboo, for eating is reduced to the confrontation of two machines, the human-body machine and the animal-body machine, under the detached gaze of a disembodied, self-determining subject—the cogito. Such a subject cannot be undermined by eating: the horrors and the dangers, but also the pleasures, of the transmutation of nonself into self are constitutionally unknown to it. Food concerns the body, not the soul; *res cogitans* is radically separated from *res extensa,* so that the kinship between the soulless animal and the soulful human can be severed at the root. The drama of eating in the enchanted world is lost in a Cartesian world, prescient of Chicago stockyards, where the animal scream is no more a sign of pain, of the pain that we also feel, than ticking is a sign that a clock is alive.[5]

The Cartesian formulation of this ideology may appear quaint to us now, but the ideology is still very much with us in practice; it is the unstated premise of our relationship with the living species which we consider as purely utilitarian. Machines or not, we make sure that their screams do not matter, or at least that we do not hear them. Of course, this attitude coexists with others that run against it, but the old Chrysippian idea of animals as meat on feet[6] and its correlate, the disembodied self, are still at the center of our alimentary modernity. It makes us deny that we can possibly be what we eat, and thus also what we do not eat, whereas, of course, we are both, just like the Huaulu.

If we are to understand why eating, and especially the eating of animals, is inseparable from the idea of taboo in Huaulu, we must forget Descartes or his residual effects on our ideas and practices. We must accept the Huaulu premise that no radical ontological difference between the human eater and the nonhuman eaten exists. At the same time, we must not remain Cartesian in the very reversal of the Cartesian ontology. That the Huaulu do not postulate an insuperable ontological barrier between animal and human does not mean that they are not preoccupied with differentiating them. On the contrary, the lack of any guaranteed, a priori difference means that the difference has to be created constantly through various cultural practices which demonstrate it. The main practice is precisely that of taboo.

But do the categories of animal and human actually exist in Huaulu thought, or am I projecting them into it? The answer is obvious with regard to "human," because there is a word for it, and a much used one at that: *manusia.* But the answer is less obvious with regard to animal. I once had a conversation with a number of Huaulu, including the somewhat more Indonesianized kamara (village head), about Huaulu classifications. I pointed out that the Huaulu language has no equivalent for the B.I. term *binatang,* "animal."[7] In fact, the Huaulu word *binatani,* although a borrowing from *binatang,* has a much more restricted meaning, since it is used only as an insult for humans who are "beastly": dirty, diseased, physically impaired.[8] The Huaulu do not like to feel inferior to any other people, and so the little group tried very hard to find an indigenous term matching binatang in its extended sense. They came up with the term peni, but then had to agree that it refers only to animals as sources of meat. Indeed, inedible animals do not fall into the category of peni.[9] They finally acknowledged that they had no word for animal, but added the usual apology that they were much debased and therefore ignorant in comparison with their ancestors, who must surely have had a word, since they had one for everything.

This conversation, while confirming that the Huaulu don't have a word for animal, strongly suggested that they have the idea, since my interlocutors could perfectly understand the problem I had raised. Of course, the understanding was aided by their awareness of the Indonesian word *binatang,* although some of the older men present could not understand the Indonesian language even in its Ambonese form. In any case, the question of "animality" took on a wholly Huaulu life in our conversation, which was conducted in the Huaulu language. It was an enumerative sort of life; that is, the idea of animal was rendered by enumerating various animal species in such a way as to suggest that they all had something distinctive in common. That the idea of animality was well understood by them was also implied by their initial suggestion that the word *peni* is an equivalent of the word *binatang.* Although peni does not include all animals, it includes only animals (defined as "any being which has flesh [ayoku]").[10] In other words, since the category peni does not include any vegetals or minerals, animality is obviously a requisite for belonging to this category. Hence, animality must be a category of Huaulu thought, even though there is no noun for it. The implicit use of this category is also demonstrated by my interlocutors' agreement with the objection that peni leaves out species which do not belong to any of the accepted vegetal categories.

To clarify the last statement, I should say that the species which we identify as vegetal are encompassed in the Huaulu language by a number of irreducible categories of various generality. These are, as

Vegetable foods are collected from the forest each day. Here, a young boy is carrying back pinang fruit and Malay apples. 1973. (Photo by V. Valeri.)

far as I could ascertain: ai (tree), aluwa (creeper), naufutu (herb), telo (banana), ulapa (mushroom), and alesa (rattan). Bamboos also form a clearly recognized group, but a linguistically covert one. Their group is identifiable, like most such groups, by comparative judgments of likeness. In addition, certain utilitarian categories (comparable to peni in the animal kingdom) exist, such as malafutu (spinach) and mauw (a creeper [and sometimes an herb] with medicinal or magical use). No species that we recognize as animal is ever included in these categories as far as I know, just as no species that we recognize as vegetal is included in the, admittedly less numerous and exhaustive, higher-order animal categories. I conclude that although vegetal and animal are covert categories, they are sufficiently recognized to avoid any obvious overlapping. Probably the intuitive basis for their contrastive recognition is that animals are capable of locomotion, whereas vegetals are not.

I never used the kinds of tests for discovering covert categories which Ellen systematically administered among the Nuaulu, but I am sure that if I had given any Huaulu, even a child, cards representing animals and vegetals, and asked him or her to divide them into two piles on the basis of similarity, all the animals would have been put together in the same pile, and no vegetal would have been in it. In any event, there is much more direct and satisfactory evidence for the existence of animal as a general category of Huaulu culture, whatever its application to concrete species.

In our conversation on the possible equivalents of *binatang,* it did not occur to my interlocutors to go beyond the realm of nouns. The reason is that *binatang* is a noun, but also, and more profoundly, that the Huaulu, just like us, tend to associate the idea of category with that of noun rather than with other parts of speech. But their language, like so many other Indonesian languages (including B.I.), makes heavy use of numeral classifiers. Whenever anything is counted, the classifier appropriate to that thing must be added to the numeral (the correct sequence is: noun, numeral classifier, numeral). Now, animals have their own classifier, *hatani* (lit., "its body"), which cannot be applied to any other living thing. One can argue, therefore, that the category of animal has its positive linguistic realization in this numeral classifier.[11] It is a much more strongly marked realization than a noun would be, because the use of numeral classifiers is extremely frequent, if not obligatory. Indeed, even if one does not know the meaning of a particular noun, one can immediately infer from the use of *hatani* that it is the name of an animal.[12]

Voiced or unvoiced, animal is in any case a privileged counterpart of manusia (human). Humanity is defined, to an important extent, by its relationship to animality. The point is made most forcefully by mythological history. In the distant past, when humans did not yet die, animals were extremely close to them; in fact, they were humans in disguise. If you only followed them back to their underground lair, you would discover that it was like a human village; if you entered their house by stealth, you would see them take off their animal kahukuam (wrapping)[13] and appear in their true human nature. Furthermore, fruitful intermarriage between them and humans of both sexes was frequent. But since humans became mortal, this intimate connection between them and the animals came to an end. The animals became more different; the kahukuam has stuck to them ever since and cannot be removed to reveal a familiar human face. The only exceptions are certain individual animals which turn out to be the illusory manifestations of anthropomorphic occult powers or even of the detached "soul" (mattiulu) of a human. They can still shed their animal body to appear as humans.

So the mythical life of the animals survives today as the animal life of occult powers. But it is not a life with which the Huaulu usually want to have much to do. While ancestral shades and sewaem may take the body of animals to help their descendants or "owners,"[14] they also take that form to harm them as a punishment. Furthermore, a majority of "false animals" are in fact the vehicles of evil powers—kinakinaem. On the whole, therefore, the confusion of animal and human represented by these beings is viewed negatively: it stands for the loss of one's human identity and ultimately for death, because without such distinct identity there is no life for humans.[15] In sum, while in mythical times the intimate relationship, the quasi-identity of animal and human, stood for immortality, now that humans are mortal it stands for death. It is as if humans had conquered their humanity at the price of mortality, or rather as if humans had become differentiated from animals the day they acquired consciousness and, with it, became aware of their death. But this is for another book.

What makes these powers bad, or else is a sign of their badness, is that they represent too close a connection between animal and human. To become involved with them is to regress to an earthly paradise that has in the meantime become hell; it is to become intimate again with animals, but only when they have become even more different from humans than they used to be. In other words, these powers represent the fatal attraction of animality for humans, and demonstrate at the same time that human identity rests on no ontological guarantee, but must constantly be asserted against what is animal in humans.

One such animalizing power is called makakalisafu. Makakalisafu appear as ordinary game animals (usually as wild pig, deer, or cassowary), but their extraordinary aspects become manifest as soon as the hunter pursues them. He can never catch up with them or stop pursuing them. Under their spell, he runs and runs, progressively losing his clothes, his speech, and other human traits. His last connection with the human world is his bush knife, symbol of a humanity that is above animals because it kills them. If he loses that too, there is no return for him. I heard one of my friends, Pulaki, narrate in all seriousness his adventure with a makakalisafu. He claimed to have pursued it for weeks or even months (he had, of course, lost count) without ever stopping. But the spell was eventually broken because he never let go of his bush knife. His grandfather nursed him back to life, but had to teach him to speak and to eat cooked food again. These things happen, Pulaki told me, only to those who transgress serious taboos. The implication seems to be that it is taboos that keep humans different from animals. If humans do not respect taboos, they find themselves insensibly reduced to animals, forever separated from human society.

Habitual disregard of taboos may animalize even without the intervention of occult powers that are the image of such animalization. Certain people may "become insane" (i mumanu). Like the victims of makakalisafu they incessantly run in the wilderness, lose the power of speech, go naked, and eat raw food. Sometimes, deep in the forest, one hears a mumanu's ululation in the distance. It grows, it approaches, suddenly he is before us, naked and wild. But he does not stop; he continues his mad run and we hear his voice disappear in the distance. He has forever become part of the forest, just like an animal, and he is himself animallike—an image of humanity lost because of loss of taboo. Then there are humans who "become witches" (i masiele). They take the form of predatory animals who devour people from the inside, in the raw, of course. Finally, I may mention the belief that a hunter who spends too much time alone in the forest, thereby rejecting social intercourse (and at the same time necessarily violating the fundamental taboo that one cannot eat one's kill), irresistibly slips into animality: he sees humans in animals and may have sexual intercourse with them, thereby falling further into an animal state. There are many stories about such cases.[16]

I could go on and on, and indeed more evidence will be presented later. But what I have said suffices for the moment to indicate the existence of a fear of "going animal," of losing the human attributes of speech, clothing, cooking, and living in villages, which evidently characterize humans in Huaulu eyes. This fear is, I would argue, alimented by a profound sense of affinity with animals. I have already mentioned the obvious grounds for this sense of affinity. Animals, particularly those with which the Huaulu have the most frequent intercourse, are physically and behaviourally similar to humans. They have similar organs, functions, desires, and sometimes even expressions. All these suggest similarity of feeling and thought. Thus animals are said to share with humans two attributes which we ourselves would Cartesianly tend to limit to humans: a mattiulu and a hali. Mattiulu is life in its organic and feeling dimensions. It is both animating principle and unconscious or semiconscious mind. It is the subject of fright and other uncontrolled emotions that are felt to be profoundly rooted in the body and intertwined with its vitality. It can become detached from the human body and enter into an animal body, animating and directing it. Mattiulu is thus a point of confusion between animals and humans, not only because they share it as an attribute, but also because it makes their mutual transmutation possible.

Although the mattiulu of animals and humans are closest, all living things have mattiulu. In contrast, only animal and humans (and occult powers) have hali, "heart," although of different kinds (hence the expressions *hali manusia,* "human heart," and *hali manusiassi,* "not a human heart," i.e. the heart of animals or of evil occult powers). "Heart" is in fact a very approximative translation of *hali.* The term is a cognate of the word for liver in other Indonesian languages (including *hati* in B.I.), but it refers to the psychic functions located elsewhere in this part of the body, not to the physical organ itself, which is called wassa. The hali, in any case, is the reification of various psychic functions and activities, just like our heart and mind. It predicates, in the third person, many of the activities which *I* would predicate in English idiom.[17] For instance, the Huaulu usually say "haliku kararihua," "my hali has forgotten," even if it is also possible to say "a kararihua," "I have forgotten."[18] Although *hali* predicates various states which we would call passions (e.g. halini sa', "his hali is angry"), it would be a mistake to identify the hali with our old "irascible soul." Indeed, it is involved in rational activity such as memorizing, reflecting, recalling (e.g. napa haliku rumrumhali hei, "let me think"; lit., "wait while my hali thinks this over, ponders").

The sharing of mattiulu and hali with animals implies, once again, that no radical ontological difference, guaranteeing a separate identity, exists between animals and humans. Because animals and humans share conscious and unconscious mental states, desires, feelings, and agency, they are not so terribly different. Moreover, they have the potential for becoming even less different. Humans can become more animallike than they already are, and animals more humanlike than they already are (indeed, they could become as humanlike as they used to be). Therefore, the contrast between animal and human must be kept, and it is indeed kept, most primordially, by taboos, which artificially create a difference where there is none or which exaggerate it where there is some. The most deliberately oppositional of these taboos guarding the "iron door" (to use a Huaulu idiom applied elsewhere) between animals and humans (or at least the Huaulu as a variety of humans, a way of being human), are the following:

1. It is taboo to have sex with animals or even speak of sexual

relations with them. The mere mention of such relations in "a curse" (i akalia, i sero) is sufficient to produce a thunderstorm and sometimes a flash flood. The reason for this taboo seems clear. Sexual relations between two individuals indicate that they are members of the same species.[19] Thus if humans were to have sex with animals they would not recognize their species difference from them. And because curses are supposed to take effect, cursing somebody by saying he or she has sex with an animal is almost equivalent to bringing about such an event. Both bestiality and its evocation in curses thus fall under the same taboo. Obviously, this taboo would not be necessary if sexual relationships with animals were not conceivable, at least at the imaginary level. And they are conceivable because animal sexuality—or better said, the sexuality of many animals—appears rather similar to human sexuality. This similarity is strongly evoked by the animals that appear most frequently in the curses. These are pythons of various species (e.g. omi iri pohi tipoloem, "fuck with the tipolo pythons"), the wormlike grubs (e.g. omi iri pohi etiem, "fuck with the grubs"), and the shrimps (okoem), which, probably because of their color and shape, are a very common metaphor for female pudenda in the Huaulu language (e.g. omi irire okoem, "fuck with the shrimps").[20] In sum, taboo arises here, as so often elsewhere,[21] as a reaction to a potential or actual point of confusion between animal and human.

2. The taboo on laughing at wild animals or in their presence is also one in which identification and differentiation are closely intertwined. Psychologically, laughing at somebody implies a degree of identification with him.[22] Thus this elementary experience motivates the conventional rule that laughing at somebody indicates closeness or even identity with him from the point of view of social categorization and interaction. Conversely, not laughing at somebody indicates distance, usually of a hierarchical kind, that is, one implying respect. In Huaulu society, some relations (for instance, those between cross-cousins) are characterized by jocularity because they connote closeness and equality (besides a certain mutual hostility); in other relations (for instance, those between in-laws) which imply distance and inequality, jokes and laughing are strictly taboo. The relationship of humans with wild animals is thus in many ways assimilated to a relationship inside Huaulu society, that is, the relationship with in-laws, as well as other relationships that are characterized by the taboo on laughter, or simply its avoidance, such as the relationship with elders, guests (who are also potential enemies), ancestors, and so on. Such assimilation and, more profoundly, the very idea of applying the signification that laughter has in human relationships to the relationship between humans and wild animals imply a subtle assimilation of the two kinds of relationships, and thus of those that are involved in it—human and animal. On the other hand, the taboo on laughing at wild animals, and even on laugh-

ing and joking in their presence, along with the fact that animals never laugh among themselves or at humans, emphasizes a profound difference between wild animals and humans, and also one between wild animals and domestic ones, since the latter, as we shall see, may be laughed at because of their closeness to humans.[23] So difference and similarity are subtly intertwined. Difference is established against a background of similarity and because of this background.

3. It is taboo to put human clothes on animals, wild or domesticated. Otherwise, violent thundering and pouring rain occurs. The motivation of this taboo should also be clear. As the beliefs concerning makakalisafu, mumanu, and so on have shown, clothing profoundly differentiates humans from animals, mainly because it covers genitalia and secondary sexual attributes. Therefore, it is the index of a uniquely human feeling (according to the Huaulu, as according to us): mukae, "shame." Putting clothes on animals would thus be denying that any difference between them and humans exists: it would amount to animalizing humans by humanizing animals.

4. It is taboo to cradle animals in one's arms, like children, and even to use the same word to refer to the two forms of cradling.[24] The taboo emphasizes a contrast between animal and human precisely where there tends to be none. Animal pets are very much like children, which is signified by our impulse to cradle them. The existence of a word for cradling animals indicates that this act is by no means rare or inconceivable (indeed, I have seen people do it). The partition between humanity and animality is very thin here. It must be reaffirmed in words at least.

5. Animals and humans are alike in having bodies, and thus in having weight, locomotion, sexual difference. Some animals, moreover, are like humans in behavior, even in such behavior as play. Since the contrast between animal and human cannot be asserted in these attributes, it must at least be asserted in their names. Hence there are different words for the weight, locomotion, play, male and female forms, and so on, of animals and humans, and it is taboo to mix them up.[25] On the other hand, the basic ground for the similarity between animals and humans—that is, the fact that both have a body—is not denied. Indeed the same word, *hata,* designates the body of an animal and that of a human. Moreover, the names of the organs shared by animals and humans (head, hair, liver, skin, and so on) are also shared. Is it too farfetched to infer from these lexical facts that the animal identifies with the bodily in humans? Indeed, one could argue that the use of *hatani* (its body) as a numerical classifier for animals exclusively confirms this identification by showing that only animals are categorically defined by the body, at least when they are counted. Put otherwise, animals can be identifed with the unmarked "body."

6. Finally, it is taboo to give the same proper names to animals

and humans (although it is not taboo to give the name of an animal species—e.g. tuyam, a green parrot—to an individual human). Personal names thus have a categorical dimension: one can infer from them whether they refer to an animal or to a human.

I believe that these taboos demonstrate that animality is a category of Huaulu culture. If it were not, the taboos could not be applied. Furthermore, the taboos indicate that animals are a privileged reference for humans in Huaulu, that in an important way Huaulu define themselves as humans, make themselves human, by contrasting themselves to animals. Many more facts could be given in support of this point. Let me just mention, in conclusion, the most banal: the use of animals as negative terms of comparison—to stigmatize human defects, moral or physical. For instance, people who are too greedy or too selfish are insultingly called fufae, "crocodile," or tekepatola, "patola python"—animals notorious for their voracity. And people who grunt or breathe heavily or are inarticulate are called hahu, "pig." Other animals provide ridiculous nicknames, castigating defects and other demeaning peculiarities. Furthermore, neighboring peoples whom the Huaulu consider subordinate or inferior to them are depicted as animallike or as having been so before being humanized, or fully humanized, by some Huaulu ancestor or culture hero. A preferred victim of such derogatory characterizations is the people of Besi (Pesiem). It is said that they did not know the use of fire before they learned it from an ancient from Makualaina (the village of a people related to the Huaulu). Until then they had eaten raw food, and as a result "they had hair on their tongue, like pigs." Analogously, the people of Manusela are said to derive from a bird whose wings and tail were cut by a Huaulu ancestor, who is also said to have turned the people of Nisawele into humans after they emerged as animals from their sacred mountain, the Murkele.

In sum, animality is the destiny not just of taboo violators but also, albeit metaphorically, of all those who fall short of a certain normative image of what it is to be human, an image which includes eating cooked food, speaking a properly articulated language, feeling shame and thus covering one's nakedness with clothing, controlling and regulating one's sexuality, living in villages, and, most important, following taboos, particularly those which assert and sustain the contrast between animals and humans.

Hunting and the Origin of Humanity

There is a myth which nicely brings together several of the points I have just made and adds some complementary ones. Appropriately, it concerns the dog, the animal which mediates animality and humanity by making the hunt possible.

The Myth of Wassulau

That giant lived at Kaffaulu. He swallowed all villages [i.e. their inhabitants] through and through. Then the [survivors of the] ipa Lafatue and of the ipa Lulumeni held a meeting regarding the dog [which had been swallowed too and which they wished to get back. One of the members of Lafatue, Manutalaka, volunteered to fight the giant. Having engaged him in combat] Manutalaka saw how things were and cut him. He cut his eight heads, eight arms, and eight legs. [The way he cut him was as follows:] He engaged him in combat. First he aimed at one head, but he missed; he aimed at an arm, but he missed; he aimed at a leg, but he missed. He tried again. [Finally] in one day he [managed to] cut one head, one arm, one leg. He tried again the next day and cut another head, another arm, and another leg [and so on; he cut one set every day until the seventh day, when] he [the giant] fell to the ground. Then the giant said [with his last mouth], "You have killed me because of the dog." From the fallen giant out came the people of Lafatue and Lulumeni who had been swallowed. Then out came Wassulau (the first dog) and its mapeam [the forest rat which is its food]. At Nusalau[26] and then at Nusa Patola[27] he [Manutalaka] gave clothing to the people who came out of the giant. To some he gave loincloths, to some pants. But there was not enough clothing. Those who had no pants were the Fatasiwa: Kururutu Kara, Ruku Haya, Luma Sokate, Uwela,[28] and first Pessere.[29] Men and women both had loincloths (akaweliem).

Wassulau went west (lau) in the direction of the sea.[30] She was a bitch and pregnant. Before leaving, Wassulau had said: "Don't eat my mapeam. It is my staple food." But Heuwe Tamatay ate it. After he ate it, Wassulau returned and asked, "Where is my mapeam?" "Heuwe ate it." "No! He shouldn't have." Then she jumped onto the Tahere Mountain.[31] And there she gave birth to eight puppies.

[Heuwe] called her [requesting one of her puppies] so that he could go hunting. The one he took ran after [a deer] as far as from here to the sea. Heuwe killed the deer and killed the dog. Three days later, [Heuwe went to Wasulau and said,] "Another dog for me." He went hunting and the dog ran after [a deer] as far as the mountain without stopping. It ran after it, barking and barking. Then [Heuwe] killed the deer and killed the dog.

Up there Wassulau [complained,] "He has killed two of my children already." Two days later [Heuwe] asked again for one dog. He went hunting with it. He went west as far as from here to the Sapulewa [River]. He followed his dog for a long time, then he heard it barking in the distance, in the direction of the sea. He shot the deer and the dog with arrows.

Two days later he called another [dog]. He went hunting with it to the Sapulewa River, and it ran as far as the mountain. He followed it, and shot the deer and the dog with his arrows.

Two days later again he repeated the whole thing. He called Wassulau: "Come!" Two days later again he called. He went hunting with it to the mountain. Suddenly he lost track of it [the dog], but he heard it again barking and barking in the direction of the sea.

Two days later he did it again. He followed it [another dog] to kill the dog and the deer with his arrows. Two days later, again he called. Two days later he again called another dog. He went hunting again with it as far as the mountain and as far as the sea. "I can't anymore!" [i.e. go any further]. And he killed the dog and the deer with his arrows.

At this point Wassulau said: "I absolutely don't want [to give him another puppy]. I only have one child left." Then Heuwe went hunting without dogs (e pakalaha). He had no more dogs left. They were finished. He went hunting and shot a wild pig. A boar with tusks three inches long (saha tolu) [i.e. a male]. It ran in the direction of the sea to its lair (hahu nifotuam). It entered and went down [to the underground village of the pigs]. He [Heuwe] followed it. The pig told him, "Extract this arrow with an iron point." As soon as he had extracted it, he ran as far as that breadfruit tree, and they began running after him. Boars with tusks three inches long, sows, and so on ran after Heuwe. He ran and ran until he climbed up a tree. He climbed up a tree; they [the pigs] felled it (ia repai). He moved to another tree [heiya: going from the branches of one to those of the other], but again they felled it. And so on and so forth until he moved to an areca tree grove (pulauw lelaam). The pigs felled them all. Then Heuwe moved to an uliam [kalondong hutan.] The pigs stabbed it but stopped because they felt a sourness on their tusks [the tree's sap is very sour]. They then lay down around him [i.e. around the tree where Heuwe was staying, waiting for him to fall down] to kill Heuwe. But he did not give up. He called, "Wassulau!" Again he called, "Wassulau!" Up there eh! you heard as far as the setting sun [i.e. so loud he called]. He called three times, "Wassulau!" And finally Wassulau [the son] came down [from the mountain. Wassulau the mother told him,] "Go down to your master, who is in the direction of the sea." When he arrived there [Wassulau exclaimed,] "Hia'! Pigs!" [Heuwe] said, "We are going to die." "No, you are not going to die, but perhaps I will." Then Heuwe said, "Why?" "The pigs are going to kill me." "Indeed!" At this point the pigs got up to catch him [Wassulau]. Some [attacked] from this side, some from that. But he barked, and they [the pigs] all died. He barked again, and they [other dangerous animals] all died. He killed that mulala,[32] that kuha,[33] female and male. The tekepatola,[34] he killed the female and the male. The kakuinam, he killed the female and the male. The pig, he killed the female and the male. The deer, he killed the female and the male.

Then Heuwe went home. He saw how things were, and went to the river Awa [near Wolu on the south coast of Seram]. There the pigs owned the fire. They said, "Wassulau stole it." The pigs went down to their lair: "Eh! our fire has already gone out. There is only a little left." The pigs blew and blew until it [the few embers that were left] was out. The children cried, "We shall eat our food raw!" Then they [the pigs] met in council: "It was indeed Wassulau who did it." "Not me." "You were indeed the one who stole it." And the pig said, "We two will be at war." "No, don't be at war with me!" Then Wassulau displayed his penis. The piglets laughed. How much they laughed! The adults asked, "Why [do you laugh]?" "It is nothing; [we laugh] at Wassulau's penis." "It is my advantage!" [said Wassulau]. Then war. From that time on the dog kills game. A war because of the penis.

[Heuwe and the other members of the Tamatay lineage] met in council and decided to kill Wassulau. He was attacked as an enemy. But he barked once inland, and they all died; once in the direction of the sea, and they all died. At which Heuwe said, "This dog has killed too many people already." Then he and his wife went to process sago pith (i weti). The husband stayed all alone hammering at the sago pith. His wife had returned home. He sat quietly hammering so that it [the dog] would come close to watch him. [When the dog did] he struck the dog's head with his hammer, but he [the dog] bit the throat of his master Heuwe. They both died. They buried them on the Tahere Mountain. They left the whole carcass of the dog to rot, except its right front paw, which they kept for the sake of its nails (tifuneniam). These became the nasinaham [headhunting power/magic] called Lafatueam. He [the dog] also gave an utuniam [magical object] of the soyam kind [also for headhunting] to the senior branch of Tamatay [Wassulau rahe kinoyem, "the magical lightning stones of Wassulau."]

The Lulumeni lineage went to the south at Wassolomina,[35] where it lived with the Matoke[36] lineage and the Lafatue lineage. Ninisau was the "father" of Lulumeni. The giant lived on top the mountain Arere (hoto Arere uluniam).[37] When he fell the island shook (ia paki nusam warua). The Lafatue people "owned" Manutalaka as their child [i.e. he was a member of their lineage]. They also owned Nusa Patola as their mountain. Lafatue and Lulumeni now live in the village of Openg [Tamatay now lives in Huaulu].

Because of its connections with Lafatue, of its ownership of parts of Wassulau's remains, and especially because Heuwe was its ancestor, the Tamatay lineage is considered the lawful owner of this myth. That it was told to me by Polonahu, a member of the Sinala lineage, not by Ilakessa, the senior Tamatay man, testifies to the myth's sacredness. Indeed, it belongs to a category of tales, the aitetukiniem (lit. "the narratives"), which, being maquwoli, cannot be told lightly and which prove fatal to the narrator should he make any mistake, however involuntarily. In fact, these myths can be narrated only by men who are advanced in age and, as such, are closer to the ancestors and also close enough to death not to have much life left to lose. A comparatively young man like Ilakessa preferred to let the opportunity to tell the tale himself pass. Instead, he allowed Polonahu, one of the oldest men in the village, to narrate it to me. But however old and sure of his knowledge Polonahu was, he insisted on certain conditions. First of all, nobody but me and my wife should be present at the narration. To this end, I should go to his house a couple of kilometers away from the village. Second, I should not tape the narration, partly because it was too sacred for that, partly because other people might hear it later. So one morning I went down to his house and had to take down the story in writing as fast as I could, since the old man could not quite understand that he should adjust his speed in talking to mine in writing. This explains in part the skimpiness of my text, but not entirely, since other narratives that he allowed me to tape are almost as skimpy and presupposing as this one (see, for instance, the origin myth of the cassowary below). The fact is one must already know these stories to understand them in the form in which they are narrated. Because their contents are taboo, the narrator does not linger on details and speaks with as much indirection as possible. Fortunately Polonahu's son, Pitere, who understood my difficulties somewhat better than his father, clarified most points in the narrative for me. Moreover, my understanding was facilitated by my having already transcribed a much longer, if rather different, version of the myth in Piliana.

I mention all this not only to situate the text as it stands in the ethnographic process, but also and especially to give an idea of its importance to the Huaulu. It is this importance that makes it sacred, and thus highly restricted. Even so, it would be wrong to infer that it is unknown to the ordinary Huaulu. On the contrary, most people know at least the gist of it, as they do of most other sacred tales. The precautions taken against its free circulation are a rhethorical signal indexing the importance of the tale and the intangibility of its ownership by the Tamatay, not a way of making its contents unknown. The issue is not knowledge, but the right to dispose of it.[38] It is, in other words, an issue of power and prerogative. That this is so is indicated by the final part of Polonahu's narration, where he traced the channels through which Wassulau's story became Tamatay's property. The basis for Tamatay's ownership is that they are the closest successors to those who were involved in the story and to Heuwe in particular. Parallelly, the ontological premise of the truth of the tale is that Wassulau is witness to it—that its telling is, in a sense, addressed to him even before it is addressed to a human public. This premise was vividly brought to my attention by the occasional invocation to Wassulau with which Polonahu punctuated his narration: "Wassulau, u koi ea, assasauw mamanissa, ooh!" "Wassulau, look at me, I tell the truth, hey!"

But let me attempt to explain the myth—that is, to show that it conveys certain categorical oppositions and transformations which legitimize the Huaulu's hunting life and life by hunting in their own eyes. The starting point of the story is just the opposite of the present that it is supposed to justify. Humans (that is the peoples of Seram and the neighboring islands) do not live by hunting but die by being hunted. An eight-headed, eight-limbed giant devours entire villages (a common theme in Huaulu sacred history). The survivors meet to find a way to remedy the situation. The giant will, of course, have to be killed, but interestingly, this is not what is foregrounded. What the reunion is supposed to be about is how to get the dog—that is, hunting—out of the giant's body. Indeed, the point is emphasized by the giant himself when, having fallen to the ground, he tells Manutalaka: "You have killed me because of the dog." But before we turn to the dog, some comment on the giant is called for. Its devouring and forced regurgitation of people and dog is an image of transformation common in Seramese and other mythologies worldwide. The transformation is initiated in the stomach of the giant but is brought to fruition by Manutalaka. In a sense, the giant is like a woman from whose belly the hero delivers (true) humans. Having been brought together in the undifferentiating space of the monster's stomach, the digested people are differentiated again, this time into the categories that still rule the world of central Maluku, namely the Siwa and the Lima and the Irianese. Such categories are generated by Manutalaka's distribution of different kinds of clothing. Polonahu alluded to this theme but did not fully develop it. As was explained to me later (and as is confirmed by other versions of the myth I heard in central Seram), Manutalaka starts with woven clothing but he runs out of it; then he continues with barkcloth, but he also runs out of that. Therefore the last humans to come out of the monster stay naked. These clothing categories are variously connected with the Siwa, the Lima, and the inhabitants of Irian. The actual connections matter less than the basic principle of hierarchy they illustrate: those who came out first are the superior ones, indexed by woven clothing; the last stayed naked and are usually identified with the inhabitants of Irian, which the peoples of Seram look down on as less human than themselves (I heard tales in Huaulu that some Irianese have tails like animals). Last in this hierarchy is indeed an animal: the dog (together with its food, the mapeam). But it is an animal that, contrary to all others, is allowed to be part of a hierarchy of humans. It is a quasi-human animal and as such destined to mediate between animal and human.[39]

A new order, then, is extracted from the giant's dismembered body. It is based on the differential negation of nakedness—that is, of a trait which evidently humans and animals shared before being devoured by the monster and clothed by Manutalaka. But clothing is just the first step in the process of humanization. The next two are the invention of hunting and the invention of cooking. The dog plays the crucial transformative part in both.

The invention of hunting reverses, as I have said, the original situation in which humans were hunted and eaten. From meat-providers, humans now become meat-eaters. The first stage of this reversal, though, is presented by the myth as too extreme and therefore ultimately unsustainable and indeed self-destructive. Heuwe, the original hunter, is quite indiscriminate in his relationship with the animal world. He does not discriminate between the animal as victim (the deer) and the animal as helper (the dog), but kills (and presumably eats) them both. Thus he successively destroys seven of Wassulau's eight puppies.[40] Forced to hunt without dogs, he is turned into a prey again: the animals he attempts to kill attempt to kill him. Indeed, this reversal—a return to the beginning of the myth in a different guise—is associated with a change in the animal adversary. Until then, Heuwe had been confronted by the more vulnerable and pavid deer, but now he finds himself challenged by the ferocious pig. Not surprisingly, given its signification of the reversibility of the relations of hunter and hunted, the pig assumes anthropomorphic characteristics. Indeed, pigs are represented in the myth as more human than coeval humans, since not only do they live in villages and, like humans, are sensitive to nakedness (as demonstrated by their laughter when Wassulau shows his nakedness to them), but also, contrary to humans, they possess fire and are therefore able to cook their food.

Pigs thus represent more than a dangerous symmetry between hunter and game; they also represent the superiority of the animal over the animal. The situation is remedied by Wassulau, that is, by an animal which, by allying himself with humans, allows them to achieve superiority over the animals, even over the more humanlike pigs, who are humanlike even in their ferocity. In calling the only surviving child of the bitch Wassulau (called Wassulau as she is and thus clearly meant to be her successor) to the rescue, Heuwe acknowledges that he cannot do without the dog, that without it he cannot be human, that is, be hunter instead of hunted. A distinction must be introduced between animals as game, as enemies (the myth clearly states that hunting is war and Wassulau is at the origin of various pieces of magic for warfare), and as friends.

The next step constitutes the logical conclusion of the process of humanization through hunting, since it is also the usual conclusion of the creation of meat through hunting: namely the acquisition of fire for cooking purposes. Here again the main antagonists are the pigs, as the animals closest to humans and therefore most threatening to humans' special status above animals. Originally, fire was owned by pigs, not by humans. It is Wassulau again who inverts this situation, by stealing the fire on behalf of his master, Heuwe. From now on, pigs will be really and fully animal, fully different from humans, because they will lack what is now uniquely human: the ability to cook the food they eat.[41]

There is a third element, besides hunting and cooking, that is alluded to here. Indeed it is fully intertwined with those two pillars of the human state. It is the element of male supremacy. Polonahu's narrative alludes to it; another version that I collected in Piliana (closer to the very location of the narrated events) makes it even more explicit.[42] It is by showing his penis that Wassulau is able to tip the scales, to get away with the theft of fire, and to initiate the eternal war between himself and the pigs that sustains (and justifies) the human hunt. Polonahu's apparently cryptic remark, "a war because of the penis," becomes perfectly transparent once the penis is viewed as the phallus, that is, as a culturally chosen and elaborated mark of manhood[43] that inextricably connects the contrast of animal and human with the contrast of man and woman.

Hunting is part of man's estate; indeed, it largely identifies with it. Women are dependent on it but excluded from it. It is on hunting, therefore, that male supremacy rests. But hunting also presupposes human supremacy over animals, which is achieved by the domestication of the dog. All these categorical oppositions are appropriately condensed in Wassulau's penis. This penis is in reality the male phallus as the pivot of culture—a pivotal role confirmed by the fact that the most sacred object in Huaulu is the Leautuam, a supposedly always living and always erect phallus descended from heaven and preserved in a special taboo house (luma maquwoliam).[44] The parallel between subordinated animals and subordinated women, which is only implicit in Polonahu's version of the myth of Wassulau, was made fully explicit in the version I heard in Piliana, according to which the pig who confronts Wassulau is female.

Another interesting point that deserves comment is that the pigs are defeated because they (or more precisely, in Polonahu's version, their children) are overcome by laughter in seeing Wassulau's "advantage" over them—that is, his penis. Laughter is taken here as a sign of defeat, because it appears as a force that dominates the body, that irresistibly runs through it. But at the same time it seems that laughter, this human trait, runs out of the pigs forever, since they are now not known to laugh. On the contrary, just like all other wild animals, they cannot tolerate laughter (which is taboo in their presence). In sum, the pigs lose their laughter and their fire at the same time: they lose out to humans by losing their own humanity on all fronts.

Hunting, cooking, and laughter are now in their human place. But something, or rather somebody, remains out of place. It is Wassulau, the dog, who, being the source of what makes humans human, is himself too human an animal to be tolerated. It is also Wassulau's counterpart, Heuwe, who acquired the characteristic human traits but was not himself fully human. These transitional and symmetric creatures must eliminate each other. The final step in the process of humanization, then, is the reciprocal neutralization of a dog and a human who are too close to each other to be compatible. Dogs have to be more animal than Wassulau, and humans more human than Heuwe. Wassulau survives only as an occult power used in war; Heuwe, as an ancestral shade that stands for Tamatay's rights and civilizing claims.

Nevertheless the myth still guarantees the special status of Wassulau's descendants. It also guarantees the correlative superiority of humans over animals and of men over women. At the same time, it subtly undermines these superiorities and suggests the residual possibility of their reversal by showing that they result from a theft. Not men's theft at the expense of women (as in other mythologies), but men's theft at the expense of animals. If being human consists in hunting wild animals and having fire to cook their meat, and perhaps even in the privilege of laughing, then humans must acknowledge that these human traits are of animal origin and are now exclusively theirs because of another animal—the dog. It seems to me that in the idea of the theft lies the recognition of the fundamental animality of humans. Animals were there first; humans were like animals, or animals like humans. And it was only because animality transcended itself in the figure of the dog that humans were finally produced. The sense of human distinctiveness is inseparable from a lingering awareness of its debt to animals, just as, perhaps, the male sense of superiority is inseparable from a residual consciousness of its debt to women.

Indigenous Principles

The basic dialectic of human and animal which I have delineated constitutes the backdrop for the more specific play of similarity and difference that determines the status, taboo or otherwise, of each animal or vegetal category. It is to these, and to animal categories especially, that I now turn. But first we must look into the main general principles which the Huaulu adduce to account for their animal taboos.

The standard reason for most taboos is, of course, "it has been that way from antiquity" (wahiamuni taka holuholu). Tradition is self-legitimating, so one can always refer to it to justify a taboo. But such justification is good mostly for getting rid of the inquisitive ethnographer. It is too trivial and self-evident to use with a fellow Huaulu. With each other, the Huaulu prefer to use pragmatic arguments, such as "*x* is taboo because it gives tropical sores." The purported objective properties of an animal are invoked to explain certain effects on those who eat it and thus why they should not eat it. But, to a surprising degree, the Huaulu do not stop at that. They frequently feel the need to give a principled justification of those properties, as if they could not be taken for granted, to a much greater degree than the properties of nontaboo things. Indeed, the tendency to reduce to principle and the concomitant tendency to generalize and systematize—however limited and often inconsistent its results—seem stronger in the realm of taboo than outside it. Leaving aside for the moment the possible reasons for this, let us consider the principles that are most frequently invoked to account for animal taboos.

1. Human aspect. Ita oi wahi manusia, ia aeressi "we don't eat it because it looks like a human being." I have heard this principle invoked to account for the taboo on dugong and monkey meat.[45]

2. Feeding. Ita umanakire, ita aeressi (*or* ita aere ia maquwoli), "if we feed them, we do not feed on them (*or* it is taboo to eat them)." This principle is invoked to account for the taboo on the domesticated animals kept by the Huaulu, particularly dog and cat, and on most wild animals that are kept as pets.

3. Voluntary ingress. If a wild animal enters the village voluntarily, without being pursued by hunters or dogs, it is taboo to eat it.

These first three principles are openly anthropocentric. Whether the animal strongly resembles humans physically, or is fed by the Huaulu, thereby becoming part of their society to some extent, or is attracted to the space where that society is located, it is too strongly associated with the Huaulu to be eaten by them. This generalization is not explicitly made by the Huaulu themselves, but it seems implicit in the three principles. Without it, it is hard to account for their existence—and coexistence.

Anthropocentricism, of a more indirect sort, can also be said to underlie the next two principles:

4. Origins. Kalu ita rahe asaleam hinira, ita aeressi, "if it is our 'origin,' we don't eat it." This is a loosely "totemic" principle,[46] but it is important to stress that ancestors need not be the transformation of the animal (or plant) that is taboo. Indeed, just the opposite may be true: the animal or plant may be taboo to the descendants of an ancestor who "transformed" (lelia) into it.[47] In this second case too the natural species is called the asale of those who follow the taboo, indicating that this notion is not quite what we understand by "origin." It refers, rather, to encounters—usually, but not necessarily, metamorphic—between a natural species (often connected with an occult power) and an ancestor. It is rarely the "origin" of a lineage in the sense that its members descend from an animal or a plant. More of this later.

5. Dream pact. If one dreams of an occult power in the shape of an animal (or, less often, in the shape of a plant), and some kind of pact or relationship is established between the dreamer and the power as a consequence, the animal or plant become taboo for him and usually also for his descendants or, if he is a shaman, for his "adepts" (mulitem). A variant of this is that the power, whatever its manifestation,

explicitly "'tells' certain taboos" (eme sali maquwoliem) as a condition of the covenant. Shamanic taboos are or were for the most part "dreamed" in this way, or such is the theory.

At least overtly, the next principles have less to do with the relationship of the tabooed animal to the Huaulu than with its "intrinsic" characteristics:

6. Color. More exactly, two colors, "black" (mete) and especially "red" (musunu), are grounds for taboo. Even more important than red is any combination of colors, or shades of the same color, which goes under the name of likalikam, "variegated"[48] or "spotted." Color is a source of taboo directly but also indirectly, when it is supposed to make shamanic familiars "afraid" (i mutau). Then what is avoided by the familiars must also be avoided by the shamans and their patients.

7. Anomaly. Amuni ita hua oiressi, "we have not seen it yet." The expression refers to an unexpected or unhabitual event, that is, an event which defies expectations as they are created by a long collective experience (hence the use of the "definitional" pronoun *ita* "[inclusive] we," rather than *ea,* "I," or *ami,* "[exclusive] we"). There is a strong implication that the habitual is the normal, the way things should be. If things behave strangely, unexpectedly,[49] they are viewed as inauspicious, dangerous, and usually also as the manifestation of an evil power. They are therefore avoided and declared maquwoli. The following extract from my field-notes may illustrate this set of ideas: "Hatupae says that he has seen an eel roll around a tamaliam fish. Although it would have been easy to pierce both with an arrow, he did not do it, because 'he was afraid.' I asked him, 'afraid of what?' 'That there was an evil power (kinakinam) [apparently in the eel], because we have never seen an eel rolled around a fish [i.e. this is an anomalous event].' Patakuru, who is present, repeats the same explanation: 'Ita mutau sepapu hua ita oiressi' 'We are afraid because we have not yet seen it before.'"[50]

8. Misoneism. A variant of the previous principle (but also, in a sense, the converse of principle number 4 is: ita kaluara (rari) pohiressi, "we have not come out (originated, become what we are) with it." This is what I would call a principle of misoneism.[51] Anything imported, new, anything that has not been with the Huaulu from the beginning of time, is suspicious, potentially dangerous, and thus taboo, especially for those who are in the closest contact with tradition and thus have the greatest responsibility for it. This principle, however, applies more to cultivated plants (i.e. rice, kasibi, "cassava," varieties of sugarcane and bananas, etc.) and inanimate substances or objects than to animals. It also applies to any tinned meat. The latter is in any case suspect, since the animal that provides it is unknown (I was even asked if it was true that tins contain the flesh of children).

9. Unfamiliarity. The principle that a relationship with the previ-

ously unknown is dangerous takes another form besides the "misoneistic" taboos: it makes a number of appropriational acts taboo until some form of acquaintance is ritually established. For instance, it is taboo to take resin for the first time from an *Agathis alba* damar before one has chewed some of the resin, and has therefore diminished the distance between the tree and oneself (perhaps to the point of establishing some consubstantiality with it). Analogously, a special binding rite (the binding of a strip of rattan around the left wrist) is necessary when one enters into a tract of forest for the first time (if one has no hereditary connection with it). It is said that in this case one runs the risk of being attacked by the kaitahu upuam (lord of the land), since the latter is not yet "used to" the intruder. One may generalize from these examples and conclude that where there is acquaintance, established relationship with a dangerous power, taboo is diminished or even removed (all other things being equal, of course). This generalization is confirmed by the belief that a menstruating woman is somewhat less polluting to her husband than to other men, because "he is already used to her" (eme piasa nika).

10. Mixture. Just as animals or plants of mixed colors ("variegated" or "spotted") are taboo, so are many other mixtures. The most clearly articulated principle of excluded mixture, however, is that animals at the two extremes of the three-tiered cosmos are taboo to eat together. Indeed, it is rare that the rules specifying that animal *x* should not be eaten with animal *y* are even enunciated without mention of this general principle. For instance: ita ae manuem pohi iyaem ia maquwoli, barani essa ia ruwe hoto aituhu, essa pale wae, "it is taboo to eat fish and fowl together, since one lives up in the trees, the other down in the water."

11. Ritual association. Finally, a principle frequently invoked is that the taboo animal or plant has some connection with a ritual activity that is itself defined by taboos. For instance, it is said that a number of birds are taboo for women to eat because "they bite the headhunters" (ia koto timatem). The expression refers to the purported power of these birds to announce the invisible presence of prowling headhunters. They can do so because of various metaphoric and metonymic associations with these hunters, as we shall see. The upshot is that the birds are closely associated with an activity, headhunting, which is strictly taboo to women. Hence the birds, too, are taboo to them.

These principles account for a number, sometimes a great number, of taboos. Even so, they often cannot be said to apply as they stand to some of the taboos that they purport to explain. Unstated principles, corollaries, or presuppositions may have to be invoked. This is very much the case, as we shall see, with principles number 1 and number 10. It also seems pretty obvious that several of the principles echo one another and imply more general ones. It is often one of these more general, unstated principles that must be invoked to make full sense of the taboos which the Huaulu attempt to explain by some stated principle, or sometimes simply do not attempt to explain. In any event, it is to these implied but unstated principles that I resort, whenever possible, in the absence of any stated ones or when the stated ones clearly do not do their job. If I must speculate, I prefer to speculate on the basis of notions that seem consistently suggested by the discourses of the Huaulu themselves. Let me briefly anticipate some of these basic notions, or implied principles. There are at least four:

i. The first stems from the "anthropocentric" and "sociocentric" criteria I have already noted, particularly in overt principles 1 through 4: this is an implied principle of excessive closeness. If an animal is too close to the Huaulu (or, more generally, human) world because of the way it looks and behaves, and especially because it lives with them and shares their food, it is intangible at least in the sense that it is not eaten. In this case, it seems not so much that one is what one eats as that one does not eat what one is. To eat oneself, however indirectly, would be to subvert the fundamental distinction between eater and eaten, between self and food.

ii. But there is a converse principle: excessive distance from the Huaulu world. Thus what is "new," "never seen before," because it belongs to a world completely different from the Huaulu one and indeed antithetical to it, cannot be eaten either (see overt principle number 8). Here, the idea that one is what one eats, and therefore one does not eat what one does not want to be (a stranger, even an anti-Huaulu), is emphasized. However, the taboos founded on this principle are less compelling and of narrower application than those founded on the previous principle—a sign of where the emphasis lies.

iii. The implied principle of the "never before seen" has another, more cognitive, application when it refers not to things that happen to belong to the foreign world, but to things of the Huaulu world that do not behave as expected. In other words, "strangeness" exists on purely empirical or accidental grounds in implied principle ii, whereas it depends on principle, or simply on ingrained expectation, in implied principle iii. The latter can therefore be called a principle of excluded anomaly. The principle that anomaly is a source of danger is directly expressed in overt principle 7, but we shall find it in many other forms, including that of anomalous species. Anomalous species are usually those that violate the principle that each animal belongs to only one of three habitats: up in the trees, down on the ground, down in the water. For instance, it is considered taboo to let the ilauwa frog come into contact with a house, because it lives both down in the water like fish and up in the trees like birds.

iv. The principle of excluded anomaly touches the principle of excluded mixing, as is shown most directly by the belief that it is just as taboo to mix species of opposite habitats as it is to eat (or come into contact with) a single species which is made anomalous by its living across such habitats. The relevant fact, it seems, is that habitats become mixed in both cases, and it is this mixing which is dangerous and should not be "introjected" through food. The principle of excluded mixing, however, is not limited to habitat in its application. It also explains why combinations of colors (the variegated or spotted forms that are called likalika) tend to be taboo (see principle 6). The misoneistic principle of taboo, insofar as it implies the separation of the Huaulu world from extraneous worlds, can also be viewed as a manifestation of the more general principle of excluded mixing. And so can all those taboos that enjoin the separation of antithetical categories (blood shed by woman and blood shed by man, things intrinsically of the mountain and things intrinsically of the sea), which rule out the inversion of the terms of a series (the marriage of the senior and that of the junior, what comes before and what comes after in a ritual process, and so on).

Mixing is, in a sense, the ultimate principle of taboo, as Douglas and Leach have insisted. But there is a limit beyond which the reduction of other principles to this one becomes highly artificial or plainly impossible. As we have seen, mixing is in no way relevant when excessive similarity is the motive for taboo. In fact, one could argue that taboo exists in this case because there is not enough mixing. More important, mixing, just as any of the other principles, cannot alone explain any of the taboos. For these principles to become operative in a particular context, that context must already have a certain value and signification; it must include phenomena that have a certain weight in the imaginative and practical life of Huaulu subjects. In other words, the symbolic value of a taboo object is not reducible to its mere classificatory status, and even less so to some very general classificatory principle. It is inseparable from the value of what it stands for and where it finds itself. It is overdetermined.

Grouping Taboos

I now turn to a discussion of the meat taboos. I have divided them into groups that correspond as closely as possible to Huaulu conceptions and practices. It seemed natural to begin with the taboos of the domesticated animals, since these are ideologically and experientially crucial, and since the Huaulu account for them with a single, clearly stated (if not completely developed) principle. Furthermore, these taboos allow us to introduce immediately two parallel oppositions of the greatest importance: between domesticated and wild animals, and between the village and the forest. Having introduced these oppositions, it seems necessary to consider the status of animals that are intermediate, either as a species or as individuals, in that they defy the strict ideological separation of human and nonhuman habitats. These animals form the second group.

The following groups of taboos concern unambiguously wild meats. Group three includes mixing taboos; group four, single-species taboos that seem motivated, by and large, by anomaly. These two groups form a unity in Huaulu thought and yet are distinguished from each other, which is indicated by their sharing of skin diseases as the consequence of violation, but skin diseases of a different kind (leprosy for mixing taboos, tropical sores and yaws for single-species taboos). Note, moreover, that the validity of group three, just like that of group one, is guaranteed by its association with an explicit principle of its own.

Given the overwhelming importance of the male/female opposition and its rich manifestations in various areas of taboo, species taboos for women also form a rather obvious grouping—the fifth. The sixth group, shamanic taboos, is also very well defined. Moreover, contrary to the previous groups, it is put to instructional use by the Huaulu themselves. In other words, it is common to hear statements of the type "the sewa pukariam has these taboos . . . ," whereas it is rare to hear: "women have the following taboos . . . ," unless the ethnographer, or any other curious stranger, asks about them. It is important to stress, however, that even if people do not spontaneously use the lists that I have categorized as groups one through five, they are quite capable of producing these lists if requested, and are even able to add new items when necessary. This suggests that my groupings are not purely analytical abstractions of my own devising. Each corresponds to one or, usually, more of the principles, overt or implied, that I have just mentioned.

But I do not wish to give the impression that all meat taboos have a principled or "structural" explanation, even if it seems immediately clear that the more widely shared a taboo is, the more likely (and in any case the easier) is its reduction to some principle.

"If We Feed Them, We Do Not Feed on Them"

All Huaulu men are, in practice and more important at heart, hunters. The great forest that surrounds them on every side teems with wild pigs, deer, cassowaries, marsupials, birds, and snakes. The numerous rivers and streams are filled with fish, eels, and crustaceans. When not engaged in their favorite activity of pursuing these animals, the Huaulu speak incessantly about it. Their bragging words find confirming echoes in the familiar smells of blood, of singed fur, of half-putrid meat smoked on the evening fires, which punctuate hunting's great passion.

But the Huaulu are hunters by obligation, and not just by inclination: like the Lele or the Bororo,[52] they may not feed on animals which they feed. Although this taboo leaves open the theoretical possibility of eating the meat of animals raised by other people, in practice it means, and has meant even more in the past, that only game animals, animals which are hunted, constitute proper food for the Huaulu. This, as they well know, puts them at odds with people such as the coastal Muslims, who, by and large, have inherited the Mosaic dietary code,[53] in which the paradigmatic food is provided by raised or even domestic animals (cattle,[54] sheep, and goats), that is, by man's companions, not by his enemies.[55]

The animal companions of the Huaulu consist of three species—the dog, the cat, and the chicken—and any individual wild animal which is raised as a pet. Among the latter are a number of parrots, plus the occasional cassowary or even feral pig captured in its immature stage. Although there are in fact various additional reasons for the taboo status of all these animals, and for that of the chicken in particular, the principle "if we feed them it is taboo to feed on them" (kalu ita umanakire ita aere ia maquwoli; or "if we raise/adopt them it is taboo to eat them," kalu ita apiaraire ita aere ia maquwoli) is generically applied to them all. The explanatory power of this principle follows from the signification given to the act of feeding/raising. By continually feeding animals, just as by continually feeding children (the words *umanaki* and *apiara* are used in both cases), one makes them into fellow social beings. One allows them into the spaces of the house and the village, and thereby makes them participate, however indirectly, in the social life that takes place in those spaces. As fellow social beings of a sort, the animals habitually fed by the Huaulu are also granted a degree of personhood that is incompatible with treating them as food. Indeed, eating means incorporating another being by destroying it, and thus reducing it to a mere thing with which no mutual relationship, however asymmetric, is possible. Kant's formula "it is impossible to be at the same time thing and person"[56] is too radical to apply to Huaulu, or to any existing human society, for that matter. But if it is modified into the formula "it is impossible to be at the same time food and person," it is a truly universal principle. For everywhere food is the contrary of person; it is the paradigmatic thing.[57] My social world ends where my food begins. This is why eating together is the most primordial act of social constitution: in it, the table companions recognize one another as persons by denying that the living being they treat as food is a person. Somebody is included by excluding somebody else, who is in fact reduced to a mere body.

Fellow social beings, then, are given at least this form of dignity: they are spared the ignominy of being treated as mere things, as food. Even if they are killed (as human enemies or some domestic animals are) they are not eaten. Under normal circumstances, cannibalism is abhorrent to the Huaulu,[58] and is identified with monstrous figures such as atalayem, "the giants" (that is, persons with a human figure, at least in part, but whose gigantic size gives them inhuman appetites), or humans who have turned to "lycanthropy" (i masiele), or "witches" (suaki, suakipatia).[59] The horror felt for cannibalism transfers to the eating of the animals that live a social life with the Huaulu. Not eating tame animals means not eating fellow beings.

As should already be clear, the generic principle "if we feed them, we do not feed on them" has different implications depending on whether the animal which is habitually fed belongs to a species that is viewed as intrinsically wild or to one that is viewed as intrinsically domesticated. In the former case, the taboo is limited to the individual animal which is fed. In the latter, it is extended to the species as a whole. Take, for instance, pigs or cassowaries, which are feral animals in Huaulu experience. If a piglet or a cassowary chick is brought back to the village to be raised as a pet or mascot (as was sometimes the case in the past) or to be sold to strangers (as is sometimes the case in the present), it becomes taboo to eat for all Huaulu. All other members of its species, however, remain edible. In contrast, if an animal of a species that is never encountered wild, such as the dog, is fed and raised by the Huaulu, the taboo extends to the species as a whole.

It seems, then, that certain animals are "adopted" as species, whereas all others can be adopted only as individuals. And that difference lies in the former's universal association with humans, in their being not just "domestic" animals but also "domesticated" ones. This universal association demonstrates that they all have, young or old, the potential for being raised by a particular class of humans—the Huaulu. Indeed, the Huaulu may buy or otherwise acquire their domestic animals from any other human group. In this sense, all individual dogs, cats, and chickens, wherever they are found, are interchangeable from a Huaulu perspective. It is precisely this claim to the species as a whole which is behind the extension of the inedibility taboo to all the species' individual members. However ethnocentric the reason for the taboo is (the Huaulu do not consider taboo the domesticated animal which they do not raise),[60] it requires a reference to mankind. By virtue of their universal association with humans, all individuals of the same species can acquire particular connections with Huaulu society. In this sense the taboo, by indissolubly linking these animals with their species, also links their masters with their own (human) species. Put otherwise, the Huaulu implicitly recognize a universal human component in themselves by implicitly recognizing that this component is present in their dogs, or cats, or chickens, since these are essentially defined as creatures that exist only in association with humans.

Because all individuals of a species that exists in an exclusively domesticated state are equivalent to one another in being fed by humans, feeding one individual establishes a relationship with all others. In contrast, feeding some individuals of a wild species can have no such effect. The universal, in this case, is not in agreement with the particular. The unfed members of the species are not interchangeable with the fed ones. In sum, when the Huaulu say, "we do not feed on them because we feed them," the referent of the second *them* is particular in the case of both wild and domesticated species, but the first *them* refers to a universal (the species as a whole) in the case of domesticated species and to a particular (the individuals fed) in the case of wild species.

This contrast between intrinsically wild and intrinsically domesticated species is made indubitable by the different extensions of the inedibility taboo attached to them, but it is not translated into verbal categories. The asymmetry is thus given a practical, but not a lexical, reality. This is a frequent phenomenon in the Huaulu taboo system. Indeed, we have seen that the contrast human/animal is more clearly sustained by a number of important taboos (such as the one on putting clothes on any animal, wild or domesticated) than by verbal categorization. Notions are sustained by taboos, and not just by words. And why not, since, after all, speech is a kind of practice, just like eating, dressing, and so on? One practice is just as good as another.

An additional qualification of the principle "if we feed them, we do not eat them" concerns birds. The Huaulu often capture birds, which they then keep in their homes until the birds die or are sold. The individual animals thus move from the category of wild to that of "fed." Yet it may happen that they are eaten if they die in captivity.[61] Only birds that have been kept as pets for a long time or who have oracular powers (as certain species are often said to) are never eaten.[62] How is it possible to explain the potential exclusion of birds from the principle "if we feed them, we do not eat them"?

The reason for this exclusion is that the principle presupposes a tacit parameter. Not all animals have the same potential for becoming social, for being assimilated to persons. Certain species are intrinsically closer to humans. This is usually the case of mammals or other large animals in which anthropomorphic or sociomorphic characters can be recognized. A consequence of this closeness is that these animals can be more easily individualized and thus integrated, through the act of feeding, to the feeder and his community, and at the same time be separated from the other members of their species that remain wild.

But birds are not easily individualized, besides being less anthropomorphic than all other animals that may be "fed" by the Huaulu. This is one reason a fed bird still tends to be seen as a member of its original "community" rather than as a member of the community of its human feeder. Another reason is that birds, in contrast with fully domesticated animals (dogs, cats, and chickens), are not usually fed with leftovers of human meals, but with their habitual food in the wild state, namely raw fruits (especially bananas).[63] They cannot, therefore, be viewed as true commensals of their masters. Their relationship is much more distant than the one established through the fireplace. This matches their only partial integration into Huaulu society.

We are beginning to see that the apparent simplicity of the statement "if we feed them, we do not eat them" hides presuppositions which vastly complicate its actual functioning. Moreover, as I have already mentioned, more than feeding is involved in making raised animals taboo. In fact, feeding is less the single principle from which inedibility and other taboos derive than a kind of shorthand for all the significant relations between the Huaulu and the animals they keep. Just as commensality is often a cipher for the totality of social relations among humans, so "feeding" an animal may be, as here, a metonymy (but also a metaphor) for all its consequences—that is, for the life that master and animal share. This life has different characteristics and different intensities—and thus also different outcomes with regard to taboo—with different animal species. Let us look, then, at some of these differences (and similarities) as they concern the three domesticated species: dog, cat, and chicken.

Dogs

The dog is the object of the strongest taboos, for it is the animal closest to humans, particularly human males as hunters. This is only to be expected in a society of passionate hunters, for whom a faithful and combative dog, a dog that "bites game" (ia koto peni), is the most valued companion.[64] I was repeatedly told: Ita makuwolira poto; sehu ita umanakira nika. Pohi manusia rahe lessiniam, "It [the dog] is extremely taboo for us, since we have raised/fed it. Moreover, it is mankind's residue." The latter statement is a reference to a myth according to which the dog was fashioned by the Creator from the residue of the substance with which he had fashioned the first human couple. The motif of the dog as residue of mankind has an obvious echo in the myth of Wassulau, in which the animal comes out of the giant's dismembered body last, after human ancestors who people Seram and adjacent islands. Both myths imply that dog and man have a common origin, although the dog, being a "residue" of its master or having emerged after him, is inferior to him. Furthermore, as Wassulau's myth indicates, the dog epitomizes the whole process of appropriation of wild animals, from their killing to their transformation into cooked food. It epitomizes, therefore, the main process that makes Huaulu social life possible—

another reason for considering the animal part of that social life and as inviolable as it.

The inviolability of the dog as a quasi-human member of Huaulu society is recognized by additional taboos that complete the one on its meat. It is taboo to strike the dog not only with a bush knife, but also with a mere broom, a bamboo poker, or especially (again an echo of Wassulau's myth) a firestick. It is also taboo to kick a dog and, for the women, to climb over one. The last taboo is meant to preserve the animal from menstrual pollution and from becoming contaminated with the alleged "heaviness/slowness" (monumonuam) of women, a most undesirable quality in the hunt. If these taboos are violated, the dogs cease to chase and bite animals, and become useless.

I was given innumerable anecdotes about the dire consequences of canine mistreatment. Laipassa, for instance, told me that when his daughter died, his heart was "chaotic," "uncontrollable," "mad" (haliku takaruwa). He diverted his fury and pain onto his favorite dog. The offended animal, who allegedly used "to kill three or four animals a day," never killed another one.

Hunters often let their favorite dogs eat from their own plates, but some people are understandably more squeamish about this form of commensality, especially if the dog is not theirs. Once, when Aipai was a child, his father's favorite dog took some food from his plate. Angered, Aipai struck the animal. His father was so incensed that he drew his bush knife and attempted to kill the boy. He was prevented by his other sons. At that, he cursed them all, promising that if they were going to eat any meat killed by a dog, their bellies would swell and they would eventually die. During my first stay in Huaulu, the first part of the curse had already taken its effect; when I returned for a second visit, the three brothers were all dead. People mentioned the story again and again to illustrate the seriousness of dog taboos, but also, perhaps, to wonder aloud about a hunter who loved his dog more than his sons—not an altogether infrequent phenomenon, I would say.

Dog-fancying is limited to those dogs who procure meat, however. About them, the Huaulu wax lyrical. Not only do their masters share their best food with them, caress and kiss them on the mouth, but they may also even sleep on the same mat.[65] But as soon as dogs fail to show courage and to bring home the bacon, this attitude changes brusquely. They are insulted, cursed, kicked, spat at, derided for their pathetic attempts to get back into the good graces of their masters. They are reminded that they eat without working, that they "steal" (i amana') food. And if these taunts are not enough to make them mend their ways, they are pointedly asked, "When are you going to die?" I dislike dogs, particularly in the scabby state in which they are often found in Huaulu, but even my heart of stone was moved to pity on certain occasions. I still remember with a pang, for instance, the miserable dog who attempted to slide silently toward his master to seize some scrap of food. The master had long seen it coming and was biding his time with sadistic pleasure. When the dog almost reached the scrap, all it got was a brutal blow, with assorted curses and this statement, delivered half in Indonesian, half in Huaulu: manusia maata', mau hidup kembali! "a dead man wants to live again!"

Even these insults and curses, however, indicate the degree to which dogs are humanized. In fact, insults and curses, along with mockery and laughter, are possible only with dogs and other tame animals, as I have mentioned. But then if these behaviors are as appropriate with dogs as they are with humans, it must be because dogs are semihuman, indeed are "residues of mankind" or are even metaphorically equated to humans, as in the above curse. If the disappointed Huaulu insult their dogs so cruelly, it is precisely because they feel betrayed by these inconstant and capricious companions, easily overcome by laziness and ill will. Our niceness to our pets is due to their being a mere appendage of ourselves, useless animals which we like precisely to the extent that they have not a will of their own, that we recognize an abyss between them and us. Our benevolence is that of the despot vis-à-vis his domestic slave.

The Huaulu attitude toward their dogs is quite different: it is molded on their attitude to fellow humans. Humans are liked and admired to the extent that they are good companions and good partners, that they give and do not just take. Dogs who cease to hunt, who are afraid of wild animals, are despised for their cowardice (the ultimate vice for a Huaulu) and for their parasitic behavior, just as certain humans are. Insulting them is not a mere discharge of ill humor; it is an attempt to remind them that they have to live up to their contract with humans. Indeed, it is believed that dogs can understand the language of their masters, although they cannot speak it. My skeptical reaction to this piece of information was often countered with the invitation to make a trial: "Let us just say in front of a dog: 'Let us kill that dog there.' You will see that it will run away immediately, because it can hear/understand (ia pulai)."

The implicit contract that is supposed to exist between the Huaulu and their dogs, with mutual obligations and duties, seems to be suggested by the disregard for and de facto suspension of some of the taboos protecting the dog from violence when the dog ceases to provide meat or, worse still, when it begins to steal it from the houses. In these cases, dogs may be beaten, even severely, and denied food. But there is a limit to the break in the relationship. Killing a dog remains an unspeakable crime, one that must be atoned for.[66] The following story was cited to me as an example of both crime and punishment. Long ago

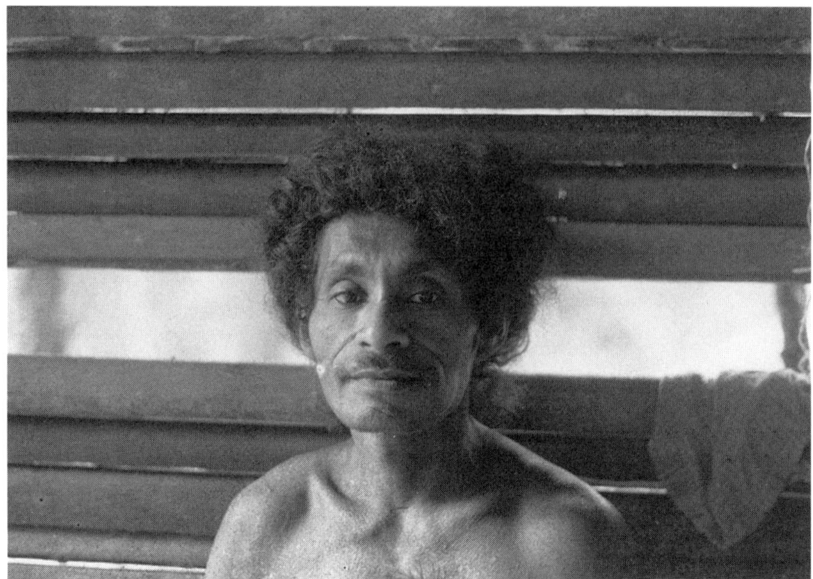

The head of the clan of wife-takers of the Huaulu, who follows some Islamic taboos and does not eat either wild boar or dog meat. 1972. (Photo by V. Valeri.)

some men from the junior branch of Tamatay (Tamatay kiitam) were so annoyed by the continual larcenies of a dog which belonged to another lineage (Allay) that they made "a trap" (susukaluam) to catch it. The dog was killed, but their punishment was not late in coming and has remained in force until this day. The members of Tamatay kiitam frequently suffer, and sometimes die, from asthma.[67] Because of this ancient crime, they are supposed never to eat the meat of animals killed with the help of dogs. They may eat only animals killed by traps. Having broken the contract with dogs by killing one, they cannot without danger attempt to benefit from the dogs' fulfillment of their side of the contract. One can receive only if one gives. Or better, receiving and giving are of the same kind: if one gives death, one receives death.

Even worse than killing a dog is eating it. This is recognized as one of the strongest taboos (ita rahe maquwoli potoam; ita maquwolire poto), and as such its violation is believed to bring about the death of the violator. It is also a taboo very much connected with the Huaulu identity as Memahem ("pagans"), and this with some reason, since the taboo indexes a whole mode of life, based on hunting, which is or was typical of the inland peoples of Seram and is rejected by the coastal cultures of Muslims and, to some extent, of Christians. Although Muslims too do not eat dog,[68] in the Huaulu view their difference, relative to Christians and pagans alike, resides in not eating pork. Similarly, although Christians are notorious antinomians and as such are reported to have no food taboos, they are differentially identified by the absence of one particular food taboo: that of dog meat. In sum, eating dog is for Christians the same thing as not eating it for pagans, and as not eating pork for Muslims. This explains why in the Huaulu view, but also to some extent in that of their Christianized mountain neighbors, a meal of dog meat marks—indeed, contributes ritually to bringing about—conversion to Christianity, a bit in the way that a meal of pork marked assimilation for the nineteenth-century Jew in Europe.[69]

According to my informants only four Huaulu ever ate dog meat, all of them on the coast, and at the instigation of people from Openg who had become Christians. Three of them died shortly afterwards. The fourth one, who claimed to have eaten dog meat "to feel how it tasted," became a living dead—paralytic and unable to provide food for himself.[70] Their memory is a permanent warning of the dire consequences of disregarding the taboo on dog meat.

Cats

Since it is also raised by the Huaulu, the cat is strictly taboo for them to eat. Like the dog, the cat is allowed to enter the houses and to move more or less freely inside them. The attitude toward the cat is, however, very different from that toward the dog. In fact the two animals are constantly contrasted in the informal narratives of everyday life and in the formal ones that are codified by the tradition. To take just one example, one of my friends, Pitere, a great hunter and dog lover, used to contrast two ideal situations. The first, and positive, one was summarized by the dictum: wassuem tutu utune u weti ipiem utuna, "if you have one hundred dogs, you may process one hundred sago palms"; that is to say, the dogs will procure you so much meat that you will have to produce an enormous amount of sago starch to eat with the meat. The second, and horrifyingly negative situation, was defined by a hundred cats and no dogs. This situation, according to Pitere, occurred in Tolatefata, a small settlement on the coast where his sister lived and waged a losing battle against the hundred cats who kept stealing the little meat she and her husband managed to procure.

A tall tale, but it makes perfectly clear that what the Huaulu object to in the cat is its "thieving" nature. Just like the dog that is no good, the cat consumes meat but does not produce it, in addition to being cleverer than the dog at stealing it. Under the circumstances, it is not surprising that few Huaulu keep cats. Or rather, no man raises cats, but a few women do, in order to keep the mouse population under control. For the "pact" between the cat and the Huaulu, a pact that makes them grudgingly accept it as a member of their society, although a lesser one than the dog, obligates the cat to hunt for mice so as to protect the Huaulu food supply. Unfortunately cats never seem happy with eating only mice, and many a cat has fallen victim to the wrath of the aggrieved meat owner. Nevertheless, I do not have any examples of people killing the family cat; only stranger cats, caught red-pawed at the meat basket, may be dispatched.

Contrary to the dog, then, the cat may be killed if it violates its side of the contract that binds it to the Huaulu, but like the dog it may not be eaten without serious consequences. Opinions differ, however, as to their seriousness: according to some people, death strikes the eater of cat meat as often as that of dog meat, unless he or she prays to the ancestors to intercede; according to others, the cat-eater may expect to get away with a mere case of "double breath" (that is, shortness of breath or asthma), just like those who kill dogs but do not eat them. The lesser severity of the cat taboo indicates the lower status of the cat in Huaulu society; still, the existence of the taboo demonstrates that feeding an animal and allowing it to live permanently in one's house, and thus also in the village, turns it into a person, at least to the extent that it cannot be treated as the ultimate thing—food.

While both dog and cat may be considered house members of a sort, their activities give them different relationships with it. From one point of view, the dog is a more intimate member of the house than the cat. But from another, it is less of a house animal than the cat, owing to its being the quintessential hunter, and thus also its association with the forest. This contrast obviously parallels that of man and woman, but also that of adult and baby or small child, since the latter are hardly allowed to leave the house or to crawl or walk on the ground, especially after dusk. The contrast between the adult dog as a forest being and the cat of all ages as a domestic one is made quite apparent by their differential treatment at death. The cat must be buried pale lohu, that is, in the ground under the house (which is on stilts) or in the ground on which a house formerly stood. To do otherwise is maquwoli. This treatment is identical to that reserved for a puppy dog which has died before being able to walk out of the house. In contrast, adult dogs must be exposed in the forest. Those which have received the title of kapitane (war leader) because of the amount of game they have killed are put on a small platform built on the branches of a tree. Common dogs are simply left on the branch of some tree or thrown under a bush.

There are some striking analogies between these rules and those that concern the disposal of human bodies. Human babies are totally domestic beings, and as such they are buried "under the house" (pale lohu) just like cats and puppy dogs. Adult human males, who as hunters are associated with the forest besides being associated with their houses, should be exposed in the forest, in a manner similar to that of the best hunting dogs. They are put in the hollow of a tree or on a platform built on its branches. The bodies of women are also disposed of in the forest, but by burial, in a lower position that can be compared with that of inferior dogs.

These various parallelisms suggest that the cat and the dog are part of Huaulu society as symbolic, and not just practical, help: they help the Huaulu to think about themselves and to classify their relations with one another. Indeed, it seems clear that, just as in Bachelard's words, "les choses mettent en ordre nos idées," and "les matières élémentaires mettent en ordre nos rêves,"[71] animals, and domestic animals in particular, put social categories in order. This ordering function is best displayed by the chickens, to which I now turn.

Chickens

"Chickens" (maulohuem) are on a very different level from dog and cat, and I mean this literally: they are never allowed into the house, and they live on the ground under it, freely roaming in the village and in its outskirts. Only at night do some householders let the chicken sit on perches under the outer edge of the roof's house, so as to protect them from predators such as pythons and civets. However, it is more usual, especially nowadays, to build coops for them under the house or close by it. Chickens, then, do not live with humans; they either have their own "houses" or perch on trees wherever they can find them. Furthermore, they feed on worms, insects, excrement, and small reptiles even more than on leftovers from human meals thrown through the split bamboo floors. For the latter, they compete with the "bad" dogs who are not admitted to their master's repast. Indeed, an unwelcome aspect of a Huaulu meal is that as soon as one sits down to it in the kitchen, dogs and chicken assemble under the split bamboo floor, and noisily fight each other even before the scraps start falling, although it must be admitted that this greatly simplifies the disposal of refuse.

Because they do not live in the house and are not necessarily or exclusively dependent on human leftovers for their food, chickens are not individually integrated into human households in the manner of dogs and cats. They maintain their own autonomous social life, although it is a life located in the village and taking place almost constantly under human eyes. It is precisely because they form a parallel society, in which Huaulu society mirrors itself in recognition and revulsion, that chickens come to be treated as fellow citizens of a sort. In contrast with dogs and cats, their letters of naturalization are obtained almost entirely on cognitive and imaginative grounds.

I am a person who likes to talk, but in Huaulu, a society of fast talkers, I have had to listen a lot. So many notions of Huaulu culture have impressed themselves on my mind even before I noticed them, because so many aimless conversations invisibly turned around them. How many times have I seen a chat shifting—because of an increase in the incessant gallinaceous clamor accompanying, like a *basso continuo,* the Huaulu day—to courtyard subjects: the ardor with which that rooster was pursuing a hen, or the bellicose spirit of that other, who had just picked a fight with a rival, or the alarmed but tough demeanor of a mature hen escorting her chicks to a safe feeding spot. Some men would even lean from the parapet of their verandas to incite two cocks sparring with each other, and then, when the less-spirited animal would flee from the onslaught of its more robust adversary, would laugh delightedly and pursue it with derisive comments. Then, the excitement subsided, the conversation would return to its ordinary, lazy flow. Little by little, as the days went by, I began realizing that chickens provided the otiose Huaulu with constant potential for spectacle, with dramas suddenly arising and picking up speed, only to peter out again in the average hum of the everyday. It became clear that chickens were fascinating to them for the same reason that the Huaulu were becoming fascinating to me, reacting to their reactions and influenced by the direction of their talk: because the chickens enacted as in an animal fable the great play of Huaulu passions—the violent fights and competitions of males, the motherliness of females, the lecherous pursuits of one sex and the somewhat dubious coyness of the other.

The society of chickens presents the Huaulu, in their words, with a particularly stark and simplified, but extraordinarily living, metaphor of one basic dimension of their own society: gender. Cocks symbolize the qualities attributed to men, or the failure to live up to the image of maleness constructed with those qualities—namely force, combativeness, courage, and the ability to defeat other males and to force females into submission (sexual submission being here the prototype of all others). Hens symbolize the qualities attributed to women: fertility, care for offspring, submissiveness with an element of resistance, and also excessive "cackling." Being animal, and being without other qualities which characterize humans and their society and which soften the above contrasts, cocks and hens present a caricatural image of gender. But it is precisely the laughter that they elicit that helps the Huaulu put some distance between themselves and the crude images of man and woman with which they clearly identify. Chickens, by caricaturing humans, allow them to be more human than they would otherwise be. There is more to chickens than this, however.

I have often wondered why Huaulu do not have, as so many other Indonesians do, formal cockfights.[72] The reason is that they prefer to have informal or rather "natural" ones. Cocks are not incited to fight in the context of human rules and for human ends. They are not reduced to appendices of individual human owners, but are allowed to have a social life of their own, and it is in this social life that the fights they choose to pick are occasionally significant to the Huaulu. This Huaulu difference in the symbolic use of cocks reflects other differences. It reflects, first and foremost, a characteristic attitude toward society itself, or, what amounts to the same thing, it reflects the specific tenor of Huaulu society. It is a society with a hierarchical ideal, but also one with an ideal of individual autonomy. The tension between the two is never resolved[73] and gives Huaulu life a peculiar tone and flow: sudden and exciting flare-ups occasionally take shape against the dull background of everyday life, where people go their own way or cautiously avoid confrontation. It is as if Huaulu men could not long be close to one another without having to confront the issue of their relative status, and therefore fight it out, one way or another.

The spectacle of chicken social life is very reminiscent of this unspoken, if crucial, aspect of Huaulu social life. Ordinarily cocks disperse over the space of the village, each watching his hens and haughtily eyeing other males from afar. But suddenly the play of checks and balances that keeps the cocks apart cannot be sustained: a hen seems to wander off into enemy territory; two cocks suddenly find themselves too close, a confrontation occurs, the outcome of which is either a clear situation of inequality (with one cock fleeing or badly battered) or, more often, a disengagement that reproduces the initial situation. All of this is a crude correlate of certain aspects of the relations between Huaulu men or between male-dominated groups—aspects predicated on competition and confrontation, often with women as the stakes. The metaphoric relation between gallinaceous social life and human social life remains unspoken, of course, (otherwise it would lose much of its force and efficacy), but its presence is indicated in speech by the frequent use of the bantam as a figure of the male human fighter and of the cockfight as an image of the war dance or of combat. Moreover, a metonymic relation between fighting cocks and fighting men also exists: the male ceremonial headdress in such occasions as dance and war, or even during the competitive song exchanges which used to take place until recently at weddings, includes the caudal feathers of cocks.

As I have indicated, the metaphoric use of chicken society not only includes elements of similarity with human society; its efficacy depends on elements of contrast as well. The dimension of contrast is especially emphasized in one symbolic valence of chickens: they stand for indiscriminate mating, for "incest." This disregard for a fundamental taboo makes them definitely nonhuman. Yet here again the contrast of chicken and human would not be efficacious if an element of similarity were not present as well, or more exactly, if the lapse into incest were not so frequent among humans, and not only in their fantasy lives. The "chickenization" of incest, if I may call it that, is a persuasive device for repressing incest in humans.[74]

Chickens are thus part of a dialectic of humanization which requires a conflicting treatment of animals, especially of those that live in close contact with humans. On the one hand, their human characters are emphasized, until these animals become living caricatures of man; on the other hand, they are animalized even further, to help bring about a radical contrast between the categories of human and animal. Ultimately, then, the humanization of domestic or paradomestic animals should not deceive us; it is just one side of the process that creates humankind by creating an artificial gulf between animals and humans.

As far as chickens are concerned, this dialectic is reflected in a number of myths. One myth, in particular, confirms that chickens evoke incest and thus also the necessity to overcome it in order to be fully human. The protagonists of this myth are two pairs in which the characters of chicken and human are combined: a brother-sister pair on earth and a brother-sister pair in heaven. The earthly brother overcomes the potentially incestuous relationship with his sister by offering her to his celestial counterpart. In exchange, he receives a piece of the moon, which is his counterpart's sister. He then returns to earth, where he is able to marry exogamously by offering the precious object as bridewealth. Before doing that, he cuts in two the ladder connecting heaven and earth, in order to prevent his excessively loving sister from following him and leaving her husband in heaven. "Chickenly" love between brother and sister is thus overcome, especially by the brother, and the two are separated as radically as heaven and earth and, one feels bound to add (since the descendants of the half-chicken man are entirely human), as humans and chickens.

Chickens are also significant in Huaulu social life as time markers. More specifically, they are connected with the transitional hours between night and day. Dawn is indicated by the expression maulohuam kessia, "the chicken comes down [from its perch]," whereas the onset of night is marked by the opposite movement: maulohuam saa, "the chicken goes up [on its perch]." Also, the cock crows three times, and always at the same hour (as I can testify, having checked it on my watch on many a sleepless night), in the latter part of the night and before dawn, as if to remind humans, and perhaps even to guarantee, that the sun will return. No wonder, then, that a mythological connection between cocks and sun exists. Indeed, in the myth that I have just mentioned, the heavenly rooster/brother is almost certainly connected with the sun, since his sister is the moon, and the Huaulu believe that sun and moon are brother and sister. Further evidence for the connection of rooster and sun is provided by the magical object which grants the

Huaulu warriors success in headhunting and war. This is the already mentioned Leautuam (seed/principle of the sun), whose name sufficiently indicates its solar origin, an origin which also seems to imply origin from a celestial rooster, because the Leautuam comes attached to the taboo on eating chicken.

The chicken's connection with sunset and sunrise explains why the animal is also involved in the dialectic of life and death. According to the myth, the earliest ancestors lived in a land where death and decrepitude had not yet become irreversible. When somebody died the survivors put a multicolored hen at the head of the corpse and a red rooster at his feet. First the hen "cackled" (tutukoko), then the rooster "crowed" (rukule), and this five times. At last the dead rose, completely rejuvenated. Death was still a form of sleep from which humans woke up, thanks to the cackling and crowing of friendly chickens. But one day Irreversible Death appeared in the form of a gigantic eagle that devoured entire villages. The ancestors decided to flee it by taking to the sea and searching for a land where the monster had not yet arrived. When ready to cast off, they discovered their chickens' disappearance. They had to wait for them to show up. The delay allowed Death to catch up with them. In sum, it is because they stuck to their chickens, these markers of time, that the ancestors fell victim to time's final injury: death.[75]

It is my contention that the taboo on eating chickens and their eggs has its roots in all the above associations and significations. But then an issue arises: How does this claim relate to the reasons for the taboo actually given by the Huaulu? Although the chickens generically belong to the category of "fed" animals, the principle "if we feed them, we do not feed on them" is not usually invoked to account specifically for the taboo on their meat—especially nowadays, for reasons that will become clear in a moment. Some people say that chickens are not eaten in gratitude for the benefits of resuscitation and rejuvenation which they bestowed in ancient times, but the most popular and compelling explanation is a different one.

Chicken meat is said to be maquwoli because eating it has some very specific consequences. If men eat it, they will cease to be able to kill in war; if women eat it, they will be afflicted with poture melekae, "long menstruation" (i.e. dysmenorrhea); and if shamans eat it, their sewa or spirit familiars[76] will forsake them. These three consequences (and thus also motivations for not eating chicken) are interconnected. The second is the logical extension of the first one, since women are afflicted with long menstrual bleedings which impair their fertility whenever they come in contact (through food, touch, sight, or even speech) with the forbidden domain of male headhunting. As for the third, it is probably the logical extension of the second: a majority of the shamanic sewa are female and thus follow women's taboos.[77] They would refuse to enter the shaman's body if chicken meat had contributed to making it.

In sum, chickens are said to be taboo because of their connection, direct or indirect, with the principle of successful killing of humans in war or headhunting (the two activities imply each other in Huaulu thought). The principle itself is given a tangible form by the already mentioned Leautuam, which has many symbolic associations with chickens. This is why the taboo on eating chicken is also explained with the argument that it is incompatible with the use of the Leautuam's powers for headhunting purposes.

The Huaulu's own account of the taboo on eating chicken also explains why the taboo ceased to be followed by all men since the mid-sixties but continues to be followed by all women and all shamans. As a man put it to me: "[In the past] if we ate chicken, we ceased to be able to kill (hita; lit., 'to cut with a machete'). But nowadays we have stopped killing because we are afraid of being caught by the police and jailed. Therefore, we have said to ourselves: 'We may as well eat it [chicken].'" Some men, though, still follow the taboo because they have not renounced headhunting in their heart of hearts and still hope to be able to practice it one day. So it is not the rule that has changed, but the set of circumstances that require its application by men. However, circumstances have not changed for women, who still want to have children and are expected to produce them in great numbers. And shamans still want to be possessed by their sewa, of course.

It must also be said that in the eighties the eating of chicken had become a battleground between traditionalists and "modernizers" (if the term is not too extreme).[78] The latter camp was mostly represented by the kamara (headman), who, having lived most of his life on the coast, had a more critical attitude toward taboo than the average Huaulu.[79] During one of his rare visits to the mountain village where I resided, the kamara attempted to spread the eating of chickens among men (no question of doing so among women) by founding a sort of chicken-eating society, of which I was immediately made an honorary member, much to my annoyance. The members of the society were supposed to put several thousand rupiahs each in a common fund which was used to buy chickens from the villagers who owned them. Then the kamara's wife would cook the meat and some rice for the members of the society. A number of men, especially young ones, participated. But most men stayed away, either because they claimed that the taboo was still in force or because they said that chicken meat disgusted them (i makapoaire), although some used lack of money as a pretext. I myself ate fish on purpose before going to the only banquet I attended, since this allowed me to decline eating chicken on the principle that fish cannot be mixed with fowl. I thus managed to stand by the tradition while at the same time avoid offending the kamara (who, however, attempted to persuade me that I ran no risk).

The kamara's attempt at proselytizing was extreme, and his taste for chicken meat may have had something to do with it. Nevertheless, it does seem likely that the contemporary emphasis on headhunting as a motive for the taboo will contribute to undermining it in the long run and may even result from a more or less conscious desire to get rid of it. But then the emphasizing of this motive would not have been possible if—for reasons that I hope to have made sufficiently clear—the chickens had not provided the weakest instantiation of the more general principle for not eating them; that is, "if we feed them, we do not feed on them."

In any case, the basic issue remains to be tackled: Why is it that in Huaulu[80] conception all the associations which motivate the chicken's taboo status are reduced to an association with headhunting or rather with its personification—the Leautuam?

One part of this question can be answered easily enough. Headhunting is the activity which condenses all or most of those associations. It is directly predicated on the necessary interdependence of life and death, since it is said to consist in feeding the Leautuam, the ancestors, and Lahatala with "human flesh," in order to avoid their feeding on the flesh of the Huaulu. It implies a strong emphasis on all the male attributes represented by the roosters, and at the same time it makes possible the female fertility that is displayed in exaggerated form by the hens. Indeed, the interdependence of killing and fertility—deemed as unproven by some anthropologists of the hypercritical school[81]—finds its expression in the idea that the Leautuam, a living phallus, becomes particularly hard, and thus sexually potent, when receiving a head. Everything happens as if the symbolic castration of an enemy turns into the symbolic raising of the collective phallus of Huaulu men.[82]

But there is another part to this question which is somewhat less easy to answer. We have seen that rooster and hen stand to each other as certain attributes of man and woman in exaggerated form. We should expect, then, the taboo on chicken to be formulated in ways that take this correspondence into account. In other words, we should expect some kind of explanation that would amount to saying that men and women cannot eat chicken because they cannot eat themselves or the opposite sex, or that one cannot threaten the intangibility of the male/female opposition by threatening the intangibility of the animals that perpetuate it by constantly presenting it to consciousness. Instead of this, we find that the taboo is justified only through the rooster, so to speak. In other words, although the significations that go into the tabooing of the chicken include female components, these are wholly subordinated to and encompassed by the male element. It is because women cannot enter into contact with what is basically a male animal—since it stands for the most male of all activities and indeed for the phallus itself—that they do not eat its meat in its male and female forms.

Perhaps the answer to this conundrum lies precisely in the caricatural nature of the chickens' relationship to humans. Roosters are exaggerated males just as hens are exaggerated females. But most important, what appears as truly exaggerated in chickens is gender asymmetry itself. Roosters dominate hens to a degree that is unknown between man and woman, but which Huaulu men imagine they approximate when they engage in headhunting. It seems possible, then, to claim that chickens do not reflect male-female relations in the human world as much as they allow men to inflect those relations in a way that makes them much more asymmetric, at least in the context of headhunting and its related cults and cultual objects. Headhunting allows men to claim to be the ultimate authors of female fertility. This is also why it allows them to obliterate the direct symbolic connections between women and hens. Man the headhunter manages to monopolize all the meanings carried by hens and bantams and thus to emphasize the bantam over the hen as he emphasizes the man over the woman. The taboo on chicken reduces, in effect, women (as givers of life) to appendices of men (as givers of death). And even in the transformed way which is gaining ground today, with only men being allowed to eat chicken, the taboo reproduces that asymmetry. In fact, it makes it worse, because it turns male supremacy into mere privilege, unpaid for by taboo and sacrificial warfare.

One question may have arisen in the mind of the reader. Dogs and cats are taboo because they are part of the inner core of Huaulu society, and chickens are taboo because their society is a metaphor for some fundamental features of Huaulu social life. But dogs and cats are useful in more than symbolic ways. Is the symbolic "utility" of chickens sufficient to explain why they are kept? To us, chickens are fundamentally utilitarian animals: there is something paradoxical in the idea of keeping them for purely aesthetic or moral reasons. I wish to reassure the utilitarian-minded: chickens and their eggs do have a nonsymbolic use in Huaulu—they are often sold to strangers. The taboo on the meat of any village animal is valid only for the Huaulu. Hence, not only chickens may be sold to strangers, but also wild pigs and cassowaries which, having been captured when very small, are sometimes raised for sale. The implicit rationale for this is that although these animals have become, in different degrees and forms, part of Huaulu society, they are not part of the society of the buyer. More to the point, Huaulu taboos are not conceived as rules of universal validity; piapia pohi eme rahe maquwoliem, "each person has his or her own taboos," is a recurrent maxim.[83] If some stranger is prepared to buy raised animals, it means that they are not taboo for him, and there is nothing wrong with the Huaulu taking advantage of it.[84]

Having reassured the utilitarian-minded, I must upset them again, however. For by all accounts the selling or giving away of chickens was of little significance in the past. Even today it does not play a great role in the mountain village, nor can it, because of the village's isolation. It makes more utilitarian sense to raise chickens in the coastal settlements, but in fact they are not as frequently kept there as on the mountain, perhaps because they are more easily stolen or wander off to other villages. Thus, even today it seems hardly possible to justify the keeping of chickens on utilitarian grounds. The Huaulu's own attitude seems to be that chickens are a necessary appendage to any village, that they are part of the way things have been since the beginning of times. Thus, no Huaulu would think of eliminating chickens simply because there are not enough buyers around. Rather, their interest in establishing property claims on specific animals and taking some care of them waxes or wanes with the need to make cash. People (particularly youngsters) who often go to the coast, where there is a market for chickens, tend to develop a more proprietory relationship with the animals that they can claim as their own. This accounts for the increase in chicken coops that I have observed since communication with the coast has become more frequent (that is, since the late eighties).

That chickens are conceived as a necessary part of society, more than as a mere source of income, is at any rate confirmed by many tales. For instance, when describing the utter destruction of a village by the enemy, narrators of a lisam (a war story) never fail to use the rhetorical formula "he did not leave a man alive, a dog alive, a chicken alive" (ia repi manusia esassi, wasu esassi, maulohu esassi), as if chickens and dogs were as much an intrinsic part of the village as humans. The formula also reflects an actual practice: Huaulu wars were not waged for exploitation but for extermination. And extermination of the enemy went with that of the animals which lived in association with him. Chicken-stealing is not the Huaulu idea of bravery. Only head-stealing (it is indeed called so: ita amana', "we steal [heads]") qualifies as such. Another telling confirmation of the logical (I should say mythological) connection of chickens and Huaulu social life is provided by the already mentioned episode of the origin myth in which the ancestors feel compelled to wait for their chickens before migrating.

The above evidence indicates that the Huaulu keep their chickens mostly for their symbolic and commemorative use, as it developed in their shared life through the centuries. Although these symbolic uses are not viewed as incompatible with the use of chickens as commodities to be disposed of outside the community, the raising of chickens in the past is represented as totally nonutilitarian. The same is true of the raising of animals such as feral pigs, cassowaries, and parrots.[85] In the distant past, the time depicted in epic narratives, these animals were occasionally captured and raised to become pets or mascots or, in the case of some parrots, as house guardians (owing to their alleged ability to foresee the arrival of strangers, that is, potential or actual enemies). A parrot and more frequently a pig could become so identified with a village that killing it was a serious insult. Indeed, it is said that such mascot pigs were killed and eaten by enemy kapitane in order to put their owners to shame and force them into a retaliatory war. Pig-raising was thus part of the competition among autonomous groups: being able to keep a raised pig, to avenge its killing, and/or to get away with killing the pig of another group were all important sources of lala, "name" (or, as we would say, "honor"). Nowadays, however, the raising of pigs is exceedingly rare. I witnessed only one case, in 1988, in the coastal settlement of Alakamat. It was raised for sale by a man whose wife was a former Christian from the southern coast of Seram.[86]

Names

Naming practices provide additional evidence for the symbolic status of dogs, cats, and chickens. Briefly put, all dogs are individually named, no cat receives a proper name, and a few chickens sometimes receive one. These differences confirm some of the points already made and allow me to expand on them. Dogs are the animals most closely integrated into human society: like their human masters, they participate in it as individuals. The main sign of individuality is the possession of a proper name. This is precisely why they all receive one. But dogs are inferior members of human society; they retain their animality even if more humanity is granted to them than to any other animal. Therefore, their names cannot be interchangeable with those of humans. Although a name that has never been used before may be bestowed on either dog or human, once it is given to one it is absolutely taboo to give it to the other. It is in any case rare that a name is equally apt for human and dog, since dog names usually have distinctive features of their own.[87]

Three of these features are particularly important: dog names evoke either exceptional force, or important events of the external world affecting Huaulu society, or, more rarely, the animal's place of birth (especially if it is a foreign village). Two typical examples of the first group of names are Motoro (motor boat) and Kotalima (five fortified villages). The first is obviously a new name; it is supposed to endow the dog with the speed of a motorboat. The second name is ancient; it is composed of a noun (kota, "fortified village") that evokes strength and of a numeral (lima, "five"), which indexes the political moiety (Lima), to which the Huaulu belong and which is supposed to have the upper hand over the opposite moiety (Siwa, "Nine").[88]

Interesting examples of the second group of dog names are Karyawan, Repelita, Pe-de-i, Pemilu, Makan Bersama. The common feature of all these names is that they come from Bahasa Indonesia, the language of the Indonesian state. The first name, Karyawan, means "white-collar worker." It was first given to a dog to commemorate the brief sojourn in Huaulu of a group of self-styled "white-collar workers" who used the dazzle of their status to acquire some cockatoos dirt-cheap (these parrots fetch a very high price in Jakarta or even in Ambon). Probably, the name was also bestowed to commemorate the very fact of having learned this fancy title, which the Huaulu had not heard before. But I also suspect that the title did not appear as fancy to them as their guests had hoped, since its bestowal on a dog rather than on a child implied a certain degree of sarcasm. Repelita is an acronym which stands for Rencana Pembangunan Lima Tahun, Indonesia's "Five-Year Development Plan," in the name of which the Huaulu have had to endure a certain number of local "projects," which usually entailed hard (and unrewarded or barely rewarded) labor. Pemilu is an acronym for Pemilihan Umum, "General Election," another nuisance which occurred at the time the dog was named. Pe-de-i is the acronym of Partai Demokrasi Indonesia. It commemorates the visit of a candidate from that party which received no votes in Huaulu, where the obligatory government party (Golkar) fetched a solid 100 percent.[89] Finally, the name Makan Bersama "eating together," was given to a dog in ironic commemoration of a district officer's policy to force the Huaulu to give up exclusive rights to their extensive sago groves on the Salawai River and to share them with their coastal neighbors from Sawai—a policy much opposed by the Huaulu and which brought them on the verge of war with Sawai in 1985.

There is not much need to give examples of the third group of dog names, but I will quote two: Kabau (from Kabauhari, a village east of Huaulu) and Sapulewa (from a river near which the dog that bore the name was born, at the time its proprietor lived there). All these names belong to those who first gave them and to their descendants. Thus, over time they become lineage property. With the passage of generations, the original meaning of the name is usually forgotten. As a result many of the ancestral names for dogs have only a diacritical value at present: they index the lineage to which the proprietor of the dog belongs. A fourth group of dog names—that is, names that are traditional in a lineage—may thus be taken into account. But because several of the traditional names whose meaning is still remembered refer to strength or a memorable event, or a place, it seems likely that in the past as nowadays these were the principal referents of dog names and thus that the first three groups I have enumerated are really the principal ones. Be this as it may, all traditional dog names are by definition evocative of effectiveness in the hunt, because, whatever their original meanings, only names of dogs that "bit a lot of game" have been given again and again. Indeed the standard answer I received whenever I asked why a traditional name was bestowed on a dog was that it was originally borne by a dog very good at killing game, and it was hoped that in bestowing it on a new dog, the latter would prove equally effective. Dogs named after a famous forebear may prove a failure, however. When this happens again and again, the name becomes devalued, and a completely new name may have to be found.

Whether it is motivated by the desire to transfer strength from an object or an event to the dog or by the desire to commemorate an event or a place, dog names seem to share a common reference to a world external to Huaulu society and yet not quite foreign to it. The names of the second group are the most interesting from this point of view: they turn the dogs into embodied chronicles of Huaulu relations with the Indonesian nation-state, its policies, and its representatives. But many of the names of the first group (e.g. Motoro) or of the third (e.g. Kabau) also evoke a world spatially and socially intermediate between the extremely distant and the extremely close, between absolute difference and absolute identity. These various forms of intermediateness seem to be analogically related to the intermediateness of the dog itself. The dog is the animal closest to human society as conceived by the Huaulu, as we have seen. Yet it does not enjoy full membership in that society, because it is not fully human, only a "residue of mankind."

Analogously, the social worlds adjacent to Huaulu society are in a sense part of it, because they communicate with it and influence it. A society's conceptual boundaries do not coincide with its physical ones, but they are determined by power relations. Thus, insofar as external human agents impinge on Huaulu society by producing powerful events that it must undergo (e.g. national elections) or powerful artifacts that it desires and attempts to incorporate symbolically (e.g. motorboats), or by furnishing means (such as the hunting dogs themselves, when they are bought from abroad) to perpetuate Huaulu social life, they are all implicitly seen as part of that life. But in another sense they are not part of it, because they escape its rules and often clash with its interests. They evoke, therefore, conflicting feelings: their power is respected and desired, and yet it is viewed as imperfectly human because imperfectly Huaulu, and in this sense as animallike. Giving the name Pemilu or Motoro to a dog, then, reflects both the recognition of an external human power and a certain scornful or ironic feeling vis-à-vis it—a sort of revenge for the sense of inadequacy or dependency it induces.[90]

While dogs are *individually* part of human society and yet not quite in it, chickens may be seen as part of it solely as a *species*, as we have seen. It is appropriate, then, that they are not individually named, with few exceptions. The exceptions, however, confirm the rule. Each lineage owns at least a pair of chicken names, one for a cock, one for a hen. These names, which may not be given separately, were originally those of the pair of magical (i.e. resuscitating) chickens, which lived with the more distant ancestors. But these ancestors, in turn, named their chickens "after their own village sites or the nearby mountains or streams" (i atemuire hini ninianiem, ulayem, waem) that served as landmarks and foraging grounds. Chickens, in sum, indexed the whole territorial counterpart of the ancient lineages. Since in those times each lineage lived alone in its own territory, it seems clear that just as nowadays the mass of nameless chickens stands for the multilineage village, so in the past the named chickens stood for the monolineage village. Furthermore, the named chickens are not named as individuals, but as a male-female couple. They form, in sum, an autonomous society in its minimal form. In this sense they are again similar to the nameless chickens, since like them they stand to the village as a society stands to another society. Finally, it must be kept in mind that in Huaulu theory the ancestors stand for all their descendants, and thus for a species or kind. Chickens named after ancestors are therefore equivalent to an entire kind. Moreover, this animal kind is the counterpart of a human one, that is, of the lineage issued from the original owners of the original chickens. By occasionally naming a pair of chickens after an original pair, then, present-day members of a lineage celebrate their own kind by celebrating its relationship with another kind—an animal one. They also commemorate names that evoke places on which they retain rights and that remind them of a time when each lineage lived autonomously in its own territory.[91] The essential point that named and unnamed chickens have in common is that both are linked to humans through place.

Chickens are, in a sense, the animal correlatives of the rootedness of a human group in its territory and especially in the site where its houses are situated. Chickens can be such correlatives because they offer the daily spectacle of a species always very close to a ground—the village ground—which they constantly and entirely occupy and from which they derive their sustenance. Chickens, then, occupy the village as a synecdoche of the wider territory at whose center the village lies—a fact made evident by the existence of chicken names referring either to village or to surrounding territory. They are the closest image of autochthony available to a people who does not claim autochthony, but the right of first occupation.

However different their cases are, dogs which receive ancestral names have one thing in common with named chickens: both implicitly index lineages parallel to the human lineages which own the right to bestow those names. Both, then, are genealogically suggestive instantiations of totemism in its Lévi-Straussian sense. Both reproduce a human-animal alliance of the past in the present. But on closer inspection the similarities between the two cases turn out to be less close than they seem at first. For the main purpose of a dog name, whatever its species associations (and we have seen that they are more varied than those of chickens), is to bestow on the dog some properties that it must possess as an individual: fierceness, propensity to "bite" game, and so on. Names of ancestral dogs are given with this purpose in mind, rather than with a purely commemorative or totemic one. Because the choice of an ancestral name is contingent on this purpose, its temporal distance from the present is largely irrelevant, and thus its species dimension (which, in Huaulu theory, is all the greater the older the name is) takes a backseat.[92]

In sum, while choices of names for chickens are past-oriented because they are species-oriented, and more precisely oriented toward a symbolic, almost totemic use of their species-being, the choice of names for dogs is present-oriented because dogs are appropriated by humans as individual agents producing concrete results, rather than as mere carriers of collective symbolic values, as species-beings. Even this contrast indicates that dogs are treated more as human beings than chickens are, because it is precisely *qua* individual agents that humans are considered members of society.[93]

As for cats, they form a somewhat intermediate case. As we have seen, the cat is an individual member of the household, like the dog, but maintains its own autonomy, like the chicken. Contrary to the chicken, however, it does not have an intense social activity, but appears to be a loner. Furthermore, its contribution to the household is not very important and is constantly undermined by its "thefts." This doubly antisocial (vis-à-vis humans and vis-à-vis other cats) individuality is disturbing to the Huaulu, and is the reason the cat is not given full recognition as a member of Huaulu society by the granting of a personal name. Cats are nameless individuals.[94]

Some Conclusions and Expansions

The analysis of the status of dog, cat, and chicken should have made it clear that major differences exist in their relationships with Huaulu society. The dog participates in Huaulu society as an individual, through its relations with a master and his household. The cat is a more autonomous loner who nevertheless lives in the house. The chicken participates in it through the contribution of its own autonomous social life. As is usually the case with all other birds, the individual is merged in the species.[95]

These differences in the social and conceptual position of the three animals account for the different intensity and character of the taboos attached to them. The most socially integrated and individualized of all three, that is the dog, is also the one that has the most numerous and the strictest taboos. In particular, besides being strictly taboo to eat, it cannot be killed or seriously harmed. In this sense, the dog is like a kinsman, who differs from a mere human in being intangible besides being inedible. Cat and chicken, in contrast, do not have the status of kinsmen, but that of humans who are not relatives, since, like them, they may not be eaten but may be killed. Nevertheless it seems that the recognition of individuality and domestic cohabitation give both cat and dog a privileged moral status which is denied to the chicken.

This is indicated by a significant difference in the way their taboos are formulated. As we have seen, the formula "If we feed them we do not feed on them" is routinely applied to dog and cat but much more rarely to the chicken. The taboo on the latter is usually justified by reference to specific dangers incurred in violating it: lack of success in war, dysmenorrhea, loss of shamanic powers. Of course, the negative consequences of violating the taboo on dog and cat can also be invoked to justify it. But it is striking that this is much less usual than in the case of chickens. The significance of this contrast should be immediately apparent. Dog and cat are said to be taboo in virtue of a principle which is moral in the sense that it is not dictated by an egoistic interest and that it shows a recognition of these animals' right to expect respect for their integrity, at least with regard to edibility. Chickens, instead, are usually defined as taboo in the more usual sense that it is dangerous to eat them. The lack of individuality and personality in chickens translates as a lesser concern for their rights and a greater concern for the eater's interests. In this respect, chickens are treated very much like most wild animals. This reaffirms their relative eccentricity: they are part of the village and yet also beyond it, as is made clear by the fact that chicken names, when they exist, are borrowed both from village sites and from surrounding landmarks. This intermediate status is, of course, reinforced by the essentially caricatural relationship that exists between the animal society of chickens and the human society of the Huaulu.

There are other, more hidden, traits which set dog and cat apart from chickens and which may contribute to explaining their much closer relationships with the Huaulu. One such trait is another consequence of their predatory character, besides the already mentioned ones of companionship, hunting, and keeping mice away from the house. As is well known, predators, together with apes, differ from all other animals but are similar to humans in that their eyes face forward.[96] Dogs and humans, cats and humans, are thus able to look each other in the eyes, and this—besides making understanding, or the illusion of it, possible among them—gives the animals something which we call the gaze—the gaze of a face—and which we feel is intrinsically human. If the eye is the mirror of the soul, then predators—especially those which, being mammal, are similar to humans in so many respects already—can be the mirrors of humans. Furthermore, a life of predation makes for cleverness: the dog and the cat are immensely more clever than the chicken, and as such humans tend to identify with them, besides being able to train them to do things on behalf of humans.[97]

"Cuddliness," another well-known trait in dog and cat, may also contribute to explaining the special favor the Huaulu show them. "In order to gain favor with human beings," Dekkers observes, "it is advisable to resemble a human being, in order to climb high up the top ten [species preferred as companions by humans worldwide] the best thing to do is to resemble a young human being, an infant. The ingredients were analysed by Konrad Lorenz as early as 1943; a round head with large eyes and a small nose, a round body with short legs and a nice soft skin."[98] We are genetically predisposed to be moved by such infantile features, it seems, because they remind us of our infants.

In Huaulu itself, the cuddliness factor is definitely more pronounced in the cat than in the dog. In other words, the cat seems to have certain characteristics of the pet,[99] although the dog too, especially the puppy dog, is occasionally treated as a pet by its master. It would be misleading, however, to consider dog and cat as substantially similar to our pets. The latter are characterized by a deliberate uselessness, whereas the Huaulu cat and especially the dog must also be useful; they are more fellow citizens than pets. Let it be noted, however, that usefulness does not mean mere utility. The Huaulu view of their dogs and cats is not crassly utilitarian; it is, rather, that the Huaulu associate them with the entire sociality and ethos involved in the activities in which they are useful (hunting, the preservation of meat, etc.). If anything, it is the bourgeois attitude to the pet which is crassly utilitarian—in negative form. Pets embody the cost of conspicuous waste; they are Veblenian servants, not fellow agents.

We have just touched on a difference between cat and dog which helps us to understand further why dog is associated with man and cat with woman. Insofar as the cat evokes the infant more than the dog does, and insofar as the care of infants is the main province of women, cats are more appropriate companions and totems for women than for men. Indeed, men affect a certain disdain for cats; one may even say that they have adopted their dogs' view of their traditional enemies. But there is another difference between cat and dog which reinforces their differential association with man and woman under Huaulu cultural conditions. Let the ethnologist quote the ethologist on this point:

> Both dogs and cats live a double life as pets. They see their owners as their parents, protectors who are always ready to feed them as if they were still puppies or kittens, even though they may be fully adult. As a result, many of their actions remain infantile throughout their lifespan. But at the same time they become sexual adults and, as they mature, develop the qualities of adult dogs and adult cats. And this is where they diverge. Mature dogs become loyal pack members, cats do not. So the adult domestic dog becomes doubly dependent, seeing its owner both as pseudo-parent and as pack leader. This has made it the ideal, devoted companion of mankind for over ten thousand years.
>
> The adult domestic cat, on the other hand, is dependent only when it acts as an "overgrown kitten." In its true adult mode it rapidly reverts to an independent, prowling hunter. To enjoy the company of a cat, therefore, we must be prepared to forgo our dominant pack leader role, and adopt a more modest position.[100]

Translated into the Huaulu situation, this analysis accounts for an important aspect of the association of men with dogs and women with cats. The dog offers men the experience of domination, which is one thing that differentiates men from women. The cat does not offer the same experience, and as such it is a more appropriate counterpart of women, who should not be in a dominant position. Women can enjoy powerlessness in their relationship with cats; men can enjoy power, willingly and even slavishly bestowed, in their relationship with dogs. Furthermore, this dimension of contrast between cat and dog correlates with the more overt dimension which, as I have shown, is at the center of the Huaulu's explicit characterization of these animals. Because they are pack animals that accept humans as their leaders, dogs' predatory instincts can be molded to serve human ends. Otherwise said, dogs can be taught to hunt for humans; male power over them is not an end in itself. In contrast, the individualistic cat can hunt only for itself, which also means that it may steal from humans instead of contributing meat to them. Hence the doglike enmity between man and cat can coexist with the more motherly feelings of women only as long as the cat's selfish hunting of mice happens to have useful side effects for the household's economy.

All the above adds to my earlier point—that life with the Huaulu charges dogs and cats with anthropomorphic characteristics—the new point that these animals could not live with the Huaulu if they were not naturally endowed with anthropomorphic characteristics to begin with. These natural and universal characteristics are not in contradiction to their cultural and particular ones; on the contrary, the latter clearly build on the former. In fact, the natural anthropomorphism of cat and dog must have been reinforced by thousands of years of life shared with humans. Culture and nature go hand in hand here, as is shown by the fact that dogs and cats have sought out humans as much as humans have sought them. It is reductive to view these and other domestic animals as passive and arbitrary recipients of human significations, for the very same anthropomorphic attributes that account for the human interest in these animals also account for the animals' acceptance of serving the interests of humans and living with them in the first place.

As for the other animals kept by the Huaulu—chickens and parrots[101]—it is striking that they all have one strongly anthropomorphic trait in common: they stand upright.[102] In addition, parrots bring food to their mouth with their paw, which therefore appears similar to the human hand.[103]

I have saved these more general traits common to Huaulu-kept animals and to their brethren worldwide for last for two reasons. The first is that their role in binding animal and human in Huaulu is more hypothetical than the role of the traits with which I have started. The second is that several of these general anthropomorphic traits are also found in wild animals that are taboo. This fact, besides strongly suggesting that the traits in question are indeed significant to the Huaulu, provides one of several bridges between the taboos on domestic animals and the taboos on wild animals, to which I must now turn.

Before I do so, however, let me reiterate that, whatever their relationship with Huaulu society, dog, cat, and chicken contribute to its continuous existence by offering a mirror for some of its most important categories together with their oppositions. Thus, man stands to woman as bantam stands to hen and as dog stands to cat; house stands to village as dog and cat (which are admitted to the house) stand to chicken (which is not allowed into the house, but freely roams all over the village ground); positive individuality stands to negative individuality as dog stands to cat; hunter stands to headhunter as dog stands to bantam; and so on. I could continue the analysis. But enough has been said to support my final statement, unsurprising as it may be. Not eating dog, cat, and chicken, as well as the wild animals occasionally fed as mascots or pets, is a powerful way of acknowledging and reasserting the intangibility of the social categories and, ultimately, the intangibility of the social world for which the "fed" animals stand, in their own eccentric and therefore enlightening way.

Omen and Taboo: Between Village and Forest

We have considered the symbolic status of all species that live in the village, in different degrees of association or even indentification with its human inhabitants. One common characteristic of all these animals is that they are tamed by the Huaulu and thus controlled by them. But what about those animals that frequent the house or the village without being tame or which occasionally enter it, in defiance of what is to be expected from wild animals?

Obviously the first animal to consider is the house mouse or rat, both called siluam and identified in regard to symbolic status.[104] Indeed, this animal is domestic but neither tame nor welcome. Instead of passively waiting to be fed, it steals human food. Furthermore, it destroys baskets and clothes, its droppings befoul the house, and it may attack babies and even sleeping adults. The animal thus frequents the house as an enemy, not as a friend, and as such it is not considered by the Huaulu as a fellow social being, even if it lives in close proximity to them. This explains why it is hardly differentiated in categorical status or in name[105] from its forest cousins and why, like them, and incidentally like other unwanted guests of the house (such as matawayam, "the cockroach"), it may be killed and even eaten, although it is considered inedible on grounds of taste.[106]

However, there are cases when the killing of domestic mice or rats is studiously avoided, and one may even speak of taboo. This is when the animals manifest some anomaly, either in color or in number. With regard to the former, white mice are supposed to be the form in which the dead of the house, especially the recently dead, return to it to visit their kin. As for number, an unusually large number of mice or rats is a sure index of the presence of topoyem, "the shades of the dead," in the house. Such infestations may occur at any time but are more frequent when somebody has recently died, since he or she will still feel the compulsion to return to the house and seek the company of living relatives. Anomalous siluem are not harmed, then, out of a complex mixture of love, respect, and fear of the dead—the relative proportion of each component varying with the identity of the dead and depending, in particular, on the time elapsed since death (the longer this time is, the less "natural" the dead person's desire to return among the living is assumed to be, and the correspondingly greater his malevolence).

In sum, while there is no taboo on ordinary house mice/rats, a white mouse or an unusually numerous bunch of mice are taboo (or simply avoided) precisely because they are not "true/ordinary rats/mice" (silu tuniem). They point to something other than themselves, the dead, who nevertheless are them in some sense. In what sense? Sometimes, the Huaulu speak as if the dead take the form (or as they say, kahukuam, "the external aspect/envelope") of rats. For instance, once when I complained to my friend Alimau of trouble I had sleeping because of the constant racket the rats made in my house at night, she commented: "Siluem te' topoyem? Ita amaneressi," "Are they rats or dead people? We don't know." Her words suggest a bodily identity between rats and the dead. But on other occasions the relationship was described as more indirect, as in the statement: Siluem matamataem i tapaleire, "The dead 'threw' the rats [into the house]." In other words, the dead drove the rats in great number into the house, to signal their own presence. These two accounts seem rather different to us, but not to the Huaulu. A signal is no mere signal to them; it implies the real presence of the signalled in the signal. To create a signal of themselves, the dead must manipulate the rats, drive them into the house. Thus the animals become possessed by the dead, a bit as the shamans become possessed by their sewaem. Just as one speaks of the possessed shamans as if they were their sewaem, so one speaks of the rats as if they were the dead who drive them. And just as a sewa may be present in several people at once, so a dead person may be present in several rats at once (although it seems that the dead always come accompanied by other dead: being a crowd is a form of their facelessness).

And why should the domestic mice or rats be associated with the dead in the first place? Like the dead, the mice prefer darkness; they come out at night. Furthermore, they tend to scurry on the beams under the roof, which is precisely the space occupied by the dead and from which they descend. More important, mice, like the dead, are part of the house, and yet their presence is unwanted because it is basically negative. Because they miss the living, the dead attempt to snatch them away, so that they can continue to enjoy their company. In a more profound sense, the dead are constantly preying on the living because of their vicarious, memorial existence, and because of the nostalgia and remorse the living feel toward them. Such remorse translates into the bites of rats which prey on the aliments of the living or even on their flesh. The Huaulu are all rat-men. Finally, the observation that mice or rats feed on corpses (all the more easily, since traditionally they were exposed rather than buried) may also have contributed to the belief that the animals are the transformed dead.

The status of the mouse/rat may be compared and contrasted with that of the suyam (indefinite form: sui), the smallest bat known to the Huaulu and the only one to enter, now and then, their houses, where they fly and screech in great numbers.[107] Just like the occasional presence of many mice, so the occasional swarming of these bats in and around the house portends the arrival of the dead. Bats being in a sense winged mice, it is not surprising that the suyem are given a roughly similar symbolic value. But there are some important differences due to the fact that bats, contrary to rats, are entirely wild animals that usually live away from human homes and swarm only in them at nightfall or soon after. Bats are thus associated with two highly dangerous transitions: from the wild sphere to the human one, and from day to night. As such, they signal the presence of a kind of dead different from the ones signalled by the rats. Rats, being familiar enemies, unwelcome, but constant, presences in the house, are associated with the family's dead, or with the dead when they are still believed to return to their home without too much danger for the living.[108]

Bats, instead, represent the most dangerous dead or the dead at their most dangerous: the stranger dead, the dead who died violently and are full of longing and desire for revenge—the wildest and deadliest of dead, who should remain confined to the forest and the night, which are their own provinces. Such dead are at their most dangerous precisely at nightfall, when the bats swarm into the houses. At this ambiguous hour when the fast boundaries between darkness (already deep in the forest) and daylight (still lingering in the village) become blurred, "the evil dead" (kinakinaem) are said to walk around seeking the living.

The bats' connection with dusk explains why they also signal (or sima, "betray," as the Huaulu more appropriately say) an attack from the most dangerous death-givers among the living: the timatem, or "the headhunters." This association with headhunters should be expected on both symbolic and practical grounds. Symbolically, headhunters are, just like the bats, a wild and extraneous force that threatens to invade the village. Practically, the risk of a headhunter's attack is greatest at dusk, when he can come closer to the village without being seen from it (since the bush in which he hides is already immersed in darkness) but can still see what goes on in it.

These facts of life and experience should make sufficiently clear why a swarming of bats is a much greater source of alarm than a swarming of mice. How many times did I hear, mingled with the animals' screeching and whirring in the rapidly falling night, the anxious voices echoing each other with the warning cry: "Suyem po'! Lailai omi taqi loli!" How many bats! Do not get away [from the house and a fortiori from the village]." Parents would call their children back into the house and if necessary go and tear them from their games on the village grounds. And I still vividly remember a terrified woman telling me, once the alarm had passed, "suyem sinahoki mataku rifurifua," "The bats awhile ago made my eyes 'flutter' [in fear]."[109]

It does not seem surprising, then, that bats, in contrast with mice, are taboo to harm and a fortiori to kill and eat (although bats are otherwise considered edible). Yet it would be wrong to jump to the conclusion that they are taboo simply because they are feared. Things are much more complex. For even as an object of fear, the bat is an object of gratitude. Indeed, the bat makes it possible to take steps against the danger of an attack from the dead or from headhunters by signalling its imminence. This is precisely why the animal that is feared as the announcer of headhunters (and thus because it is in some way identified with them) is also called, more reassuringly, makausuwa timatem, "the one which makes the headhunters go back where they come from" (since they realize that their presence has been betrayed by the animal, and their intended victims are on their guard).

Although this positive aspect of the bat is just the other face of its negative aspect, it is emphasized in the local explanation of its intangibility. In fact, many say that it is taboo to harm and eat the bat because of another property: it helps women during a difficult delivery. Although the bat, as a prolific mammalian, lends itself to a desirable association with women in childbed, such benevolence from an animal which is otherwise viewed as a forerunner of death seems paradoxical. But the paradox dissolves as soon as one looks more closely at the reasons for the bat's helpfulness. The bat is helpful only as an embodiment of the shamanic powers collectively called sewa kahianaem (child-bearing/child-delivering sewa),[110] which are in turn the transformations of the most fearsome of all dead: the muluaqinaem—the women who died in childbed. Normally the muluaqinaem attack women in childbed because they are envious of them and want them to die as they did. Therefore, they impede birth by holding the fetus inside the womb with their long nails. But some heroic shamans are capable of neutralizing them by turning them into their contrary: into facilitators of birth, into "childbearers"—into kahianaem, precisely.

The mammalian character of the bat can thus be activated as a symbol of childbirth only against a more general background of death-giving. In other words, the animal lends itself to representing some positively transformed dead because some of its attributes evoke the giving of life, although most others evoke the giving of death. In motivating the taboo on the bat one may well emphasize a positive attribute like the facilitation of childbirth. But this positive attribute, just like the "warning about headhunters" attribute, is inseparable from negative ones. One can be a signal of headhunters only if one has some connection with them. Analogously, one can be a facilitator of childbirth only if one has some connection with the impeders of childbirth—indeed only if one was, and in a sense continues to be, one of them: a muluaqina. In sum, the bat is forever condemned to have a share in the evil it signals, hence the fear that this supposedly beneficial animal arouses when it appears in and around the house.

We must now turn to wild animals whose presence in the village or in the house is absolutely exceptional, and is therefore seen as highly problematic. Minimally this implies avoidance; maximally, a formal taboo; and in most cases, also an omen—negative or ambiguous and to be further determined. I begin with what seems to be the rarest event, and also the one with the clearest consequences for taboo. Any animal from an edible species which voluntarily enters the village grounds is absolutely taboo to eat, although it may be killed.[111] If, however, the animal enters the village because it is pursued there by dogs or hunters, it may be eaten without danger. This contrast shows that it is not the physical contact with the village space that makes the animal taboo, but an internal, intentional state. In the highly anomalous case of game animals spontaneously entering the village, this state is in fact assumed to result from the intervention of a malevolent occult power: either a topoi (ghost) or a witch. Eating the meat of these animals would mean falling into the clutches of the powers that direct them. But these powers, in turn, would not be associated with the animals if the latter did not evoke the idea of danger in a more primordial sense, because they stand for the scandal of a reversal of the relative positions of wild and domestic, of animal as game and animal as friend. It is the very friendliness and sociability seemingly displayed by a wild animal that is deeply disquieting and threatening, in sum. The source of this taboo is anomaly, then, but not just any anomaly. It is an anthropocentric anomaly, one which subverts the hierarchical relationship between the human predator and his prey and which therefore evokes the possibility of a fuller reversal, in which the human predator becomes prey to his animal prey. We shall find the fear of this reversal again and again at the bottom of animal taboos and especially in their basic conceptual framework.[112]

Let us now turn to the case of animals which exceptionally visit the house, and not just the village. Like all anomalous events, such visits are treated as information—as omens; but some species invariably announce, and indeed bring, misfortune, whereas others announce an event that may be positive or negative: the arrival of visitors from outside the village. The latter class of animals includes butterflies and birds. Because their role as informers is essentially beneficial, they are seen as friendly to humans, and it is therefore taboo not only to eat them but also to kill or harm them in any way. Of course, this taboo concerns the individual animals that have entered the house, not their entire species, which is not affected by the anomalous behavior of some of their members.[113]

But why is it believed that butterflies and birds entering a house announce visitors? Almost certainly because their rare intrusions into domestic space are viewed as analogous to the equally rare intrusions of strangers. Furthermore, as far as birds are concerned, the belief that they are able to see visitors before humans can see them and to communicate the information (i sima ita, "they inform/warn us") derives from exaggerating one of their properties (they can see farther than humans because they can fly and because their eyesight is keen) and from anthropomorphizing another (their singing or screeching strikes the Huaulu as similar to human speech).

This supposed ability explains why certain birds, particularly parrots such as the kakakuam[114] and lakam,[115] which can be taught to "speak like humans" (i asasau),[116] are domesticated and permanently kept in the house for oracular purposes.[117] I can still hear their shrill screech suddenly tear the morning quiet, and see them jumping up and down excitedly on their perches. They would then twist their necks quizzically toward the chatterers they had silenced, as if to check that they were paying heed. The humans would indeed look at the birds intently, and one, breaking the suddenly heavy silence, would say, "ia koi," "It sees [somebody coming]." If visitors did arrive, people would comment that the bird had announced the event; if not, nothing was said. Like other oracles, the birds are said to be very mischievous and thus fond of deception. Thus if what they are supposed to announce does not occur, their oracular powers are not disproved in the least; rather, their mischievousness is only proved once again. And as far as odds go, a parrot cannot be more mischievous than it is oracular.

Butterflies are supposed to announce the arrival of people not only when they enter the house but even when they brush against somebody, in or outside the village ("the butterfly brushes," rifayam papa ita). Indeed, a wild animal does not have to enter the village or a house to acquire a human significance: the fact that it uncharacteristically seeks physical contact with a person is considered a sufficient indication that its behavior has something to do with humans, that it is either a message or the sign that the animal is not really an animal but an occult power. In either case, former humans—"the ancestral dead" (ailaem)—are believed to be behind it. They sometimes like to visit their descendants in this form. I witnessed one such visit in 1988, during the closing night of the kahua feast. Late that night, a large nocturnal butterfly suddenly appeared in the village hall in which the feast was taking place, and fluttered for some time along the line of dancers. People pointed at it in awe and one of the elders stopped a young dancer from shooing it away. I asked why such a precaution was necessary and was told that maybe the butterfly was an ancestor attending the feast. People were very pleased with the event, because it seemed to indicate ancestral approval of the feast and the decision to close it that night—a decision about which a lot of uncertainty and uneasiness existed at the time.

Now let us turn to the far more complex class of animals whose anomalous presence in the house is a harbinger of pure misfortune and is therefore said to be maquwoli (i.e. "it should not happen"; see chapter 3). The class includes three species of frogs and at least three chirping insects. I will describe them as the Huaulu describe them, hoping to identify in this way the traits that make them significant, and thus taboo, for the Huaulu. The three frogs are the tatauwam, the ilauwam, and the kararam.[118]

The tatauwam is described as a small frog which always lives in streams or ponds (pale wae, "below in the water," is the Huaulu expression for this habitat).[119] But it is able to make very long jumps and may thus land in a house if it happens to leave its usual habitat. Because this is a rare event, it is considered significant. It portends some misfortune, although there have been cases in which, after a tatauwam was sighted in a house, a woman dreamed of it, and in the dream the animal taught her either aitotu kahianaem (birthing/fostering medicines) or auweteam (magic for the kind of river fishing that is practiced by women).[120] Their ominous signification also applies when they touch somebody, or clothes, or get into somebody's way. Thus if the frog jumps out of the water in front of a person, it is a sign that a misfortune will strike him. If it jumps onto his right side, the misfortune may include death and is due to his own "transgressions" (rosaem). If it jumps on his left side, the misfortune is due to "other people's transgressions" (lelaki rahe rosaem). The animal is said to have a connection with the dead, and this is manifested particularly when it alights over a lamp, which is the most dangerous omen.

Perhaps because of some relationship with their sewaem, the tatauwam is absolutely taboo to eat for the members of the Tamatay clan and Sinala lineage. But members of other clans or lineages are also unlikely to eat it, unless it is offered them by some strangers, because it is taboo to kill for all Huaulu. Some Huaulu claim to have eaten it in Nisawele and to have relished it, particularly the "white juices" that exude from the animal when it cooks. Most people, however, make fun of the Nisawele, "who would eat anything," for eating it and declare that they would never dream of doing the same. Patakuru, one of my friends, explained that it smells bad, of rot (lit., fauhihina,[121] "it smells like a woman"), and Kuweyamani, another good friend and frequent commensal, said that it reminded him of a muluaqina and thus of what he would least want to touch. These associations are not idiosyncratic; they indicate that the animal is connected with the dead, and thus also with the most dangerous of them all—the ghosts of women who died in childbirth. The latter connection is confirmed by the belief that the tatauwem, just like the muluaqinaem, may be the source of aitotu kahianaem, "medicines/magic to give birth."

The kararam[122] is described as similar to the tatauwam in every respect, except size, which is said to be much smaller in the kararam.[123] Consequently, the status of the two species with regard to taboo is also similar: both should be kept out of the house and particularly off clothes and lamps. The kararam too is not eaten, although it is not formally taboo for any lineage, as far as I know.

The ilauwam[124] is usually described in terms that point to its anomalous status with regard to two basic categories of Huaulu classification: pale wae (down in the water) and hoto aitufhu (up in the trees).

Indeed, people say that because the ilauwam is wont to jump up into the trees, it lives in both habitats (ilauwam ia ruwe hoto aitufhu pohi ia pale wae, "the ilauwam lives up in the trees and down in the water"), instead of "only living down in the water" (kessa ia ruwe pale wae). Probably because of its anomalous status as species, the ilauwam is even more dangerous (or piniassi, "bad") than the other two frogs, particularly if it alights on people,[125] lamps, or clothes. If an ilauwam touches the central pillar of the house, which is its very core and foundation, somebody is bound to die.[126] Traditionally, I was told, if an ilauwam entered a single house, the entire village was abandoned as a "bad place" (tinueniam piniassi; *or* i tinuere piniassi, "they lived in a bad place").[127] Nowadays the animal must be caught and thrown out of the house, but in such way that it cannot jump back into it. It is bound with some rattan to a stick, sometimes two sticks connected in the form of a cross (sokoam, the sign of taboo),[128] then briefly roasted on the veranda's fire, and cast out. This method of disposal seems to belie my informants' claim that it is taboo to kill the ilauwam, since it practically ensures that the hapless animal will die. Yet it is true that it is not actually dispatched, and never expires in the house. And it probably falls victim to predators before it can die of its burns.[129] Although some informants claimed that the ilauwam is taboo to eat, others assured me that, just like the other two species of frogs, it is not formally taboo for the average Huaulu but is not eaten anyhow because people "feel it is disgusting" (i makapoaire).

Just like the swarming of rats and bats or the entrance of birds and butterflies, the appearance of frogs in the house is connected with the dead. But it has a specific, more intimate, and therefore more threatening implication. It signals that somebody's soul has become detached from him and that he therefore risks death. To quote the explanation I received for the ilauwam: Kalu ilauwam ia pititou ese ita, amuni ita rahe mattiulu raqia nika. Topoyam ia rapaleira mattiulu, wahi ia patihuira, "If an ilauwam jumps on us [lit., jumps and hits us], it means that the soul has already left [us]. The dead has thrown the soul [i.e. it has forced the soul into the animal, which therefore acts anomalously], as if it wanted to warn us." What is not clear in this statement is whether the dead in question is the one responsible for stealing the soul or if he is simply a warning ancestor.[130] In the first case, the dead would act inconsistently, first by stealing the soul, then by warning of its loss. In the second case, it is not clear why the ancestor is referred to with a term that puts him or her in the general category of "the shadows of the dead" (topoyem). Most probably the ambiguity of the statement reflects the fundamental ambiguity of the dead themselves. The ancestors are like all other dead in being malevolent and not just benevolent—in snatching souls as much as in warning of the deed. Analogously, the dead, even at their most malevolent, have a tendency to betray themselves, to undo their own possessive acts by making them apparent, which is inevitable, since these acts are ultimately dictated by a possessive desire and even love for the living. In any case, these theories help us understand why the anomalous events in question are not just signs, but also concurrent causes of misfortune, because what produces the message—soul loss and, beyond it, the dead who steals the soul—is also what produces the misfortune. Put otherwise, the sign is part of the cause—it is a signal.[131] From this point of view, the attempt to impede the occurrence of the omen, or to remove it if it has occurred, makes perfect sense without having to assume a confusion of the sign with its referent.

Let us now move to three chirping insects—the nayam (indefinite form: nai), the kalopoam, and the kikiam—whose presence in the house or whose alighting on a person, or on clothes, or on the house's lamps is inauspicious and should be avoided.

The nayam is a cicada.[132] When I first entered a forest in Seram I thought that the island was teeming with lumberjacks. From every direction I heard the strident noise of what sounded like power saws. But what I thought were outrageous destroyers of the wilderness in which I was plunging with delight proved elusive. Whenever I walked toward them with the intention of glaring at them, they seemed to disappear, and true to the magical aspect of the forest, they always stayed at the same distance or, even more surprisingly, reappeared behind me. I mention all this not so much to denounce, from the safety of a much later time, my urban naiveté with regard to things of the forest as to give an idea of the incredible sound of the nayam. The insect does indeed lacerate the air with a sound more like a saw than what a saw itself can produce. It can certainly saw on your nerves, but during the endless forest marches its relentless monotony acts as a powerful anesthetic by echoing the monotony of visual and muscular impressions.

So the insect's voice *is* striking, and not just for the stupid stranger, for it speaks loudly and somewhat threateningly to the Huaulu too, at least at certain moments of the day. Not surprisingly, these are moments of transition: the rising tide,[133] dawn, and dusk. And equally unsurprisingly, the transition from day to night is far more negative, dense as it is with remorse and nostalgia, than the transition from night to day. If the cicadas are heard "crying" loudly at dawn, it only means that they "ask for rain" (ia putani ala roam), and rain will fall during the day.[134] But if they are loud and insistent at dusk, then they are the "dead fathers, mothers, great-grandparents" (amai sie, inai sie, upu sie) who ask for fire,[135] and thus, one assumes, for the lost joys of warmth and commensality among the living, since evening is the time when the kitchen fires are lit to cook and the veranda's fires burn brightly for the returning hunter or gardener while he waits for dinner. But to the dead, one must give a stone instead of bread or, rather, ashes instead of fire. To send them away, to persuade them of what they cannot believe or accept—that they have to stay dead, that they must leave the living alone—the burnt-out contents of the fireplace are thrown into the air from the house.

The cicada thus seems symbolically significant because of its association with points of transition in time.[136] It signals them and may become fused with other beings, such as the dead, concurrently attached to one or more of them. The association with the dead is reinforced when the cicada anomalously enters the house—that is, when it does what the dead are supposed to wish to do but should not. Then it is believed that the cicada has stolen a soul and, therefore, that the life of somebody in the house is in danger, especially when the animal—just as in the parallel case of the frogs—lands on a lamp or a person or clothes. Therefore, killing the offending cicada is strictly taboo, because it would be killing the lost soul and thus also its owner. But one may want to ask if there is not a deeper connection between the threat of death, represented by the soul loss, and the sudden appearance in the house of an animal timepiece usually confined to the forest. Perhaps it reminds the inhabitants that the passage of time applies to them too, that their day also turns into night. Is this not what ultimately explains the belief that the voice of the cicada is the voice of death itself, speaking through the preying dead?

The kalopoam is said to be "like the nayam," but to my admittedly ignorant ears it sounded more like a cricket. Its chirping—of which my hosts frequently made me aware—is associated with the period immediately following the sunset and with the early part of the night. Some informants, however, connected the animal's "voice" (liona) with the late afternoon as well. These discrepancies are perhaps explained by the identification of different species under one name. But there is no doubting the animal's connection with the most crucial and crucially dangerous time of the day—namely nightfall. It is this connection which gives the kalopoam its reputation as a timepiece. As Kohunusa put it: "It gives us time. When it starts chirping, it is the evening. It starts after sunset." Both the connection with nightfall and that with time account for the fact that the kalopoam's presence in the house, just like that of the nayam, signifies death for one of its inhabitants and is therefore "taboo." In fact, from the symbolic standpoint, the kalopoam can be considered a somewhat attenuated form of nai.

The kikiam is, again, said to be "like the nayam" and to be the object of the same taboos, if less stringently. I never saw one, and the descriptions I have heard are somewhat confusing.[137] Visually, the animal is supposed to "resemble a large brownish [other Huaulu informants said yellow] fly with transparent wings and small black eyes." This description suggests a cicada. On the other hand, the name of the animal is supposed to be onomatopoeic in that it echoes its chirping, which we would describe as "cricri" and the Huaulu, whose language lacks consonant clusters, describe as "kiki." This suggests a cricket. In any case, what matters is that the animal is said to be wahi nayam, "like the nayam." The basis for the association is probably the kikiam's strong chirping and its complementary distribution with the nayam in time: while the nayam is heard mostly during the day and until sunset, the kikiam is heard throughout the night—or so I was told.[138]

In contrast with the above cicadas, or in any case insects compared to the nai cicada, the "field cricket" (kau lesate)[139] is not considered invariably ominous when it enters the house, perhaps owing to the relative frequency of the event. But it is believed that the kau lesate's presence is significant one way or another, which must be found out by interrogating the animal as an oracle. Questions are therefore put to it, and it is supposed to answer each with an affirmation or a negation. For instance, if one wishes to obtain information about game, one may ask: "Does the trap (into which an animal may have fallen) belong to *x*?" If the cricket continues chirping, the answer is negative; if it becomes silent, it is affirmative.[140] In the latter case, another, more specific question is asked: "Will it kill (or has it killed) a deer in growth stage *y*?"—and so on until one is satisfied or a state of indeterminacy is reached. One also asks metaquestions, that is, questions about the truth status of the oracle's answers, such as: "Are you deceiving me?" (Uqalafoka ea?) Obviously the Huaulu have never heard of Epimenides the Cretan.

If there is a strong presumption that the cricket has been "thrown by the shade of a dead" (topoyam rapaleira), a different kind of interrogation—in fact, torture—takes place. The animal's posterior legs are pulled out, then the cricket is turned on its back and its head is rubbed on the palm of one's hand. In the unlikely event that after this severe treatment the cricket "wakes up" (ia panu), its waking up means that it has not been thrown by a dead (i.e. sent as an "angel of death"), but if it dies, its death makes it iconic of the dead who "threw" it into the house. The very verb used (*rapalei*, "to throw") indicates the anomalous character of such intrusion: a cricket has to be forced into the space which is the province of humans; otherwise, it would not normally or spontaneously enter it. This potential for embodying an intrusion from the dead undoubtedly explains that the animal is considered taboo to eat (but not, evidently, to kill by torture) for the Huaulu.[141]

In conclusion, all the species of frogs and insects described above (with the partial exception of the kau lesate) are the object of the same taboo, where *taboo* means "prescribed avoidance of an ominous event," "injunction to avoid the occurrence of an event which is both the sign and the cause of a misfortune." The event in question is the entrance into the house, and more specifically the alighting on a person, on clothes, or on a lamp, of animals from those species. It is considered ominous because it is associated with an invisible counterpart: the entrance of malevolent dead into the house. While the taboo on letting the animals into the house was very strongly and clearly stated by all, there was more ambiguity with regard to edibility. Most people claimed that they would not eat them, not because they are taboo, but because i makapoaire, "they felt disgusted by them."[142] Some species were said to be taboo by authoritative men, however. This was the case, in particular, of the two species (nai and ilau), which seem to function as prototypes of their groups (insects and frogs) and which are also the most feared.

One point would seem to require some explanation. We can easily understand why the alighting of these animals on a person or on a person's clothes must be especially avoided. It indicates that the person in question, and not just somebody generically, is in danger. Instead of being diluted among all the inhabitants of the house, the danger is concentrated on one of them. But why is it that the contact with the house's lamp is so greatly feared? To answer this question we must look at the place of the lamp in the house and especially at its close relationship with the luma upuam, "the master/owner of the house."

The traditional Huaulu lamp consists of a stand (a split bamboo stuck into a base formed by a piece of a sago palm branch) on which burns a leaf-wrapped package of tree resin (kesi; B.I.: damar), mixed with ashes to slow the combustion. The flame must be kept alive by frequently poking the resin with a small segment of bamboo or rattan. The person who "tends the lamp" (ia kafe), often the master of the house, is surrounded by a circle of people—kinsmen, friends, and visitors—who converse with him during the long nights, often until dawn. The shaky light of the lamp animates and at the same time distorts the faces by impressing a continuous movement on them. The pulsation of this ever different, ever frail light opens mysterious depths in the house and liberates fantastic shapes in its darkest recesses. The small center of light becomes one with the silent beats of the congregated hearts, with the fluxes and refluxes of the conversation, with the gazes that it magnetically attracts, and with the great enveloping womb of the night—magical silences and creaks breaking out of the darkness—conjured by its radiating breath.

It is the association of the burning flame with these nocturnal scenes which turns the lamp into an outer form, an echo of the life of the house and of the people who inhabit and frequent it at the most intimate hours, when there is only space for kinsmen and friends, for those who really "belong." The flame is the soul of the house, because it is the slowly burning soul of its people as they live their nights around its luminous circle. No wonder, then, that the household lamp acquires a sort of sacredness, and that what has a negative effect on it has a negative effect on those who surround it, eyes hypnotically fixed on its flickering flame, night after night, generation after generation—time burned out in the night of times. Hence the taboo on the contamination of the lamp—whose voice speaks so purely of life and happiness—by a croaking frog or a strident cicada jumping out of the darkness, totally foreign, totally out of place, just like the sudden shock of death. Hence, also, the taboo on letting the flame become mixed with deadly darkness by a converse movement: by letting it fall through the cracks of the floor, onto the dirty ground, haunted by animals and the dead.[143] If this happens, or even if a fragment of still-burning resin falls to the ground and keeps burning there, an extremely serious taboo has been violated. The violation portends the death of the master of the house—of the man most likely to be tending its lamp and most closely identified with it. To neutralize these dire consequences it is necessary for the mistress of the house to take out an ancient heirloom, a "ceremonial cloth" (kalu makahau)[144] and, having slung it over her shoulder and across her breast, to seek the lamp or the resin fragment on the ground under the house floor. When she finds it, she must wrap it in the cloth with immense respect and carry it back to the house in the same way as she would carry her child—a demonstration and a recognition of the animated character of the lamp, evocative of its human identity and its connection with life, momentarily negated by its fall onto the dirty ground and by its dying out in the darkness, but reaffirmed by the image of a new birth, of a new baby entering the house as a new life for its master.[145]

When I first lived in Huaulu in the early seventies, only the traditional resin lamps were used. Today one also finds kerosene lamps, except in the houses containing lineage or village sacra,[146] which are incompatible with the "stinking" liquid. The taboo on frogs, cicadas, and so on, alighting on resin lamps has been extended to kerosene lamps, but not the taboo on letting the lamps fall from the house onto the ground. This difference is probably explained by the fact that a lamp preserves its signification as luminous center of the house even when it burns kerosene, but the latter substance—in contrast with the perfumed resin which is associated with the aerial sphere[147]—does not need to be kept separate from the earth, from which it is extracted.[148]

But then it is obvious that burning kerosene lamps, however practical and labor-saving, debase the house, bringing it further down to earth. The new lamp is a sadly apt symbol, in the Huaulu's own eyes, of a more general debasement of their life, of its fall from ancestral integrity. Only in the houses where the ancestral past is still present in the form of sacra can this debasement not be accepted. The religious has become divorced from the practical, although neither has yet been named.

Can we draw certain systematic conclusions from the above facts, without indulging in the vice Nietzsche denounced in systematic thinking—of treating the weak points as if they were as strong as the strong ones? We can try. Certain constants are obvious and indeed striking. The presence of the above animals in the house is usually connected with the presence of the dead, more often than not in their threatening aspect. The connecting link is provided by the idea that wild animals tend to avoid humans. If animals seek humans, if they enter humans' villages and a fortiori their houses, it must be because they are forced by a quasi-human presence, that of the dead who miss life among the living. In this sense, these animals are not true animals because they do not behave as wild animals would. They are the "external envelope" (kahuku) of the dead or at least their "sign" (tanda). It is not anomalous behavior as such, then, that is the source of taboo, but anomaly as a sign that the dead refuse to stay dead, as a sign that they desire the company of the living, to the point of snatching them away. Nor can the behavior of the dead, I think, be treated as the anomaly which is the source of taboo—that is, as merely a categorical confusion of life and death. Even if the dead's behavior were reducible to such confusion, the reaction to it could not be viewed as a mere instantiation of the general horror of categorical mix-ups—if such horror exists—for death and life are not categories like the others. Humans inhabit life and eschew death. It is their fear of dying which lies at the bottom of these taboos. It is what the Huaulu themselves tell us, for the representation of death is not mediated here by any specific disease or other misfortune, as is the case in most other classes of taboo.

Granted that all these animals are or may be, one way or another, connected with the dead—is there a way to account for their differences in dangerousness and, moreover, their attachment to different kinds of taboos? Why is it that some are taboo to eat but not to kill, whereas others are taboo to kill but not to eat, and a few are said to be taboo on both grounds? Why is it, also, that some are treated as negative omens, whereas others are viewed more ambiguously or as providers of information whose positive or negative nature must be further determined?

One great divide should be mentioned first. On the one hand are animals that are considered good to eat and are therefore treated as "game" (peni). On the other hand are animals that are said to be bad to eat—too "disgusting" (i makapoaire)[149] or "bitter" (kaatae). This contrast correlates in part with that between the animals which occasionally enter the house and the animals which enter only the village, if they enter anywhere at all. Indeed, the latter animals include those providing the most desirable meat: pigs, deer, cassowaries, civets, hornbills, giant bats, which are unable to enter the houses either because of their mode of locomotion or because they are too big (although large birds and large bats may rest on the roofs). As for the wild animals that occasionally enter the houses, none—barring several birds—are said to be good to eat, except sometimes by a few eccentrics.[150]

As we have seen in an earlier chapter, some theorists, such as Leach, treat disgust or any other judgment of inedibility as equivalent to taboo or even as an attenuated or residual form of it. This view makes light of the partial autonomy of the gustatory/culinary sphere. It is at any rate inapplicable to the present case, because by and large the taboo on eating is in complementary distribution with the taboo on killing. In other words, the weight of taboo seems to change with the gustatory status of the animal's flesh in Huaulu culture. If the animal is said to be good to eat, then it is taboo to eat but not to kill in case it enters the village; if it is said to be bad to eat, then it is taboo to kill but theoretically it is not taboo to eat if it enters the house.[151] This shift of the focus of taboo seems to me to result from, among other factors, a deliberate consideration of the gustatory, aesthetic aspect of meat-eating. What would be the point of tabooing what one would not do anyhow, that is, eating the scant and disgusting—in the Huaulu view—meat of butterflies and cicadas and even of frogs, small bats, and mice? Such "small deer," to use the Shakespearean expression, are no deer to the Huaulu, who, thank God, have better things to eat.

To our common sense, however, such talk of complementary distribution may sound like nonsense. Isn't the relationship between killing and eating one of redundancy rather than complementarity? If I cannot kill, how can I eat? Furthermore, if I cannot eat, why would I kill? Defying such apparently sound objections, the Huaulu are careful to distinguish between taboos on killing and taboos on eating. And common sense seems to be on their side. For one may very well eat what others may kill, as indeed happens when the Huaulu visit Nisawele and are offered frog meat. Moreover, one may want to kill an animal even if one has no plans to eat it. For instance, several of the large game animals which occasionally enter the village are better killed because they are dangerous in a physical and not just metaphysical sense.

In any case, the shift away from eating enables taboo to take a much more important form, and one more coherently pursued, than the avoidance of killing. It is the "avoidance" of the animal's intrusion itself. As we have seen, this avoidance is largely theoretical, since the movements of the animals are by and large beyond human control, to such an extent that it seems odd to translate *maquwoli* as *taboo* in this case (see chapter 3). But the practical impulse retreats here before the symbolic one. The important point is that the shift from the avoidance of eating to the "avoidance" of the animal's contact with the house is also a shift from the individual body to the collective one. Following Fortes' immortal dictum, one has to do one's eating oneself. However collectively shared a taboo is, its point of incidence is through the individual act of eating. In contrast, the "taboo" on the animal's contact with the house emphasizes the individual's subordination to the "house"—that is, to a physical structure which is the image of a social one.[152] Indeed, the intrusion of the animal can be dangerous for just anybody in the house; it does not have a more precisely individual focus, like the intrusion into the stomach (unless, of course, the animal happens to jump over or before somebody in particular). It is as if, then, these inedible animals, these vermin that frequent the house, displace the intangible body, which is the preoccupation of taboo, from the person in flesh and bone to the house as person. Or better said, the person in flesh and bone remains the focus of taboo, but only as he or she is encompassed by and subordinated to a larger body—the social body which is represented by the house. All taboos are thus of the body, but some are of the unmediated body, others are of the body as mediated by its container of wood, leaves, and people.

There are, of course, exceptions, uncertainties, and irregularities in the complementary distribution of the two taboos; we should never forget that the Huaulu are not as obsessed with the *esprit de système* as we might like them to be in our moments of structuralist yearning. Nevertheless, their taboos are neither as haphazard nor as redundant as an antistructuralist *parti pris* would make them. The point is confirmed by an analysis of the variables which account for the differential dangerousness of the animals' intrusion into the house and thus also for variations in their taboo status. The main variable is, quite obviously, the frequency of the intrusion. The more frequent, the less dangerous. Thus mice or rats, as habitual, if unwelcome, visitors, are not viewed as very dangerous and are not normally taboo.[153] Conversely, frogs and cicadas, whose intrusions are exceedingly rare, are the most dangerous and therefore the most strictly taboo. Somewhat intermediate, hence ambiguous or further determined by other variables, are birds and butterflies (and to a lesser extent field crickets), whose presence in the house is not so unusual.

Two important variables are whether the animal appears in the house by night or by day, and whether it is prevalently connected with the upper (sky)[154] or the lower (water) regions of the cosmos. That diurnal intrusions and a connection with the upper regions are viewed more positively than their opposites explains why the presence of wild birds and butterflies is on the whole not dangerous,[155] except in the sense that it may signal the visit of an enemy or that of ancestors always ready to criticize and punish. Conversely, the frogs' connection with water and their tendency to intrude at night (since they are attracted by lamps) make theirs the most dangerous intrusion.

There is another variable which further reinforces the dangerousness of frogs or, at the very least, of their prototype—the ilauwam. This is a species or classificatory anomaly, by which I mean not an anomaly that concerns the behavior of certain individuals (as entering the village or the houses is for wild animals), but an anomaly that is intrinsic to the situation of a species in the classificatory system. In the case of the ilauwam, the latter anomaly may ride on the coattails of the former, which was already suggested, I trust, by the fact that the ilauwam is usually defined by its odd situation in the three-tiered universe. Most people note that it is an animal of the water (ia ruwe pale wae, "it lives down in the water"), but contrary to most such animals it is also frequently found in the tops of trees (ia saa hoto aitufhu, "it keeps going up the trees"). But one informant was more explicit. He was one of those who claimed that, unlike the tatauwam (or the closely related kararam), the ilauwam is not just disgusting but also formally taboo to eat. And he volunteered the following explanation: "The tatauwam is not taboo because it only lives down in the water; instead, the ilauwam lives both up in the trees and down in the water and is therefore taboo." Several authoritative men agreed with this explanation, which anyhow is standard for a number of other taboos, as we shall see.[156] It is important to stress, however, that species anomaly is activated as a source of danger only in individuals manifesting a behavioral anomaly, that is, seeking humans in their houses or even on their paths. It acts as a supplement to but not as the main reason for the frog's dangerousness.

Anomaly plays an explicit role in the ilauwam but, given that this species is treated as the prototype of its group (as is shown by the fact that the other two frogs are defined by comparisons with the ilauwam), it may play an implicit role in all frogs, since, after all, the reason they can intrude into houses is that they can jump, besides being able to swim. Jumping, as a form of locomotion intermediate between walking or swimming in the lower regions and flying in the upper ones, may be viewed as "anomalous" in the sense that it violates the fundamental division between up and down. In this sense, there may be an element of anomaly in the cicadas too. Anomaly may also play an implicit role in the bats, since bats are like rats and yet they fly. But here again species anomaly alone would seem to be insufficient, since giant bats are perfectly edible and crickets and cicadas are not otherwise taboo. The crucial factor is behavioral and characterizes not the species but the individual: intruding into the house, jumping onto people or before them, congregating in great numbers, and so on. Some nonbehavioral, but equally individual, traits—such as color in white mice—may also play a role in motivating taboo.

A final variable to be considered is anthropomorphism. The closer the animal is to humans in anatomy or behavior, the less ominous is its presence in the house. One reason birds are the least dangerous intruders into the house is that their "vocalizations" (liona) are viewed as less different from human ones than those of frogs, cicadas, or bats. Indeed, as I noted, some birds are said to be capable of speech. Moreover, birds can sing like humans. They can also be sung to, either out of purely poetic impulse or, more frequently, to attract them so as to capture them. Another possible similarity with humans lies in the birds' bipedalism, not to mention their generic "petlike" qualities, which I noted earlier.

Intruding birds are less dangerous but are nevertheless more taboo than all other intruders. They cannot be killed and cannot be eaten out of respect. They come from the above, a superior habitat, and they are helpful and informative. The taboo on birds is motivated by respect, not fear; or rather, respect is more important than fear, since the two are always found together in something which is very respected (see chapter 3).

Fish and Fowl

The taboos treated in the previous section are, in essence, mixing taboos. The mixture they exclude, or interpret as ominous when it spontaneously occurs, is between two spheres that should remain separate: the village and the forest, respectively treated as equivalents of the living and of the dead. In this section I discuss another kind of mixing taboo. This time, the mixture to be avoided is between opposites internal to the forest and, more generally, to the wild. Briefly put, the animals that live hoto aitufhu, "high in the trees," and those that live pale wae, "down in the water," cannot be eaten together in the same meal without producing a terrible disease: koloputi, "leprosy."

To understand this taboo and the consequences of its violation, it is necessary to know something about the cosmological structure it presupposes. The Huaulu distinguish five (main) cosmic strata: hoto laliata (up in the sky), hoto aitufhu (up in the trees), pale kaitahu (down on the ground), pale wae (down in the water [fresh and salt]), and underground, for which no single general expression is used.[157] The two extreme strata, up in the sky and underground, are associated with occult powers, notably the dead. The living are situated in the three intermediate strata. Each species is usually confined to one stratum, with certain kinds of species functioning as prototypes. Eventual crossovers—either as permanently realized by a species or as realized by certain combinations of species in the human stomach—are considered dangerous or informative, or both, mostly if animals are involved, more rarely in the case of vegetals. The reason for the preponderance of animals is probably that only they are mobile enough to be capable of truly and strikingly crossing borders. Animals, in other words, have a greater potential for disorder than vegetals, not to mention the obvious fact that in this society of hunters meat is more important than vegetable food.

Not all crossovers are dangerous or equally dangerous. The most dangerous ones are between the strata that are the "natural" habitat of occult powers (sky and underground) and the strata that are the allotted habitat of the living. These crossovers often have their parallels, or visible manifestations, in crossovers inside the world of the living (or the world of ordinary beings, as it may also be called). We have seen, for instance, that when wild animals enter the village or the house they are usually treated as the signs of an invasion from the sphere of the occult. Some animals which move across habitats, such as the monitor lizard, are also frequently associated with occult powers, as we shall see. But other inappropriate movements across the three central strata do not seem to be the visible manifestations of the presence of occult powers. They are dangerous in themselves, as mixtures which threaten to diminish the clarity of the oppositional contrasts on which the order of the visible world rests. The danger arises, however, only when the two extremes "up in the trees" and "down in the water" become mixed in the stomach of humans. It is a highly relational kind of danger, then, and one that depends on human action rather than on being intrinsic to some species construed as anomalous. Much, if not exactly most, of the Huaulu sense of anomaly is therefore vested in man-made mixtures, although these ultimately presuppose ostensibly unmade incompatibilities or even hostilities.

But what constitutes a mixture exactly? What degree and form of contact must occur for the mixture to occur and the consequences to set in motion? The strongest form of mixing is, of course, the actual consumption of the incompatible foods in the same meal. But there is mixing even when one eats the incompatible foods sequentially, in two different meals taken at a short interval. In other words, as long as one food is still in the stomach it is dangerous to consume another food that is at odds with it. The mixture also occurs when the two foods are cooked in the same container (bamboo trunk or pot) or are put on the same plate even if cooked separately. Either way their "juices" (salawa) become mixed, and thus eating one involves eating the other as well. Then they fight each other in the body of the eater and bring havoc to it, beginning on its surface, on its visible part—the skin.

The resulting disease, koloputi, refers to leprosy proper (which in advanced cases implies the falling off of fingers, toes, nose, and ears), but also to various other cutaneous affections and swellings that look similar to leprosy in its initial stages and that the Huaulu, like so many other peoples,[158] do not distinguish from the dreaded disease. All these alterations of the skin are therefore viewed with extreme anxiety. From the gravity of the consequence, one can measure the gravity of the cause. Eating cannot go against the grain of the cosmos; it must respect the incompatibility of above and below, of air and water, and other subtler distinctions that immediately suggest themselves as soon as one looks at the specific applications of the taboo rule. The eater who undermines the shape of the cosmos undermines his own shape. His flesh is eaten away by the flesh he eats.

The principle of the incompatibility of up-in-the-trees and down-in-the-water is stated in abstract form and applied quite consistently to general categories. People will tell you that any bird cannot be mixed with any fish. And their insistence on always speaking of "up" in the trees and "down" in the water, as if this spatial contrast were the self-explanatory reason for the taboo, indicates that the preservation of the vertical structure of the cosmos is indeed its basic motivation. Sometimes the causal force of that vertical contrast is made more evident by borrowing the expression *sebab,* "because," from the Indonesian language. I well recall that earlier in my stay, when I was forced to eat several meals a day by the constant stream of invitations, I was often admonished to take care not to eat the two most common animal foods together, shrimp and cuscus, "because one lives in the trees, the other down in the water" (sepapu essa ia ruwe hoto aitufhu, essa pale wae). The only safe combinations, it turned out, involved animals living pale kaitahu (down on the ground) and animals living hoto aitufhu or pale wae. In other words, animals whose habitats are adjacent are compatible; animals inhabiting opposite habitats are not.[159] The reason for this difference is, quite obviously, that the system rests on its maximal opposition.

But if the principle that animals whose habitats lie at the two extremes of the three-tiered cosmos are incompatible is the base of all actual mixing taboos, it alone cannot account for them all. One reason is that some animals are anomalous in terms of the three-tiered classification in that they live in more than one habitat, contemporaneously or successively in the course of their life. Another reason is that morphological and behavioral criteria are tacitly taken into account to further segment the species included in the large habitat categories, particularly the up-in-the-trees one. Moreover, it is clear that a certain correlation between morphology and habitat is assumed to be normal, so that when a conflict between them arises, as in the case of the cassowary, the animal is singled out by special mixing taboos. Yet anomaly per se is not necessarily relevant for purposes of taboo, or it may be countered by other and more important criteria.

Let us look, then, at how these eccentric species are situated in the general system of mixing taboos, and indeed at all the rules of mixing I have been able to record from innumerable concrete instances and from elicited or spontaneously proffered generalizations (which in this field were rather common):

1. All birds (including chickens and the maleo bird, *Megapodius wallacei* [also known as the Moluccan scrubfowl],[160] but excluding the asuali, "cassowary") and their eggs, all bats, two varieties of cuscuses (ihisi makila and ihisi elahuwa), the two edible pythons (tipolo and tekepatola, *Python reticulatus*) are taboo in combination with all denizens of the water (fish, crustaceans, shells, eels), which are not otherwise taboo.
2. All birds (chickens and the maleo included, the cassowary excluded) and their eggs and all bats are taboo in combination with ihisi makila and ihisi elahuwa.
3. All birds (chickens and the maleo included) and their eggs, bats, ihisi makila, and ihisi elahuwa are taboo in combination with the cassowary.
4. All birds, the cassowary, all bats, the ihisi makila and the ihisi elahuwa, and the tekepatola and tipolo pythons are taboo in combination with the grubs of forest tree weevils (eti ai, also called eti poto, *Rhynochophorus ferrugineus*).[161]
5. The cassowary is taboo in combination with the maate' fish (herring, *Clupea schrammi*).[162]
6. The grubs of forest tree weevil are taboo in combination with fish, shrimp, shells, and eels.

These taboos may be represented synoptically by the diagram below.

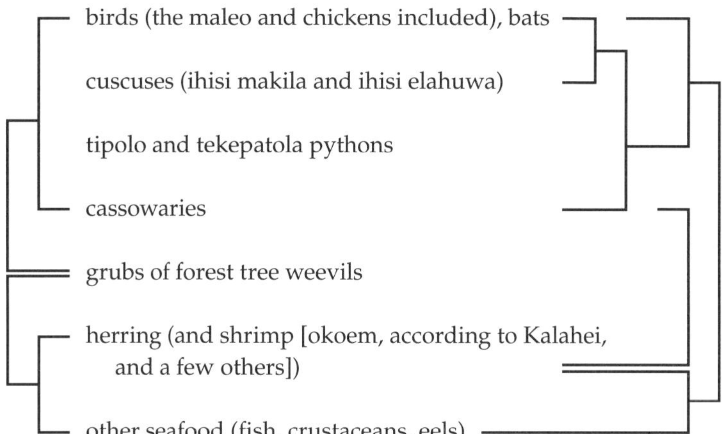

Two vegetables (pandanus seeds and matalala bananas) are also involved in this system of incompatibilities. Pandanus seeds (and the red pulp that surrounds them) should be mixed with neither the meat of the animals that live up in the trees nor the meat of the animals that live down in the water. In addition, they are incompatible with the meat of the cassowary and eti ai. Matalala bananas should not be eaten together with any of the creatures that live up in the trees or with the cassowary or eels. They are not taboo in combination with fish and shrimp, however. The tabooed mixtures result in koloputi, just like the mixtures of meats. Another dangerous mixture of vegetable and meat is that of cuscus meat and lemon (mumusi) or chili (maisa). It results in the loss of teeth rather than leprosy, which indicates that its logic is different from that of all other taboo mixtures.

In accounting for the rules that are not fully explained by the general principle already stated, it is useful to begin with those which concern the cassowary. This animal is morphologically a bird but, contrary to the other birds, it never flies; it runs on the ground. It is therefore put both in the category of manu (bird) and in that of the large terrestrial game animals to which wild pigs and deer also belong. This conflict of identities is recognized and even reflected upon by the Huaulu, as I discovered early on. When I went to Seram I had, of course, read Bulmer's classic article on why the cassowary is not a bird among the Karam of New Guinea.[163] So one day, when we had just killed a young cassowary and sat down to rest and chew betel, I slyly began to wonder aloud for all to hear about the animal at our feet that looked like a bird but wasn't one. Feigned naiveté was soon rewarded. Kuweyamani, my neighbor on the gigantic buttress of the tree on which I was perching, somewhat vulture-like, laughed and said: "It *is* a bird. Only it cannot fly. But it wasn't always that way. Haven't you heard yet the story about what happened to it?" "No," I answered, trying very badly to disguise my eagerness (I knew very well by this time that the best way to learn something from a Huaulu was to show a certain lack of interest, but none too great—just a certain absentmindedness meant to indicate that one was listening more out of politeness than out of a true desire to know). And he proceeded then and there to tell the brief story of how the cassowary fell from up in the trees to down on the ground, and has not returned to its original place ever since. I did not have a tape recorder with me at the time, but after we returned from our expedition a few days later, I went to see Kuweyamani and asked him to narrate the story again "for my tape recorder." As I was expecting (though I never gave up trying just because of that) he was frightened by the idea that his narration would become public and open to anybody's scrutiny. He told me that he was "too young to tell stories" and that I should ask an old man. Old men are both vain of their knowledge and horribly stingy with it, but I finally managed to persuade Polonahu Huaulu Kiita to let me tape the myth, which I give here exactly as he narrated it, that is, in the highly presupposing style which is typical of such stories. His son Pitere later provided missing elements, which are reported in brackets.

> That cassowary [was on top of the trees like the other birds]. The birds—one ate [a fruit] here, no way! anywhere, no way! Only the cassowary would finish them [the fruits] all. Fruits of the sago palm, of this faulu [?] tree. Anything, that bird [the cassowary]! It did not want [to let the other birds eat]! "It can't go on like this; it pushes us away too much!" [said the other birds]. The tekitekiana bird then said, "Oh dear! That much we eat! Is it possible that we go on eating without ever being able to be sated?" And the other ones: "But what can we do about it?" No more said! This tekitekiana rushed already [to the task]. It said, "Leave that to me." And those: "It won't work!" "Hm!" it said, "be patient!" No more said! What the kaa bird [*Rhyticeros plicatus*][164] eats, what this fiti bird eats, what this horu bird eats—whatever [a bird eats, the cassowary] eats it all! No, it can never be satiated. As soon a bird starts picking a fruit, hell! it has to fly away [because the cassowary chases it]. They start picking, they have to fly again. The tekitekianam then: "No more said! Let me jump here and there" [so that the cassowary will follow me, thinking that I move from fruit to fruit]. The tekitekianam [which is a very small bird] sat on a branch that was really very small! It jumped onto [another] one; this cassowary also jumps onto it. It jumps onto [another] one, no, not yet! It jumps again. What? [What goes on, why does the branch fail to break under the weight of the cassowary?] It jumps onto a very very small branch [of a supa, a banyan tree]. [This time it happens.] Just "fururuuru" [the noise of the fall]! "Te'e'e'" [scream of pain]. They say that it broke its knees [i.e. broke its legs, thus acquiring knees] [by hitting during the fall] the solamanu tree, the tupou tree, the atiana tree, the ailali tree. The end. Eh! [he corrects himself] the assafera tree [also]. It broke its knees through and through. I tell you, you would hear it [screaming in pain] as far as the sea! And how it ran! [At this point one of Polonahu's sons imitated the scream of the cassowary. Polonahu smiled and said:] I think it sounded that way. The end. [Then he started again, adding a clarification and a coda, which he had forgotten:] I think that [what happened was that] its wings broke. When the cassowary fell, the kaa (hornbill) was on the ground, and it went up the trees to take the place of the cassowary (ala ia selui asualiam).

I have kept my translation as close as possible to Polonahu's narration, to preserve some of its flavor. This also meant keeping a contradiction which Polonahu himself would have corrected had it been pointed out to him. In the coda, the kaa (hornbill) is still a bird which lives on the ground, but at the beginning of the story, Polonahu mentions it as one of the birds whose food the cassowary used to appropriate. A similar myth was recorded by Ellen among the Nuaulu of southern Seram. Because of this similarity and because the Huaulu and the Nuaulu consider each other "brothers," although they speak different languages and have rather different cultures, let me quote here the Nuaulu version:

> In former times the cassowary had wings and was able to fly as other birds. One day it rested on a banyan tree, but it was too heavy and the branch bent over as far as the ground. The cassowary fell off and broke its wings. Now the hornbill at that time was like the cassowary is now, it was unable to fly. As the branch of the banyan tree touched the ground the hornbill jumped upon it. But as the hornbill was lighter than the cassowary the branch soon rose again. Now, the hornbill could not fly—as I told you—so the cassowary offered it its wings. And that is why things are as they are today.[165]

Although the two versions seem at first quite similar, there is in fact a major difference in emphasis and elaboration between them. The Huaulu one greatly develops the first part, that is to say, the one that accounts for the cassowary's fall from the tree, but it treats the exchange of positions between cassowary and hornbill in a perfunctory way, to such a point that it almost sounds like an afterthought. Just the opposite is true of the Nuaulu version, which explains in detail the mechanism of exchange of place between the two birds but is all too brief on the cassowary's fall. Most important, it does not seem to motivate the fall. This gives it the appearance of "a perfect just-so story," to use Ellen's assessment. A just-so story explains nothing: it simply states authoritatively a sequence of unmotivated events by putting it in a narrational context. A just-so story is thus justificative only because of its illocutionary force, as a performative act ("if something is narrated it means that it is true") and not as an explicative one ("*x* happened because of general rule *y*").[166] By this definition of a just-so story, however, Ellen's characterization of the version he collected is somewhat unjust. Although it does not spell out the cassowary's fall, the story does provide a *general reason* for it; it says that the bird is always too heavy to find branches capable of supporting it. The implication is that sooner or later this conflict between habitat and body size—one that separates the cassowary from the other birds—had to become manifest, and the cassowary had to move to another habitat more consonant with its weight. The problem is that this implication is not worked out narratively, and is thus easily missed. In contrast, the explanation of the fall contained in the Huaulu version cannot be missed, because it is the story's centerpiece.

It is an explanation that makes more evident the incompatibility between the cassowary's two groups of attributes (it is a bird, but it differs from all other birds in being vastly bigger than they are) by representing it narratively as a conflict between this bird and all the others. Because of its dimensions, the cassowary is endowed with an insatiable appetite and at the same time with the means of satisfying it at the expense of all other birds. Consequently, if the cassowary were allowed to stay in the habitat of the other birds, they would die out. The conflict between the species and the class Aves with regard to dimensions would therefore be resolved by the elimination of the class. The only bird left would be the cassowary. Therefore, an anomaly destructive for the class (size) must be neutralized by adding another anomaly: a habitat anomaly. It is at this point that another implication of the cassowary's size is brought to the forefront so that it can be turned into an instrument of change. This implication is the one on which the Nuaulu version focusses immediately, without motivating its relevance in the economy of the narrative: weight. Weight will be turned against voracity and will neutralize it.

But in order to effect this transformation and, at the same time, to indicate that it is meant to put an end to a conflict with the class Aves as a whole, the cassowary must be given an antagonist. This is the tekitekiana, a species which has a relationship exactly opposite that of the cassowary with the class Aves. Indeed, the tekitekiana is the smallest bird (hence the most compatible, from the alimentary point of view, with all other birds), whereas the cassowary is the largest (and thus the most incompatible with the other birds). It is the smallness of the tekitekiana that allows it to entice the cassowary to alight on the smallest branch and thus to fall to the ground. The fall is etiological: it breaks the cassowary's wings, impeding its return up into the trees, and because of the intense pain it causes the animal, the fall turns it into the high-speed runner with the characteristic scream that Polonahu's son imitated to illustrate his father's narration. Once transformed, the cassowary is opposed to another bird. This time, it is not an antagonist but a substitute (the text explicitly states that it selui, "takes the place of," the cassowary). It is a substitute entrusted with the task of indexing the logical limit which the cassowary violated: the hornbill is the *largest possible bird* compatible with the paradigmatic habitat of the birds, namely the top of the trees. Thus the originary cassowary, which is incompatible with the other birds in their habitat up in the trees, goes through a transformation with a double outcome: the present-day cassowary and the present-day hornbill. These two outcomes are mutually reinforcing in signifying the same thing: there is an absolute limit in size for a bird to be fully a bird, that is, to have the all-important attribute of perching hoto aitufhu, "up in the trees."

The myth is more than a just-so story, then. It does more than provide a narrative account of the features of the present-day cassowary; it is a principled explanation of these features. This explanation also implies that the cassowary is perceived as an anomaly among birds. It is anomalous not so much because it is a bird that runs but does not fly as because of what explains that trait to begin with: the bird's excessive size. These dimensions make it incompatible with the other birds in their usual environment. Thus the fundamental criterion for assessing the cassowary's status among birds is neither taxonomic anomaly (runs, does not fly) nor Darwinian inefficiency (too much overweight to live up in the trees), but a sociological criterion based on an Aristophanic (rather than a Lévi-Straussian) anthropomorphization of the relations among birds. Cassowaries are not in a merely definitional conflict with their class or in conflict with the birds' environment; they are in a sociological conflict with the other birds: they are antisocial birds. The lack of sociability of the cassowary is frequently remarked upon by the Huaulu. It forms another reason for setting the animal apart from all other birds, which are perceived as highly sociable with one another and at times with humans as well. Even in myth, the cassowary is a loner and symbolizes the transgression of basic rules of social life; moreover, it is the preferred body of extremely antisocial beings such as the muluaqinaem, the already mentioned shades of women who died in childbirth.

If my analysis of the myth is correct, then, Ellen's conclusions with regard to the place of the cassowary in Nuaulu classification cannot be extended to Huaulu. He claims that in Nuaulu the cassowary is not really treated as an anomaly; rather, the coexistence of birdlike and nonbirdlike traits in the animal makes it possible to treat it sometimes as a member of the class Aves, sometimes as a member of the category peni, which in Nuaulu comprises the three large terrestrial game species: cassowary, wild pig, and deer. Thus in Ellen's view, alternate, and contextually motivated, classifications take the place of anomaly, which implies sticking more rigidly to a single classification.

This is not what happens in Huaulu, however. It is not just that the category peni (cognate of the Nuaulu *peni*)[167] is clearly not used as an alternate of manu with reference to the cassowary, or even that I was explicitly told that the cassowary is a bird despite its running on the ground like pigs and deer; it is also, and more important, that the position of the cassowary in the taboo system sets it apart from birds and pigs and deer. From the point of view of taboo, the cassowary does not have alternate values, but fixed ones,[168] which clearly indicate its anomalous status. Let us look, then, at how these taboos compare with those of regular birds and other relevant species.

Although the cassowary is considered a bird (manu), it does not share with the other birds the most important taboo of mixing: mixing with the creatures of the water. In this respect, the cassowary is like the paradigmatic terrestrial animals, the deer and the pig. But it is not quite like them either, since it has some residual taboos that indicate its birdness, taboos that pigs and deer do not have. They include the taboo of combination with one single fish species, the maate'a (herring),[169] the taboo of combination with the forest tree weevil (eti ai), and the taboos of combination with pandanus seeds and with matalala bananas (the last taboo, as I have mentioned, is explicitly said to be motivated by the fact that the cassowary is a bird). The last three taboos are fully shared with the birds; the first I would interpret as a synthetic index, both as a reminder of the cassowary's birdness (it behaves as a bird at least in combination with one fish species) and as a reaffirmation of its difference from other birds (it does not behave as a bird in combination with all other fish species). But the clearest index of the difference between the cassowary and birds is their incompatibility as food: it is taboo to eat any bird (and any other species up in the trees) with cassowary meat.

The combined effect of all these taboos is to show that the cassowary's status *is* anomalous: like birds in certain respects; like terrestrial game in others; but different from, and even opposite to, both in still other respects. In assessing the classificatory status of the cassowary, then, it is not sufficient to take into consideration how it is named or how it is described. One must pay attention to its position in the taboo system. While names and descriptions may suggest that the singular combination of traits of the cassowary is simply an opportunity for classifying it in alternate ways, taboo and myth indicate that it is in fact a problematic animal, one which must be justified discursively or singled out in practice rather than simply allocated to a category. In sum, it is impossible to decide that the cassowary is a bird or that it is not a bird depending on the contexts. It can be fixedly all those things, but this is precisely why the animal is highly problematic and thus the focus of myth and taboo. I should add that while the cassowary is regarded as anomalous in practice and in discourse by all Huaulu, there are variations in the degree to which it should be considered anomalous.

Some people insist on its birdness more than others; consequently, they say that it should be considered taboo in combination with all creatures down in the water, and not just with the herring. This is a minority opinion, however. Even those who say that the opinion may have some merit as a general principle argue that it is countered by another criterion that clearly sets the cassowary apart from the other birds and denizens of the trees. This is the experiential fact that the cassowary eats all manner of fish and shrimp: "if the cassowary eats them, it means that they are not taboo to eat with it." Thus, I was told that the cassowary is, contrary to ordinary birds, pinia, "good," that is to say, not taboo in combination with seafood. It was easy to point out that the argument is contradicted by its taboo status in combination with herring, although the cassowary also eats herring (or so was I told).[170] The argument was less convincing as a reason for the cassowary's difference from the other birds than interesting as a symptom of the feeling that it is indeed different, whatever the true reasons for its difference may be. And it was even more interesting as proof that the mixing taboos are rooted in the revulsion that animals of opposite categories feel for each other, and thus reflect the necessity in which humans find themselves of acting—or at least eating—in agreement with a cosmological order which they can know but not change. Just like language for Plato, maquwoli putatively exists *fusei* and not *thesei:* as a reflection of the order of things in the order of culture rather than as an arbitrary order in the Saussurean sense.

Let us now turn to another animal that has a very special, indeed unique, position in the system of mixing taboos—the eti ai. The word designates the larval stage of the largest weevil (kiffo poto, *Rhynochophorus ferrugineus*) known to the Huaulu. This larva infests the decaying trunks of forest trees. It is rather large (hence the alternative name eti poto, "big grub") and dark brown (a color which the Huaulu call mussunu, which also refers to what we call red). It is considered a delicacy and actively sought.

I never managed to obtain an explanation for the weevil's incompatibility with both the animals up in the trees and those down in the water from the Huaulu themselves. Yet it seems likely that the peculiar character of this animal, which begins its life wormlike on the ground and ends it as a beetle that flies and climbs on the trees, must have something to do with it. It cannot be habitat anomaly alone, though, for two reasons. The first is that habitat anomaly can explain why a grub which eventuates in a flying creature of the above is incompatible with the creatures swimming below in the water, but not why it is also incompatible with the creatures of the above. Indeed, weevils are found on the ground, not in water. Second, there is another creature, the "monitor lizard" (pue), which is even more anomalous than the eti/kiffo in terms of habitat, since it lives in all three of them, and yet has no mixing taboos.

There is one detail in the grub's list of mixing taboos which provides a clue about where the explanation is to be found. The list includes the cassowary. In other words, the cassowary is treated as a bird in relationship to the eti. This amounts to saying that morphology here takes the front seat in the definition of the cassowary and therefore also in the definition of the eti. Could it be that the same is true more generally of the eti/kiffo in its relationship with all other animals with which it is incompatible? I think so. Although the grub is found down on the ground and not in the water, its wormlike aspect suggests in many respects the creatures of the water, and this is what dictates its incompatibility with birds and the other creatures of the above.[171] Indeed, the eti contrasts with the animals typically found on the ground in not having feet. Its wriggling compares with the swimming of fish or eel or water snake. Moreover, it is born in a swarm, just like those watery creatures. One can say, therefore, that the morphology of the eti is in conflict with its habitat, or rather that the species violates the typical association of morphology and habitat found in the animals living on the ground. In this sense, the eti is analogous to the cassowary or, as we shall see, to the two edible pythons; but because the last three animals violate, to different degrees, only the contrast between up-in-the-trees and down-on-the-ground, they are still above the eti, which in addition violates the contrast between the two belows. The cassowary and the two pythons are indeed treated as creatures of the above with regard to mixing with the eti.

In sum, the eti is incompatible with both animals of the above (defined as minimally as can be) and animals below in the water because of a resonance, so to speak—because one sees in the larva both the winged creature it will become and the watery creature it should rightly be.[172] Morphology once again plays a role in taboos that are ostensibly determined by habitat alone. There seems to be a tacit association between a certain form (often with the kind of locomotion or other behaviors it dictates) and a certain habitat. Animals that violate these associations do seem to have a predisposition for taboo or other forms of symbolic use that may in turn require the creation of taboos. But then many other factors intervene to determine a specific outcome in terms of taboo. Consider, for instance, the different outcomes of three species which are anomalous in terms of the three-tiered cosmos: the tree weevil (eti ai), the sago grub (eti ipiam), and the monitor lizard. The tree weevil is not taboo in itself for anybody but only in combination; the monitor lizard is taboo in itself for sewa pukari[173] shamans; and the sago grub is completely free of taboo. How can these differences be accounted for?

Let us take the difference between monitor lizard and tree weevil first. It is true that the monitor lizard resembles the tree weevil in that both are associated with all three tiers of the cosmos. But although the monitor lizard may be found where birds perch and where fish swarm, it keeps looking like a ground animal, with four feet and a tail, thus fitted for walking.[174] This centeredness on the ground explains why the animal is associated with one of the most distinctive taboos of the most popular and widespread form of shamanism. Indeed, as I shall argue later, the monitor lizard appears as an analogue of the shaman—a solidly terrestrial being who is nonetheless capable of mediating the world he inhabits with the worlds inhabited by occult powers above and below it.

In any case, once the monitor lizard's elective affinity with shamanism is realized as taboo, its participation in other spheres, such as that of mixing taboos, becomes less likely, since such participation would diminish its ability to distinguish that particular ritual activity. In contrast, the tree weevil specializes in mixing taboos. But then there is predestination in this specialization, since the scandal of mixing is so much more profound in the tree weevil than in the monitor lizard, owing to the fact that the former animal is not morphologically stable like the latter, but successively takes two very different forms, one wormlike, the other birdlike.

An indirect proof that transformation is the strongest form of habitat mixing is furnished by the use of a transformation narrative to account for the scandal of the cassowary. Indeed there is an obvious parallelism between tree weevil and cassowary. Just as the terrestrial tree weevil turns into a flying beetle again and again, so the cassowary, once and for all, turns from a flying being into a terrestrial one.

But what accounts, then, for the fact that the other transformative species—the eti ipiam or sago grub (*Rhynochophorus bilineatus*),[175] which turns into a winged beetle like the tree weevil—is not taboo? I speculate that in this case the dangerous association of change of habitat with morphological change is countered and neutralized by other attributes. One attribute is probably size, which, as we shall see, often plays a role in differentiating similar species from the point of view of taboo. The eti ai is the larva of the biggest kiffo; but the eti ipiam turns into a much smaller beetle. It may well be, then, that the former evokes the idea of a flying, up-in-the-trees creature much more strongly than the smaller species; consequently, the larger of the two species may take on itself the whole burden of representing the violation of the three-tiered cosmos instantiated by them both. In other words, representation becomes more important here than instantiation. Or better said, the most exaggerated instantiation becomes representative, and thus the focus of the judgment of anomaly for the whole set which it represents. As anomaly is emphasized in the bigger species, it is deemphasized in the smaller, by a sort of division of labor. This confirms, by the way, that the logic of taboo is symbolic even when it is merely in the service of classification.

But the crucial attribute is probably color, or rather color as the index of an association which puts the eti ipiam beyond the sphere of taboo.[176] In contrast with the eti ai, which is mussunu, "red/brown," the eti ipiam is putia, "white/pale." Its whiteness is the whiteness of the sago starch in which the grub is born and develops. Indeed, the sago grub is not so much "hunted," like the tree weevil, as farmed by cutting down sago palms in gardens and groves and letting the trunk become infested with the animal. The grubs are then harvested with some of the tools also used to process the sago pith. In a sense the grubs are viewed as transformed sago—as one particular way of consuming sago. The association is reinforced by the fact that they are often baked inside lumps of "sago flour" (afano). Now, sago, as the absolutely basic staple, is largely exempted from taboo and in any case has no mixing taboos. It is the absolutely unmarked food, which can be combined with any other. I conclude that the sago grub takes on the same taboo-neutral character of the starch it eats. Because the principle that one is what one eats applies to animals too, staplehood is able to override anomaly.

There is one more taboo of the eti ai that needs explaining. The animal cannot be mixed with pandanus fruit. Again, no reason is proffered by the Huaulu for this taboo.[177] But it may well be that the purpose of the taboo is to dissimilate the only two species that are incompatible with all the animals up in the trees and all the animals below in the water. What is perhaps problematic about this shared incompatibility is that it occurs between two beings of a very different order: a mobile animal and an immobile vegetal. I speculate that the taboo reaffirms their difference against what negates it, that is, that sharedness. But I confess that I am at a loss to explain why the pandanus occupies the same place as the tree weevil in the system of mixing taboos.[178]

A related but nonetheless different case is that of the telo matalala. This kind of banana is incompatible with all creatures of the above (including in this case the cassowary, "because it is a bird," as it was put) but only with eels among the creatures below in the water. There is therefore no perfect parallelism between this vegetal and the eti ai, and thus, predictably in terms of my hypothesis, no need to dissimilate them by means of taboo. Indeed, eti ai and matalala bananas may be eaten together without danger. But what about the matalala's own mixing taboos—can they be accounted for in some way or must we remain agnostic as in the case of the pandanus? I believe that one trait of the matalala to which the Huaulu invariably attracted my attention offers a clue. They pointed out that the name matalala, "sky variety,"[179] refers to a peculiarity which makes this banana tree unique: the bunch is said to point to the sky instead of falling down toward the ground, as in all other varieties.[180] To the Huaulu, this indicates a connection with the above, and thus, one may infer, a confusion between above and below. However, what makes this confusion dangerous in terms of the down-in-the-water/up-in-the-trees contrast is its coexistence with an additional feature. Because of its considerable dimensions and its explicitly phallic associations,[181] the matalala evokes a penislike equivalent under water, the eel. Eating the meat of creatures up in the trees with the matalala would therefore mean bringing its underwater resonances into the mixture. Analogously, eating eels with the upward-pointing fruit, which indexically associates with the creatures of the above, would mean bringing their incompatible meats in contact, however indirectly.

We are now in a position to see that the mixing taboos form a certain hierarchy of nested oppositions. The most encompassing opposition is manifested by the tree grub, which partitions all species in the list into two exclusive categories (up-in-the-trees/below-in-the-water) with which it entertains identical relations of incompatibility. At this level, the cassowary is treated as a bird, since it is put in the up-in-the-trees category. At the next hierarchical level, the mutual incompatibility of the cassowary and herring creates two symmetric categories: the denizens of the water without the herring and the denizens of the above without the cassowary. While the denizens of the water are not further subdivided by taboos of mixing, the denizens of the above are. In relationship with the cassowary, with which they are equally incompatible, winged animals (birds and bats) and arboreal marsupials form a single category. This category is opposed to that of pythons, in that the latter is not incompatible with the cassowary. The cassowary thus helps reveal a categorical opposition, just as the tree grub does, but in a somewhat different manner. Winged animals and arboreal marsupials are in turn separated by the mutual incompatibility of their meats. Clearly, these nested taboos indicate that the irreducible core of the up-in-the-trees category is constituted by the winged animals and the arboreal marsupials. For only these are contrasted with the terrestrial bird, the cassowary, whereas the pythons are not. In fact, the pythons are incompatible with neither cassowary nor marsupials nor winged animals. As such, they neutralize their various oppositions.

All of which raises a number of problems. We may begin with the simplest one, which concerns the core category of the up-in-the-trees, namely winged animals. For all species in this category, "winged" is treated as equivalent to "able to fly." Indeed, this is what justifies the categorical exclusion (partial or total, depending on the context) of the cassowary—a winged animal which cannot fly. Why is it, then, that the chicken and the maleo bird—the latter not a flyer, the former not exactly one—are included in the category? With regard to the chicken, the problem does not really exist. Huaulu chickens, contrary to ours, are pretty good flyers if they have to be. In any case, what matters is that they fly well enough to perch on trees, as they do every night, thereby qualifying as full members of the up-in-the-trees category. Indeed, chickens, as the most familiar of all birds, are birds par excellence, as indicated by the fact that they are often called manu, "bird" (particularly when bantams are referred to), instead of the more specific maulohu. A more legitimate question about the chicken is why it appears in the list of mixing taboos at all, since it is traditionally considered taboo in itself. The obvious answer is that its inclusion is a new thing; however, the not-so-obvious implication is that mixing taboos are not a haphazard ensemble of fossilized customs, but are generated by principles which are still productive. Had it been otherwise, it would have been easier for the Huaulu, in their present mood of complaint about the excessive burden of taboo, to treat chicken meat as neutral with regard to mixing, since it was not traditionally included in the list of meats with mixing taboos. Its inclusion shows that it is the principle behind it, and not just the taboos taken singularly, which is part of the tradition. The tradition requires, then, its generative use, so that if a new animal becomes edible, one must still consider whether or not it is incompatible with others and with which ones it may be.

But what about the maleo? How can this running bird be a different case from the cassowary's? Two answers present themselves. The first is that while the cassowary never flies from the time of its birth to that of its death, the immature maleo does fly and perch on trees. The second possible answer is that we have here a case similar to that of the eti ai and the eti ipiam. In other words, when two species are similar, it is the bigger one that attracts taboo in most cases (although the converse may also be true, as we shall see). But dimension is rarely the only motivation. It seems to intervene as a caricaturing element, if one may say so. Put otherwise, when the animal is already the most representative of its group, dimension may make its prototypicality more evident, more striking. This is probably the case with the cassowary, whose dimensions magnify some of the nonbird attributes it possesses more clearly than the maleo. The result is that taboo, which derives from a sort of overestimation of contrast, is attracted to the cassowary at the expense of the maleo, which is conversely turned into a full bird with regard to mixing.

The next problem concerns the division of the creatures up in the trees in relationship to the cassowary. I have explained why the cassowary must be dissimilated from them, but why is it that the pythons are not included? Probably because, among all animals associated with up-in-the-trees, the pythons are those closest to the ground to which the cassowary has fallen. Indeed, although these animals are classified as arboreal by the Huaulu, as by other peoples,[182] they, and particularly the patola python, can also creep on the ground. It is thus clear not only that the category up-in-the-trees is further subdivided, but also that these subdivisions are ranked vertically, with the pythons at the lowest level and the winged creatures at the highest.

But here a new problem arises. For the two most proximate kinds, winged animals and cuscuses, which are treated as equivalent relative to all other animals with regard to mixing, are dissimilated by being made taboo with one another. In contrast, pythons are not dissimilated by means of mixing taboos from either of the two kinds of animals that stand above them, cuscuses and winged animals. Why this difference? For the very simple reason, I would argue, that only winged creatures and cuscuses are fully and purely creatures of the above, and are thus locked in a contradictory relationship with one another: they are identical with regard to habitat, but profoundly different with regard to morphology and locomotion (since cuscuses, contrary to birds, can climb but not fly). This contradictory proximity is treated as irrelevant when both kinds of animals are contrasted with vastly different animals, but it becomes relevant when they are related to one another directly. The rights of morphology and locomotion must then be reasserted against those of habitat in the finer definition of the difference between the two kinds, which is required when they face each other in the pot.[183] Pythons, in contrast, are more obviously and thus safely different. Their occupation of the arboreal habitat notwithstanding, they present a less burning problem of differentiation.[184] The same can be said of their relationship with the cassowary. They share with it, in part, the ground, but they are, after all, defined as animals of a different sphere—the arboreal. Thus pythons, albeit partly intermediary between up-in-the-trees and below-on-the-ground, or rather because of it and because of their peculiar morphology, present no problem of differentiation from either the cassowary or fully arboreal animals that would have to be addressed by means of taboo.

One objection may be raised against the invoking of morphology, however. Pythons are morphologically and locomotionally similar to creatures below in the water such as eels. When combined with winged creatures or cuscuses, therefore, we would expect them to evoke the lethal confusion of fish and fowl that is the keystone of the system of mixing taboos, just as the case is with the matalala banana. But the difference which in fact exists between this banana and pythons shows how important it is to take the calibration of the attributes into account when speaking of taboos. True, pythons evoke in certain respects the realm of below-in-the-water. They are, in fact, associated with water *tout court,* but it is mostly the water of above: they are connected symbolically with rain. The connection rests partly on empirical grounds, since snakes appear in great numbers when it rains,[185] partly on symbolic signatures. The latter are particularly significant for the patola pythons, in whose "multicolored" (likalika) skin is read a pattern of clouds (tuputupuem, "cloud formations," is the name).[186] In sum, its connections with the ground and even the streams notwithstanding, the patola python (and a fortiori the tipoloa, which is rarely found on the ground, as far as I could see from the hunts I took part in) is overwhelmingly a creature of the above. As such, whatever confusion of fish and fowl it may evoke, it is not as troubling as the one evoked by a species (the matalala banana) that is situated right in between fish and fowl.

The final problem raised by the list of mixing taboos is that it involves only two kinds of marsupials, although all kinds are very close in every respect. There are actually some differences among informants on the kinds involved. Everybody agrees that one is the makilam; a majority of the best informants say that the second kind is the elahuwam, but some have told me, rightly or wrongly, that it is the kapupum. These statements are in conflict but can be viewed as equally possible applications of the same principle. To understand this point and more generally why these varieties of cuscuses are the significant ones from the point of view of taboo, we must consider for a moment the Huaulu classification of the cuscuses.

There are in Seram three species of cuscuses recognized by our zoology: the *Phalanger orientalis orientalis* (Pallas), the *Phalanger maculatus chrysorrhous* (Demarest), and the perhaps much rarer *Phalanger celebensis.*[187] The Huaulu classification recognizes only the first two species. But while it names the category "cuscuses" (ihisi) as a whole, it does not name each species as such. Instead, it names the male and female in each species and, furthermore, certain stages or subvarieties of each. Thus the male of the *Phalanger maculatus chrysorrhous,* or spotted cuscus, is called ihisi makilam (or simply makilam), while its female form is called ihisi kapupuam (or simply kapupuam). As for the male of the *Phalanger orientalis orientalis,* two varieties are distinguished by color: the white one is called (ihisi) elahuwam and the beige one is called (ihisi) moliam. The female is called (ihisi) mussufam. Furthermore, all young *Phalanger orientalis orientalis,* irrespective of sex, are called (ihisi) kopakopa anam. Each of these varieties also has a name which is used in magical formulas, in poetry, or during the hunt (when using ordinary names is dangerous). These names need not be discussed here, since they do not change the ordinary classification of the cuscus.

It would be extremely incorrect to infer from these names that the Huaulu do not recognize the existence of the two species of cuscuses. They recognize them in discourse, if not lexically. But more important, this recognition is made evident by the linkage of the named kinds of cuscuses as "husband" and "wife" or as "parents" and "child." It is through these linkages that the exact boundaries of species are traced.[188] Thus the makilam and the kapupuam are said to form a husband-wife pair. As for the elahuwam and the moliam, they are both said to be husbands of the mussufam. In turn, the three of them are said to be the parents of the kopakopa anam. Thus while the species *Phalanger maculatus chrysorrhous* is defined by a relation of conjugality, the species *Phalanger orientalis orientalis* is defined both by conjugality and by filiation. The conjugal formula which characterizes the second species is defined, half in jest, as a polyandrous one: hihina esa manawa hua, "one wife for two husbands." Sometimes the formula hihina hua manawa tolu, "two wives, three husbands," is used to define the whole set of cuscuses. In this case there is no implication of a union across species. I should add that for some informants at least there is a developmental linkage between the two "husbands" of the mussufam: they recognize that the moliam is a younger stage and that the elahuwam is an elderly ("white-haired") male. Polyandry, thus, has an age dimension: one "husband" is younger than the other.

This classification is remarkable for at least two reasons. First of all, it identifies each species of cuscus by the criterion of inbreeding, which also happens to be the main criterion for establishing the conceptual boundaries between species in our natural science. The use of this criterion is implied by the definition of the species through a husband-wife pair and by the exclusion of any idea of intermarriage between males and females of two different species of cuscuses. In the second place, the classification is remarkable because it applies categories that are normally confined to humans, namely the categories manawa (man/husband) and hihina (woman/wife),[189] to two animal species. This usage sets the cuscus markedly apart from all other animals, for which specifically animal forms of *male* (*tulalam* for birds, *mossaniam* for all others) and *female* (*inaniam*) are used. It agrees with the strong anthropomorphization of the cuscuses (which has many physical traits resembling those of humans), testified by innumerable expressions, myths, and ritual usages, and also found among the Nuaulu.[190] But as is usual when an animal is strongly anthropomorphized, it serves as a distorted mirror for humans: its behavior is not fully human—only human enough to make its perversion of what is truly human more evident. This is at least the case for the *Phalanger orientalis orientalis* species, whose way of being "husband and wife" takes the culturally repellent form of polyandry—repellent because it inverts the culturally proper form of polygyny and, more profoundly, the proper hierarchical relation between man and woman (since it is assumed that if a woman marries two men she is "on top"). Indeed, whenever the expression *hihina essa manawa hua* is used to refer to this species, people laugh with the same laughter that accompanies the mention of some imaginary transgression or inversion of proper sexual behavior.

One consequence of the fact that each species is defined as a conjugal pair or a ménage à trois is that the most important member, naturally the male, can stand for the whole species as far as mixing taboos are concerned. Indeed, in response to my query about why the mixing taboos are limited to makilam and elahuwam, one of my friends said, "Because they are the two main husbands; the other cuscuses do not count."[191] Here again a strong element of anthropomorphism is involved, because in human society the husband can indeed be considered as standing for the whole family. In sum, the equivalence of part and whole allows the taboo to follow a principle of economy or, rather, to compromise between freedom and restraint in the relationship to a species or grouping of species. As we have seen and shall see again, this symbolic "economizing" is by no means infrequent. We should not be surprised. Taboo is very hard on the Huaulu, as they keep complaining, and one understands why they want to keep it to a minimum. Provided some necessary contrast, some incompatibility is sustained in some way, all the rest may be considered redundant and eliminated. This is precisely why taboo, just like language, likes to resort to marking and prototypicality. Giving mixing taboos to all cuscuses would be too burdensome, since cuscus meat is very commonly present on Huaulu tables.[192] One cannot live on symbolism and classification alone; one must eat some meat after all! Fortunately, Huaulu culture was not created by some faculty committee.

Recourse to markedness may also help explain why according to some informants mixing taboos apply not to the males of both species of cuscuses, but to one species only, in both its female (kapupu) and male (makila) forms. Indeed, the principle that one term of a pair stands for them both may be applied when the pair consists of two species of cuscuses, not just when it consists of the male and female of each species. In other words, the *Phalanger maculatus,* as the largest and most impressive cuscus, may stand for all cuscuses. Hence taboo may be limited to this species instead of being limited to the males of each of the two species. The two views of the mixing taboos, while different, presuppose the same logic.

There is a mixing taboo, however, that concerns all cuscuses indistinctly. This is the taboo on throwing their bones, after they have been cooked and eaten, into streams or ponds. Otherwise, the "master" (upu) of the cuscuses becomes angry and holds the animals back so that they cannot be procured again (massa ita oi leussi, "otherwise we do not see them again"). The reason for this anger is apparently the revulsion that the cuscuses feel for a habitat which is not theirs.[193] It is a reason that comes out more clearly and consciously here but which in fact is valid for all taboos on mixing: it is dangerous to mix in one's stomach the meats of incompatible animals, because these animals hate each other or hate each other's environment.[194] In other words, classification, which is constructed by humans, is completely reified in Huaulu consciousness. The compatibilities and incompatibilities predicated on classification become mutual hates and avoidances among species in different classes, particularly as determined by habitat. Taboo is supposed to register these objective incompatibilities and hates so that humans do not become entangled in them. But taking them into account also means showing respect for the concerns of the animals involved. This component of respect for the animal, and thus the fear of incurring its displeasure, is probably also found behind the taboo on mixing acid and "hot" condiments (lemon and chili) with the mild meat of cuscuses. The sanction for the transgression of this taboo is the loss of one's teeth and thus of the very ability to eat the meat of the offended animal. All this begins to suggest that taboo must also be understood as part of a strategy of respect and displaced avoidance of the wild animals. This strategy is not as marked as the "pact" with domestic animals, and it has different implications, but it is nevertheless quite important, as we shall see.

To conclude briefly: With regard to mixing in the human stomach, animal species are primarily defined by their situation in a three-tiered structure of habitats, generated by two intersecting oppositions: between above and below, and between what is out of water and what is in water. Besides these basic divisions others exist, based on morphological and behavioral criteria, for certain species or groupings thereof. The interference of these various criteria produces specific compatibilities and incompatibilities, and thus specific mixing taboos. These in turn seem to reassert the normalcy of the basic three-tiered classification of animals. With few exceptions, then, animals live in agreement with this cosmic structure; and humans who eat them should too. Eating is turning external flesh into one's own flesh, converting the multiplicity of animals into the unity of one's own body. This process of conversion can succeed only if it does not run against the basic structure of the cosmos, as is reflected in the compatibilities and incompatibilities of animals and thus of their flesh. To eat incompatible flesh is to tear one's own flesh apart—to fall victim to leprosy. The mixing taboos thus point to the dependence of the human body on the body of the cosmos. The two symbolize each other. This is why the analysis of these taboos must be symbolic before it can be anything else.

Turtles and Crocodiles

In the previous section, I have considered various species whose anomalous status eventuates in a peculiar list of mixing taboos. One may well ask, however, if anomaly does ever affect the status of a species as such—if it makes a species taboo in itself, rather than merely in combination with some other species.

The answer is yes. But such taboos, as already suggested by the case of the monitor lizard, are usually limited to certain social categories or even individuals—a sign that more than anomaly is needed for them to become taboo, although anomaly undoubtedly attracts this something more. Only in very few cases does anomaly seem to eventuate in intrinsic taboos that apply to all Huaulu. Yet we shall see that, even in those cases, one must invoke more than a supposedly universal reaction against anomaly because of the presence of classificatory thought in all minds. I say "seem to" because all the evidence suggests it, yet it is never explicitly acknowledged.

The most notable of the seemingly anomalous species which are taboo for all are turtles. More exactly, and puzzlingly to the Huaulu themselves, three of the four kinds of turtles they recognize are universally taboo, whereas the fourth is taboo only to women. The three turtles in question are the makopa, the henu, and the ulae.

The makopa is described as a freshwater turtle with a "black" carapace. It is obviously the *Cuora amboinensis* Guenther (Amboinian box terrapin).[195] The henu is a sea turtle with a "grayish" carapace. It is said to be identical to the animal called teteruga in the local variant of A.M. and penyu in B.I. It is probably the *Chelonia mydas* (green turtle).[196] The ulae is also a sea turtle, said to be similar to the henu, but with a likalika, "multicolored" or "variegated," carapace. It may well be the *Eretmochelys imbricata* (also called *Chelonia imbricata*), that is to say, the hawksbill turtle.[197]

The turtle that is taboo only for women is called tipope and glossed in A.M. as *teteruga salawaku.* It is said to be the largest and is probably to be identified with "the largest of the Chelonians,"[198] namely the *Dermochelys coriacea.*[199] However, it would be wrong to assume that the Huaulu, who usually live inland and allegedly abstained from fishing in the sea until a comparatively recent time, are so familiar with these species as to use the terms *henu, ulae,* and even *tipope* consistently. What really matters to them are two distinctions. The first is between the turtle most familar to them—the freshwater turtle (makopa)—and the sea turtles; the second is between the tipope turtle and all others. The second opposition is sustained by the already mentioned difference in the extension of taboo; the first by the belief that makopam ia laikana henu, "the makopa generates[d] the henu [and one assumes the closely related ulae as well]." The statement that one species "generates" others, or that it is their inaniam "mother," or upuam, "master/owner," is frequently used, as we shall have a few more opportunities to see, to refer to the relationship between one species that stands out in a grouping and all other species in it. What makes the generating species stand out is usually dimension: it is either bigger than all others or, conversely, smaller. But other factors, such as proximity to humans, also tend to be involved. More often than not, the generating species is the focus of taboo. The same is probably true of turtles. The main focus of taboo is clearly the makopa, the only animal which the Huaulu, especially in their traditional habitat, would have the opportunity to experience extensively. It is by attraction to the makopa, I would surmise, that the more distant and larger henu and ulae have become taboo.[200] In contrast, the species that is most distant from the makopa from the point of view of dimension and probably space as well is less taboo (the tipope), since it is dangerous only for those weaker beings who are more susceptible to danger—women. The smallest and the largest in the set stand opposite each other as the most taboo and the least taboo.

By this interpretation, then, a principle of economy which is both symbolic and material is again at work in determining the status of these animals. One of them stands for the whole and thus attracts, in part or entirely, the tabooness which would by right belong to the whole. This raises two questions. The first is, What characters of the whole set are at the root of the taboo? The second is, Why is it that the whole is represented by a caricature of the attributes that define it, either by blowing them up or by miniaturizing them?

The obvious answer to the second question is that both processes allow the type to become more visible. In a sense, the smaller or bigger animals are the templates of a mental construct, the type, and bear in their very dimensions a telltale sign of their mental origin and function. Certain species are not just species; they are also vehicles for cognition and other operations of the socialized mind. As such, they must be minded, which more often than not means they must be viewed as dangerous, as taboo.

Turning now to the first question: What are the taboo-inducing characters of all turtles that are magnified in the makopa by miniaturization[201]—if one may use an oxymoron—and by proximity to the human observer? If we ask the Huaulu, the answer is simple: the taboo-inducing character is the texture of the turtle's skin. Indeed, they affirm that turtles are taboo to eat because the consumption of their meat induces a large number of painful and purulent "sores" (nuka) on the surface of the body. As a result, the skin looks somewhat like the skin of turtles. In sum, it would seem that the taboo is a consequence of the operation of the analogic mind. A correspondence is established between an undesirable state of the human skin and the permanent texture of an animal's skin.[202] The permanent is viewed as the cause of the impermanent, and thus contact, as established by eating, is ruled out, is made taboo. The Huaulu do not explain why the meat of the tipope, whose skin is not different in texture from that of the other turtles, does not have the same effect, except on women. Indeed, they are themselves puzzled at the exception, since, as they say, "their aspect is the same" (ita oire sama).[203] Naturally, the exception could be explained away with the usual principle that women are more vulnerable than men, although this would still leave open the question of why tipope meat is less dangerous than that of the other three turtles. But the problem is that there are at least three other similarly scaly species—tipolo, tekepatola, and monitor lizard—which do not induce skin disease in women or shamans, for whom they are taboo. Only the crocodile seems to confirm the skin-texture theory of taboo. Leaving aside the crocodile for the moment, let us look again at the turtles. Is it possible to preserve the Huaulu explanation and yet remedy its deficiencies by adding something to it which would make it truer? In other words, is scaliness in these animals a motivation for taboo, but only because it is part of a larger complex of traits which is left unmentioned?

In order to answer this question, I must first elaborate a point that emerged from the analyses of mixing taboos in the previous section. Those analyses showed that if an animal diverges from a combination of traits typically associated with one of the three main habitats, or worse, if it combines traits that belong to different habitats, it assumes a peculiar position in the system of mixing taboos. This system, then, is in itself a strong indication for the existence of prototypical kinds, each of which is categorically associated with one of the three tiers of the cosmos because it is exclusively, or almost exclusively, found in that tier.

Birds are such prototypical animals for the up-in-the-trees habitat, and fishes for the down-in-the-water habitat. The large quadrupeds that are the main game animals (wild pig and deer) seem to be prototypical of the down-on-the-ground (or maybe one should say "down to earth") animals. Further evidence for declaring these animals prototypical in their habitat is provided by ready-made expressions such as "like the birds on top of the trees" (wahi manuem hoto aitufhu) or "like the fishes down in the water" (wahi iyaem pale wae); there are no counterparts of these expressions for animals whose habitat associations are not so clear. For instance, one would never say "like the ilauwa down in the water" if one wanted to refer to a prototypical animal living in the water. Another piece of evidence for the prototypical status of these kinds of animals is furnished by the fact that birds, fishes, and quadrupeds taken alone are lesser foci of universal taboos than animals that straddle different habitats (such as frogs) or whose somatic traits are in conflict with those that are prototypical for their habitat (as in the case of the cassowary). In sum, certain animals convey an idea of normality with regard to the association of habitat and somatic and behavioral traits, whereas others do not. The former tend to be "safe," whereas the latter tend to be dangerous. If certain species in the generically safe categories are taboo, it is for special reasons, which affect only particular individuals or categories of people. The zoologically typical is safe for the social universal.

At this point it is possible to answer our initial question. Scaliness is indeed a motivation of taboo in turtles, but only because it occurs in a paradoxical context, that is, in association with traits that are not typical for scaly animals down in the water. The archetypal aquatic animal is the fish, as we have just seen, but turtles are fishy only with regard to skin; in all other regards, they are like terrestrial animals: they walk on all fours, breathe, and are even born on land. Furthermore, they manifest other unaquatic traits such as building nests for their eggs and hissing when challenged by an enemy. I would argue, then, that skin is a trait that stands synecdochically for the whole combination of attributes which gives turtles their anomalous status of "terrestrial" animals that live in water. This anomaly's fundamentality to the turtle taboo is indirectly suggested by the fact that all other four-footed animals that live in between water and land, albeit in different degrees—frogs, the crocodile, and the monitor lizard—are taboo to some extent. Moreover, the principal focus of taboo among turtles is the makopa, that is, the species which is most frequently experienced by the Huaulu as living in between land and water, whereas the tipope, which is viewed as the most marine of sea turtles, is the least taboo.

But why is it precisely the skin, rather than any other trait, which bears the burden of representing the whole turtle status? One answer to this question is that the skin is the most visible part of an animal and wraps it entirely. Better than any other body part, then, it can stand for the whole animal or the whole set of traits that define it. Another answer is that the skin structure of turtles, however different from that of fishes, is still scaly like theirs. Thus it is also the point at which the fundamental nonfishiness of turtles becomes most apparent. In other words, what makes skin bear the burden of taboo is that it connects the two sides of the conflict which defines the turtles: it is both what makes it fishy and what reveals that it is not. But then, why is it that the official explanation stops at the skin as such and does not mention what the skin stands for? If anomaly is the real motivation of taboo, why is it that it remains unmentioned? Why is it, in fact, that the Huaulu justify the taboo simply by citing their desire to avoid turning turtlelike with regard to skin?

The failure to mention anomaly could be explained by the more general tendency for basic principles and phenomena of consciousness to remain implicit. The more categorical they are, the more one must think *with* them rather than *about* them. Indeed, most of the anomalies that the Huaulu explicitly invoke as a motivation for taboo are not of the abstract, classificatory kind (species anomaly), but relate to habitat (as we have seen) or to the interconnection of events (a thunderclap when the sky is free of clouds, rain when the sun shines, a wild animal entering the village or otherwise seeking humans, or two animals of different species found intertwined, as if coupling).

But there are other, more specific reasons why the whole burden of explaining taboo concentrates on the skin as such when turtles are concerned. Two convergent reasons seem particularly important. The first and more obvious one is that the motivation for a rule becomes confused with the motivation of an actor for not violating it. Thus when the ethnographer asks the why of the rule, he is given the why of following it instead: "We don't eat turtle because we don't want to get 'turtle skin.'" In other words, the actor's point of view is confused with that of the system; what happens because of the institution is confused with the happening of the institution. The confusion is forgivable in the informants, who usually have only a practical interest in the rule and therefore focus more on its alleged consequences (skin disease) than on its causes. But it is unforgivable in the ethnographer. Yet too many ethnographers perpetuate precisely this confusion while believing that they respect "the native point of view." Respect cannot be great if it begins by mistaking one type of answer for another. *The native point of view* is an ambiguous expression: does it refer to the point of view of individual native agents at a certain time and in a certain context or to the point of view of the cultural schemes that their statements and choices presuppose?

The second reason for the skin explanation is that the human body must be drawn in if the taboo is to have any force, if people must be made to feel that they are directly concerned by it. Attention therefore shifts from the classificatory position of the offending species to something more tangible in it, something in its body that may be of bodily consequence to humans. An analogy is isolated that connects one body to the other. The only thing in the body of turtles that allows one to trace such a connection is the texture of their skin, which recalls the diseased skin of humans. Hence this analogic element of more immediate relevance in determining action displaces the actual motive for the reaction against the turtle. But analogy is not completely able to displace motive, which leaves some tracks behind. The fact that the explanation explains too much, that it cannot explain why skin texture as such is not sufficient to make other animals taboo, or that when they are under taboo, its violation does not result in skin disease, is sufficient to indicate that something else is at work, and I have dared to speculate what it could possibly be. But I hasten to add that I would not have dared to do so if the Huaulu themselves did not insist so much on classifying animals in terms of prototypical connections between somatic traits and habitat, and if most animals anomalous in terms of this classification were not given some symbolic value and were not a focus of taboo or avoidance in various degrees.

The crocodile is another species whose meat is universally taboo. At first approximation, this taboo seems pretty much like the one on turtle meat. In both cases, local discourse focusses on the animal's skin and its alleged similarity to diseased human skin, but the context suggests anomaly as *the* reason for taboo. Moreover, this anomaly appears to exist on very similar grounds for both animals. Just like turtles, crocodiles share much of their morphology and physiology with terrestrial species, but only a certain similarity in skin structure with the prototypical denizens of their habitat—water. Yet other, more powerful associations and values enter into the taboo status of the crocodile and make it a case apart.

The most important of such associations and values center around the predatory character of the animal. Although the crocodile's victims include land animals, its diet is based mostly on fish. This, together

Fishing on the Sapulewa River by barricading it with baskets, in preparation for the collective fish poisonings. 1972. (Photo by V. Valeri.)

with the fact that it is the largest animal "down in the water," makes it the lord of rivers and of their denizens. It is not surprising, therefore, that the crocodile mediates between them and the Huaulu fisherman. Indeed, the principal deities of fishing—a class of sewa potoem[204] called telue—are said to be crocodiles. There are two such divinities, each the "property" of a different ipa. Etuainani "belongs" to the ipa Puraratuhu; Pinasainale is the "property" of the ipa Sayaramani. These two divinities divide between them the two main rivers where the Huaulu fish: Pinasainale is the "lord" (upu) of the fishes in the largest river, the Sapulewa, while Etuainani "lords" over the fishes in its affluent river, the Oni. The relative size of the two rivers parallels the relative rank of the two lineages, in that Sayaramani claims leadership of the senior section of the Huaulu clan (Huaulu potoa), whereas Puraratuhu is the leader of the junior section (Huaulu kiita). These deities receive the first fruits of fishing at each of the big, collective fish poisonings held in the rivers Sapulewa and Oni during the "dry" season.[205] They also possess the shamans just like all other sewaem. And like many of them, they combine animal and human bodies. Although basically female, both deities also combine male and female traits. Thus, when she does not take her crocodile form, Pinasainale, who lives at the bottom of the Sapulewa, wears such male insignia as a red head cloth and two red cloths crossed on her chest (the latter in the manner of officiating shamans). Moreover, when she possesses a shaman, she may manifest herself with a sonorous cock-a-doodle-doo, like a bantam. When that happens, the next day will be rainless, for the telue control the weather. Such mixtures of terms that are otherwise separated and indeed opposed are typical of sewaem, of course, since they are a function of the sewaem's various mediating roles. But they also parallel and converge with the anomalous combination of attributes that make the crocodile an anomalous species. It is clear, therefore, that this anomaly is only the base on which much more is built.

Another important feature of the telue is that "they eat human flesh" (i ae manusia). This is, of course, because they are crocodiles; or rather, the cannibalistic tendencies of so many sewaem and even ancestors find their natural expression in a crocodilian embodiment. The crocodile's man-eating propensity contributes crucially to making it taboo to eat (but not to kill). Indeed, it represents the subversion of a fundamental hierarchical relationship: that between human as predator and animal as prey. Humans become hunted by an animal, they become its game and thus lose their humanity, they become confused with the animals that fear being killed and eaten by man.[206] I think that this reversal is in itself distressing to the Huaulu and adds something to the horror of death at the hands (or rather paws) of the crocodile. This horror at becoming a hunted animal was evident, for instance, in the words a woman once used to warn me not to go alone near rivers: "When a crocodile smells us, then it runs after us on the ground. However much you will run, you will not make it; it will catch you and eat you up." I saw her shudder when she evoked for me and for herself alike the crocodile smelling human odor; it was not only the horror of being eaten that went into that shudder, but also the horror of being smelled like a beast, as human hunters smell their game. It was the horror of losing one's humanity.

A myth provides confirmation for the hypothesis that the crocodile evokes a dangerous mixing of human and animal, and that this mixing is one motivation of the taboo on its flesh. Actually the myth in question is narrated to explain another taboo, that on uttering the name "crocodile" in Salaipu, the site of one of the oldest Huaulu settlements in the mountains behind the present village.

> This ancestral village saw a dispute between two brothers of the Tapale lineage (closely related to Sayaramani, by the way) concerning whether or not it was possible to put a human loincloth on a pet pig. One brother claimed that tremendous thundering would be the consequence; another denied it. They quarrelled and quarrelled until the first brother said to the other, "Try and you will see." As the pig was girdled with a loincloth a tremendous storm broke out with extraordinary lightning and thundering. One lighting bolt struck a luhe tree nearby, and from it

> came the first crocodile. Because the crocodile is associated with lightning, uttering its name at Salaipu provokes lightning. Therefore it is taboo to utter the name of the animal.[207]

Thus the taboo on pronouncing the name "crocodile" in Salaipu presupposes another taboo: that on putting human clothes on animals. As we have seen, this is one of the taboos explicitly concerned with the confusion between animal and human, and it applies to domestic animals as much as to wild ones. The crocodile is said, therefore, to have originated as a punishment for having mixed animal and human. It symbolizes that mixing, and its bite and its variegated (likalika) skin (which the Huaulu find repellent in itself because it evokes a human skin disease) remind the Huaulu of the necessity of keeping animal and human apart.[208] Certainly, the crocodile symbolizes this mixing because people have the myth in mind. But reciprocally the crocodile was selected by the mythographer as the punishment for mixing animal and human because it already evoked that mixing in experience, as I have tried to show. Taken together, myth and experience seem to point in the same direction, which is the one of my analysis.

The man-eating character of the crocodile should not be separated from its role as fishing deity, however. On the contrary, this character allows one to understand the deity role more fully, for this deity exists in a sacrificial setting. It is because humans are occasionally eaten by the lord of the fish that fish become available to them. By this logic, everything has a price ultimately paid in human life; to eat fish one must accept being eaten by fish, even if it is through the master of fish. This human sense of being oneself a victim legitimizes, here as in other acquisitive activities of the Huaulu, the victimizing of nonhumans which is required if one is to eat. Because the crocodile represents the fundamental reciprocity between animal and human in which their asymmetries must be inscribed, it is, of course, intangible. The crocodile is beyond eating because it makes eating possible.

Besides mixing (or, from another point of view, mediating) denizens of the water and land animals, fish and fisherman, the crocodile connects what encompasses and conditions them all: the waters of above (rain) and those of below (rivers). This is sufficiently demonstrated by its control of rain as telua, but is also alluded to in the myth of Salaipu, which says that the animal, although living pale wae, "down in the water/streams," originates, through the connecting link of lightning, from the waters of above—the clouds of the rainstorm. The myth, and the attached belief in the crocodile's control of rainstorms, is rooted in the analogic integration of everyday experience. The Huaulu divine the presence of crocodiles in rivers and ponds from the shape of the clouds in the sky. They say that if the clouds have a likalika, "variegated," pattern, which is reminiscent of the variegated pattern of the crocodile's skin, it will rain until the streams overflow. Then the crocodiles will be able to come out and hunt. Indeed, experience shows that crocodiles abound when rainstorms make the rivers murky and overflow. The Huaulu infer from this that crocodiles are able to produce rainstorms when they are hungry and want to be able to come out of hiding and hunt. One can literally see them in the sky before one sees them in the streams. They once again, as in the myth, move from one to the other when the storm bursts from the sky in mighty lightning and thunder. The mixing of sky and water—these two cosmological extremes, which should stay separate—in the storm summarizes at the highest spatial level the mediating but also subversive role of the crocodile and is therefore a cipher of all that makes the crocodile fearsome.

But the horrors evoked by the crocodile are too great to be faced directly. Running through the skin as goose flesh, they transfer onto the crocodile's own skin as a mark of Cain, where they finally rest. There they hide and at the same time betray themselves by their superficiality, by making themselves deceptively but reassuringly skin-deep in the roughly textured, variegated skin of the animal and in the diseased skin of the human. Moreover, as a surface, the skin solicits the sense of sight, that is, the sense associated with the greatest distance from the object. A taboo that is in fact rooted in the frightening proximity of touch and smell (the feeling of the crocodile's and one's diseased skin; the smell and sight of the progressively opening sores, their intolerable itchiness; being smelled and seized by an overpowering beast) is explained, or explained away, in terms of a visual quality: likalikam, that is, the quality of being variegated, motley,[209] or roughly textured.

Thus taboo, in this case as in many others, realizes its mission of keeping dangerous things at a distance even before it does so by enjoining their avoidance as food. It first distances them, more subtly and more profoundly, by transforming and displacing the representations that account for their dangerousness. Such representations cannot therefore be taken at their face value, but must be seen for what they are: the complex results of the many motivations of which they bear the traces: the motivation of the rule, of course, but also the motivation of disguising that motivation and the motivation of creating a practical representation of the rule, that is, one that connects it analogically to its sanction and thus to the subjective motivations of agents in following the rule.

In sum, representations of rules such as the one given for the taboo on crocodile meat must be analyzed less as correct descriptions of motivation than as dreams: as condensations and displacements of real motives—dreams, or rather nightmares, since such representations must keep the Huaulu "awake," for they concern things to be avoided. And these things must be avoided in the most radical way known: not eaten, not incorporated, not made part of oneself. For if my analysis is correct, crocodiles evoke more than a distant classificatory disorder (à la Douglas) in which the eater wants no part; they evoke a much more important, and threatening, confusion—that between animal and human. This confusion is intrinsic to crocodile flesh and may be absorbed with it. Hence, eating crocodile means becoming partly like it; it means acquiring the texture and general appearance of its skin. It means contracting a skin disease. The "sanction" of the taboo is thus not an explanation but an index of its real motivation: the fear of a fall into animality in a humanity surrounded on every side by animals that evoke, for different reasons, similarities between humans and animals. Such dangerous similarities are due in some cases to certain animals (such as the domestic ones) becoming like humans, but in other cases to humans becoming like certain animals (such as the scaly crocodiles or turtles). Feeling human—recognizing a distinct human identity in oneself—is a very fragile feeling indeed in this society; the spectacle of too many animals makes it difficult to sustain. The feeling must therefore be fostered and protected by taboos whose disregard means the loss of human life, either because one literally dies and thus leaves the human sphere in the most radical way, or because one becomes in some respect like a beast, that is, by looking like one.

My interpretation of what is perhaps the most important strand in the taboo on crocodile meat—namely that it enables humans to obtain the meat of fish legitimately—is indirectly confirmed by the somewhat similar case of the taboo on the ihisiupu. Indeed, this animal is, as its name indicates, the lord of cuscuses, just as the crocodile is the lord of fish. In both cases, the lord is respected in order to guarantee access to the animals which are its subjects. However, the reciprocal relationship with the ihisiupu does not imply the victimization of humans as the relationship with the crocodile does.

I never saw an ihisiupu, and I am therefore uncertain about its zoological identification. I was told that it looks like a rat, that "it climbs in the trees" (ia saa hoto aitufhu), and that it resembles in its color a species of cuscus (the elahuwa, *Phalanger orientalis orientalis*) which is gray or whitish, but that it is much smaller than that cuscus. Also, contrary to this or any other cuscus, it has no marsupium. The last claim, if true, rules out any possible identification with the Seram Island bandicoot (*Rynochomeles prattorum*).[210] A likely candidate is some forest rat or even an arboreal civet, possibly one preying on cuscuses,[211] which would contribute to explaining the ihisiupu's status as "lord of cuscuses." Both in informal discourse and in myth, the ihisiupu is said to announce the presence of cuscuses. When it starts to "shout" (pamaloa), as cuscuses do, that is, by making a noise that the Huaulu describe as "tutututut . . ." and to which they refer by the onomatopoeic verb *tete*, the cuscuses respond in chorus, thereby signalling their presence to the hunters. This is supposed to justify the description of the ihisiupu as murim, that is, "herald," of the cuscuses. But in heralding the cuscuses, the ihisiupu betrays them to the human hunter, delivers them into his hands. This seems to indicate that it has mastery over them: they do its bidding, shouting—and betraying themselves to humans—when it cues them to do so. The ihisiupu is thus like other upue, "masters," of animal species, which must be respected in order not to alienate them. If they are angered, they make the animals over which they preside disappear, and the Huaulu go hungry. These upue are usually invisible, but they may become visible, or audible, in various forms: as a particularly large specimen of the species over which they preside or, as I have mentioned, the smallest or the largest species in a grouping; as meteoric phenomena; as lights of strange color; as shouts in the forest; as a "sudden flood" (hahayam). The ihisiupu is obviously a case in which the master of a grouping of species is identified with the smallest one. Or more exactly, the animal is put in the same general category of ihisi, "cuscus," because of its alleged similarities to them (particularly with regard to its call) and because it seems to have a friendly relationship with humans. Indeed, the upu of a grouping of animals is often more than their type: it represents their "huntability" by humans because of its seeming connection with this group of animals. In the case of the crocodile this component completely displaces the type component, as we have just seen.

In conclusion, the ihisiupu is taboo to eat because, as master of the cuscuses and as friendly to humans, it embodies a human interest that must remain inviolate: a steady supply of cuscuses. Here again we have an overlapping of the human and the animal; however, this overlapping results in taboo not because it is threatening to the continuity of a distinct human life but, on the contrary, because it contributes to it. In certain cases the overlapping is destructive; in the others, such as this one, it is life-promoting. In all cases, the source of taboo is the inviolability of the humanness in its Huaulu form—an inviolability that can be threatened or reinforced, depending on the animal, by an overlapping of animal and human.

Species Taboo to Women

For convenience' sake, I will classify the species taboo for women into the following groups:

1. reptiles: the two pythons tekepatola and tipolo, the tipope turtle, the pue (monitor lizard, *Varanus indicus*), and a smaller *Varanus* which lives mostly in the water (so the Huaulu claim).

2. makuwelele (civet) (*Paradoxurus hermaphroditus* and probably also *Viverra tangalunga*).[212]
3. fishes: walaka potoa, fulei (glossed as *large ikan batu*), kohi, funana, tamali, wuoi (shark).
4. birds (but not their eggs): laka (cockatoo, B.I. kakatua, *Cacatua moluccensis*), salewa (kingfisher), koka (owl), tukutuku (owl), wesiwesi, munui (hawk), and toa.
5. eels: makasusuenaka, makihoifa, kelolawali.[213]
6. reptiles (and their eggs): tipope turtle, pue (monitor lizard, *Varanus indicus*), and a smaller *Varanus* which lives pale wae.

Furthermore, the following vegetables are taboo to women:

1. tuberous plants: ihisiwaki (yam), akapa, mali.
2. pandanuses (sau): sau fina, sau tipoloa, sau malahutua—that is, all pandanuses except sau hameauwa and sau potoa.

None of these taboos (except those on eels and on the tekepatola python) is observed before the first menstruation or after menopause. But they must all be observed by a first-born woman throughout her life, "because she is the first born." Except for the tipope, whose meat gives skin diseases, the consequences of eating the forbidden species are usually said to be any (or all) of three: "longer than normal menstrual bleeding" (poture melekae), "crossed eyes" (matare kohae), and loss of hair or even "baldness" (huwemusi).[214] These consequences affect the reproductive powers of a woman, either because she cannot conceive (prolonged bleeding) or because she proves unattractive to men (crossed eyes,[215] sparse hair, or even baldness). Similar effects, and excessive menstrual bleeding in particular, occur whenever women violate the taboo on entering into contact with what is most male, that is, anything or anybody connected with war.[216] This suggests that the animals tabooed for women have a connection either with war and headhunting (or with the paraphernalia used in such activities) or, more generically, with the attributes which enable men to engage in such activities.

The suggestion finds explicit and implicit confirmations. My informants spontaneously commented that the cockatoo is taboo for women to eat because the fiery orange "plumes" (horae) that become erect on its head when angered or confronted by an enemy are used as part of the ceremonial headdress of men, which is also the war headdress. They also said that the two species of owls and the toa bird are taboo for women because they "bite headhunters" (koto timatem), that is to say, identify them by their presence.[217] Indeed, these predatory birds are so identified with the predatory "headhunter" (timata) that their

A young girl playing an arapapu (stringed instrument), with a tame cockatoo sitting beside her. 1973. (Photo by V. Valeri.)

presence axiomatically implies his presence. That identification also explains why owl feathers and apparently those of the toa as well are part of the headhunter's headdress. Another taboo bird, the salewa, "kingfisher," contributes its long caudal feathers to the same. In fact the number of salewa feathers in a headdress used to indicate the number of humans killed by the wearer. I know nothing about the wesiwesi bird, but I suspect that it is a hawk, just like the munui.[218] As a bird of prey, the latter may have been a source of feathers for the headdress of headhunters. Indeed, all birds that furnish feathers to the headhunter's (or simply the male's) headdress are either highly aggressive or predators, and thus evoke him by analogy.

We may infer that some other animals are taboo for women to eat because, being predators and aggressive, they are animals that evoke human males in the same capacities, that is, in the Huaulu view, at their most male. This is certainly the case with the civet and even more so with the frightening pythons. One of them, the *Python reticulatus,* is associated, moreover, with the highest (and therefore most ferocious) category of headhunters: those who, having killed at least 10 humans, received the title of kapitane (*or* kapitale). Indeed, the snake's skin pattern (called tuputupuem) was painted on the long frontal flap of the kapitane's ceremonial bark "loincloth" (uheli).[219] The shape of the pythons is obviously phallic, as is the shape of eels, which also happen to be very aggressive and ferocious animals. Indeed, a symbolic equation seems to exist between the phallus and the practice of violence,[220] and this is one of the probable reasons it is easy to recognize a phallic shape in several animals taboo for women to eat. Nevertheless, this shape seems a necessary, but not a sufficient, reason for the taboo. It must be combined with other qualities, such as size, texture, and color. The requirement of additional qualities is certainly suggested by the fact that only two species of eels are taboo for women. The taboo on one of the two, the makihoifa, seems to be sufficiently explained by its ability to reach considerable dimension and by its skin being likalika (which in this case refers to black spots on a yellow background). But I am at a loss to explain why the second species, the makasusuenaka, is taboo. It is neither large nor endowed with a color usually associated with taboo (spotted, variegated, or red). Perhaps its reported capability of burrowing in the sand for quite a long time may evoke analogous abilities at vaginal penetration in the human male.

I should say that my impression that these eels and snakes have phallic associations in the Huaulu mind is based on rather extended observation of women's (and indirectly men's) reaction to them. When encountered, these animals often induce in Huaulu Eves a reaction similar to that of Western women toward mice: screams of disgust and fear which sometimes seem quite spontaneous but more often look suspiciously exaggerated. I have often felt that women indulge in theatrical reactions when an interesting male audience is around, as if they want to make quite evident to men the symbolic association of the animals from which they jump away, in terrified but mock recognition of their power. I remember vividly that the woman most loudly demonstrative in her reactions to eels was also the most notorious for her sexual adventures, and was frequently accused by other women of seducing their husbands by proposing to practice fellatio on them. It was clear that the equation of the eel with the phallus was quite vivid in her mind,[221] but this personal twist would not have been possible without an audience responsive to it (men would giggle at her antics), and thus without a collective understanding of the association it presupposed.

In sum, it seems that all animals considered so far have a connection with men as killers, either because they are predators, or because they are phallic, or because they provide materials or themes for the ritual costume of warriors, or for all these reasons at the same time. Because one is what one eats, for women to eat the meat of these "totemic" animals of men at their most male—that is, in the Huaulu view, as violent bearers of the phallus—would mean losing their identity as givers of life, as mothers, by confusing it with the antithetical identity of men as givers of death, as warriors. The alleged consequences of the violation of these taboos is the loss of women's procreative powers (due to dysmenorrhea) and even the loss of their ability to attract men (due to baldness, strabismus, and similar repulsive traits). The most telling consequence is, of course, dysmenorrhea or any of the medical conditions which the Huaulu interpret as an extended, sometimes unstoppable, bleeding (poture melekae). For such extended bleeding demonstrates that women have fallen prey to men's wounding violence, that they have become part of men's world, but only in its weaker form—that of the victim. Menstruation then actualizes its potential for evoking a bleeding wound. It is this latent meaning that must be kept at bay by keeping women in the age of menarche separate from male violence and anything, including the meat of certain animals, that symbolizes it.

What then of the other animals whose meat is taboo to women—that is, a number of fishes, the tipope turtle, and the *Varanus*? Let us begin with the most difficult case, the fishes. It seems that their list includes the larger freshwater fish: tamali, walaka potoa ("big walaka"), and fulei. All these are voracious predators, as is the shark, the only marine fish in the list of female taboos. The significance here of predation and size is shown by the assocation of the tamali and the large river eel with Pinasainale, the crocodile deity of the Sapulewa River. Indeed, they are considered her helpers. It is therefore possible to infer that these animals partake of the dangers of the crocodile as predator and fishing deity. They do so to a degree which is too small to endanger men but not small enough to be safe for women, the weaker sex. The taboo status of tamali and eels for women but not for men, then, reveals the inferiority of women and ultimately their dependency on men. A contrast in size and ferociousness in the same universe of animal life (crocodile vs. the two second-largest predators in the water) is thus used as a diagram of the fundamental hierarchical contrast in human life. The same can probably be said of the shark. This dangerous predator of the sea is not considered dangerous enough for men so that it *can* be considered dangerous enough for women.[222]

And what about the taboo on the tipope turtle? I have indicated above some of the possible reasons the tipope is less dangerous than its smaller counterparts. But this lesser dangerousness only emphasizes that it is still dangerous enough to be taboo to women. This suggests that, in the last analysis, the difference between tipope and all other turtles cannot be explained with arguments taken from a classification of animals independent of a classification of humans. For the difference is probably less one between turtle and turtle than one between man and woman. It is a difference arbitrarily introduced to make women appear more susceptible than men to what is wrong about turtles. Men are exempted from one turtle taboo so as to make it possible to show that women cannot be exempted. And they cannot be exempted because they are considered weaker and therefore more vulnerable vis-à-vis the dangerous forces of the world.[223] In sum, the taboo on the tipope can be explained pretty much like the taboo on tamali and large eels. In an animal field which evokes danger as a whole, some species are identified as less dangerous in order to manifest women's greater vulnerability to danger and thus their inferiority to men. There is not so much a correspondence between the supposedly distinctly motivated domains of animal and human classification as an obvious interference of the latter in the former. Animal classifications are often, but far from invariably, human classifications in disguise. Or better said, they reveal their anthropocentric bias in their strange irregularities, which are due to a sort of action at a distance from the human world, to whose field they gravitate.

That the monitor lizard is taboo for women but not for men is again explained by the same overriding motivation of manifesting female inferiority by female vulnerability. As I have mentioned, the monitor lizard is viewed as dangerous to some extent because it violates the division of the cosmos into three tiers, albeit it is fundamentally a terrestrial animal. But its shape and size also condemn it to be compared to the crocodile. It thus assumes the role of the crocodile's junior cousin; it is a crocodilian in a minor key. As such, it is ready made to manifest the contrast of man and woman. Men and women are vulnerable to the bigger cousin, but only women are endangered by the meat of the smaller cousin.

And now the vegetals: yams and pandanuses. Here again we seem to have a case of the largest being taboo. Indeed, it is apparently the largest yams and edible pandanuses that are taboo to women. But why these vegetables? It is hard to escape the impression that they are singled out for a particular antipathy with the feminine because of their phallic shape. For women to eat them (just as to eat the phallic-shaped animals)[224] would represent a confusion of two forms of ingestion: sexual ingestion and alimentary ingestion. It would mean eating the penis with the wrong mouth, so to speak. Wrong because, contrary to the "right" mouth (the vagina), the wrong mouth (that is, the mouth proper) implies a definitive absorption and thus a confusion of the characters of man with those of woman, indeed the disappearance into woman of what makes man distinctive. Such eating, therefore, is an intolerable subversion of sexual difference. As such, it also threatens what is most female in women: the ability to procreate.

My claim that the eating of phallic species is taboo for women because it evokes a confusion of eating and copulating, which in turn evokes a collapse of gender distinctions, receives support from the strong disapproval of, but also the irresistible attraction to, fellatio in Huaulu. The ultimate stigma of perversion, for a woman, is to be accused of seducing men by such means, that is, by means that are symbolically destructive both of her femaleness and of their maleness. It is not by chance, then, that the above-mentioned woman who was accused of practicing fellatio was also considered unfeminine, malelike because of her too independent and assertive behavior, and sterile (indeed, she never had a child). She represented the confusion of male and female that is associated with "eating" men with the wrong mouth—the mouth of digestion instead of the mouth of conception.

As I have mentioned, many female taboos are meant to preserve the distinctiveness of man and woman by preserving the integrity and thus the separateness of their most qualifying activities: giving birth and giving death. From this point of view it makes sense that they are limited to the period in which a woman is capable of procreation, that is, between her first and last menstruations. But there is a core of taboos that are enforced beyond that period. We may therefore surmise that they concern the distinction of man and woman even beyond the attributes of procreation and destruction. Interestingly, these taboos concern the pythons and the eels, which may be taken as evidence that these species are ultimately avoided by women because of their phallic association. Eating them threatens male and female identities whether or not procreation is involved. Clearly, prototypicality is at work here too: pythons and eels are invariably and permanently taboo because, as the most penislike among the species incompatible with femaleness, they are prototypical for females. Moreover, prototypicality is at work not only on the animal side but on the human side as well. The first-born is the prototype of a group of siblings, and as such he or she stands for them all. This is why all the female meat taboos must be observed by a first-born woman throughout her life, not just during the reproductive stage of her life. In sum, here as elsewhere taboo is often limited to parts that stand for wholes—consisting of things tabooed or persons with taboos.

Difference and Deference: Shamanic and "Totemic" Taboos

By far the greatest number of food taboos is connected with shamanism. Few people remain unaffected by them. They are permanent for shamans and their wives, and some are even for entire lineages. They are followed by patients during the period when they are under treatment, or even for life in certain cases. If the patient is a suckling, his or her taboos must be followed by the mother too, sometimes until the child has become an adult. Since illness is very common, and most men are initiated into shamanism and must keep its taboos even if they do not commonly practice it, shamanic taboos have a profound incidence in Huaulu life. The taking up and relinquishing of them at various moments of one's life contributes to one's internal biographic sense; it diachronizes one's identity and connects the experience of taboo with that of time.

As I mentioned in chapter 1, the general name for shamanic practices is sewa. The term refers more specifically to shamanic songs and to the deities or "familiars" who possess the shamans and grant them their powers. Four varieties of shamanism are recognized. They are ranked in order of antiquity and named after the principal deities employed in them: sewa potoa ("great sewa"), sewa pukaria ("pukari sewa"), sewa ninawania ("ninawa sewa"), and sewa laufaha ("Muslim sewa").[225] They all share a basic core of taboos, but each variety also has its own. In addition, each individual deity and even "medicine" (aitotu) attached to her or him has a distinctive set of taboos. Finally, taboos are added all the time, and some are shed. The result is a veritable jungle, which cannot be reduced to an exhaustive list, let alone exhaustively accounted for by a set of principles. Also, shamans do not always agree on what is and what is not taboo. Nevertheless, the following species are usually said to be taboo for all varieties of shamanism: asuali (cassowary), makila (male spotted cuscus), kaa (hornbill), laka (cockatoo), tipolo (tree python), tekepatola (*Python reticulatus*), maulohu (chicken),[226] loku (B.I.: sayur kakatua, "cockatoo vegetable"), palaqi (papaya), peta (a yam), and two kinds of bananas—telo matalala (B.I.: tongkat langit, "the cane of the sky") and telo urifatasia (also called telo waea).[227]

Certain distinctions are immediately necessary. For instance, some say that the two kinds of banana are taboo only during the period (sometimes quite long, it is true) when a shaman treats a patient. Others claim that they are not taboo for the sewa potoa shaman. It is also said that the taboo on the cassowary is continuous for the sewa potoa shaman who belongs to the Sayaramani lineage, but that the shaman of the Purarattuhu lineage follows it only when treating a patient. Furthermore, I should point out that while seven lineages have the right to perform the sewa potoa and have established relationships with deities of this category, at the time of my fieldwork only two lineages (the above-mentioned Purarattuhu and Sayaramani) had a practicing shaman, and informants were sure only about their taboos and those of the shaman from the Tamatay lineage.

As for the additional taboos of each kind of shamanism, the most important ones are:

1. For sewa potoa: maisarale (deer), tessi and kakaku (two kinds of parrots), wala (B.I.: ikan batu, "stone fish"), laitili (the leaves of guantum), inaqaqi (taro), ala (rice), alamafu (corn), nuwefele (coconut oil) and all food fried in it, pukalawa (cloves), and black sugar (from local sugarcane, tohu).[228] In addition, "kerosene" (miniatana) cannot be used in the house of the shaman. Neither may he plant the clove tree or keep cloves in his house or even dry them in front of it, nor may he plant the papaya. He may not touch lesalesa (B.I.: rumput kuda, "horse grass" or elephant grass) or keep in his house any of the animals that are taboo for him to eat. The last taboo (and, theoretically, that on planting clove trees) applies to all members of lineages with practicing sewa potoa shamans. A number of other taboos apply only to particular lineages. Thus Purarattuhu may not plant the tuwa (tuak palm) or drink its wine, or eat or even keep sissai birds; Sayaramani may not eat a variety of sago (ipia potoa); and no Tamatay may look fixedly at the "black sunset clouds" (etelia).

2. For sewa pukaria: niapa (all bats), hahu (pig), ihisi elahuwa (white cuscus, male of the *Phalanger orientalis*), all birds except the horuwa (A.M.: burung bombo), pue (*Varanus indicus*), oko (shrimp), makihoi (all eels), tinati (a species of shellfish), pole (a conical shell), tamali (largest freshwater fish), iya wahu (A.M.: ikan julung-julung, garfish), iya kinolo (A.M.: ikan kurara, a sea fish which is all red), iya lasiani (A.M.: ikan lassi), iya lapa (A.M.: ikan rompa), peti (pike),[229] pai and matawu (two other fishes), and nine varieties of bananas (besides the two that are taboo for all types of shamans and their patients). The wild banana called telo horinoa is also taboo. Other vegetals that are taboo for all sewa pukaria are: all sau (pandanuses), ainasa (pineapple), kasibi (cassava).[230]

3. For sewa laufaha: These sewa are said to be Muslim (Laufaha) and thus to have all the taboos of the followers of Islam, as construed

by the Huaulu. In practice, this means following all the taboos of the sewa pukaria (which include most of the Islamic taboos) and a few others in addition. All cuscuses are barred, and in addition the telo poya, which is the other variety of wild banana. But, surprisingly, one Islamic prohibition is conspicuously absent: that on alcohol. On the contrary, I have often seen sewa laufaha shamans perform in a drunken state.

4. For sewa ninawania: These have the same taboos as sewa potoa and in addition taboos on the lapina (squash), ula (mushrooms), patata (sweet potato), kirama okue (*Gnetum gnemon* leaves). Moreover, these shamans may not touch the fruit of the fiauwa (*Aleurites moluccana,* candlenut) or use its oil. Touching bamboos of the awa kind is also strictly taboo because of their connection with the main familiars (called mulua awa, "girls of the awa bamboo") of ninawania shamanism. Finally, the shamans "may not step over" (ita safuruwairassi) the tokolili kai (a kind of ginger plant) or the trunk and other parts of the pahu (*Arenga pinnata*).

It is not my intention to analyze shamanic taboos in detail. Such analysis belongs with a special study of shamanic practices. I have listed the most important ones principally to give an idea of their extent and variety, and thus the burden which they represent for many Huaulu.[231] Even so, certain general observations are possible and necessary here.

If one asks the Huaulu, Why are these animals and plants taboo? the standard answers one receives are disarmingly tautological. "They are taboo because they are taboo to the sewa"; "They are taboo because they are taboo with the medicines of the sewa." This kind of answer matches the kinds of stories one hears about how the relationship between particular sewa and particular shamans was established. The basic scheme of these stories, as I have already had the opportunity to mention, is extremely simple: There is an encounter between a man (often an initiated shaman already) and a sewa, usually in the forest or in a dream; the sewa proposes or, rather, imposes a pact: "I will help you cure and so on; these are my medicines and these are my taboos [i.e. the avoidances I request]." Sometimes the man resists or the sewa does not make himself/herself sufficiently understood. Then the sewa makes the shaman sick or even kills members of his family, until the man understands or is forced to give himself up to the service of the sewa.[232] An alternative kind of story is that, by trickery or the threat of violence, a shaman forces an evil power into his service, and thus transforms it into a "good" power (good, that is, only insofar as it remains under shamanic control). Even in these cases, however, the sewa must say that he becomes a friend and must declare what his medicines and taboos are. Shamanic taboos, then, are viewed as a fundamental part of the pact between sewa and shaman. By giving up on the consumption of certain foods, the planting of certain crops, or even certain cooking, clothing, and building practices, shamans obtain certain useful powers. In the face of this central idea, all other motivations of the taboos retreat, to the point that they may indeed matter little. If the idea of sacrifice, perhaps even reduced to a *do ut des,* is sufficient to justify a taboo, then the choice of the object to taboo may be arbitrary. Moreover, where the field is as crowded as it is in shamanism, the main point seems to be to find something other, something to differentiate the new sewa, the new medicine. The situation has certain resemblances to fashion, or advertisement, or academic culture.

Nevertheless, even a cursory look at the lists of shamanic taboos cannot fail to reveal that they include many species which we have repeatedly encountered: monitor lizard, pythons, cockatoo, eels, hornbill, bats, matalala bananas, yams, and so on. This suggests that their inclusion (if not always the choice among them) is far from being arbitrary or as arbitrary as the Huaulu just-so stories seem to suggest. Granted that it is the sewaem (or perhaps better said the shaman's dreams or visions) who dictate the taboos—do we have to assume that the taboos' inclusion is totally random, that certain species do not spontaneously present themselves as natural choices, or at least as first choices? Put otherwise, is the logic of dream free of culture, and thus free of a culture's characteristic preoccupations and classifications, or is it dependent on culture to some extent? Does one dream in a universal language or in a particular one?

Supposing, then, the sewaem to be culturally informed agents—what would their choices likely be? Do these expected choices correspond in some way to the actual ones? Consider, to begin with, this fact: a large number of sewaem are female or sexually ambiguous, although the shamans are invariably male in Huaulu.[233] We may expect these sewaem, then, to require their shamans to follow the basic food taboos of women, either because as women of sorts the female sewaem would be contaminated in entering male bodies, or because their sexual ambiguity requires a corresponding ambiguity in their human vessels. For either or both reasons, these shamans must become in part female by following certain female food taboos. This explains why a number of species that are taboo for shamans—monitor lizard, pythons, cockatoo, chicken (nowadays), eels, the tamali fish, pandanuses and yams—are the characteristic food taboos of women. Note, however, that this is truer of the sewa pukaria and sewa laufaha than of the sewa ninawania and especially of the sewa potoa. Not only does the last include fewer "female taboos," but also its stronger male identification is revealed by a telling detail: The consequences for the shaman of violating the sewa potoa's taboos—falling from trees, cutting oneself, being bitten by poisonous snakes, gored by wild boars, and so on—are identical with the consequences of violating the taboos of male cults such as headhunting.[234] The reason for this identity is not just a greater emphasis on maleness, however. More important still is the special status of sewa potoa as the original, ancestral, and uniquely Huaulu form of shamanism. It is the only form, moreover, which is inherited rather than freely acceded to by co-optation. As an ancestral cult, it shares its status with the other ancestral cults monopolized by men, and its taboos mark the affinity. In contrast, the other kinds of sewa are borrowed from the neighboring eastern people or beyond and are not descent-based. Their taboos, therefore, have very different and not very characteristic misfortunes attached to them: various illnesses and, especially, loss of the relationship with the familiar deities, who refuse to possess the shaman.

A second predictable choice of taboos from the sewaem's part is that of species that are in some way the counterpart of their basic mode of existence, particularly in relationship to shamans. Indeed, it is very clear from the shamanic performances themselves, where possessed shamans act and sound like some of the taboo animals, that these animals are viewed as preferred embodiments or manifestations of the sewa. There is, in fact, such a close relationship between animals and sewaem that it can turn into virtual interchangeability.[235] For that to happen, however, it is necessary that the properties of the animal evoke either those of the shamanic familiars in general or those of particular classes or even individuals of familiars. This is verified by many taboo species. For instance, the almost universal taboo on bird meat for sewa pukari shamans seems due to the birdlike character of these sewaem (so often mentioned in their songs): like birds they descend from above and alight on the shamans. The same can be said of bats, of course, which, moreover, come out at night, just like the pukari themselves. Analogy may again explain the taboo on cuscuses and those on the other animals of the above that descend to the ground, namely the pythons. Note, however, that here we immediately encounter other forces at work besides that of analogy. For clearly there are also the perennial requirements of differentiation and economy. There is a tendency for cuscuses to be seen as analogous to sewaem, but then only the two prototypical cuscuses—both of them male—are selected. The makilam, which is the largest and most powerful (and moreover likalika, here in the sense of "spotted") is understandably taboo for all varieties of shamanism, whereas the elahuwam, the male of the *Phalanger orientalis orientalis* and second to the makilam in dimensions and power, is taboo only for the second most important sewa variety—the sewa pukaria. As for the sewa laufaha, it requires the avoidance of all cuscuses, male and female, because this is the rule for Muslims. At the same time, transferred to the Huaulu context, the rule fits with the general diagrammatic distribution of cuscus taboos and shamanic hierarchy: the inferior "Muslim" shamanism is associated with the unmarked form of cuscus avoidance, thus also with the additional avoidance of the females of the two species (kapupu and mussufa). Differentiation, but in a more elementary form, most probably also explains why only the pukari are preeminently associated with a universal bird taboo, although all sewaem have birdlike qualities and are associated with at least some birds (particularly the "messenger birds" par excellence: parrots like kakaku and tessi).

The movement from sky to ground that is so obviously the reason for bird taboos is also found behind the taboo on four plants: poi (B.I.: pisang hutan, "wild banana"), lesalesa (elephant grass), palaqi (papaya), and loku ("cockatoo vegetable"). Indeed, they are said to be taboo for the shamans and their patients because their seeds supposedly fall from the sky. They are therefore "planted by the sewa" and "belong" to them. Because of this, they cannot be appropriated by the sewa's devotees. Possession always implies some degree of identification in Huaulu. This identification is all the stronger here where it is clearly based on the analogy of movement and its signification: connecting above and below, the world of sewa and the world of humans.[236]

This "origin from the sky" may also be behind the shamanic taboo on the cassowary, although it was not directly formulated in this way. In the case of this animal, moreover, the analogy with the sewa goes beyond the simple direction of movement. Or rather, this direction is made all the more significant by the fact that for certain traits the cassowary belongs to the creatures of the above par excellence—the birds—but for other traits it is a creature of below. It is thus an almost perfect representation of the sewa and indeed of shamanism as such. This is perhaps the reason the cassowary is taboo for all varieties of shamanism and also why a "cassowary man" (i.e. a being half-human, half-cassowary) is said to be the ruler of all pukari on the mountain where they live.

The cassowary may also be seen as the more striking representative of a whole class of species that have an obvious affinity with the sewa: anomalous species. Clearly, anomaly is one of the main reasons that not only the cassowary but also its mythical counterpart, the hornbill, as well as the monitor lizard, shrimps,[237] and shellfish (in addition to several other species in which anomaly is arguably a less important component), are all taboo for shamans in one way or another. Indeed, if anomalous species have a vocation for taboo, it is one that is realized most resoundingly in the realm of shamanism. The fundamental reason for this is that these species, particularly when they connect different habitats, as is usually the case, seem the closest objective analogy one can find to the mediating role of the sewaem (and also, one may add, to the sewaem's mischievous tendency to subvert order, as is again made apparent in shamanic performances).[238]

But given that the sewaem themselves have much in common

with their antagonists—the kinakina, or "evil ones"—and may even be viewed as their transformation, the species that recall one kind of occult power may also recall the other. There is thus a fundamental ambiguity in these taboo species. The reason for their incompatibility with the shamanic cult may be equally construed as avoidance of what belongs to the sewaem or as avoidance of what the sewaem abhor. By the first interpretation, the shaman manifests his subservience to the sewaem: what belongs to the master cannot be had by the servant. By the second interpretation, the shaman shows his fidelity to the sewaem. But the two interpretations separate what is clearly inseparable and intertwined. The sewaem may avoid what "belongs" to them because the rule that one does not eat oneself is as valid for them as for humans. And they may avoid what belongs to their adversaries because it and their adversaries are strangely reminiscent of the sewaem themselves in a previous state and thus represent the threat of returning to it. In sum, the Huaulu contemplate in their sewaem a predicament that they also experience. They may not eat themselves, but they may also not eat what evokes a conflict in themselves, between their identities. Because of the multiplicity of attributes and evocations which characterizes all species, it is ultimately impossible to differentiate the two cases, although the Huaulu themselves may attempt to do so in their discourses about the sewaem, or about themselves directly. It would be foolish for us to prefer one argument to the other, rather than focussing on the underlying ambiguity.

Some of the species which are taboo for shamans may have implicit phallic associations like several of the species taboo for women. Possible examples are, besides pythons and eels, several yams, cassava, and the gigantic fruits of the matalala banana. But these associations are not exclusive of others and may in fact reinforce them or be reinforced by them. This proliferation of reasons is nothing surprising in the realm of sexuality, which is so charged with ambiguities and displacements because of repressions and prohibitions. One illustration may be the papaya. We have just seen the official reason it is taboo for shamans. But this reason does not explain the peculiar coexistence of attraction and repulsion for the tree and its fruit. It may well be that the papaya evokes a disturbing, but also deeply seductive, combination of sexuality and anomaly, its fruits recalling an obscene proliferation of both testicles and breasts.

There is more. The redness of the fruit's pulp is sometimes invoked as a reason for the taboo.[239] Redness usually means blood when taboo is invoked. But what blood—the female blood of menstruation or the male one of killing? Or is it precisely their confusion which is at issue here, a confusion made worse by the fact that the fruit also exudes a white milk and thus evokes the maternal breast at the same time as the maternal womb? And what about the fact that the tree sometimes comes in hermaphroditic form, with both male and female flowers in the same individual? It is difficult to decide which of these traits are significant to the Huaulu. But separately or in combination they all seem to refer to the most repressed area of human experience, that of sexual identity. As such, they can only be unconscious, therefore impossible to recover directly through discourse. If anything, we may expect discourse to displace such significations. But displacement rarely happens without leaving telltale traces of what is displaced. That is probably the case with the statement that the papaya is taboo because it grows from seeds fallen from the sky. Such a statement has sexual resonances for the Huaulu, because the sky is male (it is "our father," ita amare), while the earth it fertilizes with its seed is female and viewed as the "mother of us all" (ita inare). Indeed, the statement may reflect a displacement of sexuality from the human to the cosmic sphere. Perhaps, then, the papaya is such a central taboo for shamanism because it combines shamanism's two most powerful and frequently invoked forms of mediation: sexual ambiguity and the sexual union of sky and earth. In other words, the papaya may be taboo for shamans as their objective correlative, as their "totem," one is tempted to say.[240]

Many species taboo for both sewa laufaha and sewa pukaria are also taboo for Muslims. This suggests that not only the sewa laufaha but also the sewa pukaria, and perhaps all forms of shamanism, bear the mark of a coastal, Muslim-influenced origin.[241] Huaulu accounts suggest that much, and there is much evidence that they are right. To give just one example: the generic name for shaman, "lepe," is derived from *lebe,* the Moluccan reflex of B.I. *lebai,* which designates a mosque functionary.[242] But the shaman's connection with an external world dominated by coastal Islamic culture is significant for more than historical reasons: it continues to be a recognized source of his power, and it provides an analogy for his structural position between inside Huaula society and outside it, and between the visible and invisible worlds.

If the "Islamic" taboos of the sewa pukaria and the sewa laufaha seek to establish an identification with external powers, a number of taboos that are attached to the sewa potoa maintain, on the contrary, a sharp division between traditional Huaulu powers and the later, external world.[243] I call these taboos misoneistic because they are explicitly meant to isolate the sewa potoa shaman and his patients from "new things" or, as the Huaulu put it, "from things we have not come out with" (ita keluarasi pohire). Such things are incompatible with the sewa potoa, which are associated with the distant past, with the initial moment in time when the Huaulu were alone in Seram. Examples of misoneistic taboos are the taboos on taro, rice, corn, cloves, cassava,[244] and all varieties of sugar cane except two, which are the only ones said to be originary. Also misoneistic are the taboo on coconut oil and food fried in it (a coastal way of cooking) and the taboo on kerosene, and, I may add as an interested party, the taboos on using a tape recorder, a camera, and even a flashlight to look at my notebook during a seance of sewa potoa.[245] While a majority of misoneistic taboos apply to the sewa potoa (and to a lesser extent to the sewa ninawania), a few also apply to the other forms of shamanism, inasmuch as they concern plants (such as manioc, pineapple, squash, and perhaps even sweet potato) introduced after them, usually in colonial times.

Finally, it is notable that all species that are the foremost sources of food, particularly large game (cassowary, deer, and pig), marsupials, shrimp, even one variety of the sago palm (ipia potoa), and several of the most common tuberous plants (taro, cassava, some yams), are taboo for at least one kind of shamanism. This confirms a point that I have made before: one of the mainsprings of ritual efficacy is renunciation, giving up what is important in order to obtain something which is even more important. The logic of taboo shows itself to be also a logic of *sacrifice,* not just one of avoidance. Without some loss, no gain is possible. This is why the Huaulu constantly complain of the burden of taboo, but also never accepted the idea that the medicines I gave them came with no taboos attached. My patients kept clamoring for some taboo, without which, they feared, my pills would have no effect. My obstinate refusal to satisfy them forced them to follow taboos of their own choice or to surrender my medicines to a shaman, for him to administer during a seance, complete with the hoped-for taboos and much to the satisfaction of everybody concerned (except me, initially).

Better than all other cases, that of shamanism shows the incredible variety of motivations that goes into taboo. It serves as a warning, therefore, against any attempt to reduce the logic of taboo to some simple formula, classificatory or otherwise. Its luxuriant proliferation indicates that taboo does not have to be principally motivated by the thing tabooed. On the contrary, the relationship between a taboo and its object may often be arbitrary, because the fundamental motivation for choosing an object for taboo is the requirement of a cost, of a price to pay, in order to give efficacy to a cure, to mobilize the possession of a power, or whatever. That payment is more important than what one pays with. Another reason the relationship between a taboo and its object may be arbitrary is the requirement of difference. The inside has to be differentiated from the outside; the past from the present or from the more recent past; one kind of shamanism from another; one individual shaman, spirit, medicine, time, place from another; and so on. Where taboos proliferate by becoming attached to social differences, taboo tends to become arbitrary: what is tabooed matters less than the existence of the taboo. Where taboos, on the contrary, are more limited in number and concern all the Huaulu or the basic categories into which they are divided (such as male and female), they tend to be more motivated by their objects, which amounts to saying they are less prey to the vagaries and revisions of agency and interest. In moving from the taboos common to all Huaulu to the taboos of shamanism we have moved from one pole of taboo to the other: from a pole characterized by external motivation and by a global contrast between human and animal and between Huaulu and non-Huaulu, to a pole more concerned with the internal differentiation of Huaulu society and with a more selective relationship with the external, non-Huaulu world as well.[246]

I have mentioned that a few of the taboos of the sewa potoa are followed by all the members of a lineage rather than by the shaman alone. This is sufficient to indicate that his divinities are not his property but that of his lineage—that he communicates with them as its representative and not as an individual. The contrast with the other forms of shamanism, in which the sewa are individual property, is in this respect total. But these collective taboos raise another and conceptually more problematic issue. For, contrary to all other shamanic taboos, including those which are followed by the sewa potoa shaman alone, these are usually accounted for in "totemic" terms. Indeed, it is not uncommon to hear the Huaulu say that they do not eat or otherwise violate the species that are the objects of these taboos "because we have our origins in them" (barani ita rahe asale hinire). Such statements are not limited to the taboos of the sewa potoa; they are made of all taboos that apply to a lineage as a whole.

Before looking a bit closer into this matter, one thing must be made clear. Whatever this totemism may be, it is not of the Bergsonian–Lévi-Straussian kind—that is, a system of species differences correlated with a system of social differences. There are at least two reasons the diacritical theory of totemism does not apply here. First, "totemically" interpreted taboos are very few, and not all lineages have them. It is therefore impossible to speak of a "system" encompassing all basic social units, let alone all social differences. Second, some of these taboos are in fact shared by different lineages, and as a result their power of differentiation is rather scant. In fact, the Lévi-Straussian theory applies better to nontotemic taboos than to explicitly totemic ones, as we have just hinted. Consequently, Huaulu totemism cannot be considered a mere epiphenomenon of the basic phenomenon of differentiation; not only may it be in conflict with differentiation, but also it obviously adds to differentiation something specific which is not found in purely differential relationships with species (admitting but not conceding that food taboos may be construed as *only* differential rather than as *also* differential).

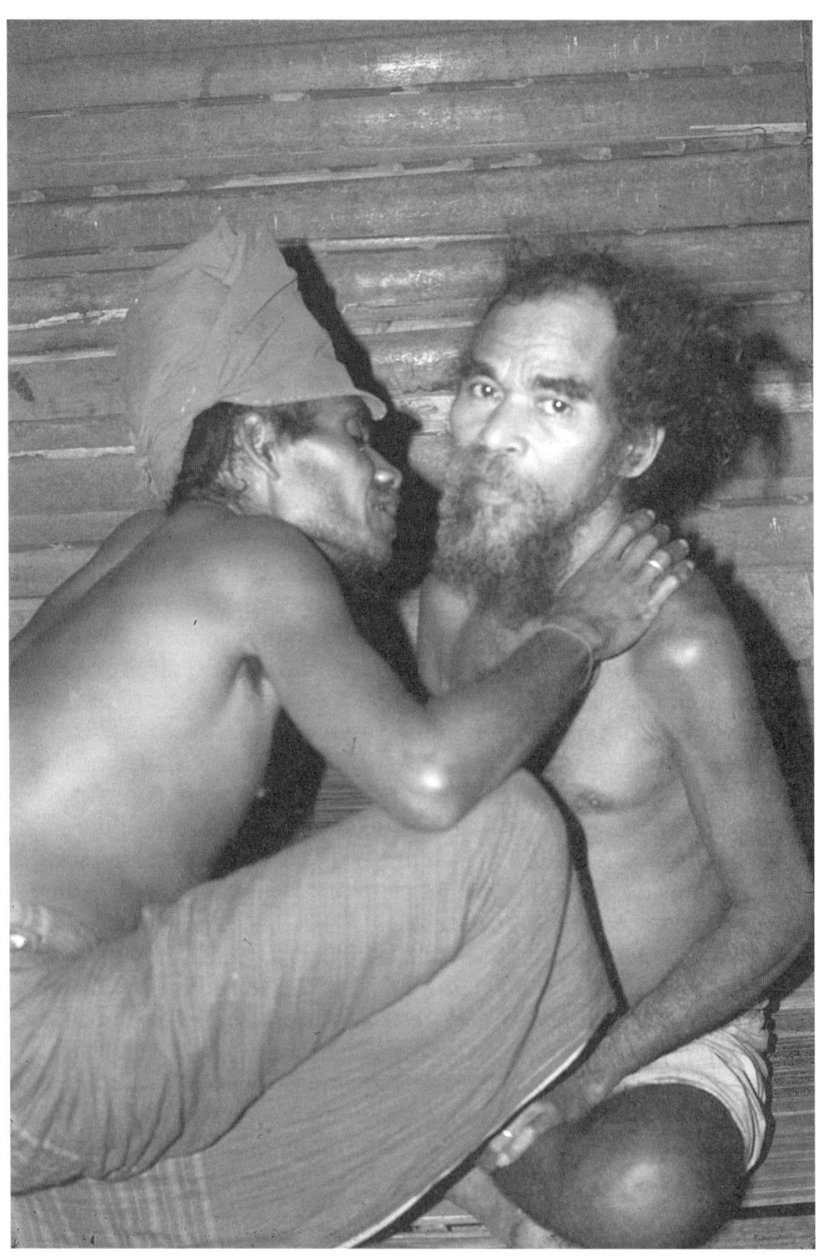

A sick man is treated by a shaman, who tries to suck out his illness. 1985. (Photo by V. Valeri.)

The crucial problem raised by the *interpretatio totemica* of taboo is: What do the Huaulu mean when they say that certain animals or plants or other natural phenomena are their "origin"? Do they mean that they descend from them? Or that they descend from certain powers (the sewaem) who can transform themselves into those animals? As a way of introducing these and related questions, I want to quote an episode from my fieldnotes. It illustrates some uses of the *interpretatio totemica* of taboo, but also its ambiguities and unclarities. It also shows that this interpretation exists in a context wider than that of Huaulu society, both because it is used to different effect by other people with whom the Huaulu are conversant and because the Huaulu apply it to their neighbors diferently from themselves. Here is the text:

> Alakamata, Sept. 5, 1986.
>
> Last night . . . while we were drinking palm wine, one of the Tanimbarese[247] who live between Openg and Alakamata (there are now four houses of them) came in [the house of Koye Sayaramani, the kamara or kepala desa of Huaulu, with whom I was staying at the time]. Seeing us drink, he said, "Palm wine is good"—a way of asking for it. He was offered one glass. While drinking it, he told us about Romian, his village in Tanimbar. . . . "My grandfather used to tell very beautiful stories. They were so beautiful that one knew they were true. He used to tell that all Tanimbarese originate in Seram, from a place which seems to be behind Sawai. . . . After they left Seram they landed on a small island on which was a wine palm. An ancestor began tapping palm wine. The sap kept coming out uninterruptedly until the island was submerged and the inhabitants scattered on different islands of the [Tanimbarese] archipelago, where they began speaking different languages. But the ritual language remained the same for everybody. It is the language which is still spoken in the island of Fordata. This is why we go on drinking palm wine."
>
> Then Koye said, "To tell you the truth, we Huaulu should not drink palm wine, because it is our origin." I thought he was deriving from the same idea (palm wine as origin) a conclusion contrary to that of the Tanimbarese. But I had heard Pulaki say that palm wine had been tabooed ever since an old lady had cursed the Huaulu for killing one another when in a state of drunkenness. So I asked Koye, "Was it tabooed because of a curse?" "No, not a curse, but the origin [is the cause]." "Then tell me the story." Koye immediately backtracked, saying: "Koa [lit., "no," but here it means "you have misunderstood me," "that's not what I meant,"] I wanted to say that whoever has his origin, for instance, in the tuwa [wine palm/palm wine], should not drink it." Then, turning to the Tanimbarese, he added, "This [i.e. the event you narrated] is already a good reason for us to consider each other pela [i.e. ritual siblings/friends]." He meant that since the Tanimbarese came from Seram, then they were related to the Huaulu [which was precisely what the narrator

> had tried to suggest to legitimize his settlement near the mouth of the Salawai River, where Alakamata and Openg are].
>
> . . . I imagined that Koye either did not wish to tell publicly the story which justified the taboo on palm wine, or abstained from telling it because it contradicted the Tanimbarese's, and he wanted to keep him happy [with the idea that he was accepted as a pela]. . . .
>
> I promised myself that I would request a clarification at the first opportunity today. So I did. Koye answered that there is no taboo on palm wine in Huaulu, and that he was speaking to the Tanimbarese "analogically and for example's sake. I only wanted to say that we too, if we have our origin in some plant or animal, don't eat it. How can we eat our origin?"
>
> The notion of origin is naturally very wide, as demonstrated by another remark of Koye's: "For instance, we (ami mani) ["we" refers to Sayaramani, Koye's lineage] don't eat the sago from the ipia potoa variety, because we have our origin in it. Indeed, one ancestor of ours was processing a sago tree of this variety [to extract its starch], when he heard a thunderclap coming out of the trunk. He went home and dreamed of a sewa potoa who lived in the sago palm. Thus the sewa potoa became ours and we stopped eating ipia potoa."
>
> He gave me this story as his answer to my question as to whether the first Sayaramani was born from (or "transformed from," lelia) the ipia potoa. He said no. Then I asked him what the origin of the latuem ["the lords," the collective title of the senior section of the Huaulu clan, of which Sayaramani is one component] was. He told me that their ancestors were human from the very beginning: "Originally the sky was on earth. Above married below (amuhoto ia pusawa amupale). When they separated, the first human came out of the earth. He was the sultan of Jailolo, the first of the seven sultans." . . .

I have quoted this text for a variety of reasons. First of all, it shows the danger inherent in taking a statement out of context and rendering it absolute. Koye in effect reacted to the Tanimbarese's story by saying something untrue—that the Huaulu have a taboo on palm wine. But then the next day he himself explained that he was not speaking literally. It seems clear that his purpose was to send the Tanimbarese a subtle hint which contradicted the message that he courteously, if in a somewhat tongue-in-cheek manner, put up front. If it was true that the Tanimbarese originated in Huaulu territory and were thus the Huaulu's relatives, with a right to settle in their territory, then why did the two people draw diametrically opposed conclusions from the idea of origin? Had the Huaulu originated from palm wine, they would not have drunk it, whereas that was precisely the reason the Tanimbarese did drink it. While proffering acceptance, Koye in fact served the bitter dish of rejection with his glass of palm wine.

It was possible for Koye to present his hypothetical argument as a factual one, since there is indeed a lineage in Huaulu for which drinking palm wine is taboo. Had I not been aware of this already, I would have extracted a wrong generalization from his rather contorted, but very Huaulu, piece of doublespeak. In the end, what matters ethnographically—and this is the second reason I quote the episode from my journal—is that Koye forcefully asserted the principle which stands behind the *interpretatio totemica* of taboo: "How can we eat our origin?" To do so—to treat as a usable, and therefore destroyable, thing the source of what one is—is to undermine oneself. Just as one cannot reveal one's name or even pronounce it, just as one cannot return to the first village site ever or even look back at it, so one cannot eat one's "origin."

But in what sense is a plant, or an animal, or any other natural phenomenon, one's origin? The text illustrates the most common kind of *interpretatio totemica,* and this is the third reason I quote it. The reason Sayaramani consider the ipia potoa (sago palm) their origin is not that they came out of it in a literal sense. Indeed, Koye, like all Huaulu, was adamant that his ancestors did not come from natural species. Only their neighbors and enemies, the Nisawele, the Manusela, and so on, did, or as the Huaulu say: "If anybody lived in Seram before us, it was animals; it is our ancestors who turned them into humans." The ipia potoa is not *the* origin, in fact, but *an* origin. It is one among several living tokens of a primordial event on which the identity and the reproductive power of Sayaramani depends. It is an origin only as a continuous condition of existence. The primordial event in question is fairly typical: it is the encounter, through the tree, between an occult power (here a sewa potoa) and an ancestor—an encounter which eventuates in a permanent relationship.

The word currently used by the Huaulu to refer to such events, *asale,* "origin," may create some misunderstanding. The word is a borrowing from Indonesian *asal,* itself derived from Arabic. *Asal* means "origin, source; beginning, cause." We ourselves associate the idea of cause with the idea of origin even more strongly than the Indonesian word. Anthropological theories of totemism do the rest. So when I first heard the Huaulu speak of plants and animals as their "origin" (asale) or even as their "ancestors" (aila), I mistakenly thought they meant that in a causal sense. I assumed that an animal or plant metamorphized into a human ancestor or gave birth to one. Hearing this interpretation applied by the Huaulu to their neighbors reinforced my error.

It was a double one. First I disregarded the fact that the Huaulu draw the line between animality and humanity much more strongly for themselves than for their "bestial" neighbors. The totemic interpretation is part of a struggle of representations which exists at a regional, not just at a local, level. Second, I disregarded the fact that causality is not the main operative concept in the Huaulu representation of the past. Origins are not so much about first causes as about first rights. But most important, I disregarded the fact that the Huaulu give the ideas of origin and ancestry a much wider meaning than they possess in English, or even in the Indonesian language, which they sometimes use. The word I translate as "ancestor" is *aiula* or *aila,* which literally means "big man," "important person," and is used as an honorific for most living adult males (me included) and as an unmarked term for all the dead ancestors, male and female.

All ancestors are indeed important persons, and most important persons are ancestors; yet the term *aila* has a wider meaning. Even in a strictly Huaulu context, it is used to refer to a person who is in some way a condition of one's existence, or somebody through whom one can trace a friendship pact or any other relationship which was not necessarily conceived in terms of blood and descent. In fact, *aila* does not even necessarily refer to a person, but may refer to what we would call a thing or a natural kind: a sago tree, as in the case discussed here, or a python, or one of the powerful fetishes called sewa utuem (the seeds of sewa) or luma upuem (the lords of the house) or both. All these "ancestors" are also referred to as origins of the particular social unit to which they are attached—a lineage or, more rarely, the Huaulu people as a whole.

In sum the totemic idea of an animal or vegetal or mineral ancestor is not applied literally to Huaulu lineages, although it may be to non-Huaulu ones. The origin of true humans such as the Huaulu is strictly human or, better, divine. Natural species or objects intervene as signs or mediators between humans and anthropomorphic occult beings with a foot in the animal or vegetal world. It is to these beings that the Huaulu properly refer when they say that a plant, an animal, a thing are their "ancestors." But even when an intellectual short circuit occurs, when the natural embodiment is emphasized to the point that it itself becomes the "origin" and the "ancestor," these notions are taken in the extremely wide sense of anything that makes the existence of a social group possible. Between such totems and their Huaulu counterparts there is no relationship which the Huaulu would qualify as one of lasi, "blood." But then, of course, the whole crux of the matter is that relatedness, kinship, does not exist by blood alone in Huaulu.[248]

Like the shamanic totems, the nonshamanic totems are very much connected with what originally constitutes the lineage and its identity. Before I give some examples, let me reiterate that there is never talk of descent from the "totem." If anything, the sign character of such totems and of the corresponding taboos is even more evident than in the case of the sewa potoa. Take, for instance, the taboos which mark the alleged former allegiance of the Tamatay lineage to Islam, which they rejected in order to live with the Latuem (the group of lineages called Huaulu).

All Tamatay may not eat "goat meat" (uneune) because this is their origin. What this means is that because goat meat is the preferred, characteristic food of Muslims in Indonesia, the Tamatay must mark their rejection of, and yet their residual identification with, their former Islamic identity by rejecting goat meat. A complementary taboo of the Tamatay, but one which need be followed by only a single member of the lineage, a man who bears the name of its prototypical ancestor (Laafale), is the taboo on pork. Here the link with Islam is commemorated positively, by a residual following of the most important food taboo of Muslims. Again we see that a principle of economy, conceptually made possible by the equivalence between the prototypical part and the whole, is at work in taboo.[249]

Examples of totemic taboos that are closer to the sewa potoa paradigm are the taboos on the maleo bird shared by the Puraratuhu and Allay. The maleo is not the body of a sewa as far as I could ascertain, but is specifically said to be taboo for those lineages because "it is their origin" (i rahe asale). What this statement refers to is an episode in the origin myth of Seram, where the ancestors of Allay and Puraratuhu met a gigantic maleo bird which built the island and its mountains just like ordinary maleo birds build their monticulate nests in real life. There are more stories linking the bird to those two lineages. Such stories in fact are part of their origin simply because they are considered their prized possessions and thus one of their enduring attributes. In a sense the totemically interpreted taboo commemorates the "birth" of the lineage, not out of the events narrated in the story, but out of the possession of the story as such.

I should say, though, that this talk of origin is ambiguous, particularly when it moves into the sphere of property—of a property which ontologically qualifies the proprietor. For sometimes to say that a particular plant is "our origin" (speaking of a lineage or village) does not imply that it cannot be eaten but, on the contrary, that it must be eaten, that it is the natural food of those who "have come out with it." Indeed, this is precisely the rationale of misoneistic taboos: one must eat what belongs to one's origin in that it was one's property from the beginning, and must refuse to eat what does not have the same status. We thus run again into the ambiguity so vividly illustrated by the confrontation between Koye and his Tanimbarese guest. One is what one is by not eating certain things but also by eating certain others. One is what one eats just as much as one is what one does not eat. Ultimately what decides that the outcome of "totemism" is avoidance or preference is always some particular story and circumstance whose occurrence cannot be predicted on a priori grounds. At best we can say that the most common foods, the staples, tend to be origins without taboo or are taboo for only selected individuals (such as pork for one particularly named

Tamatay), whereas the less indispensable foods (parrots or the tipola python,[250] for instance) tend to be origins with taboo.

From Animal to Meat, from Meat to Human

I have finished my panoramic survey of the many species that are permanently taboo for all the Huaulu or for some major category of Huaulu people. All the other species are, under normal conditions, available for eating, and are eaten if they are considered edible in an aesthetic, gustatory sense. But this freedom to eat is never full. Nothing, in fact, may be appropriated in a totally free way. If the species itself is free from taboo, then the process of appropriating it is not. Eating without some restriction, just like taking a tabooless medicine, is inconceivable for the Huaulu. There is no such thing as a free lunch, and the currency with which one pays for it is not just sweat. Sweat does not stink high enough to reach heaven; earning one's meal must ride on something more substantial—some renunciation, some giving up, some sacrifice, in a word. Another dimension of taboo will soon lie before us.

One of the first things that I said in this book, and which I will continue to say until its end, is that all Huaulu are hunters. This statement is literally true of men, who do the actual hunting, but it is also indirectly true of women. This is not only because, when given the opportunity of clubbing or slashing a small animal, a Huaulu woman will never hesitate to go ahead. It is also because the attitudes toward animals, meat, and action, which are consubstantial to hunting, permeate women's minds too. For hunting is not just a way of making a living; it is a way of life. It is a way of life in which the relationship with wild animals is, of course, central, but central intellectually and emotionally, not just practically. This is precisely why hunters constantly speak of their fights with animals; they don't just go about the silent business of killing like butchers. Hunting, like war (perhaps one should say traditional war), puts one in confrontation with an enemy, a free and resisting being; it requires knowing it or him, judging it or him by standards similar to those by which one judges oneself and one's fellow beings. Talk is integral to fighting enemies, animal or human; it is almost as if talking *about* them were the displacement of a deeply felt need to talk *to* them, and at the same time the means of repressing this need, and thus also one means of reproducing the difference between them and us, without which there would be no enemy, no animal. Speech has its part to play, then, in the dialectic of animal and human which entangles the hunter. But it is a derivative part. Talking, because it is only human,[251] is already far too far from what it flees; chasing, taking flight, turning ferociously on the attacker, killing and being killed, eating and being eaten, suffering and inflicting suffering—hunting itself—are not. This is the obscure terrain where animal and human blend to the point of confusion; this is the unspoken, indeed unspeakable, threat to a distinct sense of humanness that no narrative would be strong enough to exorcise if taboo had not taken care of it already with a few, bold strokes. It does so by two opposite means: by openly recognizing, but at the same time sharply narrowing, the area of confusion between animal and human which occurs in the hunt; by repressing human actions that betray a sense of continuity between animal and human.

The two means are complementary in establishing what is perhaps the most important of all categorical oppositions in Huaulu culture: that of animal and human. That taboos have to intervene in order to maintain this opposition shows that it is far from spontaneous or unproblematic. Indeed, it flies in the face of many experiences that keep recurring and that are evidently rebellious to their complete neutralization by cultural categories. These categories, then, do not simply or completely constitute experience; they must also fight with it. Like a good general, they use several tactics: they outflank, divide, surround, and recur to a frontal attack only where the enemy is weak. In the hunt, the enemy is strong; accordingly, the experience of continuity between hunter and hunted is contained rather than repressed, although it contradicts the sharp distinction of human and animal that is affirmed in other, more easily luminous (and therefore clearer) contexts. We have already looked at them, since they are so visible. It is time to turn to darkness, which is so much more interesting and instructive than light.[252]

The clearest recognition of the blending of human and animal in the hunt is contained in the fundamental rule of this activity: the hunter cannot eat the meat of the large game (pig, deer, cassowary) that have been killed by his arrows or his traps.[253] Should he eat it, intentionally or not, the occult powers that grant success in the hunt become very angry and deny him more game. The only part of the pig to which the hunter is entitled is totally inedible: namely, the lower jaw, which he hangs as a trophy under the roof of his house, on the kitchen side.[254] The hunter must thus give away his meat. Part of it goes to feed his family, but a good deal is given away. A small share should be given to each household in the village; the rest goes to other hunters with whom the giver is in relations of reciprocity: he gives meat to them and they give meat to him. Thus the only thing that the hunter gets for his pains, apart from the means of feeding his family, is glory, the ability to shore up his boasting narratives with the hard evidence of a row of jaws. But glory is not edible, and the *venator gloriosus* must eat the humble pie of other hunters'—his direct rivals'—meat.

The political and economic effects of the rule (which is found in many other hunter societies)[255] are thus clear: it counters the individualistic and inegalitarian potential of hunting by fostering indirect reciprocity and by making the successful hunter dependent on his rivals. Furthermore, it allows the main risk of hunting—the unpredictability of its results—to be distributed across much of the society, particularly where trapping is concerned. No doubt, these results of the rule are powerful reinforcements of it. Moreover, as ever so often, morality is decisively shaped by those who benefit from it, in this case the weak and lazy. Nobody is as vociferously in favor of the rule that good hunters have to give all their game away than the hopelessly bad or slothful hunters. Meanwhile the strong and active are caught in the snares of their own cult of glory. One of the crosses I had to bear during my fieldwork in 1985 and 1988 was having to listen to the incessant moralizing of my host, Limule, the worst hunter who ever existed and the most relentless accuser of the "stinginess" (i mokohuku) of his betters. His daily bulletin of who had gotten meat and supposedly hidden it was as tiresome as it was inaccurate.

The lazy Tersites exist everywhere and everywhere are powerful. But their noises cannot alone explain the taboo on eating one's own meat. There is something deeper in this taboo than social teleology and collective pressure. As I have hinted, it is a sense that hunter and hunted are locked in a struggle that blends them to a point, that makes them of the same kind. Eating one's meat is in reality eating one's flesh: an impossibility. This sense of continuity between animal and human is too strong to be repressed. It is thus recognized but circumscribed, limited to the actual killer or, in the case of trapping, to the actual owner of the instruments of killing. The collective identification with the animal and thus the collective guilt[256] of its consumption are displaced. In sacrificing the animal on behalf of the other members of society, the hunter sacrifices himself. But in this way he acquires a credit. This credit is repaid in the short term by other hunters who play the same role for him and thus allow him to eat meat. For a few particularly successful hunters, those who have managed to kill a very large number of animals ("at least 90," I was told),[257] the credit is repayed through the performance of a ritual that allows them to eat their own meat. It is as if one thing compensates for the other: as if the society's debt to the hunter were able to erase the hunter's debt to the animal. I am arguing, in sum, that there is a "sacrificial"[258] component to the hunt in Huaulu and that each hunter plays the role of sacrificer in turn. This sacrificial component of the hunt becomes more evident when the whole range of practices and beliefs connected with the killing, butchery, and repartition of game is considered. One practice that is explicitly sacrificial is the "offering"[259] of the skull of every butchered pig and deer to the kaitahu upuam, "the lord/owner of the land." This is his share, as the jaw is the hunter's share. The offering is effected by laying the skull on the branch of a tree, but no words, of either prayer or exhortation, are pronounced.

Let me quote from what a friend of mine, Patakuru, had to say about this practice (I summarize certain sentences but report key statements in their entirety):

> Only the akaniam, "head" [less the jaws], of wild pig and deer are put on the trees for the lord/owner of the land (si kaitahu upuam). Not that of the cassowary or of the cuscus. The jaws are hung in the kitchen for people to count them (ala i sehere, "so that they will count them"). The heads of deer and wild pig are put on the trees for the lord of the land so that he will grant game to us again (ala ia rulu ["make descend"] leku peni si ita). The deer, wild pigs, and cassowaries are the dogs of the lord of the land (kaitahu upuam ia rahe wassuem hini maisaarale pohi hahuem, asualiem). The game of the lord of the land are the humans (kaitahu upuam ia rahe peni hini manusia). His aspect is like that of humans (ita oi wahi manusia). He is like us. As big as us. Some are male, others are female. The male lord of the land fucks women and fucks men (ia polo hini hihina pohi hini manawa), because he appears deceptively (ia hali ruwana) as man or as woman. He or she appears as our husband or as our wife, just like the lusi kinaem [lit., "the evil eagles/hawks": a category of evil "spirits."] If we [men] fuck her (holo hini eme), or he fucks us [women], we are as good as dead (ita maata' naunam). After you have fucked, you don't know it anymore. You forget what happened, but then you die. Only the sewaem (shamanic spirit familiars) can discover what happened and cure us so that we do not die. (Sept. 12, 1985)

This text makes it clear that humans cannot eat the two most important game animals if they do not offer the animals' most important part, the head, to the lord of the land, who is their owner. Then it situates this practice at the juncture of two symmetric hunts: the visible hunt of humans preying on deer, wild pigs, and cassowaries, and the invisible hunt in which the lord of the land preys on humans, using deer, wild pigs, and cassowaries as dogs. Finally, it relates the two hunts by positing an equivalence between violence and sexual seduction: the former ruling in the overt hunt that where humans pursue animals, and the latter in the hidden hunt where animals or, rather, their master, the lord of the land, pursues humans. But one can immediately sense that each is the shadowy mirror image of the other.

The elucidation of the offering of the head, and of the whole complex of ideas and practices that accompanies it, must thus pass through the elucidation of this clearly capital text. Its central figure is the lord of the land, and it is from him that one must begin. I find many mentions of him in my fieldnotes. Here are some:

> Tonight I was in Hatupae's house when it began to rain and the entire village became wrapped in fog. At sunset the fog became yellow in the west. Kaalai said near me, "It is yellow on the coast [a portion of which

lies west of the village]; they must have caught a big boar." I asked him whether there is yellow light in the evening whenever a big boar has been caught, and he answered yes, without elaborating. Later, in the village hall [where I lived at the time], Pinarolo [the wife of the guardian of the hall at the time] told me that when a big peni (game animal) is killed, his master (ia rahe upuam) makes a yellow light. I asked whether he makes it because he is angry, and she said yes. I then asked Limule [Pinarolo's husband] if the master (upuam) of the boar is the same thing as the master of the land (kaitahu upuam), and he answered yes. I also asked him whether wild pig and other peni have mattiulu (soul, animating principle) like humans, and he answered yes, all animals have mattiulu. (Aug. 13, 1985)

I ask Pinarolo whether the lord of the land looks like a human being or like an animal. She gives, as usual, an answer that is no answer—a claim of ignorance: maihussu (who knows?). But then, on second thought, she adds: "I have the impression (a rasa) that he looks like a human, because he is called upuam (lord, master, owner), thus he is human (manusia)." I ask her whether when one kills too many of his creatures he makes a yellow light because he is angry and "he sets out" (ia raki) (like topoyem, "ghosts of the dead," do) to look for humans to kill in revenge. She says that she does not know, but that certainly the yellow light is due to his fury (I know, however, that when women catch too many shrimp, they risk being made ill by the shrimps' upuam,[260] who is angered. [What I imply is that the same thing probably happens here. Yellow light is a sign of approaching death or misfortune, and the master of the killed animal is angry against humans; he wants to make them sick in revenge.]). (Aug. 14, 1985)

According to Malatita [suitor and later husband of Sipinale, Pinarolo's daughter] the lord of the land is heard in either of two forms: ia rohuki, that is to say, he shouts from the depth of the forest "uuuuh!"; ia patatenu, "he echoes," our voice. When somebody leaves the house saying, "I go and check the spring traps (a tihiki supanem)," it is customary to answer him, "Come back soon because the lord of the land may kill you or make you sick." When we hear the voice of the lord of the land it means that he is angry at us either because we have taken his meat (ayokuem) or because we have wounded him unwittingly when we sank a spear or arrow (ita taafai) into the ground. Then the lord of the land may kill us. (Sept. 3, 1985)

I could go on quoting from my fieldnotes like this for a while. But the resulting collage would quickly become cumbersome and, while by present writing conventions it would breathe the spirit of authenticity into the clay of my prose, it would also generate a growing sense of opaqueness accompanied by yawns. My fieldnotes presuppose too many things, so it is just as well to say these things and construct a more explicit text, one adequate to my present purposes of communication. What I present below will thus be a comment—that is, a filling in of empty spaces—on the texts that I have just given through a reasoned summary of many more that I have not given: texts written in the pages of my fieldnotes or in my memory, things I have heard and things I have seen or inferred. And this is valid, of course, for everything that is written in this book.

Upu means any of the following: great-grandfather (mother's brother in poetic language), ancestor, master, owner. It may refer to a human being, a spirit, or a fetish. For instance, the expression *luma upuam,* "master of the house," may refer to the living owner of a house (in the plural, *luma upuem,* it may refer to "hosts"), to his dead ancestral owners, or to animated objects (i.e. fetishes), whose power in some ways constitutes, controls, and constrains the social group identified with the house. Another example of "ownership" or rather "mastery" by such fetishes is offered by the sewa upuem: heirlooms which "own" the sewa, the shamanic familiars, and which therefore allow a relationship to be maintained with them. This example shows that *upu* can also be translated by "controller."

Kaitahu means "land" in the most generic sense. But in Seram land is usually covered with wild trees; thus *kaitahuam* refers most of the time to what we would call the forest, the jungle. When a Huaulu says, "A taki roe kaitahuem," "I go out to the land," he means "I go out to the forest." When he goes only to his garden, he says, "A taki hoto ("up," or any other appropriate directional) lawa," or if he goes to his sago grove, he says, "a taki hoto somam," and so on. A kaitahu, area of land, includes, not only the trees and other plants that grow on the land, but also everything that inhabits it, game in particular. In fact, ownership of a kaitahu is less ownership of the ground than ownership of what it produces. All the land claimed by the Huaulu as their "territory" (nusam) is divided into named kaitahuem, and each belongs to a separate lineage, that is, to all the appropriate[261] descendants of the original acquirer. Some kaitahuem are transferred to wife-takers as part of marriage counterprestations from wife-givers. Human ownership can thus change; land can move from human to human by right of conquest, by inheritance, by affinal gift, or even by sale. Opposite this changing and negotiated human ownership, there is an unchanging, original, and occult ownership: that of what, for want of a better word, can be called the occult power (the "spirit," if one wishes) living in the land.

While both the human owners and the occult owners may be called kaitahu upuem, "the owners of the land," the term *kaitahu upuam* without further specification usually refers to the occult owner only. This indicates that human ownership is derivative. The real owners are occult, ultimately beyond the grasp of human agency. They transcend the human order and the arrangements made by humans, which they may always thwart. They must be pacified and cajoled, but also tricked and deceived. Humans are always squatters, they never achieve total and unchallangeable ownership of their land because this is possible only where the social order is conceptually isolated as a fully autonomous order of reality. Where social relations and social conventions exist against the background of a nonhuman world more powerful than the human one, the concept of total ownership, which wholly submits the owned thing to the owner, which in fact makes it totally a thing in the first place,[262] cannot arise. There is no notion in Huaulu of a socially guaranteed free access to what is owned, of a right of use and abuse. One always owns as part owner, as part of a superior ownership; one is forever an interloper or at best a tenant. One does not merely use but also fights to obtain: one confronts not inanimate possessed objects, but living, active beings. The owned is the vanquished, the tricked, the robbed, the prayed for, the exchanged for; it is never, or almost never, what is there to take, as an absolute given. Property is never reified to the extent that the Huaulu forget that some kind of work—and some kind of transgression (violent appropriation)—always mediates the relationship between the user and his objects. In this sense, the fetishism of property is much less blatant in Huaulu than in any bourgeois society.

This sense that one must always strike a deal, pay a price for using land, is not equally intense across all the spectrum of the land's products. Here the fact that the Huaulu are essentially hunters, on the ideological side if not always on the practical one, is quite evident. One finds none of the rituals for opening a garden, for "cooling" the land, for removing it from the control of its "spiritual" owners (as anthropologists usually call them), that exist among the horticultural or agricultural peoples of Indonesia. No first-fruit offerings of horticultural produce exist. No "payment" is exacted in this area, no "redemption" is necessary. It is true that this may indicate the lack of a well-established, guaranteed procedure more than the sense that one risks nothing in taking. In fact, it turns out that cases of attack from kaitahu upuem on those who clear the forest, who first enter it to acquire even its humblest and least valued products, abound. Such attacks take many forms: persistent nightmares, inflicting of disease, wounds that from our point of view are self-inflicted but that from the Huaulu point of view are inflicted by the occult owner of the land, and so on.

Thus a minimal condition even for entering a land without danger is to be known to the kaitahu upuam. He is supposed to dislike any stranger, any new person intruding on his domain. He must come to accept your presence, but there is no established procedure for obtaining recognition and acceptance. One must wait and see. Being a descendant of the first human occupier, of the person who first made himself known to the lord of the land and struck an implicit contract with him, usually helps. It is probably because the contract is valid for all descendants that they do not need to ask permission ritually again and again when clearing the forest for a garden or entering it for hunting and so on. Nevertheless some small prophylactic rituals may be performed. The most common one is to bind a strip of rattan to one's wrist on entering a land for the first time; it protects children or newcomers from the kaitahu upuam's attacks until he gets used to them or becomes resigned to adding them to the list of his acceptable guests. I remember, for instance, that on observing that my wife had cut herself slightly with her own bush knife on her first visit to a forest area at the beginning of our stay in Huaulu, a friend bound one of her wrists with a stripe of rattan, explaining that the kaitahu upuam had provoked her wound because he (or she) was not used to my wife yet.

This evidence indicates that even when one uses the products of the land that have less value and ideological importance, one cannot do so with total freedom and impunity, but rather runs a serious risk of paying a price with one's own life. It is nevertheless the case that the more explicit and heavy restrictions or costs concern game, particularly pig and deer, which furnish most meat. This is because meat, not vegetables, is the most valued food. Clearly, the kaitahu upuam has exactly the same values and concerns as the Huaulu. As one of the texts quoted above suggests, he does not like to see his meat (i.e. animals) taken from him, and he becomes positively angry when too much of it is stolen by humans.

The appropriation of meat thus encounters the kaitahu upuam as the major obstacle in its way. But it is an obstacle that needs to be ritually neutralized only for the largest game, whose killing engenders the greatest anger in the occult lord of the land. The neutralization is achieved through strategies of displacement and substitution, thus by a performative use of the symbolic. These strategies apply to both sides of the hunting relation: to the human side and to the animal side. On the human side, there is a displacement of responsibility. All those who partake of the meat of the animal killed should also partake of the responsibility for "stealing" it. But if this were to happen, eating meat would become impossibly dangerous. Therefore, responsibility is displaced on the most salient, the most "visible" person in the process of appropriation: not the butchers, not the cooks, not the eaters, but the killer or the owner of the trap that killed. All the danger is on him, because all the responsibility is on him. He must therefore avoid eating the meat of the animal he himself has killed. This renunciation of eating is thus both the avoidance of a danger and a revealer of the nature of this danger: the stealing of a life calls for a life in return. Were the hunter to eat his own meat, the lord of the land and master of the animal he killed would attempt to take his life, and he would become, at the very least, ill. Furthermore, he would become unable to catch any other animal.[263] Indeed, the basic symbolic condition for the appropriation of large game—that at least the killer is not allowed to eat the animal he has killed, that he shows himself "sorry"[264]—would come to an end. This symbolic condition is not just an appendage of the practical activity of hunting; it is consubstantial with it. Thus the scapegoating of the hunter, the renunciation of eating forced onto him, is the condition of possibility for all other people to eat. Here, the idiom of taboo is truly a sacrificial one.

There are cases when this strategy of displacement cannot work so easily, though. This is when the killing is too efficient. For instance, if the animal is "struck dead on the spot by the spring trap" (ia lefe tiyam), its meat is very "bad" (piniassi)—that is, maquwoli, "taboo"—not just for "the owner" (upuam) of the trap, but for all the members of his lineage. A displacement that goes further than usual is therefore necessary: the meat is entirely given to the lineage's mulua anaem (lit., "female children"), that is to say, to the sisters or daughters incorporated into their husbands' lineages and to their children or descendants. They are sufficiently "other" to be unaffected by the poison in the gift, and yet still sufficiently "close" to their lineage of origin to function as substitutes of its members, to expiate the members' "fault"—the fault of being too deadly, too successful, which turns the result of the work against the worker. Another instance where efficiency in killing is a positive danger is when too many animals have been caught; then one risks becoming a victim of the avenging fury of the lord of the land on which the animals were shot or fished. One way to reduce the ensuing danger is to share it by giving some of the meat or fish to other people. Again, it is a case of poison in the gift. But then perhaps all gifts of meat are poisoned in this way; they constitute a system for the collectivization of danger. Poison shared is poison diluted. Thus I was told that if one gets five cuscuses, one is in danger, even if as a rule it is not taboo for the hunter to eat the cuscuses he has himself killed. Accordingly, one should give away three of the five cuscuses in order to be able to eat the remaining two without fear.

This devaluation of efficiency may appear astonishing to our "modern," that is, ruthlessly and unrestrainedly aquisitive, mentality. But it is hardly surprising if one's basic value is the avoidance of hubris, itself the cardinal consequence of the idea that balance and measure should rule the relationship between the human species and the other species. Killing too many animals, cutting down too many trees, stealing too much from a world that does not belong to us, is dangerous because it brings about the reaction of those species whose continued existence is threatened.[265] The Huaulu are, as usual, lucidly aware of the profound contrast between their ideas and those of their Christian and Muslim neighbors on this score. They accuse the Christians, especially, of unrestrained, unregulated, and often useless destruction of everything living. And some also accuse them of not following the golden maxim "Live and let live." Thus Koye, who, having lived much of his adult life on the coast, is very adept at comparing what he perceives to be the Christian and the Muslim philosophies of life with the Huaulu one, told me once:

> Christians get angry with the animals that eat fruit from their trees or that eat the products of their gardens. But why get angry? This is a right given to the humans, just like the animals, by Lahatala [the sky god]. There is enough fruit for everybody. It always ends up rotting. Some time ago I became angry with the Huaulu because they wanted to put traps to catch the animals that eat langsat. What for? Take it easy. In the end, the quantity of langsat that rots is greater than the one that we manage to eat. (Feb. 25, 1988)

Huaulu are not so tolerant when less abundant goods are concerned, especially when the competitors are other humans. But Koye's words reflect a deep-seated idea regulating the relationship between animals and humans in the Huaulu view: both have a God-given right to live, and it is therefore wrong for humans to threaten the animals' life and livelihood or to kill them unnecessarily or in too great numbers.

So much for the strategy of displacement used in treating the human side. But what about the animal side?[266] Here too we find that the most salient part is substituted for the whole: the head of large game (i.e. deer and pig) is renounced by humans in order for the rest of the body to be eaten. Besides being convergent in their effects, the two substitutions are formally parallel: the noneating killer substitutes for the eaters as the noneaten head substitutes for the eaten body. In both cases, the part that carries the taboo is the whole displaced. The displacement is made possible by a severance: the head is separated from the trunk and the killer from the social body. This structure closely parallels the one found in human sacrifice (which takes the apparent form of "headhunting"): another indication that the hunt, or at least the hunt of pig and deer, must be understood in sacrificial terms.[267] This sacrificial dimension, though, is found not in the killing of the animal as such, but in the double renunciation that characterizes the disposal of its carcass: a collective renunciation of the head and the killer's renunciation of any part of the animal's trunk. I have already elucidated the signification of the second renunciation, but what about the first one? What is the source of its efficacy?

If it is indeed true that the head of the animal is the totality of its body displaced onto its most important and salient part, then an answer suggests itself: the giving of the head to the lord of the land is a symbolic return of the whole animal to him, and therefore a symbolic negation of its appropriation by the humans. This negation of the appropriation of the body of the animal thus echoes and completes the negation effected on the social body. My initial and provisional characterization of the giving of the head to the lord of the land as an "offering" should not be taken to mean that we have here a propitiatory or expiatory gift. Nothing is given to the lord of the land as far as the meat itself is concerned, since he already owns that. The offering is no gift; it is a symbolic restitution of what has been stolen, of a meat which, as our text above says quite clearly, belongs to the lord of the land. If humans give, it is not the meat, but *through* the meat. They give their renunciation of eating it; they give their symbolic negation of the appropriation of the animal, and thus their recognition of the ultimate and irreducible character of the lord of the land's mastery: mastery over the land, mastery over the animals who live on it, and mastery over the humans who hunt them. Through this deceptively simple act the Huaulu recognize themselves as intruders on a world fundamentally alien to them, a world which owns them more than they own it.

The head is not the only part of the animal's body into which the whole is displaced, and thus the appropriation of the animal symbolically negated (in the Freudian sense that saying no is one way of saying yes: the recognition of something is contained in its negation).[268] Blood is another part. A hunting and headhunting people, the Huaulu live by spilling blood, human and animal. They are thus as aware as anybody of blood's equivalence with life. Losing blood is losing the entire life; therefore, blood can be viewed as an equivalent of the animal as a whole. Furthermore, blood is the same in animals (at least in the large game whose appropriation is ritualized) and in humans; it is the closest material approximation to the idea that the hunter and the hunted share an identical life. The strategies of circumscription and displacement are thus able to converge on the blood. In it, the identity of human and animal presents itself already displaced from the whole of the body to its animating part. When blood pours out of the body—an inevitable result of butchery—the displacement is further increased. The animal is drained of its points of similarity with humans by the draining of its blood. Blood, then, cannot be appropriated without undermining the appropriation of the flesh. It is renounced.

This renunciation of blood takes two forms. The blood clots found in the carcass are put on trees like the skull or are simply thrown away. In both cases they are said to be "for the kaitahu upuam." Life is returned to its sources. The other form is characterized by renunciation pure and simple, without any explicit idea of a "return" to the kaitahu upuam: liquid blood is not collected to be eaten, but is allowed to be lost, ultimately to fall on the earth.[269]

A third part (or set of parts) of the animal's body which also seems the object of a displacement is the so-called maraissi. It consists of three small pieces of meat skewered on a thin stick or on a strip of bamboo: what looks like a heart valve; a piece of the spleen; and a piece taken from the genital area (pale kaasina, "under the buttocks," as one informant put it), which I am unable to identify. The maraissi is a maquwoli, "taboo thing," because it is marked by special restrictions and by a special destination. It is taboo to cook it in coconut milk or in anything but plain water. And it must be eaten by a person or group of persons specially designated by the owner of the animal. In one case I witnessed, the person was the owner's foster son (and also the son of his elder brother); in another, his wife and the female friends who happened to be with her when she had her meal.[270]

Although the two cases above seem fairly typical of the kind of recipient the maraissi has—namely a female or a member of a younger generation—there is no prescribed kinsman to whom this share is rendered, except when a young man catches his first large animal (pig, deer, or cassowary) in his trap. Then the maraissi is ceremonially given to his paternal aunt or, failing her, to any other married-out woman from his lineage. The piece is eaten by her with her children, and she reciprocates with a porcelain plate (at the very least), which becomes her first contribution to his future bridewealth. This rite inaugurates the young man's taboo on his own meat.

I have often asked about the signification of this "taboo share," but no informant was able (or willing) to reveal it. However, given that it is made up of three vital parts of the animal and that its preferred recipients are also bearers of life (children, wives, paternal aunts and their children, married-out sisters and their children), an analogic relationship may exist between the receivers and the thing received. I am tempted to speculate that a strategy of displacement is at work here, just as in the cases of the head and the blood. For those more directly concerned with the butchery of the animal, it would be dangerous to absorb its more vital part. But for those who have no responsibility in the appropriation of the animal's life, these parts, being full of life, are beneficial, for they promote vitality and fertility. In other words, what is poisonous (the Huaulu say "bad") for some is life-promoting ("good") for others.[271]

All the above symbolic displacements, whether they concern the animal side or the human side, are encompassed by a more fundamental displacement, which provides the frame for them all and, in a way, summarizes them all. It is taboo to butcher an animal, that is, to turn it into meat, inside the village or any other space where human houses are located. Not only, then, should species that are found exclusively outside the village be killed there, but they should also be butchered there. Even after death, animals cannot enter the village in an unbutchered state without becoming inedible: to be eaten, they must already be reduced to anonymous meat in which the animal cannot be recognized. Actually, in its strict interpretation this rule is valid only for the three largest game animals: deer, pig, and cassowary. Smaller animals, such as cuscuses, birds, and bats, are usually gutted and plucked or have their furs singed in the forest, but need not always be cut into pieces there. The same is true of snakes. The basic rule, seemingly followed for all blooded animals, is that their blood and their guts must be spilled outside the village. No butchery of wild animals should take place in it. And as for domestic animals, either they should not be killed, or if they are, they should not be butchered, because they are not eaten.[272]

What explains this taboo and its particular focus on heavily bleeding animals? The explanation can be found in the convergence of two tacit ideas: the idea that the human habitat should be associated only with life, and thus not contaminated by a death—that of the animal—which in many respects is reminiscent of that of humans; and the idea that death is made more evident by dismembering, especially by the sight of an abundance of oozing blood. Furthermore, butchery produces a lot of "dirt" (pakitayam), which, like all dirt, should be kept out of the village. But by itself, the latter motive would not be sufficient to produce the taboo, as is suggested by the fact that it is forbidden, but not taboo, to defecate inside the village. Between this "sanitary" rule and the taboo on butchering in a space permanently inhabited by humans, there is thus all the difference that exists between aesthetics and religion. Blood, even the blood of beasts, is clearly thicker than shit.

In the passage from living animal to inert meat, three categories are involved. The first one is constituted by the ensemble of all living animals considered in themselves and not in relationship to man. It is an unnamed category, as we have seen: there is no common name for wild animal or even for animal in the Huaulu language.

The second category is peni. In its extended sense, *peni* refers to all animal species that are hunted and that, therefore, furnish meat. In its narrower sense it refers—at least according to one informant (Pitere) and his sister (Saite)—to the animal after it has been butchered and even smoked in the forest, but before it has been introduced into the house. The wider sense derives from the narrower sense through anticipation: it sees the meat in the animal, so to speak, even if the animal is still alive and entire. Pitere and Saite explained the relationship between the two meanings in this way: "When we say *ita tana peni* [lit., 'we go to fetch an animal fallen into a trap'], what we really mean is 'we are going to transform an animal into meat (peni).' Hence we call the animal meat (peni)." Because the word *peni* is usually heard as part of the expression *ita tana peni,* and because that particular expression refers to butchering the three large animals (deer, pig, and cassowary) which fall into the "spring-traps" (supanem), for a long time I assumed that *peni* refers to those three animals only. This assumption seemed to find confirmation in Ellen's definition of the Nuaulu word *peni,* an obvious cognate of the Huaulu *peni:* "category of game animals, composed of pig, deer and cassowary."[273] Only little by little, during my visits to Huaulu in 1985 and 1988, did I discover and establish to my satisfaction that *peni* has in fact a much wider meaning than that. At best, one can say that pigs, deer, and cassowaries are peni par excellence; but all my informants were adamant, when explicitly questioned, that peni refers to cuscuses, snakes, birds, and so on, considered as sources of meat. "Animal that is a source of meat" is indeed the definition of *peni* on which all Huaulu would agree.

The third category is ayoku, which, strictly speaking, means "meat as it stands on the shelves above the fireplace" (or "meat on the plate"). It is often used in the definite plural form, ayokuem, "meats." *Meats* is here taken in its largest sense: any animal flesh, including seafood. As I have mentioned, *ayoku* refers to the final stage of the transformation of the animal into meat. The stage is marked by storing the meat in the kitchen, ready for cooking. Semantically, the distinction between *peni* and *ayoku* is not hard and fast. People do say "ita ae peni," "we eat peni," as much as they say "ita ae ayokuem," "we eat ayokuem" (they also say "ita ae maisarale," "we eat deer," "or ita ae hahu," "we eat pork," and so on). The distinction appears, though, at the level of taboo. According to Pitere, who claimed to describe these distinctions by category in their pristine rigor, meat in its peni stage has the same taboos as live animals. Thus one cannot laugh or joke in the presence of an animal that is being butchered or smoked in the forest. The taboo ceases to exist only when the meat has been stored in the house and has thus become ayokuam proper.

In sum, while the species name, *peni,* and *ayoku* may all be used to refer to meat, only *ayoku* means "meat" proper, not just semantically, but in its full cultural sense, which is constituted by taboos and other nonlinguistic forms of marking, such as spatial and temporal ones. Their effect is to contrast sharply the village and the wilderness outside it. The animal as living species cannot become part of the village as food until it completely loses its identity as an autonomous member of the wild and is turned into formless pieces of blackened meat on the shelf on top of the kitchen fireplace. Then it is no more a body and a quasi-person (at least as an antagonist); it has been reduced to a substance totally passive vis-à-vis the humans who eat it and turn it into their own life.

I have said that through the deceptively simple acts of renunciation and displacement detailed above, the Huaulu recognize themselves as intruders on a world that owns them more than they own it. It is in light of this recognition that we can understand why the humans'

Many detailed explanations of the logic of taboos were offered by Pitere, who is pictured here in the center of the photograph, wearing a red turban, sitting beside an older relative with a basket that holds sirih leaves and pinang nuts. 1972. (Photo by V. Valeri.)

hunt of the animals of the lord of the land is encompassed by its reversal: the lord of the land's hunt of humans. For the latter hunt is not just an imaginary expression of the principle of balance and compensation, which rules the relationship between humans and animals (and more generally all the nonhuman forms of life found in the forest); it also conveys the idea that in the end humans are defeated by a world which they cannot control and which devours them invisibly as they devour it visibly. The efficacy of ritual displacement is thus limited: the ultimate outcome of the battle with the animal is the animal's victory as a principle, a principle that takes the panic shape of the lord of the land. The displaced truth returns to center stage: killing has a price—being killed. The arrow shot at the animal bounces back at the human. But at the end of its loop, it takes a genital form: it penetrates humans at the point of their greatest vulnerability—sex. For, as the quoted and unquoted texts make clear, the counterhunt of the lord of the land uses the weapons of seduction. By appearing as a wife, or a husband, or a lover, the lord of the land persuades the victim to engage in a fatal copulation, and he or she is "fucked." Consumed by love, he or she cannot think about anything else, stops eating, and after a short time dies. Nature, defeated by man's tools, takes her revenge as sex.

But this conversion of hunting into copulation and this turning of sex, the producer of life, into a producer of death are made possible by their preexisting linkage in Huaulu thought. The linkage between hunting and sexual conquest—and the assimilation of game and erotic object, which the link implies—is extremely frequent in Huaulu discourse. I have already mentioned that this is particularly the case with cuscuses and cuscus hunting, but it is also evident for hunting in general and even for headhunting. From a male point of view (and women are largely the accomplices of men in this respect) sexuality is a game of competition and subjugation, just like hunting. Moreover, it is a game which—again, like hunting—takes place in the forest (the only place where one can find enough privacy for it). Equally evident is the linkage of sexuality with death, which I have already mentioned in connection with its emblematic figure—the chicken. It is made explicit in the myth that explains the origin of death as a contest between two sewa: one propounding a system of personal immortality through individual rejuvenation; the other—the winning one—propounding a system of species immortality through sexual reproduction.[274] These linkages are a condition of the reverse hunting practiced by the lord of the land, but they do not explain it. They do not explain, especially, why the representative of the animals defeats humans through sexuality.

The explanation is provided, I believe, by the perceived inferiority of humans vis-à-vis animals with regard to fertility and thus, allegedly, sexual potency.[275] Fertility seems so much greater in animals than in humans. This human inferiority in matters of sexual reproduction appears as a reversal of the human superiority in matters of production, food production in particular. Animals are not as good as humans at appropriating nature. And they are not as good at killing humans as humans are at killing them. The sphere of sexuality thus allows the relationship of animals and humans to be balanced, to impress on it the seal of reciprocity: the killers get killed, the devourers become "devoured." But this closing of the loop does not denote a perfect symmetry. For however valued human production is, it presupposes reproduction. Hunting is essentially killing, not creating. It transforms living animals into meat, but it cannot make them. Analogously, the hunter's activity presupposes his life; it does not make his life. Both the subject and the object of hunting, and more generally both the subject and the object of production, presuppose a reproductive (that is, self-productive) power in the matter of which humans are either dependent on animals or inferior to them. Thus in the loop opened by hunting, the sexual closing rings with more than reciprocity between human and animal; it reveals the inescapable subordination of human activity to its natural conditions—the subordination of work to sex.

The exuberant, unregulated, and polymorphous sexuality of the lord of the land embodies this complex of ideas. It accounts for the continual reproduction of animal and vegetal life on the land. It explains why he is their ultimate owner: he is their owner as the sire is the owner of the sired. At the same time, because he is partly anthropomorphic (typically, he appears to humans in human form, but his animal feet betray his animal side), he seems a guarantee of human access, however limited, to the land and its products. It is an access paid for by taboos, ritual acts, and especially the constant danger of being overpowered and destroyed by the uncontrolled, intense sexuality of the lord of the land. His animality carries away humans with it by reviving the humans' own animality, by making them forget the cultural rules and social bonds that distinguish them from animals. The seductive rape by this figure that is a blending of human and animal reveals the limits of the cultural order which the Huaulu impose on their bodies and their environment. His easiest victims are, of course, women because of their supposed weakness. The weakness, the permeability of women to rape by the lord of the land, is thus emblematic, for the Huaulu, of their general dependency on the invincible reproductive potency of the land. No formula captures more appropriately or more poignantly the Huaulu view of their relationship with this potency than the ever-present curse: maasiki kaitahu upuam ia polo ita inare, "may the lord of the land rape our mothers." Swearing, the children of the land acknowledge that they are all the bastard offspring of its half-human, half-animal lord, that a centaur or a Pan presides uninvited at their birth.

But I should again stress that although the more frequent and paradigmatic manifestation of this relation between lord of the land and humans is male, the lords of the land can be of both sexes. In fact, many of them are said to be women. And both male and female lords of the land can seduce humans. It would be a mistake, though, to transfer gender relations as they exist in the human world to the world of the lords of the land. For their more-than-human potency is also anarchic and excessive in constantly breaking down the barriers of gender. Sexual polymorphism is their basic condition: they may appear as men to women and as women to men; they are neither man nor woman, as they are neither human nor animal. Even in their ability to escape human categories they embody the transcendence, both negative and positive in its consequences, of the human order by its nonhuman, even inhuman, conditions of possibility.

The kaitahu upuam is only the most important of several occult beings who see humans as their game (the word *peni,* "game," is explicitly used). They all contribute to defining the image of reversal implicit in the hunting relation with the animal and extended in different degrees to the entire relationship of human agency with its nonhuman objects. Two are particularly significant in this context: the atalayem and the masielem. Although I have already briefly mentioned them in the introduction, they deserve a somewhat fuller discussion in this context.

The atalayem are anthropophagous giants who live in mountains, where their habitations are caves filled with treasure. Their aspect is usually human, but contrary to humans they can fly because they have wings. In fact, some of them take the body of gigantic predatory birds, especially the eagle. The atalayem are, in a sense, the lords of the mountains and, as such, counterparts of the lords of the land. As the mountains are gigantic, so are their lords. They may chase and devour humans wherever they are, but fortunately one has not seen much of them in recent times. Their presence among the Huaulu is thus narrative; nobody claims to have had direct experience of them. Still, they do not belong to a safely distant past; they may appear any time and eat up entire villages, as did the most famous and feared of them, the Hahunusa, who is in fact responsible for human mortality, as I have mentioned.

The masielam is another anthropophagous being. Like the atalayem, the masielem live in the mountains. Contrary to the atalayem, they do not inhabit caves but live in "villages like ours," built "on top of the mountains" (ulay tupem). Also, contrary to the atalayem, the masielem are still very much around, although usually invisible. They have the same aspect and dimensions as humans, but they are like animals in that smell is their dominant mode of perception. When they locate a human through smell, they silently come close to him, seize him, and devour him. They are also in the habit of "sticking their tongue out" (lewati mekune). The tip of their tongue sends a flash of light. They move it in various directions to seek their victims in the darkness. I was told that sometimes one sees flashes of light from as far away as the coast; they are produced by masielem. Humans can turn into masielem, and indeed these beings have much in common with the anthropological category of witch. As such the term *masielem* is used as a synonym of *perverted human.* I can well recall more than one elder complaining that his lineage seemed capable of generating only masielem. But I am less interested in this aspect of the masielem than in the trait they have in common with the atalayem and the kaitahu upuem, that is, their representation of a blending, situated in the wild, of the human and the animal.[276]

If my analysis is correct, this blending is the imaginary correlate of the hunt. In the hunt, animal and humans fight one another, and this mutual combat, however skewed in favor of man, gives humans a sufficient sense of similarity to produce the idea of a possible reciprocity, of a turning of the tables, between animal and humans. The sense of similarity is further reinforced by the behavioral and physical similarities between humans and animals, especially the larger mammals. Both this similarity with the animal and the reciprocity that goes with it are partly recognized, partly displaced, and in either case masked and even repressed by ritual practices, taboos, and discourses. But the frightening figures of the occult powers stand as the return of the repressed. The thought that the animals may hunt and eat humans as humans hunt and eat animals, that one is just the peni, "game," of the other, comes back to haunt the Huaulu in the guise of its premise: the blending or dissolving of the human into the animal, as represented by humanlike figures with animal feet, or wings, or animallike behaviors (protruding tongue, predominance of smell among the senses) and appetites (anthropophagy, unregulated sexuality). Atalayem and masielem represent this reversal of the eater/eaten relation between animal and human in the most direct, oral way. The kaitahu upuam represents it in a somewhat displaced form, that is, through sexuality. Ultimately, his effects are the same as those of the other two figures: the victim of one of his sexual attacks, unless cured by it, ceases to eat food (that is, the products of the wild) and "eats" himself or herself (ia malahau) instead, until death comes.

As we have seen, the strategy of displacement blends with that of sacrificial substitution. The sense of continuity between animal and human is not negated or repressed; it is neutralized by some displacement that takes on a sacrificial form. The head of the animal is sacrificed: returned to the animal's rightful owner, the lord of the land, in lieu of the whole. And the "head" of the hunting and butchering party, the man who killed the animal or who owns the trap that killed it, is also "sacrificed," or rather, he accepts sacrificing himself by not eating any meat from the animal for whose death he is responsible. Thus from the idiom of taboo ("it is taboo for the hunter to eat the animal he has killed," "it is taboo to eat the head of the animal killed") transpires a sacrificial substance which permeates other representations as well. Hunting implies the risk, and almost the necessity, of giving oneself as a return, of falling prey to the figure of a humanized animal—an animal that exacts a price, demands a revenge like a human, because it is allowed to participate, in some measure, in the moral universe of humans. To this figure of the humanized animal, the lord of the land, one may lose one's body or, even more frequently, the body of one's women.

A sacrificial component, in the primordial sense of giving up something in order to obtain something, is also present in several other taboos connected with the hunt. For instance, a condition for the efficacy of "spring-traps" (supanem) is giving up the eating of certain vegetables. One vegetable that is taboo for all Huaulu when building and maintaining spring-traps (those that strike the three largest game animals) is the lokuam, whose palmate leaves are otherwise considered quite good to eat. Other vegetables are taboos for certain lineages only. For instance, the Puraratuhu lineage has the taboos of the papaya and the ulahapam, a mushroom which is singled out as the only one, among those considered taboo, that grows on rotten wood. As for the members of the Sayaramani lineage, they cannot eat the leaves of a tuberous plant called upuam, those of "the sweet potato" (patatam), and all "the mushrooms" (ulaem). Papaya and lokuam are also taboo for everybody when making "weight traps" (sohem) for cuscuses. In addition, it is always taboo to eat the meat of any hunted animal together with the leaves of lokuam and of laitiliam (*Gnetum gnemon?*). It is even taboo to keep those leaves in the same house where some meat is kept. The standard explanation for these taboos is that they are "taboo for the mutuaulaem." Of course, this is a tautological explanation or one that simply displaces the question, Why are they taboo for the mutuaulaem?

The mutuaulaem are powers that preside over the efficacy of the hunt and are acquired by dreaming of an animal. The transmission of powers consists in a covenant whereby the dreamt animal gives the human the power to kill a certain number of animals in exchange for following certain food taboos. Because this means giving up eating vegetables or fruits that are greatly appreciated, the exchange has sacrificial connotations. From a human point of view, it makes sense to give up a less valuable food (vegetables) for a more valuable one (meat); but what is the motivation for the mutuaulaem, that is, for the animals behind these powers? I once got a very clear explanation of the matter from a woman who was visiting my former wife and myself in our house (in 1973). She noticed that we had brought back from the forest some lokuam and some laitiliam, which we used to like very much. Quite alarmed, she asked us to throw them away because otherwise "we (inclusive) will not be able to eat meat again." She went on to explain that those leaves cannot even be in indirect contact with the meat of some animal without making it impossible for the man who has gotten the meat to get any more animals in his traps. When I asked her why, she replied that those leaves are the food of the young of pig, deer, and cuscuses. If humans were to eat them, they would deprive the animals of their food and imperil their reproduction. The argument should not be confused with an ecological-utilitarian one. There are enough leaves around for animals and humans alike. Rather, the argument is that a reciprocity should exist between animals and humans, between the hunter and his game. Humans should give a token of respect to the animal, particularly to its parental feelings, by leaving the food of its young untouched. In exchange, the animals, through the mutuaulaem, will let some of them be killed by humans, so that humans can live too. Thus humans sacrifice themselves, renounce part of their food, in order that animals sacrifice themselves, renounce some individuals among them. It is not so much a *do ut des* formula as each side of a relation doing its part for its continuation.

The argument made for laitiliem and lokuem can probably be extended to the other vegetals that are taboo when making traps. Indeed, it seems that papaya and mushrooms are eaten by pigs and deer, and so of course are the leaves (in the case of the deer) and the tubers (in the case of pigs) of tuberous plants like the sweet potato and the upuam. But there is no need to postulate that every taboo plant is taboo because it is the food of some game animal. The sacrificial reciprocity is instated and maintained by the simple act of giving something up. In this case it is the renunciation itself that is the object of the sacrificial gift. Renunciation is sufficient because it is a token of respect and care. It signals that the hunter does not claim total and free possession of the animals, but recognizes his dependency on their goodwill for success in the hunt. In this respect he recognizes in the animals at least some of the attributes he recognizes in himself as a human: the ability to choose, to will, to give, or to withdraw. Such taboos, then, are a sign that animals are not reduced to mere object, that one does not see in them merely formless meat. Note that these taboos must be respected not only by the owner of the traps but by all those who benefit from them, that is to say, by all members of the owner's lineage (who should automatically receive a share of the meat caught) and by all other inhabitants of the village whose households have received shares. This basically means that almost everybody in the village must follow the taboos of everybody else when traps are set.

All the above taboos are strategies for neutralizing the moral effects of a perceived continuity between animal and human by circumscribing and displacing it through a minimal sacrificial gesture. They are acts of renunciation. Taboo is thus more than avoidance; it is also a positive gesture of giving up something in order to obtain something. Its main motivation is to maintain a relationship, to fulfill an implicit covenant with the animal species. It is a covenant which, in contrast to that with the domestic animals, does not imply that the animal lives with humans in a subordinate, but close, position. The model for the relationship with the wild animals is not the relationship with slaves (such as dogs, cats, and chickens in a sense are), but the relationship with outsiders in a regulated relation of enmity. It is war, not slavery. Enmity and parity are blended in that relationship. But whether the animals are perceived as domestic slaves or as enemy outsiders, a continuity exists between them and the Huaulu which must be neutralized by some sacrificial displacement, by some mark of respect.

To conclude this chapter, let me quote two, slightly different, taboos whose violation has a direct bearing on the supply of meat. In the first taboo, the contrast between humans and animals is expressed through a medium that indexes the human body, namely the leaves of lapuam (B.I.: daun tikar, "mat leaves," probably screwpine). These leaves are used to weave the mats on which humans sleep or sit and the "boxes" (kotale, from B.I. *kotang*) in which their clothes are stored. I speculate, therefore, that they are connected with the human body, particularly with body odor. This proves offensive to animals. Humans cannot lose their body odor, but they can keep separate from animals objects that take up their body odor or evoke it. More than the odor itself, it is the gesture of respect that matters. Correlatively, the horror that the hunted animals feel for the odor of the hunters is supposed to be displaced onto the leaves and the mats and boxes they serve to fabricate. Thus the fresh leaves of the screwpine cannot be brought into a house in which the meat of an animal killed by a spring-trap is stored. Nor may anything be woven from them in that same house. The penalty for violating this taboo is the trap's loss of effectiveness; the angry lord of the land does not let any animal fall into it. It is also taboo to burn old mats or to prepare the leaves of lapuam by heating them on a fire, either in the village or on the paths walked by those who go check the traps. The smoke will make them smell, and the lord of the animals will be offended by their odor and will not release animals.

The second taboo forbids "combing oneself in front of dying or freshly killed game" (hua holuholua). Such an act of self-ornamentation is disrespectful, because it emphasizes the contrast between the triumphantly alive hunter, pleased with himself for his victory, and the wretchedness of the bloody, defeated animal. The act implies a refusal to acknowledge that human life is made possible by animal death. It must therefore be avoided in front of the dead animal as it is avoided in front of a dead human. Both cases rule out self-exaltation, the expression of the happiness of the survivor. The parallelism implies a certain analogy between animal and human. Without a token recognition of this analogy, the appropriation of the animal is blocked. The point is illustrated by a myth, which was narrated to me to explain why the members of a certain coastal lineage became "Muslim," that is to say, in the Huaulu view, gave up eating pork, and turned it into a major taboo.

> The ancestors of this lineage were on the headwaters of the Salawai River when they ran into a pig and killed it. They had just shaved (hapa) the dead pig (before butchering it) when one of the men began grooming his hair with a comb (ipetuwam) of tomo bamboo. They told him, "Don't comb yourself; the pig is still fresh; you can only do it when its meat has become old (maka mutuaniam koni)." But he continued to comb himself. Not much time passed before total darkness wrapped them, and a terrible thunderstorm burst forth. The dead pig woke up (panua), the earth opened, and the hunters were swallowed into it. They reemerged on the coast, at Sawai, where they still live. The pig turned into stone and can still be seen today, and the bamboo comb reverted to its natural state, growing into a stand of tomoam, which has kept reproducing to the recent day. From now on they had the taboo of pork, and

> they began having children with piglike facial traits: noses similar to pig snouts and hare-lip. They changed their name and took a name which contained the word *tomoam* in it—and therefore reminded them and everybody else of their transgression and of their taboo.[277]

Myths make principles more evident and more memorable through the very improbability of what they describe. In hearing this myth, some Huaulu remarked: "How strange. The bamboo of the comb was already dry (melia) and yet it sprouted again." The narrator responded: "So that it would strike (pakina) them." A moral causality takes the place of ordinary causality to induce wonder and thus to implant memory. The miraculous reversion of an artifact to the living and continuously reproducing plant out of which it was made is "striking" enough to be a perpetual memento of the transgression which brought it about and of the animal's revenge, which threatens to "strike" again. It is only one of several inversions and exchanges of identity which signify a blocked access to pig meat: the reversion of the animal from death to life; its turning into stone, a monument to inaccessibility; the piglike traits in the members of the lineage, which make them too close to the pig to eat it. The moral of the myth seems to be: those who have denied offering token recognition of the kinship between human and animal and have therefore treated animals without respect or restraint, as if they were mere things, are condemned forever to bear witness to that kinship in their own bodies.[278]

Many more examples could be adduced to prove the pervasiveness of the idea that the appropriation of wild animals must pass through some expression of respect for them.[279] But the above will do; I do not want to be accused of pretending to say all when, as everybody knows, I would really only being boring all. Let me just conclude by bringing out the gist of my interpretation: Identification and distancing are in subtle tension in these practices. For the animal to be appropriated at all, it must be fundamentally different from humans, but this difference is never so great that an element of similarity does not remain to be overcome. It is overcome by a public act of recognition, which may take the form of a prescribed ritual act or the inchoate form of an occasional narration by which the possibility of a reversal of hunter and hunted is acknowledged.[280] The difference between human and wild animal which makes hunting possible is thus subtly inscribed in the recognition of an ultimate similarity, that is to say, the recognition of the common participation of human and animal in a moral relation. Hence the dark and multiple images of a blending of animal and human—such as lords of the land, cannibal giants, and lycanthropic witches, among others—which constantly haunt the apparent clarity of their opposition.

CHAPTER FIVE
Before Virtue

The self of the heroic age lacks precisely that characteristic which we have already seen that some modern moral philosophers take to be an essential characteristic of human selfhood: the capacity to detach oneself from any particular standpoint or point of view, to step backwards, as it were, and view and judge that standpoint or point of view from outside. In heroic society there is no "outside" except that of the stranger.

A. MacIntyre, *After Virtue*

My violated brain is rotting. Yet with what is left of it I shall try to say what is left to say. I can speak as [with the voice of] an example.

Anonymous, self-referential

Knowing a body involves sniffing its fragrance and hearing its resonances. And this I call knowledge.

F. Nietzsche, "The Immaculate Perception" in *Zarathustra*

Bien penser le réel, c'est profiter de ses ambiguités pour modifier et alerter la pensée.

G. Bachelard, *La philosophie du non*

Logic and Existence

At the end of chapter 3, I succinctly reviewed the principal areas of existence imbued with a sense of dangerousness and some of the basic reasons for this sense. But throughout chapter 4, there also was something much more important and difficult to explain: not everything at every time and for everybody is so dangerous in those areas as to require a taboo. If it were, life would simply become impossible, indiscriminately obsessed with an equal sense of danger from every conceivable side when engaged in certain activities or confronted with certain events. It would also be a mindless life, that is, one not based on the intellectual apprehension, comparison, and evaluation of objects in relationship to potentially consuming subjects.[1] The key to understanding taboo lies precisely in connecting potentially dangerous areas of existence with a logic that actualizes parts of them, that makes it possible to differentiate actually tabooed objects from objects that are not taboo, although they also belong to a generic sphere of danger. By *logic* I mean a set of coordinated principles. Such principles, and the extent to which they are actually coordinated, can be found only by an intensive study of the totality of taboos found in every dangerous area of existence.

But such study would amount to a long encyclopaedia of Huaulu culture that nobody would want to read and probably I myself would not want to write. I therefore decided to proceed otherwise: first to carry out an intensive analysis of the taboos (mostly alimentary) found in the sphere of animal-human relations; then to summarize the principles found in such a sphere and test their applicability beyond it. The first stage of the project was carried out in the necessary detail in chapter 4, the latter will be briefly carried out in this chapter, and continued in much greater detail in another book treating the highly complex and ramifying sphere of blood.[2]

The reader may recall that some way along in chapter 4, before I began considering animal taboos family by family, I reported the various principled reasons volunteered by the Huaulu to explain many of those taboos. This reporting concluded with an attempt to bring out some more generic, underlying principles that made it possible to connect the manifest ones, and thus to trace a preliminary logic in order to test and, I hope, to enrich it through the investigation of animal taboos. Again, the underlying principles in question are the principle of excessive closeness to and the principle of excessive distance from the Huaulu (or even human in general) world; the principle of excluded anomaly; the principle of excluded mixing (of antithetical categories) or mixing up (of the positions in an order of succession). The analyses of chapter 4 confirm the validity of these unstated principles and the stated ones. But they bring new aspects and elements to the fore that require new discussions and consolidations. These call for the inclusion of evidence from spheres beyond that of the bestiary.

At this stage, it seems possible and useful to encompass all the relevant principles, stated and unstated, old and new, under two much more general ones forming an opposition. Taboo is due to an excessive distance (metaprinciple 1) or an excessive proximity (or closeness) (metaprinciple 2) between subject and object, whatever they are. Primarily this distance is classificatory: it involves subject and object as representatives of various categories. But taboo may also be due to logically contingent facts: an encounter, a "falling in love" or a "falling in hate," a biographical fact which may, with time and luck, become a historical one adopted by all descendants of the one who first experienced it, and even by all the Huaulu. My use of the spatial terms *distance* and *closeness* to refer to a classificatory or biographical relationship resulting in taboo is largely due to the ability of these words (or their adjectival derivations) to cover a sufficiently great number of relevant meanings.

Distance, for instance, can refer here to a spatial or even a temporal interval between subject and object, to a categorical interval which determines similarity and difference, and to a sense of emotional or personal separation. And so do, more or less and in opposite terms, *proximity* and *closeness.* These words thus seem the most appropriate for discussing taboos in English, since they allow shifts to others whenever necessary. But they also capture a certain flavor of spatialization frequently imparted by the Huaulu to the reasons for their taboos, as must have become evident from much of chapter 4. It should by now be obvious that the widest categorical identifications that matter in taboo are defined in predominantly spatial terms or are easily convertible into them: those who live in the village and those who live in the forest, those who live up in the trees and those who live down in the water, those up in the mountains and those down, those inland and those on the coast. Even religions (Memahem, Laufaha) and ultimate political units (Siwa and Lima) are connected with distinct parts of the island and origin points. And so are, of course, lineages, villages, even different parts of the house (up and down, kitchen and veranda), and so on.

As we have seen, it is precisely sitting on different sides of these oppositions that gives the most frequent, although also incomplete, reason for being taboo one to the other, mutually or not. The reason for this is that co-residence implies co-essence, and vice versa. One must be similar enough to coexist long and tightly enough in the same place, since sharing place signifies sharing a whole mode of life and dissimilar enough to live in an antithetical place. But reciprocally, and more visibly, over time, co-residence may increase similarity (see dog and master, husband and wife, wild pet and its feeder), and residence in a different space may increase difference (hunters who live too long and too far in the forest tend to become animal-like; women given out to other villages, especially in opposed territories, tend to lose their Huaulu identity).[3]

Whether or not the basic spatial categories I have mentioned are principally or even secondarily involved, the tendency to represent taboos in spatial terms remains striking. A generic reason is that spatial relations between incompatible terms are more easily identifiable and communicable than most others which form the intricate (and often so intricate as to become invisible) complexes that determine taboo. But more important than this cognitive and communicative act is a practical one that strongly seems to reinforce it. However different their reasons, taboos share a strikingly uniform common denominator. They state a danger in predominantly spatial terms: they require the subject to maintain or create a physical distance between himself and an object, or combination of objects, or events (not to touch, pierce, penetrate sexually, eat, participate in, and so on, boiling down to requiring the subject to "stay away") .

This character of the "output" of all the reasons for taboo tends to reflect onto their representation. The invariable recommendation of keeping a distance seems to imply that there is a distance to be preserved—whatever the ultimate reasons for the distance and for the incompatibility it creates. Even when taboo seems to create distance as a reaction to closeness, it is in fact guaranteeing an already existing distance with regard to certain kinds of interactions (eating and sex), a distance all the more easily threatened by what officially motivates it: closeness in all other fields (see, for instance, the dog taboos or the sex taboos we shall return to later).[4] This coexistence of distance and closeness, however, makes us wonder if it is not also present where distance predominates. In other words: the overwhelming sense of distance one feels in the universe of taboo does not exclude its subterranean opposite. Distance may well feel more threatening because it coexists with an unacknowledged sense of closeness, just as closeness quite clearly feels more threatening because of an unacknowledged sense of distance. We would therefore do just as well to start our review of principles encompassed by the one of excessive distance and the one of excessive proximity expecting the interaction of the contraries they separate. It will appear that their separation is not absolute but, rather, due to the dominance of one contrary over a residual co-present other, without which the taboo is not fully accounted for.

Before turning to this review, however, a short preliminary summary is necessary of the reasons I have preferentially used *distance* and *proximity* in the above definitions rather than *similarity* and *difference* or other possible alternatives in English. It is because the spatial definitions give us a wider and more suitable semantic range, and because they give us the flavor of a tendency immanent in Huaulu taboo-constructing or reconstructing, although this tendency is not necessarily translated into a specific principle. Space thus suggests an ultimate framework in which different complexes of taboos can take place, whatever their motivations—this is, of course, facilitated by the easier apprehension of spatially encoded relations than of all others that motivate a taboo. But perhaps the most important reason for the tendency to spatialize cause is the invariably spatial character of the effect. All taboos prescribe or suggest or signal a spatial incompatibility; that is, they say one should not touch, penetrate, or, even more deeply, eat an object. In a way, the ultimate, if banal, explanation that suggests itself is that the distance of something, whatever it consists of, translates into an actual physical distance that should be kept as such.

I may add that when I feel tempted to use *similarity* and *difference* as the key words of my definitions—which anyhow I do whenever necessary for their application—I must recognize that they are frequently translatable into proximity and distance, because a sufficient degree of similarity is necessary to coexist in the same space (house, village, territory, or habitat), and conversely, because habitual separation is the sign of a critical amount of difference. One can even invert these propositions in some measure, because continuous coexistence may increase similarity, whereas continuous separation may decrease it or even bring it beyond the point of possible coexistence. But it is also important to stress at the outset what we shall see throughout this section: that similarity and difference cannot be radically separated—quite the contrary—in the explanation of a distance that makes co-residence impossible and a closeness that makes it possible. Distance, very small or very great, can thus aspire to the status of a unifying concept of taboo, provided one recognizes the complexity and variety of its uses.

An obvious example is that of similarity and difference, which are their nearest competitors at the level of generalization. For in most cases, continuous association in space implies a sufficient degree of similarity; and continuous dissociation in space, a sufficient difference. Moreover, the implication is mutual, especially from a Huaulu point of view. It would be impossible for dog and master to coexist if they did not share much at the categorical level, but that coexistence further adds to that sharedness, as is shown by the fact that even wild animals can become closer to humans when they are raised into pets and mascots. Conversely, the essential similarity that makes conviviality possible may be decreased by continuous spatial distance (men living alone in the forest and blending with animals; women given out in marriage to different villages; and so on). All of which seems to teach that essence and residence easily convert into each other.

The correspondence of the categorical and the spatial is also illustrated by rather rich families of taboos. If fish and fowl must remain distant in space it is because they are profoundly different, but they are different because they are normally distant in space (since space is divided into habitats which make different forms of life possible). The same applies to the taboos that separate the beings of the village from those of the forest,[5] or those of heaven from those of earth, of those of the coast from those of inland, and so on.[6] The spatialization of the reasons for taboo is not simply a consequence of the facts that most beings exist in space,[7] and that the spatial dimension of the complex relations that connect them and that are the object of evaluations ending in taboo is the easiest to apprehend and communicate.[8] It is also due to a major, and retrospectively obvious, fact: the common denominator of all taboos consists in injunctions or recommendations to keep oneself materially separate from objects that are conceptually or experientially incompatible with one's identifications.[9] Whatever the reasons for these incompatibilities, they must translate into a spatial fact to become dangerous but also avoidable. For difference to be kept at a distance, for distance to guarantee the perpetuation of difference, distance and difference must be fully convertible, but at the same time *distance* (in its actual spatial sense) must be the dominant term to sustain the notion and practice of taboo. How could I stay away from conceptual animality (i.e. not become an animal) by not touching it in a physical sense, if conceptual animality were not away from me in the same sense?[10]

Obviously, this universal translation of taboo into a spatial practice is (experientially) primarily due to forms of eating, touching, penetrating—sexually or violently—which involve a very different subject and object from the ones we are trained to believe in (even if we ourselves unconsciously violate our beliefs): a bodified subject and a subjectified object. The relationships of such terms tend to be as concrete as they are. But it does not necessarily bring practical effect and conceptual or experiential cause into agreement.[11] There is more to separation and conjunction than space, precisely because space is vested with categorical significations that can exist without it. Nevertheless, taboo cannot in the end exist without a spatial conversion of such significations at the level of practice, more exactly of certain short-distance practices. This fact at least must now keep us alert in drawing our conclusions and especially in adding to them. This is another reason I have finally preferred the contrast of *distance* and *proximity* to other terms, although I will use any of them when appropriate or convenient.

We may begin with "excessive distance" as overarching principle, not only because a majority of taboos considered in chapter 4 seem ultimately to presuppose it, but also because this very fact gives it a considerable polymorphism—its use of space included. For instance, spatial distance may be made to carry two opposite values in taboo matters. The distant object may represent a world (e.g. the coastal one, or the colonial and now national overseas) that is incompatible with or even antagonistic to the Huaulu world (or any other unit) in which the subject situates itself. Or it may not represent any antagonistic world, but only the fading away of relevance to the Huaulu one. In the former case, excessive distance results in taboo. In the latter, distance may reduce or even eliminate taboo at least for some category of subjects. One illustration of this latter possibility, and in any case of the complex relationship of distance and proximity, is the tipope turtle.

This species is, as mentioned, the most distant among all turtle species known to the Huaulu, and therefore also the least likely to be experienced. It can thus appear to contrast with the makopa turtle, which is the closest to the Huaulu world and therefore the best known. As I have attempted to show, it is precisely this relative closeness and familiarity that turns the mokopa species into the paradigmatic taboo-implying turtle. This seems confirmed by the fact that more distant turtles are equally taboo through the makopa (even if the violation of their taboo is less likely to occur for inlanders such as the Huaulu), whereas the most distant one (tipope) is not taboo for men, although it is still taboo for women. As I mentioned, this difference indicates that the tipope's dangerousness is so reduced, probably by distance, that it can exist for only the more vulnerable women. Naturally this motivation may blend with another, which is to affirm the difference between man and woman by creating a practically minimal difference between them, that is, a difference which can hardly come to frequent life, since tipope turtles are very rare indeed to eat, particularly by people who normally live inland. But this argument reinforces the first, since it presupposes it: the tipope turtle is the most distant from the Huaulu and thus the least likely to be caught by them. This distance, then, makes it possible to trace a gender difference by taboo creating too much hardship for women. It eliminates taboo for men, rather than creating one for both men and women. But in most other cases just the opposite is true: distance of objects that are highly representative of a world antithetical to the Huaulu's and therefore incompatible with it is inevitably a source of taboo—and for both sexes. This confirms that distance cannot be a merely spatial fact generating taboo; it must be the visible and moving sign of an antithetical difference that amounts to a potential Huaulu weakness. Indeed, the misoneistic taboos can all be interpreted this way.

Misoneistic taboos are found in the alimentary sphere, as we have seen,[12] but also beyond it; various artifacts and substances (e.g. kerosene, kerosene lamps or stoves, radios, tapes, guns, cameras, and so on) are taboo during the most important rituals[13] and in the ritual houses. Other new things, such as cement, electricity, and so on, are said to be constantly and universally taboo in the village proper. They may be used only in the coastal settlements,[14] none of which receives the name of niniani (village) as far as the Huaulu are concerned. Analogously, it is only on the coast that there may be a school[15] and that Huaulu schoolchildren can exist, although even that was not considered possible at the time of my first fieldwork. In fact, many Huaulu continue to declare that writing and reading are everywhere taboo for all of them, and see confirmation of this in whatever misfortune strikes those who have attended school. One reason for the literacy taboo is that the Huaulu see in it the most important difference between traditional inland people like themselves (memahe) and the people of the book, like Muslims and Christians. The taboo, then, keeps separate those who are excessively and constitutively too distant in space and time. Any contact through the objects that are the food of coastal people, or that indicate their power or their distinctiveness against a ground of similarities with the Huaulu, would undermine that distinctiveness, but only in the sense that the Huaulu would become more similar to them and finally live among them (as has been desired by the colonial and subsequently the national governments). This indicates that coastal people have become the ground against which the Huaulu figure can stand only if it does not fray its edges.

If misoneistic taboos imply the potential invasion of the Huaulu world—and thus of the village which is the center and symbol of its existence—by another social world at odds with it, taboos on animals that spontaneously enter the village or even the house imply an even more dangerous invasion from the wild world. For the invasion of foreign products that have come to identify with foreign identity can be avoided by following the necessary taboos, but invasion by wild animals is largely uncontrollable, because it is carried out by beings who share will and mobility (but not speech and common understanding) with humans. In fact, their presence in the village or the house reveals more strongly and thus threateningly this sharedness, and therefore undermines not just the distinctiveness of the Huaulu as inland people vis-à-vis the coastal peoples and the widest foreign world which they represent, but also the Huaulu's much more radical distinctiveness vis-à-vis the animal world, that is to say, their nearest cousin in the wild forest.

We have already discussed these "invasion taboos" at great length, but being able to show that there is some parallelism between them and those I have called misoneistic—a parallelism which makes their differences all the more significant—allows us to understand better why only certain objects that signify distance from what one is as a Huaulu are dangerous, or dangerous enough to be taboo. For in both cases Huaulu identity is threatened by an other that is made more powerful by its ability to invade the Huaulu world, an ability which in one case seems to show a hidden Huaulu attraction, in the other a hidden animal attraction for the Huaulu. Such attractions reveal an excess of similarity where one wants to posit an excess of difference. Identity, in sum, is both established and disestablished by relationships of contrast with comparable others. This suggests that it is not just extreme distance (or difference, if one prefers) that motivates taboo, but also its labored maintenance for a self-definition which is constantly threatened by a subterranean or implied similarity that risks coming to the surface.

In other words, we have here the possibility of a semi-Freudian (though fortunately not fully so) interpretation. Taboo is due to a fear of being dominated by something one always fights against: the sharing of attributes and desires with certain animals and certain humans. It is precisely the insistence on distance from one's body, house, and village that can reproduce one's embodied and located identity by maintaining a contrast with what is potentially able to deny it. In sum, excessive distance/difference is never alone: it always presupposes a level of similarity which can potentially take over and therefore undermine or destroy the superior identity of the taboo-follower, which is based on that difference and its hierarchical implications.[16]

The next class of phenomena that are made taboo by their "excessive distance" consists of unfamiliar events, described by such Huaulu expressions as *hua ita oiressi,* "we have not seen them before [yet]," or *ita oiriressi,* "we don't see them." Distance in these cases is thus from the expectations built on the habitually observed course of events. An already mentioned example (see chapter 4) that struck me for the particular horror and shuddering with which it was described is that of two normally separated animals—an eel and the largest river fish, the tamali—found intertwined with one another in an endless struggle. I was told that neither could be eaten. Indeed, contact or even co-presence with any unfamiliar event usually consisting of the conjunction of normally separate beings or phenomena is either taboo or ominous (and therefore to be neutralized by imprecations or more complex formulas). There is in fact a whole spectrum of such events that moves from the experientially unique to the relatively recurrent but contextually unexpected. I leave it to the former example to carry the full burden of the first extreme of the spectrum, and to the thunderclap in a cloud-free sky or rain when the sun shines to represent the other end, an end that allows us to move to the next principle, which is species anomaly—that is, a permanent and therefore expected phenomenon which is, however, unexpected from the classificatory point of view.[17] This implies that only the constant intervention of the intellect can repeatedly bring out a sense of unexpectedness and therefore give the taboo on an anomalous species some degree of subjective intensity, although never the intense one I observed in relation to unfamiliar or anomalous events.

Evidence shows that the intellect is involved and yet not quite sufficient to account for taboos and to maintain their existence through the intensity of subjective reactions. To begin with the most directly "intellectual" evidence, species anomaly seems to play the greatest role as a source of taboo in the context of mixing taboos, which are strictly and almost exclusively dependent on the classification of animals in the three tiers of the cosmos. It is precisely in these contexts that the anomalous character of those species may be commented upon, perhaps when the inquisitive stranger revives the intellectual scandal subterraneously felt by some Huaulu and certainly by those who contribute to the taboo system. Commentators may sometimes be able to rely on myths which explicitly account for the "out-of-place" character or "strangeness" of a species, as is made most evident by the origin myth of the cassowary, which, as my readers may remember, was narrated to me when we confronted the animal in the hunt. My friend who told me the story was probably thinking I would be shocked in seeing the flightless bird, and this revived his own sense of anomaly as shock to the point of telling me the myth even if it was not his place to do so, as he later remembered.

Less explicit, but no less clear, reference to species anomaly is found in a number of other myths, such as the crocodile origin myth, which I gave in chapter 4, or a number of others which I did not give (e.g. the "origin" myth of the Puraratuhu lineage from a tipolo snake descending from a tree). But however involved the intellect is in producing a sense of anomaly, it alone does not seem to be able to generate taboos. Anomaly has a propensity to generate a plethora of symbolic associations of a certain type, and these in turn may produce taboos. Indeed, the species that uniquely but permanently and vitally seem to embody the violation of an order that is followed by all remaining species tend to move (or be transferred) beyond the animal world, to be symbolically associated with other kinds of transgressors or mediators closer to the human world, and to be of greater practical significance to it. In other words, anomalous species usually enter the realm of taboo not on cognitive grounds alone, but because such grounds allow the growth of certain plants whose fruits are bitter taboos. These plants are, as we have seen, either hostile occult powers, which permanently threaten the distinction between human and nonhuman, alive and dead, male and female, and so on, or friendly occult powers (sewaem) with whom shamans momentarily identify in order to mediate between those same terms and, thus, to reproduce their distinction.

The most obvious example of this transfer and of its duality is, of course, also the most obvious example of cognitively recognized anomaly: the cassowary. As we have seen, the body of this animal tends to be assumed by the fearsome muluaqina but also by many of the shamanic powers and (indirectly) by the shamans who are possessed by them. Precisely because it appears as a striking case of successful violation of fundamental cosmological distinctions (successful because continuously embodied by a species rather than by a unique or volatile event), the cassowary can stand for the successful violation of many other distinctions on which human life depends more directly and which therefore involve a relation more visceral than intellectual. Mind becomes bowel (gut) in the cassowary's symbolic excursions into the human world, excursions which no doubt give the animal's mixing taboos some additional force—and complication.

Such excursions, as we have seen, take place in both of the directions that danger requires: existence and remedy. Existence takes the form of the cassowary's tendency to become the body of the muluaqina, an occult power made extremely dangerous by its perverse confusion of what must remain separate: living and dead, love and hate, sexual pursuit and hunting pursuit, and even male and female traits. Remedy tends to take the form of what must be remedied, because one must be able to reach it in order to reconvert it. This is why the cassowary is also a cipher of the shamanic personae which effect this reconversion—that is, a frequent embodiment of sewa pukari but also, and most tellingly, the only animal component of the chief of all such sewaem.[18] This chief is, in fact, closer to the human agent the cassowary stands for because of the animal's very anomaly which evokes mediation; the shaman reproduces crucial distinctions by provisionally negating them in the course of ritual and by permanently claiming his power to do so by means of a permanent taboo on the meat of the cassowary. This is one reason that the cassowary is directly taboo for the shaman and derivatively so for his patients.

To the unpredictable and the predictable, or occasional (eventlike) and permanent (specieslike) distance (or difference) from cognitive expectations, one must add a humanly produced violation of the fundamental classification of wild animals. I am talking, of course, of mixing taboos. These are so numerous and concerned with the core of Huaulu alimentation that they make the connection between eating and cosmic order particularly evident. But such a connection may be only transparent, perhaps, because of the extreme generality and simplicity of its cosmic referents: "up in the trees," "down on the ground," "down in the water." Humans, the consumers, are put in the middle (down on the ground), and this creates digestive compatibility with adjacent strata, but not with their combination through the combination of meats. The most generic reason is that species stand for their habitat, and their division and stratification must be accepted by humans in their very flesh. In sum, there must be a coordination of all fleshes in this world. But an additional possible reason is that the ability to move through the three strata is a privilege of human action, and thus a characteristic of the human species. If humans eat a combination that covers the entire cosmos, then, they eat themselves or, rather, a defining characteristic of themselves.[19] Hence one can say that what is too distant is also too close, and that affirming one's alimentary distance from the loss of distance between two antithetical kinds of species reestablishes one's unique position in the cosmos.

We are progressively becoming more aware that distance on one scale is often inseparable from closeness on another. But as this case shows, and as we shall better see in a while, this is hardly because a certain optimal balance of difference and similarity is necessary. The issue is in no way quantitative (as postulated by certain theories which reflect certain ideological systems)[20] but has to do with preeminent values undermined by their opposites in those crucial contexts in which taboo arises because embodied identity rests: eating, sexuality, location, and so on. In any case, we must continue with the other principles which, at least overtly, emphasize an excess of distance and/or difference and those which emphasize the opposite.

Another principle of the first kind—the distance and difference which are more prominent outside the realm of meat than inside it—is that taboo counters the inversion of normal hierarchical relations. These usually take spatial or temporal forms, and often a kinetic combination of the two. The "invasion taboos" already mentioned are obvious spatial inversions with hierarchical signification, constituted by wild animals entering human spaces, particularly the house. Such animals take the usual (and most valued) position of humans by initiating the attack and thus bringing it into human space. This puts humans and their houses or even village in the usual inferior position of wild animals. In this sense the discussion of hunting against the fear of its reversal taken up at the end of chapter 4 clarifies the sense of profound danger associated with these taboos. The fundamental hierarchical relation involved in animal taboos is precisely that of humans and animals. But it should be obvious that the principle of excluded inversion applies to an even greater extent (that is, in more articulate and clearly stated ways) beyond the bestiary to social and particularly ritual relationships. Equally obvious is the general conclusion one may draw from the danger of inversion: that animal and human, or any other terms that are constantly hierarchized by insisting on the successive order of their mutually implying actions, stand perpetually at risk of being mutually identified. In other words, if they can shift their position in the basic attacker-attacked relationship, or any other relationship that matters, then they might be considered profoundly similar.

Indeed, reversals that suggest similarity between animals and humans reinforce the whole range of beliefs and practices which suggest the same, and therefore further motivate the reproduction of the whole ensemble of animal taboos. The intrinsically bad character of the monstrous cognitive distance that the frog (ilauwam) has in relation to the human is when it enters the dimension of taboo-significant space by leaving its usual habitat and entering that of humans—the house. This very gesture makes the frog similar to the house's inhabitants to a point that demands substitution. In other words, contact with this animal that has taken your place in space and time implies your expulsion from them, and thus your death. Once again, the excessively different is taboo because a potential, subterranean sense of similarity makes identification with it excessively easy in certain contexts.

Another possible example of the principle of avoided inversion of hierarchical relations which we can find in the bestiary is offered by the predators, especially the crocodile. I have not considered the predators' category in general, because it is not explicitly recognized by the Huaulu and because the tabooness of each of its members is sufficiently explained by more particular affiliations. Nevertheless, at this level of generality, and especially after the discussion of hunting taboos and beliefs, one can observe that practically all predators whose palatability is not beyond the pale are taboo for all or for some. A possible reason is that one has no control over the kind of meat such animals eat.[21] So one may eat a tabooed meat through them. And if the animal is a bird (as is the case with the tabooed sea birds) one may violate the mixing taboos (fish and fowl) by eating its fish-fed meat.[22]

In a deeper and more general sense, however, predators evoke the idea of animals usurping the place of humans. Not only do they dominate the other animals and feed on them just as humans do, but they may even dominate men, and some (e.g. the crocodile, the patola python) also eat them. By eating these animals humans would avoid being eaten in particular cases but not in general. In fact it would increase and justify the vulnerability of humans and, indeed, their demotion in the field of relations among living things. Because of the principle that one is what one eats, eating predators would reduce humans from their uniquely human dominion over animals to being part of animal-to-animal relations—a state more open to reversal and instability. In sum, by avoiding eating animal predators, humans avoid being identified with a merely animal condition which alarmingly resembles the epitome of the cultural condition, and may therefore undermine it. This case, then, again indicates that taboo arises from an ideologically capital difference which is threatened by a deeper sense of similarity, a sense obscurely sustained by a forest of beliefs and stories, but most profoundly sustained by the experience of failure and the expectation of death.

The same basic principle—that undesirable diversity becomes a source of taboo when it can be easily transmitted to the subject because of an actual or potential similarity—is confirmed by a variety of cases less structured than those I have mentioned so far, or not structured at all, but based on biographical events. Any undesirable feature of a species (particularly one concerning its visible and overarching aspect—the skin) is a potential ground for tabooing it. But, of course, something else should be built on it for taboo to come to life. The animal's voluntary encounter with a particular individual may be enough, precisely because it is unexpected at the level of the species and thus seems to point to an unusual resemblance with the encountered. This resemblance is grounds for taboo insofar as it makes the transfer of what is undesirable much more likely. But, of course, the reasons for the encounter can be many, especially when the animal is viewed as the visible form of an occult power, friendly or unfriendly. Both attitudes are grounds for taboo. The unfriendly must be fled; one has received a particular sign of hostility and thus incompatibility. The friendly must not be fled, but it must be respected; it must not be viewed as a consumable object. Otherwise it will turn out to be as unfriendly as the unfriendly.

Let us now plunge into the "excessive closeness/similarity" series at the point of its apparently greatest difference with the one we have just finished reviewing in our final mood. In the animal sphere, which is the basis for our generalizations and exemplifications, this point is a relatively low-yield principle that can be formulated as follows: "Excessive closeness to human aspect (ita oi wahi manusia, "it looks like a human being") and/or behavior involves nonaggression and nonconsumption" (principle one). We have seen that the taboos on the "dugong" (luina) and the monkey are openly justified in this manner. The second principle is more particularistic: "Excessive closeness to the Huaulu social world involves nonconsumption" (taboo on domestic animals) and even the avoidance of killing and serious forms of violence (tabooed with regard to the dog). The third principle, "Excessive closeness of categories requires the protection of their distinction," was strikingly illustrated in chapter 4 by the dissimilation taboos that exist among certain close categories (e.g. birds and marsupials in the up-in-the-trees habitat) involved in the system of mixing taboos. This suggests that the principle applies only when excessive closeness occurs between or among categories that belong to a much wider system and therefore threatens it. Such a system, moreover, is mainly generated by the opposite principle—that of separation of excessively different and even antagonistic terms. Mere, decontextualized closeness of categories does not seem sufficient to generate taboos, at least in the animal world. It must carry a much heavier weight that depends on systemic preoccupations and/or symbolic associations.

The fourth principle is: "One cannot eat or destroy species that are associated with one's origins, either because they embody an originating power or because they are attached to it as a testimonial."[23] The obvious illustrations of this principle are the so-called totemic taboos. But some origin-proclaiming taboos, such as those of the senior Tamatay man to mark his lineage's original affiliation with Islam, cannot in any way be viewed as totemic. Furthermore, edible species connected with origins present us with a paradox: in some cases one may not eat species linked to one's origins, but in other cases such species (e.g. a certain variety of sago or a certain species of fruit tree) are eminently edible. In other words, in certain cases one does not eat what one is (since one's identity is contained in one's origins), but in others one does eat what one is (since one is what one eats). A seeming resolution of this paradox is that staples consumed as ordinary and distinctive sources of life are put in the origin category a posteriori (i.e. one has become *x* by eating it, and that has meant linking it to the origin, since what one is must be so from the beginning—existence being continuous and traditional), whereas nonstaples, and often quite rare species, are put in the origin category a priori because of their symbolic or distinctive properties.

Although the connection of both kinds of species with the hazy concept of origin is equally hazy, it seems legitimate to claim that the second kind has a much closer connection with a personalized occult power or with some radical turn of events in a lineage's history than the first one. Distinctive staples tend to have been "brought" by the ancestors. Distinctive "totems" tend to be linked to foundational encounters with occult powers. Nevertheless a certain amount of overlapping occurs and should be recognized, since it displays the fundamental antinomy which arises from the connection of being and eating: one is what one eats, therefore one must not eat what one is; but equally, one must eat what one is. Being, in sum, is an unstable balance of consumption and avoidance of symbolically significant objects—of objects which attract "foundational" associations that cannot be erased by suppression or by ritual transformations.

The fifth and final principle simply generalizes the idea that "close connection with an occult power is a source of taboo" and brings its application beyond the origins, or at least beyond the distant and fundamental ones. Indeed, it applies, sometimes alone but more usually in combination with others, to most species which stand for the relationship of shamans with their sewaem. Here again, the representation of this connection is far from clear and highly unstable. But there is no talk of reference to asale, "origin" (except for most of the taboos of the sewa potoa, since this form of shamanism is connected with the origin of the lineage that owns it), and that suffices to justify the invocation of a principle distinct from, although related to, the previous one. A further justification is provided by the many taboos that originate in encounters and pacts with nasinahe (headhunting powers), auwete (fishing powers), mutuaulae (hunting powers), and so on. In other words, while the origin taboos are fixed in number and can diminish only by erosion, "pact" taboos can be further acquired, and are therefore more likely to increase than to decrease.

One may note that four of the five closeness (or identity) principles I have just summarized fall into two classes. The first two imply respect for an other who is made close by intrinsic attributes (dugong, etc.) or by a social pact of sorts (dog, etc.), although this other is clearly inferior to oneself. The last two, on the contrary, imply the subject's dependency, that is, a strong asymmetry and even a reversal of the kind of relationship between animal and human which is covered by the first two principles. In other words, "taboos due to excessive closeness," or, better named, "identity taboos," are of two basic kinds: one implies a partial identification with a fellow creature viewed as subordinated; the other implies a partial identification with a fellow creature viewed as superordinated (because representative of a cosmic system, which must be protected through it—see principle three). There is no taboo, in this sphere, that implies an egalitarian relation—or the possible, usually long-term, reversal of an inegalitarian one, such as that with game (particularly big game).[24]

In this sphere, then, identity exists by recognizing a distorted self on opposite sides of the hierarchy—the superior and the inferior. On one side, one is what one is because of where one comes from and because of the external powers which one can use to extend one's existence; on the other, one is what one is because one is the indispensable master of an inferior but helpful dependent (the dog), or simply because of a common humanness experienced as a similarity in bodily aspect and behavior. Essentially, all these avoidances amount to a cardinal premise they share with any other: the self does not exist without the other, thus this other must be preserved in order for the self to be preserved. Animals or plants become consumable with the mouth when they cannot be consumed with the mind,[25] when they cannot be recognized as sustaining the image of the self—that is, when they cannot be viewed as others with whom comparison and contrast with oneself are possible.

This is true of all animal taboos on whatever side of the basic opposition between closeness and distance they might find their explanatory abode. Taboo, in sum, marks mental as against material consumption,[26] although the two may be in some measure mixed, as we have mentioned. Certain foods feed the body as such but also to some extent feed the body as the basis of symbolic—spoken of—existence. We have seen that this is the case with certain varieties of sago or fruit trees. We could even mention individual (and individually named) durian trees. But the most interesting case is that of the wild pig.

We should recall that the Huaulu identify with the animal's pugnaciousness and strength, which they claim to absorb by eating its flesh. But this eating assumes its full meaning when one takes into account the fact that pig-eating is tabooed for the true inhabitants of the coast, the Muslims. Eating pig thus reproduces the Huaulu's situation in a categorical system which opposes the inhabitants of inland forest to the seafarers who inhabit the coast: the former become the wild pigs, which stand in contrast with the fish of the ocean—as I had mentioned in order to illustrate, among other things, the presence of the idea that one is what one eats.

To a certain point, the pig's flesh contributes to the symbolic existence of the Huaulu subject. This implies that it is a point of intersection of opposite attributions. On the one hand, it can contribute to one aspect of Huaulu identity only by being eaten. On the other, a certain impediment to eating must emerge from the awareness of this contribution, and thus from a degree of identification. Indeed, a certain mixture of consumption and negation of consumption is quite evident in the case of pig's flesh, as we have seen at the end of chapter 4. The ambivalent status of that flesh is resolved by the fact that, for the man who killed it, it fictitiously continues to exist as living, antagonistic animal on the same level as himself. Indeed, the taboo on his eating it and all the related practices seem to negate the transition from intangible to tangible, from other to object, which makes it edible. It is such negation that allows the rest of the village to eat, as we have seen. That the meat remains the animal for one villager implies that it can be meat for all others. But this preservation is not without effects for the status of what they consume. It still remains a meat carrying the desirable properties that are supposed to make the inland, forest people superior to the coastal, beach and sea people.[27]

The ritualized appropriation of the pig and the other two largest game animals develops taboo into a clearly sacrificial direction. The skull is taboo not simply in being brought back to the village; it is taboo also in that it must be offered to the lord of the land by putting it on a tree. The same is true for the taboo on shedding the animal's blood in the village. This development, against the backdrop of the frightening narratives à la Nastagio degli Onesti,[28] raises the question of whether sacrifice is an implicit dimension of many taboos and even of the whole taboo system. There are many indications that such a dimension exists. Giving up eating a certain species that is associated with an occult power may be construed as an act of renunciation to show respect for that power. Indeed, renunciation is not mere avoidance; it is a message directed to an other on which one's existence depends. In this sense it is analogous to a sacrifice in more than the deprivative sense of Durkheim in his generalizing mood. But there is no need for a benevolent (or even malevolent) power behind the species to sustain a particle of sacrifice. This particle and the relatively respectful pretense and neutralizing effect it contains do not need an advanced personification of the species in order to exist, but rather a sense of the animal species as a necessary counterpart of the human one, and thus of the two as sharing some of each other's attributes and rights. Furthermore, the clearest sacrificial shiver is felt when one considers the whole ensemble of animal taboos.

The ensemble allows a proper relationship with the cosmos, in particular with its animal part, which is the point of closest contact with humans, to be maintained by giving up the free appropriation of many of its parts in order to retrieve it for an abundant remainder.[29] One can consume the cosmos and yet postpone being consumed by it. This complementarity of consumption and renunciation, grounded on the reversibility of subject and object positions in consumability, is precisely what makes the ritual appropriation of meat (from hunting to cooking) so crucial for the understanding of the idea of taboo, of the overwhelming rulership of rule among the Huaulu.

Taboo may be viewed, after all, as an avoidance that blends with renunciation and is thus, as I have pointed out already, a message addressed to an indispensable other. It implies an idea of self-preservation mediated by the preservation of this other, an other which must, of course, be, or ultimately become, more powerful than oneself, perhaps because it stands for the cosmos itself. Of this radical dependency of self on other I can in any case give direct evidence by moving for a moment into the social world without animal mediations. There we find a most interesting taboo: that on uttering one's own lala tuni (true/originary name, that is, the name given at birth). The taboo indicates that I can't exist as, say, Polonahu in my mouth but only in the mouths of others. Indeed, I remember how often, when I asked somebody's own name, he would turn toward those who were sitting with us and ask them to pronounce it. Or else he would give me his postnatal names, most often his shamanic one, which is in fact the name of the other on which his shamanic identity depends—the name of his most important sewa.

The common sacrificial dimension of taboos, whether their origin is more easily explainable with an excess of distance or with an excess of closeness, pushes us to explore further the points of partial neutralization and interaction between the two basic classes of principles. In other words, can we state generalizations without polarization? Is anything taboo just too dissimilar or just too similar? I begin with a point of partial neutralization of the two poles that is not without connection to the sacrificial dimension of taboo. The reader undoubtedly remembers that a fair amount of taboo is due to certain objects' connections with occult powers. These powers are officially situated on opposite sides. Some motivate taboo because they are too proximate; others, because they are too distant. In other words: some species are not eaten because of their connection with occult powers treated as "origins"; others are not eaten because of their connection with occult powers that are too different or distant not to be treated as enemies. As I had put it, the dangerousness of the latter is modelled on that of poison: it is intrinsic and permanent (irreducible), independent of the will of the occult power or else dependent on an occult power whose will is constantly malevolent. In contrast, the dangerousness of species connected with occult powers of the "origin" type is derivative: eating or killing their species is an act of disrespect that elicits their rage and desire to manifest their superiority by responding in noxious forms. On the result side, though, it is not easy to distinguish between the two forms of dangerousness. They amount to the same thing. Whatever the reason, appropriating the taboo animal has disastrous physical effects. So the idea of poison tends to dominate, together with that of the intrinsic "badness" of all kinds of occult powers.

While the mutau (avoidance) of a species should express "respect" in one case and "fear" pure and simple in the other, the two feelings are difficult to separate. To some extent, this is true of all kinds of taboo, but not enough to depolarize the Huaulu representation of their reasons. Representational depolarizing is easier when reasons come made up as occult powers. However different in moral terms, occult powers have much in common, as their stories may tell us. An element of evil may well be present in "friendly" originators, who seem in any case exceptionally jealous of their status and demanding of their descendants or dependents. Moreover, many such "originators" and "friends" happen to be transformed strangers and enemies. A contact has been established, a pact made. This pact necessarily implies certain taboos. So the taboos are represented as half-voluntary, half-forced renunciations made in order to neutralize dangers that come from a power that is never fully good. In this sense, there is a continuum, and not just a contrast, among the dangers due to fully distant occult powers and fully close ones and, through the dangers, among the powers themselves. It is a continuum which allows the ideas connected with each pole to spill over onto those connected with the other. Taboos are seen either as mere avoidances of "poison" or as propitiatory acts of renunciation. The latter are statements addressed to an other, as I have mentioned, but more easily appear when the addressee is an occult power, whatever its kind, and not an indefinite and unshadowy other.

Let us turn to another general point. A taboo is usually defined as a distance kept between a subject and an object. But such a dual relationship is the outcome of a network of others. Are these only on the object's side? Or are they on the subject's side as well? In other words, is the subject positing itself, alone and through its cognitive responses exclusively, vis-à-vis the world of consumable objects, or is this positioning dependent on his or her own position in the world of subject-to-subject relations? The facts we have considered show that both sides exist, that subject-to-object relations are mediated by both subject-to-subject and object-to-object ones. Nonetheless, they also show that the emphasis may be on one or the other in the representation of different complexes of taboo.

Mixing taboos clearly emphasize the object-to-object relationships to the point of making their violation their true and only content as taboos. Indeed, the excessive distance between a subject and a combination of objects presupposes an equally excessive distance between those objects. Violating this relational set of distances, which keeps the vertical and horizontal dimensions of the cosmos together, means making the cosmos crumble in the subject's flesh.

Mixing taboos, or any others that openly concern the interaction between the integrity of the subject and that of the cosmos, thus suggest that humans have to act in conformity with a cosmos over which they have limited power. They have to act in conformity with it, respecting its incompatibilities, if they do not want to be caught in the cross fire of their incompatibilities. Humans' primacy in the cosmos depends on their knowledge of its order—an order that implies "battle" (polemos)—and on their ability to submit their desire to this knowledge. Mixing taboos precisely perpetuate this idea or at least the sense of interdependence between subjectivity and objectivity that goes with it.[30]

Perhaps because their cosmic implications are not as wide, subject-to-subject relationships are less emphasized than object-to-object ones in mediating subject-to-object ones. But even if they are less clear-cut, they are rather pervasive, although not in the simple-minded Durkheimian or even Lévi-Straussian form. Although nowhere can a case symmetric with that of mixing taboos be found, we can use with some profit the example of female food taboos.

The proffered reason for the taboos that menstruating women have on any of the large game (particularly on eating their meat) is that their condition endangers the hunting successes of men. Women even declare that they follow these taboos because they care for men. In other words, menstruation creates a much greater distance (a notional one that is spatialized by expelling women from the village and confining them to the menstrual hut and the forest) between man and woman, that is, two categories of subjects, which results in a much greater distance between woman and game, but not between man and game, except if one considers the de facto distancing of game from hunters due to women's violation of their own taboo predicated on notional distance. In other words, man and woman are not combined in the relationship to the taboo object, in contrast with the combination of two incompatible objects in relationship to a single subject (i.e. mixing taboos). This lack of symmetry is obviously due to the presence of a hierarchical principle. Menstruation makes women not only more distant (and thus different) from men, but also inferior to them (at least in this major overt dimension). Thereby the increased asymmetry in taboo between the two categories of subjects makes more evident, and therefore reaffirms, the ordinary asymmetry between them. This asymmetry is ordinarily sustained by a number of permanent taboos for women alone. As I have mentioned, many of these taboos are due to the increased distance between man and woman that results from the headhunting activities of men.

In sum, the two contrasting states (menstruation and childbirth vs. headhunting) that create a distance to the point of incompatibility between male and female subjects also create a distance to the point of taboo toward certain objects. But it is not an equal distance for men

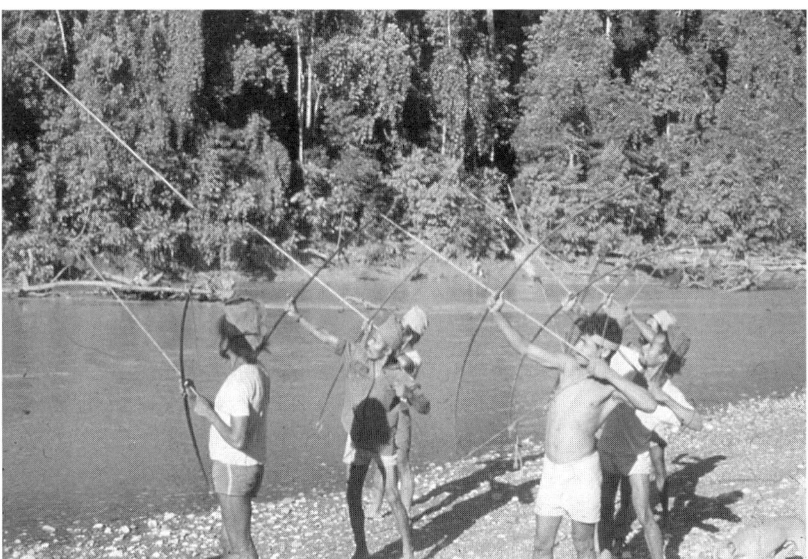

A hunting party, including Pitere, shoots arrows near the Sapulewa River to see who can shoot the farthest. Such competitions are common among men and boys. 1972. (Photo by V. Valeri.)

and women. The proffered reason is that the objects concerned are not incompatible with activities of men that are highly valued (but are completely incompatible with women), either because they result from those activities or because they evoke them (such as the owls which, being associated with headhunting, are taboo for women but not for men). Thus, it is precisely the excessive distance between the two kinds of subjects when they find themselves in their most defining states which accounts for their unequal distance from objects that stand for one of these states—those of the male subject. And this unequal distance gives, in the shade of subject-to-object relationships, the true hierarchical form of subject-to-subject relationships in this field.

The word *field* brings us to another point of irrelevance between distance/similarity and all the patent (and even mentioned) principles it contains. The answer to the question, Is anything and everything that falls under these principles taboo? is clearly no. For excessive dissimilarity or similarity, or difference in space and time, or anomaly, mixture, and inversion, or excessive closeness, and so on, to turn into the truly dangerous incompatibility of subject and object that goes under the name maquwoli, certain ontological areas, with their burden of characteristic experiences, must be crucially involved. What these areas tend to be and why they tend to be given special significance, I have sufficiently mentioned at the end of chapter 3, to give the incoming concentration on animal (mostly food) taboos its true place in the ample landscape of Huaulu taboo.

What I would like to stress a bit at this point is that these areas do not simply motivate a particular sensitivity to incompatibility between subject and object, and thus also between objects and between subjects; they may also contribute to such sensitivity when they are a natural part of otherwise shaped situations, of conceptually and institutionally important relations. Sometimes it is the importance, but also the ambiguity and therefore the vulnerability, of such relations that truly motivates the taboos that protect them. Yet a sociological or gnoseological language—in fact, language itself—does not have the same implementing or even constitutive power[31] that the experience of the body, of its substances, of its transitions and transformations—particularly the negative, not the positive ones—possesses.

The presence—almost omnipresence in certain cases—of necessary bodily activities and inevitable states (such as eating, reproducing, laughing and crying, birth and death) in most social relations, categorizations, and processes allows the translation of social phenomena into the bedrock constituted by the body in subjective experience and thus gains the innermost attention, if not always commitment, from the actual participants in society. In sum, taboo allows, and in fact requires, its analysis to transcend the antiquated separation (although of modern derivation) between individual and society, and to substitute for that separation the idea of a constant and inevitable conversion and reconversion of shared ideas and practices with inescapable, compelling, and endlessly problematic experiences situated in the concrete.[32] In fact I have treated the embodied subject as the pivot of taboo not only because the taboo is always there for somebody to follow, but also because the subject is precisely the locus of such conversions and reconversions. And it is in these that one finds one's taboo-based existence, just as taboo finds its ultimate reasons for being.

One obvious reason the taboo finds to exist and the subject finds to follow taboo in order to exist in these areas of experience is that they strongly evoke the possibility of "contagion"—that is, of an assimilation to what should remain categorically separate. I am claiming that the body, with its processes of ingestion, assimilation, loss of blood, development, decay, and so on, is a concretely experienced image of the conversion of opposites, indeed of antithetical terms (life and death, passivity and activity, etc.) which should be kept separate but ultimately cannot be. This impossibility is, of course, rooted in the nature of the body, of human life, which is an essentially paradoxical and even aporetic being when viewed in terms of thought dependent on desire.

Huaulu myths and beliefs are often articulated statements of such thought. They attempt to explain why death and life—these two antithetical and incompatible terms—are also mutually implying. We cannot be born if we do not accept one of the dates of our death proposed by Lahatala. Mortality and reproduction, accepting death by giving life, are paradoxical consequences due to the origin of death from the fatal conflict between the divinities Hahunusa and Olenusa. Every human suffers this conflict in his body and knows that Hahunusa will win again and again. These beliefs, these stories, constitute the most articulated background to the existence of and preoccupation with taboos. For taboos delay the ultimate outcome of existence and all the intermediate misfortunes that prepare it, and they testify to human weakness, which, just like its opposite (power), is due to humans' insertion in a cosmic order they do not control, or control only very partially and not indefinitely.

One could argue, therefore, that each taboo, as a reminder of human weakness and vulnerability (even when it is vulnerability relative to occult beings that lend some of their power), ultimately evokes the shade of death and arises from a particularly strong perception of that shade. This strong perception occurs whenever the object appears strongly antagonistic (potentially or actually) to the subject and whenever something allows the object facile access to the body, or to whatever extension of the body (betel basket, mat, clothes, house, village, territory, etc.) has a particular significance for the subject's self-perception (of his identity).

Empirically, it is obvious that the greatest source of danger is the bodily process that realizes the strongest form of assimilation, that is, eating. Sexual penetration is also quite dangerous, but it testifies to the primacy of alimentary ingestion, its dangerousness being frequently designated as a correlate of a form of "eating." The two are in any case mixed in the representation of the danger which humans as hunters risk vis-à-vis their animal prey—the danger of being hunted, in return, in the alimentary and sexual modes. The reason I am mentioning these two sources of taboo is not just that they are fundamental as such or that they lend some of their power, through metaphoric representations taken rather literally as beliefs, to taboos motivated by other reasons. The reason is also that they present in visible and concrete form an underlying presupposition of all contagious power attributed to objects, however distant, that threaten the subject and must therefore be kept at bay.

The presupposition is that a distant, antithetical object would be no danger if it really were so different, if it did not have a dimension of similarity to the subject that made the transfer of its qualities to the subject possible in certain forms of contact. It is precisely such presupposition that explains why taboos are activated so much in the alimentary sphere. Such activation obviously presupposes that the flesh of the antithetical animal can easily turn into that of the subject, primarily because both are flesh, but also because the subject seems to share with the object more specific attributes (e.g. skin condition), since he may acquire these attributes even if he does not eat the object. (Such is obviously the case of the crocodile, whose dangerousness lies in its skin, say the Huaulu, and in human skin's tendency to become comparable to it.)

One may well ask if the fear of the antithetical is not supported by the awareness that one has much in common with it, at least potentially. I don't have to repeat that this explains why so many antithetical beings are dangerous only to eat. I would rather reiterate that the case of meat taboos brings out more strongly a subterranean sense of similarity or even identity which coexists with the dominant sense of excessive or antinomic difference in many taboos. It is this coexistence which may make the transmission of negative/destructive qualities possible,[33] and therefore motivates the increased sense of danger whose outcome is taboo. In fact, one may argue that it also motivates the increased polarization, the excess of categorical distance that both sustains and is sustained by the taboo. In other words, certain terms become exaggeratedly different in order to suppress all the more strongly the element of similarity (and possible reversal) that is felt between them in certain relations (especially the eater-eaten relation). And I would add that corresponding to the subterranean but necessary presence of similarity when difference is dominant as an explicit motivation of taboo is the inverse combination in the taboos principally motivated by excessive closeness/similarity, although the symmetry is not total. Let's see it through an obvious example among the familiar ones: the taboo on eating dog meat.

This taboo is openly explained as a case of excessive closeness in the social and categorical, but also emotional, senses. It is hardly the logical principle of avoided identity that applies here; it is a variety of other arguments which take closeness in its various senses. I don't eat the dog because it is physically like myself, but it is like myself in the sense required, and made stronger in actuality, by the fact that it lives with me (so it is a fellow householder), hunts with me, eats with me, and is thus a friendly servant. Spatial proximity involves categorical proximity and also emotional identification—quite evident if one looks at dog-master relationships. The issue then is that this closeness requires the maintenance of a certain degree of distance. I cannot make the dog so close that, through the digestive process, it becomes my flesh. To eat its meat means to lose the meat of the animals the dog makes it possible to procure. I cannot eat myself in objective form without undermining myself in subjective form—a form which is corporeal and therefore flesh-dependent. So similarity or even partial categorical identity must be resisted and diminished by accentuating difference by means of taboo: the difference between human and animal, but also between solidarity (friendship) and enmity, and so on.

It is fundamentally in this way, as we have seen, that the difference between village (as embodiment of society) and forest (as embodiment of the contrary of society) can be maintained at the human table. In this sense, there is little difference between the coexistence of diminished similarity and increased difference in the two poles of taboo—the one emphasizing incompatibility through difference and the other incompatibility through similarity. But in another sense, there is a difference, and this lies precisely in the opposite values given to similarity/closeness and difference/distance on opposite sides of the diagram of taboo principles. When I say that an object is taboo because it is too far from the subject, I see any underlying similarity as a coadjuvant of difference in creating a danger. So both similarity and difference are negative and creators of dangers when violating the taboo. When I say that another object is taboo because it is too similar, I am seeing similarity as the value to preserve against the exaggeration of a less explicit difference (between animal and human, for instance) which incites me to deny that similarity and thus the friendship which is based on it.

Beyond and Behind the Bestiary: Identity and Difference

As I indicated at the end of chapter 3, most families of taboos are ultimately motivated by the embodiment of the subject, hence by its vulnerability to substances, forces, and processes that are external to cultural agency and thus not, or not easily, governable by it (except through avoidance). But I also recognized that this ultimate motivation may work through intermediate ones, especially that of guaranteeing an adequate and continuous performance of the various rituals and other highly controlled practices which are the active response to the threatening external forces I have mentioned.[34]

The first proposition seems to guarantee that the principles found behind food taboos can be easily extended; but the second casts doubts on whether this is so. Even by the first, one must admit that the different substances (e.g. blood) and states (e.g. dead body) attracting taboos must have some twist of their own, and are not, in any case, all so equally close to food and eating as to warrant an automatic and unmodified extension. Let us begin by looking, then, at the taboos of the corpse and at those of "female blood," the most dangerous of the three types of shed bloods, including both menstruation and childbirth. As I mentioned in my review at the end of chapter 3, all these phenomena are among the most important together with food taboos. But they are also too numerous and complex to allow me to mention more than a representative few.

Both corpses and women who menstruate or give birth are required to be expulsed from the village, since they show the incompatiblity of life and death (corpse), or life and the association of life-giving potential and the failure to actualize it (menstruation or childbirth, which is always uncertain). But there is an important difference between the modalities of their expulsion. Death occurs only once but is forever; menstrual bleeding occurs periodically, but is not permanent (there is, however, a threat that it may become so—poture melekae). We have seen this throughout chapters 3 and 4. Hence the separation of menstruating women is preventive: they must get out of the village before their state affects it and return to it after the bleeding has ceased. In contrast, the dying person is not expelled before he has reached death. The village allows him to await the end in its bosom and then postpones the expulsion of the quickly rotting corpse until the next day. But afterwards it is taboo to keep the corpse inside the village, not to mention to bring it back from the forest. The separation of corpse and village, guaranteed by taboos, is forever. In sum, in one case the taboos of separation remedy the "pollution" of death; in the other they prevent the pollution of genital bleeding.

To quote just a couple of taboos on such careful separation of the living from the dead: It is taboo to offer the corpse a cloth that one has worn, otherwise the giver will be carried away by the receiver. In other words, this separation sacrifice requires a low level of identification between sacrificer and object sacrificed. The body should not leave its imprint on the object. Contact also plays a big role in the case of the "carrying stick" (fafala) to which the corpse is bound when it is carried out of the house and to the grave or tree or cave in the forest. It is taboo for this stick to touch any part of the house during this delicate transition period. Otherwise, all its inhabitants will be carried away with the dead. Verbally, it is taboo to pronounce the word *seliam* (of the dead) about anybody's property, particularly the more intimate and "defining" properties like lukayam (the arrow), salatam (the betel basket), tupayam (the basket), kaluam (the cloth), and so on. And it is also taboo to pronounce the names of the dead; speech puts together the utterer and what would otherwise remain fully and safely distant. In sum, all these taboos undo the temptation to void the extreme distance between living and dead. We find here too, as in so many food taboos, an affirmation of extreme difference that goes against a desire, or hidden recognition, of its negation. After all, the dead may still be loved.

Much the same can be said of the taboos that separate genitally bleeding women from the village. I limit myself, again, to a couple of relevant examples. The most important one is, of course, women's confinement in a special, tightly closed, menstrual/childbirth hut (lilipossu), which is absolutely taboo for men to build or even approach (especially on the "forest" side, near its hearth), let alone visit. The hut must be built beyond the village's boundary. To move from her house to her menstrual hut, a woman must exit from the back of the house and walk beyond that boundary in order not to endanger the village. One indication that the hut implies continuity with the forest as against the village close by is that menstruating women may wander from the menstrual hut to anywhere in the forest but must absolutely stop before the village boundary.

Two other telling taboos deserve mention. Women in the lilipossu cannot "cook" (akatunu) in the full sense of the term—that is, boil a meal that consists of meat and sago porridge—not only for anybody in the village, but even for themselves. They may only grill—another indication that, whatever the distance of the menstrual hut from the village, they are conceptually associated with the forest, where the only cooking is grilling, by either men or women. Another taboo instantiates the frequent ambiguity of the reference to the principle of excessive closeness or even identity: one particular wood is said to be taboo in the construction of the menstrual hut because it is red (it would perhaps reinforce bleeding), but by contrast, it is recommended that the pieces of a red creeper be bound together, because it gives the hut its purpose, signals its identity, and keeps away anything contrasting with it. Regardless of its exact meaning, this latter example raises the wider issue of how principles apply to and through color, to which I will return later.

A final set of taboos to be mentioned concerns the relations of bleeding women with bleeding men, their activities, and the results. An obvious difference between female and male bleeding is that the latter is inflicted on other bodies, to procure meat or to procure a sacrificial head. It therefore signifies a triumph over the body, not only over the vulnerability of one's own, but also and most important over the resistance of or even attack of a powerful other. Menstrual bleeding is, of course, a sign of women's potential procreative power, but also a sign that it has not been actualized. In a sense, it is a more demeaning failure not to be able to fulfill a capacity than not to possess it (as is the case of a prepubescent girl, who is not incompatible with men's bleeding, at least as far as the hunting of animals is concerned).

How do these menstrual and funeral taboos fit the play of excessive distance and excessive proximity and the more particular principles I have extracted from animal (especially food) taboos? Both sets undoubtedly confirm the crucial importance of excessive categorical distance, as I have suggested from the beginning. The corpse is radically incompatible with the village and the living who identify with the village, because it confronts them with a state that they know they must eventually reach (which is why one lets others die in the village), but from which they want to be as distant as they can to keep on living for as long as possible. The problem that accounts for the precise "knife" of the taboo is the imprecise flesh of which humans are made. The living and the dead who have long lived together still preserve so many links, so many desires (real on one side, putative as counterpart of what is real on the other) for each other, that some brutal severance is necessary in order to go on. The living and the dead must be radically separated through a radical reclassification of the kinsman or friend who is rapidly rotting as corpse. He must be bound to the distant and multiform world of the forest, the source of everything in which everything in the end dissolves and renews. That is why he can enter the village only in a thoroughly transformed state, corresponding to what a categorical world based on human understanding guided by desire assigns it. What is threatening about the corpse is that in many ways it represents a backward transformation from village to forest, an undoing of what made a human person possible from the time he or she was born in the forest and then moved step by step to fullness in the village.

This backward transformation assimilates the corpse to the menstruating or still uncertainly delivering woman. Menstruation is the index of a power intrinsic to her body and identical to that of most animals. It belongs to the forest but not to the village because, since it did not turn into pregnancy, it signifies the defeat of the efficacious transformation that peoples the village. Even when the moment of childbirth comes, the uncertainty that surrounds its outcome (life or death for child and mother), and depends mainly on the considerable loss of blood, pulls the women toward the forest and increases the fear of the men. I have so many times seen them waiting in the village, sometimes in exhausting rows of nights and days while the woman was close to death, punctuated by screams and laments from the lilipossu and the compassionate cries of other women in response.

Men's fear is one of loss, of witnessing another death—the death of somebody who is often very close. But it is also fear of being contaminated, that is, partly assimilated to what the loss of one's blood until death signifies: being a victim and not a victor; reversing the direction of blood transformation that characterizes hunting and headhunting, and thus men's major contribution to the life of the village. This sign of failure and reversal, moreover, has not simply an analogical relation to the failures of women; it has also a syntagmatic—a causal—relation to them, because the proper handling of hunting and headhunting creates the conditions for the successful transformation of women's genital blood into living people. In other words, if men offer sufficient human sacrifice to the ultimate sources of life—the ailaem, or "ancestors" in the widest possible sense—they make it possible for women to give birth instead of wasting their blood.[35] Through their shed blood, then, enemy or stranger victims turn into Huaulu. These new Huaulu will then have to be fed by turning the largest forms of game into food for children, relatives, and friends. The causal chain of headhunting, hunting, and childbirth is thus manifestly broken if women's blood does not perennially or at least frequently turn into secure flesh for the village.

The failure women reveal, then, is an ultimate failure of men—one made all the more frequent these days with the (at least official) abandonment of headhunting and thus of the connected transformative practices vis-à-vis the village. But in women's failure there have always been other components as well: their willful resistance to men, their own indirect assertion of autonomy, and also the raging impediment of muluaqinaem—the shades of failed women who died childless or in childbed. Such occult women may well be interpreted as an openly antagonistic aspect of the female gender itself. Women who truly failed to the point of losing their life in childbed get their revenge on men; they are credited not only with blocking childbirth, with their long nails, in men's other women, but also with using the same tools to castrate men. This association seems thus to confirm that one dimension of the danger of menstruating women for men and for the village, whose existence depends on them, is castration—that is, the loss of male power to generate but also the loss of the embodied form of male claims of supremacy.[36] Women who bleed from their own genitals thus seem to threaten to make those of men bleed as well—not the remedial and once-for-all bleeding of initiation, but one that is perhaps invisible in men but becomes visible by displacement in women.

In sum, what is enormously distant from men—the bleeding that turns a vagina from a productive orifice into a wound—turns out to have to be kept distant because just below the surface it is frighteningly close to men, or rather to the state which they fear most, because it signifies unmanning.[37] Excessive distance in such matters, then, is dangerous not in itself, but because it coexists with an excessive proximity. Women are clamorously proclaimed different from men when they menstruate precisely because they are felt to be potentially or (these days) actually annoyingly close.

The basic question, then, is, Why is this closeness hidden in the open discourse? Because its acknowledgment would mean a rejection of the hierarchical opposition of man and woman. The first step in the reassertion of this opposition must thus be to keep away from consciousness what in the object negates it. Without such distance from consciousness it would be impossible for taboo to sustain the translation of mere categorical distance into an actual, existential one. In other words, taboo is only the spatial end point of a process that starts in the conflictual coexistence of recognition of similarity and desire and even duty of difference, but must move to the creation of an asymmetry between the two in consciousness. Closer to consciousness, difference is predominant or total, just like the result sought through taboo, while similarity is secondary or nonexistent. Yet the fact that the next step is recourse to the yes-or-no construction of taboo is an index of ambiguity. The effort of consciousness is not enough to keep the subversive identity of bleeding woman and man away. This is precisely why taboo proliferates, giving a very physical, and indeed spatial, existence to the dangerously unstable dimension of categorical distance in pure mental space.

We find here, in more evident form than elsewhere, that taboo is not the mere translation of a *va de soi* categorical distance. Practice, physical acts, spatial relations, and substantive connections add something more. They make it possible to disambiguate distance when it is at its most ambiguous at the mental and emotional levels. In the predominantly spatial and bodily world of taboo, one cannot be and not be at the same place at the same time; one cannot eat and not eat at the same time. The translation into taboo is thus the most effective way of eliminating the element of similarity that coexists with that of difference. But what is eliminated at the concrete level of taboo cannot be eliminated at the motivating level of the mind; otherwise the leap into the world of taboos will be unnecessary. Taboo is thus the practical, unambiguous end point of a process which begins with a contradictory mental positioning of an object relative to a subject (too distant/too close), moves on with an insufficient mental resolution that consists in making one categorical positioning take over without completely displacing the other (too distant to be treated as too close; too distant; not really close, although . . .), and ends up with an invariable negation in space and bodily contact.

This ambiguity, to be resolved by taboo at the most bodily level, throws into deep doubt Testart's theory of avoided summation of ontological identicals. Identity and difference seem to coexist and take different forms in practice and consciousness depending on the case and stage. Moreover, the theory founders against the fact that the relationships among the three kinds of blood (of menstruation, of the hunt, and of the headhunt) are inseparable from their differential relationships with the village, which makes them not even symmetrical with one another. It is therefore impossible to view the taboos that separate the three kinds of blood from one another merely as ways to avoid summations of the same substance (blood). If anything they are attempts to avoid reducing to sameness things that should stay different—and should in fact become even more different—in the face of a fear of convergence. Moreover, the main fear of convergence exists between the two stronger opposites—male bleeding and female bleeding—with female bleeding causing the fall of male bleeding to the female kind, and male bleeding causing, to a more limited extent, a further fall of female bleeding in the form of a longer state. But I must stop here in consideration of the very complicated matter of gender, which I have repeatedly touched on elsewhere and even in this chapter. I have treated it more fully on its own terms[38] rather than incidentally as part of our attempt to reach generalizations about taboo here. Let us continue with that attempt.

Like food—and more generally animal—taboos, menstrual and corpse taboos indicate the extreme vulnerability of an embodied subject, and the village-materialized society in which he is categorically located, to life and death processes of the body. But by now an important difference between food taboos and the others should have become apparent. It is a difference that depends on the different nature of the underlying bodily processes.

The bodily processes that end in death (for everybody) and those that involve genital bleeding (periodically or repeatedly in women)[39] cannot be avoided by those who undergo them. One cannot escape from one's body, except by death itself. The only partial escape is, of course, preventive, since premature, unexpected death and long or fatal bleeding in women may result from violating certain processual taboos that can be strictly observed. So this is a first difference from food taboos; if food taboos were like menstrual or death taboos, it would be as if the dangers of eating were independent of what is eaten and dependent only on the processes of digestion, which cannot, of course, be escaped as unwelcome food can. But there is another and more striking difference: as we have seen, the consequences of eating dangerous (and therefore tabooed) food do not usually extend beyond the person who does the eating. Although eating is a social act, it is also a curiously individual one as an existential drama confronting the eater and the eaten. This is probably why only very close relatives may sometimes suffer the consequences with or without the eater.

In contrast, a single individual's menstrual or parturitional bleeding, or dying and becoming a corpse, has dangerous consequences for the whole village indiscriminately, and even more intensely for certain relatives. This is precisely why the sources of these dangers have to be expelled from the village, and momentarily or permanently avoided by all its members or all its men. One not only avoids external danger, then, but is avoided *as* an external danger, and must even avoid being a danger to others. The distant symmetry between animal and human which has appeared as a hidden limit to the power of distancing danger in eating and hunting is matched here by a much closer symmetry. It is because only human-to-human relations are concerned, even if these relations are far from always being equal, that the suffering other can be a danger to those who do not suffer yet or never will (as is the case with men vis-à-vis women).

The contrast with food taboos—where keeping apart is only from the individual body and its failure does not affect others, let alone the village—therefore reveals a strong participatory and identificatory character in menstrual and death taboos. It is because we will all die and all menstruate or confront menstruation—as a failure of our reproductive hopes in ourselves, our mothers, or our wives—that we identify with corpses and even bleeding women. The inevitable limitations of the body relative to culturally shaped desires and hopes therefore cannot be avoided, either in oneself or through others. Menstruating women and corpses of either gender must therefore be kept apart from subject and village. They must be treated like external animals viewed as taboo, but contrary to such animals they themselves feel worthy of taboo, because they are conscious of the shared consciousness of their state. It is the presumption of this shared consciousness (but I have often witnessed its reality) that lies behind the operational form of the taboo in the case of corpses and obviously and visibly in the case of women. Women are not violently expelled from the village (although they would be if they did not cooperate), but are expected to guarantee their separation from it, and the integrity of their relation with their husbands, by following a number of taboos whose execution is quite difficult for men to check. They are not just objects of taboo like animals, then, but also subjects. As I mentioned, they may even declare that they follow certain taboos out of compassion for their men.

This brings me to another difference between these interhuman taboos (even if they concern the fall into what is most animal in humans) and food or animal taboos. The latter are overtly treated as guarantees of a merely exclusive opposition: *x* is taboo to *y* because its properties undermine and eventually destroy *y*. The interhuman taboos are overtly treated as guarantees of a complementary opposition: that between man and wife, male and female, or between the living and the dead, the ancestors and the descendants, and so on. I say "overtly," of course, because each of these oppositions coexists with a hidden form of the other: the alimentary incompatibility with an animal species may in fact be due to its backgrounded symbolic consumption which turns its relationship with the subject into a complementary one. A certain form of complementary opposition (subject *x* is like this because it is inseparable from its contrast with *y* and vice versa) may thus generate an exclusive opposition[40] at the categorical level to better justify a taboo at the alimentary level (better, since care and concern of the complementary other can hardly be felt when this other is a wild animal). Reciprocally, a certain form of exclusive opposition (death and life) can generate a complementary one to better justify taboos that aim at certain results: productive husband-wife (and more generally man-woman) relations, village solidarity based on the reproduction of its population, the limitation of death or infertility or unsuccessful parturition, and so on.

Finally, I should observe that the use of the term *pollution* in cases such as menstruation or death seems far more appropriate than it would be when talking about the bad effects of taboo food. For bad eating tends to have an individually limited effect of a very concrete bodily nature—and one that is delayed or never arrives in those who are strong or lucky. The extension of these effects beyond the transgressor is rare and limited, as we have seen. Delayed individual effects of a concrete bodily nature may also occur as a result of the violation of menstrual and corpse taboos, but their main effect is a conventional state immediately and automatically extended to a whole community or category of people. Such a state can be identified only by disqualification from certain activities, and thus more in agency than in the body that experiences sickness or health.

Misoneistic taboos land us in a third case of distance, not in the sense of intensity, but in the sense of the mode. It seems a mode very similar to that of dangerous wild species, since it has to do with categorically distant objects that one should keep at the spatial distance into which the categorical distance translates. But these objects are always man-made or man-produced and therefore rooted in human bodies. In this sense, they and their expulsion are reminiscent of some aspects of bodily phenomena that require expulsion from the village and distance, either from both sexes or from only men. But there are also important differences with such phenomena: misoneistically approached objects are produced intentionally and by people who are strangers to the village. Furthermore, contrary to the fixed (continuous or periodic) character of the species or bodily phenomena that we have considered, those that are the objects of misoneistic taboos imply a temporal dimension—one which is spatialized again, so that the Huaulu self-defining distance is from a possible future, which so far is realized only in the coastal areas beaten by the powerful waves from overseas.

Misoneistic taboos were all listed together in the previous section, since it seems impossible to separate new foods and other new objects. It is true that they all evoke the antithetical world that begins on the coast and extends overseas. Nevertheless, they may enter the Huaulu world in different ways, with different (and socially differentiating) consequences in terms of taboo. All artifacts and two agricultural products, rice (ala) and cloves (pukalawa), enter only as commodities bought in coastal shops or from peddlers; all other plants (kasibi, alamafu [corn], lapina [squash], etc.), through the adoption of their cultivation. It is precisely those that become in some way available through either means that can be the object of taboo. The confrontation, the temptation, and the thought that some kind of rejection is necessary make taboo grow. For that to arise, plants or artifacts must stand for the foreign, antithethical world which attracts and repels at the same time. In recent years, it has become especially frightening because its obviously increasing dominance runs against the Huaulu claim of enduring superiority (hence misoneism).

Both the locally uncultivated rice and cloves and the cultivated lapina and so on are unequally taboo as aliments, as I mentioned in the previous section of this chapter. How and whether they are taboo depends on their particular symbolic values, but especially on the identity of the subject for whom the taboo arises. That subject is usually somebody who is representatively situated at the center of Huaulu culture. The more distant one is from what is not fully Huaulu, the more one must defend Huaulu by defending that distance through a negation of one's absorbing body. On such taboos, then, rest coordinated differences inside Huaulu society and between that society and the one it posits as antithetical to it—the coastal/overseas one. It is as if the cultivating of such foreign foods were made possible in order to make the internal difference possible in coordination with the external one.[41]

But why is it that since rice and cloves are consumed to a degree of selectivity equal to that of all imported vegetals, only rice and clove trees are absolutely and universally taboo to cultivate for all Huaulu, and can therefore be acquired only as commodities, just like artifacts? There are two converging reasons: Rice cultivation requires a calendrical investment of time and work that becomes and supports a whole system of life—the system of most of the external world (especially most of Indonesia) known to the Huaulu. The other, convergent, reason is that commodity acquisition implies a much diminished closeness to that world. Let me say a few more words about each of these reasons, based as they are on Huaulu experiences, which allow them to compare their life form with that of the world that repels and attracts and rejects them as much as they do that world.

Generally speaking, the mode of acquisition of the object depends on the object's nature and on Huaulu abilities. Most of the artificial objects that characterize the outside world in its contrast and implicit superiority to the Huaulu world—kerosene lamps and stoves, radios, tape recorders, cameras, and guns—are fabricated in ways that are inaccessible to the Huaulu. These objects can therefore be acquired only from traders. Their commodity character may make them relatively accessible to people who have no connections or weak ones with the core of distinctive Huaulu characteristics and powers, in contrast with elders, men with priestly functions, and so on. The reason for this has to do with Huaulu awareness that buying an object does not create the same degree of identification with it and what it stands for as making or producing it does. If the Huaulu were to produce the only two things they could learn to produce—rice and cloves—they would let themselves be invaded by the world they have always wanted to keep at a distance, given the centrality and constitutive character of these crops for coastal areas in the Moluccas: one (the clove tree) feeding trade with the world for centuries, the other (rice) feeding the traders. Taboo then displaces its emphasis on production, because in these cases there is an alternative between buying, which as they know helps maintain a distance, and producing. Rice bought in coastal stores or from coastal middlemen may therefore be eaten by people who are not the custodians of Huaulu identity and powers on behalf of others. And the same is true of cloves, although there has been a change in recent years, as we shall see later.

But why is it that the adoption of a foreign form of production is a much greater invasion than the consumption of its products? The reason should be rather obvious. Rice production, especially, indexes a whole form of life viewed by the Huaulu as opposite to theirs. It requires more work and more servitude to the plant throughout time and, in any case, techniques and relations that one learns from others and that partly turn one into those others (an agriculturalist or planter of a commercial crop instead of a hunter). In contrast, merely buying rice or cloves, just like any other product one finds in the market, allows one to maintain a greater distance to ensure one's identity.[42] But such distance remains below the taboo level only if the symbolic use of the object is minimal.

In other words, it is not the commodity character in itself that makes the object incompatible with the Huaulu world. It is the object's strong association with the image of the world from which it comes and its power to substitute the objects on which the Huaulu image of its own identity rests (e.g. a petroleum lamp substituting for a damar lamp). We should not attribute to commodities experienced by the Huaulu the purely functional and commercial identity which we ourselves attribute, in total error, to the commodities we experience. Functions and values do not exist in a cultural vacuum. Yet relating to objects by buying from and selling to strangers, rather than producing them with or for friends, creates new alternatives for taboo. The distance it introduces may be a reason for keeping them out of the sphere of taboo, but it may also be a reason for introducing them into it. A distant world of exchange is both a convenient contrast with the proximate world and an annoying, because subversive, one. The latter view introduces new taboos—the taboos of the new; the former makes it possible for them to be applied—to what, for whom, and to what degree—in highly variable ways.

One most important variable that takes off from the production of rice and cloves but goes well beyond it when considered from another angle is the mimetic function. Cultivating rice means letting oneself be invaded by the undermining other by replicating the process on which its life rests. The more one imitates rice producers, the less one stays Huaulu. The loss of Huaulu identity, or more exactly the loss of the absolute control of the images on which it rests, may also be due to the appropriative use of certain image-making machines: cameras, videos, tape recorders, and so on. To make images of the Huaulu—or of the Huaulu at their most identity-building and -preserving, for instance by means of rituals—to record their stories, and so on, are taboo in different degrees. But ultimately, as I have repeatedly experienced, it is ethnography as a whole—the reproduction of Huaulu life to bring it away from the Huaulu, to let other people see and know it—that is fundamentally taboo. A taboo fundamentally violated or narrowed down as much as possible, or desirable, in my case. Still, a taboo that gave away a basic piece of Huaulu mind: that replication of or by the correlative other breaks down or progressively reduces Huaulu difference, and thus existence.

The Huaulu may eat rice but not become rice farmers; and they may look at some worn-out photographs of themselves but not at the vivid images of what they do, or of what their fathers and mothers did, which are in possession of strangers. That would be discovering that the ritual acts or ancestors, which or whom they believe to belong to a certain time and place, as they must, are now in fact timed and placed as strangers want. The discovery of the illusionistic ethnography of the CD ROM, if it is ever brought to them (I didn't), will translate into the end of any possible ethnography—however reduced and mediated like mine—not because of increased taboos, but perhaps because they might stop doing anything to set more protective taboos about. What for, if others have already stolen everything, or stolen the possibility of everything, through its images (since images are fully equivalent to what they represent)?

Many misoneistic taboos, then, seem based on opposite (but equivalent in their identity effects) mirrorings. The Huaulu side should not replicate what is most defining of the antithetical side in activities of production or consumption, and should not itself be replicated at its most defining (or sometimes in every case) by means of tape recorders, cameras, and even writing. All these alien and alienating objects, all these image-making and -replicating objects characterizing the overseas world whose waves reach the coasts of Seram, must be kept out of Huaulu. They must neither be used by the Huaulu nor be directed against them by strangers. The two worlds should be kept separate, on behalf of the Huaulu one, because of the perceived superior power of the overseas one—a superiority that denies the overt passionate assertion of Huaulu superiority. Huaulu, in the end, can defend this assertion only if it defends itself by means of taboos, and thus by avoiding confrontation.

These taboos also reveal the more usual dimension of the interaction of distance and closeness into which we keep running. The possession and use of artificial objects of foreign manufacture seem often the source of an exhilarating sense of difference from other Huaulu obtained by diminishing the sense of difference from the foreign world. It is the antisocial, inegalitarian character of this difference through the formidable other that is dangerous and is therefore marked and discouraged by taboo.

The whole area of "unfamiliar," "out of place," "anomalous," and "mixing" certainly needs some adaptation or even consolidation in order to apply beyond human-animal relations (or those of any other natural phenomena). This is particularly the case with directly social relations without any or much natural mediation. But even our immediate sense that these principles apply to some of the lapses into the bodily realm, with which we started this section, should be somewhat checked. Take, for instance, the case of a "bad death": the corpse of a man who died by a fall or a woman who died in childbirth. Can they be construed as unfamiliar? Perhaps yes, in the merely empirical sense of how many times one individual has been able to witness it. But does this mean that the phenomenon is not well known? Certainly not, because there is an extended knowledge about it transmitted by tradition. It is certainly not expected at the time it occurs, but it is generically believed that it will occur at some point. Timing is thus the only lack of knowledge—a lack of knowledge remedied by various shamanic attempts to discover occult agents behind the occurrences. The basic point, though, is that it is not that lack of knowledge and any anxiety due to it which explains, or in any case principally explains, the taboos that separate the phenomenon from the village. It is the social evaluation of its categorical position vis-à-vis the categorical position of the village. What makes them incompatible is not that one is "out of place" in terms of occurrence or "anomalous" in terms of categorization. It is, rather, that the corpse exists because of the supreme and devastating loss of control over one's body. And it is the categorical contrast of such lack of control and the control ideally located in a village that is prone to lose it which explains the taboos involved in keeping the corpse and its personal extensions away from the village.

That neither "out-of-placedness" nor "anomaly" really explains those taboos is demonstrated by a difference between two kinds of "badly dead" bodies which seem identical from the purely cognitive point of view of out-of-placedness or anomaly (since they are both referred to as the result of a fall): that of the woman who died in childbirth (pukua ria ninianiam, "she fell in the village") and that of the man who died in a literal fall or in other ways considered equivalent to one (pukua, "he fell"). If a woman dies in childbirth in the menstrual hut, her corpse may be brought back to her house for the funeral rites that she requires, since the entire village is already contaminated by the spatial closeness of her death.[43] The next day, she is buried in the forest at a respectable distance from the village. Then the village ceases to be contaminated by death. But if a man dies as a result of a mishap in his defining activities of hunting or headhunting (by falling from trees or rocks, by being gored by a wild pig, or bitten by a poisonous snake, or struck by lightning), his body must be left at the place of death, where special neutralizing rites are performed. If it is introduced into the village, or if even its smallest personal belonging is, the village becomes permanently contaminated with misfortune and death, so that its inhabitants must immediately abandon it and never return to it. It is taboo to use the space itself, just as it is taboo to use the land where the "bad death" occurred and to eat the fruits of the trees that grow on it.

No such difference between male and female corpses exists when death occurs in any other form. So what explains the difference in cases of bad death? Male bad death inevitably occurs in the course of hunting and headhunting, which are considered men's most defining activities and make more important and necessary contributions to the life of the village in that even the defining activities of women (giving birth) depend on them (through food and sacrifice). So women's total failure (death in childbirth) is not as dangerous for the village as men's total failure; but given this, women's partial failure (bleeding in menstruation) or uncertainty of success (bleeding in childbirth) are more dangerous than the negative side of men's successes (i.e. killing game or victims is necessary to the life of the village but involves certain dangers which require certain separations from the village).[44] Both asymmetries, in sum, proclaim the putative superiority of men over women in their contribution to the life of the village. And incidentally, blood alone, which is abundantly spilled in both female and male cases of bad death, does not suffice to explain these differences. Nor can the mixture of village and various other terms opposed to it be seen as a threat to mere classificatory difference rather than a threat to a system of operations and transformations which is imbued with the asymmetries of value and the power of men to make them lean in their direction.

What resembles the anomalous in its cognitive sense—a sort of cassowary in the form of an event that summarizes and fossilizes to the level of the species a human life through its brutal end—is thus far from contributing to the explanation of its treatment in the world of taboos. It may nevertheless produce some reinforcement, just as the sense of anomaly may conversely be reinforced by its utilization in a symbolic field which always goes beyond mere classification or any other basis for a sense of regularity or normality.

An example is provided by the red moon. The moon's unusual association with red is not enough to turn it into an inevitably bad omen, which is made slightly more surprising by the usual association of red with danger. A further degree of anomaly (or rather, rarity of occurrence)—namely when the red moon is "high in the sky and in the east" (aroeni)—seems to make the difference, as my friend Pulaki pointed out. It is considered a bad omen, that is, something equivalent to taboo in the realm of events that one cannot avoid but can interpret in order to take neutralizing or remedial steps. The reason for this is that this particular red moon is supposed to be the initial phase of an eclipse, a phenomenon of great rarity. Yet the eclipse itself would not be particularly threatening and requiring of remedial rites that are taboo not to perform were it not inseparable from something human (but antisocial) that it has come to symbolize: incest. Indeed, the Huaulu believe that all eclipses are caused by the sexual union of moon and sun, who are sister and brother. The darkness they create to make their union invisible must be pierced with many bonfires and with the tremendous noise of as many gongs as one has around to beat. Brother and sister will then feel discovered and thus ashamed enough to separate again.

As usual, then, it is the accumulation of meanings which anomaly makes possible that allows it to appear as a reason for taboo. But apart from the fact that anomaly is never alone, it can usually participate in the creation of taboo because of its elective affinities with human violations of normality (as in the case of incest) or with mediating activities of the shamanic type. The apparent impossibility of any such association leaves the "anomalous" or "out of place" tabooless or omenless. An example of the tabooless is the frigate bird (whose anomaly is clearly commented upon), and one of the omenless is the shooting stars.

If the application of the notion of anomaly as a taboo-producing factor is not without problems in areas that have much in common with the animal world we have studied in chapter 4, it is even more problematic in predominantly interpersonal areas, without any or much natural mediation.[45] Of course, one may be tempted to say that any ritually intermediate state between usually separate or incompatible categories (e.g. boy and initiated adult, nonshaman and shaman in the initiation rites) is anomalous. But in fact such anomaly can hardly be compared with the permanent one attached to the species; moreover, even as a transitional phenomenon it hardly deserves an identification with anomaly, since it does not happen against human expectations and ideas of order but, on the contrary, is voluntarily and predictably made by humans as a way of realizing order over time. In other words, nothing could be more normal and expected and familiar, even if it is an initiatory event that does not happen every day.

What makes such transitions hedged with taboos is that they are recognized mixtures of opposite categories, which ritual must scramble in relationship to an individual in order to move him from one category or status to the other. As long as they last, these mix-ups must be marked, and viewed as confusions and uncertainties that are not perpetuated without danger, without the risk of becoming anomalies proper, thereby subtracting any form of acceptable identity from the subject involved. However great their danger, they are not viewed as worth fleeing—quite the contrary (unless they occur at the wrong time or last beyond the required time span). An artificially and voluntarily produced mix-up may in fact be the condition of success for a ritual or magical formula. The most dramatic example is provided by the sailoa, an ancient ritual now discontinued (but not normatively, it could still happen, according to many Huaulu),[46] which consisted of, among other things, collective meals that had to include all species and that therefore involved the violation of all food taboos, as well as the violation of all taboos of commensality. The reason was that food taboos reflect both social and cosmological differences. Their associated suspension indicated the correlation of cosmos and society and the correlation of all species, natural and social, in forming a whole that had to be reproduced by differentiation of this undifferentiation (the most powerful symbol of unity). The sailoa was also a defying claim of Huaulu control of the cosmos, not only because it was reconstituted by differentiation from its ritually produced undifferentiation, but also because it suspended any danger inherent in taboo animals. Such a claim of control, however, was limited in its fullness to the ritual context, and is one that has now been abandoned, reinforcing the sense of impotence and danger that the hunter and his wife experience in entering the forest. Only the village, an artificial object which is the transformation of objects from the forest and which therefore evokes a triumph over it, and which also contains even more artificial acts without uncontrolled objectual counterparts, returns the Huaulu to part of his sense of domination and control.

Yet even in the village one has to face dramatic events of limitation, a clear sense of defeat before a reclaiming forest. We have already discussed the twin events of death and birth processes that imply death, in the short or the long run. But even these do not easily or immediately fit any of the principles in which excessive distance realizes itself with regard to animal food. The closest is perhaps "out of place," both because death and menstruation and childbirth must be distanced from the village to which they are declared not to belong and because—like a thunderclap in a clear sky or a frog in the house—they are known to occur but are not quite predictable.

It is possible to find other counterparts of the set of principles that go from ita hua oiressi, "we haven't seen them yet," to anomaly in the stricter sense. But they are even less numerous than in the case of natural phenomena considered in chapter 4 and in the summary of principles attempted in the previous section of this chapter. The fundamental reason for this difference in quantity that leaps into quality (since, as I have said, the principles—even that of anomaly—cannot be applied unchanged to extrabestiary and more generally extranatural phenomena) is that unfamiliar, unexpected, permanently irregular (anomalous) phenomena can mostly occur in a world distant because beyond human control and action: the world of thunder and sky, of upper and lower strata of the cosmos, of lords of the land and animals. Village life ultimately depends on this distant world and is threatened by its irregularities or novelties because it defies culturally shaped human knowledge as the main organon of defense.

While the same (dependence on this distant world) can be said of phenomena of the human body (birthing and death and so on), it cannot be said of many of the phenomena produced by human society. The equivalent of a thunderclap in a clear sky may be a sudden quarrel or explosion of violence. But these depend on forces and reasons that can be easily identified and countered and which anyhow do not imply a sense of generalized impotence. They therefore do not give rise to omens or taboos. And even less likely is the existence of a threatening anomaly in this social world, since it is produced and managed in a ritual context, as I have mentioned. Even truly mysterious anomalies—such as Hari's curious disgust for the Huaulu staple, sago—or somewhat less mysterious ones—such as mumanu (madness)—do not attract avoidances of the taboo type vis-à-vis one's fellow villagers.

We are at the right point now to stress a tendential difference between taboos principally motivated by phenomena that are not produced by human society (even if they are symbolically used by it) and phenomena that are. While in both cases taboo may generically be said to be due to a mismatch, to pairing phenomena that do not go well together, to the point of damage and destruction for the taboo-bearing subject, the reason for this mismatch may be quite different in each case. In the case of most animal taboos, the incompatible object is intrinsically so; the human subject has little power to turn it otherwise, because he does not produce it. In the case of most purely social taboos—that is, taboos that concern the association of terms which are equally produced by humans, the subject himself or fellow members of society—

incompatibility evokes less the sense of distance of the uncontrollable, the extrasocial, from the subject than an inappropriate conjunction of homogeneous terms.

In other words, taboo consists less in avoiding a poisonous, perhaps even persecuting, object than in combining things in the wrong way or not combining them or producing one in the wrong context (although the result is ultimately the same: encountering a "poison" at least as an effect). Naturally, this is just a pole that situates itself opposite the pole of principles that primarily cover the world of the forest, the sky, and the waters. Most taboos in fact are dynamically situated between the two, directly or indirectly, because the very idea of taboo seems motivated by the inevitable interaction of a humanly dominated order and an inhumanly dominated one.

And what about the equivalents of mixing taboos—that is, of improper mixtures due to human action rather than intrinsic mixtures found at the level of the species? The fear of mixing terms that are rooted in antithetical spheres analogous to those of up-in-the-trees and down-in-the-water (inland and sea,[47] living and dead, men and women,[48] and various forms of up and down)[49] is ultimately the underlying premise of many rituals. Ritual (i.e. highly appropriate) behavior either consists in avoiding such mixing or is a more complex defensive mode against it—a series of positive actions which are nevertheless encompassed, and therefore preferentially defined, by their negative counterparts. The *do not* defines a *do* by saying that avoiding the latter consigns one to the misfortunes it is supposed to neutralize.

For instance, the innumerable taboos of a shamanic ritual keep it going in the proper order, but the true subjective motivation for this going is the hope of resisting a degradation of the body that is in turn produced, one way or another, by the invasion of an incompatible object. So ultimately all nonobjectual taboos are grounded in objectual ones. They keep together a defensive whole which would otherwise have no efficacy. Of this artificial whole the cosmic whole, whose respect motivates the mixing taboos, is a counterpart but not a mere replica. Between different wholes complex transformations exist. To go into them would be to go into detailed analyses of rituals or ritualized interactions, which we cannot do, or redo, here.

Next, what about reversal taboos? As I have announced, these are much more numerous beyond the alimentary expression of the bestiary, because any reversal in the course of ritual action—particularly the reversal of a closing act—is the most extreme and visible subversion of order-building. A striking example is provided by sewa ninawani shamanism. If the shaman undoes his white headdress to reassume his red, ordinary one, he terminates the seance until the next night. It is taboo for him to return to it on the same evening, reknotting what he has just unknotted. Tabooed reversal can also take a spatial or, more exactly an orientational form,[50] such as carrying the corpse out of the house with his face looking backward toward the living left in it. This looking backward is an announcement of return, of the undoing of the funerary process through which the dead is supposed to have been irreversibly separated from the living and their village.[51] Any reversal of anything which is part of such movements from the undesired (or bad) to the desired (or good, or better) is taboo. But any reversal that guarantees return to the appropriate situation is not taboo; on the contrary, it is taboo not to do it. For instance, if a damar lamp falls across the floor down to the underhouse ground, it is prescribed, rather than proscribed, to eliminate the event by a reversing act of bringing the lamp back into the house. Moreover, the reversal may be required at the beginning of a process, in order to put a stop to it. For instance, if on leaving the house for a hunt, or a trip or whatever is long and dangerous, I "stumble" (taatime), I should immediately return home, thereby smothering the expedition at its birth. I shall try starting another one at some other time.

Tabooed reversals or inversions abound in the domain of kinship, perhaps because it is a field structured by hierarchy but also characterized by the movement of people through it over time with potential (or simply premature) exchange of their positions. So the right kinds and times of movement should be preserved where it is possible or necessary. An obvious example is the taboo on inverting the order of occurrence of ateha (the marriage ceremony, including payments, that brings about the incorporation of the wife)[52] for father and children and for senior and junior siblings. If a son went through the ateha before his father, he would take his father's position in the hierarchy by taking his position in which this fundamental kind of event is performed. Furthermore, he would assess his autonomy and priority relative to the father, since the father is not able to claim his children as his property if he does not perform the ateha. Analogously, he would exchange position with his senior brother were he to make the ateha before him. Such reversals are tabooed by tabooing the reversal of the timing of the ceremony that makes them possible. In fact, a further attempt at stressing any such reversal is the additional taboo that father and son, elder and younger sibling, should not ateha one after the other, but be mediated by the ateha of another lineage.[53] External equalization is thus used as a means of further internal unequalization—as a way of making seniors' position as impregnable as possible.

Another set of kinship taboos can be viewed not as taboos on reversal or inversion, but as taboos on equalizing what should remain intrinsically hierarchical. Such tabooed equalization consists in addressing or referring to parents, grandparents, and elder siblings in the same way they are allowed to address or refer to children, grandchildren, and younger siblings—namely by using the most intimate names, that is, the names given at birth (lala tuni, "true/original name"). This lack of reciprocity (taboo on one side, nontaboo on the other) contrasts with the negative reciprocity between in-laws, for both of whom the use of the lala tuni for the other is taboo. This reciprocal taboo fits the more general reciprocal reserve characterizing a relationship of tension and negotiation, such as alliance, rather than one of mere and unchangeable authority, such as that of consanguines of different generations.[54]

In sum, reversal seems to be the strongest manifestation of the subversion of order,[55] although sometimes it can even be a way of preserving it. The same eloquence of the extreme is also evident in what we found with some scarcity among food taboos (and perhaps even as a component of name-calling taboos): proximate difference. One striking example we found in the previous chapter was the taboo on mixing the meat of cuscus and birds, that is, the closest animals from the point of view of all oppositions and distinctions involved in the mixing taboos. Another example concerns the relationships of the Huaulu people with another one, Openg, which is considered historically close but still different—a point that often brings about puzzlement and argument and is always in need of determination. The situation is somewhat analogous to, but far more extreme than, that of the lineages inside Huaulu. When difference is just a comma in a similarity, then one must stick to that comma. Names, customs, and properties cannot be borrowed without risking an increasing loss of distinctive identity, either as lineage members or as niniani, "village" (i.e. ethnic group), members. I remember all the emphasis put on descriptions of the distinctive initiation rites abandoned by the people of Openg ("that would be taboo for us") and their still-living feast for the first time a child comes down from the house ("not just not our 'custom' [adat], but a taboo for us").

Another telling example of a taboo that arises from a preoccupation with proximate difference is the taboo on using the B.I. term *balai desa* to refer to the Huaulu luma potoam. The use is really a misuse, but the Huaulu's obvious preoccupation with it indicates the existence of a certain latent categorical opposition between sacred and profane. Indeed, as the Huaulu themselves point out, accepting this shift or claiming the equivalence of the two names means accepting the equivalence of two categories of village houses—one dedicated to the Memaha cult, the other to political encounters. It means, therefore, the loss of Huaulu difference—its dissolution into the wider colonial and postcolonial world of the Moluccas.

Another interesting example is the night kahua dance that characterizes the luma potoam. There are rules for who may dance side by side with each other and who may not. For "daughter-in-law" (hihina-

The luma potoam, or Huaulu "big house," is the village temple and ceremonial center, but it is taboo to refer to it with the Indonesian term *balai desa*. 1972. (Photo by V. Valeri.)

oto) and "father-in-law" (tameniam) and for son-in-law and "mother-in-law" (tameniam), it is strictly taboo, because proximity has sexual connotations, and these are incompatible with those relatives. The danger of proximate difference may also be behind the taboo on falling asleep near the leftovers of food, for sleeping and eating are the two main activities of life in the house. They should be kept apart in order to keep alive their distinct identity in the scheme of things. But also, and most important, sleep puts one in a vulnerable position near living beings that one has violated by eating and that are never completely reduced to inert matter. Bitten meat recalls the biting animal that takes its toll whenever it sees an opportunity. In other words, one fears a reversal here too: the eater may become eaten.

From all these examples one can infer that not only the cuscus-bird combination is one of the mixing taboos, but also most terms in a categorical relationship of proximate difference may pass as such.[56] The reason for this is that a collapse of categorical distinction is as significant and as possible in the combination of two categorical neighbors as it is in the combination of two categorical opposites. In other words, neighbors and enemies are crucial, but equally dangerous, terms of subject definition.

There seems to be enough evidence, at this point, to support generalizations that bring us beyond mere comparison. Reversal taboos are just the most extreme and thus visible manifestations of the ideal of completeness, in action and result. Indeed, if the action does not continue toward its end, it becomes incomplete to the point of self-annihilation. The taboo, then, suppresses the incomplete to sustain the complete, by sustaining the continuity of action. Another taboo that has the same effect is the mere premise of the reversal taboo—the interruption taboo.[57] Stopping in the middle of an action makes it momentarily or even permanently incomplete. Finally, a third consequence of the idea of completeness is the taboo on not including every thing or act that is the necessary part of the whole. In sum, completeness can take an enumerative and temporal form besides a directional one. Other kinds or aspects of completeness-sustaining taboos could be mentioned, but clearly the most important ones are sufficient for our comparison between principles of species taboos and principles of action taboos, with the principles of bodily taboos as intermediate.

But what about mixing taboos and proximate difference taboos? They presuppose not completeness in a plan of construction followed by human action, but integrity in a categorical system of large scale. In other words, the external object's limiting power over the subject is emphasized, especially, as we have seen, when the relationship with the object is alimentary. Although there is no necessary or even extreme separation of these two cases, they form a tendential pole: one that emphasizes human vulnerability to external objects that do not fit with it in the categorical framework and that the subject can flee but not control; the other that emphasizes the internal vulnerability of humans—that is, their potential failure to perform, alone or in cooperation, the rites or any other actions ruled by images of completeness.

Having said this, I feel ready to move into the last principle, which is, at this point, the most obvious and diffuse, without many differences in different fields or even between distance and closeness. I have called it the principle of experience—that is, that of any reason for following a taboo (or not following it) based on one's own direct experience or the experience of an ancestor from whom it derives. Encounters with occult powers (whether in dreams or direct vision), eating of certain objects with certain consequences, testing a general principle to find exceptions in particular cases, and so on—all these differences are apparently irreducible to one another. This ideological irreducibility should be taken seriously from the interpretive point of view, even if analytically it is obvious that individual invention is largely subordinated to collective presuppositions, for the sake of self-persuasion and the persuasion of others. It should be taken seriously because it allows the use of taboo as a self-specification in which the individual becomes a one-member species. In other words, a dimension of individualization, rooted in the ultimate unicity of experience,[58] is felt always to add as a legitimate potential to the ordinary one of classification.

The spectrum of taboo, in sum, parallels the tension between autonomy and heteronomy, which characterizes Huaulu social life when authority and power are involved.[59] Let me give just two illustrations. The first one is situated in the category of the young and is offered by the case already mentioned regarding Hari's individually asserted taboo on what would seem very odd to avoid—namely, the staple sago. Not to eat sago is to refuse some degree of commonality with practically all other Huaulu. The second illustration is situated in the category of the elderly of great experience, such as Kalahei, who claimed that there were no mixing taboos necessary between a number of birds and fish or crustaceans, on the basis of his own observation of the habits of those birds and his own daring alimentary experiences. Most people find this stress on one's individuality through stressing the individuality of relations between certain species too daring to be acceptable. Generalizations without exceptions, in any case, create a common practice on which one can rely—and which affords room for froggy people who do not wish or manage to let their differences stick out of the collective pond.

The most obvious area in which the principle of excessive similarity is applied beyond the animal kingdom is that of sexuality and its social enshrinement in marriage—what anthropologists (and I am an anthropologist) like to call the incest taboo. In fact the incest taboo partly complements, partly parallels, the taboo on eating dog meat, which I have repeatedly considered. In both cases, excessive similarity/closeness is strongly emphasized as the reason for the taboo, with the effect of making another, ultimate reason invisible. That is to say, closeness becomes a motivation for taboo only if it involves an activity (eating or sex) that is in blatant antithesis to other ones (friendship or kinship) that truly define the relationship between subject and object in these cases. Eating the dog (or simply killing or maiming it) is the most extreme form of antithesis to procuring food with the dog, which implies a pact of indissoluble friendship. Of course, one could ask why eating one particular dog really threatens the procuring of meat, since one can get more dogs to continue hunting. Why is it that the whole species is carried along, that one dog is never separated from all others, however different the sense of closeness to or distance from different ones?

The basic reason is that the relationship is so continuous and fundamental that it involves the subject's most general self-definition relative to it. I can be a species only relative to a species. This is true of wild species as well as domestic ones, although in very different degrees of generality with regard to self-definition. Hence, whatever the concrete feelings that may exist between a subject and his dog and any other dog, their differences do not count at the level of taboo. Taboo always turns a matter of degree at the level of perception and experience or even evaluation into a neat yes or no. I am either hunter or not; so I just do not eat dog meat or not.[60] And the alternative is purely theoretical, since being a Huaulu means being a hunter, directly as a man or indirectly as a woman. Women indeed may help men hunt minor game and not just consume it.[61]

In sum, the identification of the dog with the hunting it helps make possible, and thus with the entire form of life that defines the Huaulu, is a symbolic consumption of the animal. Such symbolic consumption is at odds with the alimentary one, for eating is destroying and thus undermining what one should permanently be. One does not eat what one is. And yet it is also true that one is what one eats because the dog has helped one to eat. It would seem, indeed, that the two inextricably bound mottoes find their point of coexistence in the difference of their point of application. If a possible food object, such as the dog, represents the subject in a relatively global form, then it is taboo. If it does so only by attributes or partial aspects, it is not. In the first case, the symbolic appropriation of the animal, not to mention its cooperation, is emphasized over the digestive one; in the second, vice versa.

Excessive closeness thus translates a complex process, including excessive distance of activity categories or general states that cannot be left out of its account. Game and hunter, meat and meat producer, enemy and friend, and so on, are founding oppositions that cannot be undermined by treating those who belong to one term as if they were of the other. In other words, it is taboo to treat the dog as food because it is identified as food maker, and as enemy because it is identified as friend. From this point of view, excessive closeness is not grounds for taboo as such and certainly not generically, but rather because it requires respect for an opposition in which subject and object participate. If the dog is very close to me as hunter, then going after it as if it were game would undermine the categorical opposition which allows me to feel very close to it (the dog). To identify the dog as a friend implies not treating it in a dissonant key, as an enemy one is free to pursue, and so on. All of which seems to point to the conclusion that taboo is due not to a metaphysical rejection of the summation of identicals, but to a preoccupation with preserving oppositions (enemy/friend) on which order is based. If the dog is too much like me in a certain respect, how can I treat it as completely different, to the point that it becomes a symbolically inert piece of meat? Stressing similarity, closeness, and so on, between two members of the same category, then, is also silently stressing their categorical differences from, indeed radical oppositions to and incompatibilities with, the members of opposite categories. The two operations are inseparable, since identity cannot be established by similarity alone.

Nevertheless, this preoccupation with difference in the preoccupation with similarity, or even identity, remains implicit for reasons I have already alluded to. The main reason is that the dog evokes a type, the hunter, with which the Huaulu closely identify. Moreover, dogs, just like cats, chickens, kept birds, and so on, escape a purely categorical assessment because one constantly lives with them, and they thus become friends in more than an abstract sense. Emotions, a sense of belonging to the same house, habits, and so on, bind their owners to them. And, of course, this emotional connection takes the forefront in representation, just as in motivation. Even so, it would never grow if it were not made possible by the antitheses I have alluded to.

This is also true of the sense of closeness from which the incest taboo alone is supposed to arise—by negation. What are the antitheses which hiddenly feed this closeness, and why does this closeness feed its negation in the field of sexuality? Obviously the two questions have one basic answer in common. It is precisely sexuality that gives shape to the antithetical relationship with the closest and most continuous stability—that provided from birth by consanguinity. The reason for this sense of incompatibility is that sexuality seems to provide affection and solidarity, just as kinship does, but in a fundamentally labile way. The intensive passion of a few months or even years may end up in its opposite, or in mere routine if the two lovers have become spouses. Sexuality, in sum, evokes ups and downs, and especially a sense of inner conflict between man and woman. This is or becomes a conflict between all allies when the relationship of two of their members is actually marital. In fact, the strongest opposition is that between marriage and consanguinity.[62]

From all these difficult, unstable relationships, which often border on fight even among groups, derives a stronger sense of the durability, unchangeability, and sense of identity which make kinship relations even more incompatible with sexual, not to speak of affinal, ones. Even psychologically, then, the idea of an extreme closeness that alone is said to motivate the incest taboo does not exist alone. What is destined to be incompatible with the sense of an extreme closeness, and thus indicates being quite distant, is already there as a source of that sense. There is thus a psychological circle that reinforces a stated categorical one. The elements of passion and discord, or even renovation, that sex and especially marriage bring cannot be introduced into a relationship that is supposed to remain steady and reliable forever. Just as I cannot eat a dog without breaking the relationship with it forever, so I cannot have sex or even marriage with a sister without breaking or undermining what I can expect and request from her forever (as a consanguine).

It would be erroneous, however, to see the antithesis between consanguine and affine as one of good and bad, or to exchange a total incompatibility of individuals in those contrasting categories with a total incompatibility of the two categories as applying to shifting individuals. What I am referring to here is the positive counterpart of the negative incest taboo. Consanguinity is unchanging in its positive and negative senses. One can always trust it, and one always searches the expression of unchangeability relative to the tradition through it. But such unchangeability also means an inability to react to new conditions. Alliance thus introduces an external, even if traditional, element which legitimizes changes at least in the sense that it shows the different virtues of people who compete in order to realize the reproduction of the lineage under their name. In other words, there is an implicit opposition between a static, purely internal reproduction of consanguinity, which ultimately undermines it, and an externally mediated reproduction through marriage. The dynamism of the latter is a positive justification for the incest taboo, which is then both a way to keep consanguinity out of a practice that undermines it and a way to ensure its reproduction by incorporating female nonconsanguines who give consanguines (in the form of children) to their husbands.

In this sense, there is an obvious parallelism between the taboo on eating the dog and the taboo on "eating" the sister. Just as endophagy would make exophagy impossible, so endogamy would make exogamy impossible. In both cases, the laziness of not looking out—for keeping the body in life and for reproducing it—would reduce the possibility of staying alive in its fullest sense. Ideologically speaking, one emphasizes the negation of intimacy, because this allows one to reinforce consanguinity as an object of respect at the same time as one secures renovating adventure. The sense of parallelism between the two cases, but also the primacy of hunting, is indicated by the venatorial images of sexual pursuit.

Both cases, then, show that excessive similarity is a motive for taboo only with regard to certain crucial activities (eating and sex) which are incompatible with excessive similarity between subject and object, pursuer and pursued. The reasons for this incompatibility are the extreme distance between certain categories, not just extreme similarity. But such extreme categorical distance is not outside the realm of desire. Inside that realm, such distance may produce an even keener sense of similarity between subject and wrong object, and thus it is this sense of similarity that is the reason for taboo. It certainly is, but let me insist once again that it would not be without a sense of extreme categorical distance (incompatibility) between one relationship (e.g. kinship closeness) and another (e.g. sexual pursuit).

That excessive similarity as a source of taboo implies its contrary[63] is also shown by the case of taboos due to excessive closeness to origins. These are very similar to taboos on original or recent encounters with occult powers considered "exceptionally distant" (but having become much closer through a pact). The only major difference that has pushed me to classify them on two opposite sides of a rather rough and provisional divide is that, once again, one kind of taboo emphasizes difference even if it recognizes its diminution, whereas the other—excessive closeness to origins—emphasizes closeness due to direct, even if temporally more and more distant, origin from these powers.

The most obvious point of transition from one side to the other is provided by the so-called totemic species[64] or any object which stands for the origin of the subject by way of descent directly or indirectly (that is, through full incorporation by adoption or marriage).[65] As I have explained at some length, the representations of origin and descent from such beings, not to mention their relationship with the species that stand for them, are usually irreducible to totemism as practiced elsewhere or imagined by anthropologists. More often than not, such beings are connected with origins because of originary encounters which shape and continue to condition the mode of being of those who identify their essence with them. This is precisely why, by an apparent paradox, their case is not so different from that of beings which are still considered too distant and yet have made themselves closer through a voluntary encounter.

This closeness creates its own dangerousness, which is that of a vindictive return to an excessive distance, where the ultimate dangerousness (because of uncontrollability) lies. Put otherwise: if the being sees that a pact is broken, it returns to its former enemy status or actualizes it if it was only potential. In the case of "totemic" taboos, there is hardly such a return: or else it is not emphasized, because the relationship was established long ago, at the stage in which irreducible identity took shape through a variety of encounters that froze encountered objects out of consumption simply because they became semisubjects. Time, in fact, has made them even more so. Hence it is closeness, indeed identity, that is seen as the fundamental motive for the taboo, not difference into which one can easily fall back. Yet this difference is also present, at least as a radical loss of self, precisely because these totemic taboos are identity taboos. The transitional point between the two series, in sum, allows us to see even better, and in any case to start proclaiming, that the two series can be constructed not because each is characterized by one term (e.g. excessive distance/similarity) to the exclusion of its opposite (excessive closeness/difference), but because either term dominates to the point of hiding the opposite it needs in order to be dangerous.

That mere summation of similars or identicals is not in itself a source of taboo is also demonstrated by its dependence on the initial value of what is added. If it is good for certain purposes, then, far from being taboo, its reinforcement by summation becomes a magical prescription. If it is bad, then its reinforcement by summation makes it even worse, and thus taboo. An example of the latter is the eating of peanuts (which are dry) when one has a dry cough—a negative state, the fate of which one wants to diminish by the addition of an opposite quality, and not to increase by the addition of an identical quality. An example of the opposite (summation of identicals is positive) is smearing the fat of tekepatola (the most biting of all snakes) on a bush knife to increase its "sharpness" (moiya).[66]

We must distinguish, finally, positive and negative summation. Only negative summation gives rise to taboo. Moreover, it seems that summation has something in common with eating and its fundamental discriminatory criteria—namely, reinforcing highly valued qualities of the body by eating foods that carry those qualities. One could even say that in the most generic sense, much good eating—and some bad eating—is subject-object summation. To return to the patola python, it is optimal food for hunters, since it allows them to increase their ferocious hunters' hearts. Likewise, good eating for a mother who has just given birth is the meat of a kapupu, a cuscus female, like herself. It will add milk to milk, thereby making it more abundant for the mother at the time when this is necessary. Plants that grow quickly will add to the quickness of babies' growth.

Beyond a certain point, though, similarity summation through eating or other forms of intimate relationship between subject and object is dangerous and thus a source of taboo. Where is the point passed? Probably at that of form. The obvious case is the dog as, among other things, an animal with a number of somatic characteristics reminiscent of humans. And maybe also a degree of anthropomorphism explains why a number of plants which have palmlike or palm composite leaves (reminiscent perhaps of the hands of humans) are taboo at least for shamans and trap owners—that is, people who live in the dangerously intermediate border between human and nonhuman and must therefore be more careful than others in approaching and using objects that stand on the same border.

There are other forms of summation, or rather of coexistence of excessively close beings, that motivate taboos. One of them is that of powerful identicals, namely sewaem. More than one cannot be in the body of a shaman at the same time; however, the shaman may call them at the same time in defiance of the tremendous danger of becoming their battlefield. This case introduces a much more general one. Force, within the subject relative to other subjects or to objects, is a criterion that transcends the categorical one. Or rather, it allows the run of the risks involved in such attempts at transcendence. Interestingly enough, the postulate of a certain amount of force and competition among people introduces fundamental distinctions among different cases of relationships with the very close or identical. While it is taboo to have sex with and marry a sibling or any other consanguine, it is not taboo to kill him or her. The latter is referred to as piniassi, "not beautiful," but not as maquwoli, "taboo." We shall have to return below to the noncorrespondence between force and categorization.

We may end this section with what seems to be the most dangerous pairing with the excessively close—a pairing with a replica of oneself. Such a replica should be avoided, its production made impossible, and, if not, it will be necessary to confront the results of a loss of identity. To the traditional and more limited kinds of replication new ones have been added, with the result of further feeding the misoneistic taboos. These new ones are images produced with cameras, videos, and tape recorders. The presence of these tools and their results is tabooed, at least during important events, when people are more vulnerable, because the original, the true, loses itself, becomes indistinguishable from something else that looks like it. Hence the idea that the camera catches and assumes control of the "soul" (mattiulu). One's soul becomes confused with the image—and is carried away with it.

Traditional forms of dangerous replication[67] are: using the same name (since the name is made to coincide with the totality of the person or thing); acting in an "as if" form vis-à-vis somebody (since this postulates an image that superimposes itself on him—for instance, treating him as a dead person); lighting at the same time two damar lamps in a single house; watching (thereby giving them reality by recognition) "dark sunset clouds" (eteli), which are supposed to be images of one's parents, so that they will die if they are not already ancestors. Through all these forms of replication, the death or destruction of the replicated will ensue, since it will become impossible to distinguish it from its supposedly animated portraits. This is precisely why the association with an excessively close thing or person, coming to the point of identity, means death and must therefore be taboo in the extreme. Here again, nothing like danger of summation, but a danger of confronting with replication, which removes as much of me as it replicates or makes its connection with me much less firm.

It is about time to stop the free but complicated meanderings made possible by the comparison of principles. I feel that enough ground has been covered kangaroo-style (perhaps because I wished to finish this book in Australia), moving from spot to spot and leaving out the grounds of so many taboos. But before turning to completion through generalization rather than empirical enumeration, I feel that I have to give a telling ethnographic response to any possible accusation of having seen too many principles because of too little principle in my review of taboo. The Huaulu themselves may not search for abstractions, if by that we mean equivalents for words like those we like to employ in anthropology, but they do in fact formulate taboos in ways that reflect certains principles and certain forms of generalization. There are even forms of "concrete abstractions," as I like to call them—that is, uses of empirical qualities of rather general character, that is to say, attributes that lend themselves to the expression of general ideas.

The most obvious and important case is that of colors. When colors are invoked, they are invoked as if they were the only reason for taboo, but in fact color is a reason in which many others are usually condensed. Indeed, the very contrast and formulation of excessive similarity and excessive difference as the most encompassing principles of taboo are suggested in chromatic form. For instance, Patakuru told me that the mixing of cassowary and sau (pandanus) is taboo because the two have radically opposite colors (red and black). But he attributed the same effect to the combination of two identically colored animals (makila plus eel), both of which are "multicolored" (likalika).[68] Of course this is only a supplementary explanation, since creatures of the trees and creatures of the water are generically taboo to combine. But for some exceptionalists (such as Patakuru or Kalahei) this explanation is the only one that really persuades them not to eat that particular bird or marsupial together with that particular seafood. Or there is a stronger reason which is, obviously, much more extreme than the topological one (up in the trees, down in the water)—extreme because color is found everywhere and can therefore express a much more general idea of incompatibility (even if more selective) than that expressed by vertical location (space).

Colors, moreover, stand for certain obvious categories and represent their interconnection in semi-abstract form. For instance, red is usually connected with males because it is primarily connected with the blood of hunting and that of headhunting. Hence it is taboo for women to be associated with it. It is also taboo for young males before they have killed large game—if not a human as a sacrifice. Only afterwards can they wear red cloth, particularly in the form of the turban, which marks them as full men. Alternatively, they may wear the red turban of manhood after having their first steady sexual relationship with a girl, namely after having established some control over her potentially fertile blood. That red is usually associated with males is confirmed by frequent remarks on its extension to the most humanly invested animals. Male cassowaries, for instance, are said to have reddish feathers, whereas females have blackish-bluish ones. And the tekepatola's head is red in its male (mossani) form, black in its female (inani) form. As for varied colors and textures, they are particularly prone to taboo because they lend themselves to representing the idea of mixture and confusion of opposites. But because this mixture may in fact be

The latunusa ("lord of the land") instructs young men dancing in the village square during the initiation ceremony. All of the cloth worn by initiates is red. 1972. (Photo by V. Valeri.)

exceptionally sought after in ritual contexts, it may also be mandatorily associated with red. This was certainly the case in headhunting rituals, which were in fact sacrificial ones. For instance, a leaf from a special red plant (sole) and one from a plant (suli) which is the epitome of the multicolored had to be put together with a severed head. And the two plants had to be planted on one side of the luma potoa, which was the seat of the head offering and is still the seat of the dance feast that once followed that offering (and is now performed at male initiations). Moreover, in all romuromuem tales, which narrate the process of resurrection and rejuvenation supposedly practiced in ancient times, one finds the same association: red bantam at the feet of the corpse, multicolored hen at the head.

In sum, the red of men and the multicolored of what stands at the boundaries of opposites are closely associated, because multicolor represents something that can be a mediation of extreme opposites if controlled by the blood-shedding activities of one side—the male one. All of which seems to suggest that color is not an elementary and further unanalyzable reason for taboo, but a sign of deeper reasons. And it is a sign both of a native attempt at abstraction and in the ordinary sense (for an anthropologist) of a carrier of multiple unaware or unstated associations. The native translation of taboo motivations into color motivations is thus a systematizing and abstracting effort which points to the same interpretive path we have taken and justifies our favorite talk of "concrete abstraction."[69]

Conclusions and Additions 1: Logic and Pragmatics

It is time to draw a few, but important, conclusions from the few, but not indifferent, facts and principles considered. What holds all those principles together, if anything? Throughout the book I have insisted on what the Huaulu themselves insist upon when they speak of their endless taboos and their deep preoccupation with them: avoiding the consequences of taboo violation. I have, of course, not gone as far as the Huaulu in confusing the reasons that taboos exist with the reasons for following them. The confrontation with the reasons that so many specific taboos exist seems to have revealed a subtler, more hidden, but no less strong, reason for their existence as a whole.

What is this reason? Primarily, taboos abound to help maintain a global order of which the subject is as much a part as the object. The subject cannot therefore violate the taboo without violating itself. However central the subject's position is, however anthropomorphic this anthropocentric order is, it is an order in which the subject does not rule and can advance for a while only by knowledge and avoidance or remedy or precaution. But what kind of knowledge? A knowledge of incompatibility between subject and object inside the classificatory and augmented order of which they are both part. Such incompatibility is due to the attribution of qualities and values, which may be learned from tradition or from experience or even by experiment. But it is hardly total. It usually exists relative to certain forms of consumption—eating, having sexual intercourse, and so on—and more generally to certain forms of contact—speech (talking of something, naming it, and thus putting it in one's mouth), touch, looking at, laughing at or about, and so on. Such forms of interaction with or consumption of certain objects are ruled out not only because these objects carry values and attributes at odds with the subject's own, but also because they make a profound ambivalence possible. As I have shown, closeness or distance may be emphasized, but each coexists with its contrary and may be mixed up with it. Hence there is instability—dangerousness for the subject's symbolic existence.

The forays beyond the bestiary have also taught us, however, that there is more in taboos than a reference to the external, objectual world on which the subject sustains itself by consuming what is appropriate and in the way it is appropriate. The subject is not just part of a classificatory order with animals and plants; it is also part of an order which is essentially human, internal to society and its acts. And the subject participates in that order by much more than the avoidance it entertains with food species—fleeing from them or keeping them away. Such avoidance is an avoidance of inappropriate consumption, whereas an avoidance centered on openly social acts is an avoidance of inappropriate performance. This means that taboo is, in this case, the negative and protective counterpart of a positive and assertive part. Taboo signals that one should not avoid engaging in certain actions but should, in fact, perform them appropriately. The appropriate way is a complete one; that is, it contains all the acts and words and so on that are necessary for proper function. Moreover, completeness also implies the idea of order, since something is ordered only if it misses nothing and if everything exists in the right position in space and time.

In sum, the comparative study of taboo seems to reveal, or to make much clearer, two fundamental poles in the subject's subordination to order. One pole emphasizes object consumption and determines which object is compatible or incompatible with the subject. The other one emphasizes the subject's performative ability or competence and determines which actions are compatible with which others and with which other participants. The former pole involves the subject's subordination to an order felt as external to society, one to which society (or the subject as its member) must conform in his or her consumption, particularly in his or her alimentary consumption. The latter pole implies the subject's subordination to an artificial, man-made order internal to Huaulu society. This—and the fact that many acts of which the internal order consists are ritual responses to the threatening phenomena of the outside world or of the body as participating in it—shows that the external order is felt to be more encompassing than the internal one. Although human order is at the center of the cosmos and is a response to it, that order is in the end dominated by the cosmos just as it is contained in it. Hence, any adequate form of relationship with the cosmos requires an adequate knowledge of it and the inference of what forms of contact and behavior are necessary.

One may be tempted to reduce one pole to the other, mostly in reducing the consumption of an inappropriate object to the inappropriate performance of a ritual or any other formally marked activity, since all taboos have to do with kinds of activities. But these activities are more or less loaded with objects or with subjects and are characterized by complexity or simplicity. Eating is conceived as a simple activity; thus its main characteristic is the choice of an object. A funeral, on the contrary, has much to do with adequate action: if it is done properly in all its aspects it guarantees success, that is, that the dead will keep away. Even more characterized by adequate performance are the male initiation ritual and the kahua feast connected with it. Furthermore, these activities correspond to different degrees of human control: at one extreme, mere avoidance of an external phenomenon in whose existence and form one has no part; at the other, avoidance of error in the activity that makes it possible to cope with the phenomenon, or error even in an activity without any such purpose. The reduction of pole to pole is self-contradictory, because such reduction demonstrates the possibility of taboos born owing to identity as against those born owing to difference, since there is no need to maintain difference or resist it.

The claim that all taboos have to do with performance may thus be true in an irrelevant or simplified sense.[70] They concern performance in different degrees and cannot therefore all be defined by the performance concept alone. Moreover, even performative acts can be viewed as acts of consumption, not only because ritual acts use objects extracted from the world, but because many (if not most) such acts have safe consumption (including the ability to pursue its conditions, such as hunting or headhunting) as their final aim. Drawing the contrast between consumption and performance is thus necessary in order to analyze and classify taboos. The frequent inseparability of these two types of taboos in concrete interaction should not be confused with the possibility of equating them or, moreover, with the reduction of the sphere of eating to the sphere of performance. This simplistic, forced reduction impoverishes interpretation rather than enriching it. As I mentioned, performative views are more appropriate for subject-object relations largely constituted by human action and are thus intrinsically temporal.[71] They are much less appropriate for taboos of a cosmological or experiential sort, which imply the predominance of relationships with a frozen and ultimately unknown world in which animals and occult powers swarm and mix. This is why, incidentally, the overtly universal character of taboo, namely negative expression, takes a more literal form in food taboos than it does in taboos that define the performance of ritual actions.[72] If eating is conceived as a success or a failure of performance, then it must be stressed that success in this kind of performance consists in making the right choice of the materials eaten. Doing is prevalently doing *not* by one's choice but rather as dictated by a situation one has not made or chosen. Yet it is not an instance of cuisine (a creative combination of objects that stimulates eating), but a collection of defensive and also identifying negations, that defines the subject as eater. Fortunately subjects do not exist merely by not eating, yet the acceptance of this negation constitutes a crucial and primordial act, performed daily, which makes it possible for them to exist.[73]

That consumption cannot be dissolved into performance is further and perhaps even better shown by the Huaulu tendency to use part-whole relationships in very different ways.[74] Consumption taboos often operate on the principle that one part, or a limited number of parts, can stand for the whole. Quite the contrary for performance taboos, which, as we have already mentioned, tend to imply that the maintenance of the whole requires the maintenance of all its parts and in a given temporal, spatial, and social order. The reason for this difference is the form of existence assumed by the whole. In one case, the whole exists by itself, "naturally," and the issue is thus the avoidance of its undoing by humans through consumption. In the other case, the whole exists only as a complete set of exclusively human acts. While taboo keeps the whole intact in both cases, it does so by bringing it into existence in one case and by not bringing it out of existence in the other. In other words, what exists through a human act does not exist if the subject does not act fully and properly. Put differently, the same acts that make objects exist are also negations of what makes them not exist; acts that make the object lose its existence, in part or in whole, cannot in turn bring it into existence. In one case, taboo guarantees a form of making; in the other case, it guarantees the partial or full loss of beings whose existence is not produced by humans or necessary for human existence.

The relationship of parts and whole tends to be different in the two cases precisely because in one case existence does not precede human intervention, whereas in the alimentary consumption of wild animals it does. In the case of eating, what is taboo is what is made to stand for the whole to which it belongs. By being equivalent to this whole, the not eaten *x* makes the rest of the parts edible. In the case of a whole that exists only or mainly by human action,[75] it is not sufficient (or much less often so) to produce its most important parts, those that are most symbolic of the whole. In one case, the whole exists only by human action, and cannot thus be thought to exist in full without full human creation. In the other case, the whole has its own autonomous existence. Humans do not make it but may threaten it by their acts of unmaking (consumption). The paradox revealed by this contrast is that the connection between parts and whole is predominantly symbolic in the domain of consumption (especially eating) and predominantly factual in the domain of execution.[76] To preserve a purely human creation in its entirety one must not jump over certain of its defining parts, as one can when it is a "natural" (animal, vegetal, etc.) creation that is involved in taboo. The apparently paradoxical consequence is that the symbolic relationship of part and whole is stressed in the consumption of natural objects, whereas it is not in the performance of artificial ones. Naturally, the contrast is more typological than empirical.

Eating may be part of a complex ritual, and a complex ritual may have eating as its final (and finally established) act.[77] Even so an underlying tendential contrast between consumption of the given and production of the nongiven must be recognized in order to account for the range of applications of taboo. We have already seen some manifestations of this contrast, but the part-whole manifestation is the main one, since it corresponds to two implicit definitions of the whole: an order of succession in time and of coexistence in space which is exclusively constituted by humans; and an order exclusively inherent to the world, but whose implications for human consumption must be limited to parts particularly evocative of the whole and its relatively mutual relationship with the human world.[78]

I have often been impressed by the deliberate expression of totality: by a gesture that moves up and down a whole body or object and whose repetition combines space and time. But this image of totality may be used for subtraction rather than addition; it may simplify the range of taboos rather than keeping its complexity or even adding to it. For when the interconnection of all parts in a whole is stressed, then one can as well say that some parts guarantee the achievement of the whole or that all parts are, on the contrary, necessary for it. In fact, the apparently contradictory coexistence of the two views permeates the field of taboo. We have seen how often certain parts can stand for the whole when one has to find out what to eat without danger. We could say the same of more complex actions, such as rituals, although the risk is much greater in them, precisely because of their complexity. This is why totality in an enumerative sense is stressed in them. It also allows us to speak a posteriori of failure to follow certain taboos in order to account for the failure to obtain those ends for which the ritual was performed.

The duality of the part-whole relationship, and thus the coexistence principles of economy and waste in the determination of taboos of performance and consumption, should be investigated in depth. But this would require detailed analysis of sufficiently diverse taboo-governed acts. Here, I can only remind the reader of how pervasive the principles of economy of food taboos are. I call them principles of economy not because they presuppose an agent who maximizes profit (or minimizes loss), but because they are the necessary tempering correlate of principles of taboo that tend to extend too far to make eating possible. So the vast extension of these principles and the limitations of human consumption are stressed at the same time as one escapes them or makes certain members of society escape more than others. Indeed, the "economy" in the use of taboo-generating principles takes the form of differentiating the eaters and not just the eaten.

I must remind the reader, very briefly, of the logic of limitation that is part of the generation of food taboos. It is not just that the various principles were encountered separately in the course of the analyses in chapter 4, but also that a summary is necessary in order to show that the same logic is used to limit the application of taboos that it has already helped to generate and that this logic offers a respite from the

Huaulu's increasing sense of burden under the rule of taboo, and also from the as yet unchanged view that they exist by and because of those taboos.

It should be obvious that by creating unequal closeness or distance between things the conceptual, symbolic, and experiential apprehension of the world creates the possibility of unequal application of the principle of substitution. Two things that are close together make it possible to treat one as the equivalent of the other, and thus as its substitute in relationship to all others. The degree of this closeness and substitutability changes with the others to which they are referred. Thus one needs no fixed and no "strong" principle of order to construct the two complementary faces of taboo and limitation. Nevertheless, it should also be obvious that the more involved a principle of order is, the stronger the consequences for subjects in relationship to objects. Either no substitution is possible, or no change is possible in what the substituting—or substitutable—terms are. I hope that this was shown, once again, by the most classificatory parts of Huaulu taboos, particularly by that of the three-tiered cosmos or the cosmos that depends on the structuration of space centered on the village and its opposition to the forest and more generally the outside world. In sum, classification implies much more rigid repression than mere experience does. It implies that the world forms a whole and that such a whole should not be undermined by freely playing with its parts, as confirmed by tradition—that is, the collective experience of the past consigned to the present and shown by the present to be homogeneous with the experience of the ancients.

The importance of classification in establishing the idea and importance of the whole should not suggest, however, that there is no whole without classification. On the contrary, wholes are part of the everyday experience of concrete bodies, locations, stones, parts of the forest, and are properties of objects made by humans—houses, bows, arrows, and loincloths. They are also part of any appropriate action that we like to put under the name of ritual and which the Huaulu punctuate with that of maquwoli. When any mental act of value attribution (dependent or not on classification) creates the idea of what these wholes and their integrity should actually be, taboo enters into its offensive/defensive play. In other words, there is a complex, reciprocal interaction between the mental apprehension of the form (natural or humanly produced) of an object and the human actions (consumption and production) involved in it. A natural object on which human values are projected because of its form and texture becomes a whole to be protected in its entirety, in a literal or nonliteral sense. The literal sense concerns all the parts of the object: they are equally taboo. The nonliteral sense implies either the subject or the object alone, or both, and may imply that either a single part (the only one to be taboo) or the whole except for one part is treated as equivalent to the whole.

An instantiation of these attributions and equivalences based on the part-whole apprehension was already furnished above by the example of large game. A pig is perceived and treated as a quasi-human person, a whole that exists only as such and in a rather individual form relative to zoological classification, since it hardly belongs to a higher class (except the extremely vast and generic one of peni). So it is a whole that must in some way be kept entire, but only relative to a subject—the hunter killing it—who, in turn, stands for the whole consuming population. His denial of the act of appropriation is supposed to efface the act of killing and thus fictitiously preserve the whole of the pig's life. But this equivalence of part and whole coming from the subject's side is too weak; an "objective" one is needed. As we have seen, parts of the body (upper part of the head, blood) that stand for the whole are returned to the animal principle and as such allow the reconstitution of the animal, if not its continuous existence in the eyes of such a principle (part of the "lord of the land" that "owns" the animal). In sum, two corresponding parts—in the consumer and consumed domain—stand for a whole body that requires integrity just like that of the humans. But there are cases where it is the whole that must literally stay intact, or where the whole is consumable by only a small part of the population (a sister incorporated into another lineage and her children).[79]

Certain parts of the body of the pig or other large animals are more evocative of the whole because of their recognizable shape and position (the head), uniform presence through it (blood), and apparent vital function inside (not only blood but also the parts of the maraissi which must be offered to the conveyors of life in society, that is, women given out). The taboos on these parts therefore confirm that the preservation of the whole motivates them and that differences in the ability to evoke the whole, without actually undermining its consumption, are the main reason for choosing them. But the service of parts as apt substitutes for the whole may depend on criteria that are not so transparent, and thus appear as much more arbitrary or economically motivated. Further transparence, however, can be found in the exclusively human world of the village. There, one house may be seen as structurally equivalent to all others, although not all are seen as equally equivalent to the ideal house and therefore to the village in which only such houses should be built (and still were through my last fieldwork there). The existence of this equivalence makes it possible for a house to substitute for all others with regard to certain taboos directly concerning them and more generally concerning the taboos of the inhabitants (since house and inhabitants are equivalent, and house is the materialized whole of their relations). An obvious example is the luma maquwoliam. The name of this house—the house of taboo—has become even more appropriate recently than it ever was before, because it keeps more and more of the stock of taboos relating to the principle of misoneism for the rest of the village. (The principle is not uniform, however, since similar houses exist for each of the "village parts" [ipae] and not for the village as a whole.) The luma maquwoliam will always follow the fundamental principle of being built away from running water (river or sea), which washes away mountain essence and brings to it, in opposite movement, overseas essence. And it will cease to exist, bringing Huaulu traditional existence to expiration, if there is any future use of electricity, which was explicitly said in Huaulu conversation when the idea was presented to them because of the imminent arrival of logging companies.

I have evoked these examples to explain both the motivations and the possibilities of the equivalence of parts and whole. Such equivalence is made possible in them by analogies and made necessary by the conflict between action (tangibility) for purposes of consumption and nonaction (intangibility), that is, nonconsumption of certain beings on which human life depends. The equivalence of part and whole thus implies another paradox: their disconnection from the concrete point of view of the acting subject. The examples therefore show the compromise and the tense character in the subject's recourse to part-whole equivalence. This character explains the extreme diversity and modifiability of such equivalences, particularly where they are not much fixable in unmodifiable structural differences and where sociologically expressive or practical motivations dominate. We have seen examples of both in chapter 4, but let us look at a few more examples, more revealing ones.

A particularly striking case I saw developing over the years, although it became quite apparent and was specifically theorized by most Huaulu during my last sojourn there, is that of "cloves" (pukalawa; B.I.: cengkih). Traditionally, the cultivation of such plants characterized the central and northern Moluccas, which largely lived on the trade of their cloves. The Dutch destruction of the populations that cultivated clove trees (especially in the Hoamoal Peninsula) and the flight of the survivors eastward into the island's interior may have motivated the Huaulu's refusal to identify with their practices, although these fleeing people may have included the ancestors of the Huaulu. In a sense, tabooing the cultivation of cloves was a way to reject the coastal world and its perils under the domination of the Dutch colonial power. In a way that is not totally unusual, a Huaulu taboo concurred with the dangerous colonial "order," at least until 1864. But the taboo existed and survived to define Huaulu identity in contrast with those coastal people who had cultivated cloves and, after independence, returned to cultivating them as their main source of commercial life. When I first did fieldwork in Huaulu (in the early seventies) I heard of the taboo on cultivation and even consumption only for a number of ritual specialists who are in stronger connection with the past than ordinary people are. My subsequent trips back in the eighties showed that the clove tree was becoming increasingly important.

The process was started by the son of the Dutch-designated kamara, who, after his father's death, seemed ready to innovate when money was involved. One of his daughters died in the lilipossu, and this awful misfortune was interpreted by some members of the public as demonstrating the validity of the taboo. But he continued cultivating cloves and denied that his misforune was related to his new form of cultivation (no words from him or his family about that death). The counterexperience was provided by the amount of money he made and the growth of the clove trees that made it. The more money became important (relatively speaking), the more people started a few trees in their old gardens or along paths to the village. During my last stay, I saw a fair amount of cloves drying on mats before various houses—signs of a conversion to cultivation that came out in visual fact if not in words. But, at the same time, people were talking about it and attempting to justify it to me, knowing that I had known a different past and different words. They admitted that it had been considered (and was still seen so by some) a dangerous activity that risked death (by falling from trees, and so on), but they pointed to their own supposedly accident-free experience. In other words, it was worth running the risk of taboo violation to find out if the tradition was correct or continued to be so in changing times.

Some people told me that the ancestors must have been wrong, but it was only in recent times that their descendants had the occasion to doubt them and experiment with cloves. But others, especially those who were a priori excluded because of their function and the houses they inhabited, pointed out that the kamara's experience should be a warning to them, since the death of his daughter was terrible. The response of others to this argument was that she died not because her father cultivated cloves, but most probably because of incest. The response to the response was obviously that reasons combine. And so continues the subterranean flow of arguments, which here are principally oriented, as frequently happens nowadays, by interest and the varying possibilities of realizing it. Many people are nevertheless still fearful that the violation of a capital taboo and the partial overlap with the coastal world of trade will have bad consequences like the misfortune traditionally expected. For there are cases when that has happened.

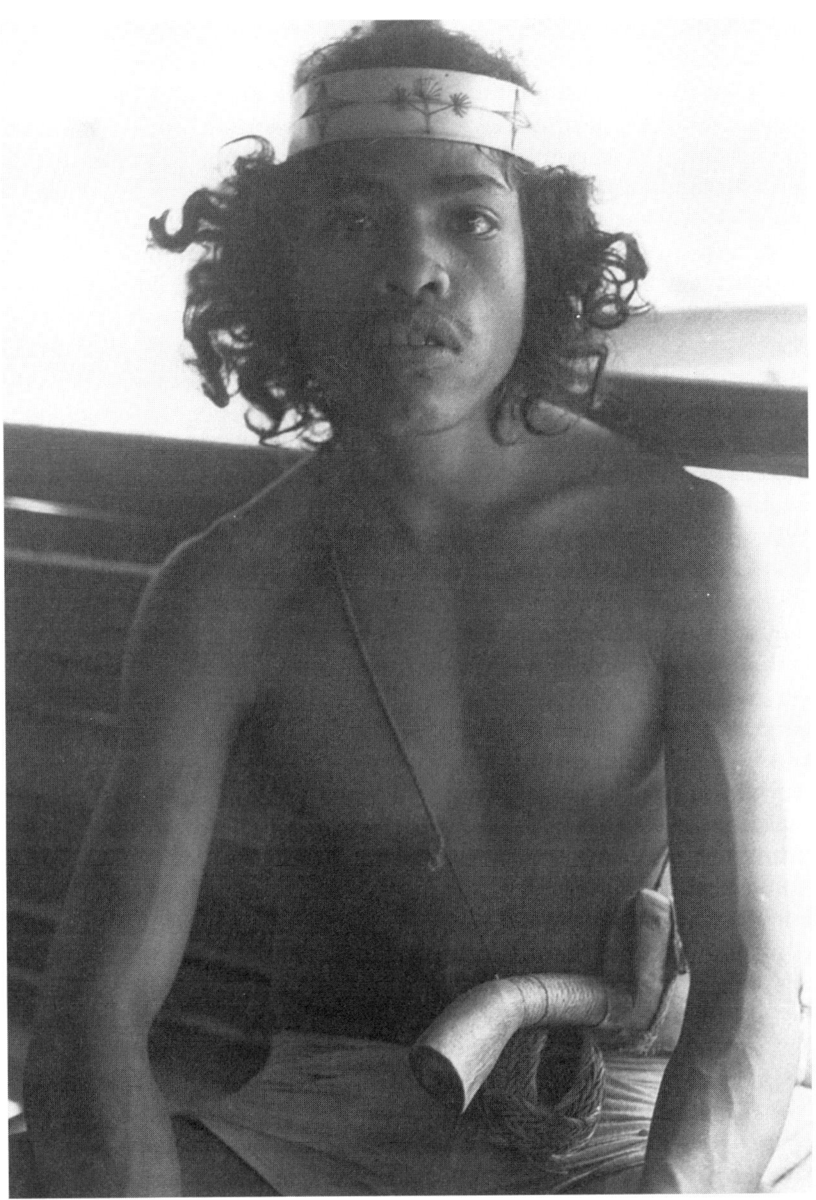

This young man of the Huaulu clan has just been inititated (as is shown by his carved bamboo headband) and told not to continue his studies along the coast. 1972. (Photo by V. Valeri.)

One case that I know well, and the reader already has a memory of it to build on, was the violation of the taboo on literacy even beyond the sending of some children to primary school. The man who had been kepala soa (B.I.: "head of the clan," an administrative office of the local Indonesian government) during my earliest fieldwork had decided to send his brightest son to secondary school in Wahai (the district headquarters). Before long, the boy was struck down by what we would call an accidental death (he fell from a truck). The entire family, who had all moved to the coast to send the children to school and adapt to the newly forming world of Indonesia, interpreted this death as a sign of the seriousness of the taboo they had violated. By provoking the death of their young descendant, the ancestors made very clear that they did not want anybody to move away from Huaulu. For the father, this meant that even the compromise situation of Alakamat had to be abandoned. The children were all taken out of primary school, and the family returned to the mountain village—the only true Huaulu—for good. From their point of view, they had to return to the original place because they had to return to the full Huauluness it still represented.

In other words, a further extension of the part for the whole made it even more vulnerable and open to nullification in all its dimensions, including the lowest and more fictitious ones (primary schools teach very little beyond working for the teacher and a few things that do not always penetrate Huaulu heads or stay in them for a long time). True reading and writing, in sum, remain taboo. Indeed, the taboo was often reformulated as a taboo on moving to middle school to become truly literate. It is clear that the taboo on literacy has been run around through a number of part and whole relations with a number of additions relative to those exemplified by the previous alimentary example. For instance, the children who do not go to school make up a decreasing part that stands for an increasing one (i.e. those who *do* go do so invisibly, because they are made up for by those who don't go). We have here relationships between proportions, one of which must stand for the whole on increasingly fragile grounds. It is even more difficult for all those who do not go beyond primary school to function as the whole that allows a very small part to do so. For this semiliterate part can hardly function as the ideal whole of the Huaulu that must be taken care of (i.e. illiterate culture), because they themselves are made possible by the decreasing part that has the closest relationship with that ideal whole (the fully illiterate).

The part that stands for the whole, making antiwhole exceptions possible, is becoming less and less noticeable to the occult powers presiding over such a whole, which makes its contrary increasingly noticeable and thus more open to attack by these occult powers. Or put otherwise, beyond belief but closer to belief alteration or even formation, a conflict between two definitions of the whole (and thus of *pars pro toto* identification or location) inevitably forms, or will have to: on the one hand, the old, eroded one—parts that stand for the tradition are exchanged for parts that don't, but up to an increasingly ineffective level; on the other, an emerging (for some people at least) whole defined in connection with the literate one. The present majority of school-goers makes the tolerance (hiding from the eyes of the national state) of school-avoiders possible. But this situation is likely to crack open at some point. In any case, inversion of these substitution relations, or rather their coexistence in inverted form, is quite possible. It is not just that the boy who went to Wahai is hidden from the cracking Huaulu whole by the semiliterate and illiterate majority; this schoolboy also represents them all, turning them into a somewhat different totality: one that looks forward with different hopes and ideas in relation to a more advanced school—the Indonesian state, with a more directly telling but also more distant connection with a winning otherness.

Subtraction and Negation

Interestingly enough, a very partial subtraction of what is commonly whole helps create the only tolerable new or exceptional-purpose whole even in traditional contexts. For instance, those who die a bad death cannot be ritually handled if the old man who must sing a special song does not halve his hearing by stopping one ear, and if his public, which is only male, does not stop both ears. The ritual for the dangerousness of these dead can thus take place only if its songs are not heard in their entirety. The whole that must exist is one that exists not by itself but only in relation to the living Huaulu. But the Huaulu make it exist in a largely negative way: by creating incompleteness, partiality, and thus distance from the dead.

The relationship of part and whole can thus be much more than a symbolic substitution which makes it possible to consume or do something necessary in exchange for something unnecessary or less necessary. It may also be the creation of actual ritual existence by removing some of the parts of material and social existence (singing, hearing in equal degrees, participating, and so on). That these removals are said to be constitutive of the thing as totality may seem strange or even contradictory, but only if we do not take seriously the expression of ritual in terms of taboo, that is, in terms of negation. In fact, the example of the artificially truncated or even completely suppressed in the rite for the male bad death shows in even stronger terms what is true, in different measures, of all rites: None is whole if the prescribed or necessary incompleteness is not created by the absence or half-absence of a certain action. On the other hand, an absence or nonaction which is taboo undoes that completeness. In other words, anything ritual or relational is a whole if the combination of contact and noncontact is realized, through doing and not doing, eating and not eating, and so on. Nevertheless, this realization of totality is possible only in negative terms. Why more emphasis on negation than on affirmation, especially if anything negative can be expressed through a positive, or vice versa? I shall return briefly to this fundamental issue, because, being a most general one, it is the final one that we must address. Here I think one must go further into a fundamental issue most directly experienced and discussed, however incompletely from our reflective point of view, by the Huaulu themselves.

The issue starts from the frequent use of the *pars pro toto* principle nowadays to diminish or even eliminate taboos, as was already indicated. This seems to explain why the principle is also increasingly used to explain the genesis of taboos. Reduction or elimination cannot be easily accepted if it is not consonant with increase or creation. The principle of existence is, for the taboo at least, the principle of nonexistence. Or better said, the principle of movement and transformation from existence to nonexistence and vice versa, when human action or self-definition through consumption is principally involved, contributes to making taboos so important but also easily reducible or even dispensable in altered conditions. The same can be said of another variable that, as we have already seen in chapter 3, is always potentially behind taboos, particularly when considered as sets. It is the variable of force. Just like the whole-part relationship, this variable must, of course, enter into consideration in explaining taboo, just as it must in finding out who may be exempted from taboo and when and where. We have here again a dynamic involving proportional and, in any case, relative calculation. The stronger a given subject, the easier for it to consider itself exempt from certain taboos (if not all). But force never exists alone. The weaker part will take the place of the stronger one because the relationship between object and subject can rarely be purely dyadic and autonomous. A subject is rarely defined independently of his ipa (lineage) or any of his relatives, allies, and so on. This contributes to the invocation and more generalized use of the *pars pro toto* principle and especially to the view of taboo as contributing to preserving totality and integrity in relation to humans and in diminishing danger for them both.

That force plays a role in the definition of subject identity, and thus of the whole of identity, is indicated not only by the wider exemptions of the stronger's taboos in relation to the whole, but also by a compensatory variety of shifts toward these taboos by the weaker who become his dependents. This paradoxical combination of stronger ones who follow their taboos less than the weaker ones who come to them (and thus help the stronger *not* to follow their own taboos by substituting for them as weaker subordinates) is best illustrated by wives, who always come from lineages with different shared taboos but must shift to the shared taboos of their husbands. Of course, this is part of the incorporation of wives, and it is a part whose evidence can make them stand for the whole (into which they are incorporated). More generally speaking, they illustrate an underlying principle which is always on Huaulu ordering lips when they see a stranger or neighbor from another ethnic group coming to reside with them, however briefly. For it is an affirmation of their lordship over the territory they occupy to request outsiders, for as long as they reside with them, to follow its basic territorial taboos, such as not hunting or even capturing for purposes of sale, and so on. The principle applies both to lineages into which one marries or comes to reside and to the village as a whole. Indeed, the two basic conditions of the Huaulu for accepting my residence among them when I arrived were that my wife had to use the menstrual huts outside the village and that we build only a house identical to all others in the village. This territorial principle of taboo linked to some basic acts of negation through which the group constitutes itself is spoken of often in taboos that the Huaulu themselves have to undergo these days when residing on the coast, at Alakamat, in Opengese territory. The place contains a particularly dangerous occult power, a lord of the land whose permission is needed to live there; but this permission belongs to Openg to begin with. To follow its taboos is to acknowledge Openg's primacy in that place, just as the Opengese recognize that the Huaulu follow their taboos in their own mountain village.

As I have already had occasion to mention, reference to the part-whole relation does not carry implications that may seem Dumontian.[80] On the contrary, the ambiguous and plastic potential of parts to wholes is always evident and quite often exploited. For one thing, the displacement of the value of the whole from part to part may generate two opposing ideas of superiority. Either superiority consists in renunciation of others, or superiority consists in heightened consumption rendered possible by the renunciation of others or, better, by one's strength, which makes it possible to have a greater resistance to danger while usually imposing the contrary on others. The results are less a mere hierarchy than a battle. On the one hand, hierarchy is in these cases reduced to strength: the strong, particularly men, limit the taboo's applicability to women and weaker men, who are their inferiors. On the other hand, strong men may be said to be dependent on women, who, precisely because of their weakness, must take taboos more literally than the men on whom they depend. If totality depends on not eroding its living components because they stand unequally for the whole, then women are superior to men precisely because their weakness keeps them from running away from undermining consumption.

In sum, the connection of taboo with superiority/inferiority is far from simple. Moreover, its results depend on its connection with other concepts. Women's help to men may be conceived as a result of their dependent state and thus their inferiority to the opposite sex, or such help may be conceived (as women in the lilipossu told me) as an expression of superior goodness (or "love") relative to men. Contrariwise, if force alone is considered, men's superiority is beyond doubt, since it allows them to shed blood. They can eat more of the whole because they can more easily escape from the dangers involved in its undermining. But then somebody or something must protect them from such undermining. One may say that strength is less "morally" positive than renunciation is, but also that renunciation is less pragmatically effective than strength. It is difficult to decide what takes over for good in the eyes of the two sexes, and even in the eyes of all individuals. The fact remains that total displacement onto or delegation to others, or on behalf of others, is impossible.

Women cannot take over all taboos for men, nor can men accept or impose this because of an absolute claim of strength, of the ability to resist danger. Not only do they have purely male activities from which females are excluded, but even in what they share with women they must, just like women, not consume certain things. For instance, different phases in time can function as differential equivalents of the whole. One can say that the past can function as the whole and thus make the present partly free of taboo. As I mentioned above, having obtained over time a certain number of trap-victims, the hunter can be said to have been liberated from the taboo on eating them.[81] But this is never possible when game are killed with the bow and arrows. Something "hard" (conceptually but not under the teeth) has to stay, whatever the contribution of subordinates or superiors. Demonstratively, the principle is equally true of male and female relations to the tabooness of certain species or other things. Take, for instance, the female taboo on eels. Women cannot eat eels, as we have seen. But although they cannot eat the meat of eels, they can eat its broth cooked in disguise, that is, in leaves (vegetables). It seems then that it is the vegetalized dissolution of certain meats (especially the water food that has the closest resemblance to land meat) that exempts the eater from taboo, since the taboo is centered on the meat. Which arises the more general issues: What *type* of part is most likely to stand for the whole? And what types of people who are part of Huaulu society are likely to be affected by this society?

The first question should find an answer in many of the analyses carried out in chapter 4, which made clear the importance of certain basic devices: prototypicality, markedness, spatial centrality, spatial upperness or temporal precedence, morphological complexity or simplicity, noticeability due to either bigness or smallness in a series of species, and so on. Such devices would require a long repetition in a theoretical tarantella, danced with Lakoff or Quintilian or Wittgenstein.[82] No room (alas), but also no necessity, in this book's context. Let me stress again, however, that these devices are used to generate taboos as much as to limit their applicability. And this, in turn, demonstrates the ambivalence vis-à-vis taboos—what makes them proliferate in forms guaranteeing limits, and sometimes imparting ignoring as much as following.

The second question can hardly be separated from the first. For the applicability of the above principles of selection of parts for the whole (and thus of rejection of a literal whole that would be unbearable) extends to the subjects. In other words, as I have so often repeated, the choice of particular species or any other object of taboo for any subject may depend on the subject just as much as on the object. We have seen this in the differences that exist between men and women (which imply affinities or counteraffinities with certain kinds of objects), but also, and particularly among men, in the differences in their social functions, many of which are in turn based on age and rank. In other words, the logical principle of selection often has its sustaining force in something that is not logical, but rather social or political and even—more and more so these days—related to general attitudes toward taboos and their sustenance. One rather obvious component of these attitudes revealed by the *pars pro toto* principle is the sacrificial component into which we have kept running throughout this book. If the consumption of a whole is made possible by the renunciation of a part that stands for all the rest (either because it is a vital or upper part, as in large game, or because it is seen as equivalent to all other similar parts), then taboo evokes an implicit exchange with an implicit other. This other clearly emerges in certain cases, and generically emerges in the notions of "ancestors," "lords of the land," various animals, and so on, but it is also present in a more indefinite form throughout much of taboo, and even in the most alimentary.

I could multiply the examples of *pars pro toto* devices of taboo and show that they are—and are becoming even more these days—some of the life-bloods of taboo's doing and undoing. I could go on with more detailed aspects of the logic of taboo—of the system of equivalences and thus substitutions that makes it concretely possible and acceptable to those who must undergo it. But by bringing us back to the general and silent principle of silent sacrifice, the *pars pro toto* and affine principles bring us to where we must return: to a final generalization about taboo. Furthermore, it is time to remind ourselves that we have followed our itinerary through taboo, choosing our examples with the same *pars pro toto* principle which we have now encountered operating in taboo from classification to action. To have reached the principle in

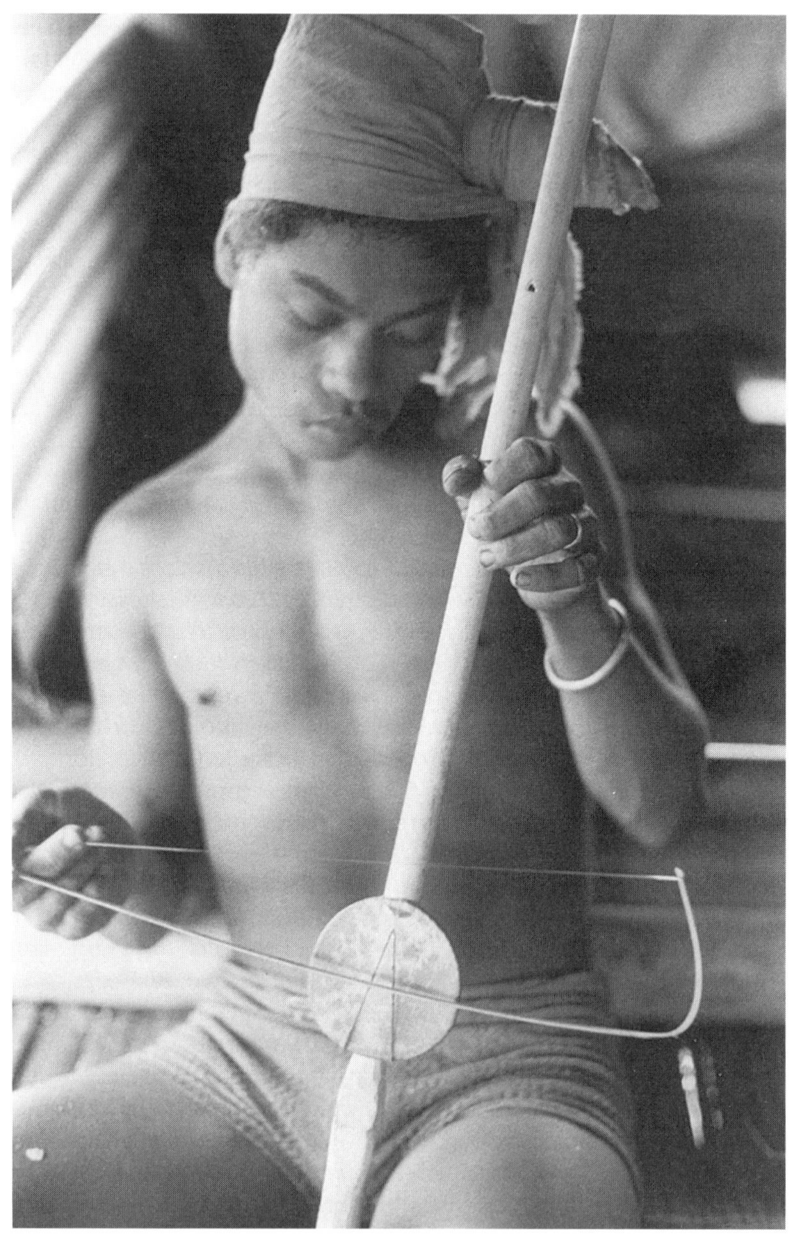

It is taboo for a young man to wear a red turban until he has killed large game (*peni*) or established a steady sexual relationship with a girl. In both cases, male control over blood must be demonstrated first, before the dress of manhood is assumed. 1972. (Photo by V. Valeri.)

this way means, arbitrary as it is, finding ourselves back at our starting point and yet at a different level which calls for a final summary. Let us attempt to provide it pure and naked, even if sometimes with visible new additions.

Conclusions

The obvious starting point is a summary definition of maquwoli, "taboo." Equally obvious is that taboo in Huaulu, as in so many other parts of the world, translates an incompatibility or improper combination between or among terms, but only in connection with certain activities or substances or modes of relationship. Such activities concern human bodies, which are strongly affected by them, and must therefore be protected from them when they are vulnerable. Protection is primarily offered by avoidance, that is by staying away from anything incompatible which might cause disease or death. But it may also be offered by properly doing what one should avoid not doing, that is, not fully performing certain ritual or fundamental acts. Devastating bodily consequences of violating these taboos (which put in the negative what could be put in the positive, that is, fully and properly performing the rites) may seem like artificially produced sanctions against a violation, but in fact are more a naturally emerging danger from which the rite is supposed to protect. These ritual acts, however, are often protective or constructive means of defense against dangers to the body or relations like those managed by mere avoidance or escape. Thus these rituals too can be seen as a form of staying away. It is a staying away, rather than mere physical detachment, that requires the transformation of subjects and objects. Pure physical danger does not seem to attract taboo, however.

The body must be attacked and undermined as a repository of identity, and thus by species or events that carry values in conflict with it. The material, here, inevitably involves the symbolic. What I must avoid through taboo is a category of animal, or whatever, which is symbolic of qualities in conflict with those of mine that I should stick to. The dangers connected with taboo, then, have a radical character: they involve my existence not as a purely physical being but neither as a purely symbolic one. Taboo thrives on the confusion of and the bridge across the two, on a view of the world which requires respecting it, but does not imply being respected by it.

But how is the compatibility or incompatibility to the point of taboo identified in animals, plants, and so on? As the previous analyses, but especially those of chapter 4, indicate, the main sources are classification, experience (individual or collective over time), and analogy or contrast. But all these causes have no effect in terms of taboo if they do not carry relevant symbolic values. Mere classification or rhetorical figures are insufficient. Taboo belongs to a world that is definable by neither one nor the other. It requires, moreover, a high coefficient of transferability, without which its viable existence becomes strictly impossible. In other words, the logic that constitutes the actual, more determined taboos from a classificatory starting point must be present beyond classification and tradition. We have seen various examples of what this diminutive logic is and that the most important one is the equivalence of part and whole. That such equivalence has a narrowing power but also a power to confirm the complementarity of social categories (men and women to begin with) needs no further comment and examples.

Chapter 4 and the above discussion help generalize on the relationship between individual and species in the domain of taboo. An individual, both on the object and subject sides and these usually in complex correlation with one another, can stand for the species as a whole or for itself alone. But even standing for the species, it can take two forms: an instantial and repetitive one (i.e. each individual is taboo because it belongs to a species) or a substitutive one (certain individuals are taboo instead of the species). And we have also seen that the more species-linked a taboo is, the more universal it also tends to be, although species are often scaled, especially with regard to the social oppositions of male and female, adult and young, senior and junior.

Another point necessary to remember in order to make any synthetic excursion through the logic of Huaulu taboo is the much more difficult and mobile of the types of action or relation that connect subject and object. Not just eating, taking or giving or sharing blood (in a variety of activities: hunt, war, sex, generation), having sex, touching, laughing at an object or in its presence, but also crying, spitting or sneezing, gazing, naming or even speaking of or listening to. It is clear that such actions and relations directly or indirectly (through equivalence) connect subject and object in a radical because substantial way. Anything that connects body to body is more threatening—and relevant for an embodied subject that finds correspondences with the bodies of nature—than anything that does not. It is not only food or blood that can move from body to body, but other substances (spit) or substantially incarnate ones (speech,[83] view). Moreover, all these substances are indexes of potential, partial or total, loss of control (laughter, crying, loosened speech). They are therefore indexes of vulnerability to one's body and thus, a fortiori, to forces that can overpower it, for instance, in revenge attack.

If we take into account all the substances or bodily related phenomena that actualize the taboo potential, two conclusions seem to impose themselves. The first is that such phenomena form a range that moves from principally consumption of natural objects to principally undoing of the performance of interhuman acts (mostly ritual). Both coexist, but in different proportions from one pole to the other. These phenomena therefore furnish further evidence that this polarity must be kept in the analysis of taboos.

The second conclusion is more general: there is a difference between conceptual and practical reasons in bringing about taboos. In the extreme form of consumption—eating—the tabooed object is explained by the relative position of subject and object in a classificatory system, that is, a conceptually inspired and in any case conceptually knowable system. In contrast, in the extreme form of the practical, it is the doing of certain things—that is, bringing about certain interactions between subject and object—that creates their incompatibility, and thus the dangers involved (e.g. smoke produced in the presence of the source of danger).[84] Of course the contrast is not absolute but variably relative. Or better still: one feels that most taboos are generated both ways: through knowledge of a knowledge-like order of the world, and through interacting or acting in such ways as to create dangerousness (i.e. a quarrel between subject and object). It is just that the relative importance of each of the two principles might vary considerably. Of course, the not doing of certain things ultimately presupposes a certain definition of that doing and of those things. Even so, it is the doing that creates such dangerousness. It is as if a person or an object became unfriendly only if unfriendly acts were committed against it, or as if a rite lost its existence if one kept doing certain taboo things. In sum, there is on one side the taking over of a performative mechanism, because what is involved in taboos exists only if people follow them (how could an initiation exist if people were not constrained to perform it?), and on the other side the taking over of an intellectually determined system of relations.

In sum, in one case the object and its dangerousness exist whether or not the subject consumes the object; in the other case, what exists is largely made by the making, since it exists as an idea but not as a concrete reality. Dangerous animals are not made dangerous by human acts, from which they are largely independent. The undoing or not doing of an initiation rite or a marriage rite or even behavior, on the contrary, exists only in and by human action, and is therefore dependent on it. Taboo thus applies to action on which states of being depend positively, whereas in consumption, taboo is an action (usually merely eating) on which being depends negatively—that is, action as destruction and not (or just through a sacrificial process of give and take, as we have seen) as construction or, more frequently, as performance.

To repeat myself in conclusion, then, the polarity of consumption and performance remains a valid one and is indeed further demonstrated by the phenomena and ideas I have just alluded to. But it should also be evident that distinction is not equivalent to separation pure and simple, just as it does not, or does not simply, call for separation. The objects of taboo can be neither the mere failure to do something nor the mere failure not to do something. Nor are actions completed or not completed reducible to a homogenized broth, since not consuming is the performance of the single act suggested by food taboos, whereas incomplete or failed performance of a whole complex of distinct acts is suggested by performance taboos. This difference is a function of a categorical difference I have already mentioned: man-made being and man-made undoing. Consumption taboos are about the protection of being made by external powers, not by human powers (except, and in part, if abstention is lived as part of a sacrificial circle); performance taboos are double negations that amount to an affirmation: do what can be done only by you. But one must be aware that this distinction is also the basis of a mutual implication, which is the true system. Without the largely man-made beings it would be impossible to maintain a consumption pattern with the external world. But reciprocally and inversely, it would be impossible to perform the purpose of existing in a predominantly human and conventional way if one did not also rely on an eating and "eating," on a taking of animals, fruit, trees, and so on, from the forest.

The validity—however partial—of the polarity between consumption and performance taboos is further confirmed by the tendential polarity in their respective effects in case of violation. If taboos are predominantly on the consumption of natural, not man-made,[85] species, then they concern dangers that involve direct ingestion or touching or even observation. One consequence of this is that such dangers cannot be transmitted to another person, except if this person can very closely stand for the violator, is much weaker than he, and undergoes, usually instead of him, the exact consequences of violating the taboo on eating an exact species or combination of species. This amounts to saying that there is no great applicability of the notion of pollution here. Such a notion, indeed, implies that a single "dirtying" is the underlying danger of all taboo violations. This abstract notion is measured more by an easily transmissible disqualification from ritual or even from community than by a specific or even generic disease or bodily modification.[86] The former condition—exclusion from ritual—for pollution's credible existence is found in Huaulu too, since it is essentially qualified by a conventional, humanly established, order and orders of accomplishment. But however much disqualification from them may be invoked, what remains most important is—just as in consumption taboos, which remain the basic model, since they provide basic experiences—a complex of dangers different for each sphere (e.g. generation and headhunting) and for each subject or at least type thereof (e.g. men and women). However great the convention and social solidarity (participation) which occurs in the dominantly performative areas, then, they are not radically distinct from areas of consumption.[87]

Conclusions and Additions 2: Taboo and Pollution

The idea of "dirt"—of something that must be washed away[88] or in any case thrown out of the village—seems to apply somewhat to the inherent failures of the human body (menstruating, dying), but not to many other fields. In any case, what matters, and justifies to some extent a comparison with "pollution," is not what its etymology suggests (since *polluere* can still be translated as "making dirty" and *being polluted* as "being made dirty"), but is the contamination of all fellow members of a category through the space that contains them. As we have seen, if a menstruating woman enters the village all men are contaminated and in danger. If a human of either sex dies in the village or is brought into it as a corpse, everybody is contaminated by death until the corpse is brought out of the village in the appropriate ritual way. The village space thus seems a conveying medium. The idea is not that a man who has been "polluted" by a menstruating woman is able to "pollute" another man. All other men become contaminated because of their contact with the village. A fortiori, the corpse does not pollute a person who pollutes another one, and so on in a chain, but pollutes the village as a whole[89] and thus pollutes an object of inevitable consumption or, better said, of use for everybody in the village.

The particularism of consumption is thus, as in consumption but much more, balanced in such taboos by categorical appurtenance. Moreover such appurtenance is translated into spatial terms: I am a villager of Sekenima, I am more a villager than women are, and so on. The cause of danger transmission is the shared participation in space, not the direct contact of subject with subject. The "polluted" is not "polluting"—a fact which makes the use of this term inappropriate from a comparative point of view (see, for instance, an author who claims that there is no idea of pollution in Islam because there is no idea of an endless contamination chain).[90]

Nevertheless, *pollution* can be used in certain cases as a term specifically connected with the generic term *dirt*. The menstruating woman implicitly "dirties" a man because she makes him a lesser man by contaminating him with what is most characteristic of woman. Although the Huaulu do not really use any term that openly refers to "dirt" in this as in other taboo contexts, its interpretive and descriptive use can be defended here by reference to ritual practice. A man contaminated by the menstrual blood of a woman can be "washed" by her beyond the village's boundaries, using river water, that is, water that evokes the carrying away toward the sea.[91] Men returning from having buried a corpse or set it inside the trunk of a very large tree must accurately wash their parang and their hands in a stream before reentering the village. Not to do so is taboo because it brings the "dirt" of the dead back into the village. It is interesting that the abstract idea of dirt and the temptation to use the derived term *pollution* with the conceptual counterparts *purity* and *purification,* exist in these spheres of Huaulu life, conceptually if not lexically.

Yet I must stress that the basic consumption model remains influential here, because the dirtied person does not become himself dirtying. For instance, the man contaminated by menstrual blood does not go on a headhunt, not because he contaminates the other hunters, but because his state assures him of total failure and even makes him a likely victim of those who should be the victims of the hunt. This excludes him, even in the interest of the whole party—in fact, of the community itself—but not because they are afraid of becoming like him, only because they do not wish their community to lose a member, acquire the reputation of a loser, and offer the enemy an image of weakness rather than protective strength. Purely mechanical ideas of "contamination" are thus far from being systematically applied in the interhuman realm. The subject and its direct confrontation with danger and the externally produced objects that are danger's source remain the dominant focus even when social interaction appears fundamental to the Huaulu themselves.[92] Which brings us to another identification of maquwoli through difference. The difference in this case is not with another taboo system, but with other systems *tout court* in Huaulu itself.

Conclusions and Additions 3: Taboo and the Spectrum of Morality

The most obvious difference is with the mukae, "shame," system or, better said, the areas of application of this notion. Strictly speaking, mukae is most often used as a verb (ita mukae, "we are ashamed"), an expression which offers a self-referential definition of the Huaulu, meaning that in supposed contrast with other people in the neighborhood the Huaulu are sensitive to what one should feel ashamed of. *Mukae* has at least two partial opposites. One is *akatea,* which, contrary to *mukae,* implies indifference to or defiance of the public judgment or evaluation of one's action. The other refers to what is lost if one has some reasons for feeling "ashamed": *lala* (lit., "name," and thus reputation, in an exclusively positive sense). Lala is much desired by the Huaulu, particularly men. Their cultural ideal is therefore to avoid its loss and having to feel ashamed, that is, as the unwilling recipient of a negative look. Feeling ashamed, ita mukae—a feeling which takes a number of conventionally understood bodily poses and attitudes[93]—is therefore an important motivation for not doing certain things or not continuing to do them.[94]

To understand fully the Huaulu notion of shame we would have to delve into many details and study revealing cases. That would be very interesting but very consuming of space and time. And such details would not add much to the role of shame in defining the uses of maquwoli. Because we are trying to understand maquwoli here, let us make only a few useful general points on shame, mukae.

We have already seen that the family of maquwoli moves from the consumption of externally produced objects to the performance of acts, with or without connections (particularly implications) with the extra-village world. Shame is a further step toward purely human relations. One is not ashamed of eating certain foods or bringing about a conflict with nonhuman forces, as is the case even in the most performative realm of taboo. Shame applies to only certain areas of the world of exclusively human relations—that is, those that do not involve "poison" or that involve only semi-anthropomorphic beings as layers and protectors of order. To shame, only the appreciation or lack of appreciation of other humans matters. Furthermore, these other humans must be Huaulu, like the misbehaver, or friendly neighbors who share certain basic values with the Huaulu.

What are the principal areas of social relations where shame may arise? Let me briefly summarize those I have noticed: (1) relationships of deference to parental authorities and more generally elders endowed with prestige; (2) relationships between allies, particularly with regard to the give and take of objects, payments, and so on (sex and food are more in the sphere of maquwoli, although both mukae and maquwoli may be involved); (3) the relationship to one's model of person, as a Huaulu or even as a human—a model which always involves relationships with other people. Failure to realize these models or to realize them properly creates a pattern of avoidance by other members of the community. The subject that is or should be ashamed has an empty house, because he has no guests. Indeed, a full house is considered a sign of lala, "name," while an empty one is a sign that the "name lacks or falls" (lalana pukua); (4) overstepping one's position. Women, for instance, say that they do not do things that are in the province of men, because i mukae, "it is shameful" (if these things are not taboo, which further reinforces their avoidance); (5) adultery (if it becomes public through the discovery of one of the two legitimate spouses).

Shame in all these cases entails acceptance of the public view[95] that one is not worthy of respect because one does not respect those persons who should be respected. Absence of shame in the same situations, on the other hand, may be an affirmation that one is endowed with great superiority relative to all others mostly from the point of view of strength. But such theoretical arrogance hardly works, not only for the young, but also for mature and prestigious people. Thus the guardian of the village temple declared himself ashamed, after initially refusing to do so when he was caught in adultery. To eliminate that shame and the accompanying hostility, he paid a substantial fine. Fines are indeed methods for eliminating shame or at least the hostile avoidance of others.

The use of shame implies a less evanescent and mysterious sphere of human action than the use of maquwoli involves. Feeling shame is less mysterious, closer to the visible surface, than undergoing a particular disease or a particular failure. It is inseparable from being seen by those one does not wish to be seen by, and therefore it is also showing that one is worried and embarrassed. Being unashamed in the eyes of the others may occur just like being unafraid of becoming sick in taboo. In other words, strength may make it possible, up to a point, to resist control, so that the resistance to control is itself a proof of strength. Nevertheless, and obviously, resistance to purely human and in fact purely Huaulu control is much less impressive and thus unable to guarantee the collective attribution of extraordinary or superior strength. At any rate, the loss of public appreciation, even an appreciation limited to a show of strength, is not effective for obtaining prestige and power over the other Huaulu. A warrior may pretend to be unashamed of the negative appreciation of his fellow villagers, but he is certainly worried about it when it affects his activities. The more the conflict between a certain display of indifference and an inner peace exists, and the more important the sphere of its arousal is, the more closeness to or even mixture with taboo comes into being.

Apart from headhunting (which would have to be treated at too great length to use as an example here), affinal relations are the most frequent and observable cases. Between wife-givers and wife-takers there is shame and taboo and even superimposition of the two. For instance, the violation of certain taboos among affines has classical consequences for taboo (individual disease or misfortune of the violator). But it is also connected with a deeper emotion than the fear attached to taboo; because he has done something unacceptable among allies which may affect them all, the violator must pay a fine. This result is unusual for taboos, since the fine eliminates both the reasons for feeling ashamed (i.e. "I recognize I was wrong, inappropriate; let me give you a compensating payment")[96] and those for feeling afraid of bodily consequences of the disease type. Even more than performance taboos this mixture of shame and affinal taboo brings us further away from consumption taboos. But it shows that these rules and the attached representations form a vast family, whose numerous interconnections seem to require a common name: morality—a name reflecting another theme far too complex and comparative for us (for us anthropologists in the company of philosophers) to be treated here at the end of my space and time.

We may, however, briefly touch two notions and accompanying practices that, being even further away from taboo than shame[97] is, bring Huaulu closer to us still, or at least to parts of our past. I am referring to the notions of hukum, "law," and of pinia, "beautiful/ good," and their mostly adjectival contraries (hukumussi and piniassi), which are connected with sala, "wrong," and rosa, "culpability" (rather than "guilt"; see chapter 3).

Pinia is a notion as Platonic as it could be, that is, such that it does not truly differentiate what is good from what it does to our senses and what is good from what it does in and for our human interaction. In a sense, we have here something that can be compared with maquwoli insofar as it brings together consumption and performance—object goodness and subject-to-subject goodness (or badness, of course). Such convergence or even confusion points to a fundamental sense that what is good, in an aesthetic as in a moral sense, is what corresponds to or does not threaten an order permeating the universe in one case and human society in the other. What violates the latter—if it can ultimately be distinguished from the former at all—is humanly and not cosmically handled like a taboo violation. This handling takes place through public opinion and its expression. The beautiful appearance or acting will be praised, will acquire a lala, "name"; its contraries will be put to shame, that is, subjected to a reflected, interiorized act, but made externally visible just like a skin affection produced by taboo violation. Indeed, I may say that taboo, shame, and ugliness are in different ways displayed on the body's most total and most visible part: the skin that covers and unifies the entire body.

But it is not just a reproaching gaze, introjected as a sense of shame, which puts down the absence of goodness. This may also be done through an empirical punishment, fine, or expulsion, which the community administers after having reached an agreement.[98] Such an agreement, and the punishment to be administered to the author of "ugly" actions, is legitimized by reference not to sentiment but to explicit rules. The rules are traditional, and thus have their source in more or less ancient ancestors. But they have basically been nameless until terms like *adat* and *hukum* have become available from Bahasa Indonesia.[99] The use of such terms to refer to these traditional rules is a clear indication of their perceived equivalence with the notion of law. Because such reference to Huaulu "law" is made so as to specify what taboo is by contrast with what it is not, we may ask ourselves where their difference lies, and whether or not we can apply our definitions of law to what the Huaulu are talking about, or presupposing, in their practices of collective judgment and punishment.

We may as well start with a quotation from our ranks, then. It comes from Spinoza's *Tractatus Theologico-Politicus* (caput IV):

> The word "law" in the widest sense means a rule in accordance with which all individual things, or all things of the same species, or some of them, act in one and the same fixed and determinate way; and this either by natural necessity or by the will of men. A law based on natural necessity is one which follows necessarily from the actual nature or definition of the thing in question; while a law based on the will of men—more properly called an ordinance[100]—is one which men prescribe for themselves and others in order to live in greater security and comfort, or for some other purpose."[101]

This definition is reflected by more recent ones, and even by those used by anthropologists such as Mary Douglas,[102] who ultimately views taboo as reified and thus failed law. Such failure, she says, is due to the absence of a sufficient power in society to sanction the law and to inflict punishment on its violator, hence the idea that danger for him or her comes from the law's natural objects or correlates—from their "polluting" powers.[103]

That taboo is simply reified, because failed, social law is hardly acceptable even in the general framework of *Purity and Danger,* where this thesis coexists with another one which contradicts it. As we have seen, this other thesis holds that taboo arises from the intellectual apprehension of the classificatory order of nature. So in a sense "law," if used, should also apply—as in Spinoza—to nature, but nature as it denies its laws, in that it produces anomalies. Furthermore, Douglas's position is that ultimately even this natural sense of law goes back to its social sense: it is a socially functional use of law that may support itself by reification and naturalization. And at any rate, does this notion of taboo as failed and reified law[104] agree with the Huaulu facts—their actions, reactions, and conceptions?

Throughout chapter 4, we have seen that the notion of anomaly (and thus of nature as violating its own rules) is vastly insufficient to explain, or explain alone, consumption taboos. Analogously, the only evidence that seems to support in some measure the idea that taboo is just reified human law (even when it presents itself as resulting from natural law) is vastly insufficient to demonstrate it. The evidence in question is the potential use of *adat* (as in other parts of Indonesia) to encompass all forms of customary behavior and thus of maquwoli too. But in reality, even when *adat* is used to refer to taboo, it is at best used with foreigners with whom one speaks some Indonesian. Among

Huaulu who converse in their own language, I heard *adat* used rarely and generally, rather than specifically, in reference to taboo. Moreover, such use implies that, whatever their reason, over time taboos become custom, so that one may also follow them to identify as a Huaulu or a member of a particular subgroup. The character of custom is thus one that the taboos share with many other habits and rules, but this by definition does not imply that they have the same cause, that they are all laws, more or less reified. Even if one were to disregard this, one would have to acknowledge a profound difference between what can be called law and what is called maquwoli. The difference is that the law is characterized by a precise definition that cannot be changed or argued about. What can be argued about is its applicability to a particular situation. Alternatively, its diminished acceptability may be said to be due to conflicts with other laws.

In other words, there is no doubt that parts of Huaulu custom correspond to some crucial aspects of what we call law: they are not just based on "knowledge" of the world's order or properties, which imply compatibilities or incompatibilities with us as humans, but are also based on human (even if now sacralized in the notion of ancestors) will to constitute a certain distinctive form of order; they are contained in actual verbal formulas which are the basis of arguments about their applicability, especially during trials in which the whole male community participates (e.g. divorce). This notion of law appears most at trial, as I have said, and indeed this is an aspect of what they have borrowed, that is, the word *hukum. Hukum* may refer to what we ourselves would call law, and is produced or sustained by collective will or by the will of a divinity (Lahatala) who stands for the community.[105] Nevertheless, such a notion is never applied to taboos. The transgression of taboo remains an individual or only partly collective act, because such are also its effects. Moreover, such effects concern the body as an entity that undergoes pain, lack of integrality, and death. The same consequences are hardly the case for Huaulu law, which the community uses only to impose fines or expulsions.

Much more could be said, but what I have said is sufficient to argue that the notion of law is not all-encompassing in Huaulu. It basically leaves taboo and even "shame" or "name" out. Certain aspects of taboo have acquired, precisely because of their shared use, a community dimension but not a legal one. The latter implies community judgment and punishment, whereas the former does not. Furthermore, community-based trials show that the area of law exclusively concerns a few interhuman, almost contractual, relations in which the community has fundamental interest and a right to intervene: adultery, divorce, breaking of engagements, chiefdom required by the Indonesian national government, and so on. In this sense, law and its administration at best complement what falls under the notions of taboo and shame, which are much more fundamental and involve self-definition through the body and its relationships with other bodies, human and nonhuman. As such, the taboo cannot possibly—that is, logically—be said to be reified, because impotent, human law. Taboo is, rather, the result of an awareness of the subject's dependency—for life and symbolic definition—on the world at large, which cannot be conceived as having humanly made laws.[106] Taboo is based more on knowing than on making. That is also why it is all expressed in not making—as negation.

That negation primarily or most evidently comes from the avoidance of danger cannot be denied after the many analyses contained in this book. But much can be built on this bedrock, which makes negation more worthy of attention than affirmation. Affirmation usually translates what is habit, and is thus less the object of reflection and delimitation than negation requires or suscitates, precisely because of the threatening world it brings to attention. The negative thus stands in clear-cut opposition to the mass of the neutral-positive world of habit. It is therefore the best way to elicit attention and sustain self-definition, for each and all the Huaulu. What is founded on danger, then, turns into a much wider world of preferential applications.[107] And these applications and their motives may contribute to explaining dangerousness and sometimes be its main reasons, as we have seen in considering the social and especially hierarchical reasons for several food taboos.

Let us see if we can, in conclusion, generalize by looking at some of these and additional reasons for the preponderance of negation in articulated discourse and visible consumption or interaction.[108]

The Practice of Negation (or No-Practice and the Practice of No)

Let us begin with the summary of an argument which I consider fundamental in explaining the preferential recourse to negation. I quote from one of my old notes:

> It is easier to identify something by what is *not* done relative to it than by what is done (or might be done). Doing in a positive sense has less shape, less predictability, less distinctiveness, than *not* doing. Not doing contains an explicit contrast to doing, whereas doing does not directly evoke not doing. Positivity (Affirmation?) is an impediment to communicability, to distinctiveness. Negativity (Negation?) is always more precise, more informative, less ambiguous, neater: "I don't do *x*, whatever that is." "I do *x*," instead, forces me to engage, to realize *x* in the world, and thus to become involved in something that may turn out one way

> or another, and which is therefore more difficult to identify in a precise way. Acting is in any case vaguer than nonacting and thus one is paradoxically less performatory in doing than in not doing. Moreover, to act is always more dangerous than not to, since activity means becoming involved in all kinds of unknown, unpredictable forces. Thus in abstaining from doing I am more in control than in doing. Doing involves me in a causality I cannot ultimately control, so that not doing makes me more master of the situation, even if at a loss. But it is a predictable loss—not an unpredictable one, which may be greater, and not just smaller, as happens when I engage in action rather than in nonaction. Hence: distinctiveness, mastery, imperviousness, integrity, can all be better experienced by not doing than by doing. "I am what I am not" implies that I have to worry about what others are. I exist by positing myself as not-them: "You eat *x*, I don't." Which amounts to recognizing that self-identification by negation (in contrast with self-identification by affirmation) always explicitly implies the Other—particularly the one one talks to. Taboo is a very relational notion; it affords a very relational way of being by being distinct. "I am what I do" involves me in confusion, and thus perplexity, because it is also intrinsically solipsistic. Being by acting implies a claim that I can be by my own devices. Cooperation with others in action, moreover, confuses me with them. The confusion with others thus adds itself to the confusion with objects. If one accepts this taboo-generating view, one must conclude that action is a lesser means of being, except where there is a strongly individualistic ideology, a strong division of labor (especially where distinct roles exist for each participant in cooperative action, and a science and technology which give the sense of mastery over causality).[109]

I have quoted this rapidly and remorselessly written note because I need the brevity of something demonstrated without care and without a response, explicit or implicit, to obvious objections. To justify it fully and answer these objections would require a whole book, whereas I am only—and at present want only to be—at the end of one that has started the path of my inquiry on the relative roles of affirmation and negation in the moralities of different cultures or historical periods.[110] Affirmation, for instance, is becoming somewhat more important in Huaulu, accompanied as it is by the decline and fall of some constitutive negations (i.e. taboos) due to the slow and cautious entrance into a different, sea-frontal world. In sum, taboo, and therefore self-definition and realization based on it, has a history—a history whose mechanisms (such as the use of the generative equivalence of part and whole for an undermining required by a different, inexorably forming, form of life) have only very partially been discussed or even alluded to in this book. But besides this obvious point, I have to make other ones briefly.

As we have seen throughout the examples offered in this book, there is more than a single motivation—namely, the subject's self-definition—for the preponderance of negation which takes the form of taboo. And one can realize such motivations, whatever they are, because of the possession of certain general or even universal features—a universal feature referred to by Freud, not in theoretical texts (which are his main source of export from psychoanalysis), but in the case history of Dora, where he reports the different relations that exist between the unconscious and "yes" and "no." There is an unconscious "yes," he says,[111] but "no such thing at all as an unconscious 'No.'"[112] This may well be one reason there is a preferential connection between negation ("saying no," having a taboo on an object) and purported rationality or intellect. The Huaulu connection of taboo and cosmos demonstrates this, as does the explicit negative status that many implicitly desired things—objects of an unconscious yes—have (as we have seen in the previous sections of this concluding chapter). What one can conclude now is that the general tendency to put the appropriate in no (in taboos) depends on no's disconnection (or perhaps we should say greater disconnection) from the unconscious (and thus the uncontrolled).

The unconscious is desire, and thus indirectly expresses itself in yes, not in no. As an explicit counterdesire, no is the calculating or rational and thus what is ideally attached to the subject. But it is also—and this brings us to another motivation for negation to which we have come from different angles throughout this chapter—partial (i.e. sacrificial) renunciation and thus saying no to one's desire to say yes to one's desire of the other, the other on whom one depends for the altruistic exchange involved in alimentary consumption. This "sacrificial" dimension of taboo is also the expression of a fundamental contradiction: to say yes to oneself silently, one must loudly say no. Or better, a subject that depends on the other must appear as sacrificing himself to that other, saying yes to him by saying no to himself. So the negation cannot even exist without the affirmation of the other and his superiority over the self. Or to put it in Freudian terms, the superior consciousness that expresses itself through the negation of the subject's unconscious reaches consciousness in displaced form, and so says yes to its own desires, which are achieved by denying the subject. In other words, it is one's yes, expressed as the yes of an other, that can make the superior no—and thus the subject—exist. The superior value of negation's agency presupposes the ontological superiority of a spontaneous tendency imputed to affirmation (which, moreover, can appear as such only in a displaced, usually animal form).[113] Unconscious desire as pure yes is given the socially inferior position that must be negated in part (by taboo) in order to achieve its hidden positive primacy.[114]

At this point we might as well move to the perhaps more easily intelligible reasons for the primacy of negation as it expresses itself in the tendency to construct taboos. One obvious reason—namely, marking—noted by Greenberg for language alone, can probably be applied to the world of defining rules: "The negative always receives overt expression while the positive usually has zero expression."[115] I could quote many Huaulu linguistic examples that confirm this, but what is striking here is that most of the explicitly formulated rules are negative. As I have already mentioned, even essentially positive rules seem to be invariably expressed in negative form; that is to say, they are negations of negations by being the negations of acts which are incompatible with the acts that should be accomplished (as is the case in ritual). We may ask, however, why marking is so important as to use negation in rule enunciation. The reason is probably that affirmation would be a mere translation of habit into words. Not only is it more difficult to be fully aware of what one does habitually and automatically, but it is also hardly necessary to point it out or even order it. The world of tabooed things is indeed a world from which one should intentionally keep away in order not to threaten the world in which one usually finds oneself. But it is the occasional violation of that ordinary world that makes it more apparent and defensible. Perhaps, then, the interest in (or invention of) negation is one of the harder modes of existence for otherwise fragile habits. One should also add, perhaps, that negation, being not only clearer than habits in consciousness, but also more limited in the number of its realizations (taboos, etc.), can more easily be memorized, thereby allowing the subject to define itself fully by defining its exact position. All these cognitive facts are not sufficient to explain the preponderance of negation as a social fact, but nonetheless give some fundamental "natural" conditions for that fact to be(come) possible.[116] Negation is easier to formulate and remember than affirmation can ever be, in sum.

What then is the social fact achieved or made possible by the preponderance of negation? It is apparently a self-definition by contrast (with another person, or category of person, or entire community), which can more easily exist by negation of what all others do, by an enumeration of taboos rather than by the half-conscious or unaware set of one's positive practices. One is what one is, in sum, by virtue of a certain amount of conscious and intentional nonbeing, which contrasts the subject to other subjects by contrasting (through taboos used as marks in Greenberg's sense) the opposed relations of different subjects to external objects (animals, plants, and so on).

Just as negation is closer to consciousness and intention (and thus also to self-definition through consciousness and practice based on it), so is it closer than affirmation to continuous existence through space and time. Let me introduce the point through a simple illustrative example: During the kahua feast (which, as in 1987–88, can last for much more than a year) it is taboo to clean the soil under the community's house in which much of the feast takes place. Already in 1973, this noncleaning appeared to me as a device for maintaining total continuity for the feast throughout the period in which it was held. The continuity is in theory one of common eating and dancing, but can in fact take that form for only a few weeks at a time throughout the official period of kahua feasting. These weeks keep returning throughout the period, especially at the beginning and at the end, as I could witness in 1988. It would be difficult, or perhaps impossible, to find a positive activity going on, without interruption, for a year and a half. But abstention does that most easily. Dirt accumulates under the village temple, and this accumulation is the positive side of a dominant negative one. Moreover, it is positive in a purely symbolic sense, as a growing sign of temporal continuity and a stable spatial coverage of the temple as site of the feast.[117] In sum, it is no surprise that prescribed nonactions (taboos) are usually considered the negative part that allows one to speak of a ritual whole (just as of a whole person) as a unity to be preserved over time. This demonstrates, in the end, that nonaction must presuppose action in order to accomplish its enduring and totalizing function. If kahua did not go on—even if at its necessary intervals—the continuity of not cleaning under the place it is performed, the duration apparently ensured by taboo, would not in fact exist.

The coexistence of affirmation and negation in the variety of forms it takes is thus ultimately the mechanism by which identity is constituted. Negation plays the dominant role against a necessary background of positive habits. It is by negating them in part that a subject consciously and visibly emerges.[118] In a sense, taboo is symbolic consumption made possible by the negation of alimentary or other kinds of material consumption. For a species to continue to symbolize my own attitudes (most often by negating them) and therefore bring the components of my being to consciousness, I must negate any possible habit of simply eating it. My biting mouth must give the species up so that the speaking mouth can utter my name and the hearing ear seize its sound. I will thus be able to perceive myself as a peculiar lowering of consumption. Indeed, it is by such varied diminution of a rather stable list of items that people acquire difference, in contrast with our world, where identity is given by consumption increase, by addition of new items to the consumption list, which keeps growing.

Finally, it seems possible to understand something important of Huaulu taboos by contrast with our consumer society, ruled by the rallying cry "Shop until you drop."[119] In Los Angeles, where most of this book was revised and this final chapter written, consumer society appeared to me in its most extreme forms.[120] Such forms made clearer what our outrageous, continuously growing consumption contributes to our identity. The more we consume, the more we add to the collective list of objects to buy, use, and throw away (or give away) after a while. Through the visible (or apparent) consumption of these goods, we acquire collective existence, or rather existence through the collective that observes us. The more we consume, the more we are noticed, watched and talked about. Most of us do not feel existence in any other way. In Huaulu, there is also no existence for us without the talking and observing of others. But such a life-giving gaze is obtained by subtracting something—and often something more than dictated by tradition—from the limited, quasi-fixed list of usables delivered by cultural logic and individual experience and biography. In a certain way, I have had the best sense of understanding Huaulu in my fieldnotes by wandering in the streets of the capital of consumption. Each one appeared as negation of the opposite other: Huaulu of Los Angeles, and Los Angeles of Huaulu. Neither knows of the other's name or existence. They coexist, in an eternal struggle but with the kind of conceptual commonality that goes with it, only in my brain. I have used this struggle to pursue some understanding of what it is to be Huaulu by taboo, but perhaps the battle was delineated only in my brain and made the obvious logical continuation—understanding what it is to be through the indefinite expansion of consumption—impossible. Some will have to look, one day, at the symmetry of early and late history—at the subject's social existence by hypertaboo or by hyperconsumption and by increasing symbolic consumption in both cases.

I have to end this long conclusion without a sense of an ending. So I will let the curtain close behind two ancient compatriots who will never die: "Non ho avuto tempo di esser breve" (G. B. Casti);[121] *"Chi mi sa dir s'io fingo?" (Gianmaria Ortes).*[122] *Or perhaps I should even add, with the positive Balzac, what I may have partly achieved by considering native abstractions by means of anthropological ones: "À l'abstraction commence la Société. . . . De l'Abstraction naissent les lois, les arts, les intérêts, les idées sociales."*[123]

Notes
Bibliography
Index

NOTES

Introduction

1. Valeri 1992c:33.
2. Valeri 1966, 1968, 1970.
3. Valeri 1992c:38.
4. Valeri 1992c:32.
5. Valeri 1996a.
6. Valeri 1968.
7. Valeri 1976b.
8. Valeri 1992c:38.
9. Valeri 1992c:39.
10. Valeri 1992c:39.
11. Valeri 1992c:37.
12. Valeri 1992c:37.
13. Valeri 1981a.
14. Valeri 1996c.
15. Valeri 1992c:37.
16. Valeri 1999.

Preface

1. Although these powers may have been put in the thing or person by an external agent, divine or human, for protective purposes.
2. Dodds 1951:36.

Chapter 1: In the Heart of the Forest, at the End of Trade Routes

1. The main village on the plateau of inland central Seram.
2. Two villages of the Nisawele people, the eastern neighbors of the Huaulu.
3. See Upton Sinclair, *The Jungle.*
4. The *I* indicates the subject who speaks, remembers, and interprets today but who was inseparable at that time from his wife, Renée. It is her coexistence that explains the descriptive *we* of my fieldnote quotations here. Nevertheless I cannot speak for her now. Nor could she speak for facts, feelings, and events in subsequent field research in which she did not participate and which, therefore, require the *I* at the descriptive as well as the interpretive level.
5. A stringed instrument adapted, in nature and name, from a rebab.
6. Wessing 1977:293–303.
7. Although they themselves sometimes idealize the Nuaulu, their cousins on the southern coast, and turn them into their absolutely traditional alter egos. It seems that one's "purity" always resides in somebody else.

8. The definite suffixes *-am* (sing.) and *-em* (pl.) are usually found at the end of Huaulu nouns. From now on, they will not always be included, only in contexts where the Huaulu themselves would normally use them, or to give a sense of Huaulu alternative usage and sometimes meaning. (See chapter 3 for a fuller discussion of linguistic issues.)

9. The primary meaning of *Laufaha* is "people from the coast," who in Seram are usually Islamic. That is why their name is not given a form analogous to the names of the Christians and mountain people.

10. From the Bahasa Indonesia (henceforth B.I.) *agama,* itself derived from Sanskrit.

11. See the final section of Valeri 1996b ("Temps mythique et temps historique").

12. Huaulu is the name of a people, of its domain, and of the village that is its official (and ceremonial) center. Its specific reference can usually be gathered from the context.

13. Sachse 1907:1.

14. Ellen 1978:7.

15. C. A. Fischer 1964:40.

16. Sachse 1907; cf. Ellen 1978:214.

17. Reiner 1956:47, 50.

18. This is also used for suicide.

19. Based on my census of gardens in 1972–73, the average size of gardens was a paltry 184.45 square meters. Only two new gardens were opened over a period of 17 months, and during that same period exactly half (11) of all households had no garden to rely on, and most of the other half had gardens that were not very productive.

20. This was the case until recently almost everywhere in Seram (see map in Ellen 1978:6–7).

21. Javanese have been settled by the government east of Wahai. It is the more recent phenomenon.

22. Assemblage of wild, not human-set, trees.

23. C. A. Fischer 1964:43.

24. Merrill 1945:xiv.

25. Their population oscillated between 141 and 144 during my first sojourn in 1972–73. How do these population figures compare with the average ones in the district of northern Seram? Census figures from Dutch times cannot be directly compared with census figures after the Indonesian independence, since, as I have mentioned, the Onderafdeeling Wahai was larger than the Kecamatan Seram Utara now is.

The first Indonesian census in the area was in 1970; 12,045 inhabitants were recorded. At the time a second census was taken in 1980, the population was 15,443—an increase of 2.77 percent over 1970. Since the number of desa, administrative villages (often including several separate settlements), is 21 in the district of northern Seram, the average population per desa was 573 inhabitants in 1971 and 735.4 in 1980. For administrative purposes, Huaulu is considered a desa. Its population was thus considerably below that of the average desa. However, the administrative repartition of the population into desa is highly arbitrary. Actual villages (i.e. settlements called kampung in Indonesian and niniani, amani, or yamano locally) are the only significant units in indigenous terms. Furthermore, the coastal desa, some of which (such as Malako) include exclusively immigrants, are considerably more populous, since they live off trade, cash crops such as copra, and a fairly intensive horticulture. More significant is the comparison between the population of Huaulu and the average population of actual mountain villages and of coastal settlements of mountain origin, which have no or few immigrants. I do not have complete data on all such villages in the district of Wahai. In particular, I lack data for a few villages west of Sawai. I will therefore consider only the villages east of Sawai, for which I have population data obtained in the administrative headquarters of the Kabupaten at Masohi. These were collected at the time of the 1970 census.

The mountain or mountain-originated villages in my sample number 24. Their total population was 4,126. The average population per village was thus 171.9. Huaulu's population was still inferior to the average, but closer to it than to the average population of northern Seram villages. I have no comparable figures from the 1980 census, or from the time of my last field trip in 1988, but I suspect that Huaulu has grown closer to the average.

26. See Sachse 1907: map facing p. 140.

27. Ellen 1975:143–144.

28. In more recent years, gardening and coconut planting for copra have developed among the Huaulu who live on the coast (for reasons to be explained later), but in the mountain village conditions are still close to those observed during my first period of field research.

29. Collins 1984:87. There are 50 languages in the central Moluccas as a whole (Stresemann 1923).

30. Collins 1983:19.

31. Collins 1983:20.

32. De Vries 1927; Jensen 1949; Grzimek 1991.

33. I follow the Huaulu renderings of these names.

34. Stresemann 1923.

35. See Ellen 1978:11.

36. Collins 1983:37.

37. Collins 1983:37.

38. Collins 1983:109.

39. Collins 1983:102.

40. Collins 1983:102.

41. Frassen 1987:34.

42. In the last few years, though, prices have fallen precipitously all over Indonesia because of overproduction.

43. See Roeder 1948; and my fieldnotes.

44. Officially at least, the Bati are now (at the end of the eighties) generically converted to Islam.

45. Valeri 1989.

46. In fact, the Lima territory does not extend indefinitely toward the west, for the people of western Seram declare themselves Siwa. Nor do the Siwa occupy the whole of the island east of Huaulu, for the Maneo consider themselves Lima. The Huaulu extend to the whole of Seram what is in fact true of central Seram exclusively.

47. On the coexistence of hierarchy and agonistic equality in Huaulu society generally, see Valeri 1990a.

48. Although there was an unsuccessful parenthesis in the midnineteenth century (Willer 1849).

49. In 1922, when the first relatively reliable census was taken, the total population of the island numbered 81,225. Of these, 4,305 were classified as "nonindigenous"; 42,776, as Muslim; 12,719, as Christian; and 21,435, as pagans. Most of the inland population was then pagan. It is now, for the most part, Christian. According to unpublished census reports to which I was given access in Masohi (the capital of the Kabupaten Maluku Tenggah), the only groups still identified as pagan in 1971 were in central and eastern Seram. The largest numbers (true or false, I do not know) given concerned the Bati people and the Masiwang-Bobot people of the district of Werinama in eastern Seram. It was claimed that there were 694 of them, found in 19 different settlements (although the number of pagans was 1 in each of two settlements!). In north-central Seram, pagans were found in Huaulu (who according to the 1971 census numbered 139) and in the Seti area, where they were supposed to be about 70. To this I would add about 40 people from Openg. In south-central Seram, there were allegedly about 150 left in the hinterland of the bay of Taluti (communities of Ekano, Hilamatan, and Mangadua). Farther west, 200 more were listed in the village of Yalahatan, and most of the 496 Nuaulu of the villages of Bunara, Niamonai, and Ruhuwa were given as pagans (population figures for the Nuaulu are corrected on the basis of information provided by Ellen 1978:12). In sum, there were approximately 1,789 pagans left in 1971 within a total population 164,626. Since then, their number has, officially at least, further diminished. Practically all Openg have become Christian, several Nuaulu were reportedly converted to Christianity and even to Islam. The inhabitants of Hilamatan and Mangadua, now reunited in the new village of Amahena near the southern coast, are registered as Christian. And I have been told that most Bati are now officially Muslim, at least in the view of the coastal people of Kiandarat and Kianlaut.

50. On Sahulau, see Valentijn 1862 and Rumphius [1679] 1983.

51. Interestingly, the contrast between the two categories of religion is usually reinforced by a linguistic asymmetry. The definite article which may be attached to *Laufaha* is not often used, whereas the reverse is true of *Memaha*, which is usually employed with either the singular (*-am*) or plural (*-em*) article.

52. Furthermore, just as in the case of the Siwa/Lima opposition, local relations often were more important than those generically induced by categorical oppositions. The Huaulu were and are on friendly terms with at least one Laufaha people on the northern coast of Seram: the Saleman. With another people, the Besi (Pesiem, in the Huaulu language), the relations were more complex. They were often raided, yet they were considered a "client" people, to be protected against the encroachments of others. Note also that if the oppositions Memahem/Laufaha and hoto mui/lau tasiam imply a certain generic solidarity of inland people against coastal ones, they do not prescribe it, nor do they of course, exclude, conflicts among inland peoples. Finally, the overlapping of the Siwa/Lima opposition with the other two should be considered part of the picture. The greatest enemies that the Huaulu have among the Laufaha, namely

the people of Sawai and Wahai, are in the Siwa category, although the Huaulu seem to pay attention to their Laufaha identity only.

53. See Howell (1989:44) on Allah Ta'Allah, from the Arabic *Allah Taala,* "God most high." *Ta'Ala* is also added to *Allah* as "praised" (Echols and Shadily 1989:13).

54. See De Martino 1976 on the Judaeo-Christian inspiration of Durkheim.

55. See Endicott 1979:124 and Howell 1989. Their use of the term *superhuman* goes back at least to Robertson Smith (W. R. Smith 1984:151, 447), although in him it is merely an alternate to *supernatural*—another misleading term, as demonstrated by Renan (1885:257), followed by Durkheim (1915) and Lévy-Bruhl (1931).

56. For longer developments of this point, see Valeri 1990a:58–62 and Valeri 1996b:108–110.

57. See the classification of "spirits" by their supposed relation to humans in Kodi (Hoskins 1993, 1998).

58. Through some Indonesian language, the word *sewa* ultimately derives from Sanskrit *seva,* "service, attendance; worship, homage, reverence; practice, frequent enjoyment; resorting (to), frequentation" (Gonda 1973:482).

59. I may perhaps be allowed to refer to two stages of my conception of sacrifice: Valeri 1985, 1994c. The latter specifically treats the Huaulu case.

60. As is well known, negative expressions are always marked as opposed to positive or affirmative ones (Horn 1989:154ff.). Thus *manusiassi,* "nonhuman," is the marked term which presupposes its opposite, *manusia,* as its unmarked ground.

61. The Huaulu do not make any conceptual distinction between war and headhunting. Both are referred to as lisam, "war." It is understood that in war one takes heads and that one may make war to obtain heads. Yet one may specifically speak of amana' akaem, "stealing heads," when the purpose is exclusively to obtain heads.

62. As such, witches are also put in the general category of kinakinaem. Mumanu are humans who are driven to madness by occult powers appearing to them in the form of game animals. Mumanu pursue the animals endlessly in the forest, until they lose their humanity and finally their life.

63. After their conversion to Islam, these rulers acquired the title of sultan. Thus the title soltane may be used instead of kolalem to refer to the shamanic familiars modelled after them. The acclimatization of these external political powers as shamanic familiars is not a unique phenomenon in the area of their former influence (e.g. Wana) and has parallels elsewhere (e.g. Zanzibar and Madagascar).

64. I should say that axiomatically witches are considered non-Huaulu and thus enemies or in any case unreliable outsiders.

65. Valeri 1990a.

66. See Valeri 1975, 1976a, 1980, 1994a.

67. See Valeri 1975, 1976a.

68. See Valeri 1996c.

69. This title, which has wide currency in Seram, is of Portuguese origin. It goes back to the council of native chiefs (camara, or "chamber") organized by the Portuguese in Ambon in the sixteenth century.

70. Valeri 1990a.

71. This community hall (luma potoam, lit., "the big house," often called the baileo in other parts of the Moluccas) is referred to as the village temple in other sections of this book. It is a single structure with many uses.

72. Rumphius [1679] 1983, 1705; Valentijn 1862; Knaap 1987a.

73. Hooyer 1895–97, 2:156; Seran 1922.

74. There are several references to this post in the company's reports. See, especially, Knaap 1987b, passim.

75. Where it goes under the name of rumah obat.

76. In Haitiling, on the site of present Wahai.

77. Hooyer 1895–97, 1:35.

78. The post of Wahai was established in 1829 (Seran 1922:74). It became a meeting point and supply producer for ships whaling in the Pacific.

79. Although military expeditions against them proved necessary in 1875 (Hooyer 1895–97, 2:156; Seran 1922:75) and in 1908 (Seran 1922:266–267).

80. I have been unable to establish the date of this move. The *terminus a quo* is 1911, when the German naturalist Tauern found their mountain village still inhabited (Tauern 1918).

81. Seran 1922:75.

82. Seran 1922:200.

83. Seran 1922:74.

84. See Roeder 1948 on Piliana.

85. Sachse 1907:75–76.

86. On this whole period see the important study by Chauvel (1990).

87. Much more so than the Nuaulu and other such small traditional groups.

88. Valeri 1975, 1976a, 1980, 1989, 1990a.

Chapter 2: Taboo in Anthropology

1. Aquinas, *Summa Theologica* 1.49.2.

2. See Gauchet 1979.

3. Frazer 1911:224, cit. in Steiner 1956:98–99.

4. W. R. Smith 1894:153.

5. W. R. Smith 1894:153.

6. W. R. Smith 1894:466.

7. Durkheim 1896:5. ["... terrible powers which ... react, with automatic necessity, against everything that offends them, just as do the physical forces" (Durkheim 1963:18).]

8. Durkheim 1915:428–30.

9. Radcliffe-Brown 1948:272.

10. Radcliffe-Brown 1965:135. Although Radcliffe-Brown prefers *ritual sanction* (i.e. a sanction effected by the belief that a misfortune, usually an illness, will occur) to *ritual pollution,* he occasionally uses the two terms interchangeably, as when he writes that in many "simple societies," "sickness—for instance leprosy among the Hebrews—is often regarded as similar to ritual or religious pollution and as therefore requiring expiation or ritual purification" (1965:207).

11. Steiner 1956:147, 114–115.

12. Ricoeur 1969:25–29; Dodds 1954; Moulinier 1952; Vernant 1980; Parker 1990; Douglas 1966. Moreover, in claiming that "primitive culture is pollution-prone whereas ours is not" (Douglas 1966:73), Douglas shows herself in a straight line of descent from Frazer's, Robertson Smith's, and Durkheim's evolutionary problematic of taboo.

13. The equation of taboo and obligation is found in Fortes 1967.

14. Again, *mystical retribution* is the preferred term of Fortes (1967:11).

15. For an example of this empirical, rather than imperative, ideology of taboo, see Laderman 1981.

16. "Defilement . . . is . . . a something that infects by contact. But the infectious contact is experienced subjectively in a specific feeling which is of the order of Dread. Man enters into the ethical world through fear and not through love" (Ricoeur 1969:29–30).

17. As Steiner puts it, "Taboo is a single, not an 'undifferentiated,' concept" (1956:34). Cf. Valeri 1985, ch. 2.

18. See Horn 1989:154ff.

19. Frazer 1928:19.

20. Frazer 1928:19.

21. Frazer 1928:49.

22. Frazer 1928:19–20.

23. Horton 1970.

24. Michaux 1949:27.

25. There have been a number of recent "Frazerian" studies of taboo: Laderman 1981; Rozin and Nemeroff 1990.

26. Durkheim 1896:5.

27. This theory seems to be directly derived from the Old Testament, where sex with kinswomen is banned on the grounds that one cannot see the blood of kin. Durkheim was himself the son of a rabbi (Lukes 1973).

28. Durkheim 1896:40–41, 53, 47ff.

29. Durkheim 1896:53.

30. "L'expiation doit se produire d'elle-même et comme mécaniquement" (Durkheim 1896:5). ["The expiation must be produced out of itself and, as it were, automatically" (Durkheim 1963:19).]

31. Durkheim 1896:54–57.

32. Durkheim 1896:56–57. ["We leave something of ourselves wherever we pass; the spot on which we tread, or where we place our hand, retains as it were a part of our substance, which in this way disperses itself without impoverishing itself. Like everything else, it comes from the divine. It permeates into everything that approaches it; it is even endowed with a higher contagion than that of purely human properties, because it has a much greater power of action" (Durkheim 1963:70–71).]

33. Durkheim 1968:463.

34. For "les êtres sacrés sont, par définition, des êtres sépares" (Durkheim 1968:428). ["By definition, sacred beings are separated beings" (Durkheim 1915:337).]

35. Durkheim 1968:430. [". . . useful maxims, the first form of hygienic and medical interdictions" (Durkheim 1915:339).]

36. "La notion toute laïque de propriété," to quote Durkheim's own untranslatable words (1968:431).

37. Again, the biblical inspiration is quite evident.

38. Durkheim 1968:432ff.

39. Durkheim 1968:431.

40. Durkheim 1968:452.

41. "Il n'y a pas . . . d'interdit dont l'observance n'ait, à quelque degré, un caractère ascétique" (Durkheim 1968:444). ["There is no interdict, the observance of which does not have an ascetic character to a certain degree" (Durkheim 1915:350).]

42. Durkheim 1968:452. ["It is an integral part of all human culture" (Durkheim 1915:356).]

43. "Le culte positif n'est donc possible que si l'homme est entraîné au renoncement, à l'abnégation, au détachement de soi et, par conséquent, à la souffrance" (Durkheim 1968:451). ["The positive cult is possible only when a man is trained to renouncement, to abnegation, to detachment from self, and consequently to suffering" (Durkheim 1915:355).]

44. Durkheim 1968:452; my translation.

45. Radcliffe-Brown 1965:139 ("Taboo").

46. Radcliffe-Brown 1965:151 ("Taboo").

47. Radcliffe-Brown 1948:275.

48. Radcliffe-Brown 1965:150 ("Taboo").

49. Radcliffe-Brown 1965:152 ("Taboo").

50. Radcliffe-Brown 1965:143 ("Taboo").

51. Radcliffe-Brown 1965:143 ("Taboo"). In what follows, I expand on Radcliffe-Brown's own treatment of this example.

52. Radcliffe-Brown 1948:269.

53. Radcliffe-Brown 1948:402–403.

54. "The social value of anything" is defined as "the way in which that thing affects or is capable of affecting social life" (Radcliffe-Brown 1948:264).

55. At the same time as he uses the notion of value quantitatively, Radcliffe-Brown fails to attach any criterion of measurement to it, as Leach (1971:46) notes. See also my more extended criticism of Radcliffe-Brown's calculus of social value, in Valeri 1981b.

56. Radcliffe-Brown 1948:269.

57. Radcliffe-Brown 1948:269. This second principle comes dangerously close to the idea (already formulated by Cicero *De natura deorum* 1.36.101) that only animals that are useful are imbued with sacred/dangerous qualities.

58. Leach 1971:41, 43.

59. See Leach 1971:38.

60. This, however, seems to run astray from Radcliffe-Brown's own emphasis on social value as the expression of the moral force of society, since it is based on utilitarian facts conceived in a socially decontextualized way: the actual, physical danger represented by an animal; a matter of taste (preference for fatty foods). Of course, it is possible to argue that these material or sensorial facts acquire social value by virtue of existing as givens for a society; but perhaps they may be further analyzed in more cultural terms—that is, as socially constituted and not simply as socially assumed. But then if food preferences are

to be explained in social terms, how can they explain, in Radcliffe-Brown's manner, the degree of social value that is attached to them? The explanation would become, once again, dangerously circular, with social value explaining social value.

61. Radcliffe-Brown 1948:218.

62. See Leach 1971:30 and his references to the myths transcribed by Man and Radcliffe-Brown. The reason the civet cat and monitor lizard are the most important of these beings, from which all living things descend, is that they straddle different habitats and can therefore represent all species living in those habitats (see Radcliffe-Brown 1948:346–348 and Leach 1971:392).

63. Radcliffe-Brown 1948:266–268. Danger is indicated by the word for heat (*kimil*) in the language of the Andamanese groups studied by Radcliffe-Brown (see Leach 1971:22).

64. Radcliffe-Brown 1948:268.

65. The principles stressed by Radcliffe-Brown—"desirability" and "fearsomeness" of the animal—may indeed play a role, but then in conjunction with this idea of retribution. The greater the pleasure the eater extracts from the animal, the greater the animal's moral claim on him; and the more powerful and ferocious the animal is, the more seemingly real the danger that it will be able to exact reciprocation.

66. Radcliffe-Brown 1948:268.

67. Radcliffe-Brown 1948:313–314.

68. Radcliffe-Brown 1948:314.

69. Radcliffe-Brown 1948:313.

70. Thus protective ornaments are fashioned from their bones (Radcliffe-Brown 1948:273–274).

71. The taboos on these animals become total, rather than simply conditional on not using other precautions such as painting one's body with clay, when the person is in a state of particular vulnerability. This happens in rites of passage and when one has committed murder (note how the murder of a human is subtly linked, through these taboos, to the "murder" of an animal).

72. "The prohibited desire in the unconscious shifts from one thing to another" (Freud 1950:34).

73. Freud 1950:34–35. A lot of importance is given by Freud himself (p. 66), and consequently by his critics, to the thesis that parallelisms exist between the thought processes that underly the existence of taboos and the thought processes that underly neurotic avoidances. These parallelisms, if they exist, are of little interest to the present discussion and are not, in my opinion, what is significant in Freud's contribution to the topic of taboo.

74. Freud 1950:68.

75. On this interpretive strategy, see Skorupski 1976 and Valeri 1981a, 1992b.

76. Valeri 1985, conclusions.

77. Valeri 1992b.

78. Leach 1964:30.

79. In his privileging of results over the processes and conditions that bring about the results, Leach shows himself to be the functionalist that he always claimed to be.

80. Leach 1964.

81. The point was seen well by Philo, who claimed that Moses tabooed the most delicious foods so that the Israelites would learn moral discipline (Douglas 1966:44, quoting from Stein 1957:141ff.). As a blanket explanation for the prohibitions of Leviticus, Philo's principle is, of course, wrong. But it captures the fundamental point that what has to be given up must have some value if the giving up is to have some value. Hence, tabooed foods must be good to eat or at least considered edible. Interestingly, one Buginese (thus Muslim) peddler I met in Seram explained the taboo on pork in his religion with a story that starts from the same premise as Philo's.

82. Leach 1964:23.

83. Leach 1971:44.

84. Leach 1964:35 (see diagram).

85. Leach 1964:37.

86. Leach 1964:23.

87. Leach 1964:39.

88. Leach observes that in English "obscenity," that is, the breaking of verbal taboos, falls into three classes: "1) dirty words—usually referring to sex and excretion; 2) blasphemy and profanity; 3) animal abuse—in which a human being is equated with an animal of another species" (Leach 1964:28). He professes to know nothing about the reasons for this, but surely there must be a reason why the "mixings" that taboo represses all concern the contrast between higher and lower categories, and not just any categories. The taboos of the first class repress the mixing of higher and lower functions of the body; those of the second class and third classes, the mixing of higher and lower beings (respectively, gods and humans; humans and animals).

89. Leach makes no attempt to explain these differences. But in his theoretical framework only one explanation seems possible: that some cultures are better at categorizing than others; that is, they devise categories that fit perception better and thus leave fewer residues to taboo. Implicitly, then, Leach's theory is still in the line of the ethnocentric-evolutionary approach of Frazer and his kind.

90. As perhaps happens when the elements that do not fit preexisting *Gestalten* are suppressed and are thus not perceived at all.

91. Indeed this suppression would seem to be required by Leach's own claim that we can perceive as things only what our categories allow us to perceive as such. As he writes, the "world is a representation of our language categories, not vice versa. Because my mother tongue is English, it seems self evident that *bushes* and *trees* are different kinds of things. I would not think this unless I had been taught that it was the case" (Leach 1964:34). Nothing is left in between bushes and trees, then.

92. "It is crucially important that the basic discriminations should be clear-cut and unambiguous" (Leach 1964:35).

93. See Lakoff 1987.

94. Wittgenstein 1958; Needham 1975; Ellen 1993a:129.

95. Mayr 1984:647.

96. See Bulmer 1967.

97. Leach 1964:45–46.

98. E.g. Leach 1964:25, 45.
99. E.g. Leach 1964:40, 45.
100. Leach 1964.
101. Leach 1964:43.
102. Leach 1964:44.
103. Leach 1964:44.
104. Leach 1964:45.
105. Leach 1964:53.
106. See Leach 1964:41, table 1.
107. Things may change in other cultures, which shows that any simple generalization about what "generates" taboo is inherently questionable.
108. Leach 1971:24, 29.
109. Radcliffe-Brown 1948:348.
110. Radcliffe-Brown 1948:348.
111. Radcliffe-Brown 1948:348.
112. Leach 1971:29ff.
113. In what way, for instance, are sharks, which are a strong focus of taboo, anomalous?
114. Leach 1971:30.
115. For the turtle, see Leach 1971:29. The reason why honey (as a product of bees) may be viewed as anomalous is not spelled out by Leach. Presumably it is anomalous because it is the only kind of animal secretion (or even "excrement") that is good to eat.
116. Although as Radcliffe-Brown pointed out, as we have seen, he had an unduly restrictive and utilitarian view of such value and considered it a variable independent of cosmological classification.
117. Indeed, the turtle, along with the dugong, which is also a focus of taboos, is the sea animal most important for humans and is also anthropomorphic in many of its traits. Among the land animals, the pig's importance for humans and its anthropomorphism are unrivalled. As for bees, they produce the most valued substance among those that can be obtained from the creatures up in the trees. And probably, their social life strikes the Andamanese, as it does so many other people, as being similar to human social life.
118. "Pollution" in Douglas 1975b:54.
119. "The danger [of pollution] replaces active human punishment" (Douglas 1966:134; see also pp. 14, 142).
120. Douglas 1975b:54. The idea goes back to Durkheim (1896:5), as we have seen.
121. Douglas 1966:4.
122. Douglas 1966:35; "Pollution" in Douglas 1975b:50. On the idea of dirt as "matter out of place," Douglas (1966:164) also quotes James (1902:129).
123. Douglas 1966:35.
124. See Valeri 1985: ch. 3 and Valeri 1990b, for Polynesian and Indonesian examples, respectively. An obvious Indian example is the cow, which is eminently pure but is eminently polluting if approached or used inappropriately (i.e. killed, flayed, eaten; its skin used as leather, and so on). See Stevenson 1954:63.
125. In formulating her general theory of pollution, Douglas seems to

forget what she herself notes at one point with regard to the use of the English adjective *dirty* in certain contexts: "Shoes are not dirty in themselves, but it is dirty to place them on the dining table; food is not dirty in itself, but it is dirty to leave cooking utensils in the bedroom, or food bespattered on clothing; similarly, bathroom equipment in the drawing room; clothing lying on chairs; outdoors things in-doors; upstairs things downstairs; under-clothing appearing where over-clothing should be, and so on" (Douglas 1966:36).

126. Here again, she converges with Leach.

127. On this filiation see Valeri 1979.

128. Marrett 1914:80–84, cit. in Steiner (1956:102–103).

129. See Neusner 1973 and I. M. Lewis 1991.

130. It should be clear that the transgression of a rule of avoidance is a secondary and derivative form of disorder. It presupposes the disorder intrinsic to what must be avoided. The latter is structural, in the sense that it reveals a failure in the principles that constitute the system—their inability to classify reality without residues. Douglas's theory of pollution as systemic residue threatening the system applies only to this primary, structural disorder.

131. As in the Greek notion of miasma, where the murderer, for instance, is stained by the blood of his victim until the latter is appeased.

132. An excellent example is the miasma of the ancient Greeks (see Parker 1990).

133. Douglas 1966:2.

134. Indeed, many pollutions simply mark off an offender for a conventional time and automatically cease to exist at the expiration of that time. For instance, according to Leviticus (11:24–25, 27–28, 30–31), whoever touches the carcasses of winged insects or of quadrupeds "that go on their paws" (27), and of a variety of other animals, becomes automatically unclean, but this uncleanness lasts only until evening. The conventional character of pollution is made even more evident when an actual misfortune is involved in it, as in the case of leprosy. As Lewis notes, "If someone plucked out the signs of uncleanness [of leprosy], the white hairs, or cauterized quick flesh before he came to the priest, he was clean; but if he did so after he had been certified unclean, he was still unclean" (G. Lewis 1987:597).

135. Perhaps because pollution beliefs in complex societies are in obvious contradiction to her evolutionary view that only "primitive culture is pollution-prone" (Douglas 1966:73). Certainly not always the most "primitive" cultures (i.e. "undifferentiated"; see Douglas 1966:77), as the three examples below in the text demonstrate.

136. Dodds 1951; Moulinier 1952; Rudhardt 1958; Vernant 1980; Lloyd-Jones 1971:55–78; Parker 1990.

137. Dumont 1959; Harper 1964; Orenstein 1965, 1970a, 1970b; Madan 1985, 1991.

138. Neusner 1973, 1975; Levine 1974.

139. To be sure, Douglas does not really distinguish between different kinds of classification. But it seems that the reason she focusses on taxonomy is that it manifests in the highest degree a preoccupation with "neatness" and avoidance of ambiguity, which, in her view, is the source of the classificatory

impulse as such. Taxonomy thus reveals the essence of classification. This argument, though, is never fully developed or justified by Douglas.

140. Sperber 1975:12. On the intrinsically Aristotelian character of taxonomy, see Ellen 1993a:218ff.

141. This is a very strange definition, since all insects have six legs. What is probably meant—as Soler (1973:952) surmises—is that these insects walk like quadrupeds, whereas they should only fly, since they have wings.

142. Douglas 1966:48.

143. This view is brought to the most extreme conclusion by Kristeva, who extrapolates: "La loi, ce qui freine le desir de tuer, est une taxinomie" (Kristeva 1980:130). ["The law, in other words what restrains the desire to kill, is a taxonomy" (Kristeva 1982:112).]

144. Douglas 1972.

145. Hunn 1979:109; Kirk 1980:44–45.

146. Douglas 1966:55.

147. The only species that is demonstrably anomalous in the list is the bat, which is assimilated to a bird because it flies, but is otherwise like a terrestrial animal. Alter (1979:49) notes that there are two birds—chicken and duck—which can be construed as anomalous but are not taboo.

148. Kirk 1980:45.

149. Soler 1973:948–949; Hunn 1979:111; Kirk 1980:45–46.

150. As one of the three interpretations puts it (Kirk 1980:45).

151. I interpret this expression as a reference to felines and canines, not to the list of animals (weasel, mouse, crocodile, etc.) which Douglas (1966:56) attaches to it. In any case, it is agreed that the list of taboo animals includes carnivorous mammals, at least by implication (Hunn 1979:112).

152. Of the 20 birds mentioned, 15 are birds of prey, "probably barring from the table every known species of the orders Falconiformes and Strigiformes. Three additional categories eliminate the genus *Corvus,* all birds of scavenging propensities, and the fish-eating storks, herons, and cormorants. Thus 18 of 20 birds cited are meat and fish eaters" (Hunn 1979:111).

153. Kirk 1980:45–47.

154. Douglas herself, however, does not develop this interpretation and seems even to rule it out by writing that nothing is said in the Bible about predatory habits and scavenging as reasons for animal taboos (Douglas 1966:55).

155. Kirk 1980:45–46.

156. Stein 1957:146.

157. Douglas 1966:55.

158. Soler 1973.

159. Soler 1973:944.

160. Soler 1973:944–946.

161. I.e. when an individual animal does not fully correspond to its type, either by defect or because it has traits in conflict with its type.

162. Soler 1973:951.

163. Soler 1973:949. Bulmer notes that in New Guinea "both dogs and pigs interfere with trapping by consuming game before the hunter has had a chance to recover it" (Bulmer and Tyler 1968:337 n. 5).

164. Héritier in Introduction to Vialles 1987.

165. A key is not necessarily a taxonomy, but a taxonomy can function as a key. My point is that the biblical text develops a taxonomy in this case, but not out of a taxonomic impulse, only as a special kind of key, for that is its essential purpose.

166. "Cloven hoofed, cud chewing ungulates are the model of the proper kind of foods for a pastoralist" (Douglas 1966:54).

167. This seems Douglas's own view when she wraps the whole analysis up: "If the proposed interpretation of the forbidden animals is correct, the dietary laws would have been like signs which at every turn inspired meditation on the oneness, purity and completeness of God" (Douglas 1966:57). This would be true only in the sense that God sanctifies and personifies a lot that is socially and pragmatically true of his worshippers.

168. As Bulmer (1967:21) believes it must be for the taboo on the pig.

169. We have already encountered this term in the Andamans; it also exists in Groote Eylandt (Worsley 1982:72) and, as we shall see, in Huaulu.

170. Douglas 1966:55.

171. Soler 1973:951–952.

172. Soler 1973:952.

173. Douglas 1966:56.

174. Douglas 1966:56.

175. Douglas 1966:56.

176. Douglas (1975:285) herself has later recognized that this was "a too facile solution."

177. This last point has been made very well by Sperber (1975), following, in part, Leach (1971:44). However, Sperber's motivation of the normative impulse in purely cognitive terms (as a yearning for neatness where none can be found), and thus as belonging to a "symbolic apparatus (dispositif)" conceived as ancillary to the taxonomic and encyclopaedic ones, appears to me to reproduce the shortcomings of Douglas's theory at a higher level of rigor (i.e. he does not confuse taxonomic statements with normative ones). Sperber misses the fact that it is what animal types stand for in terms of moral and social types that makes them rigid and generates the fear of anomalies. It is not in an abstract cognitive function but in concrete social evaluations that one must look for an answer to the issue of normative ideals in animal classifications.

178. The only purely taxonomic motivation I can think of for adhering rigidly to the definition of each group of animals by the prototypes bird, quadruped, and fish is that these prototypes are related systematically. Indeed, wing, foot, and fin form a series of variations inside the same category—the organ of locomotion. Any redefinition of each group that abandons these traits in order to accommodate more species would break this systematicity. One can well suppose that a desire for intellectual order also plays a role here.

179. Hunn 1979:113.

180. Bulmer 1967:19.

181. Bulmer 1967:18.

182. Tambiah's 1969 article, reprinted in Tambiah 1985a.

183. Tambiah 1985a:204.

184. Douglas 1970:270.

185. Douglas 1975:263–273.
186. Douglas 1975:304.
187. But see perhaps Douglas 1975:280–281.
188. Douglas 1975:285.
189. Douglas 1975:289–313.
190. See I. M. Lewis 1991.
191. As claimed by Douglas: "Any given system of classification must give rise to anomalies" (Douglas 1966:39). The point is repeated, more or less, in Douglas 1992:25.
192. Douglas 1975b:288.
193. Of which exogamy is said to be the most primitive form (Durkheim 1896:28).
194. Durkheim 1896:53.
195. Lévi-Strauss 1969.
196. Héritier 1979; Gomes da Silva 1983, 1984; Testart 1985, 1991.
197. Héritier 1979:233.
198. Héritier 1979:233.
199. An illustration is famously provided by Ayurvedic medicine, which even violates the ordinary rules of purity to reestablish the necessary balance in the body (see Zimmermann 1982).
200. Héritier comes closer to Leach when she adds that the taboo on the association of identicals is all the stronger when there is a certain ambiguity between difference and identity (Héritier 1979:232). Taboo disambiguates by emphasizing identity (and thus prohibition) over difference in such mixed cases. Note that for Leach, on the contrary, taboo disambiguates by emphasizing difference, contrast. Even when they come closest, Leach and Héritier reveal their fundamental differences.
201. Interestingly, it is most developed in cultures that have been influenced, directly or indirectly, by the related medical doctrines of Greeks, Arabs, and Indians. See, for instance, Zimmermann 1982 (on India) and Laderman 1981 (on Malaya).
202. Héritier 1984.
203. "Le tabou consiste en la séparation du même avec le même" (Testart 1985:385; see also p. 401). ["Taboo consists in separating same from same, that is, in separating one thing from being united with itself" (J.H.).]
204. Testart is therefore the theoretician of taboo who is closest to Durkheim's view of taboo (especially in his 1896 essay) as creator of difference in the face of the undifferentiating tendencies of the sacred.
205. He thus accepted Laura Lévi Makarius's generalization of Durkheim's theory of the taboos of menstruation and incest to all taboos (Makarius 1974:22–23).
206. Testart 1985:397.
207. Testart 1985:413.
208. Testart 1985:413.
209. Hence, Testart assumes that iron, hair, fire, and so on, are really blood in disguise, which explains, in his view, why they must frequently be kept separated from blood.
210. In fact, he is quite ready to acknowledge that "il est rare que les

croyances fassent explicitement référence au sang" (Testart 1985:417). ["Beliefs rarely make explicit reference to blood" (J.H.).] But he argues that if the manifest discourse of society seems bloodless, its latent meaning has always to do with blood (p. 400). This must remain a postulate, however.

211. Testart 1985:413.

212. Testart 1985:397.

213. Testart 1985:389.

214. "Le sang est antinomique avec lui-même" (Testart 1985:462). ["Blood is an antinomy to itself" (J.H.).] "Le tabou ne consiste pas à séparer deux choses différentes qui s'opposeraient par l'essence, il vise à séparer deux choses similaires, essentiellement identiques, parce qu'elles sont toutes deux en contact avec le sang" (p. 355). ["Taboo does not consist in separating two different things that are already essentially in opposition, it instead tries to separate similar things, essentially identical, because they are both in contact with blood" (J.H.).]

215. Which is therefore not so different from that of Douglas and Leach, at least in the context of his explanation of why blood signifies transgression/subversion.

216. Testart 1991:66.

217. The separation is, in fact, of man and woman because of their opposite relationships to the bleeding animals: positive in men (who do not bleed), negative in women (who do bleed).

218. Testart 1985:453.

219. "La structure économique du communisme primitif et la structure de l'idéologie du sang expriment, chacun dans son domaine propre, la nécessité d'une même disjonction. Ce sont deux structures isomorphes. Elles ont la même armature logique" (Testart 1985:452). ["The economic structure of primitive communism and the ideological structure of blood express, each within its own domain, the necessity of disjunction. These are two isomorphic structures. They have the same logical armature" (J.H.).]

220. "La nature profonde du tabou . . . consiste en un mouvement centrifuge—mouvement par lequel le producteur est dessaisi de son produit, mouvement par lequel le même est éloigné du même" (Testart 1985:463). ["Taboo's most profound nature . . . consists in a centrifugal movement by which the producer is released from his product, a movement in which same is separated from same" (J.H.).]

221. Testart 1991.

222. Testart 1991:96.

223. Testart 1991:129.

224. Gomes da Silva 1983, 1984.

225. This is basically her response to Needham's skeptical consignment of the anthropological class of "incest" to nonexistence (Needham 1971).

226. Gomes da Silva 1983:74.

227. Gomes da Silva 1984:122. ["An identity crisis is produced as soon as another person either becomes too similar to me, or becomes too different, since the two produce the same effect, that is, depriving me of another presence, another image, another difference. The problem therefore is not simply to avoid excessive similarities, but also to prevent dangerous disjunctions" (J.H.).]

228. "Tout ce que l'on essaie de réaliser, c'est un état d'équilibre entre la

similitude et la différence" (Gomes da Silva 1983:76). ["Everything that we try to do, is in a state of equilibrium between similarity and difference" (J.H.).]

229. Gomes da Silva 1984:119. ["The language of pollution among the Trobrianders articulates the rules of social identity: it recreates a differential scale when an intolerable proximity is affirmed" (J.H.).]

230. Gomes da Silva 1984:121. ["Some of the distinctions used in pollution function to impose rules on the universe of similarities"(J.H.).]

231. "La pollution permet d'établir des différences, mais elle le fait à partir de la reconnaissance d'un réseau de similitudes préalables" (Gomes da Silva 1984:123–124). ["Pollution makes it possible to establish differences, but only on the basis of the recognition of a network of pre-established similarities" (J.H.).]

232. Devyer 1973. The fear of pollution of the French aristocracy was limited to the pollution of blood through marriage with outsiders.

233. Lévi-Strauss 1966:115.

234. Radcliffe-Brown 1952.

235. Fortes 1967:8. The last point has been much developed by Testart (1985).

236. Lévi-Strauss 1966:116.

237. Lévi-Strauss 1966:109–110. The food exchanges in question include the "imaginary" ones that exist among clans each of which has the ritual guardianship of a species. On these imaginary exchanges, see Lanternari 1982.

238. Lévi-Strauss 1966:116–117.

239. Lévi-Strauss dismisses the claim that totemism involves not just significations but also moral rules (such as the prohibition on marrying persons with the same totem or eating or touching the totem) with the curious argument that moral prescriptions are not always found connected with totemic classifications (1966:97). This is again an essentialist argument, but with a peculiarly unacceptable twist. It assumes that if one phenomenon is (at least overtly) less general than another with which it is associated, then this phenomenon is irrelevant to the interpretation of that other phenomenon. The argument confuses the interpretation of a phenomenon with that of its most commonly realized feature. Moreover, Lévi-Strauss reduces some of those moral phenomena—particularly the taboos—to mere devices for creating signification (see 1966:102–103, and my discussion below). He thus incurs in the *petitio principii* that everything "totemic" about totemism must be of a purely semiotic nature.

240. Or also, as he says, "supplementary" or "complementary" (Lévi-Strauss 1966:103).

241. "The fact that some species are forbidden and others permitted is not attributable to the belief that the former have some intrinsic physical or mystic property which makes them harmful but to the concern to introduce a distinction between 'stressed' and 'unstressed' species (in the sense linguists give to these terms). Prohibiting some species is just one of several ways of singling them out as significant and the practical rules in question can thus be thought of as operators employed by a logic which, being of a qualitative kind, can work in terms of modes of behavior as well as of images" (Lévi-Strauss 1966:102; see also pp. 103, 108).

242. Lévi-Strauss 1966:106–108.

243. Lienhardt 1961:165–166; Fortes 1967:13, 14.

244. For instance, the color and shape of houses among the Tallensi.

245. Fortes 1967:16.

246. Lévi-Strauss 1966:117, 130–131.

247. I am purposely brief here, for these points will be developed at length in the analysis of Huaulu food taboos.

248. Gell 1979:137.

249. To put it differently: A category of persons exists precisely because they are the only ones to observe a certain taboo (Gell 1979:136).

250. Note that Gell treats ego, self, personality, and subject as interchangeable concepts. It may be argued that they are inseparable but not identical. But in the context of the present discussion, it is not necessary to revindicate their difference.

251. Gell 1979:137.

252. Gell 1979:145–147.

253. Which is indeed defined as the projection of the paradigmatic axis onto the syntagmatic one. See Jakobson 1960.

254. Gell 1979:139.

255. Gell 1979:144 n. 1.

256. It cannot explain either, because it cannot explain both, as we have seen.

257. In other languages, including the Huaulu language, the use of the word for "eating" to refer to killing and copulating is metaphoric. A clear indication of this is that there are more specific and more common words for killing and copulating. Gell could prove that *tadv* has no privileged relationship with eating in Umeda only if there were no other words referring specifically to killing and copulating.

258. Gell 1979:135.

259. See also Bataille 1973.

260. Meigs 1978:312.

261. Which she has herself studied in the field (see Meigs 1978).

262. Meigs 1978:313 (emphasis removed).

263. Meigs 1978:315.

264. Indeed, Meigs uses the classical diacritic model to separate "mess," "dirt," and "pollution" (1978:314–315).

265. "Our instinctive recoil from contact with other persons' emissions reflects our fear of their decaying power" (Meigs 1978:312). Contrary to this view one can adduce what Sartre says of the revulsion felt for viscousness: that it cannot be explained except if the moral qualities attributed to viscousness are present in its experience from the very beginning (Sartre 1980:696). Viscousness "manifeste une certaine relation de l'être avec lui-même et cette relation est originellement *psychisée* parce que je l'ai découverte dans une ébauche d'appropriation et que la viscosité m'a renvoyé mon image" (p. 703). [". . . manifests a certain relation of being with itself and this relation has originally a psychic quality because I have discovered it in a plan of appropriation and because the sliminess has returned my image to me" (Sartre 1966:779).]

266. Note that Meigs purports to describe only the ideas of pollution of the Hua and of North Americans. That these two peoples have extremely different ideas in every respect except pollution, however, seems to suggest that

they are not alone in sharing the same basic view of the phenomenon—indeed, that such a view is of extreme generality. Meigs could hardly expect us to believe otherwise, since she derives the Hua-American view of pollution from a very immediate, "instinctive" psychological phenomenon of revulsion for substances which evoke death.

267. Meigs 1978:313.

268. Although Meigs is right to object to Leach's purely cognitive view of such ambivalence.

269. Because bodily emissions can be transferred from body to body or those of one body can become mixed with those of another body, they always in some measure evoke the danger of identity loss. This danger is present even when the relationship with the other is "positive."

270. Meigs 1978:313.

271. Kristeva 1980.

272. For details, see Kristeva 1977:232–234, 228–229.

273. Kristeva 1980:87. [". . . having areas, orifices, points and lines, surfaces and hollows, where the archaic power of mastery and neglect, of the differentiation of proper-clean and improper-dirty, possible and impossible" (Kristeva 1982:72).]

274. As is well known, Freud speaks of a phallic stage for both males and females, because for him the same and only organ, the phallus, matters for them both. The phallus has a symbolic and not an anatomical reality. Lacan views it as a "signifier of desire" (quoted in Kristeva 1985). The resolution of the Oedipus complex constitutes the subject in relationship to the phallus, and thus, symbolically, to the father (Laplanche and Pontalis 1974:311–312).

275. Kristeva 1980:87. ["If language, like culture, sets up a separation and, starting with discrete elements, concatenates an order, it does so precisely by repressing maternal authority and the corporeal mapping that abuts against them" (Kristeva 1982:72).]

276. Kristeva 1980:88; my translation.

277. Kristeva 1980:88. ["Through language and within highly hierarchical religious institutions, man hallucinates partial 'objects'—witnesses to an archaic differentiation of the body on its way toward ego identity, which is also sexual identity. The *defilement* from which ritual protects us is neither sign nor matter. Within the rite that extracts it from repression and depraved desire, defilement is the translinguistic spoor of the most archaic boundaries of the self's clean and proper body. In that sense, if it is a jettisoned object, it is so from the mother" (Kristeva 1982:73).]

278. Kristeva 1980:82.

279. Kristeva 1980:83. ["One encounters it as soon as the symbolic and/or social dimension of man is constituted" (Kristeva 1982:68).]

280. Kristeva 1980:79. ["The function of these religious rituals is to ward off the subject's fear of his very own identity sinking irretrievably into the mother" (Kristeva 1982:64).]

281. Kristeva (1980) even invokes residues of "matrilineality."

282. Kristeva 1980:79–80. [". . . does not succeed in differentiating itself as *other* but threatens one's *own and clean self,* which is the underpinning of any organization constituted by exclusions and hierarchies" (Kristeva 1982:65).]

283. Kristeva 1980:123. [". . . the admixture, the flow, the noncompliant,

converging on that 'improper and unclean' place, which is the maternal living being" (Kristeva 1982:104).]

284. Kristeva 1980:123. ["Defilement will now be that which impinges on symbolic oneness, that is, sham, substitutions, doubles, idols" (Kristeva 1982:104).]

285. Kristeva 1980:130. This point is, of course, derived from Douglas: "If the proposed interpretation of the forbidden animals is correct, the dietary laws would have been like signs which at every turn inspired meditation on the oneness, purity and completeness of God" (Douglas 1966:57).

286. "L'alimentaire, quand il déroge à la conformité exigible par la logique des séparations, se confond avec le maternel comme lieu impropre de la fusion, comme puissance indifférenciée et menace, souillure à retrancher" (Kristeva 1980:124). ["The dietary, when it departs from the conformity that can be demanded by the logic of separation, blends with the maternal as unclean and improper coalescence, as undifferentiated power and threat, a defilement to be cut off" (Kristeva 1982:106).]

287. The prepuce is often seen as a feminine part in the masculine organ par excellence (see Eilberg-Schwartz 1990:173).

288. There is, in fact, as Soler (1973:946) notes, a strict correspondence between three "cuts": a cut in the continuum of the body (circumcision), a cut in the continuum of time (the sabbath), and a cut in the continuum of food (holy and unholy foods). All these cuts are complementary and interchangeable. They define the Hebrew identity against an original lack of differentiation.

289. Kristeva 1980:124 (emphasis removed) ["are based upon the prohibition of incest" (Kristeva 1982:105)]; see also 118–119. Kristeva finds confirmation for her view in the centrality of the biblical taboo on seething the meat of an animal in the milk of its mother (Exod. 23:19 and 34:26; Deut. 14:21)—a clear metaphor of incest, as recognized by Soler (1973:953) and (Eilberg-Schwartz 1990:129). Some scholars even find traces indicating that this taboo was originally one of the Ten Commandments (Frazer 1918, 3:iii).

290. And, one may add, is himself a violation of the principle underlying all taboos: the separation of man and God. As *persona mixta,* Christ can only be the ultimate abomination, from a Judaic point of view (see Soler 1973:953).

291. Kristeva 1980:135–136.

292. Here Kristeva echoes Freud's argument (in *Moses and Monotheism*) that Christianity is a compromise between Judaic monotheism and pagan polytheism, that is, between the father principle and the mother principle (see Kristeva 1980:138).

293. Kristeva 1980:138 ["rent between two potentialities, demoniacal and divine" (Kristeva 1982:117).]

294. Indeed, there is a devil represented as a logician by Dante in his Hell: "Forse tu non pensavi ch'io loico fossi!" (*Inferno* 27:122–123). ["Perhaps you did not think that I was a logician!"(J.H.).]

295. Of course the Christians should not be confused with their teacher. I am reminded of Kierkegaard's Simon leprosus: "Simon *leprosus* was a Jew; if he had lived in Christianity, he would have found an utterly different kind of sympathy. Whenever in the course of the year there is a sermon about the ten lepers, the pastor affirms that he too, has felt like a leper—but when it comes to typhoid . . ." (Kierkegaard 1988:234).

296. See Obeyesekere 1990.

297. See G. Lewis 1987.

298. Kristeva 1980:87.

299. The primitiveness of this pollution is double. It corresponds to the presymbolic topography of the body which forms, through frustrations and prohibitions, in the child's relationship with its mother (Kristeva 1980:87). It also corresponds to the cultures in which this presymbolic topography, and thus the maternal principle, predominates. Kristeva believes, in sum, in the correspondence of the "culturally primitive" and the "psychologically primitive" and even in the correspondence of both to the social predominance of women (or even to what she calls "survival of a matrilineal society," pp. 85–86; my translation).

300. Feeley-Harnik 1981; Kristeva's contrast of Christianity and Judaism applies only if "Judaism" is made to stand for the priestly religion as enshrined in the so-called Priestly Code of the Old Testament. It is inapplicable if "Judaism" refers to the religion of the Qumran and to that of the rabbi (see Eilberg-Schwartz 1990, ch. 8).

301. Kristeva 1980:117–118.

302. See Alter 1979.

303. See Ellen and Reason 1979. If anything, the Levitican taboos are part of what Eilberg-Schwartz (1990) has called "the savage in Judaism," that is, what in Judaism parallels the supposedly less exalted "savage" religions.

Chapter 3: Maquwoli in Huaulu

1. Echols and Shadily 1989:272. *Pemali* is the eastern Indonesian equivalent of *pantang* in western Indonesian Malay dialects. Related concepts in Seramese languages are *holiate* in western Seram (Jensen 1949) and *monne* in Nuaulu (Ellen 1993a:171).

2. Just like definite articles in Romance languages, these suffixes are the abbreviated forms of demonstrative pronouns (*amuni* in the singular, *emuni* in the plural). The latter may still be used instead of their abbreviations when they follow the predicate of the noun (see examples below).

3. *Anasokoam,* literally, "child of the fork," can be translated as "appendage of the off-limits signal."

4. The reason these diseases are believed to follow from the violation of food taboos will be given later in this chapter.

5. These snakes are not supposed to act in their usual way, though, when they attack trespassers. Rather they bite and eat their flesh invisibly. There is a close connection between reptiles and skin diseases, as we shall see.

6. Anasokoem are the property of lineages.

7. See Ellen 1993a:251.

8. Probably the death adder, *Aspidomorphus muelleri* (see Ellen 1993:78).

9. It could be that the anomaly is more apparent than real, for the connection between the expressions *i soko asie,* "they make them off limits," and *asie i maquwoli,* "they are taboo," is only indirect. In other words, *i soko asie* describes the production of one result, which is the *premise* for another one. By convention, when the spouses have been sokoi, the taboos (maquwoliem) among them and their affines follow by implication. This explanation is not completely con-

vincing, however, because it does not take into consideration the fact that the rite i soko asie includes a formula which consists of the declaration that the bride and bridegroom are barred from using the personal name of the speaker (u pete ea leusi!). In other words, i soko asie is essentially an action which declares that a person (or his name) is maquwoli to somebody else. There is thus an undeniable, and paradoxical, intertwining of soko and maquwoli.

10. One hardly ever says *kaitahu maquwoliam,* "taboo land," preferring *kaitahu kinaam* or *kaitahu kinakinaam,* "bad [*or* really bad] land." The propositional meaning of these expressions is identical.

11. As does Dodds for the comparable Homeric use of *eidenai* (to know) in contexts where "character behavior" is described (Dodds 1951:16–17). This use according to him anticipates Platonic intellectualism in morality (one cannot but do the good if one truly knows it). Williams has criticized Dodds on the grounds that he projects into *eidenai* later meanings: "A better interpretation is that *eidenai* in Homer has a less specific sense, roughly, 'to have something in mind,' 'to have thoughts of a certain kind,' a sense that later contracted into the notion of knowledge" (Williams 1993:28). In Huaulu, the use of the verb *mane* implies the notion of learned ability, of something mental that has become a habitual disposition to action, which we would express with the noun *will.* For instance, the expression *emane kae ainafuem* (lit., "he knows how to eat langsat [a fruit]") translates as "he is able to eat langsat," "he is used to eating langsat," "he habitually eats langsat," "he has no problem eating langsat," and so on. Insofar as it refers to a mental disposition that blends with a disposition to action, *mane* can also be used in reference to a character trait. For instance, *emane halini* (lit., "he knows his own heart") translates as "he is steady," "he is courageous," "he is cunning."

12. As claimed by MacIntyre for "heroic society," that is, the type to which Huaulu also belongs: "Morality and social structure are in fact one and the same in heroic society. There is only one set of social bonds. Morality as something distinct does not yet exist. Evaluative questions *are* questions of social fact. It is for this reason that Homer speaks always of *knowledge* of what to do and what to judge" (1981:116).

13. See Ryle 1949 and Valeri 1994c.

14. Cicero *De natura deorum* 2.28.72.

15. Benveniste 1969, 2:267–272.

16. My translation of "è per cosí dire li rileggevano attentamente" (Abbagnano 1961:743).

17. See also what Dumézil has to say on the matter: "Le mot qui a fini par désigner l'ensemble des rapports de l'homme avec l'invisible, *religiones, religio,* quelle qu'en soit l'etymologie, a d'abord désigné le scrupule: non pas un élan, ni aucune forme d'action, mais un arrêt, l'hésitation inquiète devant une manifestation qu'il faut avant tout comprendre pour s'y adapter" (Dumézil 1966:57). ["The word which finally designated the whole of man's relationship with the invisible, *religiones, religio,* whatever its etymology, originally expressed caution: not a flight of the spirit, or any form of activity, but a halt, the uncertain hesitation in the face of a manifestation which one must first understand fully before one adjusts to it" (Dumézil 1970, 1:40).]

18. See also the expression *tepi omi leasi,* "don't stray" (from the path that one follows in following taboos).

19. *Taluwa* is often abbreviated to *talu.*

20. Incidentally, *sala* is not a borrowing from Indonesian *salah.* Its equivalents are found in many Indonesian languages (e.g. Laboya: *hala;* see Geirnaert-Martin 1992:429) and Polynesian languages (e.g. Haw: *hala;* Tahitian: *hara;* on the latter see Babadzan 1993:116).

21. The use of *taluwa* seems to connote a misfired action whose bad consequences directly concern the body of the actor. Thus, to say "I missed the target with my arrow," I wouldn't say *a ana* [I shot an arrow] *taluwa,* but *a ana sala.* Conversely, I never say *a hita ea* [I cut myself] *sala,* but *a hita (ea) taluwa,* where *ea* is pleonastic precisely because *taluwa* implies that the action falls onto the actor. *Taluwa* may also be used when a person (even if it is not the doer) is the victim of the erroneous action. An example is *wasuam ia koto ea taluwa,* which means "the dog bit me by chance/mistake," and also, of course, "the dog bit me inappropriately" (dogs are supposed to bite game and enemies, not humans with whom they are acquainted).

22. As in *ia kana sala pohi ea,* "it disagrees with me" (said of a taboo food).

23. See, for instance, de Heusch's criticism of Evans-Pritchard in *Sacrifice in Africa* (1985).

24. Another is *'awon,* "tortuous road," which is parallel to Latin *error.*

25. From which the Latin *peccatum.*

26. On these words, see Kittel 1985 and Ricoeur 1969:71–72.

27. Echols and Shadily 1989:103.

28. Zimmermann 1982:53.

29. Obeyesekere 1990:193.

30. See Reynolds and Levin 1985:213.

31. It cannot be denied that some of the flavor of modern Indonesian "sin"—with its biblical and koranic connotations—is slowly penetrating areas of Huaulu moral discourse precisely because of the recognized correspondence between Indonesian *dosa* and Huaulu *rosa.* Still, the Indonesian-derived expression *ita bardosa* (from *kita berdosa*), "we sin," is rarely used, and when used it is often with the sense of violating a taboo. The idea that the Christian notion of dosa—or rather the specific dosa ("sins") enumerated by Christians—applies to the Huaulu is strongly resisted by the latter, who point out that to kill or to steal is no sin for them. The use of rosa in a sense closer to that of "sin" is more in evidence when the Huaulu speak of their Christianized neighbors (who are after all the main source of the notion) than when they speak of themselves. For instance, I have heard it said that the reason the (now Christian) Nisawelem have lost so much of their population through disease and a low fertility rate is that they are being punished by (their present) God for the "sins" of their ancestors, namely excessive head-taking. This argument is all the more paradoxical, since for the Huaulu headhunting remains the most prestigious and valued action, even though they have stopped engaging in it. But after all *they* have not become Christians. Sin applies only to those who believe in it.

32. Schauer 1991:4.

33. On these and related issues, to which I shall return, see Wright 1963b: 115–117, 1963a:39–42; Kenny 1966:642–656.

34. The implied prescription may be made explicit by prefacing the statement with *tepi,* "don't." Statement 1, then becomes "tep' om' ae iyaem pohi manuem, ia koloputi." *Ia maquwoli* is usually dropped, because it is pleonastic.

This does not indicate that it means "it is prohibited," however, since *tepi* does not necessarily indicate prohibition. It may convey a recommendation, an exhortation, or simply indicate that the speaker instructs the hearer.

35. For instance, in Madagascar, see van Gennep 1960; Rudd 1960.

36. Borrowing the comparison of taboo with allergy from Smith and Izard (1979:13).

37. Ordinary feelings of aversion or "disgust" (i makapoi) do not rate as a maquwoli relationship to the loathed objects.

38. Incidentally, it was widely recognized that Hari had a rather obsessive personality.

39. Note that *piniassi,* "not good," in the aesthetic/moral sense is contrasted with *ohossi,* which refers to inefficiency or incompetence.

40. See the famous controversy between Malinowski (1948) and Radcliffe-Brown (1948) as well as Homans' (1988) attempt at reconciling them. See also Valeri 1992b.

41. Parker 1990:8-10.

42. Neusner 1973:1; Cazelles 1975.

43. Reinhardt 1990:3–4.

44. Orenstein 1965; Khare 1976; Madan 1985.

45. The positive counterpart is *katharmos* or *hagnos* (ritually pure) (Parker 1990:4) in Greek; *tohar* (purity) in Hebrew; *tahir* (state of purity) with its abstract form *taharah* in Arabic; *suddhi* or *sauca* (purity) in Sanskrit (Madan 1985:17).

46. Furthermore, in another contrast with the Greek, Hebrew, Arabic, and Hindu cases, most of these misfortunes are feared as such and not (or at least much less so) for the social or ritual exclusions that they may motivate.

47. Or else anomalous thundering, such as a thunderclap in a clear sky.

48. A "thunderclap" (lilaham) is expected after a flash of lightning, which is called matalilaham, "eye of the thunder."

49. Tuniem, "true" or "original ones," or lelakissi, "those who are not different."

50. There is no Huaulu word for incest. This does not mean that they do not have the idea (see Needham 1971), or that the idea is not given a specific expression. What I call incest is what the Huaulu call lassi essa ia pusawa lassi essa, "one blood marries [or has sexual contact] with another," an event which they say is maquwoli.

51. The association of name-uttering and spittle-mixing indicated by the fact that betel and food-sharing taboos are put in the same class as name-uttering taboos may seem surprising, but is not so from a Huaulu point of view. Words are breath and spittle for them; personal names are ontologically connected with the individuals who bear them. Hence by pronouncing the name of a relative, one mixes spittle with him or her.

52. Koloputi includes other severe diseases that resemble leprosy but are not medically leprosy (see G. Lewis 1987).

53. Kekuem are assimilated to a state of ugliness/badness of the entire body, because they may spread all over it: ita hatare piniassi, kekuem, "our bodies become bad, [covered] with tropical sores."

54. Also, a permanent alteration of the skin of some descendant becomes possible. This loss of pigment is evidently assimilated to a kind of skin disease.

55. Purely superficial skin diseases, however unpleasant and disgusting, such as leukoderma and ringworm, are said to be due not to taboo violation but to diet, heredity, or curses. These diseases may have their own avoidances, but the latter are not called maquwoliem. For instance, those who are afflicted by ringworm, which is said to be caused by an excessively fat diet, should avoid eating iham (kanari) because of its richness in fats. I repeatedly asked if this was a maquwoli, but was assured that it was not.

56. This is the most dangerous of all poisonous snakes. Its bites invariably result in death, I was told.

57. See Valeri 1996c.

58. Not because they are unable to, but because of "shame" (i mukae).

59. Both activities are taboo to them.

60. In general, men are more exposed than women to the dangers of forest, travel, and war, since they spend more time than women far away from the village.

61. For instance, there are many narratives about women being killed by headhunters, but the cause is always said to be women's stupidity or carelessness or vulnerability due to their isolation in menstrual huts, not their transgressions.

62. If these kinsmen are dead the effect is more likely to be consumption, as I mentioned.

63. The relationship between cause and effect in taboo thus belongs to the same family of phenomena (the moralization of misfortune) that has given rise elsewhere to the classical problem of the "delays of divine justice" (see Plutarch's essay of the same title).

64. In fact, it regulates action mostly through the regulation of interpretation.

65. The most determinate relationship is perhaps found in the domain of meat taboos. As I have said, eating certain kinds of taboo meat (to be specified in the next chapter) produces a limited number of effects that are all closely and patently related: ulcers on the surface of the body. This explains why these taboos are among those that are less differentiated, in Huaulu discourse, from avoidances based purely on dietetic considerations.

66. Some people even advocate killing the people afflicted with ringworm, out of fear of contagion. They claim that that is what the ancestors used to do and what their descendants should continue doing in order to keep the society free of the disease.

67. Of sun and moon in the eclipses, say the Huaulu; of heaven and earth in earthquakes, since the earth, which is the basis on which heaven rests, is shaken; and of land and sea in tidal waves.

68. In this case there is more than analogy between natural anomaly and human transgression, since the eclipse is considered the incestuous intercourse of sun and moon, who are brother and sister.

69. In 1985, an eclipse of the moon was attributed to the fact that an old man told me a secret story, moreover erroneously, as it was rumored.

70. The signs of leprosy are, according to the Huaulu, itching so intense that one cannot sleep, then swelling of the affected body part.

71. Thus they say that if one eats the flesh of turtles and crocodiles one

"contracts scabies" (ita nuka), which is reminiscent of the skin of these animals. Man ist was man isst.

72. The same reciprocity is expressed in a different form by loss of teeth, and thus of the ability to eat, as a consequence of eating marsupial meat with lime or chili. The combination is offensive to the marsupials, probably because their meat is bland, whereas lime and chili are, respectively, acid and hot.

73. Sontag 1978:67.

74. I remind the reader that the contrast of lelaki (other) and lelakissi (not-other) corresponds to our contrast of nonkin and kin (see Valeri 1994a).

75. Ita saa alakaniem ohossi, "we can't go uphill well."

76. The fact that these other afflictions are not as serious as malahau (although short breath may in fact be related to TB, just like malahau) indicates that affinal relations are considered much more important than consanguineous ones.

77. Note, in this connection, that "descent groups" (ipa) are compared to "houses" (luma), which in turn are compared to the body: lumam wahi manusia, "the house is like a human being."

78. Both women and men in that state are referred to with the same expression: i apure pokopoko, "their belly is excessively swollen." The condition in women may also result from walking on betel nut used for offerings to the ancestors (and even peels from it or spittle from the men who chewed it sacramentally). In men it may also result from hunting in a tract of forest where some man fell to his death (thereby indicating that he had violated the taboos of male sacra or other taboos equally important for the definition of maleness).

79. This is why it is taboo for women to engage in these preparations when they menstruate. But accusations that they deliberately disregard the taboo to make their husbands sick are frequent. If accepted by the all-male village assembly, these accusations are grounds for divorce.

80. Men's red spittle and women's genitally shed blood are sufficiently close for the former to function as a (retroactive!) conductor of the latter.

81. Also by short-sightedness and blindness. Being short-sighted, I was myself suspected of being careless with menstruating women.

82. As an effect of taboo violation, blindness parallels the impairment of breath (and thus also of speech). In both cases, the effect reaffirms the separation inherent in the taboo by making it more extreme. Just as the "breathing out" of a forbidden name makes all further breathing more difficult, so coming into contact with forbidden blood makes further contacts more difficult by attacking the organ that makes contact possible even at distance—that is, sight. The disease shows itself as symbolically related to the taboo because it exaggerates, in subjective and bodily forms, the separation that the taboo demands.

83. As the Huaulu like to repeat, manusia huruf pohi manusia buta huruf lelaki, "literate people and illiterate people are different."

84. An example is shamanic curing, an activity permeated with taboos. Most of these taboos correspond to specific "medicines" (aitotuem) administered for specific diseases. It is therefore understandable that the main consequence of the violation of these taboos is the recrudescence or even the incurability of the disease under treatment. In this case, then, any disease may be viewed as the effect of taboo transgression, although a characteristic effect may

also occur—namely, nightmares, which are interpreted as the persecution of the patient by the curing sewa, enraged that the patient does not follow the taboos that go with the cure (and with his aitotuem in particular: i ae maquwoliem, i mini leku i rahe aitotuem, "when they eat taboo food, they then dream their medicines"). This effect, then, is of the same type as those that attempt to persuade the patient to mend his ways.

85. For instance, I was told by one of my friends that when he discovered his brother had violated the taboo on eating dog meat, he beat him up with a bundle of arrows. But this was presented less as a punishment than as the expression of anger and dismay. The violation's true punishment was death due to sudden disease.

86. Such fines are paid exclusively from affine to affine (when, for instance, one calls the name of an affine) or from adulterer to wronged party. These fines are supposed to remove the misfortunes that may follow from the commission of the tabooed act.

87. The same is true of the taboos that must be followed by the shaman's wife at the same time as her husband and by the mother of the patient when the patient is an infant.

88. This is why it is also said that it becomes maquwoli (here in the primordial sense of "dangerous") for the guest to leave if anybody in the host's house sneezes or eats or asks dangerous questions. The violation of the taboo on leaving then falls directly on the violator, of course.

89. A bush knife (tuta) does "bite" (koto) or "eat" (kae) in the Huaulu view. These usages are not metaphors, but literally designations of cutting.

90. Lilaham kae eme, "lightning ate him," means "lightning struck him."

91. Which is said to be held back by muluaqina, the evil power into which a woman who died in childbirth, or childless, turns herself.

92. Kaitahuam kae eme, "the land ate him."

93. See Valeri 1994b.

94. Note that the term *ayoku*, "meat," encompasses the flesh of fish.

95. "Why look at animals?" in J. Berger 1980:2. Berger should be partly corrected. The attitude became dominant in nineteenth-century Europe, but it goes back to Descartes (see below) in the modern period and has its antecedents, like almost everything, in antiquity; witness Chrysippus as reported by Cicero: "Sus vero quid habet praeter escam? cui quidem ne putesceret animam ipsam pro sale datam dicit esse Chrysippus" (Cicero *De natura deorum* 2.64.160 [1933]). ["Of what use is the pig, except to be eaten? Indeed Chrysippus says that the life in a pig is merely the salt which prevents it going bad" (Cicero 1972: 187).] For an ironic dig at Chrysippus's anthropocentricism in the nineteenth century precisely, see Leopardi 1940, 1:842.

96. Of course, for Descartes the human body differs from the animal body in that it is animated by a soul. But *qua* body, it is a machine just like the body of animals.

97. Through bodily fluids such as saliva and (menstrual) blood, or simply through manipulation or ownership.

98. Valeri, in prep.

99. See Valeri 1990b.

100. And even to the isolated house or shed in the forest.

101. The same term, *usawa,* is used in polite language to refer to both.

102. These include, incidentally, the initiation of boys, which is permeated with an idiom of violent blood-spilling, although both circumcision and headhunting are now disconnected, and the presence of shed blood has become purely notional (see Valeri 1996c).

103. As usual, women are weaker and therefore submitted to more taboos than men. They may follow the taboos for eight days, that is, for the entire transitional period when their dead relative is in between the living and the dead.

104. Thus "the clothes of the dead" (kaluseliem) are taboo for the members of their lineage.

105. One of the many ways to ensure this severance is the taboo on offering to the dead clothes already used by the living, and therefore identified with them.

106. See Valeri 1990, 1992b, and Obeyesekere 1990.

107. But then there is a great deal of overlap between these powers and the dead.

108. Van Gennep 1960.

Chapter 4: Zoology and Meatology

1. Indeed, *akatunu,* the word for cooking sago, is synonymous with preparing/consuming a full meal, that is, one that includes meat.

2. Later, I was told that the taboo was based on experience: some soldier had photographed a pig killed by a trap, and since then the owner of the trap had failed to get any animal and, indeed, had ended up dying. "Pardon, but we don't want to die of hunger," they concluded. I never took a picture of a trap and its victims. But I was able to take pictures of the butchery of hunted animals, since it is not taboo to do so.

3. I borrow the term *meatology* from Fiddes (1991).

4. "Après l'erreur de ceux qui nient Dieu, laquelle je pense avoir cidessus assez réfutée, il n'y en a point qui éloigne plutôt les esprits faibles du droit chemin de la vertu que d'imaginer que l'âme des bêtes soit de même nature que la nôtre" (Descartes 1974:166). ["For after the error of those who deny the existence of God, an error which I think I have already sufficiently refuted, there is none that is more powerful in leading feeble minds astray from the straight path of virtue than the supposition that the soul of the brutes is of the same nature with our own" (Descartes 1912:46).]

5. "Les coups égraines par le timbre d'une pendule," says L. Ferry in Ferry and Germé 1994:iii. ["The blows which resonate in the striking of a pendulum" (J.H.).]

6. Again, see n. 95 on p. 443.

7. Both the B.I. term *binatang* (meaning "animals" in general) and the more specific *hewan* (meaning "domesticated animal") are missing in Huaulu.

8. It is especially used for humans who have a serious and generalized skin disease, in particular for lepers. This confirms the interpretation of skin disease as a form of animalization, especially since it is the consequence of ingesting taboo animals.

9. According to another informant, Kalahei Tamatay, peni includes all edible animals minus birds and etiem (grubs). In Nuaulu we also find the word *peni,* but with an even more restricted meaning, since there it refers only to the three largest game animals, those that furnish most meat: deer, pig, and cassowary (Ellen 1993a:115).

10. Note that humans that are preyed upon in headhunting raids are metaphorically referred to as peni.

11. A similar argument has been advanced by Tambiah for Thai (Tambiah 1985a:195).

12. Two qualifications are necessary. The first is that *hatani* may also refer to a piece of garment (i.e. a sort of additional body to humans); the second is that when fish are counted, the classifier *usena* may be used, although, if I am not mistaken, only for preserved fish.

13. *Kahukuam* was indeed glossed as *sarong binatang,* "animal wrapping" in A.M.

14. Indeed, my friend Aipai ventured the generalization that such powers "are animals because from animals come the life and warmth of humans." This is so, but at the same time the mixing of animal and human is feared.

15. It is advisedly that I speak in universalistic terms, that I say "humans" rather than, more modestly, "Huaulu." For it is the Huaulu themselves who generalize, who use manusia as the subject of all these discourses.

16. I have summarized one in Valeri 1990b.

17. See the thumos of Homer (Dodds 1951; Onians 1954; Snell 1953; Bremmer 1983).

18. Cf. the English expression *learning by heart.*

19. The idea is illustrated, by the way, by the definition of each of the two species of cuscuses by a marriage relationship between its male and female forms. The idea that individuals of the same species (or, as it should perhaps be said, terminal category) are interfertile seems to exist in Huaulu, as it exists in Nuaulu (Ellen 1993a).

20. That shrimps and tipolo pythons are paradigmatic animals in sexual curses is also indicated by their presence in the following magical formula, which is pronounced three times to prevent the effects (thunderstorm, flash flood, and so on) of such curses:

Maasiki akalia te', i sero te'
(Let them utter a sexual curse with impunity, let them curse)
Pohi okoem te', tipoloem te'
(the shrimps or the tree pythons)
leuwo afufo, leuwo leana mani.
(then I spit [the chewed bark of the alam tree], then let it be nice weather).
(fieldnotes, Oct. 27, 1985)

21. See Dekkers 1994:55.

22. Freud 1916; Bergson 1959; Valeri 1981b.

23. Laughing is a distancing mechanism that presupposes closeness and identification. Laughter at wild animals is taboo because it makes those that are distant close, but laughter at domestic animals is allowed because it distances those that are close. From this point of view, laughter at domestic animals is a milder equivalent of the taboo of laughing at the wild animals. As we shall see, domestic animals represent aspects of human behavior and activities in a dis-

torted, and thus inherently caricatural, form. The potential for laughing at them is thus always present. This is particularly true of their sexual behavior. In fact, through laughing at a degraded, caricatural state of human behavior as represented by their domestic animals, the Huaulu teach themselves to avoid such degradations. Domestic animals thus function a bit like clowns at court; they make the humanity of their masters shine by contrast with its loss in themselves. It is another of their contributions to Huaulu self-humanization.

24. *I taanai* refers to the cradling of humans, whereas *i sikui* refers to the cradling of pets.

25. Weight: human, paatina'; animal (and unmarked), moonua. Play: human, aluwae; animal (and "transhumans"), (p)amaloa. Male: human, manawa; animal: mossaniam (quadrupeds, etc.), tulalam (birds). Female: human, hihina; animal (all), inaniam.

26. Presumably Nusalaut, an island south of Seram.

27. A mountain belonging to the Lafatue lineage, now living in Openg (see end of the myth).

28. Lumamole, Waraloina, Sowa Huwe', and Matapae were later added to this list by Polonahu's son, Pitere.

29. Said to be in Irian, or "Irian" itself.

30. Lau relative to Huaulu, where the speaker finds himself. This implies that Wassulau finds himself in the southern part of the island (which is indeed the myth's locale) and goes farther west, on that part of the coast which faces Ambon and the Uliase archipelago.

31. Polonahu, the narrator, said this mountain is situated west of Huaulu, but according to Pitere, his son, it lies east.

32. A very poisonous snake.

33. A small python.

34. *Python reticulatus.*

35. The site is said to be near to the place where the people of Besi lived before moving north, across the mountains.

36. Matoke is the title of the senior branch of Tamatay.

37. According to Pitere, it lay on the southern part of the island, where the people of Openg once lived.

38. See Valeri 1994c.

39. On the place of the dog in the beliefs, practices, and mythologies of Indonesian peoples, see the classic studies of Kleiweg de Zwan (1915) and Kruyt (1937).

40. There is here an interesting parallelism with Manutalaka's cutting seven pairs of limbs from the eight-paired monster. The parallelism is emphasized by the fact that the monster's eighth head announces the dog—a bitch who produces a transformative dog, which will turn out to be the eighth in a series. The parallelism suggests what the rest of the story confirms: Wassulau the son is not just a Promethean figure benefitting humankind, he is also a destroyer of humans. As a transformative figure, he partakes of the destructive and devouring character of the monster.

Insofar as it represents the opposite of what the giant represents, insofar as it is the order of hunting to the giant's order of being hunted, the dog stands parallel to the giant, who, with Manutalaka's maieutic help, gave birth to it. As the giant multiplies by eight; so does the dog. It is true that this multiplication is through reproduction, but it is a strange, parthenogenic one, since no male mate of the bitch Wassulau is ever mentioned in the myth. Furthermore, there is equivalence and even interchangeability between Wassulau and her offspring, or at least her last born, who is called as she is. And just as Manutalaka cuts all limbs of the giant but one (which he cuts after some delay), so Heuwe kills all the children of Wassulau but one (which he kills later anyhow).

Wassulau is, in sum, the antigiant, but by the same token is also a parallel of the giant. As we have known since Aristotle, any opposition implies comparability, and thus a certain commonality—a commonality which will eventually require the elimination of Wassulau too. He is, in some measure, monstrous like the giant who "generated" his mother.

41. That eating cooked food is considered a distinctive mark of humanity is confirmed by the myth of Ayafu to which I have previously alluded. The people to whom he brings fire are animal-like, in that eating raw food has given them piglike tongues. They also ignore proper childbirth and are thus unable to reproduce themselves effectively. In this they are inferior even to animals (see Valeri 1990a).

42. See Valeri 1990a.

43. See Valeri 1996c.

44. See Valeri 1990a.

45. The latter is a purely hypothetical taboo, since there are no monkeys in Seram. But the Huaulu are aware of them from animal fables and have seen a few in Wahai, where they are occasionally brought by itinerant performers.

46. For instance, various members of the Puraratuhu lineage told me, "Ami rahe asale hini tipoloam, barani ita aeresi," "Our origin is in the tree python, as demonstrated by the fact that we do not eat it."

47. Thus the ipa Hunipotoam in Openg has a taboo on niapam because "one ancestress of theirs metamorphosed into a bat" (i rahe pinamutuam lelia hini niapam).

48. Variegated skin frequently goes with roughly textured skin; the two characteristics are often inseparable in Huaulu eyes.

46. The diagnostic reaction toward such things is the worried, but also almost indignant, utterance of the expression *sahule'?* "what is it/what happens/why does this happen [since it should not]?"

50. Fieldnotes, August 1985.

51. Or neophobia, the expression preferred by Visser (1991).

52. Douglas 1963:5; R. G. Willis 1974:30.

53. Cook 1987.

54. "They will come to avail themselves of many a benefit, and to pronounce on the appropriate days the name of God over the cattle which He has given them for food" (The Koran 22:27, Dawood translation, p. 334).

55. See Soler 1973. The same preference for raised animals is found in the Hindu alimentary code and perhaps even that of its Indo-European ancestor (see B. Smith 1994:254).

56. Kant, *Eine Vorlesung über Ethik*, p. 207 (cit. in A. Philonenko 1972:486).

57. Cannibalism may seem an exception, but is in fact the best confirmation of this principle. For by treating somebody as food, one signals that he or

she is beyond one's community, either below it (humiliative cannibalism) or above it (sacrificial cannibalism), and more often both.

58. The only partial exception allegedly was, in former times, the licking of some of the blood dripping from the severed head of a conquered enemy. This blood could even be consumed by mixing it with baked sago (afano).

59. See chapter 1 for a definition and description of these figures.

60. Thus the "goat" (uneune), which they know only in a domesticated state, is not taboo for them because they do not raise it. But it is hardly eaten anyhow.

61. Adults, however, usually abstain from eating such birds. It is said that they are eaten mostly by young boys, who do most of the capturing of the birds. My observations bear that out.

62. Some species are taboo for entire lineages and, out of respect for the lineages, may not be killed or eaten by the members of other lineages as well. But then these taboos exist whether the animal is fed or not. In fact, the birds in question may not be fed by those who have these taboos. The taboos are connected with shamanism and will be treated later with the other shamanic taboos.

63. Only very rarely is a cooked plantain given to certain birds, particularly young cockatoos.

64. The dog is even an analogue of the human hunter, as indicated by various parallels established between a good hunting dog and a good hunter or even headhunter. Like the latter, a good dog may have his lussiem, that is, eagle spirits that enter it and give it the extraordinary *furor* which allows it to attack the fiercest game fearlessly. Also, a dog which has killed a great number of animals is given the title of kapitane, which in the human sphere is attributed to a warrior who has killed at least 10 humans. Note also that hunting stories narrate the exploits of dogs almost as often as the exploits of men.

65. The emotional bond between dog and master appears to be reciprocal. A dog, or at least a good dog, is extremely reluctant to be parted from its master and refuses to be left behind when he leaves the village. The only way the master can persuade it to stay behind is to leave his "betel box" (salatam) behind. The dog sniffs it and feels reassured by the odor of its master. It also realizes that he will return, since even a dog cannot fail to observe that a Huaulu is never long parted from his betel box.

66. The dog is the only animal whose killing induces a sense of revulsion in the Huaulu. A man who in 1986 lived on the coast told me that he had seen there some Tanimbarese immigrants beating a dog to death to eat it (a common way of dispatching dogs in eastern Indonesia). He commented, "I could not watch it; I was sickened."

67. This punishment identifies the victim of the crime. Dogs are supposed to have "two breaths," since they allegedly breathe both from the mouth and from the anus. It is this additional breathing power that makes them able to run fast and long. An extreme shortness of breath may seem a suitable punishment for a crime committed against a creature that has an extremely long breath.

68. But note that they do not eat dog for quite different reasons. The Huaulu do not eat it because they raise it; the coastal Muslims cannot eat it for

the same reason they cannot raise it: it is an impure animal which must be avoided in every respect.

69. See Lukes's biography of Durkheim (Lukes 1973).

70. The first two men died of illness; the third (who had been beaten up by his older brother with a bunch of arrows on learning of his transgression) died falling from a tree. The man who became a paralytic was still alive during my first fieldwork.

71. Bachelard 1942b:182. [". . . things put our ideas in order, elemental materials put our dreams in order"(J.H.).]

72. See Geertz's vivid essay on Balinese cockfights (Geertz 1973).

73. See Valeri 1990a.

74. Another powerful one, as we shall see, is the eclipse of the sun or moon (chapter 5).

75. See Valeri 1996c.

76. In the introductory chapter, I have defined these as "occult powers."

77. In addition certain sewa potoem may take the form of a chicken, among others. For instance, Pinasainale, whose principal body is the crocodile, often manifests itself by crowing like a rooster when possessing the shaman. Generally speaking, it seems that all the chickens which were the companions of the earliest ancestors have acquired sewa potoa status.

78. The opposition between traditionalists and modernizers was implied but not used by the Huaulu themselves (at least until 1988).

79. He vaunted his ability to diminish taboo in persuasive ways. His insistence on chicken-eating may also have been due to his desire (and official duty) to create a major impediment to the resumption of headhunting. Certain men showed a desire to return to the practice, as is discussed in the pages to come.

80. See Valeri 1996c.

81. Needham 1976.

82. See Valeri 1996c.

83. Note that the pronoun *eme* can refer only to a human person. In contrast, *ia* can refer to an object which is taboo or a relationship to a subject, and can therefore be said to be "endowed" with taboo (what is taboo to some humans as a totality of a group).

84. However, I very much doubt that any Huaulu would sell a dog to people who plan to eat it.

85. I never heard that deer were tamed in ancient times. Nowadays, they may be raised for sale to non-Huaulu, but I never saw any.

86. This pig was kept in a pen near the house of its owner. I was surprised by this, because in 1972 my best informant told me that pigs could not be raised in the village but were allowed only in garden pens. The owner of the pig denied that this was true, however, and his view seems to be supported by the former existence of pet pigs freely roaming in the village. Unfortunately my informant of 1972 was absent in 1988, and I could not discuss the discrepancy with him.

Some lineages cannot raise some animals. Thus Tamatay potoam (Matoke) cannot raise the pig because one of its sewa takes "the bodily form" (kahukuam) of a pig. It also cannot raise tessiem and kakakuem (two species of parrots), apparently for a similar reason. Tessiem and sissayem (a bird with two beautiful caudal feathers used in the headhunter's headdress) are also taboo, for the same reason, for the Puraratuhu lineage. Nowadays, members of these lineages who capture these parrots for sale on the coast must keep them in the houses of people of lineages free from these taboos.

87. The only case I witnessed of an uncertainty concerning the allocation of a name between dog and human was as follows: My friend Kuweyamani, after having heard the myth of a kapitane named Wakuku, told me that he would give the name to a dog "or better, to a son." But then he thought the matter over and decided to do neither, because he thought it likely that the name belonged to the lineage of the man who had narrated the myth.

88. See Valeri 1989.

89. Golkar stands for "Golongan karya" or "group of functionaries," and is the government party which is obligatory for state functionaries. Although a majority of the Huaulu did not bother to go to the coast to vote in person, the police obligingly cast the vote for them, a humane gesture for which the absentees are still very grateful.

90. This analysis is confirmed, I believe, by the Japanese totemic association with the dog during their occupation of Seram. I was told that they descend from this animal. Both Japanese rule and the rule of the Indonesian state are characterized, in the Huaulu view, by a forceful ("male," or "kasar," as they say) interventionism in Huaulu affairs. In contrast, Dutch rule is remembered as a laissez-faire one, or, as they say, a "female" (pemerintah perempuan) and "alus" one (a very retrospective view!). It makes sense, then, that both the Japanese occupiers and the events produced by the Indonesian nation-state are associated with the dog, that is to say, with a greater closeness to Huaulu society but also with a greater animality.

91. Indeed, the stated purpose of this "naming after" (atemu) is to avoid forgetting the names of those sites with which the present lineages still identify and through which they identify themselves.

92. The only species attribute to be emphasized is that of effectiveness in the hunt; thus certain dogs of old (for example, Maloiloi) are considered the ancestors of a progeny which tends to inherit its prized characteristic as a hunting dog. The "totemic" element of this name is not so important.

93. I must mention a case of chicken-naming which seems, on first inspection at least, to form a parallel with the canine sphere. It is a case which concerns myself and my wife at the time, who was with me during my first fieldwork in Huaulu. One of our neighbors then, a rather crusty lady who was my wife's best friend, paired two of her chickens under the names Swedia (a hen) and Italia (a bantam), after the names of our countries of origin. This was, I think, an innovation. It reproduced one main feature of the traditional chicken names: the pairing of male and female names. But in another respect, it reproduced a feature of dog-naming, in that it commemorated a contemporary event: the presence of my wife and myself in the village. Yet I am not sure that commemoration was the main motivation for this choice of names. Things look quite different if seen within the framework of the Huaulu origin myth, as adapted to make sense of our presence in Seram. As I shall report elsewhere, the Huaulu identified different districts of the ancestral lands they inhabited

before coming to Seram with my former wife's and my countries of origin. From this point of view, the names Swedia and Italia were less an innovation than a recovery of a forgotten past revealed by the ethnographers' presence; they were our friend's attempt to claim ownership of forgotten ancestral place names that connected her society to ours.

94. My analysis converges with certain aspects of Lévi-Strauss's famous chapter on bird, dog, horse, and cattle names in French (Lévi-Strauss 1962:266–277). There are, of course, no cattle and no horses in Huaulu. But as in the system delineated by Lévi-Strauss, the main contrast between dog and bird—the chicken in the Huaulu case—is that the former has a mostly metonymic relationship with human society, whereas the latter has a mostly metaphoric one with it. Like the Lévi-Straussian birds (themselves strongly reminiscent of the Aristophanean ones), the Huaulu chickens form a society parallel to that of humans. But contrary to those birds (see Lévi-Strauss 1962:270–271), the chickens have strongly anthropomorphic features and differ from all their local brethren in being found right in the middle of the Huaulu village, where they provide a human, an all-too-human, spectacle for their masters.

95. The chicken is considered a bird by its association with the term *manu,* which means both "chicken" and "bird." This merging was erroneously considered by Bergson to be a characteristic tendency in the human perception of all animals (Bergson 1959).

96. Dekkers 1994:59–60.

97. Dekkers 1994.

98. Dekkers 1994:61.

99. Since the distinguishing feature of a pet is that it is treated as a child throughout its life (see Serpell 1986:63–64). Indeed, in our society one frequently hears pets referred to as "my baby." Various examples of pet-raising in "tribal societies," especially in South America, are discussed by Serpell 1986: 48–58.

100. D. Morris 1994.

101. Note that the chicken belongs to the category of "bird" (manu). In fact, it is the antonomastic bird, since *manu* may be used to refer to the chicken, particularly to the bantam.

102. Dekkers 1994:60. Note that dogs and cats are also capable of standing upright if required (p. 61).

103. Dekkers 1994:60.

104. I am uncertain about the species of domestic mice and rats found in Huaulu. They probably include, as in Nuaulu, the *Mus musculus,* the *Rattus rattus rattus,* and the *Rattus exulans ephippium* (Pacific rat) (see Ellen 1993b:29, 44–47).

105. They are both called siluam, although it is possible to add the qualifiers *malawahuam* ("small") for the house mouse/rat and *kahulassam* for the forest rat.

106. The meat of both domestic and forest siluem is said to be inedible, and even a hazard, because of its supposed "bitterness" (kaata'). But this is also what makes it an antidote against poisoning and persistent coughing (which is usually due to poisoning, especially "poisoning" from menstrual blood due to contact with women). Interestingly, the same bitterness and the same curative

virtues (at least as far as poisoning from snake bites is concerned) are attributed to "the cockroach" (matawaiyam), the other major house pest and predator. Rat-eating may also be shunned because the Huaulu are well aware that their eastern neighbors and traditional enemies slanderously accuse them of indulging in it (see story told me in Piliana). The only persons who occasionally eat rat meat are little boys, who shoot forest rats with toy bows and arrows.

107. Possibly the *Macroglossus minimus* (see Ellen 1993a:54). The name is supposed to be onomatopoeic, the screech of the animal being described as "sui, sui, sui."

108. Although when there are *many* rats in the house the symbolic scales fall on the negative, hostile side.

109. The word *rifurifua* (fluttering) is also used to refer to the flying here and there of the bat or bird. This seems to confirm that the causal relation is made to rest here on an analytic one.

110. Indeed, were the bats to be eaten or even harmed, the sewa kahianaem would "go back where they belong" (leuwe), and their help would be lost.

111. I have witnessed only one such case. A makuwelele (civet) was caught hiding inside a hollow trunk in a corner of the village. It was killed and thrown away, although some said that it might have been eaten because it was not quite inside the village. The case being uncertain, it was preferred not to run risks.

112. A case somewhat similar to that of wild game spontaneously seeking humans in their village is that of a species of spider which tends to weave its cobwebs between trees standing on opposite sides of a path. A path is a human space, even an extension of sorts of the village. The animal has voluntarily occupied it, put itself in harm's way. This is precisely why it must have harmful intentions and should not be meddled with. It is, in fact, taboo to destroy the cobwebs; one must duck under them or let the unwary foreigner (especially if he is tall, like myself) go first and tear them off with his head. Again, a friendly behavior coming from an unfriendly (i.e. wild) creature is deeply suspected. It may be truly friendly, but more likely it is deceptively so, just a ploy. Indeed, I was repeatedly told that destroying the cobwebs of the spider is taboo precisely "*because* it bars our way" (sepapu ia pakaleti ita). What seemed to me a very good reason for destroying them was for the Huaulu reason enough not to destroy them. Seeing me astonished at this explanation, they usually added that to do otherwise would mean to incur rosa (ita rosa, ita tana rosa). But as it turned out, this confused me even further, because at that time I still uncritically translated *rosa* with its B.I. equivalent, "sin." I therefore thought that the rosa incurred came from destroying the cobweb, not from weaving it across the path—from the spider. Only much later did I realize that *ita tana rosa* can also mean, as I think it does here, being on the receiving end of the hostile actions of others. In others words, the anomalous character of this spider (combined with a bit of anthropomorphism, since the spider weaves and wraps itself in woven stuff like humans) evokes a reversal of the usual and proper relationship between human and wild animal, and therefore it also evokes the potential victimization of humans. Put in overt terms, the animal becomes a figure of the persecuting ghost, of the witch, or even of the sorcerer.

It is not really an animal and it is not really a human either; it is the deceitful violation of the order of things.

In one respect, the case of these spiders is quite different from that of game found in the village. The spontaneous encroaching of spiders on paths is very frequent, but it concerns a space which is only travelled through and where humans are not permanently located. The case of wild animals spontaneously entering the village is just the reverse. It is exceedingly rare, but it concerns the most humanized of all spaces. Accordingly, more danger is involved in the second case than in the first. Moreover, while the destruction of cobwebs may be avoided, the spontaneous entrance of wild animals into the village may not. The uncontrollable is more dangerous than the controllable.

113. It should be noted that in general very few bird species are taboo to eat for all the Huaulu, although some are taboo for particular lineages, usually because of their connection with sewa potoem. Butterfly species are not taboo to eat either, but then they are not considered tasty or substantial enough to be eaten. So those which enter a house are taboo to harm but do not need to be made taboo to eat.

114. *Lorius domicella;* see Ellen 1993b:69.

115. The *Cacatua moluccensis* (cockatoo; B.I.: kakatua). See van Bemmel 1948:371.

116. The kakakuam can be taught when adult, but the cockatoo must be captured as a chick and fed by its master to be taught to speak by him.

117. The kakakuam is kept to keep track of visitors; the tuyam (a green parrot) is used as a hunting oracle (when it "speaks," it is also supposed to announce a death). Both parrots are very loquacious. Whereas the kakakuam announces the arrival of visitors when it spontaneously becomes excited and sings in a very high pitch, the tuyam must be interrogated in the usual way of oracles. Thus one recites in front of it a series of questions relating to game. For instance: lekelekeam? "an adult male deer?"; inaniam? "an adult female deer?"; and so on. If the bird stops singing after one of the questions, the answer is affirmative. The kind of game referred to in the question will then be found in one of the questioner's traps, or it will be killed by him in the course of a hunt.

Among the birds that are not domesticated but have oracular powers, two are particularly important. The tukutukuam announces the presence of headhunters; the ekam announces the presence of game, strangers, enemies, and so forth. The tukutukuam is one of two varieties of owl. It is distinguished from the other variety (called kokam) by its very long nails, which probably motivate its association with the human predators, the headhunters (it takes one to announce one). This owl can be magically induced to keep the headhunters away by constantly signalling their presence and thus by letting them know that their would-be victims are on their guard. The magical formula simply consists in saying, "Omi oto timatem tutu waikiyai," "Bite the headhunters until dawn." When the birds hear these words, they perch on "the rafters" (silimataem) of the house or on the branch of a nearby tree, and they hoot throughout the night. To make them stop, one says, "Topoyem tepi u koto mani," "Don't bite the shade of the dead." The dead would seem to be associated with the enemy headhunters in this context: both are figures of pure malevolence and terror. Like "the bats" (suyem), which as we have seen have an analogous signalling and deterring function, the tukutukuem are given the epithet makaussuwa timatem, "those that make the headhunter go back" (lit., "those that 'return' the headhunters"). Another important oracular bird is the loam. If it "croaks" (keke ala) before a Huaulu who is on his way out of the village, "it reveals/announces" (i sima hini ita) that the man will incur a misfortune if he does not immediately return home.

118. These names are all translated by the B.I. words *kodok* and *katak,* both of which mean "frog." *Katak* also means "toad," and one informant who claimed a better knowledge of Indonesian contrasted the ilauwam, which he translated as *kodok,* to the other two species, which he translated as *katak.* I doubt, however, that this indicates any conceptual contrast between the two, but rather an attempt to show knowledge of Indonesian through hypercorrection.

119. I am unable to identify the animal zoologically. I never saw it, although I was present one night when it jumped on a pregnant woman and disappeared forthwith.

120. In this case people say that the frog may have come to "visit" the woman it has elected. Thus its presence is not a negative omen. But in the only case of such an event that I witnessed, people differed for a long time about the interpretation to give. The optimist claimed that the frog was visiting a girl to whom it had recently given knowledge; the pessimists claimed that it was portending trouble for her. Contact with unordinary powers is at any rate dangerous even in the best of cases. I was told that the frog can teach fishing magic because "it knows them because it lives down-in-the-water" (ia ruwe pale wae, ia manei). Only women receive such knowledge, because it concerns forms of fishing practiced by them. Even so, there seems to be a similarity or affinity between women and frogs. This is confirmed by the fact that it is usually women who run the greatest risk from contact with these animals when the frogs enter the house or alight on them.

121. *Fauhihina* is an allophon which is increasingly used to emphasize badness and a partly obscene connection with women and female bad smells.

122. Probably the *Lytoria amboinensis* (see Ellen, Stimson, and Menzies 1976:136).

123. In one case I witnessed, people were uncertain about whether the intruding animal was a tatauwam or a kararam. It should also be kept in mind that the intruding animals are sometimes hardly seen or seen only by certain people. They may only be heard. Hence, a lot of inference is involved in their identification.

124. Probably *Lytoria infrafrenata* (see Ellen, Stimson, and Menzies 1976: 136).

125. Ia pititou ese ita, "it jumps and hits us."

126. The same happens when the animal peers into the house from the branch of a nearby tree.

127. The Huaulu always illustrate such principles with concrete examples which are presented as evidence of their validity. Ilakessa told me that Ahamati, one of the most respected citizens in Huaulu, died because of a fall from a tree soon after an ilauwam had touched the central pillar of his house.

128. This obviously indicates that the animal should not be touched if found (see the discussion of soko in chapter 3).

129. Although the ilauwam may theoretically be killed when encountered in its proper habitat, it is usually left alone, since people would not eat it. I was told of only one use for the animal: as a bait for fishing for eels. In this case, the fisherman dips the point of his arrow into the frog's blood. This is supposed to attract the eels. Another and (I was assured) better method consists in binding the frog to a piece of bamboo and then attaching it to the point of a rod or stick. The fisherman waves the cane, keeping the frog under water. This attracts eels, which feed on frogs, and when they are present, the fisherman spears them with an arrow.

130. Who is then said to "produce a sign" (eme kopai tanda).

131. That a signal is both sign and cause can be illustrated by a train signal. By giving the trains the permission to depart, the signal also causes their departure.

132. It is probably a *Dandubia* or the empress cicada (*Pomponia imperatoria*) (see Ellen 1993a:80).

133. The insect is supposed to be silent during low tide and to begin "crying" with the rising tide.

134. Since the cicadas are supposed to start crying with high tide, one may say that they are generally connected with an increase in the level or amount of water: with rainfall or with high tide, both of which have the effect of raising the level of rivers.

135. Cf. the analogous belief of the Nuaulu, who say that the sound of the nayam is "the cry of the ancestors" (Ellen 1993b:160).

136. Seasonal associations hardly play a role, as far as I am aware. This is in sharp contrast with what is the case among the Andamanese (Radcliffe-Brown 1948).

137. Ellen, Stimson, and Menzies (1976) include kiki in their list of frog names from Piliana. In view of the fact that the Huaulu and Piliana peoples speak closely related dialects of the same language, I doubt that this is correct. In any event, the kikiam was never described as a frog in Huaulu.

138. Another cicada sometimes mentioned was isiisi, which may or may not be equivalent to the Nuaulu sisie. Ellen reports that this term is "used polysemously to refer to cicadas in general (distinguished by their distinctive sound-production) and to *Baeturia* in particular" (Ellen 1993b:160). It is possible that the same ambiguity exists for isiisi, although the people whom I interrogated seemed to give it only a restricted meaning, since they were uncertain whether it was taboo or not to let an isiisi into a house. I presume, though, that all cicadas are suspect because they cannot easily be distinguished from one another when they are heard inside the house.

139. Like its Nuaulu cognate (*nesate* or *kau nesate*), this name is applied to large bush crickets (see Ellen 1993b:156).

140. This oracle, just like the bird oracles, is thus based on an analogy between animal voice and speech.

141. It is allegedly eaten by the Nisawele.

142. Deed followed word—at least if I can trust my observations. I never saw these animals eaten.

143. The ground under the house is malodorous with animal excrement, human urine (people piss through the kitchen floor), kitchen waste, and bones

and food scraps thrown to dogs and chickens through the cracks in the split bamboo floor. Bones and excrement are periodically cleared by women, but the smell, with its negative associations of corruption and death, remains.

144. This term refers to the famous kain patola (silk cloths from Gujarat) or to their locally produced imitations or derivations, whose production has long been discontinued in Huaulu and elsewhere in Seram (see Niggemeyer 1952).

145. The lamp's embodiment of the continuity of the house is also indicated by another taboo. When a package of resin is almost extinguished, it is removed from the lamp stand and a new package is lighted with the still flickering flame of the old one. It is strictly taboo to let the flame become extinguished in the old package before it burns brightly in the new one.

146. In 1988 there were seven such houses.

147. This association is explained by the fact that the resin is extracted from tall trees (which are therefore closer to heaven); in addition, the best resin is extracted from trees that grow at high altitude. More generally, perfumes belong to the air, not only because they travel through it, but also because flowers, resins, and so on, grow on trees. In contrast, stinks paradigmatically belong to the earth, which the Huaulu view as the place of corruption and generation inextricably intertwined.

148. Kerosene is called miniatana from the B.I. *minyak tanah,* "earth oil."

149. Literally, "they [human subjects] feel a sense of disgust for them [always objects]." In the Huaulu language, contrary to the English one, it is impossible to say that the tabooed object has a taboo for somebody, only that it is taboo (for some subject).

150. This leaves out two residual categories: animals bad to eat which enter the village, and a few animals good to eat (such as birds and pythons and the occasional edible bat) which may enter the houses. The first category is easily dealt with. "Disgust" redundantly adds to taboo as a motivation for not eating the animal. The second category is more complicated. Birds are a special case which I will consider in a moment. Information on what may happen if a python or an edible bat enters the house was confused and commingled with particular taboos which individual lineages may have in regard to these animals and which other lineages sometimes respect out of respect for those lineages. As for observation: I witnessed only one case of a python entering a house (I actually saw it slide on a beam a few centimeters over my head). It was small and I think not one that the Huaulu would normally eat. But it was carefully removed from the house by holding it with sticks, brought to the outskirts of the village, and there killed. I took this to be some sort of ritual killing, but I could not obtain any interpretation of what was done. A lot of tension and even fear accompanied the whole proceeding.

151. Obviously, this eating is purely theoretical because it implies two conditions: one likes most what most people dislike; the animal is killed by a person who does not have the taboo or who does not care about following it.

152. See Carsten and Hugh-Jones 1995.

153. As for the reptile which is a permanent inhabitant of the house, the gecko, it is sometimes said to be taboo to hurt because of its communicative powers, which come (they say) from heaven (Lahatala). Taboo or not, the gecko

remains untouched and must be respected by knocking the wood of the house if it makes its noise when a human says something that is to be judged as true or false. The noise of the gecko indicates the truth of what has been told.

154. This is why birds are in a special category.

155. But this is also why they are taboo *both* to kill and to eat: the greatest value and respect given to the above, since they are messengers from the above. This solves the problem of simultaneous identification and repulsion (mentioned on p. 97).

156. We have already considered a taboo explained by the requirement of keeping up and down separate. It is the taboo on letting the damar lamp, or any of its burning combustible, fall from the house to the ground.

157. Rather, one specifies what kind of underground place one refers to. Usually it is the lairs or "villages" of occult powers in animal form. Thus one speaks of the underground with such expressions as *pale ia rahe nifotuam,* "down in its lair" or *pale i rahe nifotuam ninianifafam,* "down in their lair village."

158. Including the ancient Hebrews, as testified by biblical and rabbinical texts (G. Lewis 1987).

159. Were we to follow the theories of Leach or Douglas, we would expect to find incompatibility between adjacent categories, where boundaries are an issue, rather than between opposite ones. The frustration of our expectations is perhaps an additional reason for not following those theories, at least as they stand.

160. Ellen 1993a:21. Roy Ellen is a researcher who has specifically identified the forest animals of Seram.

161. Ellen 1993a:78, 264.

162. Ellen 1993a:208. *Clupea menuria* is supposed to be found in Wahai (Weber and de Beaufort 1913:73).

163. Bulmer 1967.

164. Stresemann 1914:90.

165. Ellen 1975:214.

166. See Tambiah 1985c.

167. I give the more recent spelling used by Ellen. In his 1975 article he spells it *pene* (p. 215).

168. Although there are some differences of opinion about what these fixed values are. See below in text.

169. The Huaulu explain the choice of this creature with one of their general principles for avoidance: the herring, they say, is taboo with the cassowary because it is likalika, "variegated, versicolor." This trait may explain why it is that this water creature and not another has been chosen as the fish taboo of the cassowary, not why the cassowary is the only terrestrial animal (from a Huaulu point of view) that has a fish taboo.

170. One could also object that because the cassowary eats fish, it should be even more dangerous for humans, since such feeding habits define its meat as a mixture of fish and fowl. Indeed, this may be a reason that marine predators such as the frigate bird are taboo to eat. However the "argument by eating" is used ad hoc and without worrying about consistency.

171. See also the fact that crustaceans creep in the water just as grubs creep on the land.

172. The right way for the eti to grow would be to become fully a worm or snakelike creature of the water (such as an eel or a sea snake.)

173. On these sewa pukaria shamans, see chapter 1.

174. It is indeed defined as a "terrestrial reptile" by the *Encyclopaedia Britannica,* 11th ed., s.v. "Reptilians," Macropaedia.

175. Ellen 1993a:264. Sago grubs are considered a great delicacy to be eaten raw (when the animal is still wriggling) or barely grilled.

176. There is also the principle of size. Here, the big and dark brown one of the pair is taboo, while the other is not.

177. Probably because it was long considered self-evident to the point of finally becoming a mere habit or totem. The interest in the bodily consequences of violation is more permanent and searching than the interest in the reasons for the taboo.

178. The plant is, of course, noticeable among those with edible fruits, in that it bears male and female flowers on different trees. It is possible that this situates it in between maleness and femaleness, an opposition which is correlated with that of the dry above and the wet below.

179. Which they also glossed with A.M. *mata tongkat langit.*

180. Or so the Huaulu claim.

181. Sufficiently indicated by the metaphoric expression *oko teloem,* "bake bananas" (i.e. have sexual intercourse). No banana is more phallic, and more the object of bawdy jokes for that, than the matalala, which is by far the largest of them all.

182. See Menzies 1991:9. The patola is not infrequently found coiled around the house's beams (see Wallace [1869] 1962:228–229).

183. I once heard it said that the cuscus was originally a bird or was generated by a bird (I am not sure). Unfortunately I could not confirm this information, let alone obtain any elaboration of it, for it was treated as a secret. If confirmed, the information would provide additional evidence for the sense that the two kinds of animals are in need of dissimilation—both very close and irredeemably different, just like the cassowary and the birds on another register.

184. It may also be that here a favorite empirical criterion of the Huaulu—who eats whom?—happily overlays subtler and more inchoate considerations of classification. For the pythons eat winged creatures and cuscuses indiscriminately and thus practically demonstrate that their difference is no difference relative to them—that is, to their stomach.

185. Wallace [1869] 1962:184.

186. Incidentally, patterns similar to those of the python's skin and with the same name were painted on the frontal flap of the loincloth of kapitane (master headhunters), whose powers were connected with the above and who are said to have been able to make rain to confuse and scatter pursuing enemies.

187. Ellen 1972:226, 1975:204. Ellen (1993a:235) lists only two species: *Phalanger orientalis* and *P. maculatus.* He notes that sexually dimorphic species are recognized by two separate terms (1993:121) in Nuaulu as in Huaulu.

188. In other words, here "terminal taxa"—that is, "units with no standard named subdivisions" (Bulmer 1970:1074)—are not as relevant classificatorily as the unnamed units which they presuppose, and which happen to correspond closely to the two species of cuscuses identified by zoologists. One may

ask why, if they are more important than their gendered subdivisions, they are not named. The question makes sense only if one takes for granted the axiom that what is important must be made explicit. But this is an axiom only for scientific culture. Huaulu classifications are part of a natural language, not an artificial one. In a natural language, what is most important is also what is in everybody's mind and thus what is less in need of being named for purposes of communication. It is evident that gender makes sense only if the notion of a gendered species is presupposed. So what is the use of naming it? The moral of this is that terminal taxa should not always be viewed as the logical equivalents of the biologist's "species," as Bulmer (1970:1072) seems to propose. Only the use of terminal taxa in discourse can indicate whether this is the case or not. In the Huaulu case, the terminal taxa for cuscuses are in no way conceptual equivalents of species. They presuppose instead two such equivalents which remain unnamed and which also happen to be coextensive with two concrete species distinguished by zoologists.

189. Note also that *mussufam* and *kapupuam* are used figuratively to refer to girls and *makilam* is used to refer to boys. This is especially the case when gossiping or ironizing about their sexual adventures. The term *ihisiam* ("the cuscus" in general) is used as a metaphor of the female genitalia. "Hunting for the cuscus" (saa ihisiam; lit., "mounting on a tree to kill the cuscus" but also "mounting a cuscus") is used by males to describe the seeking of sexual adventures in the forest.

190. See Ellen 1972.

191. The informant was Pulaki Isale, the most knowledgeable and intelligent Huaulu. Other informants answered my question by using the standard explanation based on color. Thus one informant said that the makilam was involved in the taboo because it was likalika (spotted). In this case as in the case of crocodiles and turtles, the explanation is unsatisfactory, but one can see why it came about. It is unsatisfactory because, of course, it cannot explain why the elahuwam, the white cuscus, is also taboo (indeed, another informant, at a loss to explain this fact, which I pointed out to him, finally invoked a principle that I had never heard before and never heard again: "it is taboo because it is white"). But it makes some sort of instructional and minatory sense, because the spotted fur of the makilam evokes, like all things called likalika, the leprosy that is said to be the consequence of violating the taboo of mixing the meat of this species with the meat of birds.

192. A more strictly utilitarian form is given to this argument by Ellen (1993a).

193. This hostility also explains another taboo, concerning the makilam alone: It cannot be boiled in a bamboo pot, like the other meats; if it is, "it will stink." It must be smoked instead.

This taboo adds a further hierarchical contrast, that between makilam and all other cuscuses, to the hierarchical contrast of makilam and elahuwam, on one side, and all other cuscuses, on the other.

194. The character of the environment is, of course, inseparable from that of its animal inhabitants. It is in this sense that they may be mentally and practically commutable.

195. See Burkill 1966, 2:2207, and Ellen 1993b:81–82.

196. See Burkill 1966, 1:529.

197. See Sachse 1907:57. It was glossed as *penyu karang* (coral reef turtle) by some.

198. Burkill 1966, 1:795.

199. See Stresemann 1927:61.

200. Note that the *Chelonia imbricata* is "the smallest of sea turtles" (*Encylopaedia Britannica,* 11th ed., vol. 27, s.v. "Tortoise").

201. As Ellen (1993b:81) notes, the freshwater turtle "is much smaller than the marine turtles with a shell length of little over 20 cm."

202. Many taboos worldwide can be explained by this analogic interconnection between the surface of the eater and that of the eaten. For instance, the Luvale say that genet meat is taboo to the boys who are initiated, because otherwise they would contract leprosy, which is evoked by the animal's spotted skin (Lévi-Strauss 1966:98). On the predominance of the analogic mind, see the classic (and classically criticizable) studies of Lévy-Bruhl and more modern ones, especially G. E. R. Lloyd 1966. For me, though, such predominance is essentially context-dependent and not general as such.

203. *Sama* as used here is a borrowing from Ambonese Malay, but also from Bahasa Indonesia, where it means "same." The original Huaulu word *sama* means "to give as a gift" (see Valeri 1994a). Perhaps the borrowing was made possible by the fact that for the Huaulu the gift equalizes or requires an ultimate equalization at a certain fundamental level.

204. For the basic facts on sewaem, see chapter 1.

205. Nowadays, fish poisoning is rarer on the Sapulewa River, owing to the amount of work and thus the number of people who are required to do it on this river.

206. Analogously, South American Indians do not eat the jaguar because the jaguar eats them (see Testart 1991:210 n. 43).

207. Narrated by Kuweyamani, Sept. 6, 1985.

208. From the identity of the tree which transforms into the first crocodile, a stronger idea may be inferred. The luhe is a large tree that develops cavities, into which the bodies of the dead were (and still are to some extent) placed. One can argue, therefore, that the crocodile results from the "coffin" of humans, that it results from the "eating" of human bodies. The animal is, in sum, human death; it is essentially defined as a man-eater.

209. Strictly speaking, the crocodile is not always "motley" in the sense of multicolored, especially in its adult stage. In Huaulu, however, the category likalikam, which I translate as "motley" or "variegated," includes, besides the association of different colors, spottedness and variations of the same color, a rough, patterned texture, like that of crocodile skin. All these qualities are in fact equated on the symbolic plane. Thus it is said that the patola python, whose skin is in different colours, "is likalika like the skin of the crocodile." Turtles, eels, spotted cuscuses are all likalika. This quality of likalikam is disquieting to the Huaulu and is often invoked to explain why an animal or a plant is taboo. The likalika quality of crocodile and python skins often produces a shudder of horror, particularly in women, but also in men. I have heard many people say that they are "afraid" (mutau) of it.

210. Le Souef and Burrell 1926:311; see also Ellen 1975:205.

211. See Ellen 1993b:35–36.

212. See Ellen 1993b:35.

213. But vegetables cooked in eel broth may be eaten.

214. Not all informants were as categorical or precise with regard to the consequences of violating these taboos. For many people, the basic fact of life is that certain species are taboo; they are less interested in the exact consequences than in the fact that there will be bad consequences.

215. Obviously, in this, Huaulu taste does not agree with that of the ancient Greeks or of Louis XV.

216. See Valeri 1990b, and below in text.

217. Alternatively, it is said that these birds "see the war" (i oi lisam) (i.e. a party of warriors bringing war).

218. *Munui* probably corresponds to the Nuaulu *muinu toa,* which refers to Accipitridae, for all hawks and eagles, or specifically to *Accipiter novaehollandiae* (see Ellen 1993a:241).

219. This flap covers the area of the penis but evokes it at the same time (Valeri 1996b).

220. This equation is discussed at some length in Valeri 1990b and especially Valeri 1996b.

221. A recent student of bestiality informs us that there are "women [who] stuff an eel into their vagina—it wriggles as well as a snake, is pleasantly slippery and is not as dangerous" (Dekkers 1994:57). I don't know if there are such women in Huaulu, but the *idea* seems to be there.

222. I can't say why the other two fishes (kohi and funana) are also taboo. Perhaps the stripedness of the kohi plays a role, since this is a criterion often invoked by the Huaulu themselves.

223. A view shared by both men and women, I should insist.

224. Or at any rate animals which evoke male sexual potency. This is probably the case for male crocodiles and monitor lizards, whose courting behavior and exuberant—in fact, rather violent—sexuality may evoke human male sexuality in caricatural form. This interpretation is at any rate justified by many myths that narrate sexual liaisons or marriages between women and monitor lizards or even crocodiles (although the latter are painted in more negative terms than the former).

225. Also called sewa wahako' (*or* waeko'). The latter was allegedly introduced into Seram by a shaman named Salem from Ternate. It was brought to Huaulu by Paielesiwa, a Huaulu man who is said to have been one of his pupils. The introduction is thus quite recent (the forties?).

226. According to some informants, the eggs of chickens are taboo for the shaman only for the period when a patient is being cured by him.

227. In addition, all sewaem seem to have an aversion for the leuw (*Casuarina*) tree. The bark of this tree is used to make straps for carrying the "panniers" (sapey) used by women. These panniers are carried on the back, and the strap rests on the front. Because the akara (doubles of the sewaem) that protect the patients enter from their head, women in whose bodies the akara are present cannot carry those baskets.

228. The two varieties tohu metea and tohu likalika are excepted. Note that in the latter case it is exceptional that a species qualified as likalika is not taboo.

229. See Ellen 1993a:208.

230. The leaves are taboo to eat for all shamans while they are curing a patient; the tuber is taboo for only some shamans.

231. While some sewa potoa taboos are a burden for many people, it is said that this variety of shamanism is the least burdensome for the shaman himself, because it does not have as many taboos as the other three. On the other hand, the more burdensome taboos of the sewa pukaria (such as those on such common foods as shrimp, pork, cuscus), and to some extent those of the sewa ninawania, can be ritually removed from the shaman and his wife after he has practiced his art for some years. In contrast, the taboos of the sewa potoa are permanent and may never be removed.

232. Note, in this respect, that the original meaning of *sewa* in Sanskrit, preserved and even emphasized in Javanese, is "service."

233. There is no explicit prohibition on women practicing shamanism. Women themselves, however, declare that they do not practice "out of shame" (ita mukae). Traditionally, women from the communities east of Huaulu have had no such qualms. In fact, the sewa ninawania was taught to various Huaulu men by a woman from Roho. In the eighties, my old friend Pulaki married with a practicing shamaness from a Manusela-speaking community in south Seram. I have seen her practice occasionally, but on the coast and in the style of her own village (although shamanism is on the whole fairly uniform throughout central Seram, particularly among the speakers of Manusela dialects).

234. On the other hand, the consequences of the violation of lineage-wide sewa potoa taboos are different. Foods taboos have "tropical sores" (kekuem) attached to them. If a Tamatay looks at the black clouds of sunset, he will die.

235. Generally speaking, the sewa control the animals, and this is why possessed shamans are often able to predict when and where to find game and why each shamanic performance ends with a long prayer in which the sewa are asked to make hunting successful.

236. Note also that other taboos may be considered the logical consequence of some of the vegetal taboos listed above. For instance: is deer taboo for all sewa poto shamans because its main food is the taboo lesalesa—because it is lesalesa turned into meat? There are other reasons, of course, but this one seems close to the surface of Huaulu logic, for which "who eats what?" is a fundamental criterion of orientation in the realm of taboo.

237. Like many animals down-in-the-water that are taboo, shrimps walk instead of swimming, in contrast with the prototypical fish. Moreover, they walk backwards. Another inversion is that they defecate from the head. Bats too may be seen as anomalous because they fly like birds but are mammals with bodies more reminiscent of those of rats or marsupials than those of prototypical birds.

238. See Valeri 1994c.

239. Note that the color of this pulp is called *mussunu,* "red," and that this color is constantly invoked as a reason for the taboo.

240. Because the papaya represents the mediation of the sexes in an intersexual form, not just hermaphroditic, it may also be seen as a blatant evocation of sexual intercourse. The taboo on the papaya would then also imply a displaced form of sexual asceticism for the shaman. The same could also be said of the taboo on the shrimp, which is an explicit metaphor of female pudenda.

In actual life, however, sexual asceticism is necessary only for the initiation into shamanism. It is explained by the pervasive notion that nothing can be obtained for nothing, particularly in the realm of the occult to which the shaman dedicates himself.

241. See Roeder 1948.

242. Echols-Shadily 1989; Knaap 1987a:xxviii.

243. For other manifestations of this contrast between outward-looking and inward-looking forms of knowledge in Huaulu, see Valeri 1994c.

244. Although this is followed only by the Puraratuhu shaman among the sewa potoa cultors.

245. The principle of misoneism also explains why the sewa potoa shamans must build their house with a roof in the authentic, traditional Huaulu shape. This is much more difficult to build than the present shape, imported from Openg. When I first lived in Huaulu, everybody used the traditional roof. In 1988 only very few stuck to it. Among them were the two officiating sewa potoa shamans and the guardian of the luma maquwoliam—the "taboo house" par excellence, where the most important heirlooms connected with the war rituals are kept.

246. On this, see my papers: Valeri 1989, 1999 (Siwa/Lima).

247. Migrants from the Tanimbar archipelago in the southern Moluccas have been coming to Seram, not always to stay. They fish, open gardens, cut wood for sale, and their women sell locally the textiles which they weave.

248. I cannot linger here on this point, which I have made more amply elsewhere (Valeri 1975, 1976a, 1980), and which I have developed at great length in Blood and Money (Valeri, in prep.).

249. Cases similar to that of Laafale are those of individuals named after one of the totems of their lineage. They cannot eat it. No such taboo exists for those who are named after a natural species which is not a lineage totem. Totemic names reveal that there are more totems than meet the eye, totems that become apparent only when somebody is named after them. This is not in contradiction to the association of totemism with lineage organization in Huaulu. It is just that in the case of less important totems, one individual (whose name gives him a closer connection with the totem) takes on himself the burden of following the corresponding taboo on behalf of the entire lineage. Here too, then, the part stands for the whole. The same argument could perhaps be made for the individual taboos of the sewa potoa shaman. Only to a few core totems is the principle of substitution inapplicable. Some taboos must be shared by all for the totems actually to belong to all.

250. Besides being generically taboo for all shamans, this snake is specifically taboo for the Puraratuhu lineage, whose origin it is said to be.

251. At best, as we have seen, the Huaulu believe that animals (or some of them) can overhear humans. They are listeners but not speakers. There is therefore no such thing as talking to one another, contrary to what happens among humans and therefore reveals their distinctiveness from animals.

252. These last, linked sentences—just like others in this book—have been found unclear and in need of substitution by exclusively text-oriented editor friends. I feel therefore that I have to explain to the general reader what has finally persuaded my friends: namely, that now and then I intentionally seek to

use a poetic series of enunciations that move from the simple and therefore clear to the complex and therefore unclear. I want to give a sense of what one faces or prefers to face in the interpretation or even the creation of taboos. The poetic strategem cannot be asked to bear its fruits immediately—quite the opposite. It should sustain the interest but also the sense that it is not sure of the answers that are finally reached.

253. I have also observed that in many cases the hunter does not participate in the butchery of the animal, although he is present at it. There is no taboo on this, though, only restraint.

254. Before the jaw is hung, it is left for some time on the shelf on top of the kitchen's fireplace. It is believed that from there "the animal [more exactly, its soul] calls its spouse," so as to enjoy its company. The spouse is thus enticed into the traps of the man who owns the jaw. The belief testifies to the similarity of humans and animals, since the human dead also attempt to entice their living companions into death because they miss them. More important, the belief testifies to the idea that in renouncing his eating of the animal he has killed, a renunciation demonstrated by his possession of the jaw, the hunter guarantees his future success.

I shall return to the case of these jaws of wild pigs, which are the only ones appropriated by the hunter who kills them. They are attached to his house's cooking fireplace. The most significant hunting parts of deer and cassowaries are also collected by the noneater: the antlers for deer (which can nowadays occasionally be sold and thus exported from the village only for money), and the frontal bone together with the tail feathers for cassowaries. The largest river fish is also nailed to the external part of the central division of the house's thatch. And so are some other animals, including the most important snakes. These objects affixed on the hunter's house are rarely seen these days and signal noneating for the man who owns the house. Only the pig's jaws and skull have kept their fuller importance.

255. See Testart 1985, 1986a.

256. I am not using the term *collective guilt* to describe a psychological state, but a kind of self-judgment—almost a verdict. The term, after all, has a juridical origin (see Ross 1975 and Valeri 1994b).

257. But others mentioned higher numbers: from 100 to 200.

258. I am using *sacrificial* loosely, to indicate a ritualized form of killing. As I have attempted to show elsewhere (Valeri 1985, 1994b), there is much to be lost in separating the ritualized killings of the kind found in Huaulu from those classically referred to as sacrificial because they involve an offering. For one thing, there is an offering component in the Huaulu ritualized appropriation of animals, as I shall show in a moment.

259. I use the quotation marks advisedly, since the Huaulu never refer to this act by a name that means "gift" or by a verb that means "giving." Only *tepi si,* "laying for," is used.

260. His name is Okosopa. I was told that he is the lord of shrimps, as the crocodile is the lord of fish.

261. "Appropriate" descendants can be patrilineal, matrilineal (owing to uxorilocal marriage), the result of adoption, and whatever else is used.

262. In Latin *res* (thing) is the thing owned (see the English expression

real estate). Our notions of thing and reality derive from the Roman notion of ownership. See "The Human Thing," by Kelly and P. Grossi, in *Dizionario di Legge*.

263. The loss of luck at getting game ultimately goes back to the lord of the land and of the animals that live on it. But it manifests itself as a loss of effectiveness in the mutuaulaem, that is, the powers (usually embodied in small fetishes) involved in hunting magic. On these powers, see below.

264. Here again I am talking of performative (ritual) acts, not of mental states.

265. Women are particularly aware of the constant danger of overstepping the bounds of what may be safely appropriated, because their allotted mode of appropriation of animals (fishing shrimps and small fish in the rivers with bow baskets) often makes them ill owing to long immersion in cold water. Furthermore, they are constantly threatened by sudden "flash floods" (hahay) during the rainy season. It is no wonder, then, that one of the most frequent causes of illness for women that comes up in shamanic seances is attack from the irate Okosopa (lord of the shrimp). This lord of the shrimp is in fact viewed as one of the most malevolent among the various lords of the wild, as a true kinakinam (lit., "evil evil," but a generic appellation for malevolent, occult agents). A little dialogue between myself and my landlady of 1985 (Pinarolo) may perhaps serve as an illustration. One day she apologized for having served me only very few shrimps because she and her companions "had not been able to get many" (ami hitissi). I answered, to be polite, but also to test information previously received: "That's fine; if you had gotten many, the lord of the shrimp would have made you fall ill." Pinarolo looked at me for a moment, perhaps for a test of her own (was I pulling her leg? she knew I considered her a lazybones), but I kept a straight face. Reassured, she turned to Ratifala, who was weaving a basket at some distance in the house, and commented: "E manei! Huauluam mamanissa," "He knows! He is a true Huaulu." Then she added to me, with some heat, "These Huaulu nowadays fill their baskets to the brim!" What she meant was that, although she was accused of being lazy, she was in fact following the traditional rule that you should not take too much from the wild, that you should never fill your basket to the brim. An excuse, of course, but one that made the principle behind the excuse quite clear.

Let me also quote a personal experience demonstrating the pervasiveness of this principle of limited appropriation. In 1985, one of my daily pleasures was to take long showers at a delicious fountain in an idyllic little valley close to the village. An old lady, who never washed, was very disturbed by this constant challenge to her habits. To reach the fountain, I had to pass every time behind her house, and she would ask from her kitchen: "Bathing again? Aren't you ever cold?" I extolled in response the virtues of cold baths. When I fell ill, she recommended that I not bathe again at that fountain. It was clear to her that it was its upuam (occult owner/master) who had made me ill, since he disliked me intensely for overusing his fountain. One must indeed tread very carefully everywhere in Huaulu—even in the bath. The abundance of the water springing at my favorite fountain was no reason for believing that I could enjoy my showers without restraint and fear of offending some hidden owner (not to speak of the not-so-hidden old crone).

266. Needless to say, "the animal side" receives the displacement from humans. The animal is not treated as an autonomous subject who creates the displacement, but as an object that helps generate the subject by being subject to humanly produced displacements.

267. See Valeri 1994c and McKinnon 1996.

268. See Freud 1953b.

269. The Huaulu see similarities between their treatment of the animal's blood and the Islamic treatment, which is based, as they are well aware, on the idea that blood belongs to God. They therefore resent the coastal Muslims' refusal to eat the meat of deer killed by Huaulu traps. They point out that the blood of the butchered animal falls onto the ground, and thus "God has his share." The Muslims refuse to eat the meat on other grounds, however: the animal has not been killed in the Islamic way and it has been butchered by people polluted by unlawful food.

270. There is no linkage between the animal's sex and that of the recipient.

271. Besides the skull, the blood, and the maraissiam, there are other parts of the carcass that, while not taboo, are not eaten by humans or are eaten with some reluctance. The genitals and parts of the lumbar and anal areas are always given to the dogs. If a wasu kapitane (captain dog, i.e. a dog which is particularly successful in hunting) is present, the genitals of a male animal are given to him, so as to keep him courageous and aggressive (in a word, "male"). If he is not present, the genitals are given to the next best dog. Of the viscera, only the "liver" (wassa) is always eaten by humans. Much of the rest is not appreciated as food and is often given, in part or all, to the dogs to eat. I have witnessed only a few cases when lungs, stomach, and bowels were divided among the presents for eating. In this respect the Huaulu are a bit like Americans: they prefer to eat the muscle and reject the "innards" as inferior parts. Is this judgment also due to the innards' evocation of the living animal (and thus ourselves), whereas muscle can be cut into shapeless pieces, into mere "meat"?

272. The only occasional exception, especially nowadays, is the chicken, which may be slaughtered in the village to feed some distinguished visitor or peddler. The visitor or peddler is likely to be a Muslim, however, and thus highly unlikely to accept any cooked food (or any fresh meat for that matter) from a Huaulu. He would thus do his ritual killing, butchery, and cooking himself, and with his own implements and pots, brought for the purpose. Otherwise he would be polluted by contact with the implements of the abominations-eating Huaulu.

273. Ellen 1978:232.

274. See Valeri 1990b, 1996c.

275. This idea that the animals are sexually more potent than humans is of course a fantasy, but then its existence is all the more significant for that. The only empirical evidence on which it is based is that animals are usually more prolific than humans. The Huaulu constantly bemoan their lack of fertility—the fact that they reproduce much less than they need to in order to be strong. Young couples, especially women, are frequently exorted to laikana, "make children."

276. The same blending of human and animal is represented by the mu-

manu, a mad person or the being that possesses this person and makes him or her mad.

277. Saying more on the name of this lineage would identify it, which would be a bad idea in view of the fact that the lineage in question may not take kindly to its characterization by the Huaulu myth-makers.

278. It is perhaps necessary to stress that while the effect of this semitotemic explanation of the taboo on pork may be seen as derogatory, the intention behind it is not. The myth is, rather, an example of symbolic appropriation of a foreign practice for demonstrative purposes internal to Huaulu culture. Nevertheless, I must admit that the Huaulu are not above exploiting the malicious potential of the *interpretatio totemica* of the Islamic taboo on pork. For instance, the ancestors of the Islamic people of Besi, whom the Huaulu consider their dependents and inferiors, are said to have had "hairy tongues like pigs," because they did not know fire and ate raw food like animals. The conceptual leap from "they were like pigs" to "that is why they have the taboo on pork" was often made. These malicious arguments must be viewed, however, as a response to the coastal Muslims' own identification of the pig-eating Huaulu with pigs. Pork is thus the currency for claims and counterclaims of status in this part of Seram, and probably elsewhere in the island.

279. We have seen that marks of respect are stronger and more formalized vis-à-vis the larger animals which provide most meat. But they are also quite noticeable vis-à-vis the animals that are more powerful and dangerous for humans. Principal among the latter is the patola python, which is eaten by males. One must follow various rules of avoidance and respect in its presence. For instance, the taboo on laughing at the animal, especially when it is in the throes of death, is exceptionally strong in its case. Its name, like that of several wild animals, cannot be pronounced in vain. So in the forest the name tekepatola is camouflaged and becomes tekele. In this distorted form it is not recognized by the animal, which will not be angered by hearing its name called. Another rule of respect is that one should never show one's backside to a patola python. Otherwise, matana mukae, "its eyes are ashamed [it is ashamed by what it sees]" and, angered, it attacks the offender. Incidentally, this belief confirms the phallic connotation of the python: Why would it otherwise be so ashamed when seeing a bit of buttock? Is it not because the sight reminds it (and the Huaulu) of what it could do to the buttock? In a way, the python is a biting penis, to be avoided by women and not to be approached in a "feminine" way by men.

280. Among the many beliefs or practices that testify to this potential for reversal, and thus to the risk that the hunter pays a personal price for the animals he kills, let me quote two that are particularly telling. It is believed that in going to "check his traps" (tihiki supanem), a man runs the risk of becoming sick and even dying. So when somebody says, in leaving the village, "A tihiki supanem" (I go to check [lit., "visit"] the traps), it is polite to answer back, "U leu sipi sipi ala kaitahu upuam" (Come back quickly, because of the lord of the land [because he is likely to be around the traps, angered that you have put them up, and even more so if an animal has fallen into them, so he will make you sick or kill you]). Another risk run by the hunter, or simply by anybody who appropriates things in the forest, is that the weapons of his appropria-

tion (machete, knives, traps) are turned against him (more rarely: her) by the angry spirits who own the forest and its products, particularly the animals. Self-inflicted wounds are interpreted in this way. It thus makes sense that invocations to stop the flow of blood in these cases are addressed to the very spirits—auwetem and mutuaulaem—who preside over fishing and hunting, respectively. For instance, when Kaalai seriously wounded himself and the bleeding would not stop, I heard Laamese addressing the shamans and their spirits in this guise: "Omi rahe / auweteanaem / mutuaulaem / ala riki'" (Yours / little spirits of successful fishing / spirits of successful trapping / stop [lit., "cut"] the flow of blood). A man (the orai tua) added, addressing himself to the spirits alone: "Leu riki' mani / Omi hulaissi?" (Then stop the flow of blood indeed! Can't you hear?)

Eventually the shamans diagnosed two causes for Kaalai's wound and unstoppable hemorrhage: (1) One of his traps killed a deer on the hala potoam, that is, instantaneously and therefore improperly, because too effectively. Hence the lord of the land wounded him in revenge. (2) The soul of Kaalai's wife, which had left her body as a consequence of her constant quarreling with Kaalai, was keeping the wound open, so as to kill her husband in revenge.

Thus in this case, as in many others, a phenomenon of reciprocity between persons was fused with a phenomenon of reciprocity between persons and animals—another proof that animals participate in some measure in the moral universe of humans.

Beyond this, going to the forest always implies the risk of running afoul of the lord of the land. A sure sign of this is when his voice is heard. Then it means that he is angry at humans because their spears or arrows have struck him (he is invisible, so he can always be struck by mistake) or because his ayoku "meat" (i.e. animals) has been taken by them.

Chapter 5: Before Virtue

1. But taboos are also explained by forces not reducible to purely intellectual ones, as we have seen (social forces, embodiment of identity, and so on).

2. Valeri, in prep.

3. Their heads can thus be taken by their brothers/father, foreign (or rather foreignized) and autonomous. Thus I was told that one could hunt the head of a sister or daughter given in marriage out of Huaulu. The reason is that such marriages imply a ritually effected taking away of the bodily identity of Huaulu.

4. See Valeri 1983, 1987.

5. Note that this opposition goes well beyond specific taboos. The tendency to identify the village space with the cultural normality the Huaulu must inhabit has the effect of expelling or keeping out of the village any phenomenon that defies the village's sense of order, even if its cultural sources (originally encompassed by principles 3 and 4 [see page 198]) remain largely unrecognized when they apply to the forest and its inhabitants. From this point of view, there was already some truth in my original observation that those two principles have something in common with the second one I had formulated early in chapter 4.

6. The greater this difference, at least in certain areas of life, the greater the spatial distance must be. Terms different to the point of incompatibility cannot occupy the same space, because each space is identified with a certain form of life. This was amply illustrated by taboos appearing in the two relevant dimensions of spatial distance: the village/forest contrast, and the up-in-the-trees/down-in-the-water contrast. A human cannot live with a frog for the same reasons a bird cannot live with a fish (although some birds can live by eating fish; but then they all seem taboo for the Huaulu to eat, for the same reason they do not eat fish and bird together). In both cases, the habitual correlation of a certain habitat with a certain form of living denies the spatial and a fortiori substantial association of beings belonging to incompatible habitats. For this reason, there is no possible convergence over time. In sum, continuous coexistence in space and a fortiori the most intimate connection created by eating are impossible.

7. Space must be viewed as an index of distance from values based on one's location, and thus also on the identification of that location with a certain culture, with a certain way of relating to the cosmos, which implies values antithetical to those of the Huaulu.

8. Even taboo-generating temporal differences tend to be reduced to spatial ones, as I have tried to show in Valeri 1996b.

9. Rough convertibility of location and classification and practical invariance of all taboos (separation from object) create a tendency to view taboo as preserving a preexisting physical/spatial distance which is part of the structure of the cosmos in which the subject must take a right place. But such generic tendency is more easily applied to rough, very general categories with which the subject may more easily relate through his own general identifications (villager, gender, and so on). Preexisting existence may become more vague for more specific categories and a more specific subject. Moreover, as I noted in chapter 3, human agency can create difference and not just reproduce it, so that the practice of taboo is not only cognitively based; it cannot be reduced to mere respect for a fixed cosmos.

10. If, in other words, the concepts of object and subject in the sphere of taboo hardly existed beyond their embodied form? And if the forms of contact in taboo—eating, piercing, penetrating—did not always involve body-to-body symbolic identifications?

11. However, this does not mean that the distance required by a taboo is necessarily congruent with the distance that generates it, both in the literal and in the metaphoric sense of such distance (see text below for examples).

12. Kasibi (casava), alamafu (corn), ala (rice), lapina (squash), pukalawa (cloves).

13. As I well know from unfortunate ethnographic experience, during a sewa potoa performance, tape recorders and even flashlights are strictly taboo. As a result, I could only take notes in a little notebook in semidarkness (any form of lamp is in fact taboo because only the fireplace is to be kept). Such notes were only memory help for subsequent developed descriptions of what I had heard and seen. Sometimes I had the help of the shaman or of spectators for filling in. But I thought I should mention my necessary ethnographic tools and even myself as objects of misoneistic taboos. In a sense, ethnography itself is

felt to be incompatible with Huaulu identity, at least in what the Huaulu believe to be their identity's innermost ritual and mythical core. The ultimate taboo that separates the inside from the outside takes the form of secrecy. I hope I will be able to talk at length about this, and thus about the position I felt I was attributed in relationship to Huaulu, and about some attempts to articulate that position for me during later trips that reinforced or changed local attitudes to my insistent and endless search for knowledge in Huaulu.

14. During my last trip in 1988, I was surprised to hear from the heavily coastalized kamara that if the logging company would come to Huaulu (as they had heard) and offer cement houses in exchange for trees, a cement village could be built at the foot of the hill on which the present one is built, and thus near the river Eha. I was surprised because there is a taboo on building villages or even individual houses near rivers (mostly rationalized as due to dangers of flooding) but also and most important because there is a taboo on building cement houses in Huaulu territory (Alakamat, where they were beginning to be built, is a foreign territory belonging to Openg). Even the kamara's proposal, which was ill-received by the inhabitants of Huaulu, had to create some compromise by limiting the latter taboo to the upper area where the village still was in 1988 and by maintaining a certain continuity with it through a number of ritual houses to be built in the traditional style. Unfortunately, or perhaps fortunately, I don't know if the kamara's project has since been realized. I only wish to remember the angry comment of a woman who told me that she wanted to continue living "in the houses of the Romuromuem," that is, the ancestral beings that are the protagonists of Huaulu mythology (see Valeri 1994b).

15. Or that imposed (and American) missionaries were reluctantly tolerated in more recent years.

16. Put another way, what makes the excessively distant bad is that it can too easily be inappropriately close. But closeness is inappropriate because distance happens to be strongly defining for the Huaulu subject: "I am not what they are."

17. As we have seen in chapter 4, the most frequent anomalous species are asuali (cassowary), niapa (all bats), tipolo (turtle), makihoi (eel), oko (shrimp), makila (cuscus), telo matalala (matalala banana).

18. The lord of all sewa pukarie is half-human, half-cassowary, thereby making the mediating role of a shamanly significant cassowary imaginarily visible.

19. But note that this combination must come from them (i.e. from their voluntary or involuntary mixing of animals from the two extremes) to make them vulnerable to it. This seems to indicate a certain component of responsibility in mixing taboos. Humans are solidary with the articulation of the universe. If the combination is inherent in a species (and it is fully so only in the monitor lizard), the species tends to become taboo in certain contexts and for weaker (women) or specialist of mediation (shamans) people. Only shamans, in other words, can fully identify with the monitor lizard and receive the taboo from this identification, rather than from a willed unordering of the cosmos which unorders the unordered eater.

20. See Héritier and my earlier criticism. The balance theory no doubt applies in rough approximation, but fits best Hellenic culture or early Indian ide-

ology, particularly in its medical variants (see Zimmermann's 1982 description).

21. Predators may be taboo also because they often overlap with scavengers, which eat dirty or tabooed food.

22. I have in fact had contradictory information about the sea predators with which the Huaulu have very little contact—namely manutalala (frigate bird) and paikoli. The statement that they are not taboo may well be motivated by the fact that their symbolic potential can hardly be actualized by the mountain Huaulu.

23. On the wideness of the Huaulu notion of origin and ancestry, see Valeri 1990b.

24. Equality can be implied in this case only if the dimension of time (separating the two inverse relationships) is ignored. In any case, wild animals that are hunted are not taboo or are so only for the hunter who kills them. The latter taboo indicates partial identification, as I mentioned in the last section of chapter 4.

25. Or they can be consumed with the mind only in a minor, undifferentiated way common to all local food species.

26. A point I already made long ago (Valeri 1985).

27. That one is what one eats, and therefore eats what one is (although never in a literal sense, of course) or wants to be (and usually with a potential for the development of contradictory taboos), is confirmed by many alimentary practices, particularly in ritual context. For instance, the food prepared for headhunters must be cooked in such a way as to impart to it the mobility that the headhunter must carry. So the housewife "prepares it" (afanoe) by constantly moving it when cooking.

28. Boccaccio 1987:V.8. On the numerous medieval antecedents, see Branca's footnote 3 in Boccaccio 1987:670–671; see also pp. xcix–c.

29. A proof of this dependency of consumption in general on renunciation of consumption in particular is one generic, all-encompassing consequence of the violation of sewa potoa food taboos—namely constant coughing. This coughing is obviously associated with food remaining stuck in the throat, an occlusion which makes difficult or even impedes any further eating. In chapter 3, I mentioned that this instructively discourages the violation of the taboo. I can now add that it shows the dependency of eating all free foods on not eating the unfree ones, and thus shows the generic sacrificial flavor of safe eating.

30. Stating that taboos share, albeit in different degrees, a sacrificial dimension means that taboo transcends the basic polarity (too close or similar, and too far or different) under which all principles of taboo considered so far take repair. This obvious transcendence further raises a lingering question: Are the two polar principles the ultimate, inescapable source of all taboos? To put it more concretely, is anything that is taboo too dissimilar or too similar? And conversely, is anything that is taboo just too dissimilar or just too similar? And similar or dissimilar in relationship to what or to whom?

Given our definition of the two ultimate principles, the last question hardly seems worth asking. Of course, an object's distance (i.e. the common metaphoric measure of similarity and difference) necessarily relates to a subject in order to translate into a taboo for him. But we should never forget that this distance is the result of their positions in a complex set of relationships because of classification or biographical events (with time—and luck—turned into historical events). Moreover, some of these relationships may themselves turn into the object of taboo, so that various distances between objects must be considered before arriving at the subject. This is particularly true of food taboos, since eating usually involves cooking, which frequently involves mixing different kinds of species. As mixing taboos have shown us at great length, the excessive distance between a subject and a combination of objects presupposes an equally excessive distance between those objects.

31. In this sense taboo is very different from law, as we shall see in the text below.

32. See Valeri 1992b.

33. "Contagion" is in reality the possibility of assimilation.

34. Even so, I must add that taboo as pure and simple fleeing, if possible, is the end resource of any of these active responses, since they ultimately fail before the limitations of existence.

35. If a woman menstruates instead of giving birth, then her husband is seen as having been "cut" instead of having "cut" others. It is interpreted as a failure of his own headhunting. When a man is unsuccessful in shedding blood, his wife sheds blood in his place, which recalls the bleeding of his own genitals in castration. In sum, in childbirth women's shedding of blood is seen as equivalent to men's shedding of blood, but in menstruation, women's shedding of blood is equivalent to men's castration. It is a case of a taboo resting on a hidden identification of the female bleeding vagina with the male wound of castration.

36. Needless to say, this idea is confirmed by the embodiment of the village's invulnerability in the penis that descended from heaven and has become the main instrument of victorious headhunting (i.e. confrontation with enemies).

37. One may even speculate that manhood lies in the phallus—the symbolic transformation of the mere penis—only because of the bleeding vagina. In other words, it is the latter that is the most powerful motivating image. A bleeding vagina may well evoke the wound resulting from the cut of protruding genitals, and thus the loss of a manhood which primarily consists of that protruding difference.

38. Valeri, in prep.

39. Men experience this process only once in a lifetime, when forced into circumcision. But it is an experience that creates a certain conceptual distance, as I have argued elsewhere (Valeri 1990a, 1996c).

40. An exclusive opposition is an opposition between two terms that exclude each other (e.g. death and life). A complementary opposition, in contrast, is one of mutual dependence on each other's attributes. An exclusive opposition attempts to bring the other out of contact if not out of existence; a complementary opposition implies an ideally mutual recognition of the need of the other's existence for one's own.

41. On other uses of such method, particularly at a higher level, see Valeri 1989.

42. Note, however, that consumption is not as tabooed as production in at least one crucially self-identifying case. Eating store-bought rice is not as taboo as cultivating it because of the intensely self-defining character of this ac-

tivity in Indonesia. Production, then, creates a greater identification, and thus conflict between identifications that are at odds with one another (hunting and cultivating rice), than commercial acquisition does. The Huaulu seem aware of the alienating and distancing character of selling and buying (see Valeri 1994a). They frequently visit (or have to experience) the coastal market (or shop) culture. This is precisely why they can make a symbolic use of what is extrasymbolic in the world in which it exists (there is here a parallelism with aspects of marriage prestations—see Valeri 1994a).

43. Indeed, it is commonly said that a woman who died in the menstrual hut turns the village into a "village that belongs to the dead" (niniani selelalia), just as a man who died a bad death in an area of the forest turns it into a "land that belongs to the dead" (kaitahu selelalia). The village remains selelalia until the funerary rituals are finished; the land where the man died remains kaitahu selelalia, "of the dead" (and thus also deadly for the living), even after his funerary rites are performed *in loco.*

44. Another possible argument for the lack of a taboo on bringing into the village the corpse of a woman who dies in the lilipossu is that the hut is nowadays so close to the village that her death is already enough to pollute it, since it has increased her polluting powers beyond those of shed blood. This interpretation is apparently confirmed by their description as pukue pale ninianiam, "fallen into the village." But the expression points even more to an interpretation that assumes a comparative judgment with men's bad death, since it parallels the expression pukue pale kaitahu, "fallen to the ground in the forest," used to refer to men who die of that death. Moreover, the expression *pukupukuem,* "the fallen," refers only to men, who are thus the paradigmatic fallen, on which even the death of women is modelled.

45. The question is, ultimately, whether we want to give the notion of anomaly a very narrow or a very wide definition.

46. I heard the orai tua say after the conclusion of the 1988 kahua, "If only we had made a greater effort it would have become a sailoa." The premise is that the sailoa is closer to completeness—to perfection and thus strength—than the kahua.

47. One obvious example is the taboo on bringing luma upuam to the coast, as happened at Loulehali. As I was repeatedly told, "Our ancestors should not hear the sea" or "Our ancestors should not see the sea." Oppositions can become criss-crossed or combined, of course.

48. For instance, the taboo on women singing afinem, the male art practiced during the kahua dance.

49. For instance, up in the house, down on the ground, connected by what stands for up in the house, that is, the damar lamp, as we have seen. Other substantial objects of up-in-the-house should not be allowed to fall down-on-the-ground below the house. A child accompanied by sewaem and medicines cannot walk pale lohu at night. Otherwise they are abandoned pale lohu. Other categorical spatial oppositions are also linked to taboos. For instance, nobody can enter the earliest settlement place of the ancestors without dying through the loosening of the belly button. And in the lower ancestral village site, one cannot combine with the sea even by means of language (i.e. it is taboo to utter the name of sea and of some of the sea's characteristic objects).

50. The reversal of direction may sometimes be due to the eating of a particular food followed by the accomplishment of a certain action. For instance, I was told that eating sugar cane before going hunting is taboo because if one has to climb a tree, he would reverse the direction of the coming of the plant to earth (from sky).

51. A similar case is that of the people who give the prestation to incorporate the bride and regain the bridegroom. All these transitions/transactions are governed by the taboo on turning to look behind (a perceptive return to before), an inversion of their action, which betrays reluctance to accomplish it.

52. See Valeri 1994a.

53. Four or five lineages may ateha at the same time but no more than one person in each lineage. Also see Valeri 1994a.

54. The inferior and distant, then, addresses the superior as if he were equal and closer.

55. It is actually taboo to invert any significant order of relations, particularly with regard to exchange and hierarchy.

56. In contrast with the relations of wider difference, such as animal of down-on-the-ground and animal of up-in-the-trees. Such differences easily protect themselves without human abstinence.

57. In order to reverse one's movement, one must first stop it, of course. Hence interruption is either taboo in itself, or it reinforces a reversal taboo by striking its necessary premise.

58. It is so recognized by the Huaulu, or often recognized in conversation.

59. See Valeri 1990b.

60. I express myself in a double negation on purpose, for reasons that will be expressed further on. Put in a simpler, positive way, I can say, "So I simply do not eat dog meat or I do."

61. Women may sometimes kill an edible animal such as a cuscus but only by a stick and if on the ground. As for women's help, if it exists at all, it consists in camping stuff in a family expedition whose main purpose is a sojourn in forest's residence (with attached small garden).

62. Taboo concerns consanguinity (same blood) but also its equivalents: sharing of milk (creates taboo for three generations) and sharing parent as feeder.

63. Basically, what Testart conceives as a consequence of identity alone is in fact an already existing component (difference) which must be preserved for the subject-object relationship to remain. So in this case again, taboo enshrines a cause of alimentary or sexual incompatibility rather than being a mere consequence of pure avoidance of identicals.

In any case the feared result of marriage with close consanguines is to mix up marriage and descent, the unstable and negotiated with the stable and hereditary. One may object, of course, that the Huaulu preoccupation with keeping consanguinity and affinity separate and complementarity presupposes, but does not really explain, their existence. But the objection is easily defeated by the fact that this difference is, throughout Huaulu mythology and cosmology, the necessary beginning of the world. Just as the cosmos is based on a complementary relation, so is society based on the complementarity of affine and consanguine, of sex instability and (supposed) descent stability. If one introduces sex not with stranger but with sister, one may lose what one can expect of sister. Testart argues that ontological identity should not be replicated by marriage. (I should not marry my sister because otherwise two identicals would be combined, violating the ontological A + A is forbidden.) However, contrary to his argument, there is no identity to be found behind the incest taboo, only the preservation of a dualistic complementarity necessary to the existence of Huaulu and Huaulu-conceived society.

64. Thus the Puraratuhu claim that their taboo on the tipolo python demonstrates that it is their origin: "Ami rahe asale hini tipoloam barani ita aeressi," "We have our origin in the tipolo, since we don't eat it." This apparently literal statement is not quite supported by the origin myth. In any case *asale,* "origin," may mean rather different things. For instance, the Matoke have a taboo on pig meat because "it is their origin" (ia rahe asale). But this origin refers to the taboo itself: following it commemorates having originally been Muslim. But the same Muslim origin is also indicated by the taboo on uneune (goat meat), which is the most common and ideal meat for Muslims nowadays. While this taboo indicates the passage of time, separating Matoke from Muslim, the other taboo indicates the continuous connection of Matoke with Muslim.

65. Some animals are universally taboo in the village, not because they are the origin of everybody, but out of respect for the clans that claim origin from them. For example, tessi and kakaku are taboo to eat for all Huaulu because of their respect for the Sinalam and Tamatay, who regard these birds as their origins.

66. As I showed earlier, another possible and, if true, most interesting case is provided by what the same informant told me. She said that it is taboo to build menstrual huts with poles of malotu "because it is red." At the same time she said that the only creeper one can use to put together the pieces of the same hut is a kiele tapu, which is also red. In the first case, the summation of identicals is taboo because it may increase bleeding in the hut. In the second case, though, it is necessary; perhaps what keeps the hut together must be of the same nature as what the house is for. Hence summation is a contradictory principle because it may be tabooed and required at the same time, although different meanings must be emphasized.

67. See Kierkegaard on replication (Kierkegaard 1983).

68. The same effect was attributed by Kalahei to the mixing of two equally red species: tuy and oko.

69. I have returned in some detail to the taboo on dog-eating as a premise for finding out how similar the incest taboo is to it. The basic initial question is: Why is sexuality, accompanied by marriage or not, a raiser of taboo, just as eating is? And the basic answer seems to be that they both establish the closest connection between two beings, although they are, of course, of rather different natures. Eating means absorbing the eaten, fully reducing it to oneself (if one manages to digest). A sexual relationship is less assimilative, but one which implies the absorption of the male semen by a woman. In a sense, she eats. But this exclusively female eating is made possible by an exclusively male feeding. Such feeding has no counterpart in the animal-to-human sphere. It is as if food voluntarily offers itself to the eater with the purpose of appropriating her/him in part to its attributive domain.

This emphasis, or perhaps overemphasis, on closeness explains why it may seem the only reason for the incest taboo. No doubt closeness brings the strongest emotional and stative weight to the explanation.

70. Performance as a universal criterion may be more prestigious in somewhat graying anthropological circles but requires instead a good shake in connection with the Huaulu system. The applicability of the performance criterion implies the essentially affirmative character of the rituals covered by negative expressions (i.e. taboos). The pure avoidance of doing, in contrast, cannot bring performative interpretation very far, since success simply consists in not moving, in not doing. If food taboos were negation as an indirect expression of affirmation, as indexes of culinary recipes, they would not raise the problem they raise: Why is it that the dominance of actual negation which they usually represent is extended to the whole ritual realm? In a sense, this question may be translated into, or constantly bound to, the fact that it is not cuisine but a collection of true and often individual negations that defines the subject as eater. In other words, food taboos do not seem to be the simple counterparts of recipes. One is a Frenchman, American, or Chinese not so much by a combination of what one is supposed to eat as by what food one potentially refuses to eat—as a category, species, or individual.

The interconnection of the two cannot be confused with the identity (and therefore redundancy) of one relative to the other. This reduction implies a radical simplification. No doubt eating can be seen as a success or a failure in some generic type of performance ("eating" itself, or "eating the right food with the right people"). But success in these kinds of performances consists mainly in an appropriate choice of what to eat and, more important, what not to eat.

While there is no doubt, then, that a dimension of performance can be found, especially when one wants, in all taboos and thus also in the alimentary consumption taboos, it is even less doubtful that the relative importance of such dimension must be taken into account. Consumption is usually much more defining in a variety of acts, and in eating more than any other.

71. Tambiah 1985c. The contrast between the taboos of consumption and those of execution defines a polarity which allows us to identify various aspects of concrete taboos, since these are not completely separable. Keeping danger away may be keeping away from an object (usually a species) that produces it; or it may be keeping away from one's own failures in performance. In a sense, the former can be converted into the latter: eating can be seen as a success or a failure in performance, but the success in this kind of performance consists mainly in an appropriate choice of what to eat and what not to eat, which in fact is more important. It is not cuisine but a collection of negations that defines the subject as eater. Such negations emphasize the subject's identity by his recognition and keeping of his place in a world defined by a classificatory system but also by initiatives of contact or distance between more personalized terms (occult powers and subjects as shamans, or headhunters, or hunters, or fishermen, and so on). So in a sense taboo is always about performance, but this component takes first place only when much more complicated relationships with external objects exist than eating, or when the relationship is far more indirect and mediated, and the relationships with other subjects and the formal qualities of the action are focussed on.

72. The universal character of maquwoli—that is, negation as the expres-

sion of both the other side of any affirmation and of negation as such—is found as the latter in consumption taboos more often and more densely than in performative ones.

73. In performative taboo, the other side of negation—affirmation—is often well ahead of taboo's literal meaning (not to do this, not to do that).

74. The relationship between parts and whole, the way it is used and described, tends to differ between predominantly consumption taboos and predominantly action ones. This confirms that a generic difference beween the two kinds of taboos exists and must be taken into account for interpretive purposes, just as it is locally for practical purposes.

75. There are objects that exist only because they are made by humans. Their existence or continuity thus requires the totality of the acts of making.

76. Which is mostly symbolic of other things. That is, internal symbolic connections do not translate into empirical equivalences; what takes ontological effect is the symbolic connection with an external effect, short term or long term.

77. The most obvious because most grandiosely blatant example is that of the kahua, where eating is part of the final stage of festivities.

78. This is at least what one must deduce at the level of concrete acting. What is taboo in one case, then, is to consume a whole whose enjoyment usually exists as the exclusion of incomplete performances—that is, acts defined by a whole series of what exclusively or primarily exists by human action. The reason is that the whole's continuation as a whole (species, genus, or even the entire classificatory system) usually explains the taboo, but it is not sufficient to account for limiting nonconsuming taboos to certain parts of the animal. Execution-linked ("performative") taboos, in contrast, tend to refer to the totality of the parts that make up, rather than stand for, the whole. The reason for this contrast is the contrasting nature of the whole in the two cases. In one case, the whole exclusively exists in the acts performed by human agents. In ritual, for instance, whole is completeness of human action, an action that implies the use of nonhuman objects, but mostly as parts of what is artificially constructed by human subjects.

The contrast between taboos predominantly of consumption and taboos predominantly of performance is paralleled by the obvious difference between taboos that rest on the respect of the whole as a complete series of components and those that rest on the respect of the whole as equivalent to certain of its parts. The former is dominant in purely human acting and making (rituals, etc.); the latter is dominant in pure consumption.

79. As we have seen in chapter 4, this is the case of game that died a strange, usually immediate, death.

80. Dumont 1966; see also Valeri 1989, 1983.

81. This reaffirms the internal segmentation of the superior world of men, although the taboo is lifted only if the other hunters agree to perform the special ritual which actually allows him to remove the taboo. On the internal and external segmentations see the rather extraordinary draft by Kierkegaard, ex-pupil of Hegel: Kierkegaard 1983, "Repetition." See also Sartre 1966:44ff.

82. Many of their descendants, ancestors, or enemies might also want to join the dance, particularly in certain rooms of the anthropological house.

83. One can argue, in fact, for a correspondence between speech and spit.

Spit is, in a sense, a more concrete and visible state and form of speech. Or reciprocally, speech is a more abstract and invisible form of spit. But speech is also an articulate function, whereas spit is an inarticulated one (so it lends itself either to multiple meanings or to one only).

84. Since smoke objectively connects the smoke-maker (human) with the smoke-receiver (external to the human but capable of influencing or even undoing him or her). Moreover, it is a connection which goes out of hand—easy to produce but difficult or impossible to direct. It is thus an undeniable sign of human weakness seen at the margins of the most primordial sign of human power and identity—fire-making.

85. A man-made species refers to objects and events which are, just like natural ones, classifiable in kind.

86. Some examples, such as Jewish or Arabic (Chelhod 1987; Reinhardt 1990; Cook 1987; M. Philonenko 1967; Henninger 1982; Bousquet 1958; *New Encyclopaedia of Islam* 1965), Greek (Rudhardt 1958; Lloyd-Jones 1971; Vernant 1980), Brahmanical (Zimmermann 1982; Orenstein 1965, 1970a, 1970b; Madan 1985; Harper 1964; Malamoud 1996; Simoons 1967, 1968, 1974).

87. The true difference between the two is the much more collective character, not the unification of performance taboos—in contrast with consumption taboos—under the notion of "dirt" or some other generalizable effect that can be transmitted into a social evaluation implying exclusion/expulsion (directly or through the pretext of a taboo-violation-derived disease, such as leprosy according to the Talmudic culture), but the social sharing of the dangerous state or, better, the failure effect (of what one pursues by pursuing taboo in the sense of "ritual") which may be due to a crowd of different errors by different participants or to the error of just one single person.

88. Literally true in a purification ritual in which a menstruating woman who contaminated a man washes him.

89. To some extent also the territory, as indicated by the taboo on hunting and in any case the impossibility of finding game when somebody has died.

90. See Valeri 1995.

91. More generically, one can say, with Bachelard, that "l'imagination matérielle trouve dans l'eau la matière pure par excellence, la matière naturellement pure" (Bachelard 1942b:181; emphasis removed). ["Material imagination finds in water purity par excellence, the only naturally pure matter" (J.H.).]

92. The true polarity difference between taboos of consumption pure and simple and taboos of performance is the taboo violation's tendency to have individually limited effects or to extend these effects to categories of people who are related to the transgressor or who are merely coexisting with him in space or time. Interestingly enough, and in contrast again with the systems that have truly reached the notion of pollution as a human act running into a divine or objectively unified order, the most generalizing, immediate, and automatic "pollution" (or what is comparable to pollution proper) is intermediate between the consumption of the humanly unmade and the performance of the humanly made. It is the human bodily failure (centered on genitalia, i.e. the organs for reproducing, or on the failure of the entire body) rather than the failure of humans as agents, and it is an unwilled and a priori uncontrollable bodily condition of agency. This automatically concerns the entire community as reminders that they all share these phenomena.

93. One of the most common is "spitting" on the person who is ashamed or who should feel ashamed. Spitting on the face confirms the centrality of the visible skin and that of the face as site of the greatest emotional expression.

94. Nevertheless, there is hardly complete symmetry and logical or ideological complementarity between "name" and "shame." For Near Eastern examples of the analogous relative (and even absolute) disconnection of "honor" and "shame," see Wikan 1984 and Stewart 1994, ch. 11.

95. Shame "introduces the notion of an audience, for feeling shame is connected with the thought that eyes are upon one" (Taylor 1985:53).

96. Such fine payments are very different from ordinary affinal payments in that they are not reciprocal.

97. Note, by the way, that shame is a reaction of the skin or, rather, *on* the skin, thus perfectly visible and evaluable by the community, just like so many dangers attached to taboo violation. But shame is inseparable from an actual communal judgment. Like a performance taboo, it exists only by an actual social act. But in taboo this act is that of the performing subject, whether this is known by the public or not. Shame, in contrast, has the collective reaction as the only true base of existence. One does not feel ashamed for violating a social rule, even if that is the condition for a shame-inducing judgment. One feels ashamed exclusively when one has been uncovered and feels exposed to a strong collective evaluation. Thus it is the latter, it is its impact, that is the source of shame. In sum, we move from a class of taboos (consumption) whose negative consequences for the body exist whether people know of it or not (such knowledge is totally irrelevant); to another one where the transgression is due to a culturally established order but whose negative consequences do not come from the act of collective judgment; and finally to an area (shame) whose existence as the subject's reaction to his transgression exclusively depends on a collective judgment. The latter judgment could be called performative, which perhaps indicates that the notion of "performative" is overused throughout the spectrum far from the law which was its original starting point.

Further arguments can be found in a number of works which, in my opinion, bring out a rather puzzling phenomenon: the predominance of shame in Melanesia and the predominance of taboo in places like Huaulu and, on the whole, traditional Seram. On Melanesian anthropological essays and more general ones, see H. Morris 1976; Herzfeld 1980; P. Berger 1970; Fajans 1983; Read 1955; Epstein 1984; Blok 1981; Wikan 1984; Gilsenan 1985; Piers and Singer 1971; Hogbin 1947; Strathern 1977; Wyatt-Brown 1982.

98. An example of expulsion—on which, however, his violent words hardly reached consensus—was given me in Pulaki's proposal to get rid of two "ugly" (because invaded by kolikoliam [ringworm], a disfiguring and stinking skin disease) brothers.

99. Note that the Huaulu refer to the Indonesian language as one of peace, that is, of law-regulated and controlled social order. It is noncomprehension due to the speaking of traditional languages by each tribe or even each lineage that produces conflict. The theory can thus be extended to internal relations.

100. *Jus* in Latin. Further important discussion on the notion of law and its relations with others is found in Hart 1961; D. Lloyd 1972; Perelman 1945; Austin 1975; Kelsen 1961; Douglas 1973b; Glucklich 1984, 1988:10; Benveniste

1969, 2:99ff.; Kelley 1990:41, 37–38, 49–61; Dumézil 1966. On the connection with Indian law, see Harper 64:171–172; Mauss 1938, 1990; Hubert and Mauss 1899. See also, of course, Hegel 1957.

101. Spinoza 1958.

102. Douglas 1966.

103. This is another example of the functionalist theory of taboo coexisting in Douglas 1966 with the cognitive one. The two are never really or convincingly reconciled.

104. A longer debate on law and its similarity or differences with Huaulu taboo would require a number of important books and essays which have to do with the fundamental rule on rules: Austin 1975; Kenny 1966; Black 1962; Bouveresse 1995; Deleuze 1971, 1985; Dworkin 1978; Howell 1981; Hart 1961; Hegel 1957; D. Lloyd 1972; Kelsen 1961; Raz 1980, 1979; Ross 1968, 1975.

105. A most telling example of hukum as a prescription originating from Lahatala's will and action is his impediment to human birth if the fetus does not make a choice on the duration of his own life. In other words, it is impossible to be born without accepting that the life one obtains implies death. This "natural" fact is viewed and described as Lahatala's law (i.e. a prescription initiated according to his will). It is true, of course, that in Lahatala the order of nature and the order of society converge as both willed, and therefore deserve the idea of law. But "law" enters into Huaulu discourse only if there is punishment. To those who do not choose the length of their life, Lahatala inflicts the punishment of nonbirth.

106. Adat and sometimes even hukum (when Lahatala is involved) are applied to maquwoli simply because taboos have become part of the tradition, and thus part of collective will, even if they are not produced/caused by it. The major difference with law/custom is that the consequences of taboo violation are always attributed to intrinsic powers that do not depend on social action, and certainly not on those that resemble a trial and to which alone the *hukum* term is really applied.

107. But the fact that what is dangerous is more noticeable and clear-cut than what is not is the ultimate reason for many definitional and self-definitional uses of negation, of taboo.

108. That knowledge and avoidance of danger are its basic motivation is not the only reason for the use of negative expressions. The transition from this reason for the preponderance of negation, taking the form "don't eat," "I do not eat," "I do not touch," and so on, as avoidance of the dangerous, to the reason that it is easier and more precise to define oneself through what one doesn't than through what one does, should already be clear. But it has to be spelled out briefly as one of the adding parts of these conclusions.

109. From my notes on law and shame, where it is argued that shame is second only to taboo in Huaulu as a mechanism of the law. See also Mead 1934: 502; Parker 1990:257; Bachelard 1942b; Harper 1964; Kristeva 1980; Wyatt-Brown 1982; Pitt-Rivers 1977; Taylor 1985; Ross 1975.

110. For some published but partial anticipation of my thoughts on this in more fields than taboo, see Valeri 1992a.

111. It is not a direct "yes," though, but one expressed through associates.

112. Freud 1963a:75.

113. This could be construed as the hidden subjective reason for the importance given to the animal/human distinction in so many Huaulu taboos and probably underlying all of them (see beginning of chapter 4).

114. On this yes that can carry over into the no of consciousness, see Freud's essay "Negation" (1953b:235ff.).

115. Greenberg 1966:50, cit. in Horn 1989:156.

116. To borrow from Sartre: "Le non-être apparaît toujours dans les limites d'une attente humaine" (1980:41). ["Non-being always appears within the limits of a human expectation" (Sartre 1966:38).] This is one possible, but not sufficient, starting point for a view of the dominance of negation.

117. As should be evident, my explanation of the use of negation in this case is only apparently similar to that of Lambek (1992). For him, negation has more continuity than action, which is visibly punctual. But, it seems to me, if one considers the occasions in which one is confronted with doing or not doing, then there is no absolute difference between action and negation, since in both cases a decision implies moving from one state to another: from a positive relation to a negative one or vice versa, or from no reaction to reaction of one kind or the other. Note that even the choice of continuing nonaction creates an interruption, since it has to be declared or recognized as such, and thus begins at the time of decision, just like the opposite movement. The contrast exists only if we consider content—for instance, the already mentioned kahua taboo on cleaning under the house. Here an act of not doing can be continuous from beginning to end. But formally, negation and affirmation imply a share of discontinuities at the level of decision and requirement of choice, which keep coming to consciousness, and thus even more to negation than to action (the latter being quite often habitual and thus not conscious or hardly so).

118. In this sense, the logic of taboo for purposes of identification calls for some drawing from Hegelian water, except that one hardly finds a synthesis of affirmation and negation—only an unresolved dialectic of the two, with negation always being at a higher level of consciousness and always presupposing affirmation as a starting point. See Gadamer 1976; and many others.

119. See S. Willis 1991.

120. As it already appeared to Adorno (1974), whose magical *Minima moralia* anticipated for me since the sixties the world of Los Angeles. I was sort of aware of it without knowing that I was, but I immediately recognized it upon my actual encounter.

121. Casti [1802] 1987:6, preface. ["I did not have the time to be brief" (J.H.).]

122. Gianmaria Ortes, "Calcolo sopra la verità dell'istoria" (1755), in Ortes 1984:75. ["Who can tell me if I'm feigning?" (J.H.).]

123. Louis Lambert in *La comédie humaine* (Balzac 1980:687). ["Society begins with abstraction, and from abstraction are born laws, arts, interests, and social ideas" (J.H.).]

BIBLIOGRAPHY

Abbagnano, N. 1961. *Dizionario di filosofia.* Turin: Unione Tipografico-Editrice Torinese.

Abdurachman, P. R. 1978. Moluccan responses to the first intrusions of the West. In *Dynamics of Indonesian history,* ed. H. Soebadio and C. A. du Marchie Sarvaas, 161–188. Amsterdam, Oxford, and New York: North-Holland Publishing Company.

Adorno, T. W. 1974. *Minima moralia: Reflections from damaged life.* Trans. E. F. N. Jephcott. London: Verso.

Adorno, T. W. 1994. *Hegel: Three studies.* Trans. S. W. Nicholsen. Cambridge, Mass.: MIT Press.

Alter, R. 1979. A new theory of Kashrut. *Commentary* 68 (2): 46–51.

Andaya, L. Y. 1993. *The world of Maluku: Eastern Indonesia in the Early Modern period.* Honolulu: University of Hawaii Press.

Austin, J. L. 1975. *How to do things with words.* Cambridge, Mass.: Harvard University Press.

Babadzan, A. 1993. *Les dépouilles des dieux.* Paris: Fondation de la Maison des sciences de l'homme.

Bachelard, G. 1940. *La philosophie du non: Essai d'une philosophie du nouvel esprit scientifique.* Paris: J. Corti.

Bachelard, G. 1942a. *Fragments d'une poétique de l'espace.* Paris: Presses universitaires de France.

Bachelard, G. 1942b. *L'eau et les rêves: Essai sur l'imagination de la matière.* Paris: J. Corti.

Bachelard, G. 1980. *La formation de l'esprit scientifique: Contribution à une psychanalyse de la connaissance objective.* Paris: J. Vrin.

Bachelard, G. 1986. *La flamme d'une chandelle.* Paris: Presses universitaires de France.

Bachelard, G. 1988. *La poétique de l'espace.* Paris: Presses universitaires de France.

Balzac, H. de. 1980. *La comédie humaine.* Paris: Editions Pléiades, Gallimard.

Barnes, R. H. 1980. The meaning of corporations in eastern Indonesia. In *The meaning of marriage payments,* ed. J. L. Comaroff, 93–124. Studies in Anthropology, 7. London and New York: Academic Press.

Bataille, G. 1967. *La part maudite: Précedé de la notion de dépense.* Paris: Editions de Minuit.

Bataille, G. 1973. *Théorie de la religion.* Collection Idees, 306. Paris: Gallimard.

Bataille, G. 1976. *La limite de l'utile* [fragments d'une version abandonnée de "La part maudite"]. In *Oeuvres complètes,* Vol. 7, pp. 181–280. Paris: Gallimard.

Bataille, G. 1986. *Théorie de la religion.* Paris: Gallimard.

Bean, S. S. 1981. Toward a semiotics of "Purity" and "Pollution" in India. *American Ethnologist* 8 (3): 575–595.

Benveniste, E. 1969. *Le vocabulaire des institutions indo-européennes.* 2 vols. Paris: Editions de Minuit.

Berger, J. 1980. *About looking.* New York: Pantheon Books.

Berger, P. 1970. On the obsolescence of the concept of honor. *Archives européenes de sociologie* 11:339–347.

Bergson, H. 1959. *Les deux sources de la morale et de la religion.* In *Oeuvres*, 979–1247. Paris: Presses universitaires de France.

Berlin, B. 1992. *Ethnobiological classification: Principles of categorization of plants and animals in traditional societies.* Princeton, N.J.: Princeton University Press.

Berlin, B., D. E. Breedlove, and P. H. Raven. 1966. Folk taxonomies and biological classification. *Science* 154:273–275.

Berlin, B., D. E. Breedlove, and P. H. Raven. 1968. Covert categories and folk taxonomies. *American Anthropologist* 70 (2): 290–299.

Berlin, B., D. E. Breedlove, and P. H. Raven. 1973. General principles of classification and nomenclature in folk biology. *American Anthropologist* 75 (1): 214–242.

Berry, M. E. 1987. Giving in Asia, A symposium: Introduction. *Journal of Asian Studies* 46 (2): 305–308.

Biro Bina Pemerintahan Desa (Maluku). 1984a. *Himpunan Peraturan dan Surat—Surat Ederon, Instruksi Petunjuk Dalam Penyulanggaran Pemerintahan Desa.* Bulletin 1 and Bulletin 2, First Level Region. Maluku: Kantor Gubernur.

Biro Bina Pemerintahan Desa (Maluku). 1984b. *Penj Umum dan Petunjuk Tekhuis Peloksenaan Undang—Undang Nomar 5 Tahun 1979 Tentang Pemerintahan Desa.* First Level Region. Maluku: Kantor Gubernur.

Biro Pusat Statistik. 1986. *Registrasi Penduduk Okhir Tahun.* Jakarta: Biro Pusat Statistik.

Black, M. 1962. The analysis of rules. In *Models and metaphors: Studies in language and philosophy*, ed. M. Black, 95–139. Ithaca, N.Y.: Cornell University Press.

Blok, A. 1981. Rams and billy-goats: A key to the Mediterranean code of honour. *Man*, n.s. 16 (3): 427–440.

Blust, R. 1981. Linguistic evidence for some early Austronesian taboos. *American Anthropologist* 83 (2): 285–319.

Boccaccio, G. 1987. *Decameron*, ed. V. Branca. Turin: Einaudi.

Bodson, L., ed. 1988. *L'animal dans l'alimentation humaine: Les critères de choix: Actes du colloque international de Liège, 26–29 Novembre 1986.* Anthropozoologica, Numéro spécial, 2. Liège: Anthropozoologica.

Boetzelaer van Dubbeldam, C. W. T. 1906. *De Gereformeerde Kerken in Nederland en de zending in Oost-Indië in de dagen der Oost-Indische Compagnie.* Utrecht: P. den Boer.

Boetzelaer van Dubbeldam, C. W. T. 1947. *De Protestantsche Kerk in Nederlandsch-Indië, haar ontwikkeling van 1620–1939.* The Hague: Martinus Nijhoff.

Boisvert, C. 1987. De la pêche aux stupéfiants (Indonésie). In *De la voûte céleste au terroir, du jardin au foyer: Mosaïque sociographique: Textes offerts à Lucien Bernot*, ed. B. Koechlin, F. Sigaut, J. M. C. Thomas, and G. Toffin, 267–276. Paris: Editions de l'Ecole des hautes études en sciences sociales.

Bolens-Duvernay, J. 1983. Avatars mythiques du poison de pêche. *L'Homme* 23 (1): 45–59.

Bosquet, G. H. 1958. Des animaux et de leur traitement selon le Judaïsme, le Christianisme et l'Islam. *Studia Islamica* (Paris) 9:31–48.

Bouveresse, J. 1995. Règles, dispositions et habitus. *Critique* 51 (579–580): 573–594.

Boyer, P., ed. 1993. *Cognitive aspects of religious symbolism.* Cambridge and New York: Cambridge University Press.
Boyer, P. 1994. *The naturalness of religious ideas: A cognitive theory of religion.* Berkeley: University of California Press.
Bredekamp, H. 1995. *The lore of antiquity and the cult of the machine.* Princeton, N.J.: Markus Wiener.
Bremmer, J. N. 1983. *The early Greek concept of the soul.* Princeton, N.J.: Princeton University Press.
Brightman, R. A. 1991. *Grateful prey: Rock Cree human-animal relationships.* Berkeley: University of California Press.
Brown, C. H. 1984. *Language and living things: Uniformities in folk classification and naming.* New Brunswick, N.J.: Rutgers University Press.
Brown, C. H., J. Kolar, B. J. Torrey, T. Truong-Quang, and P. Volkman. 1976. Some general principles of biological and non-biological folk classification. *American Ethnologist* 3 (1): 73–85.
Bruun, O., and Kalland Arne, eds. 1992. *Asian perceptions of nature.* Nordic Proceedings in Asian Studies, 3. Copenhagen: NIAS.
Buckley, T., and A. Gottlieb, eds. 1988. *Blood magic: The anthropology of menstruation.* Berkeley: University of California Press.
Bukowski, C. 1995. *Living on luck: Selected letters 1960–1970s,* Vol. 2. Ed. S. Cooney. Santa Rosa, Calif.: Black Sparrow Press.
Bulmer, R. N. H. 1967. Why is the cassowary not a bird? A problem of zoological taxonomy among the Karam of the New Guinea highlands. *Man,* n.s. 2 (1): 5–25.
Bulmer, R. N. H., and M. J. Tyler. 1968. Karam classification of frogs. *Journal of the Polynesian Society* 77 (4): 333–385.
Bulmer, R. N. H. 1970. Which came first, the chicken or the egghead. In *Echanges et communications: Mélanges offerts à Claude Lévi-Strauss,* ed. J. Pouillon and P. Maranda, Vol. 2, pp. 1069–1091. Studies in General Anthropology, 5. The Hague and Paris: Mouton.
Bulmer, R. N. H. 1974. Folk biology in the New Guinea highlands. *Social Science Information* 13 (4–5): 28.
Burkill, I. H. 1966. *A dictionary of the economic products of the Malay peninsula.* 2d ed. 2 vols. Kualu Lumpur: Published on behalf of the Governments of Malaysia and Singapore by the Ministry of Agriculture and Co-operatives.
Carroll, M. 1977. Leach, genesis and structural analysis: A critical evaluation. *American Ethnologist* 4 (4): 663–677.
Carruthers, P. 1991. *The animals issue: Moral theory in practice.* Cambridge and New York: Cambridge University Press.
Carsten, J., and S. Hugh-Jones. 1995. *About the house: Lévi-Strauss and beyond.* Cambridge and New York: Cambridge University Press.
Cartry, M., ed. 1987. *Sous le masque de l'animal: Essais sur le sacrifice en Afrique noire.* Bibliothèque de l'Ecole des hautes études. Section des sciences religieuses, 88. Paris: Presses universitaires de France.
Casti, G. B. [1802] 1987. *Gli animali parlanti,* ed. L. Pedroia, 6. Testi Documenti di Letteratura e di Lingua, 9. Rome: Salerno.
Cazelles, H. 1979. Pureté et impureté dans l'Ancien Testament. *Supplément au dictionnaire de la Bible,* ed. L. Pirot, Vol. 9, pp. 398–554. Paris: Letouzey et Ané.
Chauvel, R. 1978. Their myths and our reality: A review of the debate in the

Netherlands on the South Moluccan question. *Review of Indonesian and Malaysian Affairs* 12 (1): 67–94.

Chauvel, R. 1980. Ambon's other half: Some preliminary observations on Ambonese Moslem society and history. *Review of Indonesian and Malaysian Affairs* 14 (1): 40–80.

Chauvel, R. 1985. Ambon: Not a revolution but a counterrevolution. In *Regional dynamics of the Indonesian revolution: Unity from diversity*, ed. A. R. Kahin, 237–264. Honolulu: University of Hawaii Press.

Chauvel, R. 1990. *Nationalists, soldiers and separatists: The Ambonese Islands from colonialism to revolt, 1880–1950.* Verhandelingen van het Koninklijk Instituut voor Taal-, Land- en Volkenkunde, 143. Leiden: KITLV Press.

Chelhod, J. 1964. Les structures du sacré chez les Arabes. Paris: G.-P. Maisonneuve et Larose.

Cherno, M. 1963. Feuerbach's "Man is what he eats": A rectification. *Journal of the History of Ideas* 24:397–406.

Chiva, M. 1979. Comment la personne se construit en mangeant. *Communications* 31:107–118.

Chlenov, M. A. 1980. Cultural vocabulary as an indicator of inter-ethnic relations: Eastern Indonesian evidence. *Bijdragen van het Koninklijk Instituut* 136: 426–439.

Chlenov, M. A., and U. Sirk. 1973. Merger of labial phonemes in Ambonese language. *Acta et commentationes Universitas Tartuensis, Oriental Studies* 2 (1).

Cicero. 1933. *De natura deorum.* Loeb Classical Library. Cambridge, Mass.: Harvard University Press.

Cicero. 1972. *The nature of the gods (De natura deorum).* Trans. H. C. P. McGregor. Harmondsworth: Penguin.

Classen, C., D. Howes, and A. Synnott. 1994. *Aroma: The cultural history of smell.* London and New York: Routledge.

Cole, C. 1984. Taxonomy: What's in a name? *Natural History* 93:30–34.

Collins, J. T. 1983. The historical relationships of the languages of central Maluku, Indonesia. Materials in languages of Indonesia, 13. Pacific Linguistics, series D, no. 47, W. A. L. Stokhof, series ed. Canberra, Australia: Research School of Pacific Studies, Australian National University.

Collins, J. T. 1984. Linguistic research in Maluku: A report of recent fieldwork. *Oceanic Linguistics* 21 (1–2): 73–150.

Cook, M. 1987. Early Islamic dietary law. *Jerusalem Studies in Arabic and Islam* 7: 217–277.

Coon, C. S. 1976. *The hunting peoples.* Harmondsworth: Penguin.

Corbin, A. 1986. *The foul and the fragrant: Odor and the French social imagination.* Cambridge, Mass.: Harvard University Press.

Csordas, T., ed. 1994. *Embodiment and experience: The existential ground of culture and self.* Cambridge and New York: Cambridge University Press.

de Heusch, L. 1985. *Sacrifice in Africa: A structuralist approach.* Bloomington: Indiana University Press.

de Heusch, L., M. Douglas, and J. M. Lewis. 1993. Hunting the pangolin (comment). *Man*, n.s. 28 (1): 159–166.

Dekkers, M. 1994. *Dearest pet: On bestiality.* Trans. P. Vincent. London and New York: Verso.

Deleuze, G. 1971. Humor, irony, and the law. In *Masochism: An interpretation of coldness and cruelty,* trans. J. McNeil, together with the entire text of L. von Sacher-Masoch, *Venus in furs,* trans. J. McNeil from the French translation by A. Willm, 71–78. New York: George Braziller.

Deleuze, G. 1983. *Cinéma,* Vol. 1: *L'image-mouvement.* Paris: Editions de Minuit.

Deleuze, G. 1985. *Cinéma,* Vol. 2: *L'image-temps.* Paris: Editions de Minuit.

De Martino, E., ed. 1976. *Magia e civiltà: Un antologia critica fondementale per lo studio del concetto di magia nella civiltà occidentale.* Milan: Garzanti.

Dermout, M. 1983. *The ten thousand things.* Trans. Hans Koning, afterword E. M. Beekman. Amherst: University of Massachusetts Press.

Descartes, R. 1912. *A discourse on method.* Trans. J. Veitch. New York: E. P. Dutton.

Descartes, R. 1974. *Discours de la méthode.* Paris: Editions de la Pléiade.

De Vries, G. 1927. Bij de Berg-Alfoeren op West-Seran: Zeden, gewooten en mythologie van een oervolk. Zutphen: Thieme.

Devyer, A. 1973. *Le sang épuré: Les préjugés de race chez les gentilshommes français de l'Ancien Régime, 1560–1720.* Université libre de Bruxelles, Faculté de philosophie et lettres, 55. Brussels: Editions de l'Université de Bruxelles.

Digard, J.-P. 1982. *Le cuisinier et le philosophe: Hommage à Maxime Rodinson.* Paris: G.-P. Maisonneuve et Larose.

Dodds, E. R. 1951. *The Greeks and the irrational.* Sather Classical Lectures, 25. Berkeley: University of California Press.

Dodds, E. R. 1954. *The soul.* Berkeley: University of California Press.

Douglas, M. 1963. The Lele of Kasai. In *African worlds: Studies in the cosmological ideas and social values of African peoples,* ed. D. Forde, 1–26. London: Oxford University Press.

Douglas, M. 1966. *Purity and danger: An analysis of concepts of pollution and taboo.* London: Routledge and Kegan Paul.

Douglas, M. 1970. *Natural symbols: Explorations in cosmology.* New York: Pantheon Books.

Douglas, M. 1972. Deciphering a meal. *Daedalus* (special issue on myth, symbol and culture), 68–81.

Douglas, M. 1973a. Critique and commentary. In *The idea of purity in ancient Judaism,* ed. J. Neusner, 137–142. Studies in Judaism in Late Antiquity (Haskell Lectures, Oberlin College, 1972–73), 1. Leiden: Brill.

Douglas, M. 1973b. *Rules and meanings: The anthropology of everyday knowledge.* Harmondsworth: Penguin Education.

Douglas, M. 1975a. Couvade and menstruation: The relevance of tribal studies. In *Implicit meanings: Essays in anthropology,* 60–72. London: Routledge and Kegan Paul.

Douglas, M. 1975b. *Implicit meanings: Essays in anthropology.* London and Boston: Routledge and Kegan Paul.

Douglas, M. 1982. Food as a system of communication. In *In the active voice,* 82–124. London: Routledge and Kegan Paul.

Douglas, M. 1992. *Risk and blame: Essays in cultural theory.* London and New York: Routledge.

Douglas, M. 1993. In the wilderness: The doctrine of defilement in the Book of Numbers. *Journal of the Study of the Old Testament,* suppl. ser. 158.

Douglas, M., and D. Hull, eds. 1992. *How classification works: Nelson Goodman among the social sciences.* Edinburgh: Edinburgh University Press.

Douglas, M., and A. Wildavsky. 1982. *Risk and culture: An essay on the selection of technical and environmental dangers.* Berkeley: University of California Press.
Dumézil, G. 1966. *La religion romaine archaique.* Paris: Payot.
Dumézil, G. 1970. *Archaic Roman religion.* Trans. P. Knapp. 2 vols. Chicago: University of Chicago Press.
Dumont, L. 1959. Pure and impure. *Contributions to Indian Sociology* 3:9–39.
Dumont, L. 1966. *Homo hierarchicus: Essai sur le système des castes.* Paris: Gallimard.
Durkheim, E. 1896. La prohibition de l'inceste et ses origines. *L'Année sociologique* 1:1–70.
Durkheim, E. 1915. *The elementary forms of the religious life.* Trans. J. W. Swain. New York: Allen & Unwin.
Durkheim, E. 1963. *Incest: The nature and origin of the taboo.* Trans. E. Sagarin. New York: Lyle Stuart.
Durkheim, E. 1968. *Les formes élémentaires de la vie religieuse: Le système totémique en Australie.* Paris: Presses universitaires de France.
Dworkin, R. M. 1978. *Taking rights seriously.* Cambridge, Mass.: Harvard University Press.
Dwyer, P. 1976. Beetles, butterflies and bats: Species transformation in New Guinea folk classification. *Oceania* 46 (3): 188–205.
Echols, J. M., and H. Shadily. 1989. *An Indonesian-English dictionary.* Ithaca, N.Y.: Cornell University Press.
Eilberg-Schwartz, H. 1990. *The savage in Judaism: An anthropology of Israelite religion and ancient Judaism.* Bloomington: Indiana University Press.
Ellen, R. F. 1972. The marsupial in Nuaulu ritual behavior. *Man,* n.s. 7 (2): 223–238.
Ellen, R. F. 1973. Nuaulu settlement and ecology: An approach to the environmental relations of an eastern Indonesian community. Ph.D. diss., University of London.
Ellen, R. F. 1975. Non-domesticated resources in Nuaulu ecological relations. *Social Science Information* 14 (5): 51–61.
Ellen, R. F. 1978. *Nuaulu settlement and ecology: An approach to the environmental relations of an eastern Indonesian community.* Verhandelingen van het Koninklijk Instituut voor Taal-, Land- en Volkenkunde, 83. The Hague: Martinus Nijhoff.
Ellen, R. F. 1986. Ethnobiology, cognition and the structure of prehension: More general theoretical notes. *Journal of Ethnobiology* 6:83–98.
Ellen, R. F. 1988a. Foraging, starch extraction and the sedentary lifestyle in the lowland rainforest of central Seram. In *Hunters and gatherers,* ed. T. Ingold, D. Riches, and J. Woodburn, Vol. 1: *History, evolution and social change,* 117–134. Oxford and New York: Berg.
Ellen, R. F. 1988b. Ritual, identity, and interethnic relations in Seram. In *Time past, time present, time future: Perspectives on Indonesian culture: Essays in honour of Professor P. E. de Josselin de Jong,* ed. H. J. M. Claessen and D. S. Moyer, 117–135. Verhandelingen van het Koninklijk Instituut voor Taal-, Land- en Volkenkunde, 131. Dordrecht, Holland, and Providence, R.I.: Foris Publications.
Ellen, R. F. 1993a. *The cultural relations of classification: An analysis of Nuaulu animal categories from central Seram.* Cambridge: Cambridge University Press.
Ellen, R. F. 1993b. *Nuaulu ethnozoology: A systematic inventory.* CSAC Mono-

graphs, 6, South-East Asia Series. Canterbury, United Kingdom: Centre for Social Anthropology and Computing, University of Kent.

Ellen, R. F., and D. Reason, eds. 1979. *Classifications in their social context.* Language, Thought, and Culture. London and New York: Academic Press.

Ellen, R. F., A. F. Stimson, and J. Menzies. 1976. Structure and inconsistency in Nuaulu categories for amphibians. *Journal d'agriculture tropicale et de botanique appliquée* 23:125–138.

Ellen, R. F., A. F. Stimson, and J. Menzies. 1977. The content of categories of experience: The case of some Nuaulu reptiles. *Journal d'agriculture tropicale et de botanique appliquée* 24:3–22.

Endicott, K. 1979. *Batek negrito religion: The world-view and rituals of a hunting and gathering people of peninsular Malaysia.* Oxford: Clarendon Press; New York: Oxford University Press.

Epstein, A. L. 1984. *The experience of shame in Melanesia: An essay in the anthropology of affect.* Royal Anthropological Institute Occasional Paper, 40. London: Royal Anthropological Institute of Great Britain and Ireland; Atlantic Highlands, N.J.: Humanities Press.

Fajans, J. 1983. Shame, social action, and the person among the Baining. *Ethos* 11 (13): 166–180.

Farge, A. 1976. Signe de vie, risque de mort: Essai sur le sang et la ville au XVIIIe siècle. *Urbi* 2:15–22.

Farge, A., ed. 1988. *Affaires de sang.* Mentalités, 1. Paris: Imago.

Farnell, L. R. 1918. Purification (Greek). In *Encyclopaedia of religion and ethics,* ed. J. Hastings, Vol. 10, pp. 482–488. New York: Scribner's.

Feeley-Harnik, G. 1981. *The Lord's Table: Eucharist and Passover in early Christianity.* Philadelphia: University of Pennsylvania Press.

Ferry, L., and C. Germé. 1994. *Des animaux et des hommes: Anthologie des textes remarquables, écrits sur le sujet, du XVe siècle à nos jours.* Livre de poche. Biblio essais; Librairie européenne des idées, 4164. Paris: Le livre de poche.

Feuerbach, L. 1957. *The essence of Christianity.* Trans. G. Eliot. The Library of Religion and Culture. New York: Harper.

Feuerbach, L. 1972. *Das Geheimnis des Opfer, oder der Mensch ist, was er isst.* In *Kleinere Schriften (1851–1866),* Vol. 4, pp. 26–52. Berlin: Akademie Verlag.

Fiddes, N. 1991. *Meat, a natural symbol.* London and New York: Routledge.

Fischer, C. A. 1964. *Southeast Asia: A social, economic and political geography.* London: Methuen.

Fischer, J. M., ed. 1993. *The metaphysics of death.* Stanford Series in Philosophy. Stanford, Calif.: Stanford University Press.

Fortes, M. 1967. Totem and taboo. *Proceedings of the Royal Anthropological Institute of Great Britain and Ireland for 1966,* 5–22.

Forth, G. 1989. Animals, witches, and wind: Eastern Indonesian variations on the "Thunder Complex." *Anthropos* 84: 89–106.

Frassen, C. F. van. 1987. Ternate, de Molukken en de Indonesische Archipel. 2 vols. Ph.D. diss., University of Leiden.

Frazer, J. G. 1891. Taboo. In *Encyclopaedia Britannica.* 9th ed. Edinburgh: A. and C. Black; Philadelphia: Maxwell Sommerville.

Frazer, J. G. 1911. *The golden bough.* Part II: *Taboo and the perils of the soul.* London: Macmillan.

Frazer, J. G. 1918. *The golden bough: A study in magic and religion.* 3d ed. 12 vols. London: Macmillan.

Frazer, J. G. 1928. *The golden bough: A study in magic and religion.* Abridged ed. New York: Macmillan.

Freeman, D. 1968. Thunder, blood, and the nicknaming of God's creatures. *Psychoanalytic Quarterly* 37 (3): 353–399.

Freud, S. 1916. *Wit and its relation to the unconscious.* London: Fisher and Unwin.

Freud, S. 1939. *Moses and monotheism.* New York: Knopf.

Freud, S. 1950. *Totem and taboo: Some points of argument between the mental lives of savages and neurotics.* Trans. J. Strachey. New York: Norton.

Freud, S. 1953a. Civilization and its discontents. In *The standard edition of the complete psychological works of Sigmund Freud,* Vol. 21, pp. 59–157. Ed. and trans. J. Strachey. London: Hogarth Press.

Freud, S. 1953b. Negation. In *The standard edition of the complete psychological works of Sigmund Freud,* Vol. 19, pp. 235–239. Ed. and trans. J. Strachey. London: Hogarth Press.

Freud, S. 1957. *The future of an illusion.* Garden City, N.Y.: Doubleday.

Freud, S. 1963a. *Dora: An analysis of a case of hysteria.* New York: Collier.

Freud, S. 1963b. Obsessive acts and religious practices (1907). In *Character and culture,* ed. P. Rieff, 17–26. New York: Collier.

Gadamer, H.-G. 1976. *Hegel's dialectic: Five hermeneutical studies.* Trans. P. C. Smith. New Haven, Conn.: Yale University Press.

Gadamer, H.-G. 1986. *Truth and method.* New York: Crossroad.

Gauchet, M. 1979. *L'origine de la religion.* Paris: Presses universitaires de France.

Geertz, C. 1973. Deep play: Notes on the Balinese cockfight. In *The interpretation of cultures,* 459–490. New York: Basic Books.

Geertz, C. 1983. Local knowledge: Fact and law in comparative perspective. In *Local knowledge: Further essays in interpretive anthropology,* 167–234. New York: Basic Books.

Geirnaert-Martin, D. 1992. *The woven land of Laboya.* Leiden: Centre for the Sociology of Nonwestern Societies.

Gell, A. 1979. Reflections on a cut finger: Taboo in the Umeda conception of the self. In *Fantasy and symbol: Studies in anthropological interpretation,* ed. R. H. Hook, 133–148. New York: Academic Press.

Gelman, R., E. Spelle, and E. Meck. 1983. What preschoolers know about animate and inanimate objects. In *The Acquisition of symbolic skills,* ed. D. Rogers and J. A. Sloboda, 297–326. NATO Conference Series 3, Human Factors, 22. New York: Plenum Press.

Gernet, L. 1917. *Recherches sur le développement de la pensée juridique et morale en Grèce (étude sémantique).* Bibliothèque de la Fondation Thiers, 37. Paris: E. Leroux.

Gilsenan, M. 1985. Lying, honor and contradiction. In *Transaction and meaning: Directions in the anthropology of exchange and symbolic behavior,* ed. B. Kapferer, 191–219. London: Academic Press.

Glucklich, A. 1984. Karma and pollution in Hindu Dharma: Distinguishing law from nature. *Contributions to Indian Sociology* 18 (1): 25–43.

Glucklich, A. 1988. *Religious jurisprudence in the Dharmasastra.* New York: Macmillan.

Gomes da Silva, J. C. 1983. Nous-mêmes, nous autres. *L'Homme* 23 (3): 55–80.
Gomes da Silva, J. C. 1984. Versants de la pollution. *L'Homme* 24 (3–4): 115–129.
Gomes da Silva, J. C. 1989. *L'identité volée: Essais d'anthropologie sociale.* Brussels: Editions de l'Université de Bruxelles.
Gompertz, G. S. G. M. 1980. *Chinese celadon wares.* London and Boston: Faber and Faber.
Gonda, J. 1973. *Sanskrit in Indonesia.* 2d ed. New Delhi: International Academy of Indian Culture.
Grossi, P. 1981. *An alternative to private property: Collective property in the juridical consciousness of the nineteenth century.* Trans. L. G. Cochrane. Chicago: University of Chicago Press.
Grunfeld, I. 1982. *Dietary laws regarding forbidden and permitted foods, with particular reference to meat and meat products. The Jewish Dietary Laws.* 3d ed. Vol. 1. London and New York: Soncino Press.
Grzimek, B. 1991. Social change on Seram: A study of ideologies of development in eastern Indonesia. Ph.D. diss., London School of Economics.
Grzimek, B. 1996. Sacrificing to authority: From ancestors to the Protestant Tuhan Allah. In *For the sake of our future: Sacrificing in eastern Indonesia,* ed. S. Howell, 304–317. Leiden: Centre for the Sociology of Nonwestern Societies.
Harper, E. 1964. Ritual pollution as an integrator of caste and religion. In *Religion in South Asia,* ed. E. Harper, 151–196. Seattle: University of Washington Press.
Hart, H. L. A. 1961. *The concept of law.* Oxford: Clarendon Press.
Hegel, G. W. F. 1957. *Hegel's philosophy of right.* Trans. T. M. Knox. London and New York: Oxford University Press.
Hell, B. 1985. *Entre chien et loup: Faits et dits de chasse dans la France de l'Est.* Collection Ethnologie de la France, 0758–5888. Paris: Editions de la Maison des sciences de l'homme.
Henninger, J. 1982. Nouveaux débats sur l'interdiction du porc dans l'Islam. In *Le cuisinier et le philosophe: Hommage à Maxime Rodinson,* ed. J.-P. Digard, 29–40. Paris: G.-P. Maisonneuve et Larose.
Héritier, F. 1979. Symbolique de l'inceste et de sa prohibition. In *La fonction symbolique: Essais d'anthropologie,* ed. M. Izard and P. Smith, 209–243. Bibliothèque des sciences humaines. Paris: Gallimard.
Héritier, F. 1984. Le sang du guerrier et le sang des femmes: Notes anthropologiques sur le rapport des sexes. *Cahiers du GRIF* 29:7–21. Paris: Edition Tierce.
Héritier-Augé, F. 1985. Le sperme et le sang. *Nouvelle revue de psychanalyse* 32: 111–122.
Herrenschmidt, O. 1979. Sacrifice symbolique ou sacrifice efficace. In *La fonction symbolique: Essais d'anthropologie,* ed. M. Izard and P. Smith, 171–192. Bibliothèque des sciences humaines. Paris: Gallimard.
Herzfeld, M. 1980. Honour and shame: Problems in the comparative analysis of moral systems. *Man,* n.s. 15 (2): 339–351.
Hogbin, I. 1947. A study of social conformity in a New Guinea village. *Oceania* 17 (2): 273–289.
Homans, G. 1988. *Sentiments and activities: Essays in social science.* New Brunswick, N.J.: Transaction.

Hooker, M. B. 1972. *Adat laws in modern Malaya: Land tenure, traditional government and religion.* Kuala Lumpur and New York: Oxford University Press.

Hooker, M. B. 1978. *Adat law in modern Indonesia.* Kuala Lumpur and New York: Oxford University Press.

Hooyer, G. B., ed. 1895–97. *De Krijgsgeschiedenis van Nederlandsch-Indië van 1811 tot 1894.* 3 vols. The Hague: Van Cleef and Batavia: G. Kolff.

Horn, L. R. 1989. *A natural history of negation.* Chicago: University of Chicago Press.

Horton, R. 1970. African traditional thought and Western science. In *Rationality,* ed. B. R. Wilson, 131–171. Oxford: Blackwell.

Horvatich, P., comp. 1993. *Maluku: The history, societies, and cultures of an Indonesian province: A bibliography of texts in the English language.* Southeast Asia Paper, 37. Manoa: Center for Southeast Asian Studies, School of Hawaiian, Asian and Pacific Studies, University of Hawaii at Manoa.

Hoskins, J. 1993. *The play of time: Kodi perspectives on calendars, history, and exchange.* Berkeley: University of California Press.

Hoskins, J. 1998. *Biographical objects: How things tell the story of people's lives.* New York: Routledge.

Howell, S. 1981. Rules not words. In *Indigenous psychologies: The anthropology of the self,* ed. P. Heelas and A. Lock, 133–143. London: Academic Press.

Howell, S. 1985. Equality and hierarchy in Chewong classification. In *Contexts and levels: Anthropological essays on hierarchy,* ed. R. H. Barnes, D. de Coppet, and R. J. Parkin, 167–180. JASO Occasional Papers, 4. Oxford: JASO.

Howell, S. 1989. *Society and cosmos: Chewong of peninsular Malaysia.* Chicago: University of Chicago Press.

Hubert, H., and M. Mauss. 1899. Essai sur la nature et la fonction du sacrifice. *L'Année sociologique* 2:29–139.

Hunn, E. 1976. Toward a perceptual model of folk biological classification. *American Ethnologist* 3 (3): 508–524.

Hunn, E. 1979. The abominations of Leviticus revisited: A commentary on anomaly in symbolic anthropology. In *Classifications in their social context,* ed. R. F. Ellen and D. Reason, 103–113. Language, Thought, and Culture. London and New York: Academic Press.

Hunn, E. 1982. The utilitarian factor in folk biological classification. *American Anthropologist* 84 (4): 830–847.

Hutchinson, S. 1992. "Dangerous to eat": Rethinking pollution states among the Nuer of Sudan. *Africa* 62 (4): 490–504.

Isenberg, S. R., and D. E. Owen. 1977. Bodies, natural and contrived: The work of Mary Douglas. *Religious Studies Review* 3 (1): 1–17.

Jakobson, R. 1960. Closing statement: Linguistics and poetics. In *Style in language,* ed. T. Sebeok, 350–377. Cambridge, Mass.: MIT Press.

James, W. 1902. *The varieties of religious experience.* New York: Henry Holt.

Jensen, A. E. 1947. Wettkampf-Parteien, Zweiklassen-Systeme und geographische Orientierung. *Studium generale* 1:38–48.

Jensen, A. E. 1949. *Das religiöse Weltbild einer frühen Kultur.* 2d ed. Frobenius Institut: Studien zur Kulturkunde, 9. Stuttgart: A. Schröder.

Jensen, A. E., ed. 1978. *Hainuwele.* New York: Arno Press.

Kant, I. 1997. *Lectures on ethics.* Trans. P. Heath. New York: Cambridge University Press.

Karim, W. J. B. 1981. *Ma' Betisek concepts of living things.* Monographs on Social Anthropology, 54. London: Athlone Press.
Kelley, D. R. 1990. *The human measure: Social thought in the Western legal tradition.* Cambridge, Mass.: Harvard University Press.
Kelsen, H. 1961. *General theory of law and state.* Trans. A. Wedberg. 20th Century Legal Philosophy Series, 1. New York: Russell and Russell.
Kenny, A. J. P. 1966. Intention and purpose. *Journal of Philosophy* 63 (20): 642–656.
Kenny, A. J. P. 1994. *Action, emotion and will.* Bristol: Thoemmes Press.
Khare, R. S. 1976. *Culture and reality: Essays on the Hindu system of managing foods.* Simla: Indian Institute of Advanced Study.
Khare, R. S., and M. S. A. Rao, eds. 1986. *Food, society and culture: Aspects in South Asian food systems.* Durham, N.C.: Carolina Academic Press.
Kierkegaard, S. 1983. *Fear and trembling.* Trans. H. V. Hong and E. H. Hong. Princeton, N.J.: Princeton University Press.
Kierkegaard, S. 1988. *Stages on life's way.* Trans. H. V. Hong and E. H. Hong. Princeton, N.J.: Princeton University Press.
Kiernan, V. G. 1988. *The duel in European history: Honour and the reign of aristocracy.* Oxford and New York: Oxford University Press.
Kirk, G. S. 1980. Some methodological pitfalls in the study of ancient Greek sacrifice (in particular). In *Le sacrifice dans l'antiquité: Huit exposés suivis de discussions: Vandoeuvres—Genève, 25–30 août 1980,* ed. J. P. Vernant, 41–80. Entretiens sur l'Antiquité classique, 27. Geneva: Fondation Hardt.
Kittel, G. 1985. *Theological dictionary of the New Testament.* Trans. G. Brownley. Grand Rapids, Mich.: Eerdman's.
Kleiweg de Zwan, J. P. 1915. De hond in het volksgeloof der inladers van de Indischen archipel. *De Indische gids* 47 : 173–201.
Knaap, G. J. 1987a. *Kruidnagelen en Christenen: De Verenigde Oost-Indische Compagnie en de bevolking van Ambon 1656–1696.* Verhandelingen van het Koninklijk Instituut voor Taal-, Land- en Volkenkunde, 125. Dordrecht, Holland, and Providence, R.I.: Foris Publications.
Knaap, G. J. 1987b. *Memories van Overgave van gouverneurs van Ambon in de zeventiende en achttiende eeuw.* Rijks Geschiedkundige Publicatieen, Kleine Serie, 62. The Hague: Martinus Nijhoff.
Knaap, G. J. 1989. *Transport, 1819–1940.* Changing Economy in Indonesia: A selection of statistical sources material from the early 19th century up to 1940, P. Boomgard, series ed., 9. Amsterdam: Royal Tropical Institute.
Kristeva, J. 1977. Le sujet en procès: Le langage poétique. In *L'Identité: Séminaire interdisciplinaire,* ed. C. Lévi-Strauss, 223–246. Quadrige, 48. Paris: Presses universitaires de France.
Kristeva, J. 1980. *Pouvoirs de l'horreur: Essai sur l'abjection.* Collection Tel quel. Paris: Editions du Seuil.
Kristeva, J. 1982. *Powers of horror: An essay on abjection.* Trans. L. S. Roudiez. New York: Columbia University Press.
Kristeva, J. 1984. Histoires d'amour. *ICA Documents* 1 (Desire): 18–21.
Kristeva, J. 1985. *Au commencement était l'amour: Psychanalyse et foi.* Textes du XXe siècle. Paris: Hachette.
Kruyt, A. C. 1937. De hond in de geestenwereld der Indoesiers. *Tijdschrift voor Indische taal-, land- en volkenkunde* 77 (4): 535–589.

Küchler, S. 1988. Malangan: Objects, sacrifice and the production of memory. *American Ethnologist* 14 (4): 625–637.
Laderman, C. 1981. Symbolic and empirical reality: A new approach to the analysis of food avoidances. *American Ethnologist* 8 (3): 468–493.
Laderman, C. 1983. *Wives and midwives: Childbirth and nutrition in rural Malaysia.* Comparative Studies of Health Systems and Medical Care. Berkeley: University of California Press.
Lakoff, G. 1987. *Women, fire, and dangerous things: What categories reveal about the mind.* Chicago: University of Chicago Press.
Lakoff, G., and M. Johnson. 1980. *Metaphors we live by.* Chicago: University of Chicago Press.
Lambek, M. 1992. Taboo as cultural practice among Malagasy speakers. *Man,* n.s. 27 (2): 245–266.
Lambek, M. 1993. *Knowledge and practice in Mayotte: Local discourses of Islam, sorcery, and spirit possession.* Toronto: University of Toronto Press.
Lancy, D. F., and A. J. Strathern. 1981. "Making twos": Pairing as an alternative to the taxonomic mode of representation. *American Anthropologist* 83 (4): 773–795.
Lanternari, V. 1982. *Le societa pastorali.* Rome: Goliardica.
Laplanche, J., and J. B. Pontalis. 1974. *The language of psychoanalysis.* Trans. D. Nicholson-Smith. New York: Norton.
Laurie, E. M. O., and J. E. Hill. 1954. *List of land mammals of New Guinea, Celebes, and adjacent islands, 1758–1952.* London: British Museum of Natural History.
Leach, E. R. 1961. *Rethinking anthropology.* London: Athlone Press.
Leach, E. R. 1964. Anthropological aspects of language: Animal categories and verbal abuse. In *New directions in the study of language,* ed. E. H. Lenneberg, 23–63. Cambridge, Mass.: MIT Press.
Leach, E. R. 1971. Kimil: A category of Andamese thought. In *Structural analysis of oral tradition,* ed. P. Maranda and K. E. Maranda, 22–48. Philadelphia: University of Pennsylvania Press.
Leopardi, G. 1937. Operette morali. In *Tutte le opere,* Vol. 1, pp. 810–1068. Ed. F. Flora. Milan: Mondadori.
Le Souef, A. S., and H. Burrell. 1926. *The wild animals of Australasia, embracing the mammals of New Guinea and the nearer Pacific islands.* (With a chapter on the bats of Australia and New Guinea by E. Le G. Troughton.) London: G. G. Harrap.
Levine, B. A. 1974. *In the presence of the Lord: A study of cult and some cultic terms in ancient Israel.* Studies in Judaism in Late Antiquity, 5. Leiden: Brill.
Lévi-Strauss, C. 1962. *La pensée sauvage.* Paris: Plon.
Lévi-Strauss, C. 1966. *The savage mind.* Chicago: University of Chicago Press.
Lévi-Strauss, C. 1969. *The elementary structures of kinship.* Trans. J. H. Bell, J. R. von Sturmer, and R. Needham. Boston: Beacon Press.
Lévi-Strauss, C. 1982. *The way of the masks.* Trans. S. Modelski. Seattle: University of Washington Press.
Lévy-Bruhl, L. 1931. *Le surnaturel et la nature chez les primitifs.* Travaux de *l'Année sociologique.* Paris: F. Alcan.
Lewis, G. 1987. A lesson from Leviticus: Leprosy. *Man,* n.s. 22 (4): 593–612.
Lewis, I. M. 1991. The spider and the pangolin. *Man,* n.s. 26 (3): 513–525.
Lienhardt, G. 1961. *Divinity and experience: The religion of the Dinka.* Oxford: Clarendon Press.

Lloyd, D. 1972. *The idea of law.* Harmondsworth: Penguin Books.
Lloyd, G. E. R. 1966. *Polarity and analogy.* Cambridge: Cambridge University Press.
Lloyd, G. E. R. 1979. *Magic, reason, and experience.* Studies in the Origin and Development of Greek Science. Cambridge and New York: Cambridge University Press.
Lloyd, G. E. R. 1983. *Science, folklore, and ideology: Studies in the life sciences in ancient Greece.* Cambridge and New York: Cambridge University Press.
Lloyd-Jones, H. 1971. *The Justice of Zeus.* Sather Classical Lectures, 41. Berkeley, Los Angeles, and London: University of California Press.
Lukes, S. 1973. *Emile Durkheim: His life and work: A historical and critical study.* London: Allen Lane.
MacIntyre, A. C. 1978. What morality is not. In *Against the self-images of the age: Essays on ideology and philosophy,* 96–108. Notre Dame, Ind.: University of Notre Dame Press.
MacIntyre, A. C. 1981. *After virtue: A study in moral theory.* Notre Dame, Ind.: University of Notre Dame Press.
MacIntyre, A. C. 1988. *Whose justice? Which rationality?* Notre Dame, Ind.: University of Notre Dame Press.
McKinnon, S. 1996. Hot death and the spirit of pigs: The sacrificial form of the hunt in the Tanimbar Islands. In *For the sake of our future: Sacrificing in eastern Indonesia,* ed. S. Howell, 337–349. Leiden: Centre for the Sociology of Non-western Societies.
Madan, T. N. 1985. Concerning the categories subha and suddha in Hindu culture. In *Purity and auspiciousness in Indian society,* ed. J. B. Carman and F. A. Marglin, 11–29. Leiden: E. J. Brill.
Madan, T. N. 1991. Auspiciousness and purity: Some reconsiderations. *Contributions to Indian Sociology* 25 (2): 287–294.
Makarius, L. L. 1974. *Le sacré et la violation des interdits.* Collection Sciences de l'homme. Paris: Payot.
Malamoud, C. 1989. Action en retour et mécanisme du sacrifice dans l'Inde brahmanique. In *Cuire le monde: Rite et pensée dans l'Inde ancienne,* 195–210. Textes à l'appui: Histoire classique. Paris: La Découverte.
Malamoud, C. 1996. *Cooking the world: Ritual and thought in ancient India.* Trans. D. White. Delhi: Oxford University Press.
Malinowski, B. 1948. *Magic, science and religion.* Glencoe, Ill.: Free Press.
Malinowski, B. 1959. *Crime and custom in savage society.* Totowa, N.J.: Littlefield, Adams.
Manderson, L. 1986. Food classification and restriction in peninsular Malaysia. In *Shared wealth and symbol: Food, culture, and society in Oceania and Southeast Asia,* ed. L. Manderson, 127–143. Cambridge and New York: Cambridge University Press; Paris: Editions de la Maison des sciences de l'homme.
Manu. 1991. *The laws of Manu, with an introduction and notes.* Trans. W. Doniger and B. K. Smith. Harmondsworth: Penguin Books.
March, K. S. 1980. Deer, bears, and blood: A note on nonhuman animal response to menstrual odor. *American Anthropologist,* n.s. 82 (1): 125–127.
Marett, R. R. 1914. Is taboo a negative magic? In *The threshold of religion,* 73–98. Rev. 2d ed. London: Methuen.

Mauss, M. 1938. Une catégorie de l'esprit humain: La notion de personne, celle de "moi." *Journal of the Royal Anthropological Institute* 68:263–281.

Mauss, M. 1950. *Sociologie et anthropologie.* Paris: Presses universitaires de France.

Mauss, M. 1969. *Oeuvres,* ed. V. Karady. 3 vols. Paris: Editions de minuit.

Mauss, M. 1990. *The Gift: The form and reason for exchange in archaic societies.* Trans. W. D. Halls. Foreword by M. Douglas. New York: Norton.

Mayr, E. 1984. *Conceptual issues in evolutionary biology.* Cambridge, Mass.: MIT Press.

Mead, M. 1934. Tabu. In *Encyclopaedia of the Social Sciences,* ed. R. A. Seligman and A. Johnson, Vol. 14, pp. 502–505. New York: Macmillan.

Méchin, C. 1992. *Bêtes à manger: Usages alimentaires des Français.* Nancy: Presses universitaires de Nancy.

Meigs, A. S. 1978. A Papuan perspective on pollution. *Man,* n.s. 13 (3): 304–318.

Meigs, A. S. 1984. *Food, sex, and pollution: A New Guinea religion.* New Brunswick, N.J.: Rutgers University Press.

Menzies, J. L. 1975. *Handbook of common New Guinea frogs.* Wau, Papua New Guinea: Wau Ecology Institute.

Menzies, J. L. 1991. *A handbook of New Guinea marsupials and monotremes.* Madang, Papua New Guinea: Kristen Press.

Merrill, E. D. 1945. *Plant life of the Pacific world.* New York: Macmillan.

Merleau-Ponty, M. 1976. *Phénoménologie de la perception.* Collection Tel, 4. Paris: Gallimard.

Michaux, H. 1949. *A barbarian in Asia.* Trans. S. Beach. New York: New Directions.

Morris, D. 1994. Cats. *New York Review of Books,* Nov. 3, pp. 16–17.

Morris, H. 1976. *On guilt and innocence: Essays in legal philosophy and moral psychology.* Berkeley: University of California Press.

Moulinier, L. 1952. *Le pur et l'impur dans la pensée des Grecs d'Homère à Aristote.* Etudes et commentaires, 11. Paris: C. Klincksieck.

Needham, R. 1964. Blood, thunder and mockery of animals. *Sociologus* 14 (2): 136–149.

Needham, R. 1971. Introduction *and* Remarks on the analysis of kinship and marriage. In *Rethinking kinship and marriage,* ed. R. Needham, xiii–cxvii, 1–34. London: Tavistock.

Needham, R. 1975. Polythetic classification: Convergence and consequences. *Man,* n.s. 10 (3): 639–649.

Needham, R. 1976. Skulls and causality. *Man,* n.s. 11 (1): 71–88.

Needham, R. 1979. *Symbolic classification.* Goodyear Perspectives in Anthropology Series. Santa Monica, Calif.: Goodyear Pub. Co.

Nemeroff, C., and P. Rozin. 1988. Sympathetic magic in kosher practice and belief at the limits of the law of Kashut. *Jewish Folklore and Ethnology Review* 9 (1): 31–32.

Nemeroff, C., and P. Rozin. 1989. "You are what you eat": Applying the demand-free "impressions" technique to an unacknowledged belief. *Ethos* 17 (1): 50–69.

Neusner, J. 1973. *The idea of purity in ancient Judaism.* With a critique and commentary by Mary Douglas. Studies in Judaism in Late Antiquity (Haskell Lectures, Oberlin College, 1972–73), 1. Leiden: Brill.

Neusner, J. 1975. The idea of purity in ancient Judaism. *Journal of the American Academy of Religion* 43 (1): 15–26.

The new encyclopedia of Islam. 1965. Ed. B. Lewis, Ch. Pellat, and J. Schacht. Leiden: E. J. Brill.

Niggemeyer, H. 1952. Baumwollweberei auf Ceram. *Ciba Rundshan* 106:3870–3897.

Obeyesekere, G. 1990. *The work of culture.* Chicago: University of Chicago Press.

Onians, R. B. 1954. *The origins of European thought about the body, the mind, the soul, the world, time, and fate: New interpretations of Greek, Roman, and kindred evidence, also of some basic Jewish and Christian beliefs.* Cambridge: Cambridge University Press.

Orenstein, H. 1965. The structure of Hindu caste values: A preliminary study of hierarchy and ritual defilement. *Ethnology* 4:1–15.

Orenstein, H. 1968. Toward a grammar of defilement in Hindu sacred law. In *Structure and change in Indian society,* ed. M. Singer and B. S. Cohn, 115–131. Viking Fund Publications in Anthropology, 47. Chicago: Aldine.

Orenstein, H. 1970a. Death and kinship in Hinduism: Structural and functional interpretations. *American Anthropologist* 72 (6): 1357–1377.

Orenstein, H. 1970b. Logical congruence in Hindu sacred law: Another interpretation. *Contributions to Indian Sociology,* n.s. 4:22–35.

Ortega y Gasset, J. 1972. *Meditations on hunting.* Trans. H. B. Wescott; Introd. P. Shepard. New York: Scribner.

Ortes, G. 1984. *Calcolo sopra la verita dell'istoria e altri scritti.* Ed. B. Anglani. Testi della cultura italiana, 6. Genoa: Costa and Nolan.

Overing, J., ed. 1985. *Reason and morality.* A.S.A. Monographs, 24. London and New York: Tavistock Publications.

Ovid. 1926. *Amores.* Loeb Classical Library. Cambridge, Mass.: Harvard University Press.

Parfit, D. 1984. *Reasons and persons.* Oxford: Clarendon Press.

Parker, R. 1990. *Miasma: Pollution and purification in early Greek religion.* Oxford: Clarendon Press.

Perelman, C. 1945. *De la justice.* Brussels: Offices de la publicité.

Peristiany, J. G., and J. Pitt-Rivers, eds. 1992. *Honor and grace in anthropology.* Cambridge Studies in Social and Cultural Anthropology, 76. Cambridge and New York: Cambridge University Press.

Philonenko, A. 1972. Note sur les concepts de souillure et de pureté dans l'Idéalisme allemand. *Les études philosophiques* (Issue entitled "Souillure et pureté") 4:481–493.

Philonenko, M. 1967. Le décret apostolique et les interdits alimentaires du Coran. *Revue d'histoire et de philosophie religieuses* 47 (2): 165–172.

Piers, G., and M. Singer. 1971. *Shame and guilt: A psychoanalytic and a cultural study.* New York: Norton.

Pitt-Rivers, J. 1977. *The fate of Shechem or the politics of sex.* Cambridge: Cambridge University Press.

Plotinus. 1957. Impassivity of the unembodied. In *The Enneads.* Trans. S. MacKenna. New York: Pantheon Books.

Radcliffe-Brown, A. R. 1914. The definition of totemism. *Anthropos* 9:622–630.
Radcliffe-Brown, A. R. 1948. *The Andaman Islanders.* Glencoe, Ill.: Free Press.
Radcliffe-Brown, A. R. 1952. The comparative method of social anthropology. *Journal of the Royal Anthropological Institute* 81:15–22.
Radcliffe-Brown, A. R. 1965. *Structure and function in primitive society.* New York: Free Press.
Rawls, J. 1955. Two concepts of rules. *Philosophical Review* 64:3–32.
Raz, J. 1979. *The authority of law: Essays on law and morality.* Oxford: Clarendon Press; New York: Oxford University Press.
Raz, J. 1980. *The concept of a legal system: An introduction to the theory of legal system.* 2d ed. Oxford: Clarendon Press; New York: Oxford University Press.
Read, K. E. 1955. Morality and the concept of the person among the Gahuku-Gama. *Oceania* 25 (4): 233–282.
Reiner, E. 1956. *Die Molukken.* Ergänzungsheft zu Petermanns geographischen Mitteilungen, no. 260. Gotha: Hermann Haack.
Reinhardt, A. K. 1990. Impurity/no danger. *History of Religions* 30 (1): 1–24.
Renan, E. 1885. *Vie de Jésus.* Paris: Calmann Lévy.
Reynolds, F. E., and R. Levin, eds. 1985. *Cosmogony and ethical order: New studies in comparative ethics.* Chicago: University of Chicago Press.
Reynolds, R. 1946. *Cleanliness and godliness.* Garden City, N.Y.: Doubleday.
Ricoeur, P. 1969. *The symbolism of evil.* Trans. E. Buchanan. Boston: Beacon Press.
Roeder, J. 1948. *Alahatala: Die Religion der Inlandstamme Mittelcerams.* Frankfurt am Main: Frobenius Institut, Bamberger Verlagshaus, Meisenback & Co.
Ross, A. 1968. *Directives and norms.* London: Routledge and Kegan Paul.
Ross, A. 1975. *On guilt, responsibility and punishment.* Berkeley: University of California Press.
Rozin, P., and C. Nemeroff. 1990. The laws of sympathetic magic: A psychological analysis of similarity and contagion. In *Cultural psychology: Essays on comparative human development,* ed. J. W. Stigler, R. A. Shweder, and G. H. Herdt, 205–232. Cambridge and New York: Cambridge University Press.
Rudd, J. 1960. *Taboo, a study of Malagasy customs and beliefs.* Oslo: Oslo University Press.
Rudhardt, J. 1958. *Notions fondamentales de la pensée religieuse et actes constitutifs du culte dans la Grèce classique: Etude préliminaire pour aider à la compréhension de la piétéathénienne au IVème siècle.* Geneva: E. Droz.
Rumphius, G. E. [1679] 1983. *Ambonsche Landbeschrijving.* Reprint. Jakarta: Arsip Nasional Republik Indonesia.
Rumphius, G. E. 1705. *D'Amboinsche Rariteitkamer.* Amsterdam: Francois Halma.
Ryan, A. 1987. *Property.* Minneapolis: University of Minnesota Press.
Ryle, G. 1949. *The concept of mind.* London: Hutchinson.
Sabbath, D., and M. Hall. 1977. *End product: The first taboo.* New York: Urizen Books.
Sachse, F. J. P. 1907. *Het eiland Seran en zijne Bewoners.* Leiden: E. J. Brill.
Sarte, J. P. 1966. *Being and nothingness: A Phenomenological Essay on Ontology.* Trans. H. E. Barnes. New York: Washington Square Press, Pocket Book Library.
Sartre, J. P. 1980. *L'être et le néant: Essai d'ontologie phénoménologique.* Bibliothèque des idées. Paris: Gallimard.

Schrieke, B. O. J. 1921–22. Allerlei over de besnijdenis in den Indischen archipel. *Tijdschrift voor Indische taal-, land- en volkenkunde* 60:373–578; 61:1–94.

Seran. 1922. *Mededeelingen van het bureau voor de bestuurszaken der buitengewesten bezittingen bewerkt door het encyclopaedisch bureau, aflevering XXIX.* Weltevreden: O. Kolff.

Serpell, J. 1986. *In the company of animals: A history of human-animal relationships.* Oxford and New York: Basil Blackwell.

Schauer, F. F. 1991. *Playing by the rules: A philosophical examination of rule-based decision-making in law and life.* Oxford: Clarendon Press.

Shweder, R. A. 1985. Menstrual pollution, soul loss and the comparative study of emotions. In *Culture and depression: Studies in the anthropology and cross-cultural psychiatry of affect and disorder,* ed. A. Kleinman and B. Good, 182–215. Berkeley, Los Angeles, and London: University of California Press.

Sillitoe, P. 1979. Man-eating woman: Fears of sexual pollution in the Papua-New Guinea highlands. *Journal of the Polynesian Society* 88 (1): 77–97.

Simoons, F. J. 1967. *Eat not this flesh: Food avoidances in the Old World.* Madison: University of Wisconsin Press.

Simoons, F. J. 1968. *A ceremonial ox of India: The mithan in nature, culture, and history, with notes on the domestication of common cattle.* Madison: University of Wisconsin Press.

Simoons, F. J. 1974. Fish or forbidden food: The case of India. *Ecology of Food and Nutrition* 3:185–201.

Sinclair, U. 1985. *The jungle.* New York: Penguin Books.

Singer, I. B. 1993. *The certificate.* Trans. L. Wolf. New York: Plume.

Skorupski, J. 1976. *Symbol and theory: A philosophical study of theories of religion in social anthropology.* Cambridge: Cambridge University Press.

Smith, B. 1994. *Classifying the universe: The ancient Varna system and the origins of caste.* New York and Oxford: Oxford University Press.

Smith, W. R. 1894. *Lectures on the religion of the Semites.* London: A. and C. Black.

Smith, P., and M. Izard, eds. 1982. *Between belief and transgression: Structuralist essays in religion, history and myth.* Trans. J. Leavitt. Chicago: University of Chicago Press.

Snell, B. 1953. *The discovery of the mind: The Greek origins of European thought.* Cambridge, Mass.: Harvard University Press.

Soler, J. 1973. Sémiotique de la nourriture dans la Bible. *Annales* 28:943–955.

Sontag, S. 1978. *Illness as metaphor.* New York: Farrar, Straus and Giroux.

Sowerby, J. C., and E. Lear. 1872. *Tortoises, terrapins and turtles drawn from life.* London, Paris, and Frankfurt: H. Sotherman, J. Baer and Co.

Sperber, D. 1975. Rethinking Symbolism. Cambridge: Cambridge University Press.

Sperber, D., and D. Wilson. 1986. *Relevance: Communication and cognition.* Language and Thought Series. Cambridge, Mass.: Harvard University Press.

Spinoza, B. 1958. *The political works.* Ed. and trans. A. G. Wernham. Oxford: Clarendon Press.

Stein, S. 1957. The dietary laws in rabbinic and patristic literature. *Studia patristica* 64:141–154.

Steiner, F. B. 1956. *Taboo.* London: Cohen and West.

Stevenson, H. N. C. 1954. Status evaluation in the Hindu caste system. *Journal of the Royal Anthropological Institute* 84:45–65.

Stewart, F. H. 1994. *Honor.* Chicago: University of Chicago Press.
Stoker, Bram. 1995. *Dracula.* Oxford: Oxford University Press.
Strathern, A. 1977. Why is shame on the skin? In *The anthropology of the body,* ed. J. Blacking, 99–110. London: Academic Press.
Stresemann, E. 1914. Die Vögel von Seran. *Novitiates Zoologie* 21:25–153.
Stresemann, E. 1923. Religiöse Gebrauche auf Seran. *Tijdschrift voor Indische taal-, land- en volkenkunde* 62:305–424.
Stresemann, E. 1927. Die Lauterscheinungen in den ambonischen Sprachen. *Zeitschrift für Engeborenen-Sprachen* 10.
Tambiah, S. J. 1985a. Animals are good to think and good to prohibit. In *Culture, thought, and social action: An anthropological perspective,* 169–211. Cambridge, Mass.: Harvard University Press.
Tambiah, S. J. 1985b. From Varna to caste through mixed unions. In *Culture, thought, and social action: An anthropological perspective,* 212–251. Cambridge, Mass.: Harvard University Press.
Tambiah, S. J. 1985c. A performative approach to ritual. In *Culture, thought, and social action: An anthropological perspective,* 123–166. Cambridge, Mass.: Harvard University Press.
Tauern, O. D. 1918. *Patasiwa und Patalima: Von Molukkeneiland Seran und seinen Bewohnern.* Leipzig: Voigtlander.
Tauern, O. D. 1928–31. Beitrag zur Kenntnis der Sprachen und Dialecten von Seran. *Anthropos* 23:100–120; 24:953–981; 25:567–578; 26:109–139.
Taylor, G. 1985. *Pride, shame and guilt: Emotions of self-assessment.* Oxford: Clarendon Press.
Testart, A. 1985. *Le communisme primitif.* Paris: Editions de la Maison des sciences de l'homme.
Testart, A. 1986a. *Essai sur les fondements de la division sexuelle du travail chez les chasseurs-cueilleurs.* Cahiers de l'homme, n.s. 25. Paris: Editions de l'Ecole des hautes études en sciences sociales.
Testart, A. 1986b. La femme et la chasse. *La recherche* 17 (181): 1194–1201.
Testart, A. 1987. De la chasse en France, du sang, et de bien d'autres choses encore (à propos de Bertrand Hell, *Entre chien et loup*). *L'Homme* 27 (2): 151–167.
Testart, A. 1991. *Des mythes et des croyances: Esquisse d'une théorie générale.* Paris: Maison des sciences de l'homme.
Valentijn, F. 1862. *Oud en Nieuw Oost-Indien.* Amsterdam: J. C. van Keesteren & Zoon.
Valeri, V. 1966. Marcel Mauss e la nuova antropologia. *Critica storica* 2:677–703.
Valeri, V. 1968. Natura e cultura: Introduzione alla teoria dello scambio e della parenteta di Claude Lévi-Strauss. Ph.D. diss. (philosophy), University of Pisa.
Valeri, V. 1970. Struttura, transformazione, "esaustivita": Un' esposizione di alcuni concetti di Claude Lévi-Strauss. *Annali della Scula normale superiore di Pisa: Lettere, storia, filosofia,* series 2, 39:347–375.
Valeri, V. 1975. Alliances et échanges matrimoniaux à Seram central (Moluques), part 1. *L'Homme* 15 (3–4): 83–107.
Valeri, V. 1976a. Alliances et échanges matrimoniaux à Seram central (Moluques), part 2. *L'Homme* 16 (1): 125–149.

Valeri, V. 1976b. Le brûlé et le cuit: Mythologie et organisation de la chefferie dans la société hawaiienne ancienne. Ph.D. diss. (ethnology), Université René Descartes, sciences humaines Sorbonne, Paris.

Valeri, V. 1979. Feticcio (Fetish). In *Enciclopedia,* Vol. 6, pp. 100–115. Turin: Einaudi.

Valeri, V. 1980. Notes on the meaning of marriage prestations among the Huaulu of Seram. In *The flow of life: Essays on eastern Indonesia,* ed. J. J. Fox, 178–192. Cambridge: Mass.: Harvard University Press.

Valeri, V. 1981a. Pouvoir des deux, rire des hommes: Divertissement théorique sur un fait hawaiien. *Anthropologie et sociologie* 5 (3): 11–34.

Valeri, V. 1981b. Rito. In *Enciclopedia,* Vol. 12, pp. 209–243. Turin: Einaudi.

Valeri, V. 1983. How can the part be the whole? Siwa/Lima dualism in the central Moluccas (Indonesia). Conference on Dual Organizations, Jerusalem. June 18–23.

Valeri, V. 1985. *Kingship and sacrifice: Ritual and society in ancient Hawaii.* Trans. P. Wissing. Chicago: University of Chicago Press.

Valeri, V. 1987. Comment on "Anthropology as Interpretive Quest." *Current Anthropology* 28 (3): 355–356.

Valeri, V. 1989. Reciprocal centers: The Siwa-Lima system in the central Moluccas. In *The attraction of opposites: Thought and society in a dualistic mode,* ed. D. Maybury-Lewis and U. Almagor, 117–141. Ann Arbor: University of Michigan Press.

Valeri, V. 1990a. Autonomy and heteronomy in the Kahua ritual: A short meditation on Huaulu society. *Bijdragen tot de taal-, land- en volkenkunde* 146 (1): 56–73.

Valeri, V. 1990b. Both nature and culture: Reflections on menstrual and parturitional taboos in Huaulu (Seram). In *Power and difference: Gender in island Southeast Asia,* ed. J. Atkinson and S. Errington, 235–272, 440–442. Stanford, Calif.: Stanford University Press.

Valeri, V. 1992a. Credenze e culti. In *Enciclopedia delle scienze sociali,* Vol. 2, pp. 565–575. Rome: Istituto della enciclopedia italiana.

Valeri, V. 1992b. If we feed them, we do not feed on them: A principle of Huaulu taboo and its applications. *Ethnos* 57 (3–4): 149–167.

Valeri, V. 1992c. On the train to Chicago, via Paris, or: Confessions of an idiosyncratic anthropologist. *Anthropolognytt* (Institute for Social Anthropology, University of Oslo, Norway) 4 (December): 31–44. (Republished in *Fragments from forests and libraries,* Durham, N.C.: Carolina Academic Press, 1999).

Valeri, V. 1994a. Buying women but not selling them: Gift and commodity exchange in Huaulu alliance. *Man,* n.s. 29 (1): 1–26.

Valeri, V. 1994b. Our ancestors spoke little: Knowledge and social forms in Huaulu. In *Halmahera and beyond: Social science research in the Moluccas,* ed. L. Visser, 195–212. Leiden: KITLV.

Valeri, V. 1994c. Wild victims: Hunting as sacrifice and sacrifice as hunting in Huaulu. *History of Religions* 34 (2): 101–131.

Valeri, V. 1995. Miti cosmogonici e ordine. *Parole Chiave* 7/8: 93–110.

Valeri, V. 1996a. Il futuro degli antropologhi: La ricerca sul campo ieri e oggi. *Promoteo: Rivista trimestrale de scienze e storia* 14 (54): 42–57. (Republished as

"The future of anthropologists: Fieldwork yesterday and today," trans. J. Hoskins, in *Fragments from forests and libraries,* Durham, N.C.: Carolina Academic press, 1999).

Valcri, V. 1996b. Les formes temporelles de la société: Temps chronologique et temps subjectif, temps mythique et temps historique chez les Huaulu (Indonésie orientale). In *Constructions sociales du temps,* ed. F. Piron and D. Arsenault, 105–129. Montréal: Septentrion.

Valeri, V. 1996c. Those who have seen blood: The memory of sacrifice in Huaulu initiation. In *For the sake of our future: Sacrificing in eastern Indonesia,* ed. S. Howell, 282–302. Leiden: ACSW.

Valeri, V. 1999. *Fragments from forests and libraries.* Durham, N.C.: Carolina Academic Press.

Valeri, V. In prep. Blood and money: Being and giving among the Huaulu of the Moluccas. Book manuscript in preparation. Edited with an introduction and conclusion by M. Feldman and R. Stasch.

van Bemmel, A. F. C. 1948. A faunal list of the birds of the Moluccan islands. *Treubia* 19:323–401.

Vandenbosch, A. 1941. *The Dutch East Indies: Its government, problems, and politics.* Berkeley and Los Angeles: University of California Press.

van Gennep, A. 1904. *Tabou et totémisme à Madagascar: Etude descriptive et théorique.* Bibliothèque de l'Ecole des hautes études; Section des sciences religieuses, 17. Paris: E. Leroux.

van Gennep, A. 1960. *The rites of passage.* Trans. M. B. Vizedom and G. L. Caffee. London: Routledge and Kegan Paul.

Vernant, J.-P. 1980. The pure and the impure. In *Myth and society in ancient Greece,* 110–129. Trans. J. Lloyd. Brighton: Harvester Press.

Vialles, N. 1987. *Le sang et la chair: Les abattoirs des pays de l'Adour.* Collection Ethnologie de la France, 8. Paris: Editions de la Maison des sciences de l'homme.

Visser, M. 1991. *The rituals of dinner: The origins, evolution, eccentricities, and meaning of table manners.* New York: Grove Weidenfeld.

Wallace, A. R. [1869] 1962. *The Malay archipelago: The land of the orangutan and the bird of paradise: A narrative of travel, with studies of man and nature.* Reprint. New York: Dover.

Weber, M., and L. F. de Beaufort. 1913. *The fishes of the Indo-Australian archipelago.* Leiden: E. J. Brill.

Webster, H. 1942. *Taboo, a sociological study.* Stanford, Calif.: Stanford University Press; London: H. Milford, Oxford University Press.

Wessing, R. 1977. The position of the Badui in the larger Javanese society. *Man,* n.s. 12 (2): 293–303.

Wikan, U. 1984. Shame and honour: A contestable pair. *Man,* n.s. 19 (4): 635–652.

Willer, T. J. 1849. Aanteekeningen amtrent het Noorder-Schiereiland van het eiland Halmaheva. *Indisch Arduef* 1 (1): 343–398.

Williams, B. 1993. *Shame and necessity.* Sather Classical Lectures, 57. Berkeley: University of California Press.

Willis, R. G. 1972. Pollution and paradigms. *Man,* n.s. 7 (3): 369–378.

Willis, R. G. 1974. *Man and beast.* New York: Basic Books.

Willis, R. G., ed. 1994. *Signifying animals: Human meaning in the natural world.* London: Routledge.

Willis, S. 1991. *A Primer for daily life.* New York: Routledge.

Wilson, R. 1987. "Is this a holiday?" Shakespeare's Roman carnival. *ELH* 54:31–44.

Wittgenstein, L. 1958. *Philosophical investigations.* Oxford: Basil Blackwell.

Worsley, P. 1982. Groote Eylandt totemism and *Le totémism e aujourd'hui.* In *The structural study of myth and totemism,* ed. E. Leach. London: Tavistock.

Wright, G. H. von. 1963a. *Norm and action: A logical enquiry.* New York: Humanities Press.

Wright, G. H. von. 1963b. *The varieties of goodness.* New York: Humanities Press.

Wright, G. H. von. 1971. *Explanation and understanding.* Ithaca, N.Y.: Cornell University Press.

Wyatt-Brown, B. 1982. *Southern honor: Ethics and behavior in the Old South.* New York: Oxford University Press.

Zimmerman, F. 1982. *La jungle et le fumet des viandes: Un thème écologique dans la médecine hindoue.* Hautes études. Paris: Gallimard, Le Seuil.

Zuesse, E. M. 1974. Taboo and the divine order. *Journal of the American Academy of Religion* 42 (3): 482–504.

INDEX

abjection, 105–111
adat (B.I. custom). *See* custom
agency: and occult powers, 25–30; and patients, 152–156
Alakamat (Huaulu coastal settlement), 1–34, 41–42, 222, 297–298, 393, 470
alliance, xvi, 34–35; opposed to consanguinity, 373–374
Ambon, 11, 18, 40
American food taboos, 434–435; and junk food, 103
ancestors, 26–27, 300–301, 352–353; and clouds, 377
Andaman islanders, 44, 53; Radcliffe-Brown on food taboos, 54–58; Leach's reanalysis, 65, 68–70, 427
animals, mixed with human, 145, 162; as a category in Huaulu, 74–174, 181–184, 302–334, 444
anomaly and the classificatory theory of taboo, 66–67; in Huaulu, 199–202, 244–245, 250; in relation to the cassowary, 255–258; and the turtle, 271–272; shamanic taboos, 291–292; as a principle of taboo, 326, 333–334, 361–366
Aquinas, Thomas, 43
Aristotle: hierarchy of classes, 65, 256, 429; idea of substance, 90
Aru, 20
Australian aborigines, 53–54

Bachelard, G., 23, 325, 478
Badui, people of west Java, 8
bananas, 261–262, 287, 288, 291, 292
Banda, 20
bats, 232–233, 290
Benveniste, L., 120
Berger, J., 162
Bergson, H., 295
Besi, 17, 179, 189, 420–421, 467
birds: Douglas on, 76–78; Huaulu on, 206–207, 449–450; lucrative trade in, 223; and speech, 234–236, 453–454; in the house, 247–248; in mixing taboos, 251; and cassowaries, 252–264; and maleo, 263–264; taboo to women, 280–284; shamanic taboos, 287–290, 291; Lévi-Strauss on, 451
blood and pollution, 48–49, 349–350; and menstruation, 50, 83–84, 168, 472; and Testart's theory of taboo, 86, 91; and male/female difference, 148–149, 152–153; and fluidity, 163–165, 444; and kinship, 300, 463, 468; and killing, 312–315; and the ritual use of red, 378–379
body: as a symbolic vehicle, 48; and pollution, 102–105, 434–435; dissolved in abjection, 106–109; and the inarticulate, 110–111; and the constitution of the subject, 111–113, 346–349; contrast with animal body, 188, 313–315, 466; taboos on dead bodies vs. bleeding female bodies, 349–357, 401–402; shame on the skin, 403–455, 479
Bolton, R., xix
Bulmer, R., 81, 252, 429, 430

calendars, absent in Huaulu, 358–359
cannibalism, 205, 447–448
cash economy: and clove cultivation, 19; and coastal settlement, 31
cassowary, 251; relation to birds, 252–58, 362, 457; myth of origin, 253–254, 333–335; shamanism, 286, 291–292; and hunting, 305, 314–315, 334; and mixing taboo, 378; red feathers on males, 378
cats, 211–213; compared to dogs, 228–230
chickens, 213–222; names, 224–226, 450–451; and mixing taboos, 262–264; and shamanism, 289; and burial practices, 379; and sacrifice, 466
childbirth, 152–153, 163, 234, 256, 480; taboos relating to death in, 362–363
Chinese shopkeepers, 17
Christianity: resistance to conversion, 8–9, 41–42, 310–311, 331–332, 439; evangelization, 22, 41, 420; compared to Judaism, 109–110; and dogs, 210–211
cicadas, 239–240, 455
Cicero: on the etymology of "knowledge," 120; on religion, 438; on pigs, 443
civet, 278–279, 280, 282–283

clans, 33; and alliance, 35–38
classification: of social groups in Seram, 16–23; as a theory of taboo, 61–83, 326–327; and totemism, 93–97; opposed to experience, 385–386
cloth: ritual use of, 243, 456; taboos on death cloths, 350
cloves: and Dutch monopolies, 19; and coastal trade, 23; misoneistic taboos, 357–359; new cultivation, 387–388
cockatoo, 280–282, 286
cognition, in the theory of taboo, 64–65, 70–76, 426
Collins, J., xix, 3, 7–20
colonial history, 9, 18, 38–40, 387–388, 450
colors: as grounds for taboo, 199, 363, 366–367, 475; as concrete abstractions, 378–380
commodities, 358–360, 412–413
consumption, opposed to production, 358–360; opposed to performance, 399–401, 478; in Los Angeles, 412–413
contagion: related to pollution, 44–45; arbitrary, 50–51; and Freudian views of repression, 58–61
cooking: rules to cook meat, 170–172; taboos on frying in coconut oil, 287, 294; boiling opposed to grilling, 351; dissolves taboos, 394; and headhunting, 471
crickets, 240–241
crocodile, 269, 270, 273–279, 336–337, 348, 460–461
culture, 133
cuscus: and mixing taboos, 248–252, 265–268; and shamanism, 286, 289, 290–291, 458–459; and hunting, 310, 317, 321; and childbirth, 376
custom (adat B.I.), 133, 368, 405–407, 480

dance. *See* kahua feast, circle dance
danger: in relation to taboo, 44–46, 55–58, 116, 126–127, 134–135; and symbolic mismatches, 136–137
Dante, 436
dead, shades of the (topoyem). *See* ghosts
death: taboos related to, 165–166, 244–245; and menstruation, 349–357; "bad" death, 361–362
deer, and hunting offerings, 304–306, 311, 314–315, 321–322
Dekkers, M., 228, 451, 461
Descartes, R., 180, 185, 444
desire: in Freudian theories of repression, 58–61; and consumption, 101–102; and abjection, 105–111
Deuteronomy, 44, 75–80
dirt, 70–72, 83, 106–107, 401
diseases, totemic classification of, 141–151
Dodds, E. R., xxii, 45, 438
dogs: used to hunt on the river, 174–175; in myth, 189–197; taboo to eat, 198, 348–349; value of, in Huaulu, 207–211, 327; names, 223–225; compared to cats, 228–230; and human sexuality, 371–372, 376, 475–476
domestic animals, 203–207. *See also* cats; chickens; dogs
Douglas, M., 45–46, 61, 70–76, 86, 91–92, 103, 106, 108, 110, 202, 278, 406, 428–430, 436, 457, 480
dream pact, 198–199, 370
dualism and moeity organization (Siwa/Lima), 20–23
Dumézil, G., 438
Dumont, L., xv, 393, 477
Durkheim, E., 24, 44; view of taboo as religious prohibition, 49–50, 63, 71, 82, 431; theory of primitive religion, 51–52; similarities to Freud, 59–60; separation of collective psychology and individual psychology, 61; on the prohibition of incest, 83–84, 88; on the logic of sacrifice, 341, 344, 421
Dutch: demarcation of Huaulu territory, 14; movement of populations, 17, 139; titles used in administration, 37
Dutch East India Company: wars fought to maintain cultivation monopolies, 19, 38

earth goddess (Puhum, Mother Earth), 15, 24, 25, 157–158
eating, 169–179; Fortes' dictum, 246; and sex, 328, 372; as performance, 383–384, 476
eels, 280–286, 287, 289, 292, 378, 394, 461
egalitarianism, xv, 33
Eilberg-Schwartz, H., 437
Ellen, R., xix, 183; on the cassowary, 253–254, 256; on game, 315, 420, 429, 437, 445, 451, 452, 455, 457, 460, 461
Endicott, K., 421
English taboos, 66–68, 70–71, 428
ethics, xxii
experience: as a principle of taboo, 370;

individual autonomy vs. heteronomy, 371–373; opposed to classification, 385–386

feeding, 198; as basis for taboo on domestic animals, 203–207
Feeley-Harnik, G., 110, 437
Ferry, L., 444
Fiddes, N., 173, 444
fire, origins of, 190–197; and resin lamps, 242–243; and smoke, 478
fish and fish poisoning, 12, 158; and crocodiles, 273–275; and mixing taboos, 248–268; taboo to women, 280, 283–284; and occult powers, 339
forest: impressions of, 3–5; tree species, 13; opposition between village and forest, 14–15, 349; and the lord of the land (upu kaitahu), 307–309; and menstruation, 352–353
Fortes, M., 93–94, 97, 162, 178, 246, 433, 434
Foucault, M., xvii
Frazer, J., xxii, 43, 44–49, 53–54, 71, 144, 436
Freud, S.: influence on Valeri, vii; on the role of emotions in taboo, 48; on the expression of the repressed, 58–61, 63, 108, 130, 332, 425; on morality, 106–107; on negation, 312, 410–411, 481; on the phallic stage, 435
frogs: in relation to desire, 60; and taboos, 236–239

game (peni in Huaulu), 181, 184–185, 244–245, 256, 303, 306, 314–315; humans as the "game" of the occult powers, 317–322, 340; and human-animal relations, 386
gardening, 13
Geertz, C., 449
Gell, A., 97–101, 434
ghosts (topoyem), 24, 165–166; and rats, 231–232; and bats, 232–234, 235–236; and frogs, 238–239; and cicadas, 241; and birds, 453–454
Gomes da Silva, 91–93, 94, 431–433
Greenberg, J., 411
guilt, xxiii

Hatu, 3
Hatumete, 3, 19
Hawaii, xv, xvi
headhunting, 16, 23, 24–25, 200; and chicken eating, 218, 220–221, 233, 235; and cockatoos, 280–282; and shamanism, 290, 421, 444, 449; and sacrifice, 311–314, 379; and women marrying out, 327, 468; and occult powers, 339; and the incompatibility of male/female, 344; and menstruation, 352–355, 402, 472; and death, 362; and the color red, 378; desire to resume the practice, 449; and preparation of food, 471
Hebrew: ideas of pollution, 43; food taboos, 75–83, 86–91, 110, 429–430
Héritier, F., 84–86, 91, 94, 431, 470–471
hierarchy: as reversible in the Siwa/Liwa opposition, 20–23; contrasted to egalitarianism, 33–38, 154–155, 159; of nested oppositions, 262–265; and taboo, 336–337; subverted, 368, 393, 474
hornbill, 255–258, 286, 287, 291
Hoskins, J., 421
house: as a symbolic structure, 5–7, 23, 246, 456; "big house" (luma potoam), 368–369; "house of taboos" (luma maquwoliam), 386–387; condition of residence, 393
Howell, S., 421
Huaulu: population, 13; origins, 20–23, 418–419
humanism, critique of, xvii
humans: as a marked category, 27–28; defined in opposition to animals, 179–189, 198, 201, 275–277
hunting, 14, 16, 49, 97, 220; and menstruation, 87–88; and eating, 88–89, 98–101, 185, 203–244; and taboos on the hunter's wife, 155–156; and the lord of the land, 158, 339; shedding blood, 164–165; with spring traps, 172–173, 444, 467–468; with bow and arrow, 173–174, 394; with dogs, 174–176; mythic origins, 190–197; and male supremacy, 196–198; and blending of human and animal, 302–334; and copulation, 316–317, 318–321; dying while hunting, 362; taboos on the hunter, 394, 442

identity: and difference, 83–111; and shamanic taboos, 286, 300
incest: and the theory of taboo, 83–84, 86–91, 88, 109; punishment of, in Huaulu, 143, 160; and chickens, 216; and sexuality, 371–375, 421; punished by death, 388; no Huaulu word for, 440

Indonesia: language, 11, 405, 479; authority established in 1960s, 40; elections in, 223; taboo on name of big house, 368–369; government, 407
initiation, 379, 399
Irian (East New Guinea), 194
Islam: resisting conversion to, 8–9, 420; influence on shamanic familiars, 301, 421

Jakobson, R., 99
Japanese occupation, 450
Java, transmigration from, 13, 17
Judaism: pollution, 43; food taboos of, 75–83, 86–91, 110, 429–430, 436, 478; compared to Christianity, 109–110, 437

kahua feast, 31; circle dance, 38, 117–118; and butterflies, 236; and the sailoa, 364, 473; rules for dancing, 368–369; and cleaning, 411–412, 481; and eating, 477
kamara (village chief): introduced by the Dutch, 37; and chicken eating, 218–219; and clove cultivation, 388; and headhunting, 449
Kanike, 4
Kant, I., 204
kapu (Polynesian "taboo"), 113, 119
Kei, 20
kerosene, 456; subject to misoneistic taboo, 199, 293–294, 357–359
Kierkegaard, S., 436, 475, 477
kinship: taboos, 367–368, 373; opposed to alliance, 373–374
knowledge: opposed to wealth in the creation of inequality, 36–38; and consciousness in Huaulu, 120, 133; and taboo, 161
Kojève, A., xxiii
Kristeva, J., 105–111, 429, 435–437

Lacan, J., 105, 435
Laderman, M., 431
Lahatala. *See* sky god
Lambek, M., 481
lamps: taboos on, 199–200; kerosene vs. damar, 293–294, 357–359; taboo on flashlights, 294; reversal of fallen lamp, 367, 473; taboo on two lamps, 377; continuous light, 456
languages: on Seram, 16–19
Latunusa ("priest of the earth," ritual office), 37, 154, 379
Laufaha. *See* Muslim peoples, of Seram
laughter: directed at animals, 143
law, xxii-xxiii, 405–408
Leach, E.: on Radcliffe-Brown, 56–69; definition of taboo, 61–62; theory of taboo, 62–69, 81, 83, 86, 91–92, 103–104, 202, 245, 424, 431, 457
leprosy, 23, 124, 126–127, 138, 144, 248–250, 441, 459
Lévi-Strauss, C., xiv, xv, xvii, 84, 88; on totemic classification, 93–97, 98, 101, 226, 256, 295, 344, 451; dismissal of taboo's moral dimension, 433
Leviticus, 44, 75–80, 106–107, 109, 426, 428, 437
Lévy-Bruhl, L., 421, 460
Lewis, I. M., 82, 428, 431, 457
Lienhardt, G., 434
lineages, 33, 368, 392–393, 474; and names, 40
liver, as a focus of taboo, 56–58
lizards, 259–260
Lloyd, G. E. R., 460
logging, in the interior of Seram, 40
lord of the land (kaitahu upuam), 304–309, 314–322, 339–340. *See also* occult powers
Lorenz, K., 228

MacIntyre, A., 325, 438
magic, 12, 24, 37; as part of the same domain as taboo, 46–49; Durkheim's views on, 51–52; and morality, 53–54; and the body, 111–112
Makarius, L. L., 431
maleo bird, 263–264, 301
Malinowski, B., 48, 440
Manusela, 4, 18–19, 42, 189, 462
maquwoli: uses in Huaulu, 114–124; classes of misfortunes, 139–141
marriage: prohibitions, 66–67, 83, 85–86, 143–144; chickens as a play on human marriage, 213–222; polyandry among cuscus, 266–267; passion in, 373; opposed to consanguinity, 373–374; adultery, 403–444; women marrying out, 468
Marx, K.: on money and commodities, 89; and Lévi-Strauss, 97
Mauss, M., xiii
meat: as a Huaulu category, 169–172; negative qualities, 178–179; rules for hunters, 309–311; categories of, 312–315

Meigs, A., 102–105, 434–435
Melanesia, 479. *See also* Irian
menstrual hut (lilipossu), 351–356; red wood used, 6, 75; death in, 362, 388; condition for residence, 393, 473
menstruation, 50, 83–84, 85, 87, 109; and blindness/short-sightedness, 148–149, 150; and selective dangers, 152–153, 163–165, 168, 200, 208, 431; sexual asymmetry, 344–345; and death, 349–356, 401, 472; and rats, 451–452; and headhunting, 472; and purification, 478
misoneistic taboos (neophobia), 199, 200, 293–294, 301, 331–333, 357–361, 387, 447, 463, 469–470
missionaries: New Tribes Mission, 41, 470
mixing taboos, 200, 249–268, 335–336, 343–344, 366, 370, 473
moeties, in the Moluccas: Siwa/Lima, 20–23
Moluccas: as a region, xiv, 11; and the Siwa/Lima opposition, 20–21; and trade, 36–38
money, 89
moon, 363
morality: related to magic, 53–54; related to taboo, 59–60; related to classification, 79–80, 82; and male/female, 106–107; relation to social identity, 152–156, 405–408; negation, 408–413; dismissed by Lévi-Strauss, 433; in "heroic society," 438
Morris, D., 229
Muslim peoples: of Seram (Laufaha in Huaulu), 17, 22–23, 179, 210–211, 286, 287–288, 327, 331–332, 340, 475; and shamanism, 290–291, 293–294, 420–421; and hunting, 310–311, 466, 467
myth: of the origins of hunting and humanity, 189–197; of the origin of the cassowary, 253–254, 333–334; of the origin of the crocodile, 275–277; of the origin of palm wine, 297–299; of the lord of the land, 305–307; of the origin of the taboo on pork, 323–324, 467; of olden times, 470

naming, of domestic animals, 222–226
negation: a phenomenon of markedness, 46; as a characteristic of taboo, 132, 373, 408–413, 474; in Freud, 312, 466
Nietzsche, F., 25, 244, 325
Nisawele, 237, 245, 455
Nuaulu, xix, 14, 17, 20, 21, 253–256, 266, 315, 417, 420, 451, 455
Nusawele. *See* Nisawele

occult powers, 25–30; and dreams, 198–199, 370; and shamanism, 286, 291–293, 334; and hunting, 303–344; and the lord of the land, 307–309, 318–322, 339–340
Openg (or Opin), 17, 20, 116, 211, 297–298, 368, 393, 420, 446, 470
opposition: of Huaulu and non-Huaulu, 7–8; village and forest, 9, 14–15; of Siwa/Lima, 20–23; complementary vs. exclusive, 356–357, 472
origins, 198, 297–299, 475; of hunting and humanity, 189–197; of the cassowary, 253–254, 333–334; of crocodiles, 275–277; of palm wine, 297–299; of the lord of the land, 305–307; of taboo on pork, 323–324, 467; of olden times, 470

pagan: populations in Seram (Memaha in Huaulu terminology), 8–9, 22–23, 179, 210; marker of Huaulu difference, 368, 420
papaya, 292–293, 462–463
Parker, R., 45
part-whole relations: and Huaulu identity, 37–38; and subject/object relations, 383–388; and negation, 391–397
penis: in myth of hunting, 190–197; as phallus (Leautuam), 196, 219; as python, 467; descended from heaven, 472
performance and ritual actions, 382–383; as a dimension of taboo, 383–384; polarity with consumption, 399–401, 404, 478, 479
phallus: relation to headhunting, 196, 219, 472; relation to fruit taboos, 285–286; relation to shamanic taboos, 292–293
philosophy, as a field, xiii
photography taboo: for animals in spring traps, 172–173, 444; for shamanic seances (sewa potoam), 294, 360–361; capturing the soul, 377
pigs: jaw as hunting offering, 287, 303, 304–307; and sacrifice, 314–315, 321–322; as part of Huaulu subject constitution, 340–341, 386; Cicero on, 443
Piliyana, xvi
Plato, 258, 405
pollution, 44–45, 69–72; and taxonomy, 73–76, 91, 406; and the body, 102–105;

pollution (*continued*)
and abjection, 105–111, 112–113, 427; of menstruation and death, 349–356, 401–402, 478
population, fluctuations of, and smallpox and influenza epidemics, 39
pork, taboo on eating: among Muslims, 62, 467; among Andaman islanders, 69–70, 426; for Hebrews, 74; Huaulu shamans, 287–288; and pig jaws, 303–304
postmodernism, critique of, xvii
pregnancy, false, 148, 442
prohibition, 61–62, 126, 131
Puhum. *See* earth goddess
pukari (shamanic seance). *See* shamanism
python, 251, 259, 264, 279–280, 282–283, 286, 292, 302, 376, 456, 458, 460, 467, 475

Radcliffe-Brown, A. R.: on ritual prohibitions of food, 44–45, 54–58; on ritual value, 52–54; and Leach, 61, 66, 422, 424–425, 427; on Australian totemism, 93–95; on fear, 440
rain and magic, 12, 276–277
rats, 231–233
religion: Durkheim's views on, 51–52, 63, 71, 82, 431; Cicero's etymology of, 120; on the island of Seram, 327; Dumézil's etymology of, 438
repression, 58–61, 63–65, 70–71, 385, 425
reversal taboos, 366, 369–370
rice: subject to misoneistic taboo, 199, 293–294, 357–359; eaten but not grown, 359–360, 472–473
Ricoeur, P., 45, 439
ritual: as defined by Radcliffe-Brown, 53–55; as defined by the Huaulu, 132; taboos on the ritual association, 200, 366; defined by the author, 366; performative wholeness, 384, 477
Robertson-Smith, W. *See* Smith, W. Robertson
Roho, 4, 462
ruler. *See* kamara (village chief); Latunusa ("priest of the earth"); lord of the land (kaitahu upuam)
rules: prescriptive vs. descriptive, 125; and taboos, 135, 411–412

sacrifice and taboo, 77, 81, 161; of the head, 304–310; of the body, 311–324, 464, 466; and sexuality, 320–322; as a dimension of the taboo system, 341–342, 395; of humans, 378
sago grub, 260–262
sago mush (ipia kouwam): personal taboo on, 124, 129–130, 371; as staple, 170–172, 315, 351, 365, 444
sago palm, 13, 129–130, 151, 298–300
Sahlins, M., xvi
Sanskrit dosa ("trouble"), 124; asaucya (impure), 138, 440
Sartre, J.-P., 481
Saussure, F., 258
Sawai: language of Muslim coastal people, 17; military post, 38, 179; war with, 223; coastal area, 297
schooling, 31, 389, 390
Seram: general characteristics of, xv, xvi, 3–4, 8; languages, 7–20, 437; trade, 9, 23; geography and climate, 11–12; eastern parts, 19–20; origins of the island in Huaulu traditions, 20–23
Serpell, J., 451
sewa spirit familiars. *See* shamanism
sexuality: as "eating," 98–101; in the conjugal relationship, 155–156; relation to death, 165; and eels, 280–286, 287, 289, 292, 461; and papayas, 293, 462–463; and violence, 305, 316–317; and reproduction, 317–318, 320, 466; and incest, 371–374, 475–476
shamanism, xvi, xxi, 8, 24; and occult powers, 26–30, 118–119; and language, 123; and ritual, 132, 151; medicines and cures, 155–156, 442–443; sewa potoam (most important seance), 161; taboos, 203; and food taboos, 286–295, 334–335; and turbans, 378–379, 396; and Islamic influences, 421, 461; and hunting, 467–468
shame, xxiii, 402–405, 479, 480
shrimp, 12, 306, 462, 465
sin, xxiii, 107–108, 123, 439
Siwa/Lima (Nine/Five) opposition, 20–23, 194, 222, 327, 419, 420–421
Skorupski, J., 425
sky god (Lahatala, Father Sky), 15, 24, 25, 157, 219, 311, 347, 407, 480
Smith, W. Robertson, xxii, 43–44, 46, 421
Soler, J., 76–79, 108, 429–430, 436
Sontag, S., 145–146
Sperber, D., 73, 429, 430
spiders, 452–453

Spinoza, B., 406
spirits, 23–30
Stein, S., 426
Steiner, R., 44–45
structure and structuralism, 246
subject: constitution of the, xvii; in relation to humans and animals, 57–58, 101–102; dissolved in abjection, 106–109; and the inarticulate, 110–111; and body, 111–113; and object, 130–131, 326–327, 330; polarities in subordination to order, 381–382

taboo, definition of the, xxii, 43–46; relation to magic, 46–58; defined by Leach, 61–62; and classification, 61–83; and incest, 83–84; 86–91, 88, 109, 421; and totemism, 93–97; and abjection, 105–111; and the constitution of the subject, 111–113; as a covenant with the occult powers, 322–324
Taluti, 3, 10, 17–19, 420
Tambiah, S. J., 81, 430, 445, 476
Tanimbar, 297–298, 301, 463
tape recorder, as taboo for shamanic seances (sewa potoam), 294, 360–361
taxonomy, 73–76, 94, 429
territory, 13–14, 419
Testart, A., 86–91, 109, 354, 431–432, 464, 474–475
topoyem (shades of the dead). *See* ghosts
totemism, 93–97; and diseases, 141–151; and names, 226; and taboos, 286, 295–302; and the principle of origins, 338–339, 375–376
turtles, 268–273; taboo to women, 284; paradigmatic taboo on, 330–331

unfamiliarity, 199–200
universals, xviii

Van Gennep, A., 167
Vernant, J. P., 45
village (niniani), 30–38; opposed to forest, 14–15, 349, 355, 364–367; part-whole relations, 386–387
village chief/headman. *See* kamara

Wahai, 12, 17, 38–40
war (lisam): eruption in 1985, 14, 24; and knowledge, 37; and taboos on blood, 149, 156–157, 160–161; and headhunting, 421
war leader (kapitane), 24–25, 37
weevil, 258–259
wild foods, 15
witches: in eastern Seram, 19; fought by shamans, 29; in Huaulu, 421, 452–454
women: in conjugal relationship, 155–156; and chicken sexuality, 214–216, 317; species taboo to, 279–286, 330–331; marrying out, 327, 329, 468; and genital bleeding, 350–351; and shamanism, 462; and shrimp fishing, 465

Zimmerman, F., 451, 471